Sacred Texts of the World
A Universal Anthology

SACRED TEXTS OF THE WORLD
A UNIVERSAL ANTHOLOGY

EDITED BY
NINIAN SMART &
RICHARD D. HECHT

CROSSROAD · NEW YORK

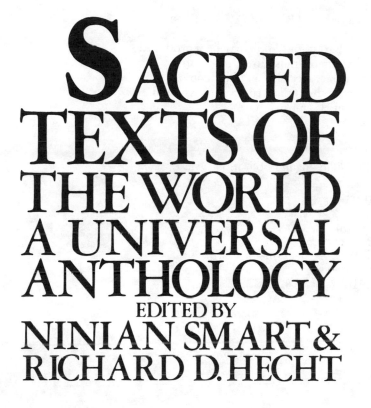

This printing: 1998

The Crossroad Publishing Company
370 Lexington Avenue, New York, N.Y. 10017

PRINTED IN U.S.A.

Library of Congress Cataloging in Publication Data

Main entry under title:

Sacred texts of the world.

1. Sacred books. I. Smart, Ninian, 1927–
II. Hecht, Richard D.
BL70.S247 291.8'2 82–7375
ISBN 0–8245–0483–6 hc AACR2
ISBN 0–8245–0639–1 pbk

Contents

ISLAM

HINDUISM

BUDDHISM

JAINISM

TAOISM

CONFUCIANISM

SHINTOISM

SIKHISM

SMALL-SCALE TRADITIONAL RELIGIONS

NEW RELIGIONS

SECULAR WORLDVIEWS

Illustrations

Acknowledgements

We wish to thank those who have helped in the preparation of the text, especially Māra Vilčinskas and Penelope Allport of Macmillan Press, Margot Levy, Juliet Brightmore and, in Santa Barbara, Randi Glick, Steven Konstantine and Libushka Smart. We are also grateful for advice from Joseph Adler and Wilbur Fridell of the Department of Religious Studies in the University of California Santa Barbara.

NINIAN SMART
RICHARD HECHT

June 1982

Introduction

It is a commonplace notion that there is in the great religions of the world a vast body of sacred literature – the Bible, the Vedas, the Qur'ān, the Lotus Sutra and so on. Great oral traditions – myths and other constellations of old lore – although not technically scriptures, for they are not written documents, have a similar place in the spiritual universe of the people who treat them as sacred. The world's sacred texts are potent sources of inspiration and behaviour and, more importantly, they play a crucial part in the formation of peoples' perception of reality. They may be thought of as somehow revealed, or as expressions of revelatory experience, and typically they are treated as possessing authority. For a community that is shaped by a religious tradition, it is vital to be clear about which texts or documents are authoritative, and so it is not unusual for scriptures to be defined as canonical, that is, belonging to a collection seen as a canon.

If we are to understand the nature of scriptures, we need to be clear about certain basic ideas – text, scripture, sacred, authority, revelation, inspiration and canon. Let us look briefly at each of these.

A body of lore can sometimes function like a scripture even if it is not written down. There are few non-literate peoples left on the globe, but until quite recently it was common to encounter traditional ethnic groups who possessed no writing. Occasionally a great and complex civilization, such as the Incas of Peru, may possess only the most rudimentary system of recording ideas, yet have a very rich oral heritage. Some of the great sets of scripture were originally transmitted by word of mouth – by systematic chanting, for example. This is true of the Pali Canon, the scripture of Theravada Buddhism, which for several centuries was handed down by generations of monks, versed in memorization. Similarly, the Hindu Vedic corpus was transmitted orally. Behind nearly every one of the great religious canons of the world there lies a mass of oral material, often with a very long history. The investigations of folklorists over the past 20 or 30 years indicate that oral traditions, however extensive they may be, are far less susceptible to error than written traditions. Thus we can make a broad distinction between spoken texts which are handed down orally and those which are found in written form, but here we use the word 'text' in its wider sense, encompassing oral traditions.

What is it for a text, an oral tradition or a scripture to be sacred? Holiness or sacredness is difficult to define in a conventional way, but that which is sacred or holy is thought to contain some kind of divine power or influence, and as being such that its sacredness must not be violated, or treated with disrespect. It is a serious blasphemy to put a Qur'ān on the floor, or to place other books upon the Hebrew Bible. That which is sacred often has a divine or transcendent origin, or so it is thought. The sacred text is one which, so to speak, has its roots in heaven, and it may even be regarded, like the earthly Qur'ān, as the copy of a heavenly original. Indeed, one of the most common symbols in the religions of the world is the heavenly book delivered to man by God or by other divine beings. It is through its originally being divine property, or because it is a direct copy of the divine book, that your text is sacred. However, the main features of the sacred are that it has beneficial power, and

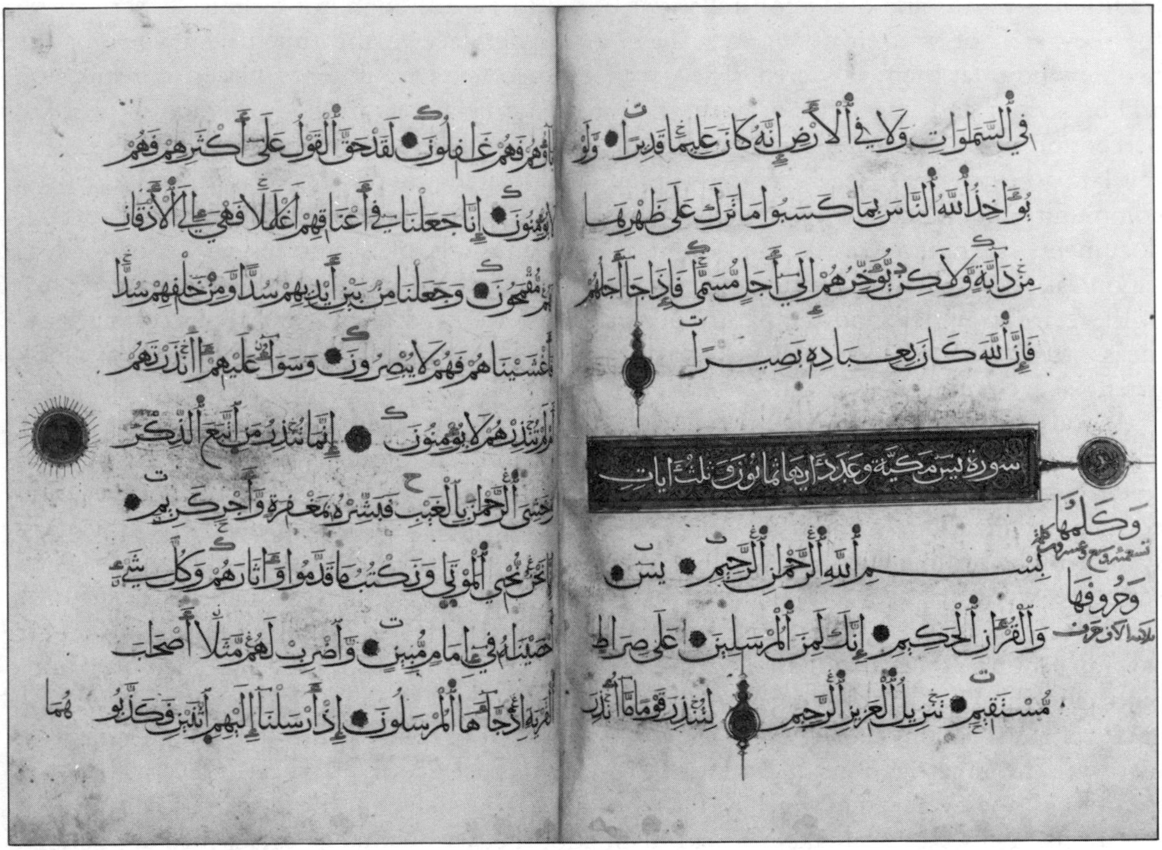

*A variety of scripts and decorative patterns is used in transcribing the Qur'ān. This page from a 14th-century Arabic manuscript shows the opening of Sura 36 (*see page 150*). Orthodox Muslims believe that only the original Arabic expresses the eternal revelation of the Qur'ān to Muhammad.*

that it is not to be treated with disrespect: thus it is customary in some Christian countries to take an oath on the Bible. When this sacredness is translated and perceived in the form of a book, it quite clearly indicates that everything of importance is contained within it and can be applied to all aspects of human life.

Something can of course be sacred without being what we would call a scripture. Any writing, such as a hymn, which is sufficiently often associated with the divine, can acquire a certain sacredness. Thus hymnbooks and missals are given a certain status and sanctity by their use and near proximity to sacred texts. It is in any event difficult to draw an absolutely clear line between a holy book and a secular one. However, what is most centrally a sacred text is one which has special authority for the community that uses it. It is in this sense that we can point to the Qur'ān, the Bible, the Vedas and so on as most typical of the genre. But even here there are problems. A number of communities may see a specific text, such as the Bible, as authoritative, but each may understand its content differently, and the very order and number of books within it may vary within each community's perception.

The authority of a sacred scripture may derive from its origin – from its being created or revealed by God, for instance, or because it expresses insights received by holy men or by a Buddha, and so forth. But this authority also consists in the fact that the scripture is normative for life in various ways. It often has a liturgical use: it may be recited and otherwise used in the context of praise and worship, and may even be a form of sacred decoration, like the Arabic calligraphy carved into stone. The repetition of sacred texts is sometimes an aid not only to worship, but also to meditation. Furthermore, sacred writings often contain laws, or at least the basis upon which laws are formulated, as in the case of the Torah, the Vinaya of Buddhism, and so on. Thus the scriptures of a particular community are normative for its worship, for doctrine and for behaviour.

Where there is an idea of God, it is usual to think that the authority of scriptures arises from the fact that God has created or revealed the texts. Where there is a less sharply defined sense of a personal creator, the scriptures are thought of not so much as revealed as somehow perceived by those with special insight and powers, or as based on the deliverances of those with special insight and powers. It is not unusual to see revelation in terms of some kind of inspiration or 'breathing in' of the words into the minds of the writers of scripture or the transmitters of sacred and authoritative words. In this case, the words and the writers or transmitters become one and the same, so that the writers or transmitters become living embodiments of sacred words.

Inspired writings are often themselves thought to be inspiring, and a main reason for reading scriptures is that they are thought to have deep inspirational value. Certainly, there are key portions of sacred writings which have strong spiritual impact and meaning. Other portions may not be particularly inspiring: thus, various stretches of Deuteronomy or the Vinaya are not so much edifying or exciting, as significant because they set forth norms of behaviour in some detail.

So far, then, we may look at sacred texts as being those which contain a power and authority and are given a certain status within a given community. Such communities and traditions are held together most typically through liturgical acts, which help to focus life upon that which is ultimate and to which the sacred texts give testimony. The status of the sacred text is canonical: as well as being normative for a community or tradition, it is also that community or tradition's canon or canonical text. The term 'canon' has a variety of meanings, but in the context of sacred texts it means the defined grouping of texts for the community or tradition.

Canon, unlike a list or a catalogue, is first and foremost a closed set of texts. Things may not be added to or subtracted from the contents of the canon, and the fact that it is closed and fixed implies that the community or a group within the community has established what constitutes its content. The history of many religious traditions indicates that at specific moments groups or councils were called together to determine what constituted the authoritative canon of sacred texts. Decisions as to what belonged in the canon were taken on different grounds – in some cases it may have involved a matter of authorship, in others the decision-making process may have involved doctrinal clashes – but canon is always the result of some conscious choice, either by one person or by selected individuals. Even extensive oral traditions are essentially canonical: one does not add to or substract from them. While the canon of written scriptures is dependent on a decision of members of the community and then subsequently upon the activity of scribes and still later printers, the 'canonicity' of oral traditions depends on the decisions of those who transmit them and instruct others in their mastery.

Thus canon always implies a community of individuals charged with the responsibility for establishing the rationale for the contents of the canon, and engaged in discerning the applicability of canonical materials to all aspects of human life. These are essentially interpretive activities, in which the repeated question is how the limited number of laws, narrative and other items within the fixed canon are to be related or extended to an unlimited number of situations outside it. It is therefore impossible to understand sacred texts without taking into consideration the activity of commentators and exegetes within religious traditions, although not all the materials collected within the canon need be understood as having equal authority.

In this anthology we have used scripture and canon as the main yardsticks for selecting sacred texts, but we have also ranged more widely. We have included oral as well as written texts, and inspirational literature lying outside the main canonical traditions. The aim is to look to what each tradition tends to revere as normative and from which it has drawn power and insight. We have tried to be balanced. To this end, we have looked at sacred texts in the light of the six-dimensional analysis of religion propounded in Ninian Smart's *Religious Experience of Mankind* (1969). Religion can typically be seen as involving various dimensions – myth (or sacred narrative), doctrine, ritual, social and institutional expression, experience and ethics. We have grouped texts under these six headings. Thus, first, we have drawn sacred narratives from each of the main traditions – stories which unfold the nature of the divine beings, or indicate how the world came into existence, and so on. Such narratives are technically referred to as myths, whether or not they have a historical basis. But since in English 'myth' often means 'false story' we have not used this word. It is not for us to judge whether the stories in this volume are true or not. It is their power to move people that counts, and we have brought them together in order to give insight into this power.

Second, we have tried to illustrate the doctrinal dimension of religion: for religions, in reflecting about the world, come to formulate teachings, philosophies, dogmas and systems which delineate the nature of the world and of the ultimate. Sometimes such systems of thought only arise after the scriptures have become fixed, but typically the sacred texts include the beginnings of such reflections about reality.

Third, we see the narratives and doctrines in the practical context of the ritual dimension. It is by worship, meditation, services, rites, pilgrimages and other such activities that human beings relate themselves to God and the gods, and prepare themselves for redemption and liberation. So in each chapter the third section concerns such ritual acts, and the practical ways in which men have worked out belief in activity.

Rituals, doctrines and myths usually imply institutions, which carry on the traditions of belief and practice. Religions, in organizing themselves, acquire a social or institutional dimension. So, fourthly, we have gathered passages to illustrate the institutional expression of each main tradition.

The fifth dimension of religion is the experiential. Religious ritual is often a means of expressing and helping to generate feelings of awe, serenity and inner insight; often the great figures of the religious traditions are those who have had spiritual experiences of great drama and depth. So, fifthly, we have attempted to delineate the inner feelings and intuitions which each tradition points to.

Finally, there is the ethical dimension. For many people this may be the most important part of religion – the way it teaches wisdom as to what is right and wrong, and looks to such ethical attitudes as love and compassion and brotherhood. We have here drawn together some of the most significant values of the various faiths.

The idea of the six dimensions of religion may provoke too a question of definition. If we use the six dimensions to define what religion is, do not secular ideologies, such as Marxism, perhaps turn out to be like religions? It would be foolish to try to settle the question here, but we have thought it wise to give some expression to secular beliefs. Although the texts of such traditions are not perhaps thought of as sacred, they sometimes in fact function to guide and inspire people in much the same way as traditional religious texts. Secular beliefs are part of the human search for ultimate meaning.

In two respects we must, in creating an anthology such as the present one, be somewhat controversial. First, although the aim is to make a balanced choice, choice there must be. We hope that we have managed to present both what is familiar and what is unexpected. Second, although our main stress is on the great traditions, we have paid attention to mankind's whole experience, and so both religious traditions which have passed out of existence and the latest new religions will be represented. Included here will be some documents drawn from secular ideologies which have importance in the existential experience of modern people; thus Mao has a place beside the Tao.

But mostly those who look to an anthology like this one have two needs: one is for a work which serves as an informative anthology of the world's most important and normative sacred texts; the other is for a handbook of spiritual messages. For it is through the sacred texts of the world that cosmic reality is somehow indicated to the mind of the human race. Whether the texts be seen as coming from the Beyond, or only from the constructive powers of the human mind, they are a strange and rich testimony to the spiritual imagination which lies at the heart of our many-cultured human heritage.

The Hall of Judgment from the Egyptian Book of the Dead. *The nobleman Ani and his wife stand by the scales on which the heart, the supposed seat of intelligence, is weighed against a feather, symbolizing Truth. Watched by Anubis, the jackal-headed god of the necropolis, and Thoth, the ibis-headed recording god, Ani recites the negative confession of the dead* (see page 37).

The Powerful Dead

Introduction

We begin our anthology of sacred texts of the world with a representative selection of religious documents from the great urban civilizations of ancient Egypt, Mesopotamia, Greece and Rome,and the Maya and Aztec of Mesoamerica. The emergence of these great urban civilizations was due in great part to the agricultural revolutions which took place in the ancient Near East in the 4th and 3rd millennia BCE, and during the first five or six hundred years of the Common Era in the New World of the Americas. These revolutions in the sources of food and its cultivation allowed humans to live in new and larger social configurations. Urbanization, with all the complexities of city life and intricate social differentiation, is mirrored in the religious traditions of these civilizations. We should recall that by the middle of the 3rd millennium BCE the Old Kingdom of Egypt was firmly established, and that at a roughly contemporary period in Mesopotamia, the Sumerian city-states of Uruk, Kish and Ur had become major cultural and political centres. In the 2nd millennium, Knossos, Mycenae and Troy in the eastern Mediterranean had begun to form the foundations of ancient Greece. Early in the 1st millennium, Carthage emerged as a major cultural centre in the western Mediterranean and the year 753, by our best estimates, saw the founding of Rome. By the end of the same millennium, much of the power of Egypt and Mesopotamia had given way to Greece and Rome, and the Maya had emerged in southern Mesoamerica. The destiny of Zoroastrianism, the major religious tradition of ancient Persia or Iran, is somewhat different from its Mesopotamian neighbours. It was given its initial formulation in the hymns of Zoroaster (called Zarathustra in Old Iranian), who lived probably in the 6th century BCE. Zoroaster was a priest of the older Persian religion, which contained many elements similar to the Vedic tradition of India, and his reformulation was based in great part on his visionary experiences with Ahura Mazda, the Wise Lord. His tradition was enlarged and reinterpreted by the Magi and other later reformers until Iran was conquered by Islam in 635 CE. The Zoroastrian tradition, along with Judaism and Christianity, was tolerated in the expanding Muslim world because of its monotheism and its sacred books. However, from the 10th century onward, Zoroastrians emigrated to India, where they are called Parsees and now number approximately 100,000 in and around Bombay. The religious tradition of the Parsees in modern India represents an important continuation of the ancient religious tradition of Zoroaster.

Each of these civilizations had its own history; there were periods of conflict, both internal and external, and periods of cultural regeneration. Often the history of one civilization impinged upon those around it; this was especially the case around the Mediterranean. Each civilization flourished and declined, but the power of its religious traditions continued to exercise considerable force long after the civilization had passed away or been absorbed by another. The great political and cultural synthesis of east and west envisioned by Alexander quickly fell in pieces after his death, but the ideal of the *cosmopolis*, the true universal city, continued throughout much of late antiquity. Greeks and Romans were more than a little fascinated by what they saw of the Near East and Egypt.

Often the religious traditions of these civilizations, in traditional or new guises, found their way into the Greek city-states or to Rome itself, and they were often considered equal or superior to the traditional Greek and Roman religions. The synthesis of these civilizations and their religious traditions in late antiquity provided the cultural matrix of much of our history in the West. Indeed, the histories of both Judaism and Christianity are dependent upon their interaction with the religious traditions of these civilizations. The power was such that geographical distances separating one civilization from another were often obliterated by philosophical and religious reflection. That the distance between Jerusalem and Athens could easily be overcome is suggested by the famous statement of Numenius of Apamea, a thorough-going Platonist of the late 2nd century CE, 'What is Plato, but Moses speaking in Attic Greek.'

The power of these religious traditions was not limited to their immediate successors. They have been equally powerful in their rediscovery. The rediscovery of classical traditions from ancient Greece and Rome during the Renaissance and the recovery of ancient Mesopotamian and Egyptian texts in the 19th century have been crucial influences in the formulation of the modern spirit of humanism. These religious traditions, now separated from us by at least 2000 years, have continued to exert their power in the way we construct our history and identity. Likewise, the religious traditions of the Maya and Aztec have continued to inform and shape the histories and identities of modern Central American cultures and nations.

Many of the problems that we have identified in the Introduction concerning the nature of sacred texts are most difficult to address in the context of the powerful religious traditions of the past. For example, in what way can we speak of a 'canon' of ancient Mesopotamian or ancient Egyptian literature? Lists of authoritative texts may have existed at one time but they are now beyond our grasp. Many of the documents collected here are found in forms which differ considerably from the forms found in Judaism, Islam or Hinduism. Some have been found in tombs and pyramids, others represent the formulations and descriptions of churchmen who were ambivalent about the meaning of Aztec religion, but nevertheless thought it merited collection and transmission, and at least one text reproduced here is drawn from something we might immediately recognize as a novel or short story. We begin the dimension of sacred narrative with a description from Zoroaster on the primordial choice between life and non-life which strikes the initial dualism between Ahura Mazda and Ahriman, between good and evil. The dualism between good and evil was to have an impact upon ancient Israel, Judaism, Christianity and Islam. Second, we include a selection from the ancient Babylonian creation narrative, the *Enuma Elish*, in which the young Marduk, charged by the assembly of the gods to wrest divine authority and the Tablets of Fate from Tiamat and Kingu, slays them both, creates the world or cosmos from the body of Tiamat and human beings from the dust and blood of Kingu. Human beings, 'the black-headed ones' as the text calls them, contain within them the rebelliousness of Tiamat's consort, and are created for only one purpose, to serve the gods. Third, we have included a short selection from Hesiod's *Theogony* in which the epic poet describes the generation of the first gods. Lastly, we have chosen a short selection from the Mayan *Popol Vuh*, which similarly describes the creation of the first semi-divine beings and the world.

We have illustrated the dimension of doctrine first by Akhenaten's great hymn to the Aten or solar disc. This Egyptian text from the 14th century BCE represents one of the greatest religious documents in human history. The Aten is described as the totally transcendent god whose providence extends to all peoples. Next we include a Zoroastrian text describing the judgment of the soul after death. Our third selection is a short segment of Plato's dialogue 'The Timaeus' in which Socrates asks Timaeus to explain his thoughts on god and creation. Unlike many other Platonic dialogues, Socrates does not offer corrections to Timaeus' observations, and this description stands at the heart of many later western reflections on the nature of god and creation. Last, we include a short selection from one of the many narratives concerning Quetzalcoatl, one of the most important divine figures of the ancient Maya and Aztec. Here, we learn how Quetzalcoatl descends into the realm of the dead in order to retrieve the bones of man and ultimately becomes the benefactor of humans.

We begin the dimension of ritual with a text taken from the Pyramid of Unas at Saqqara. Here, we find a description of the Pharaoh's ascent to the assembly of the gods. This text properly belongs in this dimension in that along with many other so-called Pyramid Texts it formed the liturgy of the Pharaoh's burial, and its recitation ensured the Pharaoh's immortality. Second, we include an ancient Zoroastrian hymn of sacrifice to the sun, a ritual in which older, pre-Zorastrian deities, such as Mithra, continued to persist after Zoroaster's cultic reforms. Third, we have included a short selection from the late 3rd century-Neoplatonist, Iamblichus, in which he describes the nature and function of true prayer. Lastly, we have chosen the description of one of the most important rituals surrounding the Aztec god Tezcatlipoca, from Fray Bernardino de Sahagún's 16th-century *General History of the Things of New Spain*. His description of this sacrifice and many other aspects of Aztec religion and daily life remain among our best documents for reconstructing the religious worldview of the Aztec.

The dimension of institutional expression is illustrated first by an ancient Egyptian hymn to Osiris and Horus. Here we learn something of the sacred narrative of Osiris, but also something of the nature of kingship in ancient Egypt. Second, we have reproduced part of the ancient Babylonian epic of Gilgamesh, in which this king is brought to understand the real responsibilities of kingship. Third, we reprint a section of Virgil's *Fourth Eclogue*, in which the poet envisions a new age under the leadership of Augustus. Lastly, we include a very short description from Sahagún on the city of Teotihuacan, the first Aztec capital and 'city of the gods'. This description underscores the importance of cities, not only in Mesoamerica, but throughout the history of religious traditions, as the centres of ritual activity and the places which connect the world of human beings to the world of the gods.

Our first text representing the dimension of experience is a prophetic text from ancient Egypt in which the lector-priest, Neferti, is asked to describe either what has already happened or what will happen. He then offers a description of the future in which the land will be destroyed by chaos, and things will only be restored through the intervention of a future king. Second, we include a Sumerian lamentation over the destruction of Ur. This text presents us with one of the most forceful descriptions of the human experience of being cut off from the gods and the divine realm. Our third text is from Apuleius' *Metamorphoses*. Here Lucius, who much earlier has been transformed into an ass, is rescued by the goddess Isis. This text is taken from a popular novel of the 2nd century CE, but it nevertheless presents us with one of the most detailed descriptions of the epiphany of this Egyptian goddess. Our last selection is once again drawn from Sahagún, and describes how the ancient Aztecs sought confession for their transgressions. The similarity between the Aztec world and Sahagún's own Christianity at this point must have impressed him greatly, and we can still detect how the Aztec understood this experience as one which re-created him as he was at the beginning of time.

We have chosen to illustrate the dimension of ethics first by a representative text from the Egyptian *Book of the Dead*. Here, the nobleman Ani recites a negative confession, attesting that he has not committed any transgression. Our second example of the ethical dimension is taken from the very beginning of the law code of the Babylonian King Hammurabi. This is one of the oldest legal documents from the Ancient Near East, and its specific laws formed the basis of all ethical conduct for the ancient Babylonians. This code of law was not understood as a simple human creation, but as something inspired by the sun god Shamash himself. Violation of the law was thus not only a violation of proper human conduct, but also a violation of the divine will. The third selection is taken from the beginning of Plotinus' *Enneads*. Here, this very important philosopher in the tradition of Plato, who has often been understood as a mystic, describes the highest virtues, those which affect the higher mind and allow human beings to become like the gods. The last text is taken from Sahagún and describes the ethical function of the Aztec wise man. Here, we quickly realize that ethics meant something more comprehensive that ethical action: indeed, the wise man was the very centre of all life and the guarantor of proper human existence.

Sacred Narrative 1

The Primordial Choice: Gāthā: Yasna 30

One of the most fundamental aspects of Zoroaster's thought in the 6th century BCE was the opposition between good and evil. This dualism is articulated in the opposition between Ahura Mazda, referred to in this text as the Wise One, and Angra Mainyu or Ahriman, the chief servant of the *Druj* or Lie. Ahura Mazda is surrounded by six or seven beings called Amesha Spentas, 'the Beneficent Immortals', who often appear as hypostatizations of his goodness, omnipotence and omniscience. Angra Mainyu is the full embodiment of the principle of evil. According to this text, there was a meeting of the two spirits at the very beginning of time. They were free to choose between 'life and non-life', and this choice gave birth to the fully actualized principles of good and evil, corresponding to the Kingdom of Justice or Truth and the Kingdom of the Lie. This text indicates that human history is a re-enactment of the very same choice between good and evil. The hymn then encapsulates time from the beginning to the end, for in the end human beings will be judged according to the choice they have made in life.

Now will I speak to those who will hear
Of the things which the initiate should remember,
The praises and prayer of the Good Mind to the Lord
And the joy which he shall see in the light who has remembered them well.

Hear with your ears that which is the sovereign good;
With a clear mind look upon the two sides
Between which each man must choose for himself,
Watchful beforehand that the great test may be accomplished in our favour.

Now at the beginning the twin spirits have declared their nature,
The better and the evil,
In thought and word and deed. And between the two
The wise ones choose well, not so the foolish.

And when these two spirits came together,
In the beginning they established life and non-life,
And that at the last the worst experience should be for the wicked,
But for the righteous one the Best Mind.

Of these two spirits, the evil one chose to do the worst things;
But the most Holy Spirit, clothed in the most steadfast heavens,
Joined himself unto Righteousness;
And thus did all those who delight to please the Wise Lord by honest deeds.

Between the two, the false gods also did not choose rightly,
For while they pondered they were beset by error,
So that they chose the Worst Mind.
Then did they hasten to join themselves unto Fury,
That they might by it deprave the existence of man.

And to him came Devotion, together with Dominion, Good Mind and Righteousness;
She gave perpetuity of body and the breath of life,
That he may be thine apart from them,
As the first by the retributions through the metal.

And when their punishment shall come to these sinners,
Then, O Wise One, shall thy Dominion, with the Good Mind,
Be granted to those who have delivered Evil into the hands of Righteousness, O Lord!

And may we be those that renew this existence!
O Wise One, and you other Lords, and Righteousness, bring your alliance,
That thoughts may gather where wisdom is faint.

Then shall Evil cease to flourish,
While those who have acquired good fame
Shall reap the promised reward
In the blessed dwelling of the Good Mind, of the Wise One, and of Righteousness.

If you, O men, understand the commandments which the Wise One has given,
Well-being and suffering – long torment for the wicked and salvation for the righteous –
All shall hereafter be for the best.

Sacred Narrative 2

Marduk Creates the World: The Enuma Elish Tablets

This text is taken from the Akkadian epic, the *Enuma Elish*, 'When on High', and perhaps dates back to the Old Babylonian period in ancient Mesopotamia at the beginning of the 2nd millennium BCE. The myth describes how the assembly of the gods was overturned by Tiamat and her consort Kingu, and the gods were forced to call upon a young, strong god, Marduk, to regain their position. We join the narrative as Marduk and Tiamat enter into combat. Tiamat and Kingu are ultimately vanquished and Marduk creates the world from the body of Tiamat, and man from earth and the blood of Kingu. This narrative may have served in the ancient Babylonian New Year festival as the liturgy of the king, who each year became Marduk, vanquished the enemies of the gods, and set the Tablets of Fate for the coming year.

Stand thou up, that I and thou meet in single combat!
When Tiamat heard this,
  She was like one possessed; she took leave of her senses.
In fury Tiamat cried out aloud.
To the roots her legs shook both together.
She recites a charm, keeps casting her spell,
  While the gods of battle sharpen their weapons.
Then joined issue Tiamat and Marduk, wisest of gods.
They strove in single combat, locked in battle.
The lord spread out his net to enfold her,
  The Evil Wind, which followed behind, he let loose in her face.
When Tiamat opened her mouth to consume him,
  He drove in the Evil Wind that she close not her lips.
As the fierce winds charged her belly,
  Her body was distended and her mouth was wide open.
He released the arrow, it tore her belly,
  It cut through her insides, splitting the heart.
Having thus subdued her, he extinguished her life.
He cast down her carcass to stand upon it.
After he had slain Tiamat, the leader,
  Her band was shattered, her troupe broken up;
  And the gods, her helpers who marched at her side,
  Trembling with terror, turned their backs about,
  In order to save and preserve their lives.
Tightly encircled, they could not escape.
He made them captives and he smashed their weapons.
Thrown into the net, they found themselves ensnared;
  Placed in cells, they were filled with wailing;
  Bearing his wrath, they were held imprisoned.
And the eleven creatures which she had charged with awe,
  The band of demons that marched . . . before her,
  He cast into fetters, their hands . . .
For all their resistance, he trampled them underfoot.
And Kingu, who had been made chief among them,
  He bound and accounted him to Uggae.
He took from him the Tablets of Fate, not rightfully his,
  Sealed them with a seal and fastened them on his breast.
When he had vanquished and subdued his adversaries,
    Had . . . the vainglorious foe,
  Had wholly established Anshar's triumph over the foe,
  Nudimmud's desire had achieved, valiant Marduk
    Strengthened his hold on the vanquished gods,

And turned back to Tiamat whom he had bound.
The lord trod on the legs of Tiamat,
With his unsparing mace he crushed her skull.
When the arteries of her blood he had severed,
The North Wind bore it to places undisclosed.
On seeing this, his fathers were joyful and jubilant,
They brought gifts of homage, they to him.
Then the lord paused to view her dead body,
That he might divide the monster and do artful works.
He split her like a shellfish into two parts:
Half of her he set up and ceiled it as sky,
Pulled down the bar and posted guards.
He bade them to allow not her waters to escape.
He crossed the heavens and surveyed the regions.
He squared Apsu's quarter, the abode of Nudimmud,
As the lord measured the dimensions of Apsu.
The Great Abode, its likeness, he fixed as Esharra,
The Great Abode, Esharra, which he made as the firmament.
Anu, Enlil, and Ea he made occupy their places.

He constructed stations for the great gods,
Fixing their astral likenesses as constellations.
He determined the year by designating the zones:
He set up three constellations for each of the twelve months.
After defining the days of the year [by means] of [heavenly] figures,
He founded the station of Nebiru to determine their [heavenly] bands,
That none might transgress or fall short.
Alongside it he set up the stations of Enlil and Ea.
Having opened up the gates on both sides,
He strengthened the locks to the left and the right.
In her belly he established the zenith.
The Moon he caused to shine, the night to him entrusting.
He appointed him a creature of the night to signify the days:
'Monthly, without cease, form designs with a crown.
At the month's very start, rising over the land,
Thou shalt have luminous horns to signify six days,
On the seventh day reaching a [half]crown.
At full moon stand in opposition in mid-month.
When the sun [overtakes] thee at the base of heaven,
Diminish [thy crown] and retrogress in light.
[At the time of disappearance] approach thou the course of the sun,
And [on the twenty-ninth] thou shalt again stand in opposition to the sun.'

[The remainder of this tablet is broken away or too fragmentary for translation.]

When Marduk hears the words of the gods,
His heart prompts him to fashion artful works.
Opening his mouth, he addresses Ea
To impart the plan he had conceived in his heart:
'Blood I will mass and cause bones to be,
I will establish a savage, "man" shall be his name.
Verily, savage-man I will create.
He shall be charged with the service of the gods that they might be at ease!
The ways of the gods I will artfully alter.
Though alike revered, into two [groups] they shall be divided.'
Ea answered him, speaking a word to him,
Giving him another plan for the relief of the gods:
'Let but one of their brothers be handed over;
He alone shall perish that mankind may be fashioned.
Let the great gods be here in Assembly,
Let the guilty be handed over that they may endure.'
Marduk summoned the great gods to Assembly;
Presiding graciously, he issues instructions.
To his utterance the gods pay heed.
The king addresses a word to the Anunnaki:
'If your former statement was true,
Do [now] the truth on oath by me declare!
Who was it that contrived the uprising,
And made Tiamat rebel, and joined battle?
Let him be handed over who contrived the uprising.
His guilt I will make him bear. You shall dwell in peace!'
The Igigi, the great gods, replied to him,
To Lugaldimmerankia, counsellor of the gods, their lord:
'It was Kingu who contrived the uprising,

And made Tiamat rebel, and joined battle.'
They bound him, holding him before Ea.
They imposed on him his guilt and severed his blood [vessels].
Out of his blood they fashioned mankind.
He imposed the service and let free the gods.
After Ea, the wise, had created mankind,
Had imposed upon it the service of the gods –
That work was beyond comprehension;
As artfully planned by Marduk, did Nudimmud create it –
Marduk, the king of the gods divided
All the Anunnaki above and below.
He assigned them to Anu to guard his instructions.
Three hundred in the heavens he stationed as a guard.
In like manner the ways of the earth he defined.
In heaven and on earth six hundred thus he settled.
After he had ordered all the instructions,
To the Anunnaki of heaven and earth had allotted their portions,
The Anunnaki opened their mouths
And said to Marduk, their lord:
'Now, O lord, thou who has caused our deliverance,
What shall be our homage to thee?
Let us build a shrine whose name shall be called
'Lo, a chamber for our nightly rest';
Let us repose in it!
Let us build a throne, a recess for his abode!
On the day that we arrive we shall repose in it.'
When Marduk heard this,
Brightly glowed his features, like the day:
'Like that of lofty Babylon, whose building you have requested,
Let its brickwork be fashioned. You shall name it "The Sanctuary".'
The Anunnaki applied the implement;
For one whole year they moulded bricks.
When the second year arrived,
They raised high the head of Esagila equalling Apsu.
Having built a stage-tower as high as Apsu,
They set up in it an abode for Marduk, Enlil and Ea,
In their presence he adorned it in grandeur.
In the base of Esharra its horns look down.
After they had achieved the building of Esaglia,
The Anunnaki themselves erected their shrines.
[. . .] all of them gathered,
[. . .] they had built as his dwelling.
The gods, his fathers, at his banquet he seated:
'This is Babylon, the place that is your home!
Make merry in its precincts, occupy its broad [places].'
The great gods took their seats,
They set up festive drink, sat down to a banquet.
After they had made merry within it,
In Esagila, the splendid, had performed their rites,
The norms had been fixed [and] all [their] portents,
All the gods apportioned the stations of heaven and earth.
The fifty great gods took their seats.
The seven gods of destiny set up the three hundred [in heaven].
Enlil raised the bow, his weapon, and laid it before them.
The gods, his fathers, saw the net he had made.
When they beheld the bow, how skillful its shape,
His fathers praised the work he had wrought.
Raising it, Anu spoke up in the Assembly of the gods,
As he kissed the bow: 'This is my daughter!'
He named the names of the bow as follows:
'Longwood is the first, the second is [. . .];
Its third name is Bow-Star, in heaven I have made it shine.'
He fixed a place which the gods, its brothers [. . .]
After Anu had decreed the fate of the Bow,
And had placed the exalted royal throne before the gods,
Anu seated it in the Assembly of the gods.
When the great gods had assembled,
And had [. . .] the fate which Marduk had exalted,
They pronounced among themselves a curse,
Swearing by water and oil to place life in jeopardy.
When they had granted him the exercise of kingship of the gods,
They confirmed him in dominion over the gods of heaven and earth.
Anshar pronounced supreme his name Asaruluhi:
'Let us make humble obeisance at the mention of

his name;
When he speaks, the gods shall pay heed to him.
Let his utterance be supreme above and below!'

Most exalted be the Son, our avenger;
Let his sovereignty be surpassing, having no rival.
May he shepherd the black-headed ones, his creatures.
To the end of days, without forgetting, let them acclaim his ways.
May he establish for his fathers the great food-offerings;
Their support they shall furnish, shall tend their sanctuaries.
May he cause incense to be smelled, . . . their spells,
A likeness on earth of what he has wrought in heaven.
May he order the black-headed to revere him,
May the subjects ever bear in mind their god,
And may they at his word pay heed to the goddess.
May food-offerings be borne for their gods and goddesses.
Without fail let them support their gods!
Their lands let them improve, build their shrines,
Let the black-headed wait on their gods.
As for us, by however many names we pronounce, he is our god!
Let us then proclaim his fifty names . . .

Sacred Narrative 3

Creation according to Hesiod: Theogony

Here, the epic poet Hesiod (*c* 750 BCE) describes the generation of the cosmos from the void, the first gods and the castration of Sky (Uranus) by his son Cronus. Hesiod's narrative continues beyond this point to describe how Zeus escaped the attack of his father Cronus and the final victory of Zeus andthe Olympian gods over the Titans.

First of all, the Voice (Chaos) came into being, next broad-bosomed Earth, the solid and eternal home of all, and Eros (Desire), the most beautiful of the immortal gods, who in every man and every god softens the sinews and overpowers the prudent purpose of the mind. Out of Void came Darkness and black Night, and out of Night came Light and Day, her children conceived after union in love with Darkness. Earth first produced starry Sky, equal in size with herself, to cover he on all sides. Next she produced the tall mountains, the pleasant haunts of the gods, and also gave birth to the barren waters, sea with its raging surges – all this without the passion of love. Thereafter she lay with Sky and gave birth to ocean with its deep current. Coeus and Crius and Hyperion and Iapetus; Thea and Rhea and Themia (Law) and Mnemosyne (Memory); also golden-crowned Phoebe and lovely Tethys. After these came cunning Cronus, the youngest and boldest of her children; and he grew to hate the father who had begotten him.

Earth also gave birth to the violent Cyclopes – Thunderer, Lightner, and bold Flash – who made and gave to Zeus the thunder and the lightning bolt. They were like the gods in all respects except that a single eye stood in the middle of their foreheads, and their strength and power and skill were in their hands.

There were also born to Earth and Sky three more children, big, strong, and horrible, Cottus and Briareus and Gyges. This unruly brood had a hundred monstrous hands sprouting from their shoulders, and fifty heads on top of their shouders growing from their sturdy bodies. They had monstrous strength to match their huge size.

Of all the children born of Earth and Sky these were the boldest, and their father hated them from the beginning. As each of them was about to be born, Sky would not let them reach the light of day; instead he hid them all away in the bowels of Mother Earth. Sky took pleasure in doing this evil thing. In spite of her enormous size, Earth felt the strain within her and groaned. Finally she thought of an evil and cunning stratagem. She instantly produced a new metal, grey steel, and made a huge sickle. Then she laid the matter before her children; the anguish in her heart made her speak boldly: 'My children, you have a savage father; if you will listen to me, we may be able to take vengeance for this evil outrage: he was the one who started using violence.'

This was what she said: but all the children were gripped by fear, and not one of them spoke a word. Then great Cronus, the cunning trickster, took courage and answered his good mother with these words: 'Mother, I am willing to undertake and carry through your plan. I have no respect for our infamous father, since he was the one who started using violence.'

This was what he said, and enormous Earth was very pleased. She hid him in ambush and put in his hands the sickle with jagged teeth, and instructed him fully in her plot. Huge Sky came drawing night behind him and desiring to make love; he lay on top of Earth stretched all over her. Then from his ambush his son reached out with his left hand and with his right took the huge sickle with its long jagged teeth and quickly sheared the organs from his own father and threw them away. The drops of blood that spurted from them were all taken in by Mother Earth, and in the course of the revolving years she gave birth to the powerful Erinyes (Spirits of Vengeance) and the huge Giants with shining armour and long spears. As for the organs themselves, for a long time they drifted round the sea just as they were when Cronus cut them off with the steel edge and threw them from the land into the waves of the ocean; then white foam issued from the divine flesh, and in the foam a girl began to grow. First she came near to holy Cythera, then reached Cyprus, the land surrounded by sea. There she stepped out, a goddess, tender and beautiful, and round her slender feet the green grass shot up. She is called Aphrodite by gods and men because she grew in the froth, and also Cytherea, because she came near to Cythera, and the Cyprian, because she was born in watery Cyprus. Eros (Desire) and beautiful Passion were her attendants both at her birth and at her first going to join the family of the gods. The rights and privileges assigned to her from the beginning and recognized by men and gods are these: to preside over the whispers and smiles and tricks which girls employ, and the sweet delight and tenderness of love.

Great Father Sky called his children the Titans, because of his feud with them: he said that they blindly had tightened the noose and had done a savage thing for which they would have to pay in time to come.

Sacred Narrative 4

Creation according to the Popol Vuh

The *Popol Vuh* is the most important surviving text of the ancient Maya. It was copied down after the Spanish conquest of Mesoamerica in the 16th century. Here, in the first chapter of this lengthy narrative, only the sea and the expanse of heaven exist in tranquillity at the beginning of time.

Admirable is the account – so the narrative opens – admirable is the account of the time in which it came to pass that all was formed in heaven and earth, the quartering of their signs, their measure and alignment, and the establishment of parallels to the skies and upon the earth to the four quarters thereof, as was spoken by the Creator and Maker, the Mother, the Father of life and of all existence, that one by whom all move and breathe, father and sustainer of the peace of peoples, by whose wisdom was premeditated the excellence of all that doth exist in the heavens, upon the earth, in lake and sea.

Lo, all was in suspense, all was calm and silent; all was motionless, all was quiet, and wide was the immensity of the skies.

Lo, the first word and the first discourse. There was not yet a man, not an animal; there were no birds nor fish nor crayfish; there was no wood, no stone, no bog, no ravine, neither vegetation nor marsh; only the sky existed.

The face of the earth was not yet to be seen; only the peaceful sea and the expanse of the heavens.

Nothing was yet formed into a body; nothing was joined to another thing; naught held itself poised; there was not a rustle, not a sound beneath the sky. There was naught that stood upright; there were only the quiet waters of the sea, solitary within its bounds; for as yet naught existed.

There were only immobility and silence in the darkness and in the night. Alone was the Creator, the Maker, Tepeu, the Lord, and Gucumatz, the Plumed Serpent, those who engender, those who give being, alone upon the waters like a growing light.

They are enveloped in green and azure, whence is the name Gucumatz, and their being is great wisdom. Lo, how the sky existeth, how the Heart of the Sky existeth – for such as the name of God, as He doth name Himself!

It is then that the word came to Tepeu and to Gucumatz, in the shadows and in the night, and spake with Tepeu and with Gucumatz. And they spake and consulted and meditated, and they joined their words and their counsels.

Then light came while they consulted together; and at the moment of dawn man appeared while they planned concerning the production and increase of the groves and of the climbing vines, there in the shade and in the night, through that one who is the Heart of the Sky, whose name is Hurakan.

The Lightning is the first sign of Hurakan; the second is the Streak of Lightning; the third is the Thunderbolt which striketh; and these three are the Heart of the Sky.

Then they came to Tepeu, the Gucumatz, and held counsel touching civilized life; how seed should be formed, how light should be produced, how the sustainer and nourisher of all.

'Let it be thus done. Let the waters retire and cease to obstruct, to the end that earth exist here, that it harden itself and show its surface, to the end that it be sown, and that the light of day shine in the heavens and upon the earth; for we shall receive neither glory nor honour from all that we have created and formed until human beings exist, endowed with sentience.' Thus they spake while the earth was formed by them. It is thus, veritably, that creation took place, and the earth existed. 'Earth,' they said, and immediately it was formed.

Like a fog or a cloud was its formation into the material state, when, like great lobsters, the mountains appeared upon the waters, and in an instant there were great mountains. Only by marvellous power could have been achieved this their resolution when the mountains and the valleys instantly appeared, with groves of cypress and pine upon them.

Then was Gucumatz filled with joy. 'Thou art welcome, O Heart of the Sky, O Hurakan, O Streak of Lightning, O Thunderbolt!'

'This that we have created and shaped will have its end,' they replied.

Doctrine 1

Akhenaten's Great Hymn to the Aten: From the Tomb of Amarna

Perhaps the most interesting figure in ancient Egyptian history is the so-called 'renegade' Pharoah, Amun-Hotep IV (1370–1353 BCE) who changed his name to Akhenaten, 'The Spirit of Aten', totally reorganized the Egyptian cult around the sun-disc, Aten, and moved his capital from Thebes northward to Akhetaten, 'The Horizon of Aten' (the modern Amarna). This was a major revolution in the religious history of ancient Egypt, although it was not, as many have suggested, a complete monotheistic revolution. This lengthy hymn from one of his courtiers describes the Aten's life-giving powers in nature, Aten as creator of the universe, Aten as creating and sustaining all people, and as the true universal deity who protects foreign peoples as well. There are similarities of thought between this text and Psalm 104 of the Hebrew Bible (pages 68–9), but one should not construe these similarities as 'borrowings' or the result of some direct contact between the reform-minded Pharoah and the poets of the Psalms.

Adoration of Re-Harakhti-who-rejoices-in-lightland, In-his-name-Shu-who-is-Aten, living forever; the great living Aten who is in jubilee, the lord of all that the Disc encircles, lord of sky, lord of earth, lord of the house-of-Aten in Akhet-Aten; and of the King of Upper and Lower Egypt, who lives by Maat,[1] the Lord of the Two Lands, Neferkheprure, Sole-one-of-Re; the Son of Re who lives by Maat, the Lord of Crowns, Akhenaten, great in his lifetime; and his beloved great Queen, the Lady of the Two Lands, Nefer-nefru-Aten Nfertiti, who lives in health and youth forever. The Vizier, the Fanbearer on the right of the King, [Ay]; he says:

Spendid you rise in heaven's lightland,
O living Aten, creator of life!
When you have dawned in eastern lightland,
You fill every land with your beauty.
You are beauteous, great, radiant,
High over every land;
Your rays embrace the lands,
To the limit of all that you made.
Being Re, you reach their limits,
You bend them for the son whom you love;
Though you are far, your rays are on earth,
Though one sees you, your strides are unseen.

When you set in western lightland,
Earth is in darkness as if in death;
One sleeps in chambers, heads covered,
One eye does not see another.
Were they robbed of their goods,
That are under their heads,
People would not remark it.
Every lion comes from its den,
All the serpents bite;
Darkness hovers, earth is silent,
As their maker rests in lightland.

Earth brightens when you dawn in lightland,
When you shine as Aten of daytime;
As you dispel the dark,
As you cast your rays,
The Two Lands are in festivity.
Awake they stand on their feet,
You have roused them;
Bodies cleansed, clothed,
Their arms adore your appearance.
The entire land sets out to work,
All beasts browse on their herbs;
Trees, herbs and sprouting,
Birds fly from their nests,
Their wings greeting your *ka*.[2]
All flocks frisk on their feet,

[1] Justice or Rightness, which is understood as something which pervades the cosmos.
[2] *Ka*: vital force.

All that fly up and alight,
They live when you dawn for them.
Ships fare north, fare south as well,
Roads lie open when you rise;
The fish in the river dart before you,
Your rays are in the midst of the sea.

Who makes seed grow in women,
Who creates people from sperm;
Who feeds the son in his mother's womb,
Who soothes him to still his tears.
Nurse in the womb,
Giver of breath,
To nourish all that he made.
When he comes from the womb to breathe,
On the day of his birth,
You open wide his mouth,
You supply his needs.
When the chick in the eggs speaks in the shell,
You give him breath within to sustain him;
When you have made him complete,
To break out from the egg,
He comes out from the egg,
To announce his completion,
Walking on his legs he comes from it.

How many are your deeds,
Though hidden from sight,
O sole God beside whom there is none!
You made the earth as you wished, you alone,
All peoples, herds, and flocks;
All upon earth that walk on legs,
All on high that fly on wings,
The lands of Khor and Kush,
The land of Egypt.
You set every man in his place,
You supply their needs;
Everyone has his food,
His lifetime is counted.
Their tongues differ in speech,
Their characters likewise;
Their skins are distinct,
For you distinguished the peoples.

You made Hapy in *dat*,[3]
You bring him when you will,
To nourish the people,
For you made them for yourself.
Lord of all who toils for them,
Lord of all lands who shines for them,
Aten of daytime, great in glory!
All distant lands, you make them live,
You made a heavenly Hapy descend for them;
He makes waves on the mountains like the sea,
To drench their fields and their towns.
How excellent are your ways, O Lord of eternity!
A Hapy from heaven for foreign peoples,
And all lands' creatures that walk on legs,
For Egypt the Hapy who comes from *dat*.

Your rays nurse all fields,
When you shine they live, they grow for you;
You made the seasons to foster all that you made,
Winter to cool them, heat that they taste you.
You made the far sky to shine therein,
To behold all that you made;
You alone, shining in your form of living Aten,
Risen, radiant, distant, near,
You made millions of forms from yourself alone,
Towns, villages, fields, the river's course;
All eyes observe you upon them,
For you are the Aten of daytime on high. . . .
You are in my heart,
There is no other who knows you,
Only your son, Neferkheprure, Sole-one-of-Re,
Whom you have taught your ways and your might.
[Those on] earth come from your hand as you made them,
When you have dawned they live,
When you set they die;
You yourself are lifetime, one lives by you.
All eyes are on [your] beauty until you set,
All labour ceases when you rest in the west;
When you rise your stir [everyone] for the King,
Every leg is on the move since you founded the earth.
You rouse them for your son who came from your body,
The King who lives by Maat, the Lord of the Two Lands,
Neferkheprure, Sole-one-of Re,
The Son of Re who lives by Maat, the Lord of crowns,

[3] *Dat*: the Netherworld. Hapy is the inundating Nile which emerges from the Netherworld to nourish the Egyptians.

Akhenaten, great in his lifetime;
And the great Queen whom he loves, the
Lady of the Two Lands,
Nefer-nefru-Aten Nefertiti, living forever.

Doctrine 2

The Činvat Bridge: Mēnōk i Khrat

A fundamental idea in the Zoroastrian tradition as it developed in history is the judgment of the soul after death. On the fourth day after death the soul faces judgment on the Činvat Bridge, 'The Bridge of the Requiter', where Ahura Mazda weighs the soul's good and evil deeds. The good enter the kingdom of everlasting joy and light, while the evil are dragged into the regions of horror, punishment and darkness. However, the 'nethermost hell' to which the demon Vizarsh drags the evil soul is not eternal, for at the end of time all bodies will be resurrected and joined with their souls. This final, all-encompassing purgation will affect all souls, so that all may enter into paradise.

And when the soul of the saved passes over that bridge, the breadth of the bridge appears to be one parasang broad. And the soul of the saved passes on accompanied by the blessed Srōsh. And his own good deeds come to meet him in the form of a young girl, more beautiful and fair than any girl on earth. And the soul of the saved says, 'Who art thou, for I have never seen a young girl on earth more beautiful or fair than thee.' In answer the form of the young girl replies, 'I am no girl but thy own good deeds, O young man whose thoughts and words, deeds and religion were good: for when on earth thou didst see one who offered sacrifice to the demons, then didst thou sit (apart) and offer sacrifice to the gods. And when thou didst see a man do violence and rapine, afflict good men and treat them with contumely, and hoard up goods wrongfully obtained, then didst thou refrain from visiting creatures with violence and rapine of thine own; (nay rather,) thou wast considerate to good men, didst entertain them and offer them hospitality, and give alms both to the man who came from near and to him who came from afar; and thou didst amass thy wealth in righteousness. And when thou didst see one who passed a false judgment or took bribes or bore false witness, thou didst sit thee down and speak witness right and true. I am thy good thoughts, good words, and good deeds which thou didst think and say and do. . . .

But when the man who is damned dies, for three days and nights does his soul hover near his head and weeps, saying, 'Whither shall I go and in whom shall I now take refuge?' And during those three days and nights he sees with his eyes all the sins and wickedness that he committed on earth. On the fourth day the demon Vizarsh comes and binds the soul of the damned in most shameful wise, and despite the opposition of the blessed Srōsh drags it off to the Bridge of the Requiter. Then the righteous Rashn makes clear to the soul of the damned that it is damned (indeed).

Then the demon Vizarsh seizes upon the soul of the damned, smites it and ill-treats it without pity, urged on by Wrath. And the soul of the damned cries out with a loud voice, makes moan, and in supplication makes many a piteous plea; much does he struggle though his life-breath endures no more. When all his struggling and his lamentations have proved of no avail, no help is proffered him by any of the gods nor yet by any of the demons, but the demon Vizarsh drags him off against his will into nethermost Hell.

Doctrine 3

Timaeus on the Creator and Creation

Perhaps one of the most influential texts in the West is Plato's dialogue, *The Timaeus*. This text has informed much Jewish, Christian and Moslem reflection on God and the nature of the created world. Here, we print the beginning of Timaeus' discussion of how the creator fashioned the world.

TIMAEUS: Let me tell you then why the creator made this world of generation. He was good, and the good can never have any jealousy of anything. And being free from jealousy, he desired that all things should be as like himself as they could be. This is in the truest sense the origin of creation and of the world, as we shall do well in believing on the testimony of wise men. God desired that all things should be good and nothing bad, so far as this was attainable. Wherefore also finding the whole visible sphere not at rest, but moving in an irregular and disorderly fashion, out of disorder he brought order, considering that this was in every way better than the other. Now the deeds of the best could never be or have been other than the fairest, and the creator, reflecting on the things which are by nature visible, found that no unintelligent creature taken as a whole could ever be fairer than the intelligent taken as a whole, and again that intelligence could not be present in anything which was devoid of soul. For which reason, when he was framing the universe, he put intelligence in soul, and soul in body, that he might be the creator of a work which was by nature fairest and best. On this wise, using the language of probability, we may say that the world came into being – a living creature truly endowed with soul and intelligence by the providence of God.

This being supposed, let us proceed to the next stage. In the likeness of what animal did the creator make the world? It would be an unworthy thing to liken it to any nature which exists as a part only, for nothing can be beautiful which is like any imperfect thing. But let us suppose the world to be the very image of that whole of which all other animals both individually and in their tribes are portions. For the original of the universe contains in itself all intelligible beings, just as this world comprehends us and all other visible creatures. For the deity, intending to make this world like the fairest and most perfect of intelligible beings, framed one visible animal comprehending within itself all other animals of a kindred nature. Are we right in saying that there is one world, or that they are many and infinite? There must be one only if the created copy is to accord with the original. For that which includes all other intelligible creatures cannot have a second or companion; in that case there would be need of another living being which would include both, and of which they would be parts, and the likeness would be more truly said to resemble not them, but that other which included them. In order then that the world might be solitary, like the perfect animal, the creator made not two worlds or an infinite number of them, but there is and ever will be one only-begotten and created heaven.

Now that which is created is of necessity corporeal, and also visible and tangible. And nothing is visible where there is no fire, or tangible which has no solidity, and nothing is solid without earth. Wherefore also God in the beginning of creation made the body of the universe to consist of fire and earth. But two things cannot be rightly put together without a third; there must be some bond of union between them. And the fairest bond is that which makes the most complete fusion of itself and the things which it combines, and proportion is best adapted to effect such a union. For whenever in any three numbers, whether cube or square, there is a mean, which is to the last term what the first term is to it, and again, when the mean is to the first term as the last term is to the mean – then the mean becoming first and last, and the first and last both becoming means, they will all of them of necessity come to be the same, and having become the same with one another will be all one. If the universal frame had been created a surface only and having no depth, a single mean would have sufficed to bind together itself and the other terms, but now, as the world must be solid, and solid bodies are always compacted not by one mean but by two, God placed water and air in the mean between fire and earth, and made them to have the same proportion so far as was possible – as fire is to air so is air to water, and as air is to water so is water to earth – and thus he bound and put together a visible and tangible heaven. And for these reasons, and out of such elements which are in number four, the body of the world was created, and it was harmonized by proportion, and therefore has the spirit of friendship, and having been reconciled to itself, it was indissoluble by the hand of any other than the framer.

Now the creation took up the whole of each of the four elements, for the creator compounded the world out of all the fire and all the water and all the air and all the earth, leaving no part of any of them nor any power of them outside. His intention was, in the first place, that the animal should be as far as possible a perfect whole and of perfect parts, secondly, that it should be one, leaving no remnants out of which another such world might be created, and also that it should be free from old age and unaffected by disease. Considering that if heat and cold and other powerful forces surround composite bodies and attack them from without, they decompose them before their time, and by bringing diseases and old age upon them waste away – for this cause and on these grounds he made the world one whole, having every part entire, and being therefore perfect and not liable to old age and disease. And he gave to the world the figure which was suitable and also natural. Now to the animal which was to comprehend all animals, that figure would be suitable which comprehends within itself all other figures. Wherefore he made the world in the form of a globe, round as from a lathe, having its extremes in every direction equidistant from the centre, the most perfect and the most like itself of all figures, for he considered that the like is infinitely fairer than the unlike. This he finished off, making the surface smooth all around for many reasons – in the first place, because the living being had no need of eyes when there was nothing remaining outside him to be seen, nor of ears when there was nothing to be heard, and there was no surrounding atmosphere to be breathed, nor would there have been any use of organs by the help of which he might receive his food or get rid of what he had already digested, since there was nothing which went from him or came into him, for there was nothing besides him. Of design he was created thus – his own waste providing his own food, and all that he did or suffered taking place in and by himself. For the creator conceived that a being which was self-sufficient would be far more excellent than one which lacked anything, and, as he had no need to take anything or defend himself against anyone, the creator did not think it necessary to bestow upon him hands, nor had he any need of feet, nor of the whole apparatus of walking. But the movement suited to his spherical form was assigned to him, being of all the seven that which is most appropriate to mind and intelligence, and he was made to move in the same manner and on the same spot, within his own limits revolving in a circle. All the other six motions were taken away from him, and he was made not to partake of their deviations. And as this circular movement required no feet, the universe was created without legs and without feet.

Such was the whole plan of the eternal God about the god that was to be; he made it smooth and even, having a surface in every direction equidistant from the centre, a body entire and perfect, and formed out of perfect bodies. And in the centre he put the soul, which he diffused throughout the body, making it also to be the exterior environment of it, and he made the universe a circle moving in a circle, one and solitary, yet by reason of its excellence able to converse with itself, and needing no other friendship or acquaintance. Having these purposes in view he created the world a blessed god.

Doctrine 4

Quetzalcoatl Creates Man: The Manuscript of 1558

One of the most important Mayan and Aztec deities was Quetzalcoatl, the plumed serpent, who functions as a creator, king and priest, culture-hero, and founder of cities. Much of what is known about this figure is presented in the chronicles produced by Catholic priests and Spanish administrators in New Spain in the 16th century. This manuscript describes Quetzalcoatl's journey to Mictlan, the region of the dead, in order to search for the bones of man so that man might be recreated to inhabit the world. Miguel Leon-Portilla, one of the greatest interpreters of ancient Mesoamerican religions, indicates that narratives such as this reflect the philosophical speculation of the ancient Aztecs. Hence, Mictlantecuhtli's imposed conditions reflect a dialectic process within the divine concerning the creation of man.

And then Quetzalcoatl went to Mictlan. He approached Mictlantecuhtli and Mictlancihuatl [Lord and Lady of the region of the dead]; at once he spoke to them:

'I come in search of the precious bones in your possession. I have come for them.'

And Michtlantecuhtli asked of him, 'What shall you do with them, Quetzalcoatl?'

And once again Quetzalcoatl said, 'The gods are anxious that someone should inhabit the earth.'

And Mictlantecuhtli replied, 'Very well, sound my shell horn and go around my circular realm four times.'

But his shell horn had no holes. Quetzalcoatl therefore called the worms, who made the holes. And then the bees went inside the horn and it sounded.

Upon hearing it sound, Mictlantecuhtli said anew, 'Very well, take them.'

But Mictlantecuhtli said to those in his service, 'People of Mictlan! Gods, tell Quetzalcoatl that he must leave the bones.'

Quetzalcoatl replied, 'Indeed not; I shall take possession of them once and for all.'

And he said to his *nahualli* [double], 'Go and tell them that I shall leave them.'

And the *nahualli* said in a loud voice, 'I shall leave them.'

But then he went and took the precious bones. Next to the bones of man were the bones of woman; Quetzalcoatl took them . . .

And again Mictlantecuhtli said to those in his service, 'Gods, is Quetzalcoatl really carrying away the precious bones? Gods, go and make a pit.'

The pit having been made, Quetzalcoatl fell in it; he stumbled and was frightened by the quail. He fell dead and the precious bones were scattered. The quail chewed and gnawed on them.

Then Quetzalcoatl came back to life; he was grieved and he asked of his *nahualli*, 'What shall I do now?'

And the *nahualli* answered, 'Since things have turned out badly, let them turn out as they may.'

And he gathered them . . . and then he took them to Tamoanchan.

And as soon as he arrived, the woman called Quilaztli, who is Cihuacoatl, took them to grind and put them in a precious vessel of clay.

Upon them Quetzalcoatl bled his member. The other gods and Quetzalcoatl himself did penance.

And they said, 'People have been born, oh gods, the *macehuales* [those given life or "deserved" into life through penance].'

Because, for our sake, the gods did penance!

Ritual 1

Unas Comes to Re-Atum

The Pyramid Texts are carved into the walls of the royal chamber within the pyramids of Saqqara. This text is from the Pyramid of Unas, the last king of the Fifth Dynasty (*c*2450–2300 BCE), and describes King Unas' ascension into the heavens and his entrance into the company of the immortal gods. This text and hundreds like it were recited by the priests during the king's burial and the subsequent funerary rituals performed at the pyramid.

Re-Atum, this Unas comes to you,
A spirit indestructible
Who lays claim to the place of the four pillars!
Your son comes to you, this Unas comes to you,
May you cross the sky united in the dark,
May you rise in lightland, the place in which you shine!
Seth, Nephthys, go proclaim to Upper Egypt's gods
And their spirits:
'This Unas comes, a spirit destructible,
If he wishes you to die, you will die,
If he wishes you to live, you will live!'
Re-Atum, this Unas comes to you,
A spirit indestructible
Who lays claim to the place of the four pillars!
Your son comes to you, this Unas comes to you,
May you cross the sky united in the dark,
May you rise in lightland, the place in which you shine!
Osiris, Isis, go proclaim to Lower Egypt's gods
And their spirits:
'This Unas comes, a spirit indestructible,
Like the morning star above Hapy,
Whom the water-spirits worship;
Whom he wishes to live will live,
Whom he wishes to die will die!'

Re-Atum, this Unas comes to you,
A spirit indestructible
Who lays claim to the place of the four pillars!
Your son comes to you, this Unas comes to you,
May you cross the sky united in the dark,
May you rise in lightland, the place in which you shine!
Thoth, go proclaim to the gods of the west
And their spirits:
'This Unas comes, a spirit indestructible,
Decked above the neck as Anubis,
Lord of the western height,
He will count hearts, he will claim hearts,
Whom he wishes to live will live,
Whom he wishes to die will die!'

Re-Atum, this Unas comes to you,
A spirit indestructible
Who lays claim to the place of the four pillars!
Your son comes to you, this Unas comes to you,
May you cross the sky united in the dark,
May you rise in lightland, the place in which you shine!
Horus, go proclaim to the powers of the east
And their spirits:
'This Unas comes, a spirit indestructible,
Whom he wishes to live will live,
Whom he wishes to die will die!'

Re-Atum, your son comes to you,
Unas comes to you,
Raise him to you, hold him in your arms,
He is your son, of your body, forever!

Ritual 2

A Zoroastrian Sacrifice to the Sun: Khorshed Yasht

While Zoroaster himself introduced a number of new religious ideas to the ancient Persian religious tradition in his hymns, he also reformed the cultic life of Achaemenid Persia. He prohibited all sacrifices to Ahriman and the Daevas or hostile deities in the service of evil. This no doubt arose from his qualified monotheism. However, he did not abolish all animal sacrifices or the *haoma* ritual (the ancient Iranian parallel to the Vedic Soma sacrifice), but only their most extreme forms. He also retained the ancient fire sacrifice, which was later extended and systematized by the priestly Magi, and has persisted among the Parsees. Zoroaster's reform of the cult was not complete or total, and earlier deities often found their way into his new formulation. In this text taken from the *Yashts*, that section of the Avesta composed of hymns addressed to different deities, the pre-Zoroastrian god Mithra (the ancient Iranian parallel to the Vedic god Mitra), 'the Lord of Wide Pastures', is identified with the escorting entities of Ahura Mazda. Mithra was a true solar deity, specifically identified with the sun, and was to have a long history after the time of Alexander the Great. The cult of Mithra was particularly popular among the Roman legions: he gradually became identified with *Sol Invictus*, the Unconquered Sun, and with later Roman emperors.

We sacrifice unto the undying, shining, swift-horsed Sun.

When the light of the sun waxes warmer, when the brightness of the sun waxes warmer, then stand up the heavenly Yazatas, by hundreds and thousands,; they gather together its Glory, they make its Glory, they make its Glory pass down, they pour its Glory unto the earth made by Ahura, for the increase of the world of holiness, for the increase of the creatures of holiness, for the increase of the undying, shining, swift-horsed Sun.

And when the sun rises up, then the earth, made by Ahura, becomes clean; the running waters become clean, the waters of the wells become clean, the waters of the sea become clean, the standing waters become clean; all the holy creatures, the creatures of the Good Spirit, become clean.

Should not the sun rise up, then the Daevas would destroy all the things that are in the seven Karshvares, nor would the heavenly Yazatas find any way of withstanding or repelling them in the material world.

He who offers up a sacrifice unto the undying, shining, swift-horsed Sun – to withstand darkness, to withstand the Daevas born of darkness, to withstand the robbers and bandits, to withstand the Yâtus and Pairikas, to withstand death that creeps in unseen – offers it up to Ahura Mazda, offers it up to the Amesha-Spentas, offers it up to his own soul. He rejoices all the heavenly and worldly Yazatas, who offers up a sacrifice unto the undying, shining, swift-horsed Sun.

I will sacrifice unto Mithra, the lord of wide pastures, well struck down upon the skulls of the Daevas.

I will sacrifice unto that friendship, the best of all friendships, that reigns between the moon and the sun.

Ritual 3

Iamblichus on Prayer: On the Mysteries

Iamblichus (*c*250–325 CE) was one of the greatest Neoplatonist philosophers of the late 3rd century. His book *On the Mysteries* is a defence and explanation of late Hellenic ritual practices, in particular, theurgy or inducing the presence of the gods. Many scholars have suggested that Iamblichus' theurgy is the darker, superstitious side of Platonism as it developed in the late Roman Empire. Here, Iamblichus describes three different forms of prayer. Prayer is understood as an essential act which 'opens up to men the realm of the gods'.

Since prayers are by no means the last part of sacrifice, but instead contribute something that is essential to its completion and thus supply to the whole rite its power and its effect, [and] since, moreover, they serve to enhance the general reverence for God and create a sacred, indissoluble bond of fellowship with the gods, it seems not inappropriate to say a few words upon the subject. Moreover, it is a subject that is worth knowing about in and for itself; further, it completes our knowledge of the gods. I therefore affirm that the first kind of prayer is that which brings [God and man] together, since it brings about the association with the divine and gives us the knowledge thereof. The second establishes a bond of fellowship founded upon like-mindedness and calls down gifts sent by the gods, which arrive before we can ask for them and perfect our efforts even without our knowledge. The third and most perfect form finally seals the secret union, which hands over every decision privately to the gods and leaves our souls completely at rest in them.

In these three stages, which embrace all that is divine, prayers gain for us harmonious friendship of the gods and also a three-fold advantage from the gods: the first has to do with illumination, the second with fellowship in a common task, the third with the state of being filled with the [divine] fire. Sometimes this precedes the sacrifice; sometimes it interrupts the sacred rite; sometimes it comes as its conclusion.

No sacral act can be effective without the supplication of prayer. Steady continuance in prayer nourishes our mind, enlarges the soul for the reception of the gods, opens up to men the realm of the gods, accustoms us to the splendour of the divine light, and gradually perfects in us [our] union with the gods, until at last it leads us back to the supreme heights. Our mode of thinking is drawn gently aloft and implants in us the spirit of the gods; it awakens confidence, fellowship, and undying friendship [with them]; it increases the longing for God; it inflames in us whatever is divine within the soul; it banishes all opposition from the soul, and strips away from the radiant, light-formed spirit everything that leads to generation; it creates good hope and trust in the light. In brief, it gives to those who engage in it intercourse with the gods.

Ritual 4

A Sacrifice for Tezcatlipoca: Bernardino de Sahagún, General History of the Things of New Spain according to the Florentine Codex

Tezcatlipoca was the Aztec god who symbolized creation, ritual purity and death. Here, Bernardino de Sahagún records one of Tezcatlipoca's most important rituals, in which an individual was selected to represent the god for a period of one year. At the end of the year, the chosen individual was sacrificed at the feast of Toxcatl. This sacrifice may reflect the sacred narrative of Tezcatlipoca, in which he often appears as the opposite of Quetzalcoatl and the absolute master of nature.

In the month of Toxcatl, the great feast of Tezcatlipoca was held. At that time died his impersonator, who for one year had lived as Tezcatlipoca.

And at that time once more was offered to the people his new impersonator, who would again live for one year. . . .

For he who was chosen was of fair countenance, of good understanding and quick, of clean body – slender like a reed; long and thin like a stout cane; well-built; not of overfed body, nor corpulent, and neither very small nor exceedingly tall. . . .

He who was thus, without flaw, who had no bodily defects, . . . they then looked well that he be taught to blow the flute; that he might pipe and play his flute well; and that with it he hold his flowers and his smoking tube and blow and suck upon it, and smell the flowers.

And while yet he lived and was cared for in the house of the guardian, before he appear before the people, care was taken that he might be prudent in his discourse, that he might talk graciously, converse well, and greet people agreeably on the road, if he met anyone.

For he was much honoured when he appeared as the impersonator; because he was the likeness of [Tezcatlipoca]; he was acknowledged as our lord, treated like a lord; one begged favours, with sighs; before him the common people bowed in reverence and kissed the earth. . . .

And for one year he thus lived; at the feast of Toxcatl, he appeared before the people. And when the man died who had been impersonator for one year, he who had led the way, he who had cast the spear for one year, who had given commands for one year, forthwith was one chosen to be set in his place, from all whom the temple guardians had saved and cared for at the time. . . .

Thereupon he began his office; he went about playing his flute. By day and by night he followed whatever way he wished.

His eight young men went following him . . .

And four warriors, who instructed youths in the art of war . . .

Then Montezuma adorned the impersonator well and arrayed him in varied garb; . . . he adorned him in great pomp with all costly articles, which he caused to be placed upon him; for verily he took him to be his beloved god. His face was anointed with black; it was said: 'He fasteth with blackened face.' A thick layer of black was smeared on his cheeks. White feathers were placed upon his head – the soft down of eagles. They placed it on his hair, which fell to his loins.

And when he was attired, he went about with sweet-smelling flowers upon his head, a crown of flowers. And these same were hung over both shoulders, as far down as his armpits. This was called 'the flowery garment'.

And from both ears hung curved, gold, shell pendants. And they fitted his ears with ear plugs made of a mosaic of turquoise. And he wore a shell necklace. Moreover, his breast ornament was of white sea shells. . . .

Then they placed golden bracelets on both upper arms, and on both wrists they put carved bracelets with precious stones, covering almost all the forearm. And he put on his net cape like a fishnet of wide mesh with a fringe of brown cotton thread. And his costly breech clout reached to the calves of his legs.

And then they placed his bells on both legs, all golden bells, called *oioalli*. These, as he ran, went jingling and ringing. Thus they resounded. And he had princely sandals with ocelot skin ears. Thus was he arrayed who died after one year.

When the feast of Toxcatl was drawing near, when it was approaching him, when it was coming to him, first they married him to four women whom they sought out for him. . . .

And he left off, scattered in various places and abandoned the ornaments he had had, in which he had walked about fasting, painted black. His hair was shorn; he was given a tuft of hair tied upon his forehead, like that of a war captain. Thus they bound his hair, knotting it with brown cotton thread called *tochiacatl*; and they tied to his long hair his forked heron ornament with single quetzal feathers attached.

Only twenty days he lived, lying with and married to the women. Four women he lived with, who also were cared for, for one year, in the guardian's house. . . .

And still on the eve of the feast of Toxcatl, still five days from . . . the feast day of Toxcatl . . . they began to sing and dance.

Now, during this time, Montezuma came not forth; those who had been the impersonator's companions provided the people with food and favours. . . .

They sang and dance [for four days] . . .

After they had sung and danced, then he embarked in a canoe. The women went travelling with him; they went consoling him and keeping him merry. Then the canoe arrived; then it touched the shore; then it was beached . . .

For here he was abandoned, a little distance from Tlapitzauhcan. The women then returned and only they who had freely become his pages accompanied him while he yet lived.

So, it was said, when he arrived where he was to die, where a small temple stood, called Tlacochcalco, he ascended by himself, of his free will, to the place where he was to die. When he climbed the first step, he passed one step, he there broke, shattered, his flute, his whistle, etc.

And when he had mounted all the steps, when he had reached the summit, then the priests fell upon him; they threw him on his back upon the sacrificial stone. Then one cut open his breast, seized his heart, and raised it as an offering to the sun.

For in this manner were all these captives offered up. But his body they did not roll down; rather, they lowered it. Four men carried it.

And his severed head they strung on the skull-rack. Thus he ended in the adornment in which he died. Thus he there ended his life, there he terminated his life, when he went to die. . . .

Institutional Expression 1

The Kingship of Osiris and Horus: The Stela of Amenmose

This text contains the fullest Egyptian version of the Osiris narrative. Specific events in the Egyptian narrative, especially the slaying of Osiris by Seth, were not committed to writing, but were narrated by later Greek visitors to Egypt. Here, we read a long praise of Osiris, and how he is king of the gods while his son Horus is king of the earth. Horus' kingship is directly reflected in Egyptian institutions since every living Pharaoh is Horus. Hence, praise of Horus is also the praise of Pharaoh, son of Osiris. This narrative is taken from a limestone stela that dates to the Eighteenth Dynasty (*c*1550–1305 BCE).

Adoration of Osiris by the overseer of the cattle of [Amun], [Amen]mose, and the lady Nefertari. He says:

Hail to you, Osiris,
Lord of eternity, king of gods,
Of many names, of holy forms,
Of secret rites in temples!
Noble of *ka* he presides in Djedu,
He is rich in sustenance in Sekhem,
Lord of acclaim in Andjty,
Foremost in offerings in On.
Lord of remembrance in the Hall of Justice,
Secret *ba*[1] of the lord of the cavern,
Holy in White-Wall,
Ba of Re, his very body.
Who reposes in Hnes,
Who is worshipped in the *naret*-tree,
That grew up to bear his *ba*.
Lord of the palace in Khmun,
Much revered in Shashotep,
Eternal lord who presides in Abydos,
Who dwells distant in the graveyard
Whose name endures in peoples' mouth.

Oldest in the joined Two Lands,
Nourisher before the Nine Gods,
Potent spirit among spirits.
Nun has given him his waters,
Northwind journeys south to him,
Sky makes wind before his nose,
That his heart be satisfied.
Plants sprout by his wish,
Earth grows its food for him,
Sky and its stars obey him,
The great portals open for him.
Lord of acclaim in the southern sky,
The imperishable stars are under his rule,
The unwearying stars are his abode.
One offers to him by Geb's command,
The Nine Gods adore him,
Those in *dat* kiss the ground,
Those on high bow down.
The ancestors rejoice to see him,
Those yonder are in awe of him.
The joined Two lands adore him,
When His Majesty approaches,
Mightiest noble among nobles,
Firm of rank, of lasting rule.
Good leader of the Nine Gods,
Gracious, lovely to behold,
Awe inspiring to all lands,
That his name be foremost.
All make offering to him,
The lord of remembrance in heaven and earth,
Rich in acclaim at the *wag*-feast,
Hailed in unison by the Two Lands.
The foremost of his brothers,
The eldest of the Nine Gods,
Who set Maat throughout the Two Shores,
Placed the son on his father's seat.
Landed by his father Geb,
Beloved of his mother Nut,
Mighty when he fells the rebel,
Strong-armed when he slays his foe.
Who casts fear of him on his enemy,
Who vanquishes the evil-plotters,
Whose heart is firm when he crushes the rebels.

Geb's heir in the kingship of the Two Lands,
Seeing his worth he gave it to him,
To lead the lands to good fortune.
He placed this land into his hand,
Its water, its wind,
Its plants, all its cattle.
All that flies, all that alights,
Its reptiles and its desert game,
Were given to the son of Nut,
And the Two Lands are content with it.
Appearing on his father's throne,
Like Re when he rises in lightland,
He places light above the darkness,
He lights the shade with his plumes.
He floods the Two Lands like Aten at dawn,
His crown pierces the sky, mingles with the stars.
He is the leader of all the gods,
Effective in the word of command,
The great Ennead praises him,
The small Ennead loves him.

His sister was his guard,
She who drives off the foes,
Who stops the deeds of the disturber
By the power of her utterance.
The clever-tongued whose speech fails not,
Effective in the word of command,
Mighty Isis who protected her brother,
Who sought him without wearying.

[1] *Ba*: the soul, represented as a bird with a human head.

Who roamed the land lamenting,
Not resting till she found him,
Who made a shade with her plumage,
Created breath with her wings.
Who jubilated, joined her brother,
Raised the weary one's inertness,
Received the seed, bore the heir,
Raised the child in solitude
His abode unknown.
Who brought him when his arm was strong
Into the broad hail of Geb.

The Ennead was jubilant:
'Welcome, Son of Osiris,
Horus, firm-hearted, justified,
Son of Isis, heir of Osiris!'
The Council of Maat assembled for him
The Ennead, the All-lord himself,
The Lords of Maat, united in her,
Who eschew wrongdoing,
They were seated in the hall of Geb,
To give the office to its lord,
The kingship to its rightful owner.
Horus was found justified,
His father's rank was given him,
He came out crowned by Geb's command,
Received the rule of the two shores.

The crown placed firmly on his head,
He counts the land as his possession,
Sky, earth are under his command,
Mankind is entrusted to him,
Commoners, nobles, sunfolk.
Egypt and the far-off lands,
What Aten encircles is under his care,
Northwind, river, flood,
Tree of life, all plants.
Nepri gives all his herbs,
Field's Bounty brings satiety,
And gives it to all lands.
Everybody jubilates,
Hearts are glad, breasts rejoice,
Everyone exults,
All extol his goodness:
How pleasant is his love for us,
His kindness overwhelms the hearts,
Love of him is great in all.

They gave to Isis' son his foe,
His attack collapsed,
The disturber suffered hurt,
His fate overtook the offender.
The son of Isis who championed his father,
Holy and splendid is his name,
Majesty has taken its seat,
Abundance is established by his laws.
Roads are open, ways are free,
How the two shores prosper!
Evil is fled, crime is gone,
The land has peace under its lord.
Maat is established for her lord,
One turns the back on falsehood.
May you be content, Wennofer!
Isis' son has received the crown,
His father's rank was assigned him
In the hall of Geb.
Re spoke, Thoth wrote,
The council assented,
Your father Geb decreed for you,
One did according to his word.

An offering which the king gives to Osiris Khentameniu, lord of Abydos, that he may grant an offering of bread and beer, oxen and fowl, ointment and clothing and plants of all kinds, and the making of transformations: to be powerful as Hapy, to come forth as living *ba*, to see Aten at dawn, to come and go in Rostau, without one's *ba* being barred from the necropolis.

May he be supplied among the favoured ones before Wennofer, receiving the offerings that go up on the altar of the great god, breathing the sweet northwind, drinking from the river's pools: for the *ka* of the overseer of the cattle of [Amun], [Amen]mose, justified, born of the lady Henut, justified, and of his beloved wife, [the lady Nefertari, justified].

Institutional Expression 2

Gilgamesh Discovers the Responsibilities of a King

The Epic of Gilgamesh may date back to the first half of the 2nd millenium BCE, although the most extensive versions come from the beginning of the 1st millennium. The narrative follows the journey of Gilgamesh, King of Uruk, who sets out to find the plant of immortality, 'Man Becomes Young in Old Age', after the death of his friend Enkidu. Gilgamesh finds his way to Utnapishtim, who has become immortal after the great flood. We join the narrative as Utnapishtim describes how he built his boat to float on the waters of the flood. Gilgamesh goes on to find the plant, but loses it before he can gain immortality. Gilgamesh fails to achieve his stated goal, but learns that the chief responsibilities of a king are the maintenance of the city and proper order.

Utnapishtim said to him, to Gilgamesh:
'I will reveal to thee, Gilgamesh, a hidden matter
And a secret of the gods will I tell thee:
Shurippak – a city which thou knowest,
[And] which on Euphrates' [banks] is situate –
That city was ancient, as were the gods within it,
When their heart led the great gods to produce the flood.
There were Anu, their father,
Valiant Enlil, their counsellor,
Ninurta, their assistant,
Ennuge, their irrigator.
Ninigiku-Ea was also present with them;
Their words he repeats to the reed-hut:
'Reed-hut, reed-hut! Wall, wall!
Reed-hut, hearken! Wall, reflect!
Man of Shuruppak, son of Ubar-Tutu,
Tear down this house, build a ship!
Give up possessions, seek thou life.
Forswear [worldly] goods and keep the soul alive!
Aboard the ship take thou the seed of all living things.
The ship that thou shalt build,
Her dimensions shall be to measure.
Equal shall be her width and her length.
Like the Apsu thou shalt ceil her.'
I understood, and I said to Ea, my lord:
'[Behold], my lord, what thou hast thus ordered,
I will be honoured to carry out.
[But what] shall I answer the city, the people and elders?'
Ea opened his mouth to speak,
Saying to me, his servant:
'Thou shalt then thus speak unto them:
"I have learned that Enlil is hostile to me,
So that I cannot reside in your city,
Nor set my foot in Enlil's territory.
To the Deep I will therefore go down,
To dwell with my lord Ea.
[But upon] you he will shower down abundance,
[The choicest] birds, the rarest fishes.
[The land shall have its fill] of harvest riches.
[He who at dusk orders] the husk-greens,
Will shower down upon you a rain of wheat."'

With the first flow of dawn,
The land was gathered [about me].
. . . [too fragmentary for translation]
The little ones [carried] bitumen,
While the grown ones brought [all else] that was needful.
On the fifth day I laid her framework.
One whole acre was her floor space,
Ten dozen cubits the height of each of her walls,
Ten dozen cubits each edge of the square deck.
I laid out the contours and joined her together.
I provided her with six decks,
Dividing her thus into seven parts.
Her floor plan I divided into nine parts.
I hammered water-plugs into her.
I saw to the punting-poles and laid in supplies.
Six sar [measures] of bitumen I poured into the

furnace,
Three sar of asphalt [I also] poured inside.
Three sar of oil the basket-bearers carried,
Aside from the one sar of oil which the calking consumed,
And the two sar of oil [which] the boatman stowed away.
Bullocks I slaughtered for the [people],
And I killed sheep every day.
Must, red wine, oil, and white wine
[I gave] the workmen [to drink], as though river water,
That they might feast as on New Year's Day.
I [opened . . .] ointment, applying (it) to my hand.
[On the seventh day] the ship was completed.
[The launching] was very difficult,
So that they had to shift the floor planks above and below,
[Until] two-thirds of [the structure had] gone [into the water].
[Whatever I had] I laded upon her:
Whatever I had of silver I laded upon her;
Whatever I [had] of gold I laded upon her;
Whatever I had of all the living beings I [laded] upon her.
All my family and kin I made go aboard the ship.
The beasts of the field, the wild creatures of the field,
All the craftsmen I made go aboard.
Shamash had set for me a stated time:
'When he who orders unease at night,
Will shower down a rain of blight,
Board thou the ship and batten up the entrance!'
That stated time had arrived:
'He who orders unease at night, showers down a rain of blight.'
I watched the appearance of the weather.
The weather was awesome to behold.
I boarded the ship and battened up the entrance.
To batten down the [whole] ship, to Puzur-Amurri, the boatman,
I handed over the structure together with its contents.

With the first glow of dawn,
A black cloud rose up from the horizon.
Inside it Adad thunders,
While Shullat and Hanish go in front,
Moving as heralds over hill and plain.
Erragal tears out the posts;
Forth comes Ninurta and causes the dikes to follow.
The Anunnaki lift up the torches,
Setting the land ablaze with their glare.
Consternation over Adad reaches to the heavens,
Who turned to blackness all that had been light.
[The wide] land was shattered like [a pot]!
For one day the south-storm [blew],
Gathering speed as it blew, [submerging the mountains],
Overtaking the [people] like a battle.
No one can see his fellow,
Nor can the people be recognized from heaven.
The gods were frightened by the deluge,
And, shrinking back, they ascended to the heaven of Anu.
The gods cowered like dogs
Crouched against the outer wall.
Ishtar cried out like a woman in travail,
The sweet-voiced mistress of the [gods] moans aloud:
'The olden days are alas turned to clay,
Because I bespoke evil in the Assembly of the gods.
How could I bespeak evil in the Assembly of the gods,
Ordering battle for the destruction of my people,
When it is I myself who give birth to my people!
Like the spawn of the fishes they fill the sea!'
The Anunnaki gods weep with her,
The gods, all humbled, sit and weep,
Their lips drawn tight, [. . .] one and all.

Six days and six nights
Blows the flood wind, as the south-storm sweeps the land.
When the seventh day arrived,
The flood-carrying south-storm subsided in the battle,
Which it had fought like an army.
The sea grew quiet, the tempest was still, the flood ceased.
I looked at the weather: stillness had set in,
And all of mankind had returned to clay.
The landscape was as level as a flat roof.
I opened a hatch, and light fell upon my face.
Bowing low, I sat and wept,
Tears running down on my face.

I looked about for coast lines in the expanse of the sea:
In each of fourteen [regions]
There emerged a region [–mountain].
On Mount Nisir the ship came to a halt.
Mount Nisir held the ship fast,
Allowing no motion.
One day, a second day, Mount Nisir held the ship fast,
Allowing no motion.
A third day, a fourth day, Mount Nisir held the ship fast,
Allowing no motion.
A fifth, and a sixth day, Mount Nisir held the ship fast,
Allowing no motion.
When the seventh day arrived,
I sent forth and set free a dove.
The dove went forth, but came back;
Since no resting-place for it was visible, she turned round.
Then I sent forth and set free a swallow.
The swallow went forth, but came back;
Since no resting-place for it was visible, she turned round.
Then I sent forth and set free a raven.
The raven went forth and, seeing that the waters had diminished,
He eats, circles, caws, and turns not round.
Then I let out [all] to the four winds
And offered a sacrifice.
I poured out a libation on the top of the mountain.
Seven and seven cult-vessels I set up,
Upon their pot-stands I heaped cane, cedarwood and myrtle.
The gods smelled the savour,
The gods smelled the sweet savour,
The gods crowded like flies about the sacrificer.
When at length as the great goddess arrived,
She lifted up the great jewels which Anu had fashioned to her liking:
'Ye gods here, as surely as this lapis
Upon my neck I shall not forget,
I shall be mindful of these days, forgetting them never.
Let the gods come to the offering;
[But] let not Enlil come to the offering,
For he, unreasoning, brought on the deluge
And my people consigned to destruction.'
When at length as Enlil arrived,
And saw the ship, Enlil was wroth,
He was filled with wrath over the Igigi gods:
'Has some living soul escaped?
No man was to survive the destruction!'
Ninurta opened his mouth to speak,
Saying to valiant Enlil:
'Who, other than Ea, can devise plans?
It is Ea alone who knows every matter.'
Ea opened his mouth to speak,
Saying to valiant Enlil:
'Thou wisest of gods, thou hero,
How couldst thou, unreasoning, bring on the deluge?
On the sinner impose his sin,
On the transgressor impose his transgression!
[Yet] be lenient, lest he be cut off,
Be patient, lest he be dislodged!
Instead of thy bringing on the deluge,
Would that a lion had risen up to diminish mankind!
Instead of thy bringing on the deluge,
Would that a famine had risen up to [lay low] mankind!
Instead of thy bringing on the deluge,
Would that pestilence had risen up to [smite down] mankind!
It was not I who disclosed the secret of the great gods.
I let Atrahasis see a dream,
And he perceived the secret of the gods.
Now then taken counsel in regard to him!'
Thereupon Enlil went aboard the ship.
Holding me by the hand, he took me aboard.
He took my wife aboard and made her kneel by my side.
Standing between us, he touched our foreheads to bless us:
'Hitherto Utnapishtim has been but human.
Henceforth Utnapishtim and his wife shall be like unto us gods.
Utnapishtim shall reside far away, at the mouth of the rivers!'
Thus they took me and made me reside far away,
At the mouth of the rivers.
But now, who will for thy sake call the gods to Assembly
That the life which thou seekest thou mayest find?
Up, lie not down to sleep
For six days and seven nights.'

As he sits there on his haunches,
Sleep fans him like the whirlwind.
Utnapishtim says to her, to his spouse:
'Behold this hero who seeks life!
Sleep fans him like a mist.'
His spouse says to him, to Utnapishtim the Faraway:
'Touch him that the man may awake,
That he may return safe on the way whence he came,
That through the gate by which he left he may return to his land.'
Utnapishtim says to her, to his spouse:
'Since to deceive is human, he will seek to deceive thee.
Up, bake for him wafers, put [them] at his head,
And mark on the wall the days he sleeps.'
She baked for him wafers, put [them] at his head,
And marked on the wall the days he slept.
His first wafer is dried out,
The second is gone bad, the third is soggy;
The crust of the fourth has turned white;
The fifth has a mouldy cast,
The sixth [still] is fresh-coloured;
The seventh – just as he touched him the man awoke.

Gilgamesh says to him, to Utnapishtim the Faraway:
'Scarcely had sleep surged over me,
When straightway thou dost touch and rouse me!'
Utnapishtim [says to him], to Gilgamesh:
'[Go], Gilgamesh, count thy wafers,
[That the days thou hast slept] may become known to thee:
Thy [first] wafer is dried out,
[The second is gone] bad, the third is soggy;
The crust of the fourth has turned white;
[The fifth] has a mouldy cast,
The sixth (still) is fresh-coloured.
[The seventh] – at this instant thou has awakened.'
Gilgamesh says to him, to Utnapishtim the Faraway:
'[What then] shall I do, Utnapishtim,
Whither shall I go,
[Now] that the Bereaver has laid hold on my [members]?
In my bedchamber lurks death,
And wherever I [set my foot], there is death!'
Utnapishtim [says to him], to Urshanabi, the boatman:
'Urshanabi, may the landing-place [not rejoice in thee],
May the place of crossing renounce thee!
To him who wanders on its shore, deny thou its shore!
The man thou hast led [hither], whose body is covered with grime,
The grace of whose members skins have distorted,
Take him, Urshanabi, and bring him to the washing-place.
Let him wash off his grime in water clean as show,
Let him cast off his skins, let the sea carry them away,
That the fairness of his body may be seen.
Let him renew the band round his head,
Let him put on a cloak to clothe his nakedness,
That he may arrive in his city,
That he may achieve his journey.
Let not [his] cloak have a mouldy cast,
Let it be wholly new.'
Urshanabi took him and brought him to the washing-place.
He washed off his grime in water clean as snow.
He cast off his skins, the sea carried [them] away,
He renewed [the band] round his head,
He put on a cloak to clothe his nakedness,
That he might [arrive in his city],
That he might achieve his journey.
[The cloak had not a mouldy cast, but] was [wholly] new.
Gilgamesh and Urshanabi boarded the boat,
[They launched] the boat on the waves and they sailed away.

His spouse says to him, to Utnapishtim the Faraway:
'Gilgamesh has come hither, toiling and straining.
What wilt thou give him that he may return to his land?'
At that he, Gilgamesh, raised up his pole,
To bring the boat nigh to the shore.
Utnapishtim [says] to him, to Gilgamesh:
'Gilgamesh, thou hast come hither, toiling and straining.
What shall I give thee that thou mayest return to

thy land?
I will disclose, O Gilgamesh, a hidden thing,
And [a secret of the gods I will] tell thee:
This plant, like the buckthorn is [. . .]
Its thorns will [prick thy hands] just as does the rose.
If thy hands obtain the plant, [thou wilt find new life].'
No sooner had Gilgamesh heard this,
Than he opened the [water-pipe],
He tied heavy stones [to his feet].
They pulled him down into the deep [and he saw the plant].
He took the plant, though it [pricked his hands].
He cut the heavy stones [from his feet].
The sea cast him up upon its shore.

Gilgamesh says to him, to Urshanabi, the boatman:
'Urshanabi, this plant is a plant apart,
Whereby a man may regain his life's breath.
I will take it to ramparted Uruk,
Will cause [. . .] to eat the plant [. . .]!
Its name shall be "Man Becomes Young in Old Age".
I myself shall eat [it]
And thus return to the state of my youth.'
After twenty leagues they broke off a morsel,
After thirty [further] leagues they prepared for the night.
Gilgamesh saw a well whose water was cool.
He went down into it to bathe in the water.
A serpent snuffed the fragrance of the plant;
It came up [from the water] and carried off the plant.
Going back it shed its slough.

Thereupon Gilgamesh sits down and weeps,
His tears running down over his face.
[He took the hand] of Urshanabi, the boatman:
'[For] whom, Urshanabi, have my hands toiled?
For whom is being spent the blood of my heart?
I have not obtained a boon for myself.
For the earth-lion have I effected a boon!
And now the tide will bear it twenty leagues away!
When I opened the water-pipe and [. . .] the year,
I found that which has been placed as a sign for me:
I shall withdraw,
And leave the boat on the shore!'
After twenty leagues they broke off a morsel,
After thirty [further] leagues they prepared for the night.
When they arrived in ramparted Uruk,
Gilgamesh says to him, to Urshanabi, the boatman:
'Go up, Urshanabi, walk on the ramparts of Uruk.
Inspect the base terrace, examine its brickwork,
If its brickwork is not of burnt brick,
And if the Seven Wise Ones laid not its foundation!
One sar is city, one sar orchards,
One sar margin land; [further] the precinct of the Temple of Ishtar.
Three sar and the precinct comprise Uruk.'

Institutional Expression 3

Augustus and the New Age: Virgil, Ecologues

Virgil (70–19 BCE) wrote this so-called 'messianic' eclogue in 40 BCE and it presents the hope for a new age of peace in the wake of assassination of Julius Caesar. The eclogue seems to reflect the growing power of Augustus, who would not become Emperor until 27 BCE. No other figure of the time was understood to embody full the *pax Romana*, 'the eternal peace of Rome'. Virgil's descriptions of the young Augustus and the New Age have suggested to not a few scholars the language of the Hebrew Bible and its descriptions of messianic kings.

Now has come the last age of the prophetic song of Cumae. The great cycle of the centuries is born anew. The Virgin [Justice] returns, and the reign of Saturn comes again. Now a new generation is descending from heaven. And do thou, O chaste Lucina, smile graciously upon the birth of that boy by whom the iron race shall come to an end and the golden race rise up throughout the world; for now thine own Apollo is king.

In thy consulship, in thine, O Pollio, this glorious age shall begin, and the mighty months begin their march. Under thy rule whatever traces of our guilt remain shall vanish, and free the earth from its perpetual alarm. He shall live the life of the gods, he shall see gods mingling with [ancient?] heroes, he shall himself be seen by them, and shall rule the world to which his father's virtues have brought peace.

For thee, O child, the earth, untilled, shall first bring forth everywhere, as gifts for thy childhood, foxglove and wandering ivy tendrils, and marsh lilies mingled with smiling acanthus. Untended, the she-goats shall bring home their udders swollen with milk; no huge lions shall alarm the herds; unmasked, thy cradle shall break forth with caressing blossoms. The snake too shall die, and likewise the deceitful poison-plant shall die, and scented Assyrian spice shall grow wild.

As soon as thou art able to read the praises of the heroes and the deeds of thy father, and to know what virtue is, slowly the plain shall grow yellow with soft cornspike, the purpling grape shall hang from the wild briar, and tough oaks shall drip with sweet honey.

Even so, some traces of ancient sin shall still survive, to bid men venture upon the sea in ships, to gird towns with walls, and cleave the earth with furrows. Then a second Tiphys shall appear, and a second Argo shall carry chosen heroes. New wars shall arise, and another great Achilles shall be sent to Troy.

Later on, when the strengthening years have made thee a man, even the trader shall quit the sea, and ships of pine shall no longer exchange their merchandise. Every land shall bear every fruit; the soil shall no longer suffer the mattock, nor the vine the pruning hook. The sturdy ploughman shall now loose his oxen from the yoke. Wool shall not longer learn to counterfeit various hues, but the ram in the meadows shall himself dye his own fleece, now a softly glowing sea-purple, now a saffron yellow; a natural scarlet shall clothe the lambs in their pasture.

'O ages like these, run on,' cried the Fates to their spindles, voicing in harmony the steadfast decree of Destiny.

Enter upon thy high honours, dear offspring of the gods, the destined father of an early Jupiter, for the hour is close at hand! See how the world bows beneath her rounded dome, see the wide lands and the far-flung sea and the unfathomable depth of the sky! See how all things rejoice in the age to come!

Ah, may the last days of my long life still continue, and sufficient breath to tell thy deeds! Not Thracian Orpheus, nor Linus, shall surpass me in song, though one have his mother, the other his father to aid him – Orpheus Calliope, and Linus beautiful Apollo. Even if Pan were to contend with me, and all Arcady were to be the judge, even Pan would acknowledge himself defeated.

Begin, O baby boy, to recognize thy mother with a smile, thy mother to whom ten months have brought much weariness. Begin, O baby boy! For one who has never smiled on his parents is not honoured by a god at his table or by a goddess on her couch.

Institutional Expression 4

The City of the Gods: Bernardino de Sahagún, General History of the Things of New Spain

The name of the first Aztec metropolis, Teotihuacan, meant the 'City of the Gods'. Here, Bernardino de Sahagún describes why the city was called by this name. The individual's life reflected the life of Quetzalcoatl, and in the context of this city, the individual became a celestial being. This institutional expression of the sacred narratives of the Aztec relates Teotihuacan to other great cities in human religious experience. These cities are always understood as the centre of the world, the place where heaven and earth touch, and the place where the divine is most available to human beings.

The Lords therein buried, after their deaths were canonized as gods, and it was said that they did not die, but wakened out of a dream they had lived; this is the reason why the ancients say that when men died they did not perish but began to live again, waking almost out of a dream, and that they turned into spirits or gods and so they said to the dead: 'Lord or Lady, wake, for it begins to dawn, now comes the daylight for the yellow-feathered birds begin to sing, and the many-coloured butterflies go flying'; and when anyone died, they used to say of him that he was now *teotl*, meaning to say he had died in order to become spirit or god.'

Experience 1

The Prophecy of Neferti: A Manuscript from the Eighteenth Dynasty

In this text, the lector-priest Neferti is summoned to the court of King Snefru (Fourth Dynasty, *c* 2600–2450). He speaks of the future and prophesies that the nation will be destroyed by civil war. However, redemption from this turmoil will arise with a redeemer called 'Ameny'. It has been suggested that this is not a genuine prophetic text and experience, but a text written during the reign of Amenemhet I (Twelfth Dynasty, *c*1990–1950), designed to glorify the king.

His majesty said: 'Come, Neferti, my friend, speak to me some fine words, choice phrases at the hearing of which my majesty may be entertained!' Said the lector-priest Neferti: 'Of what has happened or of what will happen, O king, my lord?' Said his majesty: 'Of what will happen. As soon as today is here, it is passed over.' He stretched out his hand to a box of writing equipment, took scroll and palette and began to put into writing the words of the lector-priest Neferti, that wise man of the East, servant of Bastet in her East, and native of the nome of On.

As he deplored what had happened in the land, evoked the state of the East, with Asiatics roaming in their strength, frightening those about to harvest and seizing cattle from the plough, he said:

Stir, my heart,
Bewail this land, from which you have sprung!
When there is silence before evil,
And when what should be chided is feared,
Then the great man is overthrown in the land of your birth.
Tire not while this is before you,
Rise against what is before you!
Lo, the great no longer rule the land,
What was made has been unmade,
Re should begin to recreate!
The land is quite perished, no remnant is left,
Not the black of a nail is spared from its fate.
[Yet] while the land suffers, none care for it,
None speak, none shed tears: 'How fares this land!'
The sun disc, covered, shines not for people to see,
One cannot live when clouds conceal,
All are numb from lack of it.

I shall describe what is before me,
I do not foretell what does not come:
Dry is the river of Egypt,
One crosses the water on foot;
One seeks water for ships to sail on,
Its course having turned into shoreland.
Shoreland will turn into water,
Watercourse back into shoreland.
Southwind will combat northwind,
Sky will lack the single wind.

A strange bird will breed in the Delta marsh,
Having made its nest beside the people,
The people having let it approach by default.
Then perish those delightful things,
The fishponds full of fish-eaters,
Teeming with fish and fowl.
All happiness has vanished,
The land is bowed down in distress,
Owing to those feeders,
Asiatics who roam the land.
Foes have risen in the East,
Asiatics have come down to Egypt.
If the fortress is [crowded] . . .
Desert flocks will drink at the river of Egypt,
Take their ease on the shores for lack of one to fear;
For this land is to-and-fro, knowing not what comes,
What-will-be being hidden according as one says:
'When sight and hearing fail the mute leads.'
I show you the land in turmoil,
What should not be has come to pass.
Men will seize weapons of warfare,
The land will live in uproar.
Men will make arrows of copper,
Will crave blood for bread,
Will laugh aloud at distress.
None will weep over death,
None will wake fasting for death,
Each man's heart is for himself.
Mourning is not done today,
Hearts have quite abandoned it.
A man sits with his back turned,
While one slays another.
I show you the son as enemy, the brother as foe,
A man slaying his father.
Every mouth is full of 'how I wish'
All happiness has vanished;
The land is ruined, its fate decreed,
Deprived of produce, lacking in crops,
What was made has been unmade.
One seizes a man's goods, gives them to an outsider,
I show you the master in need, the outsider sated,
The lazy stuffs himself, the active is needy.
One gives only with hatred,
To silence the mouth that speaks;
To answer a speech the arm thrusts a stick,
One speaks by killing him.
Speech falls on the heart like fire,
One cannot endure the word of mouth.

The land is shrunk – its rulers are many,
It is bare – its taxes are great;
The grain is low – the measure is large,
It is measured to overflowing.
Re will withdraw from mankind:
Though he will rise at his hour,
One will not know when noon has come;
No one will discern his shadow,

No face will be dazzled by seeing [him],
No eyes will moisten with water.
He will be in the sky like the moon,
His nightly course unchanged,
His rays on the face as before.
I show you the land in turmoil:
The weak-armed is strong-armed,
One salutes him who saluted.
I show you the undermost uppermost,
What was turned on the back turns the belly.
Men will live in the graveyard,
The beggar will gain riches,
The great [will rob] to live.
The poor will eat bread,
The slaves will be exalted.
Gone from the earth is the nome of On,
The birthplace of every god.

Then a king will come from the South,
Ameny, the justified, by name,
Son of a woman of Ta-Seti, child of Upper Egypt.
He will take the white crown,
He will wear the red crown;
He will join the Two Mighty Ones,
He will please the Two Lords with what they wish,
With field-circler in his fist, oar in his grasp.
Rejoice, O people of this time,
The son of man will make his name for all eternity!
The evil-minded, the treason-plotters,
They suppress their speech in fear of him;
Asiatics will fall to his sword,
Libyans will fall to his flame,
Rebels to his wrath, traitors to his might,
As the serpent on his brow subdues the rebels for him.
One will build the Walls-of-the-Ruler,
To bar Asiatics from entering Egypt;
They shall beg water as supplicants,
So as to let their cattle drink.
Then Order will return to its seat,
While Chaos is driven away.
Rejoice he who may behold, he who may attend the king!
And he who is wise will libate for me,
When he sees fulfilled what I have spoken!

Experience 2

A Lamentation over the Destruction of Ur: A Sumerian Hymn

The destruction of an ancient Sumerian temple was one of the most disastrous experiences that could befall a city and its people. Here, a text from the second half of the 3rd millenium vividly describes that experience. The temple of Ur has been destroyed and the poet appeals to the goddess Ningal that with the destruction of the temple she has abandoned the city and its inhabitants.

O queen, how has your heart led you on, how can you stay alive!
O Ningal, how has your heart led you on, how can you stay alive!
O righteous woman whose city has been destroyed, how now can you exist!
O Ningal, whose land has perished, how has your heart led you on!
After your city had been destroyed, how now can you exist!
After your house had been destroyed, how has your heart led you on!
Your city has become a strange city; how now can you exist!
Your house has become a house of tears, how has your heart led you on!
Your city which has been made into ruins – you are no longer its mistress,

Your righteous house which has been given over to the pickaxe – you no longer inhabit it,
Your people who have been led to slaughter – you are no longer their queen,
Your tears have become strange tears, your land weeps not,
Without 'tears of supplication' it inhabits foreign lands,
Your land like one who has multiplied . . . shuts tight its mouth.
Your city has been made into ruins; how can you exist!
Your house has been laid bare; how has your heart led you on!
Ur, the shrine, has been given over to the wind; how now can you exist!
Its *guda*-priest no longer walks in well-being; how has your heart led you on!
Its *en* dwells not in the *gipar*; how now can you exist!
Its . . . who cherishes lustrations makes no lustrations for you,
Father Nanna, your *ishib*- priest has not perfected the holy vessels for you,
Your *mah* in the holy *giguna* dressed not in linen,
Your righteous *en* chosen . . . in the Ekishnugal,
Proceeds not joyfully from the shrine to the *gipar*,
In the *ahu*, your house of feasts, they celebrated not the feasts;
On the *ub* and *ala* they played not for you that which brings joy to the heart, the *tigi*-music.
The black-headed people do not bathe themselves for your feast,
Like flax dirt has been decreed for them; their appearance has changed.
Your song has been turned into weeping, . . .
Your *tigi*-music has been turned into lamentation . . .

Your ox has not been brought into its stable, its fat is not prepared for you,
Your sheep stays not in its fold, its milk is not presented to you,
Who used to bring your fat, no longer brings it to you from the stall, . . .
Who used to bring your milk no longer brings it to you from the sheepfold, . . .
The fisherman who used to bring you fish is overtaken by misfortune,
The bird hunters who used to bring you birds were carried off
by the . . ., you can now barely exist,
Your river which had been made fit for the *magur*-boats – in its midst the . . . plant grows,
On your road which had been prepared for the chariots, the mountain thorn grows.
O my queen, your city weeps before you as its mother;
Ur, like the child of a street which has been destroyed, searches for you,
The house, like man who has lost everything, stretches out the hands to you,
Your brickwork of the righteous house, like a human being, cries your 'Where, pray?'

O my queen, you have departed from the house; you have departed from the city.
How long, pray, will you stand aside in the city like an enemy?
O Mother Ningal, [how long] will you hurl challenges in the city like an enemy?
Although you are a queen beloved of her city, your city . . . you have abandoned;
[Although] you are a queen beloved of her people, your people . . . you have abandoned.
O Mother Ningal, like an ox to your stable, like a sheep to your fold!
Like an ox to your stable of former days, like a sheep to your fold!
Like a young child to your chamber, O maid, to your house!
May An, the king of the gods, utter your ''tis enough.'
May Enlil, the king of all the lands, decree your (favourable) fate.
May he return the city to its place for you; exercise its queenship!
May he return Ur to its place for you; exercise its queenship!

Experience 3

The Manifestation of Isis: Apuleius, Metamorphoses

Alexander the Great envisioned a new political order, but his early death put an untimely end to his efforts to create a synthesis of east and west. Nevertheless, in the centuries that followed there was increasing cultural synthesis and interpenetration, and the native religious traditions of Egypt and Mesopotamia soon found their way to Greece and Rome. Apuleius, who lived in the 2nd century CE, was a distinguished lawyer, orator and novelist. His most popular work, the *Metamorphoses*, describes how the overly curious Lucius was transformed into an ass by a magician. The climax of the novel is Lucius' restoration to human shape. This is accomplished through the intervention of the Egyptian goddess Isis, and Apuleius' description of her manifestation indicates his thorough familiarity with the Isis mysteries. Lucius has fallen asleep on the sand of the seashore when he is shaken from his sleep; he knows that this is the hour of the goddess's greatest power.

So I poured out my prayers and supplications, adding to them much pitiful wailing, and once more fell sound asleep on that same bed of sand. Scarcely had I closed my eyes when lo! from the midst of the deep there arose that face divine to which even the gods must do reverence. Then a little at a time, slowly, her whole shining body emerged from the sea and came into full view. I would like to tell you all the wonder of this vision, if the poverty of human speech does not prevent, or if the divine power dwelling within that form supplies a rich enough store of eloquence.

First, the tresses of her hair were long and thick, and streamed down softly, flowing and curling about her divine neck. On her head she wore as a crown many garlands of flowers, and in the middle of her forehead shone white and glowing a round disc like a mirror, or rather like the moon; on its right and left it was bound about with the furrowed coils of rising vipers, and about it were stalks of grain. Her tunic was of many colours, woven of the finest linen, now gleaming with snowy whiteness, now yellow like the crocus, now rosy-red like a flame. But what dazzled my eyes more than anything else was her cloak, for it was a deep black, glistening with sable sheen; it was cast about her, passing under her right arm and brought together on her left shoulder. Part of it hung down like a shield and drooped in many a fold, the whole reaching to the lower edge of her garment with tasselled fringe. Here and there along its embroidered border, and also on its surface, were scattered sequins of sparkling stars, and in their midst the full moon of midmonth shone forth like a flame of fire. And all along the border of that gorgeous robe there was an unbroken garland of all kinds of flowers and fruits.

In her hands she held emblems of various kinds. In her right hand she carried a bronze rattle [the sistrum] made of a thin piece of metal curved like a belt, through which were passed a few small rods; this gave out a tinkling sound whenever she shook it three times with a quivering pulsation. In her left hand was a golden cup, from the top of whose slender handle rose an asp, towering with head erect and its throat distended on both sides. Her perfumed feet were shod with sandals woven of the palm of victory.

Such was the vision, and of such majesty. Then, breathing forth all the blessed fragrance of happy Arabia, she deigned to address me with voice divine: 'Behold, Lucius, I have come, moved by thy prayers! I, nature's mother, mistress of all the elements, earliest offspring of the ages, mightiest of the divine powers, Queen of the dead, chief of them that dwell in the heavens, in whose features are combined those of all the gods and goddesses. By my nod I rule the shining heights of heaven, the wholesome winds of the sea, and the mournful silences of the underworld. The whole world honours my sole deity [*numen unicum*] under various forms, with varied rites, and by many names. There the Phrygians, firstborn of men, call me the Mother of the Gods, she who dwells at Pessinus; there the Athenians, sprung from their own soil, know me as Cecropian Minerva; there the sea-girt Cyprians call me Paphian Venus; the Cretans, who are archers, call me Diana Dictynna [of the hunter's net]; the Sicilians, with their three languages, call me Stygian Proserpina; the Eleusinians, the ancient goddess Ceres. Others call me Juno, others Bellona, others Hecate, while still others call me the Rhamnusian. But those on whom shine the first rays of the Sun-God as daily he springs to new birth, the Arii and the Ethiopians, and the Egyptians mighty in ancient lore, honouring me with my peculiar rites, call me by my true name, Isis the Queen.

'I have come in pity for thy woes. I have come, propitious and ready to aid. Cease from thy weeping and lamentation, and lay aside thy grief! For thee, by my providence, the day of salvation is dawning! Therefore turn thy afflicted spirit, and give heed to what I command. The day, even the very day that follows this night, is dedicated to me by an everlasting dedication; for on this day, after I have laid to rest the storms of winter and stilled the tempestuous waves of the sea, my priests shall dedicate to the deep, which is now navigable once more, a new boat, and offer it in my honour as the first fruits of the year's seafaring. Thou must await this festival with untroubled heart and with no profane thoughts.'

Experience 4

'Now You Are Born Again': Bernardino de Sahagún, General History of the Things of New Spain

Perhaps the most appealing aspects of ancient Aztec religion for the Christian Fathers were rituals of water immersion and confession of transgression, which were immediately translated by the Fathers into 'natural' Christian sacraments. This was an *interpetatio Christiani*, but in this 'oral confession' recorded by Sahagún we see the experiential aspects of removing transgression and becoming the precious stone made by Quetzalcoatl.

The confessor speaks to the penitent saying: 'Oh brother, thou hast come to a place of great danger, and of much work and terror . . . thou hast come to a place where snares and nets are tangled and piled one upon another, so that none can pass without falling into them . . . these are thy sins, which are not only snares and nets and holes into which thou hast fallen, but also wild beasts, that kill and rend the body and the soul. . . . When thou wast created and sent there, thy father and mother Quetzalcoatl made thee like a precious stone . . . but by thine own will and choosing thou didst become soiled . . . and now thou hast confessed . . . thou hast uncovered and made manifest all thy sins to our lord who shelters and purifies all sinners; and take not this as mockery, for in truth thou hast entered the fountain of mercy, which is like the clearest water with which our lord god, who shelters and protects us all, washes away the dirt from the soul . . . now thou art born anew, now dost thou begin to live; and even now our lord god gives thee light and a new Sun; now also dost thou begin to flower, and to put forth shoots like a very clean precious stone issuing from thy mother's womb where thou art created . . . It is fitting that thou do penance working a year or more in the house of god, and there shalt thou draw blood, and shalt pierce thy body with cactus thorns; and that thou make penance for the adulteries and other filth thou hast done, thou shalt pass osiers twice a day, one through thine ears and one through thy tongue; and not only as penance for the carnal sins already mentioned, but also for words and injuries with which thou hast affronted and hurt thy neighbours, with thy evil tongue. And for the ingratitude in which thou hast held the favours our lord hast done thee, and for thy inhumanity to thy neighbours in not making offering of the goods bestowed upon thee by god nor in giving to the poor the temporal goods our lord bestowed upon thee. It shall be thy duty to offer parchment and copal, and also to give alms to the needy who starve and who have neither to eat nor drink nor to be clad, though thou know how to deprive thyself of food to give them, and do thy best to clothe those who go naked and in rags; look that their flesh is as thine, and that they are men as thou art.'

Ethics 1

A Negative Confession of the Dead: The Egyptian Book of the Dead

The *Book of the Dead* is the title now given to a great many funerary texts spanning the entire history of ancient Egypt and including hymns, prayers, litanies and incantations found in tombs on sarcophagi and rolls of papyrus. Perhaps the most famous papyrus text is the Papyrus of Ani, written for the nobleman Ani and his wife. The following selection is a negative confession to be recited before Osiris in the court of the Gods.

[The following] words shall be said by the Steward of the Keeper of the Seal, Nu, whose word is truth, when he cometh forth to the Hall of Maati, so that he may be separated from every sin which he hath committed, and may behold the faces of the Gods. The Osiris Nu, whose word is truth, saith: Homage to thee, O Great God, Lord of Maati! I have come unto thee, O my Lord, and I have brought myself hither that I may behold thy beauties. I know thee, I know thy name, I know the names of the Forty-two Gods who live with three in this Hall of Maati, who live by keeping ward over sinners, and who feed upon their blood on the day when the consciences of men are reckoned up in the presence of the god Un-Nefer. In truth thy name is 'Rehti-Merti-Nebti-Maati'. In truth I have come unto thee, I have brought Maati [Truth] to thee. I have done away sin for thee. I have not committed sins against men. I have not opposed my family and kinsfolk. I have not acted fraudulently [or, deceitfully] in the Seat of Truth. I have not known men who were of no account. I have not wrought evil. I have not made it to be the first [consideration daily that unnecessary] work should be done for me. I have not brought forward my name for dignities. I have not [attempted] to direct servants [I have not belittled God]. I have not defrauded the humble man of his property. I have not done what the gods abominate. I have not vilified a slave to his master. I have not inflicted pain. I have not caused anyone to go hungry. I have not made any man weep. I have not committed murder. I have not given the order for murder to be committed. I have not caused calamities to befall men and women. I have not plundered the offerings in the temples. I have not defrauded the gods of their cake-offerings. I have not carried off the *fenkhu* cakes [offered to] the Spirits. I have not committed fornication [or, had intercourse with men]. I have not masturbated [in the sanctuaries of the god of my city]. I have not diminished from the bushel. I have not filched [land from my neighbour's estate and] added it to my own acre. I have not encroached upon the fields [of others]. I have not added to the weights of the scales. I have not depressed the pointer of the balance. I have not carried away the milk from the mouths of children. I have not driven the cattle away from their pastures. I have not snared the geese in the goose-pens of the gods. I have not caught fish with bait made of the bodies of the same kind of fish. I have not stopped water when it should flow. I have not made a cutting in a canal of running water. I have not extinguished a fire [or, lamp] when it should burn. I have not violated the times [of offering] the chosen meat offerings. I have not driven away the cattle on the estates of the gods. I have not turned back the god [or, God] at his appearances. I am pure. I am pure. I am pure. I am pure. My pure offerings are the pure offerings of that great Benu [phoenix?] which dwelleth in Hensu. For behold, I am the nose of Neb-nefu [i.e. the lord of the air], who giveth sustenance unto all mankind, on the day of the filling of the Utchat in Anu, in the second month of the season Pert, on the last day of the month, [in the presence of the Lord of this earth]. I have seen the filling of the Utchat in Anu, therefore let not calamity befall me in this land, or in this Hall of Maati, because I know the names of the gods who are therein, [and who are the followers of the Great God].

Ethics 2

The Law Code of Hammurabi

Hammurabi was the sixth king of the old Babylonian Dynasty and ruled for approximately 43 years (*c*1728–1686). His code of law is one of the most comprehensive legal codes from the 2nd millennium, and many of the specific laws have parallels in the Books of Exodus, Leviticus, Numbers and Deuteronomy from the Hebrew Bible. This law code formed the centre of ethical life for the ancient Babylonian and was understood as something more than a 'human' code. It is written on a diorite stela now in the Louvre in Paris, and is topped by a relief showing Hammarubi receiving his commission to write the laws from the god of justice, the Sun-god Shamash. Hence, the laws embodied in Hammarubi's code have a divine origin and are not merely 'secular' laws.

1. If a seignior accused (another) seignior and brought a charge of murder against him, but has not proved it, his accuser shall be put to death.

2. If a seignior brought a charge of sorcery against (another) seignior, but has not proved it, the one against whom the charge of sorcery was brought, upon going to the river, shall throw himself into the river, and if the river has then overpowered him, his accuser shall take over his estate; if the river has shown that seignior to be innocent and he has accordingly come forth safe, the one who brought the charge of sorcery against him shall be put to death, while the one who threw himself into the river shall take over the estate of his accuser.

3. If a seignior came forward with false testimony in a case, and has not proved the word which he spoke, if that case was a case involving life, that seignior shall be put to death.

4. If he came forward with (false) testimony concerning grain or money, he shall bear the penalty of that case.

5. If a judge gave a judgment, rendered a decision, deposited a sealed document, but later has altered his judgment, they shall prove that that judge altered the judgment which he gave and he

shall pay twelvefold the claim which holds in that case; furthermore, they shall expel him in the assembly from his seat of judgment and he shall never again sit with the judges in a case.

6. If a seignior stole the property of church or state, that seignior shall be put to death; also the one who received the stolen goods from his hand shall be put to death.

7. If a seignior has purchased or has received for safekeeping either silver or gold or a male slave or a female slave or an ox or a sheep or an ass or any sort of thing from the hand of a seignior's son or a seignior's slave without witnesses and contracts, since that seignior is a thief, he shall be put to death.

8. If a seignior stole either an ox or a sheep or an ass or a pig or a boat, if it belonged to the church (or) if it belonged to the state, he shall make thirtyfold restitution; if it belonged to a private citizen, he shall make good tenfold. If the thief does not have sufficient to make restitution, he shall be put to death.

9. When a seignior, (some of) whose property was lost, has found his lost property in the possession of (another) seignior, if the seignior in whose possession the lost (property) was found has declared, 'A seller sold (it) to me; I made the purchase in the presence of witnesses,' and the owner of the lost [property] in turn has declared, 'I will produce witnesses attesting to my lost (property)'; the purchaser having then produced the seller who made the sale to him and the witnesses in whose presence he made the purchase, and the owner of the lost (property) having also produced the witnesses attesting to his lost (property), the judges shall consider their evidence, and the witnesses in whose presence the purchase was made, along with the witnesses attesting to the lost (property), shall declare what they know in the presence of god, and since the seller was the thief, he shall be put to death, while the owner of the lost (property) shall take his lost (property), with the purchaser obtaining from the estate of the seller the money that he paid out.

10. If the (professed) purchaser has not produced the seller who made the sale to him and the witnesses in whose presence he made the purchase, but the owner of the lost property has produced witnesses attesting to his lost property, since the (professed) purchaser was the thief, he shall be put to death, while the owner of the lost property shall take his lost property.

Ethics 3

Plotinus on Virtue: The Enneads

Plotinus (205–270 CE) was perhaps the greatest of all Neoplatonist philosophers and his *Enneads* have often been described as a mystical apprehension of god. Here, Plotinus argues that virtue allows us to escape the evils of this world by becoming godlike. But which god do we become like through virtue? The virtues he discusses here are not civic or moral virtues, but higher virtues. It is the 'purifying virtues' which affect the higher soul and allow us to become like the gods.

Since it is here that evils are, and 'they must necessarily haunt this region', and the soul wants to escape from evils, we must escape from here. What, then, is this escape? 'Being made like god,' Plato says. And we become godlike, 'if we become righteous and holy with the help of wisdom,' and are altogether in virtue. If then it is virtue which makes us like, it presumably makes us like a being possessing virtue. Then what god would that be? Would it be the one that appears to be particularly characterized by the possession of virtue, that is, the soul of the universe and its ruling principle, in which there is a wonderful wisdom? It is reasonable to suppose that we should become like this principle, as we are here in its universe.

But, first of all, it is debatable whether this principle has all the virtues; whether, for instance, it is self-controlled and brave when it has nothing to frighten it, for there is nothing outside the universe, and nothing attractive can come to it which it has not already got, and produced a desire to have or get it. But if this principle is in a state of aspiration towards the intelligible realities to which our aspirations too are directed, it is clear that our good order and our virtues also come from the intelligible. Has the intelligible, then, virtues? It is at any rate improbable that it has the virtues called 'civic', practical wisdom which has to do with discursive reason, courage which has to do with the emotions, balanced control which consists in a sort of agreement and harmony of passion and reason, justice which makes each of these parts agree in 'minding their own business where ruling and being ruled are concerned'. Then are we not made godlike by the civic virtues, but by the greater virtues which have the same names? But if by the others, are the civic virtues no help at all to this likeness? It is unreasonable to suppose that we are not made godlike in any way by the civic virtues but that likeness comes by the greater ones – tradition certainly calls men of civic virtues godlike and we must say that somehow or other they were made like by this kind of virtue. It is possible to have virtues on both levels, even if not the same kind of virtues. If then it is agreed that we can be made like even if that to which we are likened has not the same kind of virtue as ourselves, and we are differently related to different virtues, there is nothing to prevent us, even if we are not made like in regard to virtues, being made like by our virtues to that which does not possess virtue. How? In this way: if something is made hot by the presence of heat, must that from, which the heat comes also be heated? And if something is made hot by the presence of fire, must the fire itself be heated by the presence of fire? One might object in answer to the first argument that there is heat in fire, but as part of its nature, so that the argument, if it kept to its analogy, would make virtue something extraneous to the soul but part of the nature of that from which the soul receives it by imitation: and in answer to the argument from fire that it would make that principle virtue; but we consider it greater than virtue. But if that in which the soul participates was the same as the source from which it comes, it would be right to speak in this way; but in fact the two are distinct. The perceptible house is not the same thing as the intelligible house, though it is made in its likeness; the perceptible house participates in arrangement and order, but There, in its formative principle, there is no arrangement or order or proportion. So then, if we participate in order and arrangement and harmony which come from There, and these constitute virtue here, and if the principles There have no need of harmony or order or arrangement, they will have no need of virtue either, and we shall all the same be made like them by the presence of virtue. This is enough to show that it is not necessary for virtue to exist There because we are made like the principles There by virtue. But we must make our argument persuasive, and not be content to force agreement.

First then we must consider the virtues by which we assert that we are made like, in order that we discover this one and the same reality which when we possess it as an imitation is virtue, but There, where it exists as an archetype, is not virtue. We should note that there are two kinds of likeness; one requires that there should be something the same in the things which are alike; this applies to things which derive their likeness equally from the same principle. But in the case of two things of which one is like the other, but the other is primary not reciprocally related to the thing in its likeness and not said to be like it, likeness must be understood in a different sense; we must not require the same form in both, but rather a different one, since likeness has come about in this different way.

What then is virtue, in general and in particular? Our account of it will be clearer if we deal separately with the particular kinds; in this way that which they have in common, by which they are all virtues, will easily become clear. The civic virtues, which we mentioned above, do genuinely set us in order and make us better by giving limit and measure to our desires, and putting measure into all our experience; and they abolish false opinions, by what is altogether better and by the fact of limitation, and by the exclusion of the unlimited and indefinite and the existence of the measured; and they are themselves limited and clearly defined. And so far as they are a measure which forms the matter of the soul, they are made like the measure There and have a trace in them of the Best There. That which is altogether unmeasured is matter, and so altogether unlike: but in so far as it participates in form it becomes like that Good, which is formless. Things which are near participate more. Soul is nearer and more akin to it than body; so it participates more, to the point of deceiving us into imagining that it is a god, and that all divinity is comprised in this likeness. This is how those possessed of political virtue are made like.

But, since Plato indicates that likeness is different as belonging to the greater virtue, we must speak about that different likeness. In this discussion the real nature of civic virtue will become clear, and we shall also understand what is the virtue which is greater than it in its real nature, and in general that there is another kind different from civic virtue. Plato, when he speaks of 'likeness' as a 'flight to God' from existence here below, and does not call the virtues which come into play in civic life just 'virtues' but adds the qualification 'civic', and elsewhere calls all the virtues 'purifications', makes clear that he postulates two kinds of virtues and does not regard the civic ones as producing likeness. What then do we mean when we call these other virtues 'purifications', and how are we made really like by being purified? Since the soul is evil when it is thoroughly mixed with the body and shares its experiences and has all the same opinions, it will be good and possess virtue when it no longer has the same opinions but acts alone – this is intelligence and wisdom – and does not share the body's experiences – this is self-control – and is not afraid of departing from the body – this is courage – and is ruled by reason and intellect, without opposition – and this is justice. One would not be wrong in calling this state of the soul likeness to God, in which its activity is intellectual, and it is free in this way from bodily affections. For the Divine too is pure, and its activity is of such a kind that that which imitates it has wisdom. Well, then why is the Divine itself not in this state? It has no states at all; states belong to the soul. The soul's intellectual activity is different: but of the realities There one thinks differently, and the other does not think at all. Another question then: is 'intellectual activity' just a common term covering two different things? Not at all. It is used primarily of the Divine, and secondarily of that which derives from it. As the spoken word is an imitation of that in the soul, so the word in the soul is an imitation of that in something else: as the uttered word, then, is broken up into parts as compared with that in the soul, so is that in the soul as compared with that before it, which it interprets. And virtue belongs to the soul, but not to intellect or That which is beyond it.

We must investigate whether purification is the same thing as this kind of virtue, or whether purification comes first and virtue follows, and whether virtue consists in the process of being purified or the achieved state of purification. The virtue in the process of purification is less perfect than that in the achieved state, for the achieved state of purification is already a sort of perfection. But being completely purified is a stripping of everything alien, and the good is different from that. If goodness existed before the impurity, purification is enough; but even so, though the purification will be enough, the good will be what is left after purification, not the purification itself. And we must enquire what that which is left is; perhaps the nature which is left was never really the good; for if it was it would not have come into evil. Should we call it something like the good? Yes, but not a nature capable of remaining in the real good, for it has a natural tendency in both directions. So its good will be fellowship with that which is akin to it, and its evil fellowship with its opposites. Then it must attain to this fellowship after being purified; and it will do so by a conversion. Does it then turn itself after the purification? Rather, after the purification it is already turned. Is this, then, its virtue? It is rather that which results for it from the conversion. And what is this? A sight and the impression of what is seen, implanted and working in it, like the relationship between sight and its object. But did it not have the realities which it sees? Does it not recollect them? It had them, but not active, lying apart and unilluminated; if they are to be illuminated and it is to know they are present in it, it must thrust towards that which gives it might. It did not have the realities themselves but impressions of them; so it must bring the impressions into accord with the true realities of which they are impressions. Perhaps, too, this, as they say, is how it is; intellect is not alien and is particularly not alien when the soul looks towards it; otherwise it is alien even when it is present. The same applies to the different branches of knowledge; if we do not act by them at all, they do not really belong to us.

Ethics 4

The Tasks of the Wise Man: Bernardino de Sahagún, Codice Matriteuse de la Real Academia de la Historia

Here, Sahagún has arranged the tasks and functions of the wise men, 'Sabios o Philosophos' (wise men or philosophers), as they were given by his Aztec informants. His description of the Aztec wise men incorporates all the qualities of modern teachers, psychologists, moralists, metaphysicians and humanists.

The wise man: a light, a torch, a stout torch that does not smoke.

A perforated mirror, a mirror pierced on both sides.

His are the black and red ink, his are the illustrated manuscripts, he studies the illustrated manuscripts.

He himself is writing and wisdom.

He is the path, the true way for others.

He directs people and things; he is a guide in human affairs.

The wise man is careful [like a physician] and preserves tradition.

His is the handed-down wisdom; he teaches it; he follows the path of truth.

Teacher of the truth, he never ceases to admonish.

He makes wise the countenances of others; to them he gives a face [a personality]; he leads them to develop it.

He opens their ears; he enlightens them.

He is the teacher of guides; he shows them their path.

One depends upon him.

He puts a mirror before others; he makes them prudent, cautious; he causes a face [a personality] to appear in them.

He attends to things; he regulates their path, he arranges and commands.

He applies his light to the world.

He knows what is above us (and) in the region of the dead.

He is a serious man.

Everyone is comforted by him, corrected, taught.

Thanks to him people humanize their will and receive a strict education.

He comforts the heart, he comforts the people, he helps, gives remedies, heals everyone.

Postscript

Our understanding of the great civilizations of the Near East, the Mediterranean and Mesoamerica has been radically altered by literary and and archaeological discoveries which began in the 19th century and have continued into our own lifetime. First, the 19th century saw the beginning of the process of recovering the vast literary texts of these civilizations. The systematic translation of Greek and Latin inscriptions reinvigorated our understanding of Greek and Roman religion, and shed considerable light upon the Indo-European heritage of both cultures. In the Near East, excavations at the end of the 19th century revealed immense libraries containing thousands of clay tablets written in cuneiform script. The 19th century saw the decipherment of Egyptian hieroglyphs, which made available countless pyramid and temple inscriptions, and a growing collection of important papyrus manuscripts. The texts from Oxyrhyncus, written in Greek, Coptic and Arabic, also altered our understanding of later Egyptian life from the Ptolemies to the Muslim conquest. In addition, the end of the 19th century saw the discovery in Turkey of literary documents from the ancient Hittite civilizations. The recovery of these literary texts was of course dependent of archaeological excavations which altered our understanding of history. Schliemann was excavating Troy in the 1870s, Sir Arthur Evans was conducting excavations at Knossos in Crete, Flinders Petrie was conducting excavations in Egypt, and Jacques de Morgan was carrying forward fieldwork in Persia. These discoveries made major advances in our understanding of the religious traditions of what we call the powerful dead.

However, the tradition of Zoroaster and the Parsees of contemporary India is an exception. While it is true that we must reconstruct the sense of canon among the traditions of the ancient Babylonians, Egyptians, Greeks, Romans, Maya and Aztec, the Zoroastrians and Parsees have a specific sense of sacred and authoritative texts. The Avesta is the authoritative text, and it is divided into the following sections: the *Yasna* contains hymns recited by priests at specific sacrifices, and the *Gāthās*, made up of the hymns attributed to Zoroaster, are embedded within it; the *Visp-rat* contains additional invocations and offerings to the Lords of the different classes of beings; the *Vidēvāt* contains materials directed at the Daevas; the *Siroza* contains additional hymns; the *Yashts* contains hymns addressed to various gods, such as Mithra; the *Hadhoxt Nask* contains elaborate descriptions of the fate of the soul after death and the *Khūrda* is made up of minor texts which supplement the larger sections of the Avesta. But this sacred text is supplemented by other authoritative books, written at later periods, such as the *Dēnkart*, written in Pahlavi, the official language of the Sassanians, and the *Bundahishn*, which is the most comprehensive Zoroastrian cosmology, although intended as a commentary on the Avesta.

Bibliography

A number of very fine collections of texts from these religious traditions are available for the general reader. Among them are James B. Pritchard's two-volume collection *The Ancient Near East: An Anthology of Texts and Pictures* (1973 and 1975), Miriam Lichtheim's three-volume collection *Ancient Egyptian Literature* (1975, 1976 and 1981), Frederick C. Grant, *Hellenistic Religions: The Age of Syncretism* (1953) and *Ancient Roman Religion* (1957), Miguel Leon-Portilla, *Aztec Thought and Culture: A Study of the Ancient Nahyatl Mind*, translated by J.E. Davis (1963), Laurette Séjourné, *Burning Water: Thought and Religion in Ancient Mexico*, translated by Irene Nicholson (1957), and Jacques Duchesne-Guillemin, *The Hymns of Zarathustra* (1952).

According to age-old tradition, Zoroastrian priests learn their liturgies by heart and books are not used for daily services. However, at the seven great seasonal festivals, the priest reads aloud from the sacred Avesta. The muslin veil shields consecrated objects from the priest's breath, since anything leaving the body, including breath, is considered impure.

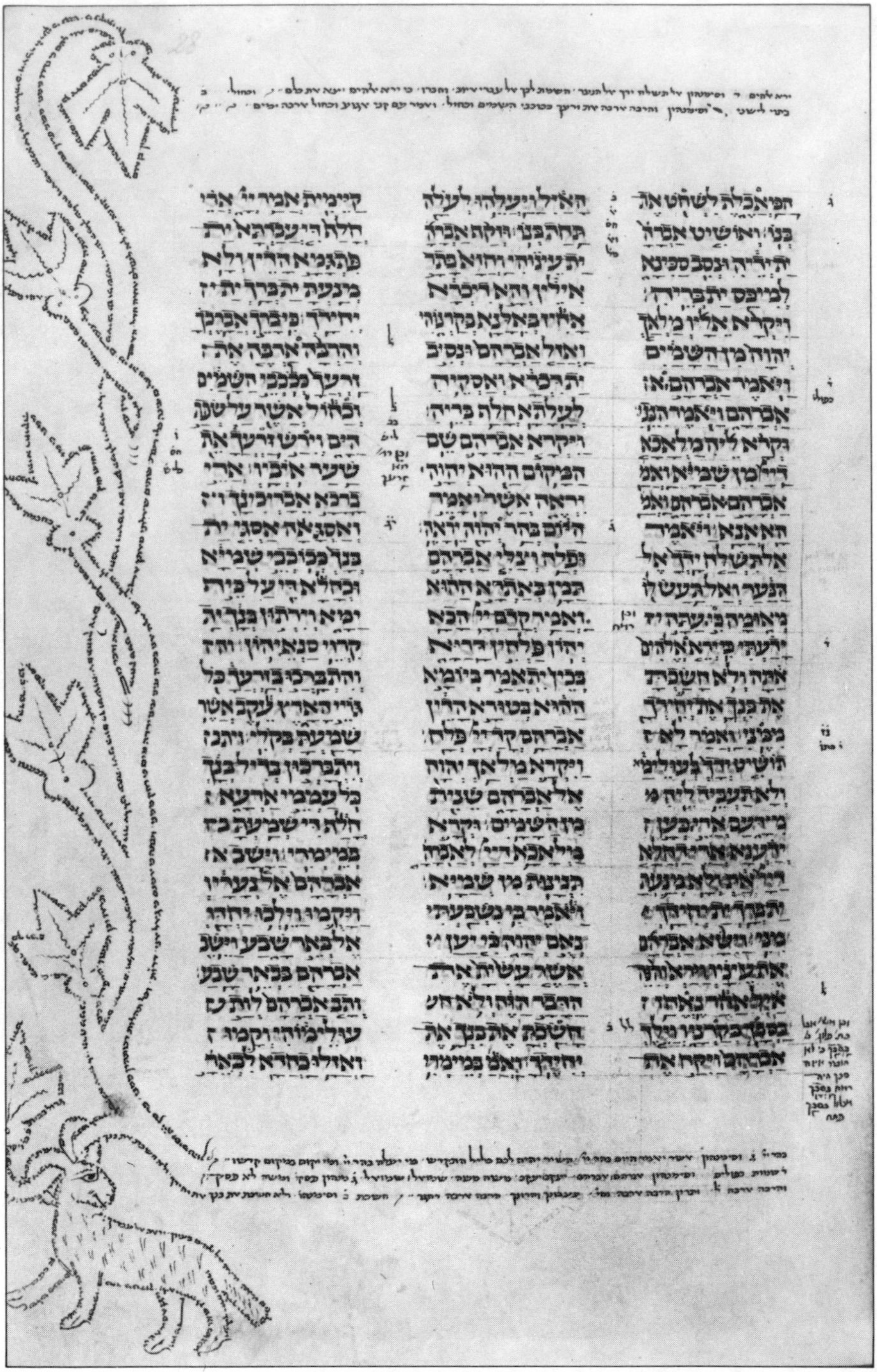

The beginning of Genesis 22, from a 14th-century manuscript of the Pentateuch. The text is surrounded by a commentary, ingeniously written in the form of line-drawings: commentary on the meaning of the scriptures is an integral part of the Jewish tradition.

Judaism

Introduction

The first issue in approaching the sacred texts of Judaism is the proper terminology used to describe the 39 books which make up the Hebrew Bible. It is quite common to find these books referred to as the 'Old Testament'. However, this designation carries with it much theological baggage; the 'Old Testament' points to the New Testament of the Christian community and implies that the old covenant has been replaced or fulfilled by the new. Such a designation should be eliminated if we want to understand the sacred writings of Judaism. A far better term to describe these books is the Hebrew Bible. Many differences exist between the Christian translations of the Hebrew Bible and the established Hebrew text. Most important in these differences are the books included within the Hebrew Bible and their order. The Catholic tradition includes such texts as First and Second Maccabees, the Wisdom of Solomon, and the Wisdom of Jesus ben Sirach as deutero-canonical texts, while these very same texts have been understood as being outside the canon of the Hebrew Bible or as apocryphal texts by Jews. Indeed, one of the important results of the Protestant Reformation was the return to the specific list of books which made up the Hebrew Bible according to Jews. The Jewish canon of the Hebrew Bible ends with the last verse of the Second Book of Chronicles, which looks forward to the rebuilding of the Temple in Jerusalem, while the Christian canon of the Hebrew Bible ends with the last verses of the prophet Malachi, serving as the theological bridge between the 'old' and the New Testament with the words, 'Behold, I will send you Elijah the prophet before the great and terrible day of the Lord comes'. The reader of this theological order then need only turn the page in order to find the fulfilment of this prophecy in the activities of John the Baptist, who within the context of the New Testament, is identified with Elijah, the herald of the messianic king.

Even the Jewish use of the term 'Bible' to refer to their sacred writings is a comparatively recent phenomenon of the past 200 years. The most accurate term for the Hebrew Bible in the history of Judaism is the term *Tanak*, an acronym made up of the first letters of the three parts of the Hebrew Bible; *Torah*, *Nevi'im* and *Ketuvim*. Torah, also described as the Pentateuch or the first five books, refers to the revelation given Moses at Mount Sinai. Even while this revelation is given well into the history of the ancient Israelites, the revelation encompasses the creation narrative, a narrative concerning the first ancestors or patriarchs, a description of Isreal's bondage under the Egyptians, the going out from Egypt, and all the legal traditions incumbent upon the community of Israel. We usually refer to these five books of the Torah through their Latin titles (Genesis, Exodus, Leviticus, Numbers and Deuteronomy), but Jews refer to these by the first major word in the Hebrew text of each book. Hence, Genesis is properly referred to as *Bereshit* ('In the beginning'), *Shemot* ('Names') for Exodus, *Vayyikra* ('And he called') for Leviticus, *Bamidbar* ('In the desert') for Numbers, and *Devarim* ('Words') for Deuteronomy. Torah is usually translated as Law, and while Torah contains laws, it is much more than simply laws as we understand the term. Many sections of the Torah are devoted to the ritual life of the community and since ancient Israel made no distinction between what we would call a civil code of law and a religious code of law, all aspects of human conduct fell within the jurisdiction of Torah. Throughout the history of Judaism, the Torah was understood to be that which is most authoritative and binding upon man. The authoritative element of Torah was extended by Rabbinic Judaism in late antiquity so that Moses received the Written Torah (*torah she-beketav*) and the Oral Torah (*torah she-ba'al peh*) at one and the same moment at Mount Sinai. Both were transmitted throughout the generations. The content of the Oral Torah is recorded in the literary productions of early Rabbinic Judaism. Hence, Rabbi Judah the Prince's collection of oral traditions called the *Mishnah* (*c*210 CE), exercises equal authority with Torah in the shaping of Jewish life. The second section of the *Tanak* is *Nevi'im* or Prophets and is made up of all the prophetic texts of the Hebrew Bible. This section is further divided into three sections: the early prophets (Joshua, Judges, First and Second Samuel, and First and Second Kings), the later prophets (Isaiah, Jeremiah and Ezekiel) and the 12 smaller prophetic books (Hosea, Joel, Amos, Obadiah, Jonah, Micah, Nahum, Habakkuk, Zephaniah, Haggai, Zechariah and Malachi). The third and final section of the *Tanak* is *Ketuvim* or writings and is made up of various forms of prose and poetic texts from different historical periods of ancient Israel. For example, *Ketuvim* includes the Book of Psalms, wisdom literature such as the Book of Proverbs, the Book of Job and the Book of Ecclesiastes, dramatic literary narratives such as the Books of Esther and Ruth, and historical texts such as Ezra and Nehemiah or First and Second Chronicles.

The process of canonizing the texts of the Hebrew Bible was exceptionally long, but three periods of crisis were instrumental in the formation of the *Tanak*. First, many of the oral and written traditions of the Torah were formalized shortly after the Babylonian Exile (*c*520 BCE), when the leadership of the Israelites taken into captivity by the Babylonians in the years 587–586 BCE returned to Judaea and figures like Ezra and Nehemiah began the reconstruction of their community. A second crisis was the confrontation between the Judaeans and the Selucid Greeks in the mid–3rd century BCE. Out of this crisis, which we know of from the apocryphal First and Second Maccabees, emerged the formalized *Nevi'im*. The third crisis was the destruction of Jerusalem and its temple in the year 70 of the Common Era. This was the major crisis in Jewish self-consciousness, for the entire religious tradition of Israel and Judaism centred upon this one institution of the Temple. Rabbinic leadership, first under Rabban Yohannan ben Zakkai and later many others, was faced with the reconstruction of a Judaism which could exist in the absence of this fundamental institution. The canon of the Hebrew Bible, in its final form, emerged from this process of reconstruction. Since we have more documents from the Rabbis of this period, we can determine some of their concerns in this final attempt to canonize the Hebrew Bible. We know that their efforts to include or exclude certain books from the canon were motivated by four concerns. First, did the specific book under consideration for canonization support or contradict something already clearly visible in the books already a part of the canon? In some cases, the contradiction was found in calendation and in still others in matters of legal interpretation for the reconstructed community. Second, was the authorship of the text clearly discernible? Some books attributed to famous personages in the past, upon closer examination were found to be pseudepigraphical or erroneously attributed to a certain well-recognized figure. Here, the language of the book in question might have been a concern, for many books which circulated in Jewish communities were now in Greek. We might assume that where no Hebrew original could be found, the book was almost immediately excluded from the canon. Third, the rabbis attempted to set as an arbitrary end to prophecy after the return from the Babylonian Exile. Originally, this may have had something to do with urbanization of Judaean society in the 4th and 3rd centuries BCE, but at the beginning of the 2nd century of the Common Era, it was also a response to the new Jewish sect, Christianity, which might have made a claim for inclusion in the canon for a new set of books about their prophetic figure, Jesus. Fourth, whether a book was included in the canon or excluded was dependent on the status of book in the contemporary community. How was a specific book used? In some cases, the popularity of a book in a non-religious context or in the everyday world was sufficient reason for excluding it.

Until recent times Jews, like Christians and other religious communities, were most familiar with their sacred writings in liturgical contexts or how the biblical text was presented in the synagogue. Early synagogues already had well-defined lectionary cycles in which the entire Torah was read in a fixed period of time. Since the Middle Ages, this time period has been one year and consequently the narrative of the Torah is divided into sections for the weeks of the year. Certain sections of the Torah are set aside for the festivals of the Jewish liturgical year. So, on the second day of Rosh Ha-Shannah or New Year, the narrative of the binding of Isaac (Genesis 22) is read in the synagogue. The sections from the Torah were supplemented with reading selections taken from *Nevi'im*, and for certain festivals of the Jewish year, whole books from *Ketuvim* are included in the reading. For example, on the festival of Purim, the Book of Esther is read and on the ninth day of the Hebrew month of Av, the Book of Lamentations, Jeremiah's lament over the destruction of Jerusalem, is read on a solemn fast day commemorating the destruction of Jerusalem first by the Babylonians and again by the Romans.

Our first selection under the heading of sacred narrative is the creation account of Genesis. Here, we have included the traditional reading selection from *Nevi'im*, Isaiah 42: 5–43: 10, in order to give the reader some flavour of how the sacred text for this section of Torah operates within its living context. The other selections within this group include the covenant made between God and Abraham from the Book of Genesis, the chronicle of oppression and liberation from Egypt from the Book of Exodus, the narrative of the death of Moses, a psalm describing the experience of exile, and a description of the messianic king from the Book of Isaiah.

The texts selected to illustrate the doctrinal dimension of the Hebrew Bible begin with the affirmation of God's oneness and unity from the Book of Deuteronomy. The second selection tells us something about the importance of wisdom in ancient Israel. This text from the Book of Proverbs has been supplemented by two rabbinic texts which first identify this wisdom with Torah and then illustrate how Torah (wisdom) was transmitted throughout the generations. The third text speaks about identity and is drawn from the Book of Deuteronomy. The fourth text, also taken from Deuteronomy, underscores the importance of land, a formal aspect of the covenant between God, Abraham, and his descendants, and proper behaviour in the land. The fifth selection is from the prophet Jeremiah and defines redemption as a critical component in Israel and Judaism.

The texts which we have selected to illustrate the ritual dimension of the Hebrew Bible begin with two texts from the Book of Exodus instituting the ritual observance of the

Shabbat or Sabbath. The Shabbat is the paradigm for all festivals during the Jewish year. The second text is from the Book of Leviticus and describes the institution of sacrifice which was the central form of ritual in ancient Israel. Here, we have included a rabbinic text which demonstrates how this ritual institution was reinterpreted and enlarged after the destruction of the Temple by the Romans. The third text describes the three festivals, Passover, Shavuot and Sukkot, which require pilgrimage to Jerusalem, and is taken from Exodus. The fourth text from the Book of Psalms represents an example of the liturgy of the Temple. The last text describes the historical moment from which the Passover ritual takes its importance and has been taken from the Book of Exodus.

The texts we have selected from the Hebrew Bible to exemplify institutional expression begin with a description of the installation of the priests from Exodus. The second text, also from Exodus, describes how the priesthood, as a symbol, is extended to the entire community of Israel. The last text in this section is also from Exodus and is the Second Decalogue which Moses receives from God after the rebellion of the Israelites in making the Golden Calf. This Decalogue is perhaps distinctive in that it contains specific laws for the community's well-being and observance.

We begin our examples of the experiential dimension of the Hebrew Bible with Moses' encounter with God at the burning bush from Exodus. This is followed by two descriptions, also from Exodus, which describe the events at Mount Sinai and the giving of Torah. The third group of texts, taken from the prophet Ezekiel, the prophet Isaiah and the Book of Daniel, describe the visionary experience which is fundamental for prophecy in ancient Israel. The fourth text is taken from the Book of Leviticus and describes some specific manners in which human life is sanctified. Lastly, we have included two texts from Ecclesiastes and Job which speak to human temporality and limitation.

The texts selected to illustrate the ethical dimension of the Hebrew Bible begin with the First Decalogue given to Moses at Mount Sinai and which he subsequently breaks in his anger at the Israelites for constructing the Golden Calf. This Decalogue, while containing some parallels to the Second Decalogue, is intensely individualistic. The second text is from the Book of Proverbs and describes the specific merits of the 'Woman of Valour'. The third text, from the Book of Proverbs as well, describes the opposing ethical standards of righteousness and wickedness. The last text from the Book of Leviticus describes the proper and improper foods for the community. These are not simply ritual requirements, but also are indicative of the expansion of ethical conduct to all aspects of human life. The separation of clean and unclean animals is directly related to the ethical requirement of maintaining the created order.

Sacred Narrative 1

Creation: Genesis 1

The narrative of creation or cosmogony of the Book of Genesis is a central text in ancient Israel and in Judaism. The first verse of the narrative has long troubled commentators since the heavens and the earth are not the first things created. Light is the first creation, and hence the first verse of the narrative is understood as a general heading, what we might recognize as a title. The narrative sets forth with unquestioned authority the order of creation, beginning with light, the firmament, the seas, the dry land, vegetation, temporal division, the sun, moon and stars, the animals of the seas, the birds of the air, and the animals of the land, man, and finally, the Shabbat. The statement that man is created in the image and likeness of God has also troubled generations of commentators. One possible understanding of this mirror likeness turns upon the term 'dominion'. Just as God exercises dominion over the cosmos, man has dominion over the created order of the world. This is a relationship of responsibility, so that God maintains the cosmos and man maintains the categories or order of reality, the sea, land and air. It should also be indicated that while this narrative is descriptive of the beginning of all things, its structure is reapplied in reflection and speculation about the end of time. Hence, the traditional prophetic reading from Isaiah 42 and 43, which accompanies this narrative in the liturgical cycle of Torah readings, not only reinterprets the Genesis creation account, but also projects it into the future.

In the beginning God created the heavens and the earth. The earth was without form and void, and darkness was upon the face of the deep; and the Spirit of God was moving over the face of the waters.

And God said, 'Let there be light'; and there was light. And God saw that the light was good; and God separated the light from the darkness. God called the light Day, and the darkness he called Night. And there was evening and there was morning, one day.

And God said, 'Let there be a firmament in the midst of the waters, and let it separate the waters from the waters.' And God made the firmament and separated the waters which were under the firmament from the waters which were above the firmament. And it was so. And God called the firmament Heaven. And there was evening and there was morning, a second day.

And God said, 'Let the waters under the heavens be gathered together into one place, and let dry land appear.' And it was so. God called the dry land Earth, and the waters that were gathered together he called Seas. And God saw that it was good. And God said, 'Let the earth put forth vegetation, plants yielding seed, and fruit trees bearing fruit in which there is seed, each according to their own kind, upon the earth.' And it was so. The earth brought forth vegetation, plants yielding seed according to their own kinds, and trees bearing fruit in which is their seed, each according to its kind. And God saw that it was good. And there was evening and there was morning, a third day.

And God said, 'Let there be lights in the firmament of the heavens to separate the day from the night; and let them be for signs and for seasons and for days and years, and let them be lights in the firmament of the heavens to give light upon the earth'. And it was so. And God made the two great lights, the greater light to rule the day, and the lesser light to rule the night; he made the stars also. And God set them in the firmament of the heavens to give light upon the earth, to rule over the day and over the night, and to separate the light from the darkness. And God saw that it was good. And there was evening and there was morning, a fourth day.

And God said, 'Let the waters bring forth swarms of living creatures, and let birds fly above the earth across the firmament of the heavens.' So God created the great sea monsters and every living creature that moves, with which the waters swarm, according to their kinds, and every winged bird according to its kind. And God saw that it was good. And God blessed them, saying, 'Be fruitful and multiply and fill the waters in the seas, and let the birds multiply on the earth.' And there was evening and there was morning, a fifth day.

And God said, 'Let the earth bring forth living creatures according to their kinds: cattle and creeping things and beasts of the earth according to their kinds.' And it was so. And God made the beasts of the earth according to their kinds and the cattle according to their kinds, and everything that creeps upon the ground according to its kind. And God saw that it was good.

Then God said, 'Let us make man in our image, after our likeness; and let them have dominion over the fish of the sea, and over the birds of the air, and over the cattle, and over all the earth, and over every creeping thing that creeps upon the earth.' So God created man in his own image, in the image of God he created him; male and female he created them. And God blessed them, and God said to them, 'Be fruitful and multiply, and fill the earth and subdue it; and have dominion over the fish of the sea and over the birds of the air and over every living thing that moves upon the earth.' And God said, 'Behold, I have given you every plant yielding seed which is upon the face of all the earth, and every tree with seed in its fruit; you shall have them for food. And to every beast of the earth, and to every bird of the air, and to everything that creeps on the earth, everything that has the breath of life, I have given every green plant for food.' And it was so. And God saw everything that he had made, and behold it was very good. And there was evening and there was morning, a sixth day.

Thus the heavens and the earth were finished, and all the host of them. And on the seventh day God finished his work which he had done, and he rested on the seventh day from all his work which he had done. So God blessed the seventh day and hallowed it, because on it God rested from all his work which he had done in creation.

These are the generations of the heavens and the earth when they were created.

Creation: Isaiah 42–43

This text is the traditional reading from *Nevi'im* which accompanies the reading of Genesis 1 in the synagogue. The test was composed, scholars believe, during the Babylonian Exile or shortly therafter by an unknown prophet who might have belonged to a group of individuals who transmitted the prophecies of the original Isaiah, but there are clear relationships between the Genesis narrative and this composition. Indeed, the prophet here uses creation as a proof for God's redemption of his scattered people.

Thus says God, the Lord who created the
heavens and stretched them out,
who spread forth the earth and what comes
from it,
who gives breath to the people upon it
and spirit to those who walk in it:
'I am the Lord, I have called you in
righteousness,
I have taken you by the hand and kept you;
I have given you as a covenant to the people,
a light to the nations, to open the eyes that are
blind,
to bring out the prisoners from the dungeon,
from the prison those who sit in darkness.
I am the Lord, that is my name;
my glory I give to no other,
nor my praise to graven images.
Behold, the former things have come to pass,
and new things I now declare;
before they spring forth I tell you of them.'
Sing to the Lord a new song,
his praise from the end of the earth!
Let the sea roar and all that fills it,
the coastline and their inhabitants.

Let the desert and its cities lift up their voice,
the villages that Kedar inhabits;
let the inhabitants of Sela sing for joy,
let them shout from the top of the mountains.
Let them give glory to the Lord,
and declare his praise in the coastlands.
The Lord goes forth like a mighty man,
like a man of war he stirs up his fury;
he cries out, he shouts aloud, he shows
himself mighty against his foes.
For a long time I have held my peace,
I have kept still and restrained myself;
now I will cry out like a woman in travail,
I will grasp and pant.
I will lay waste mountains and hills and dry up all
their herbage;
I will turn the rivers into islands, and dry up
the pools.
And I will lead the blind in a way that they know
not,
in paths that they have not known I will guide
them.
I will turn the darkness before them into light,
the rough places into level ground.
These are the things I will do,
and I will not forsake them.
They shall be turned back and utterly put to
shame,
who trust in graven images
who say to molten images, 'You are our gods.'
Hear, you deaf;
and look, you blind, that you may see!
Who is blind but my servant,
or deaf as my messenger whom I send?
Who is blind as my dedicated one,
or blind as the servant of the Lord?
He sees many things, but does not observe them;
his ears are open, but he does not hear.
The Lord was pleased, for his righteousness'
sake,
to magnify his law and make it glorious.
But this is a people robbed and plundered,
they are all of them trapped in holes and
hidden in prisons;
they have become a prey with none to rescue,
a spoil with none to say 'Restore!'
Who among you will give ear to this,
will attend and listen for the time to come?
Who gave up Jacob to the spoiler,
and Israel to the robbers?
Was it not the Lord, against whom we have
sinned,
in whose ways they would not walk,
and whose law they would not obey?
So he poured upon him the heat of his anger and
the might of battle;
it set him on fire round about, but he did not
understand;
it burned him, but he did not take it to heart.
But now thus says the Lord,
he who created you, O Jacob,
he who formed you, O Israel:
'Fear not, for I have redeemed you;
I have called you by name, you are mine.
When you pass through the waters I will be with
you;
and through rivers, they shall not overwhelm
you;
when you walk through fire you shall not be
burned,
and the flame shall not consume you.
For I am the Lord your God,
the Holy One of Israel, your Saviour.
I give Egypt as your ransom,
Ethiopia and Seba in exchange for you.
Because you are precious in my eyes,
and honoured, and I love you,
I give men in return for you,
peoples in exchange for your life.
Fear not, for I am with you;
I will bring your offspring from the east,
and from the west I will gather you;
I will say to the north, Give up;
and to the south, Do not withhold;
bring my sons from afar
and my daughters from the end of the earth,
every one who is called by my name,
whom I created for my glory,
whom I formed and made.'
Bring forth the people who are blind, yet have
eyes,
who are deaf, yet have ears!
Let all the nations gather together,
and let the peoples assemble.
Who among them can declare this,
and show us the former things?
Let them bring their witnesses to justify them,
and let them hear and say, It is true.
'You are my witnesses,' says the Lord,
'and my servant whom I have chosen,
that you may know and believe me and
understand that I am He.
Before me no god was formed,
nor shall there be any after me.'

Sacred Narrative 2

The Covenant with Abraham: Genesis 12 and 17

The first text, from Genesis 12, is the call and covenant between Abraham and God. Abram, whose name is later changed to Abraham, is called to leave his home and to enter into a covenant with God. In return, Abraham is promised descendants, land and blessing. The second text, from Genesis 17, repeats these elements of the covenant in specific formulation and institutes the ritual of circumcision as the sign of the covenant between Abraham's descendants and God.

Genesis 12:1–3

Now the Lord said to Abram, 'Go from your country and your kindred and your father's house to the land that I will show you. And I will make of you a great nation, and I will bless you, and make your name great, so that you will be a blessing. I will bless those who bless you, and him who curses you I will curse; and by you all the families of the earth shall bless themselves.'

Genesis 17:1–21

When Abram was ninety-nine years old the Lord appeared to Abram, and said to him, 'I am God Almighty; walk before me, and be blameless. And I will make my covenant between me and you, and will multiply you exceedingly.' Then Abram fell on his face; and God said to him, 'Behold, my covenant is with you, and you shall be the father of a multitude of nations. No longer shall your name be Abram, but your name shall be Abraham; for I have made you the father of a multitude of nations. I will make you exceedingly fruitful; and I will make nations of you, and kings shall come forth from you. And I will establish my covenant between me and you and your descendants after you throughout their generations for an everlasting covenant, to be God to you and to your descendants after you. And I will give to you, and to your descendants after you, the land of your sojournings, all the land of Canaan, for an everlasting possession; and I will be their God.'

And God said to Abraham, 'As for you, you shall keep my covenant, you and your descendants after you throughout their generations. This is my covenant, which you shall keep, between me and you and your descendants after you: Every male among you shall be circumcised. You shall be circumcised in the flesh of your foreskins, and it shall be a sign of the covenant between me and you. He that is eight days old among you shall be circumcised; every male throughout your generations, whether born in your house, or bought with your money from any foreigner who is not of your offspring, both he that is born in your house and he that is bought with your money, shall be circumcised. So shall my covenant be in your flesh an everlasting covenant. Any uncircumcised male who is not circumcised in the flesh of his foreskin shall be cut off from his people; he has broken my covenant.'

And God said to Abraham, 'As for Sar'ai your wife, you shall not call her name Sar'ai, but Sarah shall be her name. I will bless her, and moreover I will give you a son by her; I will bless her, and she shall be a mother of nations; kings of peoples shall come from her.' Then Abraham fell on his face and laughed, and said to himself, 'Shall a child be born to a man who is a hundred years old? Shall Sarah, who is ninety years old, bear a child?' And Abraham said to God, 'O that Ish'mael might live in thy sight!' God said, 'No, but Sarah your wife shall bear you a son, and you shall call his name Isaac. I will establish my covenant with him as an everlasting covenant for his descendants after him. As for Ish'mael, I have heard you; behold I will bless him and make him fruitful and multiply him exceedingly; he shall be the father of twelve princes, and I will make him a great nation. But I will establish my covenant with Isaac, whom Sarah shall bear to you at this season next year.'

Sacred Narrative 3

Oppression and the Youth of Moses: Exodus 1–2

This text describes how the descendants of Jacob migrated to Egypt after Joseph had prepared Egypt for the seven years of famine which devastated the surrounding lands, and how the Egyptians oppressed them. The Pharaoh, who does not remember how Joseph had managed Egyptian affairs, abruptly turns on the Israelites and enslaves them. The oppression reaches its climax with the order to kill the male children of the Israelites. This introduces the narrative of Moses, who escapes the decree of death, is brought up as a prince in the household of Pharaoh, and then must flee himself into the desert of Midian.

These are the names of the sons of Israel who came to Egypt with Jacob, each with his household: Reuben, Simeon, Levi, and Judah, Is'sachar, Zeb'ulun, and Benjamin, Dan and Naph'tali, Gad and Asher. All the offspring of Jacob were seventy persons; Joseph was already in Egypt. Then Joseph died, and all his brothers, and all that generation. But the descendants of Israel were fruitful and increased greatly; they multiplied and grew exceedingly strong; so that the land was filled with them.

Now there arose a new king over Egypt, who did not know Joseph. And he said to his people, 'Behold, the people of Israel are too many and too mighty for us. Come, let us deal shrewdly with them, lest they multiply, and, if war befall us, they join our enemies and fight against us and escape from the land.' Therefore they set taskmasters over them to afflict them with heavy burdens; and they built for Pharaoh store-cities, Pithom and Raam'ses. But the more they were oppressed, the more they multiplied and the more they spread abroad. And the Egyptians were in dread of the people of Israel. So they made the people of Israel serve with rigour, and made their lives bitter with hard service, in mortar and brick, and in all kinds of work in the field, in all their work they made them serve with rigour.

Then the king of Egypt said to the Hebrew midwives, one of whom was named Shiph'rah and the other Pu'ah, 'When you serve as midwife to the Hebrew women, and see them upon the birthstool, if it is a son, you shall kill him; but if it is a daughter, she shall live.' But the midwives feared God, and did not do as the king of Egypt commanded them, but let the male children live. So the king of Egypt called the midwives, and said to them, 'Why have you done this, and let the male children live?' The midwives said to Pharaoh, 'Because the Hebrew women are not like the Egyptian women; for they are vigorous and are delivered before the midwife comes to them.' So God dealt well with the midwives; and the people multiplied and grew very strong. And because the midwives feared God he gave them families. Then Pharaoh commanded all his people, 'Every son that is born to the Hebrews you shall cast into the Nile, but you shall let every daughter live.'

Now a man from the house of Levi went and took to wife a daughter of Levi. The woman conceived and bore a son; and when she saw that he was a goodly child, she hid him three months. and when she could hide him no longer she took for him a basket made of bulrushes, and daubed it with bitumen and pitch; and she put the child in it and placed it among the reeds at the river's brink. And his sister stood at a distance, to know what would be done to him. Now the daughter of Pharaoh came down to bathe at the river, and her maidens walked beside the river; she saw the basket among the reeds and sent her maid to fetch it. When she opened it she saw the child; and lo, the babe was crying. She took pity on him and said, 'This is one of the Hebrews' children.' Then his sister said to Pharaoh's daughter, 'Shall I go and call you a nurse from the Hebrew women to nurse the child for you?' And Pharaoh's daughter said to her, 'Take this child away, and nurse him for me, and I will give you your wages.' So the woman took the child and nursed him. And the child grew, and she brought him to Pharaoh's daughter, and he became her son; and she named him Moses, for she said, 'Because I drew him out of the water.'

One day, when Moses had grown up, he went out to his people and looked on their burdens; and he saw an Egyptian beating a Hebrew, one of his people. He looked this way and that, and seeing no one he killed the Egyptian and hid him in the sand. When he went out the next day, behold, two Hebrews were struggling together; and he said to the man that did the wrong, 'Why do you strike your fellow?' He answered, 'Who made you a prince and a judge over us? Do you mean to kill me as you killed the Egyptian?' Then Moses was afraid, and thought, 'Surely the thing is known.' When Pharaoh heard of it, he sought to kill Moses.

But Moses fled from Pharaoh, and stayed in the land of Midian; and he sat down by a well. Now the priest of Midian had seven daughters; and they came and drew water, and filled the troughs to water their father's flock. The shepherds came and drove them away; but Moses stood up and helped them, and watered their flock. When they came to their father Reu'el, he said, 'How is it that you have come so soon today?' They said, 'An Egyptian delivered us out of the hand of the shepherds, and even drew water for us and watered the flock.' He said to his daughters, 'And where is he? Why have you left the man? Call him, that he may eat bread.' And Moses was content to dwell with the man, and he gave Moses his daughter Zippo'rah. She bore a son, and he called his name Gershom; for he said, 'I have been a sojourner in a foreign land.'

In the course of those many days the king of Egypt died. And the people of Israel groaned under their bondage, and cried out for help, and their cry under bondage came up to God. And God heard their groaning, and God remembered his covenant with Abraham, with Isaac, and with Jacob. And God saw the people of Israel, and God knew their condition.

Sacred Narrative 4

The Deliverance from Pharaoh: Exodus 14–15

These two chapters describe, first in narrative style and then in poetic form, the miraculous intervention of God at the Sea of Reeds. Just at the moment when Israel seems trapped by the pursuing Egyptians and the sea, God splits the sea through the agency of Moses, Israel crosses over, and Pharaoh's troops are destroyed in the on rushing waters. This moment in the sacred narrative of Israel has shaped Jewish historical consciousness, so that this paradigm of [oppression and liberation is impressed on history itself and is also projected into the future.]

Then the Lord said to Moses, 'Tell the people of Israel to turn back and encamp in front of Pi-ha-hi'roth, between Migdol and the sea, in front of Ba'al-ze'phon; you shall encamp over against it, by the sea. For Pharaoh will say of the people of Israel, 'They are entangled in the land; the wilderness has shut them in.' And I will harden Pharaoh's heart, and he will pursue them and I will get glory over Pharaoh and all his host; and the Egyptians shall know that I am the Lord.' And they did so.

When the king of Egypt was told that the people had fled, the mind of Pharaoh and his servants was changed toward the people, and they said, 'What is this we have done, that we have let Israel go from serving us?' So he made ready his chariot and took his army with him, and took six hundred picked chariots of Egypt with officers over all of them. And the Lord hardened the heart of Pharaoh king of Egypt and he pursued the people of Israel as they went forth defiantly. The Egyptians pursued them, all Pharaoh's horses and chariots and his horsemen and his army, and overtook them encamped at the sea, by Pi-ha-hi'roth, in front of Ba'al-ze'phon.

When Pharaoh drew near, the people of Israel lifted up their eyes, and behold, the Egyptians were marching after them; and they were in great fear. And the people of Israel cried out to the Lord; and they said to Moses, 'Is it because there are no graves in Egypt that you have taken us away to die in the wilderness? What have you done to us, in bringing us out of Egypt? Is not this what we said to you in Egypt, "Let us alone and let us serve the Egyptians"? For it would have been better for us to serve the Egyptians than to die in the wilderness.' And Moses said to the people, 'Fear not, stand firm, and see the salvation of the Lord, which he will work for you today; for the Egyptians whom you see today, you shall never see again. The Lord will fight for you, and you have only to be still.' The Lord said to Moses, 'Why do you cry to me? Tell the people of Israel to go forward. Lift up your rod, and stretch out your hand over the sea and divide it, that the people of Israel may go on dry ground through the sea. And I will harden the hearts of the Egyptians so that they shall go in after them, and I will get glory over Pharaoh and all his host, his chariots, and his horsemen. And the Egyptians shall know that I am the Lord, when I have gotten glory over Pharaoh, his chariots, and his horsemen.'

Then the angel of God who went before the host of Israel moved and went behind them; and the pillar of cloud moved from before them and stood behind them, coming between the host of Egypt and the host of Israel. And there was the cloud and the darkness; and the night passed without one coming near the other all night.

Then Moses stretched out his hand over the sea; and the Lord drove the sea back by a strong east wind all night, and made the sea dry land, and the waters were divided. And the people of Israel went into the midst of the sea on dry ground, the waters being a wall to them on their right hand and on their left. The Egyptians pursued, and went in after them into the midst of the sea, all Pharaoh's horses, his chariots, and his horsemen. And in the morning watch the Lord in the pillar of fire and of cloud looked down upon the host of the Egyptians, and discomfited the host of the Egyptians, clogging their chariot wheels so that they drove heavily; and the Egyptians said, 'Let us flee from before Israel; for the Lord fights for them against the Egyptians.'

Then the Lord said to Moses, 'Stretch out your hand over the sea, that the water may come back upon the Egyptians, upon their chariots, and upon their horsemen.' So Moses stretched forth his hand over the sea, and the sea returned to its wonted flow when the morning appeared; and the Egyptians fled into it, and the Lord routed the Egyptians in the midst of the sea. The waters returned and covered the chariots and the horsemen and all the host of Pharaoh that had followed them into the sea; not so much as one of them remained. But the people of Israel walked on dry ground through the sea, the waters being a wall to them on their right hand and on their left.

Thus the Lord saved Israel that day from the hand of the Egyptians; and Israel saw the Egyptians dead upon the seashore. And Israel saw the great work which the Lord did against the Egyptians, and the people feared the Lord; and they believed in the Lord and in his servant Moses.

Then Moses and the people of Israel sang this song to the Lord, saying,

'I will sing to the Lord, for he has triumphed
gloriously;
the horse and his rider he has thrown into
the sea.
The Lord is my strength and my song,
and he has become my salvation;
this is my God, and I will praise him,
my father's God, and I will exalt him.
The Lord is a man of war;
the Lord is his name.

'Pharaoh's chariots and his host he cast into the
sea;
and his picked officers are sunk in the Red
Sea.
The floods cover them;
they went down into the depths like a stone.
Thy right hand, O Lord, glorious in power,
thy right hand, O Lord shatters the enemy.
In the greatness of thy majesty thou
overthrowest thy adversaries;
thou sendest forth thy fury,
it consumes them like stubble.
At the blast of thy nostrils the waters piled up,

the floods stood up in a heap;
the deeps congealed in the heart of the sea.
The enemy said, 'I will pursue, I will overtake,
I will divide the spoil,
my desire shall have its fill of them.
I will draw my sword,
my hand shall destroy them.'
Thou didst blow with thy wind, the sea
covered them;
they sank as lead in the mighty waters.

'Who is like thee, O Lord among the gods?
Who is like thee, majestic in holiness,
terrible in glorious deeds, doing wonders?
Thou didst stretch out thy right hand,
the earth swallowed them.

'Thou hast led in thy steadfast love the people
who thou hast redeemed,
thou hast guided them by thy strength to
thy holy abode.
The peoples have heard, they tremble;
pangs have seized on the inhabitants of
Philistia.
Now are the chiefs of Edom dismayed;
the leaders of Moab, trembling seizes them;
all the inhabitants of Canaan have melted
away.
Terror and dread fall upon them;
because of the greatness of thy arm, they are
as still as a stone,
till thy people, O Lord, pass by,
till the people pass by whom thou hast
purchased.
Thou wilt bring them in, and plant them on
thy own mountain,
the place, O Lord, which thou hast made
for thy abode,
the sanctuary, O Lord, which thy hands
have established.
The Lord will reign for ever and ever.'

For when the horses of Pharaoh with his chariots and his horsemen went into the sea, the Lord brought back the waters of the sea upon them; but the people of Israel walked on dry ground in the midst of the sea. Then Miriam, the prophetess, the sister of Aaron, took a timbrel in her hand; and all the women went out after her with timbrels and dancing. And Miriam sang to them:

'Sing to the Lord, for he has triumphed
gloriously;
the horse and his rider he has thrown into
the sea.'

Then Moses led Israel onward from the Red Sea, and they went into the wilderness of Shur; they went three days in the wilderness and found no water. When they came to Marah, they could not drink the water of Marah because it was bitter; therefore it was named Marah. And the peopled murmured against Moses, saying, 'What shall we drink?' And he cried to the Lord; and the Lord showed him a tree, and he threw it into the water, and the water became sweet.

There the Lord made for them a statute and an ordinance and there he proved them, saying, 'If you will diligently hearken to the voice of the Lord your God, and do that which is right in his eyes, and give heed to his commandments and keep all his statutes, I will put none of the diseases upon you which I put upon the Egyptians; for I am the Lord, your healer.'

Then they came to Elim, where there were twelve springs of water and seventy palm trees; and they encamped there by the water.

Sacred Narrative 5

The Death of Moses: Deuteronomy 34

The most mysterious aspect of the entire Torah is the death of Moses. Here, the one individual who is most important in the liberation of Israel from the slavery of Egypt, who transmits Torah to the community of Israel and leads them throughout the 40 years of wandering in the desert is not allowed to enter the land promised to the descendants of Abraham. Jews have thought long and hard on this short narrative; why must Moses die outside the land of Canaan, who is it that takes Moses' life, and why is it that no one knows the place of his burial? What is certain is that Moses stands out as the great prophet, unsurpassed by all the others after him. This alone has made Moses into the first sage and Rabbi of Judaism. The mysterious aspects in the narrative have suggested to certain sectors of Jewish reflection that Moses is the one who will appear at the end of time.

And Moses went up from the plains of Moab to Mount Nebo, to the top of Pisgah, which is opposite Jericho. And the Lord showed him all the land, Gilead as far as Dan, all Naph'tali, the land of E'phraim and Manas'seh, all the land of Judah as far as the Western Sea, the Negeb, and the Plain, that is, the valley of Jericho the city of palm trees, as far as Zo'ar. And the Lord said to him, 'This is the land of which I swore to Abraham, to Isaac, and to Jacob, "I will give it to your descendants." I have let you see it with your eyes, but you shall not go over there.' So Moses the servant of the Lord died there in the land of Moab, according to the word of the Lord, and he buried him in the valley in the land of Moab opposite Beth-pe'or; but no man knows the place of his burial to this day. Moses was a hundred and twenty years old when he died; his eye was not dim, nor his natural force abated. And the people of Israel wept for Moses in the plains of Moab thirty days; then the days of weeping and mourning for Moses were ended.

And Joshua the son of Nun was full of the spirit of wisdom, for Moses had laid his hands upon him; so the people of Israel obeyed him, and did as the Lord had commanded Moses. And there has not arisen a prophet since in Israel like Moses, whom the Lord knew face to face, none like him for all the signs and the wonders which the Lord sent him to do in the land of Egypt, to Pharaoh and to all his servants and to all his land, and for all the mighty power and all the great and terrible deeds which Moses wrought in the sight of all Israel.

Sacred Narrative 6

The Experience of Exile: Psalm 137

This comparatively short psalm is a vivid description of the experience of exile and was perhaps composed during the Babylonian Exile. However, while the psalm arises in one specific historical moment, it becomes the very centre of the Jewish longing for the homeland. The phrase so well-known, 'If I forget you, O Jerusalem', has reverberated in all periods of Jewish history.

By the waters of Babylon, there we sat down and wept,
when we remembered Zion.
On the willows there we hung up our lyres.
For there our captors required of us songs,
and our tormentors, mirth, saying,
'Sing us one of the songs of Zion!'
How shall we sing the Lord's song in a foreign land?
If I forget you, O Jerusalem, let my right hand wither!
Let my tongue cleave to the roof of my mouth,
if I do not remember you,
if I do not set Jerusalem above my highest joy!

Remember, O Lord, against the E'domites
the day of Jerusalem,
How they said, 'Raze it, raze it!
Down to its foundations!'
O daughter of Babylon, you devastator!
Happy shall he be who requites you
with what you have done to us!
Happy shall he be who takes your little ones
and dashes them against the rock!

Sacred Narrative 7

The Messianic King: Isaiah 11

This narrative from the prophet Isaiah describes the perfect king who will arise in Israel. He will be a proper anointed king. The term 'messiah' means 'anointed one' and here some very specific descriptions of his character are found. His kingship is projected by the prophet into the future and we are given a description of what his rule will be like; normal oppositions from our world will be obliterated and 'the leopard shall lie down with the kid'.

There shall come forth a shoot from the stump
of Jesse,
and a branch shall grow out of his roots.
And the Spirit of the Lord shall rest upon him,
the spirit of wisdom and understanding,
the spirit of counsel and might,
the spirit of knowledge and the fear of the
Lord.
And his delight shall be in the fear of the Lord.

He shall not judge by what his eyes see,
or decide by what his ears hear;
but with righteousness he shall judge the
poor,
and decide with equity for the meek of the
earth;
and he shall smite the earth with the rod of
his mouth,
and with the breath of his lips he shall slay
the wicked.
Righteousness shall be the girdle of his waist,
and faithfulness the girdle of his loins.

The wolf shall dwell with the lamb,
and the leopard shall lie down with the kid,
and the calf and the lion and the fatling
together,
and a little child shall lead them.
The cow and the bear shall feed;
their young shall lie down together;
and the lion shall eat straw like the ox.
The suckling child shall play over the hole of
the asp,
and the weaned child shall put his hand on
the adder's den.
They shall not hurt or destroy in all my holy
mountain;
for the earth shall be full of the knowledge
of the Lord
as the waters cover the sea.

Doctrine 1

The Oneness of God: Deuteronomy 6

This text from the Book of Deuteronomy contains the central doctinal affirmation of ancient Israel and Judaism, the oneness of God. It has been incorporated into the daily prayers of Jews as the *Shema* and the first of its blessings, the *Ve'ahavta*. The *Shema* is often referred to as the 'watchword' of Judaism and is perhaps the most familiar of all Jewish affirmations. The Book of Deuteronomy is important for doctrinal and liturgical formulations in the history of Judaism because the common language of the book is the transmission of sacred history from one generation to the next. Hence, this text stresses teaching and the sense that the deeds of God are present in every generation.

'Now this is the commandment, the statutes and the ordinances which the Lord your God commanded me to teach you, that you may do them in the land to which you are going over, to possess it; that you may fear the Lord your God, you and your son and your son's son, by keeping all his statutes and his commandments, which I command you, all the days of your life; and that your days may be prolonged. Hear therefore, O Israel, and be careful to do them; that it may go well with you, and that you may multiply greatly, as the Lord, the God of your fathers, has promised you, in a land flowing with milk and honey.

'Hear, O Israel: The Lord our God is one Lord; and you shall love the Lord your God with all your heart, and with all your soul, and with all your might. And these words which I command you this day shall be upon your heart; and you shall teach them diligently to your children, and shall talk of them when you sit in your house, and when you walk by the way, and when you lie down, and when you rise. And you shall bind them as a sign upon your hand, and they shall be as frontlets between your eyes. And you shall write them on the doorposts of your house and on your gates.'

Doctrine 2

Wisdom and Torah: Proverbs 8, Bereshit Rabbah, Pirke Avot

The first text from the Book of Proverbs is a example of what scholars describe as 'wisdom literature'. This form of literature, which appears in many cultures of the Ancient Near East, stresses the pursit and nature of transcendent wisdom. In this text, wisdom is speaking, describing her creation before the other elements of the ordered world. The second text is a Rabbinic interpretation of the Proverbs passage from *Bereshit Rabbah*, an exegetical commentary on the Book of Genesis, compiled in Palestine between the 4th and 6th centuries of the Common Era. Here, wisdom is identified with Torah which then serves as the cosmic blueprint for creation. The third text is from one of the most influential segments of the *Mishnah*, *Pirke Avot* or the Ethics of the Fathers. Here, we find a description of how

Torah was transmitted from Moses to the Rabbis. The usage of the term Torah without qualification indicates that both the Written Torah and the Oral Torah were given to Moses and he, in turn, transmitted both to the generations after him.

Proverbs 8:22–31

The Lord created me at the beginning of
his work,
the first of his acts of old.
Ages ago I was set up, at the first,
before the beginning of the earth.
When there were no depths I was brought
forth,
when there were no springs abounding with
water.
Before the mountains had been shaped,
before the hills, I was brought forth;
before he had made the earth with its fields,
or the first of the dust of the world.
When he established the heavens, I was there,
when he drew a circle on the face of the
deep,
when he made firm the skies above,
when he established the fountains of the
deep,
when he assigned to the sea its limit,
so that the waters might not transgress his
command,
when he marked out the foundations of the
earth
then I was beside him, like a master
workman [*amon*];
and I was daily his delight, rejoicing before
him always,
rejoicing in his inhabited world and
delighting in the sons of men.

Bereshit Rabbah 1:1

Rabbi Oshaya commenced his interpretation in this manner: 'Then I was beside him like a master workman [*amon*]' (Proverbs 8:30). *Amon* means tutor; *amon* means covered; *amon* means hidden; and some say *amon* means great. *Amon* is a tutor, as you read, 'as an *omen* [nursing-father] carries the suckling child' (Numbers 11:12). *Amon* means covered, as in the verse, '*ha'emunim* [they that were clad, i.e., covered] in scarlet' (Lamentations 4:5). *Amon* means hidden, as in the verse, 'and he concealed [*omen*] Hadassah' (Esther 2:7). *Amon* means great, as in the verse, 'are you better than No-amon?' (Nahum 3:8) which is rendered, are you better than Alexandria the Great, that is situated among the Rivers. Another interpretation: *amon* is a workman [*uman*]. The Torah declares: 'I was the working tool of the Holy One, blessed be He.' In human practice, when a mortal king builds a palace, he builds it not with his own skill but with the skill of an architect. The architect moreover does not build it out of his head, but employs plans and diagrams to know how to arrange the rooms and the doors. Thus God consulted the Torah and created the world, while the Torah declares, 'In the beginning God created' (Genesis 1:1). The word 'beginning' refers to the Torah, as in the verse 'The Lord made me as the beginning of his way' (Proverbs 8:22).

Pirke Avot 1:1

Moses received the Torah on Sinai, and transmitted it to Joshua; Joshua transmitted it to the elders; the elders transmitted it to the prophets; the prophets transmitted it to the men of the Great Assembly.

They said three things: deliberate in judgment, raise up many disciples and make a fence around the Torah.

Doctrine 3

History and Identity: Deuteronomy 26

This text from Deuteronomy is one of the earliest doxologies of ancient Israel. Its original ritual context was the offering of the first-fruits. When these had been delivered, the Israelite would recite this narrative which confirmed his place in the sacred history of Israel. It is essentially an affirmation of identity which takes precedence over the narrative of creation and the giving of Torah. To be an Israelite means to be a descendant of the wandering Aramean, Abraham, to experience the oppression of Egypt and the liberation from Egypt. This text was assimilated into the ritual of the Passover in the history of Judaism so that the Jew re-experiences these events in the Passover banquet.

And you shall make response before the Lord your God, 'A wandering Aramean was my father; and he went down into Egypt and sojourned there, few in number; and there he became a nation, great, mighty, and populous. And the Egyptians treated us harshly, and afflicted us, and laid upon us hard bondage. Then we cried to the Lord the God of our fathers, and the Lord heard our voice, and saw our affliction, our toil, and our oppression; and the Lord brought us out of Egypt with a mighty hand and an outstretched arm, with great terror, with signs and wonders; and he brought us into this place and gave us this land, a land flowing with milk and honey.

Doctrine 4

Commandments and Land: Deuteronomy 11

This text from Deuteronomy articulates the doctrinal connection between the ancient Israelites and land. The land promised to Abraham and his descendants can only be maintained by fulfilment of the commandments. Indeed, fulfilment of those commandments is not only requisite for possession of the land, but also for real human life; fulfilment of the commandments leads to blessing while disregarding them results in the curse.

'You shall therefore keep all the commandments which I command you this day, that you may be strong, and go in and take possession of the land which you are going over to possess, and that you may live long in the land which the Lord swore to your fathers to give to them and to their descendants, a land flowing with milk and honey. For the land which you are entering to take possession of it is not like the land of Egypt, from which you have come, where you sowed your seed and watered it with your feet, like a garden of vegetables; but the land which you are going over to possess is a land of hills and valleys, which drinks water by the rain from heaven, a land which the Lord your God cares for; the eyes of the Lord your God are always upon it, from the beginning of the year to the end of the year.

'And if you will obey my commandments which I command you this day, to love the Lord your God, and to serve him with all your heart and with all your soul, he will give the rain for your land in its season, the early rain and the later rain, that you may gather in your grain and your wine and your oil. And he will give grass in your fields for your cattle, and you shall eat and be full. Take heed lest your heart be deceived, and you turn aside and serve other gods and worship them, and the anger of the Lord be kindled against you, and he shut up the heavens, so that there be no rain, and the land yield no fruit, and you perish quickly off the good land which the Lord gives you.

'You shall therefore lay up these words of mine in your heart and in your soul; and you shall bind them as a sign upon your hand, and they shall be as frontlets between your eyes. And you shall teach them to your children, talking of them when you are sitting in your house, and when you are walking by the way, and when you lie down, and when you rise. And you shall write them upon the doorposts of your house and upon your gates, that your days and the days of your children may be multiplied in the land which the Lord swore to your fathers to give them, as long as the heavens are above the earth. For it you will be careful to do all this commandment which I command you to do, loving the Lord your God, walking in all his ways, and cleaving to him, then the Lord will drive out all these nations before you, and you will dispossess nations greater and mightier than yourselves. Every place on which the soles of your foot treads shall be yours; your territory shall be from the wilderness and Lebanon and from the river, the River Euphrates, to the western sea. No man shall be able to stand against you; the Lord your God will lay the fear of you and the dread of you upon all the land that you shall tread, as he promised you.

'Behold, I set before you this day a blessing and a curse: the blessing, if you obey the commandments of the Lord your God, which I command you this day, and the curse, if you do not obey the commandments of the Lord your God, but turn aside from the way which I command you this day, to go after other gods which you have not known. And when the Lord your God brings you into the land which you are entering to take possession of it, you shall set the blessing on Mount Gerizim and the curse on Mount Ebal. Are they not beyond the Jordan, west of the road, toward the going down of the sun, in the land of the Canaanites who live in the Arabah, over against Gilgal, beside the oak of Moreh? For you are to pass over the Jordan to go in to take possession of the land which the Lord your God gives you; and when you possess it and live in it, you shall be careful to do all the statutes and the ordinances which I set before you this day.'

Doctrine 5

The Promise of Redemption: Jeremiah 30–31

The great prophets of ancient Israel summon man to return to proper ethical conduct and proper relation to God. Insistent as they are on these standards, they are equally confident that this will lead to redemption. This text from the prophet Jeremiah, perhaps spoken on the eve of the destruction of the southern kingdom of Judah by the Babylonians, holds out the promise of redemption not only for the southern kingdom, but also for the northern kingdom taken into captivity at the end of the 7th century by the Assyrians. The promise of redemption and its fulfilment becomes one central component in the doctrinal dimension of ancient Israel and is transferred to Judaism, where redemption is interpreted as a historical goal.

For thus says the Lord:
'Your hurt is incurable,
and your wound is grievous.
There is none to uphold your cause,
no medicine for your wound,
no healing for you.
All your lovers have forgotten you;
they care nothing for you;
for I have dealt you the blow of an enemy,
the punishment of a merciless foe,
because your guilt is great,
because your sins are flagrant.
Why do you cry out over your hurt?
Your pain is incurable.
Because your guilt is great,
because your sins are flagrant,
I have done these things to you.
Therefore all who devour you shall be devoured,
and all your foes, every one of them, shall go into captivity;
those who despoil you shall become a spoil,
and all who prey on you I will make a prey.
For I will restore health to you,
and your wounds I will heal, says the Lord,
because they have called you an outcast:
"It is Zion, for whom no one cares!" '

Thus says the Lord:
'Behold, I will restore the fortunes of the tents of Jacob,
and have compassion on his dwellings;
the city shall be rebuilt upon its mound,
and the palace shall stand where it used to be.
Out of them shall come songs of thanksgiving,
and the voices of those who make merry.
I will make them honoured, and they shall not be small.
Their children shall be as they were of old,
and their congregation shall be established before me;
and I will punish all who oppress them.
Their prince shall be one of themselves,
their ruler shall come forth from the midst;
I will make him draw near, and he shall approach me,
for who would dare of himself to approach me?' says the Lord.
'And you shall be my people,
and I will be your God.'

Behold the storm of the Lord!
Wrath has gone forth, a whirling tempest;
it will burst upon the head of the wicked.
The fierce anger of the Lord will not turn back
until he has executed and accomplished the intents of his mind.
In the latter days you will understand this.

'At that time,' says the Lord, 'I will be the God of all the families of Israel,
and they shall be my people.'

Thus says the Lord:
'The people who survived the sword found grace in the wilderness;
when Israel sought for rest, the Lord appeared to him from afar.
I have loved you with an everlasting love;
therefore I have continued my faithfulness to you.
Again I will build you, and you shall be built,
O virgin Israel!
Again you shall adorn yourself with timbrels,
and shall go forth in the dance of the merrymakers.
Again you shall plant vineyards upon the mountains of Sama'ria;
the planters shall plant, and shall enjoy the fruit.
For there shall be a day when watchmen will call in the hill country of E'phraim:
"Arise, and let us go up to Zion, to the Lord our God." '

For thus says the Lord:
'Sing aloud with gladness for Jacob,
and raise shouts for the chiefs of the nations;
proclaim, give praise, and say,
"The Lord has saved his people, the remnant of Israel."
Behold, I will bring them from the north country,
and gather them from the farthest parts of the earth,
among them the blind and the lame, the woman with child and her who is in travail, together;
a great company, they shall return here.
With weeping they shall come,
and with consolations I will lead them back,
I will make them walk by brooks of water,

in a straight path in which they shall not
stumble;
for I am a father to Israel,
and E'phraim is my first-born.

'Hear the word of the Lord, O nations,
and declare it in the coastlands afar off;
say, "He who scattered Israel will gather
him,
and will keep him as a shepherd keeps his
flock."
For the Lord has ransomed Jacob,
and has redeemed him from hands too
strong for him.
They shall come and sing aloud on the height
of Zion,
and they shall be radiant over the goodness
of the Lord,
over the grain, the wine, and the oil,
and over the young of the flock and the
herd;
their life shall be like a watered garden,
and they shall languish no more.
Then shall the maidens rejoice in the dance,
and the young men and the old shall be
merry.
I will turn their mourning into joy,
I will comfort them, and give them gladness
for sorrow.
I will feast the soul of the priests with
abundance,
and my people shall be satisfied with my
goodness,'
says the Lord.

Thus says the Lord:
'A voice is heard in Ramah,
lamentation and bitter weeping.
Rachel is weeping for her children;
she refuses to be comforted for her children,
because they are not.'

Thus says the Lord:
'Keep your voice from weeping, and your eyes
from tears;
for your work shall be rewarded,
says the Lord,
and they shall come back from the land of
the enemy.
There is hope for your future,
says the Lord,
and your children shall come back to their
own country.
I have heard E'phraim bemoaning,
"Thou hast chastened me, and I was chastened,
like an untrained calf;
for thou art the Lord my God.
For after I had turned away I repented;
and after I was instructed, I smote upon my
thigh;
I was ashamed, and I was confounded,
because I bore the disgrace of my youth."
Is E'phraim my dear son?
Is he my darling child?
For as often as I speak against him,
I do remember him still.
Therefore my heart yearns for him;
I will surely have mercy on him,'
says the Lord.

Ritual 1

The Shabbat: Exodus 23 and 31

These texts from the Book of Exodus represent the ritual institution of the Shabbat which is the paradigm of sacred time for both ancient Israel and Judaism. The Shabbat is the ritual re-experience of God's rest at the end of creation, and in both texts is extended to all living creatures and not man alone. Also, the Shabbat becomes another sign, along with circumcision, of the covenant made between God and Abraham's descendants.

Exodus 23:12–13

'Six days you shall do your work, but on the seventh day you shall rest; that your ox and your ass may have rest, and the son of your bondmaid, and the alien, may be refreshed. Take heed to all that I have said to you; and make no mention of the names of other gods, nor let such be heard out of your mouth.'

Exodus 31:12–17

And the Lord said to Moses, 'Say to the people of Israel, You shall keep my sabbaths, for this is a sign between me and you throughout your generations, that you may know that I, the Lord, sanctify you. You shall keep the sabbath, because it is holy for you; every one who profanes it shall be put to death; whoever does any work on it, that soul shall be cut off from among his people. Six days shall work be done, but the seventh day is a sabbath of solemn rest, holy to the Lord; whoever does any work on the sabbath day shall be put to death. Therefore the people of Israel shall keep the sabbath, observing the sabbath throughout their generations, as a perpetual covenant. It is a sign for ever between me and the people of Israel that in six days the Lord made heaven and earth, and on the seventh day he rested, and was refreshed.'

Ritual 2

Sacrifice: Leviticus 1–2 and Babylonian Talmud

The central form of ritual in ancient Israel was sacrifice. Indeed, the ancient Israelite would not have understood other ritual activities, such as prayer, apart from sacrifice. The first text, from Leviticus, describes two specific forms of sacrifice, the *olah* or burnt-offering and the *Minḥah* or meal-offering. When the Temple, the institution housing this ritual and activated by a very elaborate priesthood, was destroyed by the Romans in 70 CE, the Rabbis began to extend the meaning of sacrifice beyond the physical sacrifices described by Leviticus. The second text represents such an extension of meaning and is taken from the Talmud of Babylonian Jewry (compiled in the late 7th and early 8th centuries CE). This interpretation, in which prayer and study of the institution of sacrifice are functional equivalents of sacrifice, comes as the conclusion of a long and elaborate discussion of the *Minḥah*.

Leviticus 1:1–2:16

The Lord called Moses, and spoke to him from the tent of meeting, saying, 'Speak to the people of Israel, and say to them, When any man of you brings an offering to the Lord, you shall bring your offering of cattle from the herd or from the flock.

'If his offering is a burnt offering from the herd, he shall offer a male without blemish; he shall offer it at the door of the tent of meeting, that he may be accepted before the Lord; he shall lay his hand upon the head of the burnt offering, and it shall be accepted for him to make atonement for him. Then he shall kill the bull before the Lord; and Aaron's sons the priests shall present the blood, and throw the blood round about against the altar that is at the door of the tent of meeting. And he shall flay the burnt offering and cut it into pieces; and the sons of Aaron the priest shall put fire on the altar, and lay wood in order upon the fire; and Aaron's sons the priests shall lay the pieces, the head, and the fat, in order upon the wood that is on the fire upon the altar; but its entrails and its legs he shall wash with water. And the priest shall burn the whole on the altar, as a burnt offering, an offering by fire, a pleasing odour to the Lord.

'If his gift for a burnt offering is from the flock, from the sheep or goats, he shall offer a male without blemish; and he shall kill it on the north side of the altar before the Lord, and Aaron's sons the priests shall throw its blood against the altar before the Lord, and Aaron's sons the priests shall throw its blood against the altar round about. And he shall cut it into pieces, with its head and its fat, and the priest shall lay them in order upon the wood that is on the fire upon the altar; but the entrails and the legs he shall wash with water. And the priest shall offer the whole, and burn it on the altar; it is a burnt offering, an offering by fire, a pleasing odour to the Lord.

'If his offering to the Lord is a burnt offering of birds, then he shall bring his offering of turtle doves or of young pigeons. And the priest shall bring it to the altar and wring off its head, and burn it on the altar; and its blood shall be drained out on the side of the altar; and he shall take away its crop with the feathers, and cast it beside the altar on the east side, in the place for ashes; he shall tear it by its wings, but shall not divide it asunder. And the priest shall burn it on the altar, upon the wood that is on the fire; it is a burnt offering, an offering by fire, a pleasing odour to the Lord.

'When any one brings a cereal offering as an offering to the Lord, his offering shall be of fine flour; he shall pour oil upon it, and put frankincense on it, and bring it to Aaron's sons the priests. And he shall take from it a handful of the fine flour and oil, with all of its frankincense; and the priest shall burn this as its memorial portion upon the altar, an offering by fire, a pleasing odour to the Lord. And what is left of the cereal offering shall be for Aaron and his sons; it is a most holy part of the offerings by fire to the Lord.

'When you bring a cereal offering baked in the oven as an offering, it shall be unleavened cakes of fine flour mixed with oil, or unleavened wafers spread with oil. And if your offering is a cereal offering baked on a griddle, it shall be of fine flour unleavened, mixed with oil; you shall break it in pieces, and pour oil on it; it is a cereal offering. And if your offering is a cereal offering cooked in a pan, it shall be made of fine flour with oil. And you shall bring the cereal offering that is made of these things to the Lord; and when it is presented to the priest, he shall bring it to the altar. And the priest shall take from the cereal offering its memorial portion and burn this on the altar, an offering by fire, a pleasing odour to the Lord. And what is left of the cereal offering shall be for Aaron and his sons; it is a most holy part of the offerings by fire to the Lord.

'No cereal offering which you bring to the Lord shall be made with leaven; for you shall burn no leaven nor any honey as an offering by fire to the Lord. As an offering of first fruits you may bring them to the Lord, but they shall not be offered on the altar for a pleasing odour. You shall season all your cereal offerings with salt; you shall not let the salt of the covenant with your God be lacking from your cereal offering; with all your offerings you shall offer salt.

'If you offer a cereal offering of first fruits to the Lord, you shall offer for the cereal offering of your first fruits crushed new grain from fresh ears, parched with fire. And you shall put oil upon it and lay frankincense on it; it is a cereal offering. And the priest shall burn as its memorial portion part of the crushed grain and of the oil with all of its frankincense; it is an offering by fire to the Lord.'

Babylonian Talmud, Tractate Minahot 110a

'And in every place incense is offered to my name, and a pure offering; for my name is great among the nations, says the Lord of hosts' (Malachi 1:11). What is the meaning of the phrase 'in every place'?[1] R. Samuel b. Nahmai said in the name of R. Jonathan that this refers to the students of the sages who engage in the study of Torah in every place, (and God says) I account it to them as though they burnt and presented offerings to my name. The phrase 'and a pure offering' refers to one who studies the Torah in purity; that is one who marries a wife and then studies Torah.

'A song of Ascents. Come, bless the Lord, all you servants of the Lord, who stand in the house of the Lord in the nights' (Psalm 134:1). What is the meaning of the phrase 'in the nights'? R.

[1] Each of the biblical verses brought into the discussion would seem to suggest that either the biblical narrative is contradictory (here, it contradicts injunctions within the Torah which confine sacrifice to the 'house of the Lord', i.e., Jerusalem) or that historical events, such as the destruction of the Temple, contradict the truth of the revealed text.

Johanan said that this refers to the students of the sages who devote themselves to the study of the Torah at night and the Torah accounts it to them as though they were occupied with the Temple ritual.

'Behold, I am going to build a house for the name of the Lord my God and dedicate it to him for the burning of incense of sweet spices before him, and for a continual offering of the showbread, and for burnt offerings morning and evening, on the Shabbats and the new moons and the appointed festivals of the Lord our God. This is an ordinance for ever to Israel' (2 Chronicles 2:3). R. Giddal said in the name of Rab that this refers to the altar built in heaven, where Michael, the great Prince, stands and offers up an offering. R. Johanan said that this verse refers to the students of the sages who are engaged with the laws of the Temple ritual. Scripture accounts it to them as though the Temple was built in their days.

Resh Laqish introduced another verse and asked how is it to be understood: 'This is the law for the burnt offering, for the meal offering, for the transgression offering and for the guilt offering' (Leviticus 7:37). It teaches, he continued, that whosoever occupies himself with the study of Torah is as though he were offering a burnt offering, a meal offering, a transgression offering and a guilt offering. Rabba asked, why then does the verse say, '*for* the burnt offering, *for* the meal offering'? It should have said, 'a burnt offering, a meal offering'! Rather, it means that whosoever engages in the study of Torah needs neither burnt offering, nor meal offering, nor transgression offering, nor guilt offering.

R. Isaac said, what is the significance of the verses, 'This is the law of the transgression offering' (Leviticus 6:18) and 'This is the law of the guilt offering' (Leviticus 7:1)? These verses teach that whosoever engages in the study of the law of the transgression offering is as if he offered the transgression offering and anyone who engages in the study of the law of the guild offering is as if he offered a guilt offering.

Ritual 3

The Festivals of Shavuot and Sukkot: Exodus 23

The most important ritual festivals in ancient Israel, aside from the Shabbat, were the festivals of Passover, here described as the feast of unleavened bread, Shavuot, here described as the feast of harvest, and Sukkot, here called the feast of ingathering. These festivals were distinctive in ancient Israel due to the command that on these festivals 'shall all your males appear before the Lord God'. Every male was required to journey from his place to Jerusalem in order to fulfill the commandment of appearing before God on these festivals. Their distinctive aspect was retained in the history of Judaism, and they were denoted as 'the three pilgrimage festivals'. In the modern world, the importance of these festivals has waned somewhat so that Rosh Ha-Shannah, the New Year, and Yom Kippur, the Day of Atonement, are often described as the most important festivals in the Jewish ritual year.

'Three times in the year you shall keep a feast to me. You shall keep the feast of unleavened bread; as I commanded you, you shall eat unleavened bread for seven days at the appointed time in the month of Abib, for in it you came out of Egypt. None shall appear before me empty-handed. You shall keep the feast of harvest, of the first fruits of your labour, of what you sow in the field. You shall keep the feast of ingathering at the end of the year, when you gather in from the field the fruit of your labour. Three times in the year shall all your males appear before the Lord God.'

Ritual 4

Praise of the Creator: Psalm 104

This psalm represents the poetic expansion of the fundamental themes found in the Genesis creation narrative. The psalmist describes God as master of creation; all things in the created world are dependent upon him. Indeed, this text represents one of the high points of literary creativity in ancient Israel, but the psalms, traditionally attributed to David, also represent the liturgical formulations which in many cases accompanied the rituals of the Temple.

Bless the Lord, O my soul!
O Lord my God, thou art very great!
Thou art clothed with honour and majesty,
who coverest thyself with light as with a garment,
who hast stretched out the heavens like a tent,
who hast laid the beams of thy chambers on the waters,
who makest the clouds thy chariot,
who ridest on the wings of the wind,
who makest the winds thy messengers,
fire and flame thy ministers.

Thou didst set the earth on its foundations,
so that it should never be shaken.
Thou didst cover it with the deep as with a garment;
the waters stood above the mountains.
At thy rebuke they fled;
at the sound of thy thunder they took to flight.
The mountains rose, the valleys sank down
to the place which thou didst appoint for them.
Thou didst set a bound which they should not pass,
so that they might not again cover the earth.

Thou makest springs gush forth in the valleys;
they flow between the hills,
they give drink to every beast of the field;
the wild asses quench their thirst.
By them the birds of the air have their habitation;
they sing among the branches.
From thy lofty abode thou waterest the mountains;
the earth is satisfied with the fruit of thy work.

Thou dost cause the grass to grow for the cattle,
and plants for men to cultivate,
that he may bring forth food from the earth,
and wine to gladden the heart of man,
oil to make his face shine,
and bread to strengthen man's heart.
The trees of the Lord are watered abundantly,
the cedars of Lebanon which he planted.
In them the birds build their nests;
the stork has her home in the fir trees.
The high mountains are for the wild goats;
the rocks are a refuge for the badgers.
Thou hast made the moon to mark the seasons;
the sun knows its time for setting.
Thou makest darkness, and it is night,
when all the beasts of the forest creep forth.
The young lions roar for their prey,
seeking their food from God.
When the sun rises, they get them away
and lie down in their dens.
Man goes forth to his work and to his labour until the evening.

O Lord, how manifold are thy works!
In wisdom hast thou made them all;
the earth is full of thy creatures.
Yonder is the sea, great and wide,
which teems with things innumerable,
living things both small and great.
There go the ships,
and Leviathan which thou didst form to sport in it.

These all look to thee,
to give them their food in due season.
When thou givest to them, they gather it up;
when thou openest thy hand, they are filled with good things.
When thou hidest thy face, they are dismayed;
when thou takest away their breath,
they die and return to their dust.
When thou sendest forth thy Spirit, they are created;
and thou renewest the face of the ground.

May the glory of the Lord endure for ever,
may the Lord rejoice in his works,
who looks on the earth and it trembles,
who touches the mountains and they smoke!
I will sing to the Lord as long as I live;
I will sing praise to my God while I have being.
May my meditation be pleasing to him,
for I rejoice in the Lord.
Let sinners be consumed from the earth,
and let the wicked be no more!
Bless the Lord, O my soul!
Praise the Lord!

Ritual 5

The Passover: Exodus 12

This text from the Book of Exodus describes the institution of the Passover lamb and the tenth plague which befell the Egyptians. The roasting and eating of the lamb appears as a preliminary ritual in which the Israelites are required to participate before the last plague, the killing of the first-born, settles upon the land. The ritual of the Passover lamb and the sacred narrative of God's passing over the specially prepared homes of the Israelites are re-experienced in the ritual repetition of the Passover banquet, the *seder*. Here, the symbolic foods of the roasted shank-bone and the unleavened bread, the *matzah*, represent the Passover lamb and the special preparation required for freedom from Egyptian oppression.

The Lord said to Moses and Aaron in the land of Egypt, 'This month shall be for you the beginning of months; it shall be the first month of the year for you. Tell all the congregation of Israel that on the tenth day of this month they shall take every man a lamb according to their fathers' houses, a lamb for a household; and if the household is too small for a lamb, then a man and his neighbour next to his house shall take according to the number of persons; according to what each can eat you shall make your count for the lamb. Your lamb shall be without blemish, a male a year old; you shall take it from the sheep or from the goats; and you shall keep it until the fourteenth day of this month, when the whole assembly of the congregation of Israel shall kill their lamb in the evening. Then they shall take some of the blood, and put it on the two doorposts and the lintel of the houses in which they eat them. They shall eat the flesh that night, roasted; with unleavened bread and bitter herbs they shall eat it. do not eat any of it raw or boiled with water, but roasted, its head with its legs and its inner parts. And you shall let none of it remain until the morning, anything that remains until the morning you shall burn. In this manner you shall eat it; your loins girded, your sandles on your feet, and your staff in your hand; and you shall eat it in haste. It is the Lord's passover. For I will pass through the land of Egypt that night, and I will smite all the first-born in the land of Egypt, both man and beast; and on all the gods of Egypt I will execute judgments: I am the Lord. The blood shall be a sign for you, upon the houses where you are; and when I see the blood, I will pass over you, and no plague shall fall upon you to destroy you, when I smite the land of Egypt.

'This day shall be for you a memorial day, and you shall keep it as a feast to the Lord; throughout your generations you shall observe it as an ordinance for ever. Seven days you shall eat unleavened bread; on the first day you shall put away leaven out of your house, for if any one eats what is leavened, from the first day until the seventh day, that person shall be cut off from Israel. On the first day you shall hold a holy assembly, and on the seventh day a holy assembly; no work shall be done on those days; but what every one must eat, that only may be prepared by you. And you shall observe the feast of unleavened bread, for on this very day I brought your hosts out of the land of Egypt: therefore you shall observe this day, throughout your generations, as an ordinance for ever. In the first month, on the fourteenth day of the month at evening, you shall eat unleavened bread, and so until the twenty-first day of the month at evening. For seven days no leaven shall be found in your houses; for if any one eats what is leavened, that person shall be cut off from the congregation of Israel, whether he is a sojourner or a native of the land. You shall eat nothing leavenened; in all your dwellings you shall eat unleavened bread.'

Then Moses called all the elders of Israel, and said to them, 'Select lambs for yourselves according to your families, and kill the passover lamb. Take a bunch of hyssop and dip it in the blood which is in the basin, and touch the lintel and the two doorposts with the blood which is in the basin; and none of you shall go out of the door of his house until the morning. For the Lord will pass through to slay the Egyptians; and when he sees the blood on the lintel and on the two doorposts, the Lord will pass over the door, and will not allow the destroyer to enter your houses to slay you. You shall observe this rite as an ordinance for you and for your sons for ever. And when you come to the land which the Lord will give you, as he has promised, you shall keep this service. And when your children say to you, "What do you mean by this service?" you shall say, "It is the sacrifice of the Lord's passover, for he passed over the houses of the people of Israel in Egypt, when he slew the Egyptians but spared our houses."' And the people bowed their heads and worshipped.

Then the people of Israel went and did so; as the Lord had commanded Moses and Aaron, so they did.

At midnight the Lord smote all the first-born in the land of Egypt, from the first-born of Pharaoh who sat on his throne to the first-born of the captive who was in the dungeon, and all the first-born of the cattle. And Pharaoh rose up in the night, he, and all his servants, and all the Egyptians; and there was a great cry in Egypt, for there was not a house where one was not dead. And he summoned Moses and Aaron by night, and said, 'Rise up, go forth from among my people, both you and the people of Israel; and go, serve the Lord, as you have said. Take your flocks and your herds, as you have said, and be gone; and bless me also!'

And the Egyptians were urgent with the people, to send them out of the land in haste; for they said, 'We are all dead men.' So the people took their dough before it was leavened, their kneading bowls being bound up in their mantles on their shoulders. The people of Israel had also done as Moses told them, for they had asked of the Egyptians jewellery of silver and of gold, and clothing; and the Lord had given the people favour in the sight of the Egyptians, so that they let them have what they asked. Thus they despoiled the Egyptians.

And the people of Israel journeyed from Ram'eses to Succoth, about six hundred thousand men on foot, besides women and children. A mixed multitude also went up with them, and very many cattle, both flocks and herds. And they baked unleavened cakes of the dough which they had brought out of Egypt, for it was not leavened, because they were thrust out of Egypt and could not tarry, neither had they prepared for themselves any provisions.

The time that the people of Israel dwelt in

Egypt was four hundred and thirty years. And at the end of four hundred and thirty years, on that very day, all the hosts of the Lord went out from the land of Egypt. It was a night of watching by the Lord, to bring them out of the land of Egypt; so this same night is a night of watching kept to the Lord by all the people of Israel throughout their generations.

And the Lord said to Moses and Aaron, 'This is the ordinance of the passover: no foreigner shall eat it; but every slave that is bought for money may eat of it after you have circumcised him. No sojourner or hired servant may eat of it. In one house shall it be eaten; you shall not carry forth any of the flesh outside the house; and you shall not break a bone of it. All the congregation of Israel shall keep it. And when a stranger shall sojourn with you and would keep the passover to the Lord, let all his males be circumcised, then he may come near and keep it; he shall be as a native of the land. But no uncircumcised person shall eat of it. There shall be one law for the native and for the stranger who sojourns among you.'

Thus did all the people of Israel; as the Lord commanded Moses and Aaron, so they did. And on that very day the Lord brought the people of Israel out of the land of Egypt by their hosts.

Institutional Expression 1

The Priesthood: Exodus 29

The leadership of ancient Israel was centred around and upon the activities of a clearly defined priesthood which descended from Aaron and his sons. The tension between this institution and other forms of leadership in ancient Israel, kings and prophets shaped much of the history of ancient Israel. This text describes the installation of Aaron and his sons as the priests of Israel.

'Now this is what you shall do to them to consecrate them, that they may serve me as priests. Take one young bull and two rams without blemish, and unleavened bread, unleavened cakes mixed with oil, and unleavened wafers spread with oil. You shall make them of fine wheat flour. And you shall put them in one basket and bring them in the basket, and bring the bull and the two rams. You shall bring Aaron and his sons to the door of the tent of meeting, and wash them with water. And you shall take the garments, and put on Aaron the coat and the robe of the ephod,[1] and the ephod, and the breastpiece, and gird him with the skilfully woven band of the ephod; and you shall set the turban on his head, and put the holy crown upon the turban. And you shall take the anointing oil, and pour it on his head and anoint him. Then you shall bring his sons, and put coats on them, and you shall gird them with girdles and bind caps on them; and the priesthood shall be theirs by a perpetual statute. Thus you shall ordain Aaron and his sons.

[1] The ephod was a tunic-like garment worn under the breastplate. The breastplate was made up of 12 precious or semi-precious stones representing the 12 tribes of Israel. Both were used for divinatory purposes.

Institutional Expression 2

A Kingdom of Priests: Exodus 19

While the actual priesthood was confined to the descendants of Aaron, his sons and members of the tribe of Levi, the priesthood as a metaphor was extended to all of Israel. This short text becomes vital to Jewish self-consciousness and reflection on the nature of the covenant made between God and Abraham. Israel's election is articulated through this extended metaphor of priesthood.

On the third new moon after the people of Israel had gone forth out of the land of Egypt, on that day they came into the wilderness of Sinai. And when they set out from Reph'idim and came into the wilderness of Sinai, they encamped in the wilderness; and there Israel encamped before the mountain. And Moses went up to God, and the Lord called to him out of the mountain, saying, 'Thus you shall say to the house of Jacob, and tell the people of Israel: you have seen what I did to the Egyptians, and how I bore you on eagles' wings and brought you to myself. Now therefore, if you will obey my voice and keep my covenant, you shall be my own possession among all peoples; for all the earth is mine, and you shall be to me a kingdom of priests and a holy nation. These are the words which you shall speak to the children of Israel.'

Institutional Expression 3

The Decalogue of the Community: Exodus 34

This text describes the second Decalogue Moses received on Mount Sinai after he destroyed the first set of the Ten Commandments in his anger at seeing how the Israelites had constructed the Golden Calf in his absence. While the biblical narrative assumes that these commandments are the very same as those he received on the first trip up the mountain, they are very different. In this Decalogue, the emphasis is on the community's responsibilities and hence, we might describe this as the Decalogue of the Community.

'Observe what I command you this day. 'Behold, I will drive out before you the Amorites, the Canaanites, the Hittites, and Per'izzites, the Hivites, and the Jeb'usites. Take heed to yourself, lest you make a covenant with the inhabitants of the land whither you go, lest it become a snare in the midst of you. You shall tear down their altars, and break their pillars, and cut down their Ashe'rim (for you shall worship no other god, for the Lord, whose name is Jealous, is a jealous God), lest you make a covenant with the inhabitants of the land, and when they play the harlot after their gods and sacrifice to their gods and one invites you, you eat of his sacrifice, and you take of their daughters for your sons, and their daughters play the harlot after their gods and make your sons play the harlot after their gods.

'You shall make for yourself no molten gods.

'The feast of unleavened bread you shall keep. Seven days you shall eat unleavened bread, as I commanded you, at the time appointed in the month Abib; for in the month Abib you came out from Egypt. All that opens the womb is mine, all your male cattle, the firstlings of cow and sheep. The firstlings of an ass you shall redeem with a lamb, or if you will not redeem it you shall break its neck. All the first-born of your sons you shall redeem. And none shall appear before me empty.

Six days you shall work, but on the seventh day you shall rest; in ploughing time and in harvest you shall rest. And you shall observe the feast of weeks, the first fruits of wheat harvest, and the feast of ingathering at the year's end. Three times in the year shall all your males appear before the Lord God, the God of Israel. For I will cast out nations before you, and enlarge your borders; neither shall any man describe your land, when you go up to appear before the Lord your God three times in the year.

'You shall not offer the blood of my sacrifice with leaven; neither shall the sacrifice of the feast of the passover be left until the morning. The first of the first fruits of your ground you shall bring to the house of the Lord your God. You shall not boil a kid in its mother's milk.'

And the Lord said to Moses, 'Write these words; in accordance with these words I have made a covenant with you and with Israel.' And he was there with the Lord forty days and forty nights; he neither ate bread nor drank water. And he wrote upon the tables the words of the covenant, the ten commandments.

Experience 1

The Burning Bush: Exodus 3

The first text illustrating the experiential dimension of the Hebrew Bible is from the Book of Exodus and is perhaps the most famous of all examples of the human confrontation with the transcendent. Here, Moses, tending the sheep of Jethro, is both fascinated and terrified by the burning bush. This experience is critical in Moses' life and represents his formal commission to bring the Israelites out of Egypt. The experience confirms Moses' powers to accomplish these deeds and links him to the unfolding sacred history of the descendants of Abraham.

Now Moses was keeping the flock of his father-in-law, Jethro, the priest of Mid'ian; and he led his flock to the west side of the wilderness, and came to Horeb, the mountain of God. And the angel of the Lord appeared to him in a flame of fire out of the midst of a bush; and he looked, and lo, the bush was burning, yet it was not consumed. and Moses said, 'I will turn aside and see this great sight, why the bush is not burnt.' When the Lord saw that he turned aside to see, God called to him out of the bush, 'Moses, Moses!' And he said, 'Here am I.' Then he said, 'Do not come near; put off your shoes from your feet, for the place on which you are standing is holy ground.' And he said, 'I am the God of your father, the God of Abraham, the God of Isaac, and the God of Jacob.' And Moses hid his face, for he was afraid to look at God.

Then the Lord said, 'I have seen the affliction of my people who are in Egypt, and have heard their cry because of their taskmasters; I know their sufferings, and I have come down to deliver them out of the hand of the Egyptians, and to bring them up out of that land to a good and broad land, a land flowing with milk and honey, to the place of the Canaanites, the Hittites, the Amorites, and Per'izzites, the Hivites, and the Jeb'usites. And now, behold, the cry of the people of Israel has come to me, and I have seen the oppression with which the Egyptians oppress them. Come, I will send you to Pharaoh that you may bring forth my people, the sons of Israel, out of Egypt.' But Moses said to God, 'Who am I that I should go to Pharaoh, and bring the sons of Israel out of Egypt?' He said, 'But I will be with you; and this shall be the sign for you, that I have sent you: when you have brought forth the people out of Egypt, you shall serve God upon this mountain.'

Then Moses said to God, 'If I come to the people of Israel and say to them, "The God of your fathers has sent me to you," and they ask me, "What is his name?" what shall I say to them?' God said to Moses, 'I AM WHO I AM.' And he said, 'Say this to the people of Israel, "I AM has sent me to you."' God also said to Moses, 'Say this to the people of Israel, "The Lord, the God of your fathers, the God of Abraham, the God of Isaac, and the God of Jacob, has sent me to you": this is my name for ever, and thus I am to be remembered throughout all generations. Go and gather the elders of Israel together, and say to them, "The Lord, the God of your fathers, the God of Abraham of Isaac, and of Jacob, has appeared to me, saying, "I have observed you and what has been done to you in Egypt; and I promise that I will bring you up out of the affliction of Egypt, to the land of the Canaanites, the Hittites, the Amorites, the Per'izzites, the Hivites, and the Jeb'usites, a land flowing with milk and honey." And they will hearken to your voice; and you and the elders of Israel shall go to the king of Egypt and say to him, "The Lord, the God of the Hebrews, has met with us; and now, we pray you, let us go a three days' journey into the wilderness, that we may sacrifice to the Lord our God." I know that the king of Egypt will not let you go unless compelled by a mighty hand. So I will stretch out my hand and smite Egypt with all the wonders which I will do in it; after that he will let you go. And I will give this people favour in the sight of the Egyptians; and when you go, you shall not go empty, but each woman shall ask of her neighbour, and of her who sojourns in her house, jewellery of silver and gold, and clothing, and you shall put them on your sons and on your daughters; thus you shall despoil the Egyptians.'

Experience 2

The Revelation at Sinai: Exodus 19 and 33

These two texts from the Book of Exodus describe the experience of Moses and Israel at Mount Sinai at the moment in which the Torah was given. The first text describes the preparations of the community and how the mountain, the field of this experience, is set apart from the surrounding geography. The second text describes Moses' second ascent up the mountain and his desire to see God face to face.

Exodus 19:7–25

So Moses came and called the elders of the people, and set before them all these words which the Lord had commanded him. And all the people answered together and said, 'All that the Lord has spoken we will do.' And Moses reported the words of the people to the Lord. And the Lord said to Moses, 'Lo, I am coming to you in a thick cloud, that the people may hear when I speak with you, and may also believe you for ever.'

Then Moses told the words of the people to the Lord. And the Lord said to Moses, 'Go to the people and consecrate them today and tomorrow, and let them wash their garments, and be ready by the third day; for on the third day the Lord will come down upon Mount Sinai in the sight of all the people. And you shall set bounds for the people round about, saying "Take heed that you do not go up into the mountain or touch the border of it; whoever touches the mountain shall be put to death; no hand shall touch him, but he shall be stoned or shot; whether beast or man, he shall not live." When the trumpet sounds a long blast, they shall come up to the mountain.' So Moses went down from the mountain to the people, and consecrated the people; and they washed their garments. And he said to the people, 'Be ready by the third day; do not go near a woman.'

On the morning of the third day there were thunders and lightnings, and a thick cloud upon the mountain, and a very loud trumpet blast, so that all the people who were in the camp trembled. Then Moses brought the people out of the camp to meet God; and they took their stand at the foot of the mountain. And Mount Sinai was wrapped in smoke, because the Lord descended upon it in fire; and the smoke of it went up like the smoke of a kiln, and the whole mountain quaked greatly. And as the sound of the trumpet grew louder and louder, Moses spoke, and God answered him in thunder. And the Lord came down upon Mount Sinai, to the top of the mountain; and the Lord called Moses to the top of the mountain, and Moses went up. And the Lord said to Moses, 'Go down and warn the people, lest they break through to the Lord to gaze and many of them perish. And also let the priests who come near to the Lord consecrate themselves, lest the Lord break out upon them.' And Moses said to the Lord, 'The people cannot come up to Mount Sinai; for thou thyself didst charge us, saying, "Set bounds about the mountain, and consecrate it."' And the Lord said to him, 'Go down, and come up bringing Aaron with you; but do not let the priests and the people break through to come up to the Lord, lest he break out against them.' So Moses went down to the people and told them.

Exodus 33:17–34:10

And the Lord said to Moses, 'This very thing that you have spoken I will do; for you have found favour in my sight, andI know you by name.' Moses said, 'I pray thee, show me thy glory.' And he said, 'I will make all my goodness pass before you, and will proclaim before you my name "The Lord"; and I will be gracious to whom I will be gracious, and will show mercy on whom I will show mercy. But,' he said, 'you cannot see my face; for man shall not see me and live.' And the Lord said, 'Behold, there is a place by me where you shall stand upon the rock; and while my glory passes by I will put you in a cleft of the rock, and I will cover you with my hand until I have passed by; then I will take away my hand, and you shall see my back; but my face shall not be seen.'

The Lord said to Moses, 'Cut two tables of stone like the first; and I will write upon the tables the words that were on the first tables, which you broke. Be ready in the morning, and come up in the morning to Mount Sinai, and present yourself there to me on the top of the mountain. No man shall come up with you, and let no man be seen throughout all the mountain; let no flocks or herds feed before that mountain.' So Moses cut two tables of stone like the first; and he rose early in the morning and went up on Mount Sinai, as the Lord had commanded him, and took in his hand two tables of stone. And the Lord descended in the cloud and stood with him there, and proclaimed the name of the Lord. The Lord passed before him, and proclaimed, 'The Lord, the Lord, a God merciful and gracious, slow to anger, and abounding in steadfast love and faithfulness, keeping steadfast love for thousands, forgiving iniquity and transgression and sin, but who will by no means clear the guilty, visiting the iniquity of the fathers upon the children and the children's children, to the third and the fourth generation.' And Moses made haste to bow his head toward the earth, and worshipped. And he said, 'If now I have found favour in thy sight, O Lord, let the Lord, I pray thee, go in the midst of us, although it is a stiff-necked people; and pardon our iniquity and our sin, and take us for thy inheritance.'

And he said, 'Behold, I make a covenant. Before all your people I will do marvels, such as have not been wrought in all the earth or in any nation; and all the people among whom you are shall see the work of the Lord; for it is a terrible thing that I will do with you.'

Experience 3

Prophetic Visions: Ezekiel, Isaiah and Daniel

These three texts illustrate other aspects of experience in ancient Israel. The first text, from the prophet Ezekiel, describes his vision of God's throne or chariot in the early years of the Babylonian Exile. This description became a central component of later Jewish mysticism in which the mystic attempted to glimpse the throne of God after his ascent through the heavens. The second text is the prophet Isaiah's vision of God. This vision is instrumental in Isaiah's call to prophecy. Indeed, almost all of Israel's great prophets have such intense visionary experiences and in each case, the experience functions as the formal commission of the prophet. The third text is Daniel's vision of the four beasts which are interpreted by Daniel to represent four kingdoms. While the book of Daniel was set in the second half of the 6th century BCE, the book was most likely written in the 2nd century BCE. The prophecy is then a prophecy after the fact and the four beasts or kingdoms represent the Babylonians, the Medes, the Persians and the Greeks.

Ezekiel 1:1–2:10

In the thirtieth year, in the fourth month, on the fifth day of the month, as I was among the exiles by the river Chebar, the heavens were opened, and I saw visions of God. On the fifth day of the month (it was the fifth year of the exile of King Jehoi'achin), the word of the Lord came to Ezekiel the priest, the son of Buzi, in the land of the Chalde'ans by the river Chebar; and the hand of the Lord was upon him there.

As I looked, behold, a stormy wind came out of the north, and a great cloud, with brightness round it, and fire flashing forth continually, and in the midst of it came the likeness of four living creatures. And this was their appearance: they had the form of men, but each had four faces, and each of them had four wings. Their legs were straight, and the soles of their feet were like the sole of a calf's foot; and they sparkled like burnished bronze. Under their wings on their four sides they had human hands. And the four had their faces and their wings thus: their wings touched one another; they went every one straight forward, without turning as they went. As for the likeness of their faces, each had the face of a man in front; the four had the face of a lion on the right side, the four had a face of an ox on the left side, and the four had the face of an eagle at the back. Such were their faces. And their wings were spread out above; each creature had two wings, each of which touched the wing of another, while two covered their bodies. And each went straight forward; wherever the spirit would go, they went, without turning as they went. In the midst of the living creatures there was something that looked like burning coals of fire, like torches moving to and fro among the living creatures; and the fire was bright, and out of the fire went forth lightning. And the living creatures darted to and fro, like a flash of lightning.

Now as I looked at the living creatures, I saw a wheel upon the earth beside the living creatures, one for each of the four of them. As for the appearance of the wheels and their construction: their appearace was like the gleaming of a chrysolite; and the four had the same likeness, their construction being as it were a wheel within a wheel. When they went, they went in any of their four directions without turning as they went. The four wheels had rims and they had spokes; and their rims were full of eyes round about. And when the living creatures went, the wheels went beside them; and when the living creatures rose from the earth, the wheels rose. Wherever the spirit would go, they went, and the wheels rose along with them; for the spirit of the living creatures was in the wheels. When those went, these went; and when those stood, these stood; and when those rose from the earth, the wheels rose along with them; for the spirit of the living creatures was in the wheels.

Over the heads of the living creatures there was the likeness of a firmament, shining like a crystal, spread out above their heads. And under the firmament their wings were stretched out straight, one toward another; and each creature had two wings covering its body. And when they went, I heard the sound of their wings like the sound of many waters, like the thunder of the Almighty, a sound of tumult like the sound of a host; when they stood still, they let down their wings. And there came a voice from above the firmament over their heads; when they stood still, they let down their wings.

And above the firmament over their heads there was the likeness of a throne, in appearance like sapphire; and seated above the likeness of a throne was a likeness as it were of a human form. And upward from what had the appearance of his loins I saw as it were gleaming bronze, like the appearance of fire enclosed round about; and downward from what had the appearance of his loins I saw as it were the appearance of fire, and there was brightness round about him. Like the appearance of the bow that is in the cloud on the day of rain, so was the appearance of the brightness round about.

Such was the appearance of the likeness of the glory of the Lord. And when I saw it, I fell upon my face, and I heard the voice of one speaking.

And he said to me, 'Son of man, stand upon your feet, and I will speak with you.' And when he spoke to me, the spirit entered into me and set me upon my feet; and I heard him speaking to me. And he said to me, 'Son of man, I send you to the people of Israel, to a nation of rebels, who have rebelled against me; they and their fathers have transgressed against me to this very day. The people also are impudent and stubborn: I send you to them; and you shall say to them, "Thus says the Lord God." And whether they hear or refuse to hear (for they are a rebellious house) they will know that there has been a prophet among them. And you, son of man, be not afraid of them, nor be afraid of their words, though briers and thorns are with you and you sit upon scorpions; be not afraid of their words, nor be dismayed at their looks, for they are a rebellious house. And you shall speak my words to them, whether they hear or refuse to hear; for they are a rebellious house.

'But you, son of man, hear what I say to you; be not rebellious like that rebellious house; open your mouth, and eat what I give you.' And when I looked, behold, a hand was stretched out to me, and, lo, a written scroll was in it; and he spread it before me; and it had writing on the front and on the back, and there were written on it words of lamentation and mourning and woe.

Isaiah 6:1–13

In the year the King Uzzi'ah died I saw the Lord sitting upon a throne, high and lifted up; and his train filled the temple. Above him stood the seraphim; each had six wings: with two he covered his face, and with two he covered his feet, and with two he flew. And one called to another and said:

'Holy, holy, holy is the Lord of hosts;
  the whole earth is full of his glory.'

And the foundations of the thresholds shook at the voice of him who called, and the house was filled with smoke. And I said 'Woe is me! For I am lost; for I am a man of unclean lips, and I dwell in the midst of a people of unclean lips; for my eyes have seen the King, the Lord of hosts!'

Then flew one of the seraphim to me, having in his hand a burning coal which he had taken with tongs from the altar. And he touched my mouth, and said: 'Behold, this has touched your lips; your guilt is taken away, and your sin forgiven.' And I heard the voice of the Lord saying, 'Whom shall I send, and who will go for us?' Then I said, 'Here am I! Send me.' And he said, 'Go and say to this people:

"Hear and hear, but do not understand;
  see and see, but do not perceive."
Make the heart of this people fat,
  and their ears heavy, and shut their eyes;
  lest they see with their eyes,
  and hear with their ears,
  and understand with their hearts,
  and turn and be healed.'

  Then I said, 'How long, O Lord?'
  And he said:

'Until cities lie waste without inhabitant,
  and houses without men,
  and the land is utterly desolate,
  and the Lord removes men far away,

and the foresaken places are many in the
midst of the land.
And though a tenth remain in it,
it will be burned again,
like a terebinth or an oak,
whose stump remains standing when it is
felled.'

The holy seed is its stump.

Daniel 7:1–28

In the first year of Belshaz'zar king of Babylon, Daniel had a dream and visions of his head as he lay in his bed. Then he wrote down the dream, and told the sum of the matter. Daniel said, 'I saw in my vision by night, and behold, the four winds of heaven were stirring up the great sea. And four great beasts came up out of the sea, different from one another. The first was like a lion and had eagle's wings. Then as I looked its wings were plucked off, and it was lifted up from the ground and made to stand upon two feet like a man; and the mind of a man was given to it. And behold, another beast, a second one, like a bear. It was raised up on one side; it had three ribs in its mouth between its teeth; and it was told, "Arise, devour much flesh." After this I looked, and lo, another, like a leopard, with four wings of a bird on its back; and the beast had four heads; and dominion was given to it. After this I saw in the night visions, and behold, a fourth beast, terrible and dreadful and exceedingly strong; and it had great iron teeth; it devoured and broke in pieces, and stamped the residue with its feet. It was different from all the beasts that were before it; and it had ten horns. I considered the horns, and behold, there came up among them another horn, a little one, before which three of the first horns were plucked up by the roots; and behold, in this horn were eyes like the eyes of a man, and a mouth speaking great things.

As I looked, thrones were placed
and one that was ancient of days
took his seat;
his raiment was white as snow,
and the hair of his head like pure wool;
his throne was fiery flames,
its wheels were burning fire.
A stream of fire issued
and came forth from before him;
a thousand thousands served him,
and ten thousand times ten
thousand stood before him;
the court sat in judgment,
and the books were opened.

I looked then because of the sound of the great words which the horn was speaking. And as I looked, the beast was slain, and its body destroyed and given over to be burned with fire. As for the rest of the beasts, their dominion was taken away, but their lives were prolonged for a season and a time.

I saw in the night visions,
and behold, with the clouds of heaven
there came one like a son of man,
and he came to see the Ancient of Days
and was presented before him.
And to him was given dominion
and glory and kingdom,
that all peoples, nations, and
languages should serve him;
his dominion is an everlasting dominion,
which shall not pass away,
and his kingdom one
that shall not be destroyed.

'As for me, Daniel, my spirit within me was anxious and the visions of my head alarmed me. I approached one of those who stood there and asked him the truth concerning all this. so he told me, and made known to me the interpretation of the things. "These four great beasts are four kings who shall arise out of the earth. But the saints of the Most High shall receive the kingdom, and possess the kingdom for ever, for ever and ever."

'Then I desired to know the truth concerning the fourth beast, which was different from all the rest, exceedingly terrible, with its teeth of iron and claws of bronze; and which devoured and broke in pieces, and stamped the residue with its feet; and concerning the ten horns that were on its head, and the other horn which came up and before which three of them fell, the horn which had eyes and a mouth that spoke great things, and which seemed greater than its fellows. As I looked, this horn made war with the saints, and prevailed over them, until the Ancient of Days came, and judgment was given for the saints of the Most High, and the time came when the saints received the kingdom.

'Thus he said: "As for the fourth beast,
there shall be a fourth kingdom on earth,
which shall be different from all the
kingdoms,
and it shall devour the whole earth,
and trample it down,
and break it to pieces.
As for the ten horns,
out of this kingdom ten kings shall arise,
and another shall arise after them;
he shall be different from the former ones,
and shall put down three kings.
He shall speak words against the Most High,
and shall wear out the saints of the
Most High,
and shall think to change the
times and the law;
and they shall be given into his hand
for a time, two times, and half a time.
But the court shall sit in judgment,
and his dominion shall be taken away,
to be consumed and destroyed to the end.
And the kingdom and the dominion
and the greatness of the kingdoms
under the whole heaven
shall be given to the people of
the saints of the Most High;
their kingdom shall be an
everlasting kingdom,
and all dominions shall serve and obey
them."

'Here is the end of the matter. As for me, Daniel, my thoughts greatly alarmed me, and my colour changed; but I kept the matter in my mind.'

Experience 4

The Code of Holiness: Leviticus 19

No less important than the intense experiences of Moses at the burning bush or Mount Sinai, the prophets Ezekiel and Isaiah, and Daniel, is the normal experience of the community. This text from Leviticus represents the initial segment of what scholars describe as the 'Holiness Code'. The experience of holiness is not abstract and separated from daily encounters with others. Holiness is experienced in the ethical conduct and this conduct is extended so as to incorporate all life.

And the Lord said to Moses, 'Say to all the congregation of the people of Israel, You shall be holy; for I the Lord your God am holy. Every one of you shall revere his mother and his father, and you shall keep my sabbaths: I am the Lord your God. Do not turn to idols or make for yourselves molten gods: I am the Lord your God.

'When you offer a sacrifice of peace offerings to the Lord, you shall offer it so that you may be accepted. It shall be eaten the same day you offer it, or on the morrow; and anything left over until the third day shall be burned with fire. If it is eaten at all on the third day, it is an abomination; it will not be accepted, and every one who eats it shall bear his iniquity, because he has profaned a holy thing of the Lord; and that person shall be cut off from his people.

'When you reap the harvest of your land, you shall not reap your field to its very border, neither shall you gather the gleanings after your harvest. And you shall not strip your vineyard bare, neither shall you gather the fallen grapes of your vineyard; you shall leave them for the poor and for the sojourner; I am the Lord your God.

'You shall not steal, nor deal falsely, nor lie to one another. And you shall not swear by my name falsely, and so profane the name of your God: I am the Lord.

'You shall not oppress your neighbour or rob him. The wages of a hired servant shall not remain with you all night until the morning. You shall not curse the deaf or put a stumbling block before the blind, but you shall fear your God: I am the Lord.

'You shall do no injustice in judgment; you shall not be partial to the poor or defer to the great, but in righteousness shall you judge your neighbour. You shall not go up and down as a slanderer among your people, and you shall not stand forth against the life of your neighbour: I am the Lord.

'You shall not hate your brother in your heart, but you shall reason with your neighbour, lest you bear sin because of him. You shall not take vengeance or bear any grudge against the sons of your own people, but you shall love your neighbour as yourself: I am the Lord.

'You shall keep my statutes. You shall not let your cattle breed with a different kind; you shall not sow your field with two kinds of seed; nor shall there come upon you a garment of cloth made of two kinds of stuff.

'If a man lies carnally with a woman who is a slave, betrothed to another man and not yet ransomed or given her freedom, an inquiry shall be held. They shall not be put to death, because she was not free; but he shall bring a guilt offering for himself to the Lord, to the door of the tent of meeting, a ram for a guilt offering. And the priest shall make atonement for him with the ram of the guilt offering before the Lord for his sin which he has committed; and the sin which he has committed shall be forgiven him.

'When you come into the land and plant all kinds of trees for food, then you shall count their fruit as forbidden; three years it shall be forbidden to you, it must not be eaten. And in the fourth year all their fruit shall be holy, an offering of praise to the Lord. But in the fifth year you may eat of their fruit, that they may yield more richly for you: I am the Lord your God.

'You shall not eat any flesh with the blood in it. You shall not practise augury or witchcraft. You shall not round off the hair on your temples or mar the edges of your beard. You shall not make any cuttings in your flesh on account of the dead or tattoo any marks upon you: I am the Lord.

'Do not profane your daughter by making her a harlot, lest the hand fall into harlotry and the land become full of wickedness. You shall keep my sabbaths and reverence my sanctuary: I am the Lord.

'Do not turn to mediums or wizards; do not seek them out, to be defiled by them: I am the Lord your God.

'You shall rise up before the hoary head, and honour the face of an old man, and you shall fear your God: I am the Lord.

'When a stranger sojourns with you in your land, you shall not do him wrong. The stranger who sojourns with you shall be to you as the native among you, and you shall love him as yourself; for you were strangers in the land of Egypt: I am the Lord your God.

'You shall do no wrong in judgment, in measures of length or weight or quantity. You shall have just balances, just weights, a just ephah, and a just hin: I am the Lord your God, who brought you out of the land of Egypt. And you shall observe all my statutes and all my ordinances, and do them: I am the Lord.'

Experience 5

Human Limitation: Ecclesiastes 3 and Job 38–42

These two texts illustrate additional facets of ancient Israel's wisdom literature (compare Doctrine 2, Ethics 2 and 3). The first text from the Book of Ecclesiastes underscores temporality in human existence and describes a number of human experiences which condition and structure human life. The title of this book, Ecclesiastes, is derived from the Greek translation of the Hebrew text and probably means 'the one of the congregation' or one who speaks before the congregation. The Hebrew title is Qohelet which means a speaker before a congregation or a preacher. The Jewish tradition has identified this Qohelet as Solomon the son of David, who in many ways is the paradigmatic wise man in ancient Israel. The second text is a central document in both Jewish and Christian reflection on human limitations.

Ecclesiastes 3:1–9

For everything there is a season,
and a time for every matter under heaven:
a time to be born, and a time to die;
a time to plant, and a time to pluck up what is planted;
a time to kill, and a time to heal;
a time to break down, and a time to build up;
a time to weep, and a time to laugh;
a time to mourn, and a time to dance;
a time to cast away stones, and a time to gather stones together;
a time to embrace, and a time to refrain from embracing;
a time to seek, and a time to lose;
a time to keep, and a time to cast away;
a time to rend, and a time to sew;
a time to keep silence, and a time to speak;
a time to love, and a time to hate;
a time for war, and a time for peace.
What gain has the worker from his toil?

Job 38:1–42:6

Then the Lord answered Job out of the whirlwind:
'Who is this that darkens counsel by words without knowledge?
Gird up your loins like a man,
I will question you, and you shall declare to me.

'Where were you when I laid the foundation of the earth?
Tell me, if you have understanding.
Who determined its measurements – surely you know!
Or who stretched the line upon it?
On what were its bases sunk,
or who laid its cornerstone,
when the morning stars sang together,
and all the sons of God shouted for joy?

'Or who shut in the sea with doors,
when it burst forth from the womb;
when I made clouds its garment,
and thick darkness its swaddling band,
and prescribed bounds for it,
and set bars and doors,
and said, "Thus far shall you come, and no farther,
and here shall your proud waves be stayed"?

'Have you commanded the morning since your days began,
and caused the dawn to know its place,
that it might take hold of the skirts of the earth,
and the wicked be shaken out of it?
It is changed like clay under the seal,
and it is dyed like a garment.
from the wicked their light is withheld,
and their uplifted arm is broken.

'Have you entered into the springs of the sea,
or walked in the recesses of the deep?
Have the gates of death been revealed to you,
or have you seen the gates of deep darkness?
Have you comprehended the expanse of the earth?
Declare, if you know all this.

'Where is the way to the dwelling of light,
and where is the place of darkness,
that you may take it to its territory
and that you may discern the paths to its home?
You know, for you were born then,
and the number of your days is great!

'Have you entered the storehouses of the snow,
or have you seen the storehouses of the hail,
which I have reserved for the time of trouble,
for the day of battle and war?
What is the way to the place where the light is distributed,

or where the east wind is scatttered upon the
earth?

'Who has cleft a channel for the torrents of
rain,
and a way for the thunderbolt,
to bring rain on a land where no man is,
on the desert in which there is no man;
to satisfy the waste and desolate land,
and to make the ground put forth grass!

'Has the rain a father,
or who has begotten the drops of dew?
From whose womb did the ice come forth,
and who has given birth to the hoarfrost of
heaven?
The waters become hard like stone,
and the face of the deep is frozen.

'Can you bind the chains of the Plei'ades,
or loose the cords of Orion?
Can you lead forth the Maz'zaroth in their
season,
or can you guide the Bear with its children?
Do you know the ordinances of the heavens?
Can you establish their rule on the earth?

'Can you lift up your voice to the clouds,
that a flood of waters may cover you?
Can you send forth lightnings, that they may
go
and say to you, "Here we are"?
Who has put wisdom in the clouds,
or given understanding to the mists?
Who can number the clouds by wisdom?
Or who can tilt the waterskins of the heavens,
when the dust runs into a mass
and the clods cleave fast together?

'Can you hunt the prey for the lion,
or satisfy the appetite of the young lions,
when they crouch in their dens,
or lie in wait in their covert?
Who provides for the raven its prey,
when its young ones cry to God,
and wander about for lack of food?

'Do you know when the mountain goats bring
forth?
Do you observe the calving of the hinds?
Can you number the months that they fulfil,
and do you know the time when they bring
forth,
when they crouch, bring forth their
offspring,
and are delivered of their young?
Their young ones become strong,
they grow up in the open;
they go forth, and do not return to them.

'Who has let the wild ass go free?
Who has loosed the bonds of the swift ass,
to whom I have given the steppe for his
home,
and the salt land for his dwelling place?
He scorns the tumult of the city;
he hears not the shouts of the driver.
He ranges the mountains as his pasture,
and he searches after every green thing.

'Is the wild ox willing to serve you?
Will he spend the night at your crib?
Can you bind him in the furrow with ropes,
or will he harrow the valleys after you?
Will you depend on him because his strength is
great,
and will you leave to him your labour?
Do you have faith in him that he will return,
and bring your grain to your threshing
floor?

'The wings of the ostrich wave proudly;
but are they the pinions and plumage of
love?
For she leaves her eggs to the earth,
and lets them be warmed on the ground,
forgetting that a foot may crush them,
and that the wild beast may trample them.
She deals cruelly with her young, as if they
were not hers;
though her labour be in vain, yet she has no
fear;
because God has made her forget her
wisdom,
and given her no share in understanding.
When she rouses herself to flee,
she laughs at the horse and his rider.

'Do you give the horse his might?
Do you clothe his neck with strength?
Do you make him leap like the locust?
His majestic snorting is terrible.
He paws in the valley, and exults in his
strength;

he goes out to meet the weapons.
He laughs at fear, and is not dismayed;
he does not turn back from the sword.
Upon him rattle the quiver, the flashing spear
and the javelin.
With fierceness and rage he swallows the
ground;
he cannot stand still at the sound of the
trumpet.
When the trumpet sounds, he says "Aha!"
He smells the battle from afar,
the thunder of the captains, and the
shouting.

'Is it by your wisdom that the hawk soars,
and spreads his wings toward the south?
Is it at your command that the eagle mounts up
and makes his nest on high?
On the rock he dwells and makes his home in
the fastness of the rocky crag.
Thence he spies out the prey;
his eyes behold it afar off.
His young ones suck up blood;
and where the slain are, there is he.'

And the Lord said to Job:
'Shall a faultfinder contend with the Almighty?
He who argues with God, let him answer it.'

Then Job answered the Lord:
'Behold, I am of small account;
what shall I answer thee?
I lay my hand on my mouth.
I have spoken once, and I will not answer;
twice, but I will proceed no further.'

Then the Lord answered Job out of the
whirlwind:
'Gird up your loins like a man;
I will question you, and you declare to me.
Will you even put me in the wrong?
Will you condemn me that you may be
justified?
Have you an arm like God,
and can you thunder with a voice like his?

'Deck your self with majesty and dignity;
clothe yourself with glory and splendour.
Pour forth the overflowings of your anger,
and look on every one that is proud, and
abase him.
Look on every one that is proud, and bring
him low;
and tread down the wicked where they
stand.
Hide them all in the dust together;
bind their faces in the world below.
Then will I also acknowledge to you,
that your own right hand can give you
victory.

'Behold Be'hemoth, which I made as I made
you;
he eats grass like an ox.
Behold, his strength in his loins,
and his power in the muscles of his belly.
He makes his tail stiff like a cedar;
the sinews of his thighs are knit together.
His bones are tubes of bronze,
his limbs like bars of iron.

'He is the first of the works of God;
let him who made him bring near his sword!
For the mountains yield food for him where all
the wild beasts play.
Under the lotus plants he lies,
in the covert of the reeds and in the marsh.
For his shade the lotus trees cover him;
the willows of the brook surround him.
Behold, if the river is turbulent he is not
frightened;
he is confident though Jordan rushes against
his mouth.
Can one take him with hooks,
or pierce his nose with a snare?

'Can you draw out Levi'athan with a fishhook,
or press down his tongue with a cord?
Can you put a rope in his nose,
or pierce his jaw with a hook?
Will he make many supplications to you?
Will he speak to you soft words?
Will he make a covenant with you to take him
for your servant for ever?
Will you play with him as with a bird,
or will you put him on leash for your
maidens?
Will traders bargain over him?
Will they divide him up among the merchants?
Can you fill his skin with harpoons,
or his head with fishing spears?
Lay hands on him;
think of the battle; you will not do it again!

'Behold, the hope of a man is disappointed;
he is laid low even at the sight of him.
No one is so fierce that he dares to stir him up.
Who then is he that can stand before me?
Who has given to me, that I should repay him?
Whatever is under the whole heaven is mine.

'I will not keep silence concerning his limbs,
or his mighty strength, or his goodly frame.
Who can strip off his outer garment?
Who can penetrate his double coat of mail?
Who can open the doors of his face?
Round about his teeth is terror.
His back is made of rows of shields,
shut up closely as with a seal.
One is so near to another that no air can come between them.
They are joined one to another;
they clasp each other and cannot be separated.
His sneezings flash forth light,
and his eyes are like the eyelids of the dawn.
Out of his mouth go flaming torches;
sparks of fire leap forth.
Out of his nostrils comes forth smoke,
as from a boiling pot and burning rushes.
His breath kindles coals,
and a flame comes forth from his mouth.
In his neck abides strength,
and terror dances before him.
The folds of his flesh cleave together,
firmly cast upon him and immovable.
His heart is hard as a stone,
hard as the nether millstone.
When he raises himself up the mighty are afraid;
at the crashing they are beside themselves.
Though the sword reaches him, it does not avail;
nor the spear, the dart, or the javelin.
He counts iron as straw, and bronze as rotten wood.
The arrow cannot make him flee;
for him slingstones are turned to stubble.
Clubs are counted as stubble;
he laughs at the rattle of javelins.
His underparts are like sharp potsherds;
he spreads himself like a threshing sledge on the mire.
He makes the deep boil like a pot;
he makes the sea like a pot of ointment.
Behind him he leaves a shining wake;
one would think the deep to be hoary.
Upon earth there is not his like,
a creature without fear.
He beholds everything that is high;
he is king over all the sons of pride.'

Then Job answered the Lord:
'I know that thou canst do all things,
and that no purpose of thine can be thwarted.
"Who is this that hides counsel without knowledge?"
Therefore I have uttered what I did not understand,
things too wonderful for me, which I did not know.
"Hear, and I will speak;
I will question you, and you declare to me."
I had heard of thee by the hearing of the ear,
but now my eye sees thee;
therefore I despise myself,
and repent in dust and ashes.'

Ethics 1

The Ten Commandments: Exodus 20

This text from Exodus is the first Decalogue given by God to Moses and Israel. Here, the emphasis of these commandments is upon the individual (compare Institutional Expression 3, page 72). Jewish tradition holds that the Torah contains 613 commandments which are obligatory upon man. What then is the relationship between the Decalogue and the other commandments? Jewish thinkers in the ancient and medieval periods suggested that the

Decalogue's commandments are general categories under which all the other commandments could be subsumed; the first five commandments deal with relationships between God and man and last five commandments establish general relationships between man and man.

And God spoke all these words, saying,

I am the Lord your God, who brought you out of the land of Egypt, out of the house of bondage.

You shall have no other gods before me.

You shall not make for yourself a graven image, or any likeness of anything that is in heaven above, or that is in the earth beneath, or that is in the water under the earth; you shall not bow down to them or serve them; for I the Lord your God am a jealous God, visiting the iniquity of the fathers upon the children to the third and the fourth generation of those who hate me, but showing steadfast love to thousands of those who love me and keep my commandments.

You shall not take the name of the Lord your God in vain; for the Lord will not hold him guiltless who takes his name in vain.

Remember the sabbath day, to keep it holy. Six days you shall labour, and do all your work; but the seventh day is a sabbath to the Lord your God; in it you shall not do any work, you, or your son, or your daughter, your manservant, or your maidservant, or your cattle, or the sojourner who is within your gates; for in six days the Lord made heaven and earth, the sea, and all that is in them, and rested the seventh day; therefore the Lord blessed the sabbath day and hallowed it.

Honour your father and your mother, that your days may be long in the land which the Lord your God gives you.

You shall not kill.

You shall not commit adultery.

You shall not steal.

You shall not bear false witness against your neighbour.

You shall not covet your neighbour's house; you shall not covet your neighbour's wife, or his manservant, or his maidservant, or his ox, or his ass, or anything that is your neighbour's.

Ethics 2

The Woman of Valour: Proverbs 31

This text from Proverbs describes the virtues of the ideal woman in ancient Israel. These virtues are essentially ethical in nature and serve by extension as the index of values proper to both men and women in Israelite society.

A good wife who can find?
She is far more precious than jewels.
The heart of her husband trusts in her,
  and he will have no lack of gain.
She does him good, and not harm,
  all the days of her life.
She seeks wool and flax,
  and works with willing hands.
She is like the ships of the merchant,
  she brings her food from afar.
She rises while it is yet night
  and provides food for her household and
    tasks for her maidens.
She considers a field and buys it;
  with the fruit of her hands she plants a
    vineyard.

She girds her loins with strength and makes her
arms strong.
She perceives that her merchandise is profitable.
Her lamp does not go out at night.
She puts her hands to the distaff,
and her hands hold the spindle.
She opens her hand to the poor,
and reaches out her hands to the needy.
She is not afraid of snow for her household,
for all her household are clothed in scarlet.
She makes hereself coverings;
her clothing is fine linen and purple.
Her husband is known in the gates when he
sits among the elders of the land.
She makes linen garments and sells them;
she delivers girdles to the merchant.
Strength and dignity are her clothing,
and she laughs at the time to come.
She opens her mouth with wisdom,
and the teaching of kindness is on her
tongue.
She looks well to the ways of her household,
and does not eat the bread of idleness.
Her children rise up and call her blessed;
her husband also, and he praises her:
'Many women have done excellently,
but you surpass them all.'
Charm is deceitful, and beauty is vain,
but a woman who fears the Lord is to be
praised.
Give her of the fruit of her hands,
and let her works praise her in the gates.

Ethics 3

The Wise and the Wicked: Proverbs 14

In this text, Proverbs 14:1–35, the reader is given a clear idea that pursuit of wisdom in ancient Israel led to very practical consequences; wisdom leads to the ethical life while turning away from this wisdom leads to wickedness and transgression.

Wisdom builds her house,
but folly with her own hands tears it down.
He who walks in uprightness fears the Lord,
but he who is devious in his ways despises
him.
The talk of a fool is a rod for his back,
but the lips of the wise will preserve them.
Where there are no oxen, there is no grain;
but abundant crops come by the strength of
the ox.
A faithful witness does not lie,
but a false witness breathes out lies.
A scoffer seeks wisdom in vain,
but knowledge is easy for a man of
understanding.
Leave the presence of a fool,
for there you do not meet words of
knowledge.
The wisdom of a prudent man is to discern his
way,
but the folly of fools is deceiving.
God scorns the wicked,
but the upright enjoy his favour.
The heart knows its own bitterness,
and no stranger shares its joy.
The house of the wicked will be destroyed,
but the tent of the upright will flourish.
There is a way which seems right to a man,
but its end is the way to death.
Even in laughter the heart is sad,
and the end of joy is grief.
A perverse man will be filled with the fruit of
his ways,
and a good man with the fruit of his deeds.
The simple believes everything,
but the prudent looks where he is going.
A wise man is cautious and turns away from
evil,

but a fool throws off restraint and is
careless.
A man of quick temper acts foolishly,
but a man of discretion is patient.
The simple acquire folly,
but the prudent are crowned with
knowledge.
The evil bow down before the good,
the wicked at the gates of the righteous.
The poor is disliked even by his neighbour,
but the rich has many friends.
He who despises his neighbour is a sinner,
but happy is he who is kind to the poor.
Do they not err that devise evil?
Those who devise good meet loyalty and
faithfulness.
In all toil there is profit,
but mere talk tends only to want.
The crown of the wise is their wisdom,
but folly is the garland of fools.
A truthful witness saves lives,
but one who utters lies is a betrayer.
In the fear of the Lord one has strong
confidence,
and his children will have a refuge.
The fear of the Lord is a fountain of life,
that one may avoid the snares of death.
In a multitude of people is the glory of a king,
but without people a prince is ruined.
He who is slow to anger has great
understanding,
but he who has a hasty temper exalts folly.
A tranquil mind gives life to the flesh,
but passion makes the bones rot.
He who oppresses a poor man insults his
Maker,
but he who is kind to the needy honours
him.
The wicked is overthrown through his evil-
doing,
but the righteous finds refuge through his
integrity.
Wisdom abides in the mind of a man of
understanding,
but it is not known in the heart of fools.
Righteousness exalts a nation,
but sin is a reproach to any people.
A servant who deals wisely has the king's
favour,
but his wrath falls on one who acts
shamefully.

Ethics 4

The Clean and Unclean: Leviticus 11

It is usually understood that the list of clean and unclean animals in this text from the Book of Leviticus is primarily an expression of the ritual dimension of ancient Israel. However, discrimination of animals which are clean and unclean related also to a cosmic elite in ancient Israel, since the maintenance of these distinctions reflects the distinctions made by God in the creation of the world. Hence, by scrupulous separation one maintains the categories or separations vital to the cosmic order. Israel's task is to maintain order and this finds its ethical reflection in the selection of food.

And the Lord said to Moses and Aaron, 'Say to the people of Israel, These are the living things which you may eat among all the beasts that are on the earth. Whatever parts the hoof and is cloven-footed and chews the cud, among the animals, you may eat. Nevertheless among those that chew the cud or part the hoof, you shall not eat these: the camel, because it chews the cud but does not part the hoof, it is unclean to you. And the rock badger, because it chews the cud but does not part the hoof, is unclean to you. And the hare, because it chews the cud but does not part the hoof, is unclean to you. And the swine, because it parts the hoof and is cloven-footed but does not chew the cud, is unclean to you. Of their flesh you shall not eat, and their carcasses you shall not touch; they are unclean to you.

'These you may eat, of all that are in the waters. Everything in the waters that has fins and scales, whether in the seas or in the rivers, you may eat. But anything in the seas or the rivers that has not fins and scales, of the swarming creatures in the waters and of the living creatures that are in the waters, is an abomination to you. They shall remain an abomination to you; of their flesh you shall not eat, and their carcasses you shall have in abomination. Everything in the waters that has not fins and scales is an abomination to you.

'And these you shall have in abomination among the birds, they shall not be eaten, they are an abomination: the eagle, the vulture, the osprey, the kite, the falcon according to its kind, every raven according to its kind, the ostrich, the nighthawk, the sea gull, the hawk according to its kind, the owl, the cormorant, the ibis, the water hen, the pelican, the carrion vulture, the stork, the heron according to its kind, the hoopoe, and the bat.

'All winged insects that go upon all fours are an abomination to you. Yet among the winged insects that go on all fours you may eat those which have legs above their feet, with which to leap on the earth. Of them you may eat: the locust according to its kind, the bald locust according to its kind, the cricket according to its kind, and the grasshopper according to its kind. But all other winged insects which have four feet are an abomination to you.

'And by these you shall become unclean; whoever touches their carcass shall be unclean until the evening, and whoever carries any part of their carcass shall wash his clothes and be unclean until the evening. Every animal which parts the hoof but is not cloven-footed or does not chew the cud is unclean to you; every one who touches them shall be unclean. And all that go on their paws, among the animals that go on all fours, are unclean to you; whoever touches their carcass shall be unclean until the evening, and he who carries their carcass shall wash his clothes and be unclean until the evening; they are unclean to you.

'And these are unclean to you among the swarming things that swarm upon the earth: the weasel, the mouse, the great lizard according to its kind, the gecko, the land crocodile, the lizard, the sand lizard, and the chameleon. These are unclean to you among all that swarm; whoever touches them when they are dead shall be unclean until the evening. And anything upon which any of them falls when they are dead shall be unclean until the evening. And anything upon which any of them falls when they are dead shall be unclean, whether it is an article of wood or a garment or a skin or a sack, any vessel that is used for any purpose; it must be put into water, and it shall be unclean until the evening; then it shall be clean. And if any of them falls into any earthen vessel, all that is in it shall be unclean, and you shall break it. Any food in it which may be eaten, upon which water may come, shall be unclean; and all the drink which may be drunk from every such vessel shall be unclean. And everything upon which any part of their carcass falls shall be unclean; whether oven or stove, it shall be broken in pieces; they are unclean, and shall be unclean to you. Nevertheless a spring or cistern holding water shall be clean; but whatever touches their carcass shall be unclean. And if any part of their carcass falls upon any seed for sowing that is to be sown, it is clean; but if water is put on the seed and any part of their carcass falls on it, it is unclean to you.

'And if any animal of which you may eat dies, he who touches its carcass shall be unclean until the evening, and he who eats of its carcass shall wash his clothes and be unclean until the evening; he also who carries the carcass shall wash his clothes and be unclean until the evening.

'Every swarming thing that swarms upon the earth is an abomination; it shall not be eaten. Whatever goes on its belly, and whatever goes on all fours, or whatever has many feet, all the swarming things that swarm upon the earth, you shall not eat; for they are an abomination. You shall not make yourselves abominable with any swarming thing that swarms; and you shall not defile yourselves with them, lest you become unclean. For I am the Lord your God; consecrate yourselves therefore, and be holy, for I am holy. You shall not defile yourselves with any swarming thing that crawls upon the earth. For I am the Lord who brought you up out of the land of Egypt, to be your God; you shall therefore be holy, for I am holy.'

Postscript

The process of translating the Hebrew Bible had begun during the Hellenistic period when Jews were already living outside of Judaea. The pseudepigraphical Letter of Aristeas describes how Ptolemy Philadelphus ordered a Greek translation of the Pentateuch for the Library in Alexandria between 250 and 240 BCE. 72 learned sages were invited to come down from Jerusalem to work on this translation; the 72 were rounded off to 70 and hence the name of their translation, 'Septuaginta'. This translation of the Pentateuch and later the prophetic and historical books of the Hebrew Bible enjoyed tremendous popularity among Greek-speaking Jews. Aramaic translations of the Pentateuch, called *targumim*, were begun perhaps as early as the 1st century BCE. The only extant version of this Palestinian translation is the *Codex Neofiti* and later translations of the Pentateuch, especially *Targum Onkelos* (3rd century CE), *Targum Yerishalmi* (4th century CE) and *Targum Pseudo-Jonathan* (no later than the 7th or 8th century CE) were exceedingly influential in the development of the Jewish tradition. Other influential translations were produced in the Middle Ages, among them being Judeo-Persian translations (14th and 15th centuries) and Yiddish translations beginning from the 13th century. Among the Yiddish translations, one very free paraphrase, the *Ze'enah u-Re'enah*, was particularly influential among Eastern European Jewish communities. Moses Mendelssohn's German translation of the Pentateuch (1783), the Psalms (1785), Ecclesiastes (1770) and Song of Songs (1788) was completed at the beginning of the 19th century and was first published as *Minhah Hadashah* (1805), and was later republished by Moses Israel Landau in 1833–7. Martin Buber and Franz Rosenzweig published a German translation in 15 volumes under the title *Die Schrift zu verdeutschen* (1926–37), which they believed captured the original sense of the Biblical Hebrew prose and poetry.

Bibliography

The most influential English translations of the Hebrew Bible are David Levi's Pentateuch and *haftarot*, based on the King James Version of 1611, published in 1787, Rabbi J.H. Hertz's *Pentateuch and Haftorahs* (1929–36) and the translations of the Jewish Publication Society of America, first in 1917 and a more recent translation (1962–82) adapting Jewish commentary literature and biblical scholarship into an English translation.

The opening of the Gospel of St John from the oldest extant manuscript of the New Testament, the 4th-century Codex Sinaiticus, from the monastery of St Catherine in the Sinai.

Christianity

Introduction

Basically the first scripture of the emerging Christian Church was the Greek version of the Hebrew Bible known as the Septuagint. But the Christian communities thought that they had access to inspiration through the work of the Holy Spirit. Moreover, they thought that their Lord had brought into being a new covenant, which superseded the old one. That old covenant had as its scriptural expression the books of the Hebrew Bible, now viewed as the Old Testament by Christians. The various authoritative writings which grew out of the early Church came to be formed into a new and second portion of scripture known as the New Testament. It was not till the fourth century CE that the canon was effectively settled, incorporating the 27 books since regarded as canonical (though Luther had doubts about Hebrews, James, Jude and Revelation). The tests of authenticity used by the Church were whether a given work was apostolic, showed true doctrine and received widespread geographical usage. Four kinds of writing are found in the New Testament: Gospels or works about the acts and teachings of Jesus and proclaiming his lordship; Acts, recording early missionary activity; letters or epistles, some exhibiting the development of doctrine; and an inspired visionary work, the Book of Revelation.

The following selections include two Old Testament passages. One is from Isaiah and belongs to that part which modern scholars often refer to as Second Isaiah (Deutero-Isaiah). Its importance is in the references to the Suffering Servant, interpreted by Jews as referring to Israel, but by Christians as foretelling Jesus' role. The second Old Testament passage is Psalm 22. The Psalms have figured prominently in Christian worship. This particular Psalm is important because its first line was supposedly uttered by Christ on the Cross as he was dying. Christian interpretation gave a Christ-oriented meaning to the Psalms, and so differed from Jewish interpretation.

In the following selections we have started with the figure of the Suffering Servant, who is thought by Christians to prefigure Christ. Thus we begin with a key passage in the Old Testament in the unfolding of the sacred story or myth of Christ. In some of the passages which have a special emphasis in the worship of the Church it has been thought useful to use the Authorized Version, with its more numinous and mysterious overtones, rather than the plainer version of the New English Bible which we have elsewhere followed. It must of course be emphasized that for most Christians up to the period after the Reformation, knowledge of scripture came through the liturgy, and so had a special resonance.

The other three passages relating to the sacred story are drawn from Matthew, Luke and Revelation, describing Jesus' activity as a healer and charismatic teacher, the crucifixion and resurrection, and finally a vision of Christ at the end of history, when the world is transformed and judged.

These events have to be understood in terms of their doctrinal significance, and to indicate this we have chosen passages from John, Luke, First Corinthians and Romans. The two passages from John refer to Christ as Creator and as glorified Son of Man (interpreted by the Church through the doctrine of the incarnation). The Luke passage shows how Christ's teaching was frequently through parables, emphasizing the challenge and mystery of the divine. The first passage from Paul concerns life after death, while the second concerns grace, an idea central to Christian understandings of salvation.

The ritual use of the scriptures is emphasized in our next passages. First, we include two Psalms, the first because the first line was uttered, according to the record, by Christ as he was dying on the Cross, and the second because it is perhaps the most famous of all Psalms in Christian use. For much of the Church's history the Psalms were central to sacred song: indeed Calvinism long involved repudiating any non-biblical form of hymn, in favour of the Psalms. Next we have an account of the Last Supper, from Mark, the founding in other words of the Church's most pervasive sacrament. The passage from John relates to the notion of Christ himself as food, the bread of heaven, the conception underlying the Eucharist. In the fourth passage, Paul discusses Christian worship, including speaking in tongues (a vital feature of later Pentacostalism).

It is notable that Paul sees worship as building up the Church, and the next passages relate to the institutional side of Christianity. The first, from Romans, spells out Paul's theory of the Church as a new Israel, in which the members are heirs of Abraham by faith rather than descent. The next passage, from Acts, describes the coming of the Spirit which animates the Church and consigns authority. In First Timothy, an indication of the ordering of the sacred community is given.

The worship of the community both expresses and nourishes experience. In the first of three passages there is described the transfiguration of Jesus, when he becomes awe-inspiring to his close disciples, who experience something of his glory. The second passage, from Matthew, is an account of Jesus' temptation by the Devil, which may indeed be an attempt to reconstruct something of Jesus's own experience of the struggle between good and evil. The Acts passage is the famous story of Paul's conversion.

Through, and out of, all the above flowed a new ethic. This was expressed in the Sermon on the Mount, here the first of three key passages. The second passage from James gives us an appreciation of the ideals of the early community. The third passage is the most moving of all Paul's writings, the paean to love in First Corinthians 13.

Sacred Narrative 1

The Suffering Servant: Isaiah 52–53

This belongs to the portion of Isaiah commonly seen as the second Isaiah, composed by an unknown prophet of the Exile nearly two hundred years after Isaiah (8th century BCE). Christians see it as prefiguring Jesus, the paradoxically suffering and exalted Messiah, and sacrificial lamb.

Behold, my servant shall deal prudently, he shall be exalted and extolled, and be very high. As many were astonished at thee (his visage was so marred more than any man and his form more than the sons of men), so shall he sprinkle many nations; the kings shall shut their mouths at him; for that which had not been told them shall they see, and that which they had not heard shall they consider.

Who hath believed our report, and to whom is the arm of the Lord revealed? For he shall grow up before him as a tender plant and as a root out of a dry ground; he hath no form nor comeliness, and when we shall see him, there is no beauty that we should desire him. He is despised and rejected of men, a man of sorrows and acquainted with grief, and we hid as it were our faces from him; he was despised, and we esteemed him not.

Surely he hath borne our griefs and carried our sorrows; yet we did esteem him stricken, smitten of God, and afflicted. But he was wounded for our transgressions, he was bruised for our iniquities; the chastisement of our peace was upon him, and with his stripes we are healed. All we like sheep have gone astray; we have turned every one to his own way; and the Lord hath laid on him the iniquity of us all.

He was oppressed and he was afflicted, yet he opened not his mouth; he is brought as a lamb to the slaughter, and as a sheep before her shearers is dumb, so he openeth not his mouth. By oppression and judgment he was taken away; and as for his generation, who among them considered that he was cut off out of the land of the living? For the transgression of my people was he stricken. And they made his grace with the wicked, and with the rich in his death, although he had done no violence, neither was any deceit in his mouth.

Yet it pleased the Lord to bruise him; he hath put him to grief: when thou shalt make his soul an offering for sin, he shall see his seed, he shall prolong his days, and the pleasure of the Lord shall prosper in his hand. He shall see the travail of his soul, and shall be satisfied; by his knowledge shall my righteous servant justify many, for he shall bear their iniquities. Therefore will I divide him a portion with the great, and he shall divide the spoil with the string; because he hath poured out his soul unto death, and he was numbered with the transgressors; and he bare the sin of many, and made intercession for the transgressors.

Sacred Narrative 2

Christ as Faith-Inspiring Healer: Matthew 8

The Gospel emphasizes Jesus' career as a healer. Importance is also placed on the faith of those whom he helps thus. The strange powers and authority of Jesus are reflected too in the call of Matthew and the way in which he goes beyond observance of the law and John's asceticism.

After he had come down from the hill he was followed by a great crowd. And now a leper approached him, bowed low, and said, 'Sir, if only you will, you can cleanse me.' Jesus stretched out his hand, touched him, and said, 'Indeed I will; be clean again.' And his leprosy was cured immediately. Then Jesus said to him, 'Be sure you tell nobody; but go and show yourself to the priest, and make the offering laid down by Moses for your cleansing; that will certify the cure.'

When he had entered Capernaum a centurion came up to ask his help. 'Sir,' he said, 'a boy of mine lies at home paralysed and racked with pain.' Jesus said, 'I will come and cure him.' But the centurion replied, 'Sir, who am I to have you under my roof? You need only say the word and the boy will be cured. I know, for I am myself under orders, with soldiers under me. I say to one, "Go", and he goes; to another, "Come here", and he comes; and to my servant, "Do this", and he does it.' Jesus heard him with astonishment, and said to the people who were following him, 'I tell you this: nowhere, even in Israel, have I found such faith.

'Many, I tell you, will come from east and west to feast with Abraham, Isaac, and Jacob in the Kingdom of Heaven. But those who were born to the kingdom will be driven out into the dark, the place of wailing and grinding of teeth.'

Then Jesus said to the centurion, 'Go home now; because of your faith, so let it be.' At that moment the boy recovered.

Jesus then went to Peter's house and found Peter's mother-in-law in bed with fever. So he took her by the hand; the fever left her, and she got up and waited on him.

When evening fell, they brought to him many who were possessed by devils; and he drove the spirits out with a word and healed all who were ill, to make good the prophecy of Isaiah: 'He took away our illnesses and lifted our diseases from us.'[1]

At the sight of the crowds surrounding him Jesus gave word to cross to the other shore. A doctor of the law came up, and said, 'Master, I will follow you wherever you go.' Jesus replied, 'Foxes have their holes, the birds their roosts; but the Son of Man has nowhere to lay his head.' Another man, one of his disciples, said to him, 'Lord, let me go and bury my father first.' Jesus replied, 'Follow me, and leave the dead to bury the dead.'

Jesus then got into the boat, and his disciples followed. All at once a great storm arose on the lake, till the waves were breaking right over the boat; but he went on sleeping. So they came and woke him up, crying: 'Save us, Lord; we are sinking!' 'Why are you such cowards?' he said; 'how little faith you have!' Then he stood up and rebuked the wind and the sea, and there was a dead calm. The men were astonished at what had happened, and exclaimed, 'What sort of man is this, that even the wind and the sea obey him?'

When he reached the other side, in the country of the Gadarenes, he was met by two men who came out from the tombs; they were possessed by devils, and so violent that no one dared to pass that way. 'You son of God,' they shouted, 'what do you want with us? Have you come here to torment us before our time?' In the distance a large herd of pigs was feeding; and the devils begged him: 'If you drive us out, send us into that herd of pigs.' 'Begone,' he said. Then they came out and went into the pigs; the whole herd rushed over the edge into the lake, and perished in the water.

The men in charge of them took to their heels, and made for the town where they told the whole story, and what had happened to the madmen. Thereupon the whole town came out to meet Jesus; and when they saw him they begged him to leave the district and go. So he got into the boat and crossed over, and came to his own town.

And now some men brought him a paralytic lying on a bed. Seeing their faith Jesus said to the man, 'Take heart, my son; your sins are forgiven.' At this some of the lawyers said to themselves, 'This is blasphemous talk.' Jesus read their thoughts, and said, 'Why do you harbour these evil thoughts? Is it easier to say, "Your sins are forgiven"? or to say, "Stand up and walk"? But to convince you that the Son of Man has the right on earth to forgive sins' – he now addressed the paralytic – 'stand up, take your bed, and go home.' Thereupon the man got up, and went off home. The people were filled with awe at the sight, and praised God for granting such authority to men.

As he passed on from there Jesus saw a man named Matthew at his seat in the custom-house;

[1] Isaiah 53:4.

and he said to him, 'Follow me.' And Matthew rose and followed him.

When Jesus was at table in the house, many bad characters – tax-gatherers and others – were seated with him and his disciples. The Pharisees noticed this, and said to his disciples, 'Why is it that your master eats with tax-gatherers and sinners?' Jesus heard them and said, 'It is not the healthy that need a doctor, but the sick. Go and learn what that text means, "I require mercy, not sacrifice." I did not come to invite virtuous people, but sinners.'

Then John's disciples came to him with the question: 'Why do we and the Pharisees fast, but your disciples do not?' Jesus replied, 'Can you expect the bridegroom's friends to go mourning while the bridegroom is with them? The time will come when the bridegroom will be taken away from them; that will be the time for them to fast.

'No one sews a patch of unshrunk cloth on to an old coat; for then the patch tears away from the coat, and leaves a bigger hole. No more do you put new wine into old wine skins; if you do, the skins burst, and then the wine runs out and the skins are spoilt. No, you put new wine into fresh skins; then both are preserved.'

Sacred Narrative 3

Christ's Death and Resurrection: Luke 23–24

After the trial, the Gospel describes the procession to Golgotha (the Skull), the dying words of Jesus and the subsequent events grouped as the Resurrection experience. Finally there is Christ's departure from the disciples and (by implication) his ascension.

As they led him away to execution they seized upon a man called Simon, from Cyrene, on his way in from the country, put the cross on his back, and made him walk behind Jesus carrying it.

Great numbers of people followed, many women among them, who mourned and lamented over him. Jesus turned to them and said, 'Daughters of Jerusalem, do not weep for me; no, weep for yourselves and your children. For the days are surely coming when they will say, "Happy are the barren, the wombs that never bore a child, the breasts that never fed one." Then they will start saying to the mountains, "Fall on us", and to the hills, "Cover us". For if these things are done when the wood is green, what will happen when it is dry?

There were two others with him, criminals who were being led away to execution; and when they reached the place called the Skull, they crucified him there, and the criminals with him, one on his right and the other on his left. Jesus said, 'Father, forgive them; they do not know what they are doing.'

They divided their clothes among them by casting lots. The people stood looking on, and their rulers jeered at him: 'He saved others: now let him save himself, if this is God's Anointed, his Chosen.' The soldiers joined in the mockery and came forward offering him their sour wine. 'If you are the king of the Jews,' they said, 'save yourself.' There was an inscription above his head which ran: 'This is the king of the Jews.'

One of the criminals who hung there with him taunted him: 'Are not you the Messiah? Save yourself, and us.' But the other answered sharply, 'Have you no fear of God? You are under the same sentence as he. For us it is plain justice; we are paying the price of our misdeeds; but this man has done nothing wrong.' And he said, 'Jesus, remember me when you come to your throne.' He answered, 'I tell you this: today you shall be with me in Paradise.'

By now it was about midday and there came a darkness over the whole land, which lasted until three in the afternoon; the sun was in eclipse. And the curtain of the temple was torn in two. Then Jesus gave a loud cry and said, 'Father, into thy hands I commit my spirit;' and with these words he died. The centurion saw it all, and gave praise to God. 'Beyond all doubt,' he said, 'this man was innocent.'

The crowd who had assembled for the spectacle, when they saw what had happened, went home beating their breasts.

His friends had all been standing at a distance; the women who had accompanied him from Galilee stood with them and watched it all.

Now there was a man called Joseph, a member of the Council, a good, upright man, who had dissented from their policy and the action they had taken. He came from the Jewish town of Arimathaea, and he was one who looked forward to the kingdom of God. This man now approached Pilate and asked for the body of Jesus. Taking it down from the cross, he wrapped it in a linen sheet, and laid it in a tomb cut out of the rock, in which no one had been laid before. It was Friday, and the Sabbath was about to begin.

The women who had accompanied him from Galilee followed; they took note of the tomb and observed how his body was laid. Then they went home and prepared spices and perfumes; and on the Sabbath they rested in obedience to the commandment. But on the Sunday morning very early they came to the tomb bringing the spices they had prepared. Finding that the stone had been rolled away from the tomb, they went inside; but the body was not to be found. While they stood utterly at a loss, all of a sudden two men in dazzling garments were at their side. They were terrified, and stood with eyes cast down, but the men said, 'Why search among the dead for one who lives? Remember what he told you while he was still in Galilee, about the Son of Man: how he must be given up into the power of sinful men and be crucified, and must rise again on the third day.' Then they recalled his words and, returning from the tomb, they reported all this to the Eleven and all the others.

The women were Mary of Magdala, Joanna, and Mary the mother of James, and they, with the other women, told the apostles. But the story appeared to them to be nonsense, and they would not believe them.

That same day two of them were on their way to a village called Emmaus, which lay about seven miles from Jerusalem, and they were talking together about all these happenings. As they talked and discussed it with one another, Jesus himself came up and walked along with them; but something held their eyes from seeing who it was. He asked them, 'What is it you are debating as you walk?' They halted, their faces full of gloom, and one, called Cleopas, answered, 'Are you the only person staying in Jerusalem not to know what has happened there in the last few days?' 'What do you mean?' he said. 'All this about Jesus of Nazareth,' they replied, 'a prophet powerful in speech and action before God and the whole people; how our chief priests and rulers handed him over to be sentenced to death, and crucified him. But we had been hoping that he was the man to liberate Israel. What is more, this is the third day since it happened, and now some women of our company have astounded us: they went early to the tomb, but failed to find his body, and returned with a story that they had seen a vision of angels who told them he was alive. So some of our people went to the tomb and found things just as the women had said; but him they did not see.'

'How dull you are!' he answered. 'How slow to believe all that the prophets said! Was the Messiah not bound to suffer thus before entering upon his glory?' Then he began with Moses and all the prophets, and explained to them the passages which referred to himself in every part of the scriptures.

By this time they had reached the village to which they were going, and he made as if to continue his journey, but they pressed him: 'Stay with us, for evening draws on, and the day is almost over.' So he went in to stay with them. And when he had sat down with them at table, he took bread and said the blessing; he broke the bread, and offered it to them. Then their eyes were opened, and they recognized him; and he vanished from their sight. They said to one another, 'Did we not feel our hearts on fire as he talked with us on the road and explained the scriptures to us?'

Without a moment's delay they set out and returned to Jerusalem. There they found that the Eleven and the rest of the company had assembled, and were saying, 'It is true: the Lord has risen; he has appeared to Simon.' Then they gave their account of the events of their journey and told how he had been recognized by them at the breaking of the bread.

As they were talking about all this, there he was, standing among them. Startled and terrified, they thought they were seeing a ghost. But he said, 'Why are you so perturbed? Why do questionings arise in your minds? Look at my hands and feet. It is I myself. Touch me and see; no ghost has flesh and bones as you can see that I have.' They were still unconvinced, still wondering, for it seemed too good to be true. So he asked them, 'Have you anything here to eat?' They offered him a piece of fish they had cooked, which he took and ate before their eyes.

And he said to them, 'This is what I meant by saying, while I was still with you, that everything written about me in the Law of Moses and in the prophets and psalms was bound to be fulfilled.' Then he opened their minds to understand the scriptures. 'This,' he said. 'is what is written: that the Messiah is to suffer death and to rise from the dead on the third day, and that in his name repentance bringing the forgiveness of sins is to be proclaimed to all nations. Begin from Jerusalem: it is you who are the witnesses to all this. And mark this: I am sending upon you my Father's promised gift; so stay here in this city until you are armed with the power from above.'

Then he led them out as far as Bethany, and blessed them with uplifted hands; and in the act of blessing he parted from them. And they returned to Jerusalem with great joy, and spent all their time in the temple praising God.

Sacred Narrative 4

The Last Things: Revelation 21–22

The Revelation of St. John written towards the end of the first century and perhaps the work of John, son of Zebedee, is an apocalyptic and poetic vision of the last things, when divine judgment occurs and a new age commences, conceived here as coming quickly.

And I saw a new heaven and a new earth, for the first heaven and the first earth were passed away, and there was no more sea. And I John saw the holy city, new Jerusalem, coming down from God out of heaven, prepared as a bride adorned for her husband. And I heard a great voice out of heaven saying, 'Behold, the tabernacle of God is with men, and he will dwell with them, and they shall be his people, and God himself shall be with them and be their God. And God shall wipe away all tears from their eyes; and there shall be no more death, neither sorrow, nor crying, neither shall there be any more pain, for the former things are passed away.'

And he that sat upon the throne said, 'Behold, I make all things new.' And he said unto me, 'It is done. I am Alpha and Omega, the beginning and the end. I will give unto him that is athirst of the fountain of the water of life freely. He that overcometh shall inherit all things; and I will be his God, and he shall be my son. But the fearful, and unbelieving, and the abominable, and murderers, and whoremongers, and sorcerers, and idolators, and all liars shall have their part in the lake which burneth with fire and brimstone, which is the second death.'

And there came unto me one of the seven angels which had the seven vials full of the seven last plagues, and talked with me, saying 'Come hither; I will shew thee the bride, the Lamb's wife.'

And he carried me away in the spirit to a great and high mountain, and shewed me that great city, the holy Jerusalem, descending out of heaven from God, having the glory of God; and her light was like unto a stone most precious, even like a jasper stone, clear as crystal; and had a wall great and high, and had twelve gates, and at the gates twelve angels, and names written thereon which are the names of the twelve tribes of the children of Israel: on the east three gates, on the north three gates, on the south three gates, and on the west three gates. And the wall of the city had twelve foundations, and in them the names of the twelve apostles of the Lamb.

And he that talked with me had a golden reed to measure the city and the gates thereof and the wall thereof. And the city lieth foursquare and the length is as large as the breadth; and he measured the city with the reed, twelve thousand furlongs; and the length and the breadth and the height of it are equal. And he measured the wall thereof, an hundred and forty and four cubits, according to the measure of a man, that is, of the angel. And the building of the wall of it was of jasper; and the city was pure gold, like unto clear glass. And the foundations of the wall of the city were garnished with all manner of precious stones. The first foundation was jasper, the second sapphire, the third a chalcedony, the fourth an emerald, the fifth sardonyx, the sixth sardius, the seventh chrysolyte, the eighth beryl, the ninth a topaz, the tenth a chrysoprasus, the eleventh a jacinth, the twelfth an amethyst. And the twelve gates were twelve pearls; every several gate was of one pearl. And the street of the city was pure gold, as it were transparent glass.

And I saw no temple therein, for the Lord God Almighty and the Lamb are the temple of it. And the city had no need of the sun, neither of the moon, to shine in it, for the glory of God did lighten it and the Lamb is the light thereof. And the nations shall walk in the light of it, and the kings of the earth do bring their glory and honour into it. And the gates of it shall not be shut at all by day (for there shall be no night there); and they shall bring the glory and honour of the nations into it; and there shall in no wise enter into it any thing that defileth, neither whatsoever worketh abomination or maketh a lie, but they which are written in the Lamb's book of life.

And he shewed me a pure river of water of life, clear as crystal, proceeding out of the throne of God and of the Lamb. In the midst of the street of it, and on either side of the river, was there the tree of life, which bare twelve manner of fruits and yielded her fruit every month; and the leaves of the tree were for the healing of the nations. And there shall be no more curse; but the throne of God and of the Lamb shall be in it, and his servants shall serve him; and they shall see his face, and his name shall be in their foreheads. And there shall be no night there, and they need no candle neither light of the sun, for the Lord God giveth them light; and they shall reign for ever and ever.

And he said unto me, 'These sayings are faithful and true, and the Lord God of the holy prophets sent his angel to shew unto his servants the things which must shortly be done. Behold, I come quickly. Blessed is he that keepeth the sayings of the prophecy of this book.'

And I John saw these things and heard them. And when I had heard and seen, I fell down to worship before the feet of the angel which shewed me these things. Then saith he unto me, 'See thou do it not, for I am thy fellow servant, and of thy brethren the prophets, and of them which keep the sayings of this book. Worship God.'

And he saith unto me, 'Seal not the sayings of the prophecy of this book, for the time is at hand. He that is unjust, let him be unjust still; and he which is filthy, let him be filthy still; and he that is righteous, let him be righteous still; and he that is holy, let him be holy still. And, behold, I come quickly, and my reward is with me, to give every man according as his work shall be. I am Alpha and Omega, the beginning and the end, the first and the last. Blessed are they that do his commandments, that they may have right to the tree of life, and may enter in through the gates into the city. For without are dogs, and sorcerers, and whoremongers, and murderers, and idolaters, and whosoever loveth and maketh a lie. I Jesus have sent mine angel to testify unto you these things in the churches. I am the root and the offspring of David, and the bright and morning star. And the Spirit and the bride say, Come. And let him that heareth say, Come. And let him that is athirst come; and whosoever will, let him take the water of life freely. For I testify unto every man that heareth the words of the prophecy of this book: if any man shall add unto these things, God shall add unto him the plagues that are written in this book; and if any man shall take away from the words of the book of this prophecy, God shall take away his part out of the book of Life, and out of the holy city, and from the things which are written in this book. He which testifieth these things saith, Surely I come quickly.'

Amen. Even so, come, Lord Jesus.

The grace of the Lord Jesus be with you all. Amen.

Doctrine 1

Christ the Creator: John 1

John opens with a hymn of creation and so parallels Genesis. Here Christ is the eternal word of God – a notion developed in later accounts of Christ as God. He is foretold here by John the Baptist, whose movement preceded Jesus' but was closely allied.

In the beginning was the Word, and the Word was with God, and the Word was God. The same was in the beginning with God. All things were made by him, and without him was not any thing made that was made. In him was life, and the life was the light of men. And the light shineth in darkness; and the darkness comprehended it not.

There was a man sent from God whose name was John. The same came for a witness, to bear witness of the light, that all men through him might believe. He was not that light, but was sent to bear witness of that light. That was the true light, which lighteth every man that cometh into the world. He was in the world and the world was made by him, and the world knew him not. He came unto his own, and his own received him not. But as many as received him, to them gave he power to become the sons of God, even to them that believe on his name, which were born not of blood, nor of the will of the flesh, nor of the will of man, but of God. And the Word was made flesh, and dwelt among us (and we beheld his glory, the glory, the glory as of the only begotten of the Father), full of grace and truth.

John bare witness of him, and cried, saying 'This was he of whom I spake, He that cometh after me is preferred before me, for he was before me.' And of his fullness have all we received, and grace for grace. For the law was given by Moses; but grace and truth came by Jesus Christ. No man hath seen God at any time; the only begotten Son, which is in the bosom of the Father, he hath declared him.

Doctrine 2

Christ As Incarnate God: John 13–16

This farewell discourse in John has been a main source not only for the Christian Church's development of a doctrine of Christ's divinity as redeemer, but also for that of the Holy Spirit (the 'Advocate' or Paraclete).

When he had gone out Jesus said, 'Now the Son of Man is glorified, and in him God is glorified. If God is glorified in him, God will also glorify him in himself; and he will glorify him now. My children, for a little longer I am with you; then you will look for me, and, as I told the Jews, I tell you now, where I am going you cannot come. I give you a new commandment: love one another; as I have loved you, so you are to love one another. If there is this love among you, then all will know that you are my disciples.'

Simon Peter said to him, 'Lord, where are you going?' Jesus replied, 'Where I am going you cannot follow me now, but one day you will.' Peter said, 'Lord, why cannot I follow you now? I will lay down my life for you.' Jesus answered,

'Will you indeed lay down your life for me? I tell you in very truth, before the cock crows you will have denied me three times.

'Set your troubled hearts at rest. Trust in God always; trust also in me. There are many dwelling-places in my Father's house; if it were not so I should have told you; for I am going there on purpose to prepare a place for you. And if I go and prepare a place for you, I shall come again and receive you to myself, so that where I am you may be also; and my way there is known to you.' Thomas said, 'Lord, we do not know where you are going, so how can we know the way?' Jesus replied, 'I am the way; I am the truth and I am life; no one comes to the Father except by me.

'If you knew me you would know my Father too. From now on you do know him; you have seen him.' Philip said to him, 'Lord, show us the Father and we ask no more.' Jesus answered, 'Have I been all this time with you, Philip, and you still do not know me? Anyone who has seen me has seen the Father. Then how can you say, "Show us the Father"? Do you not believe that I am in the Father, and the Father in me? I am not myself the source of the words I speak to you: it is the Father who dwells in me doing his own work. Believe me when I say that I am in the Father and the Father in me; or else accept the evidence of the deeds themselves. In truth, in very truth I tell you, he who has faith in me will do what I am doing; and he will do greater things still because I am going to the Father. Indeed anything you ask in my name I will do, so that the Father may be glorified in the Son. If you ask anything in my name I will do it.

'If you love me you will obey my commands; and I will ask the Father, and he will give you another to be your Advocate, who will be with you for ever – the Spirit of truth. The world cannot receive him, because the world neither sees nor knows him; but you know him, because he dwells with you and is in you. I will not leave you bereft; I am coming back to you. In a little while the world will see me no longer, but you will see me; because I live, you too will live; then you will know that I am in my Father, and you in me and I in you. The man who has received my commands and obeys them – he it is who loves me; and he who loves me will be loved by my Father; and I will love him and disclose my-self to him.

Judas asked him – the other Judas, not Iscariot – 'Lord, what can have happened, that you mean to disclose yourself to us alone and not to the world.' Jesus replied, 'Anyone who loves me will heed what I say; then my Father will love him, and we will come to him and make our dwelling with him; but he who does not love me does not heed what I say. And the word you hear is not mine: it is the word of the Father who sent me. I have told you all this while I am still here with you; but your Advocate, the Holy Spirit whom the Father will send in my name, will teach you everything, and will call to mind all that I have told you.

'Peace is my parting gift to you, my own peace, such as the world cannot give. Set your troubled hearts at rest, and banish your fears. You heard me say, "I am going away, and coming back to you." If you loved me you would have been glad to hear that I was going to the Father; for the Father is greater than I. I have told you now, beforehand, so that when it happens you may have faith.

'I shall not talk much longer with you, for the Prince of this world approaches. He has no rights over me; but the world must be shown that I love the Father, and do exactly as he commands; so up, let us go forward!

'I am the real vine, and my Father is the gardener. Every barren branch of mine he cuts away; and every fruiting branch he cleans, to make it more fruitful still. You have already been cleansed by the word that I spoke to you. Dwell in me, as I in you. No branch can bear fruit by itself, but only if it remains united with the vine; no more can you bear fruit, unless you remain united with me.

'I am the vine, and you the branches. He who dwells in me, as I dwell in him, bears much fruit; for apart from me you can do nothing. He who does not dwell in me is thrown away like a withered branch. The withered branches are heaped together, thrown on the fire, and burnt.

'If you dwell in me, and my words dwell in you, ask what you will, and you shall have it. This is my Father's glory, that you may bear fruit in plenty and so be my disciples. As the Father has loved me, so I have loved you. Dwell in my love. If you heed my commands, you will dwell in my love, as I have heeded my Father's commands and dwell in his love.

'I have spoken thus to you, so that my joy may be in you, and your joy complete. This is my commandment: love one another, as I have loved you. There is no greater love than this, that a man should lay down his life for his friends. You are my friends, if you do what I command you. I call you servants no longer; a servant does not know what his master is about. I have called you friends, because I have disclosed to you everything that I heard from my Father. You did not not choose me: I chose you. I appointed you to go on and bear fruit, fruit that shall last; so that the Father may give you all that you ask in my name. This is my commandment to you: love one another.

'If the world hates you, it hated me first, as you know well. If you belonged to the world, the world would love its own; but because you do not belong to the world, because I have chosen you out of the world, for that reason the world hates you. Remember what I said: "A servant is not greater than his master." As they persecuted me, they will persecute you; they will follow your teaching as little as they have followed mine. It is on my account that they will treat you thus, because they do not know the One who sent me.

'If I had not come and spoken to them, they would not be guilty of sin; but now they have no excuse for their sin: he who hates me, hates my Father. If I had not worked among them and accomplished what no other man has done, they would not be guilty of sin; but now they have both seen and hated both me and my Father. However, this text in their Law had to come true: "They hated me without reason."

'But when your Advocate has come, whom I will send you from the Father – the Spirit of truth that issues from the Father – he will bear witness to me. And you also are my witnesses, because you have been with me from the first.

'I have told you all this to guard you against the breakdown of your faith. They will ban you from the synagogue; indeed, the time is coming when anyone who kills you will suppose that he is performing a religious duty. They will do these things because they do not know either the Father or me. I have told you all this so that when the time comes for it to happen you may remember my warning. I did not tell you this at first, because then I was with you; but now I am going away to him who sent me. None of you asks me "Where are you going?" Yet you are plunged into grief because of what I have told you. Nevertheless I tell you the truth: it is for your good that I am leaving you. If I do not go, your Advocate will not come, wheras if I go, I will send him to you. When he comes, he will confute the world, and show where wrong and right and judgement lie. He will convict them of wrong, by their refusal to believe in me; he will convince them that right is on my side, by showing that I go to the Father when I pass from your sight; and he will convince them of divine judgement, by showing that the Prince of this world stands condemned.

'There is still much that I could say to you, but the burden would be too great for you now. However, when he comes who is the Spirit of truth, he will guide you into all the truth; for he will not speak on his own authority, but will tell only what he hears; and he will make known to you the things that are coming. He will glorify me, for everything that he makes known to you he will draw from what is mine. All that the Father has is mine, and that is why I said, "Everything that he makes known to you he will draw from what is mine."

'A little while, and you see me no more; again a little while, and you will see me.' Some of his disciples said to one another, 'What does he mean by this: "A little while, and you will not see me, and again a little while, and you will see me"? and by this: "Because I am going to my Father"?' So they asked, 'What is this "little while" that he speaks of? We do not know what he means.'

Jesus knew that they were wanting to question him, and said, 'Are you discussing what I said: "A little while, and you will not see me, and again a little while, and you will see me"? In very truth I tell you, you will weep and mourn, but the world will be glad. But though you will be plunged in grief, your grief will be turned to joy. A woman in labour is in pain because her time has come; but when the child is born she forgets the anguish in her joy that a man has been born into the world. So it is with you: for the moment you are sad at heart; but I shall see you again, and then you will be joyful, and no one shall rob you of your joy. When that day comes you will ask nothing of me. In very truth I tell you, if you ask the Father for anything in my name, he will give it you. So far you have asked nothing in my name. Ask and you will receive, that your joy may be complete.

'Till now I have been using figures of speech; a time is coming when I shall no longer use figures, but tell you of the Father in plain words. When that day comes you will make your request in my name, and I do not say that I shall pray to the Father for you, for the Father loves you himself, because you have loved me and believed that I came from God. I came from the Father and have come into the world. Now I am leaving the world again and going to the Father.' His disciples said, 'Why, this is plain speaking; this is no figure of speech. We are certain now that you know everything, and do not need to be questioned; because of this we believe that you have come from God.'

Jesus answered, 'Do you now believe? Look, the hour is coming, has indeed already come, when you are all to be scattered, each to his home, leaving me alone. Yet I am not alone, because the Father is with me. I have told you all this so that in me you may find peace. In the world you will have trouble. But courage! The victory is mine; I have conquered the world.'

Doctrine 3

The Religion of and about Jesus: Luke 15–16

Here Jesus addresses Pharisees and others, and there are put together various famous parables including the puzzling one about the Unjust Steward. The main emphasis of these challenging stories is to delineate the nature of God, the Kingdom and salvation. Jesus had doctrines to preach, but did so for the most part through imagery, anecdote and action.

Another time, the tax-gatherers and other bad characters were all crowding in to listen to him; and the Pharisees and the doctors of the law began grumbling among themselves: 'This fellow', they said, 'welcomes sinners and eats with them.' He answered them with this parable: 'If one of you has a hundred sheep and loses one of them, does he not leave the ninety-nine in the open pasture and go after the missing one until he has found it? How delighted he is then! He lifts it on to his shoulders, and home he goes to call his friends and neighbours together. "Rejoice with me!" he cries. "I have found my lost sheep." In the same way, I tell you, there will be greater joy in heaven over one sinner who repents than over ninety-nine righteous people who do not need to repent.

'Or again, if a woman has ten silver pieces and loses one of them, does she not light the lamp, sweep out the house, and look in every corner till she has found it? And when she has, she calls her friends and neighbours together and says, "Rejoice with me! I have found the piece that I lost." In the same way, I tell you, there is joy among the angels of God over one sinner who repents.'

Again he said, 'There was once a man who had two sons; and the younger said to his father, "Father, give me my share of the property," So he divided his estate between them. A few days later the younger son turned the whole of his share into cash and left home for a distant country, where he squandered it in reckless living. He had spent it all, when a severe famine fell upon that country and he began to feel the pinch. So he went and attached himself to one of the local landowners, who sent him on to his farm to mind the pigs. He would have been glad to fill his belly with the pods that the pigs were eating; and no one gave him anything. Then he came to his senses and said, "How many of my father's paid servants have more food than they can eat, and here am I, starving to death! I will set off and go to my father, and say to him, 'Father, I have sinned, against God and against you; I am no longer fit to be called your son; treat me as one of your paid servants.' " So he set out for his father's house. But while he was still a long way off his father saw him, and his heart went out to him. He ran to meet him, flung his arms round him, and kissed him. The son said, "Father, I have sinned, against God and against you; I am no longer fit to be called your son." But the father said to his servants, "Quick! fetch a robe, my best one, and put it on him; put a ring on his finger and shoes on his feet. Bring the fatted calf and kill it, and let us have a feast to celebrate the day. For this son of mine was dead and has come back to life; he was lost and is found." And the festivities began.

'Now the elder son was out on the farm; and on his way back, as he approached the house, he heard music and dancing. He called one of the servants and asked what it meant. The servant told him, "Your brother has come home, and your father has killed the fatted calf because he has him back safe and sound." But he was angry and refused to go in. His father came out and pleaded with him; but he retorted, "You know how I have slaved for you all these years; I never once disobeyed your orders; and you never gave me so much as a kid, for a feast with my friends. But now that this son of yours turns up, after running through your money with his women, you kill the fatted calf for him." "My boy," said the father, "you are always with me, and everything I have is yours. How could we help celebrating this happy day? Your brother here was dead and has come back to life, was lost and is found." '

He said to his disciples, 'There was a rich man who had a bailiff, and he received complaints that this man was squandering the property. So he sent for him, and said, 'What is this that I hear? Produce your accounts, for you cannot be manager any longer." The bailiff said to himself, "What am I to do now that my employer is dismissing me? I am not strong enough to dig, and too proud to beg. I know what I must do, to make sure that, when I have to leave, there will be people to give me house and home." He summoned his master's debtors one by one. To the first he said, "How much do you owe my master?" He replied, "A thousand gallons of olive oil." He said, "Here is your account. Sit down and make it five hundred; and be quick about it." Then he said to another, "And you, how much do you owe?" He said, "A thousand bushels of wheat", and was told, "Take your account and make it eight hundred." And the master applauded the dishonest bailiff for acting so astutely. For the worldly are more astute than the other-worldly in dealing with their own kind.

'So I say to you, use your worldly wealth to win friends for yourself, so that when money is a thing of the past you may be received into an eternal home.

'The man who can be trusted in little things can be trusted also in great; and the man who is dishonest in little things is dishonest also in great things. If, then, you have not proved trustworthy with the wealth of this world, who will trust you with the wealth that is real? And if you have proved untrustworthy with what belongs to another, who will give you what is your own?

'No servant can be the slave of two masters; for either he will hate the first and love the second, or he will be devoted to the first and think nothing of the second. You cannot serve God and Money.'

The Pharisees, who loved money, heard all this and scoffed at him. He said to them, 'You are the people who impress your fellow men with your righteousness; but God sees through you; for what sets itself up to be admired by men is detestable in the sight of God.

'Until John,it was the law and the prophets: since then, there is the good news of the kingdom of God, and everyone forces his way in.

'It is easier for heaven and earth to come to an end than for one dot or stroke of the Law to lose its force.

'A man who divorces his wife and marries another commits adultery; and anyone who marries a woman divorced from her husband commits adultery.

'There was once a rich man, who dressed in purple and the finest linen, and feasted in great magnificence every day. At his gate, covered with sores, lay a poor man named Lazarus, who would have been glad to satisfy his hunger with the scraps from the rich man's table. Even the dogs used to come and lick his sores. One day the poor man died and was carried away by the angels to be with Abraham. The rich man also died and was buried, and in Hades, where he was in torment, he looked up; and there, far away, was Abraham with Lazarus close beside him. "Abraham, my father," he called out, "take pity on me! Send Lazarus to dip the tip of his finger in water, to cool my tongue, for I am in agony in this fire." But Abraham said, "Remember, my child, that all the good things fell to you while you were alive, and all the bad to Lazarus; now he has his consolation here and it is you who are in agony. But that is not all: there is a great chasm fixed between us; no one from our side who wants to reach you can cross it, and none may pass from your side to us." "Then, father," he replied, "will you send him to my father's house, where I have five brothers, to warn them, so that they too may not come to this place of torment?" But Abraham said, "They have Moses and the prophets; let them listen to them." "No, father Abraham," he replied, "but if someone from the dead visits them, they will repent." Abraham answered, "If they do not listen to Moses and the prophets they will pay no heed even if someone should rise from the dead."'

Doctrine 4

Sin and Freedom: Romans 5-6

Paul elaborates the doctrines of the Fall (in Adam all sin) and Christ as the Second Adam, in solidarity with whom the faithful Christian will gain freedom from sin and death. The Jewish Law is seen as not solving the problem but as casting it into clear light. The new life is the product of grace and the Christian's justification is by faith.

Mark what follows. It was through one man that sin entered the world, and through sin death, and thus death pervaded the whole human race, inasmuch as all men have sinned. For sin was already in the world before there was law, though in the absence of law no reckoning is kept of sin. But death held sway from Adam to Moses, even over those who had not sinned as Adam did, by disobeying a direct command – and Adam foreshadows the Man who was to come.

But God's act of grace is out of all proportion to Adam's wrongdoing. For if the wrongdoing of that one man brought death upon so many, its effect is vastly exceeded by the grace of God and the gift that came to so many by the grace of the one man, Jesus Christ. And again, the gift of God is not to be compared in its effect with that one man's sin; for the judicial action, following upon the one offence, issued in a verdict of condemnation, but the act of grace, following upon so many misdeeds, issued in a verdict of acquittal. For if by the wrongdoing of that one man death established its reign, through a single sinner, much more shall those who receive in far greater measures God's grace, and his gift of righteousness, live and reign through the one man, Jesus Christ.

It follows, then, that as the issue of one misdeed was condemnation for all men, so the issue of one just act is acquittal and life for all men. For as through the disobedience of one man the many were made sinners, so through the obedience of the one man the many will be made righteous.

Law intruded into this process to multiply law-breaking. But where sin was thus multiplied, grace immeasurable exceeded it, in order that, as sin established its reign by way of death, so God's grace might establish its reign in righteousness, and issue in eternal life through Jesus Christ our Lord.

What are we to say, then? Shall we persist in sin, so that there may be all the more grace? No, no! We died to sin: how can we live in it any longer? Have you forgotten that when we were baptized into union with Christ Jesus we were baptized into his death? By baptism we were buried with him, and lay dead, in order that, as Christ was raised from the dead in the splendour of the Father, so also we might set our feet upon the new path of life.

For if we have become incorporate with him in a death like this, we shall also be one with him in a resurrection like his. We know that the man we once were has been crucified with Christ, for the destruction of the sinful self, so that we may no longer be the slaves of sin, since a dead man is no longer answerable for his sin. But if we thus died with Christ, we believe that we shall also come to life with him. We know that Christ, once raised from the dead, is never to die again: he is no longer under the dominion of death. For in dying as he died, he died to sin, once for all, and in living as he lives, he lives to God. In the same way you must regard yourselves as dead to sin and alive to God, in union with Christ Jesus.

So sin must no longer reign in your mortal body, exacting obedience to the body's desires. You must no longer put its several parts at sin's disposal, as implements for doing wrong. No: put yourselves at the disposal of God, as dead men raised to life; yield your bodies to him as implements for doing right; for sin shall no longer be your master, because you are no longer under law, but under the grace of God.

Doctrine 5

Life after Death: I Corinthians 15

Paul here elaborates what became normative doctrine – the resurrection of the body (not just as Greek thought often pictured it, disembodied survival), based on his own experience of the risen Christ.

And now, my Brothers, I must remind you of the gospel that I preached to you; the gospel which you received, on which you have taken your stand, and which is now bringing you salvation. Do you still hold fast the Gospel as I preached it to you? If not, your conversion was in vain.

First and foremost, I handed on to you the facts which had been imparted to me: that Christ died for our sins, in accordance with the scriptures: that he was buried; that he was raised to life on the third day, according to the scriptures; and that he appeared to Cephas,[1] and afterwards to the Twelve. Then he appeared to over five hundred of our brothers at once, most of whom are still alive, though some have died. Then he appeared to James, and afterwards to all the apostles.

In the end he appeared even to me; though this birth of mine was monstrous, for I had persecuted the church and am therefore inferior to all other apostles – indeed not fit to be called an apostle. However, by God's grace I am what I am, nor has this grace been given to me in vain; on the contrary, in my labours I have outdone them all – not I, indeed, but the grace of God working with me. But what matter, I or they? This is what we all proclaim, and this is what you believed.

Now if this is what we proclaim, that Christ was raised from the dead, how can some of you say there is no resurrection of he dead? If there be no resurrection, then Christ was not raised; and if Christ was not raised, then our gospel is null and void, and so is your faith; and we turn out to be lying witnesses fo God, because we bore witness that he raised Christ to life, whereas, if the dead are not raised, but he did not raise him. For if the dead are not raised, it follows that Christ was not raised; and if Christ was not raised, your faith has nothing in it and you are still in your old state of sin. It follows also that those who have died within Christ's fellowship are utterly lost. If it is for this life only that Christ has given us hope, we of all men are most to be pitied.

But the truth is, Christ was raised to life – the first-fruits of the harvest of the dead. For since it was a man who brought death into the world, a

[1] i.e. Peter.

man also brought resurrection of the dead. As in Adam all men die, so in Christ all will be brought to life; but each in his own proper place: Christ the first-fruits, and afterwards, at his coming, those who belong to Christ. Then comes the end, when he delivers up the kingdom to God the Father, after abolishing every kind of domination, authority, and power. For he is destined to reign until God has put all enemies under his feet; and the last enemy to be abolished is death. Scripture says, 'He has put all things in subjection under his feet.' But in saying 'all things', it clearly means to exclude God who subordinates them; and when all things are thus subject to him, then the Son himself will also be made subordinate to God who made all things subject to him, and thus God will be all in all.

Again, there are those who receive baptism on behalf of the dead. Why should they do this? If the dead are not raised to life at all, what do they mean by being baptized on their behalf?

And we ourselves – why do we face these dangers hour by hour? Every day I die: I swear it by my pride in you, my brothers – for in Christ Jesus our Lord I am proud of you. If, as the saying is, I 'fought wild beasts' at Ephesus, what have I gained by it? If the dead are never raised to life, 'let us eat and drink, for tomorrow we die'.

Make no mistake: 'Bad company is the ruin of a good character.' Come back to a sober and upright life and leave your sinful ways. There are some who know nothing of God; to your shame I say it.

But, you may ask, how are the dead raised? In what kind of body? A senseless question! The seed you sow does not come to life unless it has first died; and what you sow is not the body that shall be, but a naked grain, perhaps of wheat, or of some other kind; and God clothes it with the body of his choice, each seed with its own particular body. All flesh is not the same flesh: there is flesh of men, flesh of beasts, of birds, and of fishes – all different. There are heavenly bodies and earthly bodies; and the splendour of the heavenly bodies is one thing, the splendour of the earthly, another. The sun has a splendour of is own, the moon another splendour, and the stars another, for star differs from star in brightness. So it is with the resurrection of the dead. What is sown in the earth as a perishable thing is raised imperishable. Sown in humiliation, it is raised in glory; sown in weakness, it is raised in power; sown as an animal body, it is raised as a spiritual body.

If there is such a thing as an animal body, there is also a spiritual body. It is in this sense that Scripture says, 'The first man, Adam, became an animate being',[1] whereas the last Adam has become a life-giving spirit. Observe, the spiritual does not come first; the animal body comes first, and then the spiritual. The first man was made 'of the dust of the earth': the second man is from heaven. The man made of dust is the pattern of all men of dust, and the heavenly man is the pattern of all the heavenly. As we have worn the likeness of the man of dust, so we shall wear the likeness of the heavenly man.

What I mean, my brothers, is this: flesh and blood can never possess the kingdom of God, and the perishable cannot possess immortality. Listen! I will unfold a mystery: we shall not all die, but we shall all be changed in a flash, in the twinkling of an eye, at the last trumpet–call. For the trumpet will sound, and the dead will rise immortal, and we shall be changed. This perishable being must be clothed with the imperishable, and what is mortal must be clothed with immortality. And when our mortality has been clothed with immortality, then the saying of Scripture will come true: 'Death is swallowed up; victory is won!'[2] 'O Death, where is your victory? O Death, where is your sting?'[3] The sting of death is sin, and sin gains its power from the law; but, God be praised, he gives us the victory through our Lord Jesus Christ.

Therefore, my beloved brothers, stand firm and immovable and work for the Lord always, work without limit, since you know that in the Lord your labour cannot be lost.

---

[1] Genesis 2:7.
[2] Isaiah 25:8.
[3] Hosea 18:14.

Ritual 1

Despair and Deliverance: Psalm 22

This Psalm is in the category of a lament, and is especially meaningful in Christian worship because Jesus, according to Matthew 27:46 and Mark 15:84, uttered the first sentence from the Cross. By implication the Christian too shares in deliverance after going through a like sense of dereliction.

My God, my God, why hast thou forsaken me?
Why art thou so far from helping me, and from the words of my roaring?
O my God, I cry in the day-time, but thou answerest not;
And in the night season, and am not silent.
But thou art holy,
O thou that inhabitest the praises of Israel.
Our fathers trusted in thee;
They trusted, and thou didst deliver them.
They cried unto thee, and were delivered;
They trusted in thee, and were not ashamed.
But I am a worm and no man,
A reproach of men and despised of the people.
All they that see me laugh me to scorn;
They shoot out the lip, they shake the head, saying,
Commit thyself unto the Lord; let him deliver him:
Let him deliver him, seeing he delighteth in him!
But thou art he that took me out of the womb;
Thou didst make me trust when I was upon my mother's breasts.
I was cast upon thee from the womb:
Thou art my God from my mother's belly.
Be not far from me, for trouble is near;
For there is none to help,
Many bulls have compassed me;
Strong bulls of Bashan[1] have best me round.
They gape upon me with their mouth
As a ravening and a roaring lion.
I am poured out like water
And all my bones are out of joint:
My heart is like wax;
It is melted in the midst of my bowels.
My strength is dried up like a potsherd
And my tongue cleaveth to my jaws,
And thou hast brought me into the dust of death.
For dogs have compassed me:
The assembly of evil-doers have inclosed me;
They pierced my hands and my feet.
I may tell all my bones;
They look and stare upon me;
They part my garments among them
And upon my vesture do they cast lots.
But be not thou far off, O Lord:
O thou my succour, haste thee to help me.
Deliver my soul from the sword,
My darling from the power of the dog.
Save me from the lion's mouth;
Yea, from the horns of the wild oxen thou hast answered me.
I will declare thy name unto my brethren;
In the midst of the congregation will I praise thee.
Ye that fear the Lord, praise him;
All ye the seed of Jacob, glorify him,
And stand in awe of him, all ye the seed of Israel.
For he hath not despised nor abhorred the affliction of the afflicted,
Neither hath he hid his face from him;

[1] In the grasslands of north-west Jordan.

But when he cried unto him, he heard.
Of thee cometh my praise in the great congregation:
I will pay my vows before them that fear him.
The meek shall eat and be satisfied;
They shall praise the Lord that seek after him:
Let your heart live for ever.
All the ends of the earth shall remember and turn unto the Lord,
And all the kindreds of the nations shall worship before thee:
For the kingdom is the Lord's
And he is the ruler over the nations.
All the fat ones of the earth shall eat and worship;
All they that go down to the dust shall bow before him,
And none can keep alive his own soul.
A seed shall serve him;
It shall be told of the Lord unto the next generation.
They shall come and shall declare his righteousness
Unto a people that shall be born, that he hath done it.

Ritual 2

Beyond the Valley of Death: Psalm 23

The following psalm is perhaps the best-known and most used in the Christian tradition, and is a song of confidence after the travails brought on by human enemies and other dangers. Both during the medieval period and after the Reformation the Psalms represented the core of Christian devotional worship – in much of the Calvinist world, for instance, non-Biblical sung hymns were forbidden, and in effect the Psalms constituted the hymn book.

The Lord is my shepherd; I shall not want.
He maketh me to lie down in green pastures;
He leadeth me beside the still waters.
He restoreth my soul;
He guideth me in the paths of righteousness for his name's sake.
Yea, though I walk through the valley of the shadow of death,
I will fear no evil: for thou art with me;
Thy rod and thy staff, they comfort me.
Thou preparest a table before me in the presence of mine enemies:
Thou hast anointed my head with oil;
My cup runneth over.
Surely goodness and mercy shall follow me all the days of my life,
And I will dwell in the house of the Lord for ever.

Ritual 3

The Last Supper: Mark 14

The narrative here is at the core of the later Christian celebration of the Eucharist. The words 'This is my body' came to be interpreted variously either as being Christ's real presence in the bread and wine ('transubstantiated') or just as a symbolic way of affirming the spiritual bond between Jesus and his followers.

And in the evening he cometh with the twelve. And as they sat and did eat, Jesus said, 'Verily I say unto you, one of you which eateth with me shall betray me.' And they began to be sorrowful, and to say unto him one by one, 'Is is I?' and another said, 'Is it I?' And he answered and said unto them, 'It is one of the twelve that dippeth with me on the dish. The Son of man indeed goeth, as it is written of him; but woe to that man by whom the Son of man is betrayed! Good were it for that man if he had never been born.' And as they did eat, Jesus took bread, and blessed, and brake it, and gave to them, and said, 'Take, eat; this is my body.' And he took the cup, and when he had given thanks, he gave it to them; and they all drank of it. And he said unto them, 'This is my blood of the new testament, which is shed for many. Verily I say unto you, I will drink no more of the fruit of the vine until that day that I drink it new in the kingdom of God.'

Ritual 4

The Bread of Heaven: John 6

This passage includes a feeding of the multitude (as also in Mark, Matthew and Luke). Jesus gives thanks (*eucharistia*) over the bread – foreshadowing the Lord's Supper. Later, he delivers to his disciples a discourse on the bread of heaven, and how his flesh is this heavenly bread. This notion underlies the central act of worship of the Church.

Next morning the crowd was standing on the opposite shore. They had seen only one boat there, and Jesus, they knew, had not embarked with his disciples, who had gone away without him. Boats from Tiberias, however, came ashore near the place where the people had eaten the bread over which the Lord gave thanks. When the people saw that neither Jesus nor his disciples were any longer there, they themselves went aboard these boats and made for Capernaum in search of Jesus. They found him on the other side. 'Rabbi,' they said, 'when did you come here?' Jesus replied, 'In very truth I know that you have come looking for me because your hunger was satisfied with the loaves you ate, not because you saw signs. You must work, not for this perishable food, but for the food that lasts, the food of eternal life.

'This food the Son of Man will give you, for he it is upon whom the Father has set the seal of his authority.' 'Then what must we do', they asked him, 'if we are to work as God would have us work?' Jesus replied, 'This is the work that God requires: believe in the one whom he has sent.'

They said, 'What sign can you give us to see, so that we may believe you? What is the work you do? Our ancestors had manna to eat in the desert; as Scripture says, "He gave them bread from heaven to eat." ' Jesus answered, 'I tell you this: the truth is, not that Moses gave you the bread from heaven, but that my Father gives you the real bread from heaven. The bread that God gives comes down from heaven and brings life to the world.' They said to him, 'Sir give us this bread now and always.' Jesus said to them, 'I am the bread of life. Whoever comes to me shall never be hungry, and whoever believes in me shall never be thirsty. But you, as I said, do not believe although you have seen. All that the Father gives me will come to me, and the man who comes to me I will never turn away. I have come down from heaven, not to do my own will, but the will of him who sent me. It is his will that I should not lose even one of all that he has given me, but raise them all up on the last day. For it is my Father's will that everyone who looks upon the Son and puts his faith in him shall possess eternal life; and I will raise him up on the last day.'

At this the Jews began to murmur disapprovingly because he said, 'I am the bread which came down from heaven.' They said, 'Surely this is Jesus son of Joseph; we know his father and mother. How can he now say, "I have come down from heaven"?' Jesus answered, 'Stop murmuring among yourselves. No man can come to me unless he is drawn by the Father who sent me; and I will raise him up on the last day. It is written in the prophets: "And they shall all be taught by God." Everyone who has listened to the Father and learned from him comes to me.

'I do not mean that anyone has seen the Father. He who has come from God has seen the Father, and he alone. In truth, in very truth I tell you, the believer possesses eternal life. I am the bread of life. Your forefathers ate the manna in the desert and they are dead. I am speaking of the bread that comes down from heaven, which a man may eat, and never die. I am that living bread which has come down from heaven: if anyone eats this bread he shall live for ever. Moreover, the bread which I will give is my own flesh; I give it for the life of the world.'

This led to a fierce dispute among the Jews, 'How can this man give us his flesh to eat?' they said. Jesus replied, 'In truth, in very truth I tell you, unless you eat the flesh of the Son of Man and drink his blood you can have no life in you. Whoever eats my flesh and drinks my blood possesses eternal life, and I will raise him up on the last day. My flesh is real food; my blood is real drink. Whoever eats my flesh and drinks my blood dwells continually in me and I dwell in him. As the living Father sent me, and I live because of the Father, so he who eats me shall live because of me. This is the bread which came down from heaven; and it is not like the bread which our fathers ate; they are dead, but whoever eats this bread shall live for ever.'

Ritual 5

Worship in the Early Church: I Corinthians 14

Here is a vignette of early Christian worship; Paul attempts to bring order upon ecstatic utterance, important as expressing the work of the Spirit in the community, and the basis for the development of later Pentecostal movements.

I say, then, that the man who falls into ecstatic utterance should pray for the ability to interpret. If I use such language in my prayer, the Spirit in me prays, but my intellect lies fallow. What then? I will pray as I am inspired to pray, but I will also pray intelligently. I will sing hymns as I am inspired to sing, but I will sing intelligently too. Suppose you are praising God in the language of inspiration: how will the plain man who is present be able to say 'Amen' to your thanksgiving, when he does not know what you are saying? Your prayer of thanksgiving may be all that could be desired, but it is no help to the other man. Thank God, I am more gifted in ecstatic utterance than any of you, but in the congregation I would rather speak five intelligible words, for the benefit of others as well as myself, than thousands of words in the language of ecstasy.

Do not be childish, my friends. Be as innocent of evil as babes, but at least be grown-up in your thinking. We read in the Law: 'I will speak to this nation through men of strange tongues, and by the lips of foreigners; and even so they will not heed me, says the Lord.' Clearly then these 'strange tongues' are not intended as a sign for believers, but for unbelievers, whereas prophecy is designed not for unbelievers but for those who hold the faith. So if the whole congregation is assembled and all are using the 'strange tongues' of ecstasty, and some uninstructed persons or unbelievers should enter, will they not think you are mad? But if all are uttering prophecies, the visitor, when he enters, hears from everyone something that searches his conscience and brings conviction, and the secrets of his heart are laid bare. So he will fall down and worship God, crying, 'God is certainly among you!'

To sum up, my friends: when you meet for worship, each of you contributes a hymn, some instruction, a revelation, an ecstatic utterance, or the interpretation of such an utterance. All of these must aim at one thing: to build up the church. If it is a matter of ecstatic utterance, only two should speak, or at most three, one at a time, and someone must interpret. If there is no interpreter, the speaker had better not address the meeting at all, but speak to himself and to God. Of the prophets, two or three may speak, while the rest exercise their judgement upon what is said. If someone else, sitting in his place, receives a revelation, let the first speaker stop. You can all prophesy, one at a time, so that the whole congregation may receive instruction and encouragement. It is for prophets to control prophetic inspiration, for the God who inspires them is not a God of disorder but of peace.

As in all congregations of God's people, women should not address the meeting. They have no licence to speak, but should keep their place as the law directs. If there is something they want to know, they can ask their own husbands at home. It is a shocking thing that a woman should address the congregation.

Did the word of God originate with you? Or are you the only people to whom it came? If anyone claims to be inspired or a prophet, let him recognize that what I write has the Lord's authority. If he does not recognize this, he himself should not be recognized.

In short, my friends, be eager to prophesy; do not forbid ecstatic utterance; but let all be done decently and in order.

Institutional Expression 1

The New Israel: Romans 4

The Church is conceived as the new Israel, its members being descendants of Abraham, the epitome of faith. The Christian community is thus in effect constituted by faith, and as circumcision was the seal of Abraham's faith, baptism is for the Christian. Such doctrines launched a world-wide community not confined to the Jewish milieu.

What, then, are we to say about Abraham, our ancestor in the natural line? If Abraham was justified by anything he had done, then he has a ground for pride. But he has no such ground before God; for what does Scripture say? 'Abraham put his faith in God, and that faith was counted to him as righteousness.' Now if a man does a piece of work, his wages are not 'counted' as a favour; they are paid as debt. But if without any work to his credit he simply puts his faith in him who acquits the guilty, then his faith is indeed 'counted as righteousness'. In the same sense David speaks of the happiness of the man whom God 'counts' as just, apart from any specific acts of justice: 'Happy are they', he says, 'whose lawless deeds are forgiven, whose sins are buried away; happy is the man whose sins the Lord does not count against him.' Is this happiness confined to the circumcised, or is it for the uncircumcised also? Consider: we say, 'Abraham's faith was counted as righteousness'; in what circumstances was it so counted? Was he circumcised at the time, or not? He was not yet circumcised, but uncircumcised; and he later received the symbolic rite of circumcision as the hallmark of the righteousness which faith had given him when he was still uncircumcised. Consequently, he is the father of all who have faith when uncircumcised, so that righteousness is 'counted' to them, and at the same time he is the father of such of the circumcised as do not rely upon their circumcision alone, but also walk in the footprints of the faith which our father Abraham had while he was yet uncircumcised.

For it was not through law that Abraham, or his posterity, was given the promise that the world should be his inheritance, but through the righteousness that came from faith. For if those who hold by the law, and they alone, are heirs, then faith is empty and the promise goes for nothing, because law can bring only retribution; but where there is no law there can be no breach of law. The promise was made on the ground of faith, in order that it might be a matter of sheer grace, and that it might be valid for all Abraham's posterity, not only for those who hold by the law, but for those also who have the faith of Abraham. For he is the father of us all, as Scripture says: 'I have appointed you to be the father of many nations.' This promise, then, was valid before God, the God in whom he put his faith, the God who makes the dead live and summons things that are not yet in existence as if they already were. When hope seemed hopeless, his faith was such that he became 'father of many nations', in agreement with the words which had been spoken to him: 'Thus shall your posterity be.' Without any weakening of faith he contemplated his own body, as good as dead (for he was about a hundred years old), and the deadness of Sarah's womb, and never doubted God's promise, but, strong in faith, gave honour to God, in the firm conviction of his power to do what he had promised. And that is why Abraham's faith was 'counted to him as righteousness'.

Those words were written, not for Abraham's sake alone, but for our sake too: it is to be 'counted' in the same way to us who have faith in the God who raised Jesus our Lord from the dead; for he was delivered to death for our misdeeds, and raised to life to justify us.

Institutional Expression 2

The Coming of the Spirit: Acts 2

The inauguration of the Christian Church occurred at the Feast of Weeks, known also as Pentecost (the name means 'Fiftieth (day)' after Passover). The coming of the Spirit is dramatic. Peter's preaching is a statement of early Christian faith: already the Jewish Scriptures are being seen as foretelling Jesus.

While the Day of Pentecost was running its course they were all together in one place, when suddenly, there came from the sky a noise like that of a strong driving wind, which filled the whole house where they were sitting. And there appeared to them tongues like flames of fire, dispersed among them and resting on each one. And they were all filled with the Holy Spirit and began to talk in other tongues, as the Spirit gave them power of utterance.

Now there were living in Jerusalem devout Jews drawn from every nation under heaven; and at this sound the crowd gathered, all bewildered because each one heard the apostles talking in his own language. They were amazed and in their astonishment exclaimed, 'Why, they are all Galileans, are they not, these men who are speaking? How is it then that we hear them, each of us in his own native language? Parthians, Medes, Elamites; inhabitants of Mesopotamia, of Judaea and Cappadocia, of Pontus and Asia, of Phrygia and Pamphylia, of Egypt and the districts of Libya around Cyrene; visitors from Rome, both Jews and proselytes, Cretans and Arabs, we hear them telling in our own tongues the great things God has done.' And they were all amazed and perplexed, saying to one another, 'What can this mean?' Others said contemptuously, 'They have been drinking!'

But Peter stood up with the Eleven, raised his voice, and addressed them: 'Fellow Jews, and all you who live in Jerusalem, mark this and give me a hearing. These men are not drunk, as you imagine; for it is only nine in the morning. No, this is what the prophet spoke of: "God says, 'This will happen in the last days: I will pour out upon everyone a portion of my spirit; and your sons and daughters shall prophesy; your young men shall see visions, and your old men shall dream dreams. Yes, I will endue even my slaves, both men and women, with a portion of my spirit, and they shall prophesy. And I will show portents in the sky above, and signs on the earth below – blood and fire and drifting smoke. The sun shall be turned to darkness, and the moon to blood, before that great resplendent day, the day of the Lord, shall come. And then, everyone who invokes the name of the Lord shall be saved.' "

'Men of Israel: listen to me: I speak of Jesus of Nazareth, a man singled out by God and made known to you through miracles, portents, and signs, which God worked among you through him, as you well know. When he had been given up to you, by the deliberate will and plan of God, you used heathen men to crucify and kill him. But God raised him to life again, setting him free from the pangs of death, because it could not be that death should keep him in its grip.

'For David says of him:

"I foresaw that the presence of the Lord
would be with me always,
For he is at my right hand so that I may
not be shaken;
Therefore my heart was glad and my
tongue spoke my joy;
Moreover, my flesh shall dwell in hope,
For thou wilt not abandon my soul to
Hades,
Nor let thy loyal servant suffer corruption.
Thou hast shown me the ways of life,
Thou wilt fill me with gladness by thy
presence."[1]

[1] Psalm 16:8–11.

'Let me tell you plainly, my friends, that the patriarch David died and was buried, and his tomb is here to this very day. It is clear therefore that he spoke as a prophet who knew that God had sworn to him that one of his own direct descendants should sit on his throne; and when he said he was not abandoned to Hades, and his flesh never suffered corruption, he spoke with foreknowledge of the resurrection of the Messiah. The Jesus we speak of has been raised by God, as we can all bear witness. Exalted thus with God's right hand, he received the Holy Spirit from the Father, as was promised, and all that you now see and hear flows from him. For it was not David who went up to heaven; his own words are: "The Lord said to my Lord, 'Sit at my right hand until I make your enemies your footstool.'" 'Let all Israel then accept as certain that God has made this Jesus, whom you crucified, both Lord and Messiah.'

When they heard this they were cut to the heart, and said to Peter and the apostles, 'Friends, what are we to do?' 'Repent,' said Peter, 'repent and be baptized, every one of you, in the name of Jesus the Messiah for the forgiveness of your sins; and you will receive the gift of the Holy Spirit. For the promise is to you, and to your children, and to all who are far away, everyone whom the Lord your God may call.'

In these and many other words he pressed his case and pleaded with them: 'Save yourselves,' he said, 'from this crooked age.' Then those who accepted his word were baptized, and some three thousand were added to their number that day.

They met constantly to hear the apostles teach, and to share the common life, to break bread, and to pray. A sense of awe was everywhere, and many marvels and signs were brought about through the apostles. All whose faith had drawn them together held everything in common: they would sell their property and possessions and make a general distribution as the need of each required. With one mind they kept up their daily attendance at the temple, and, breaking bread in private houses, shared their meals with unaffected joy, as they praised God and enjoyed the favour of the whole people. And day by day the Lord added to their number those whom he was saving.

Institutional Expression 3

Church Order: I Timothy 2–4

In this pastoral epistle attention is paid to the way the emerging officers of the Church (bishops and deacons) should conduct themselves. The development of heresy is alluded to also, evidently some kind of Gnosticism, that is, one of a number of movements and trends of thought affirming *gnosis*, or knowledge of the Ultimate – but typically seeing the material world as evil; the author of the letter reacts against this, as God's creation is good.

First of all, then, I urge that petitions, prayers, intercessions, and thanksgivings be offered for all men; for sovereigns and all in high office, that we may lead a tranquil and quiet life in full observance of religion and high standards of morality. Such prayer is right, and approved by God our Saviour, whose will it is that all men should find salvation and come to know the truth. For there is one God, and also one mediator between God and men, Christ Jesus, himself man, who sacrificed himself to win freedom for all mankind, so providing, at the fitting time, proof of the divine purposes; of this I was appointed herald and apostle (this is no lie, but the truth), to instruct the nations in the true faith.

It is my desire, therefore, that everywhere

prayers be said by the men of the congregation, who shall lift up their hands with a pure intention, excluding angry or quarrelsome thoughts. Women again must dress in becoming manner, modestly and soberly, not with elaborate hair-styles, not decked out with gold or pearls, or expensive clothes, but with good deeds, as befits women who claim to be religious. A woman must be a leaner, listening quietly and with due submission. I do not permit a woman to be a teacher, nor must woman domineer over man; she should be quiet. For Adam was created first, and Eve afterwards; and it was not Adam who was deceived; it was the woman who, yielding to deception, fell into sin. Yet she will be saved through motherhood – if only women continue in faith, love, and holiness, with a sober mind.

There is a popular saying: 'To aspire to leadership is an honourable ambition.' Our leader, therefore, or bishop, must be above reproach, faithful to his one wife, sober, temperate, courteous, hospitable, and a good teacher; he must not be given to drink, or a brawler, but of a forbearing disposition, avoiding quarrels, and no lover of money. He must be one who manages his own household well and wins obedience from his children, and a man of the highest principles. If a man does not know how to control his own family, how can he look after a congregation of God's people? He must not be a convert newly baptized, for fear the sin of conceit should bring upon him a judgement contrived by the devil. He must moreover have a good reputation with the non-Christian public, so that he may not be exposed to scandal and get caught in the devil's snare.

Deacons, likewise, must be men of high principle, not indulging in double talk; given neither to excessive drinking nor to money-grubbing. They must be men who combine a clear conscience with a firm hold on the deep truths of our faith. No less than bishops, they must first undergo a scrutiny, and if there is no mark against them, they may serve. Their wives, equally, must be women of high principle, who will not talk scandal, sober and trustworthy in every way. A deacon must be faithful to his one wife, and good at managing his children and his own household. For deacons with a good record of service may claim a high standing and the right to speak openly on matters of the Christian faith.

I am hoping to come to you before long, but I write this in case I am delayed, to let you know how men ought to conduct themselves in God's household, that is, the church of the living God, the pillar and bulwark of the truth. And great beyond all question is the mystery of our religion:

'He who was manifested in the body,
vindicated in the spirit,
seen by angels:
who was proclaimed among the nations,
believed in throughout the world,
glorified in high heaven.'

The Spirit says expressly that in after times some will desert from the faith and give their minds to subversive doctrines inspired by devils, through the specious falsehoods of men whose own conscience is branded with the devil's sign. They forbid marriage and inculcate abstinence from certain foods, though God created them to be enjoyed with thanksgiving by believers who have inward knowledge of the truth. For everything that God created is good, and nothing is to be rejected when it is taken with thanksgiving, since it is hallowed by God's own word and by prayer.

By offering such advice as this to the brotherhood you will prove a good servant of Christ Jesus, bred in the precepts of our faith and of the sound instruction which you have followed. Have nothing to do with those godless myths, fit only for old women. Keep yourself in training for the practice of religion. The training of the body does bring limited benefit, but the benefits of religion are without limit, since it holds promise not only for his life but for the life to come. Here are words you may trust, words that merit full acceptance: 'With this before us we labour and struggle, because we have set our hope on the living God, who is the Saviour of all men – the Saviour, above all, of believers.

Pass on these orders and these teachings. Let no one slight you because you are young, but make yourself an example to believers in speech and behaviour, in love, fidelity, and purity. Until I arrive devote your attention to the public reading of the scriptures, to exhortation, and to teaching. Do not neglect the spiritual endowment you possess, which was given you, under the guidance of prophecy, through the laying on of the hands of the elders as a body.

Make these matters your business and your absorbing interest, so that your progress may be plain to all. Persevere in them, keeping close watch on yourself and your teaching; by doing so you will further the salvation of yourself and your hearers.

Experience 1

Jesus Transfigured: Mark 8–9

Peter's confession at Caesarea Philippi that Jesus is Messiah is followed by an account of what this means in practice: Jesus will suffer humiliation. Yet something glorious will happen, when the Son of Man returns. As a foretaste, the three closest disciples are taken up to a high mountain and have a fearful and numinous experience – Jesus is transfigured, and in the company of Moses, chief founder of ancient Israel, and Elijah (prototype of prophets and herald of the Messiah).

Jesus and his disciples set out for the villages of Caesarea Philippi. On the way he asked his disciples, 'Who do men say I am?' They answered, 'Some say John the Baptist, others Elijah, others one of the prophets.' 'And you,' he asked, 'who do you say I am?' Peter replied: 'You are the Messiah.' Then he gave them strict orders not to tell anyone about him; and he began to teach them that the Son of Man had to undergo great sufferings, and to be rejected by the elders, chief priests, and doctors of the law; to be put to death, and to rise again three days afterwards. He spoke about it plainly. At this Peter took him by the arm and began to rebuke him. But Jesus turned round, and, looking at his disciples, rebuked Peter. 'Away with you, Satan,' he said; 'you think as men think, not as God thinks.'

Then he called the people to him, as well as his disciples, and said to them, 'Anyone who wishes to be a follower of mine must leave self behind; he must take up his cross, and come with me. Whoever cares for his own safety is lost; but if a man will let himself be lost for my sake and for the Gospel, that man is safe. What does a man gain by winning the whole world at the cost of his true self? What can he give to buy that self back? If anyone is ashamed of me and mine in this wicked and godless age, the Son of Man will be ashamed of him, when he comes in the glory of his Father and of the holy angels.

He also said, 'I tell you this: there are some of those standing here who will not taste death before they have seen the kingdom of God already come in power.'

Six days later Jesus took Peter, James, and John with him and led them up a high mountain where they were alone; and in their presence he was transfigured: his clothes became dazzling white, with a whiteness no bleacher on earth could equal. They saw Elijah appear, and Moses with him, and there they were, conversing with Jesus. Then Peter spoke: 'Rabbi,' he said, 'how good it is that we are here! Shall we make three shelters, one for you, one for Moses, and one for Elijah?' (For he did not know what to say; they were so terrified.) Then a cloud appeared, casting its shadow over them, and out of the cloud came a voice: 'This is my Son, my Beloved, listen to him.' And now suddenly, when they looked around, there was nobody to be seen but Jesus alone with themselves.

On their way down the mountain, he enjoined them not to tell anyone what they had seen until the Son of Man had risen from the dead. They seized upon those words, and discussed among themselves what this 'rising from the dead' could mean. And they put a question to him: 'Why do our teachers say that Elijah must be the first to come?' He replied, 'Yes, Elijah does come first to set everything right. Yet how is it that the scriptures say of the Son of Man that he is to endure great sufferings and to be treated with contempt? However, I tell you, Elijah has already come and they have worked their will upon him, as the scriptures say of him.'

Experience 2

Christ and the Devil: Matthew 4

We know little of Jesus' own religious experience: but we can infer a strong sense both of the presence of his heavenly Father and of the antagonism of the Evil One. This passage illustrates Jesus' struggle not to be deflected from his appointed task. The account is sandwiched between Jesus' baptism and the launching of his ministry.

Jesus was then led away by the Spirit into the wilderness, to be tempted by the devil.

For forty days and nights he fasted, and at the end of them he was famished. The tempter approached him and said, 'If you are the Son of God, tell these stones to become bread.' Jesus answered, 'Scripture says, "Man cannot live on bread alone; he lives on every word that God utters." '

The devil then took him to the Holy City and set him on the parapet of the temple. 'If you are the son of God,' he said, 'throw yourself down; for Scripture says, 'He will put his angels in charge of you, and they will support you in their arms, for fear you should strike your foot against a stone." ' Jesus answered him, 'Scripture says again, "You are not to put the Lord your God to the test." '

Once again, the devil took him to a very high mountain, and showed him all the kingdoms of the world in their glory. 'All these,' he said, 'I will give you, if you will only fall down and do me homage.' But Jesus said, 'Begone, Satan; Scripture says, "You shall do homage to the Lord your God and worship him alone." '

Then the devil left him, and angels appeared and waited on him.

Experience 3

Paul's Conversion: Acts 9

Paul's experience of the risen Christ had a dramatic effect on him, and was in many ways the crucial turning point in the history of the earliest church, since he was the central figure in the expansion of the new faith among the Gentiles.

Meanwhile Saul was still breathing murderous threats against the disciples of the Lord. He went to the High Priest and applied for letters to the synagogues at Damascus authorizing him to arrest anyone he found, men or women, who followed the new way, and bring them to Jerusalem. While he was still on the road and nearing Damascus, suddenly a light flashed from the sky all around him. He fell to the ground and heard a voice saying, 'Saul, Saul, why do you persecute me?' 'Tell me, Lord,' he said, 'who you are.' The voice answered, 'I am Jesus, whom you are persecuting. But get up and go into the city, and you will be told what you have to do.' Meanwhile the men who were travelling with him stood speechless; they heard the voice but could see no one. Saul got up from the ground, but when he opened his eyes he could not see; so they led him by the hand and brought him into Damascus. He was blind for three days, and took no food or drink.

There was a disciple in Damascus named Ananias. He had a vision in which he heard the voice of the Lord: 'Ananias!' 'Here I am, Lord,' he answered. The Lord said to him, 'Go at once to Straight Street, to the house of Judas, and ask for a man from Tarsus named Saul. You will find him at prayer; he has had a vision of a man named Ananias coming in and laying his hands on him to restore his sight.' Ananias answered, 'Lord, I have often heard about this man and all the harm he has done to thy people in Jerusalem. And here he is with authority from the chief priests to arrest all who invoke thy name.' But the Lord said to him, 'You must go, for this man is my chosen instrument to bring my name before the nations and their kings, and before the people of Israel. I myself will show him all that he must go through for my name's sake.'

So Ananias went. He entered the house, laid his hands on him and said, 'Saul, my brother, the Lord Jesus, who appeared to you on your way here, has sent me to you so that you may recover your sight, and be filled with the Holy Spirit.' And immediately it seemed that scales fell from his eyes, and he regained his sight. Thereupon he was baptized, and afterwards he took food and his strength returned.

We stayed some time with the disciples in Damascus. Soon he was proclaiming Jesus publicly in the synagogues: 'This,' he said, 'is the Son of God.' All who heard were astounded. 'Is not this the man,' they said, 'who was in Jerusalem trying to destroy those who invoke this name? Did he not come here for the sole purpose of arresting them and taking them to the chief priests?' But Saul grew more and more forceful, and silenced the Jews of Damascus with his cogent proofs that Jesus was the Messiah.

As the days mounted up, the Jews hatched a plot against his life; but their plans became known to Saul. They kept watch on the city gates day and night so that they might murder him; but his converts took him one night and let him down by the wall, lowering him in a basket.

When he reached Jerusalem he tried to join the body of disciples there; but they were all afraid of him, because they did not believe that he was really a convert. Barnabas, however, took him by the hand and introduced him to the apostles. He described to them how Saul had seen the Lord on his journey, and heard his voice, and how he had spoken out boldly in the name of Jesus at Damascus. Saul now stayed with them, moving about freely in Jerusalem. He spoke out boldly and openly in the name of the Lord, talking and debating with the Greek-speaking Jews. But they planned to murder him, and when the brethren learned of this they escorted him to Caesarea and saw him off to Tarsus.

Ethics 1

The Sermon on the Mount: Matthew 5–7

Matthew has an expanded and rearranged version of the sayings of Jesus commonly known as the Sermon on the Mount as found in Luke. It includes the Beatitudes and Lord's Prayer, and is cast in the framework of the coming of the Kingdom.

When he saw the crowds he went up the hill. There he took his seat, and when his disciples had gathered round him he began to address them. And this is the teaching he gave:

'How blest are those who know that they are poor;
the kingdom of Heaven is theirs.
How blest are the sorrowful;
they shall find consolation.
How blest are those of a gentle spirit;
they shall have the earth for their possession.
How blest are those who hunger and thirst to see right prevail;
they shall be satisfied.
How blest are those who show mercy;
mercy shall be shown to them.
How blest are those whose hearts are pure;
they shall see God.
How blest are the peacemakers;
God shall call them his sons.
How blest are those who have suffered persecution for the cause of right;
the kingdom of Heaven is theirs.

'How blest you are, when you suffer insults and persecution and every kind of calumny for my sake. Accept it with gladness and exultation, for you have a rich reward in heaven; in the same way they persecuted the prophets before you.

'You are salt to the world. And if salt becomes tasteless, how is its saltness to be restored? It is now good for nothing but to be thrown away and trodden underfoot.

'You are light for all the world. A town that stands on a hill cannot be hidden. When a lamp is lit, it is not put under the mealtub, but on the lampstand where it gives light to everyone in the house. And you, like the lamp, must shed light among your fellows, so that, when they see the good you do, they may give praise to your Father in heaven.

'Do not suppose that I have come to abolish the Law and the prophets; I did not come to abolish, but to complete. I tell you this: so long as heaven and earth endure, not a letter, not a stroke, will disappear from the Law until all that must happen has happened. If any man therefore sets aside even the least of the Law's demands, and teaches others to do the same, he will have the lowest place in the kingdom of Heaven, whereas anyone who keeps the Law and teaches others so will stand high in the Kingdom of Heaven. I tell you, unless you show yourselves far better men that the Pharisees and the doctors of the law, you can never enter the kingdom of Heaven.

'You have learned that our forefathers were told, "Do not commit murder; anyone who commits murder must be brought to judgment." But what I tell you is this: Anyone who nurses anger against his brother must be brought to judgment. If he abuses his brother he must answer for it to the court; if he sneers at him he will have to answer for it in the fires of hell.

'If, when you are bringing your gifts to the altar, you suddenly remember that your brother has a grievance against you, leave your gift where it is before the altar. First go and make your peace with your brother, and only then come back and offer your gift.

'If someone sues you, come to terms with him promptly while you are both on your way to court; otherwise he may hand you over to the judge, and the judge to the constable, and you will be put in jail. I tell you, once you are there you will not be let out till you have paid the last farthing.

'You have learned that they were told, "Do not commit adultery." But what I tell you is this: If a man looks on a woman with a lustful eye, he has already committed adultery with her in his heart.

'If your right eye leads you astray, tear it out and fling it away; it is better for you to lose one part of your body than for the whole of it to be thrown into hell. And if your right hand is your undoing, cut it off and fling it away; it is better for you to lose one part of your body than for the whole of it to go to hell.

'They were told, "A man who divorces his wife must give her a note of dismissal." But what I tell you is this: If a man divorces his wife for any cause other than unchastity he involves her in adultery; and anyone who marries a woman so divorced commits adultery.

'Again, you have learned that they were told, "Do not break your oath", and "Oaths sworn to the Lord must be kept." But what I tell you is this: You are not to swear at all – not by heaven, for it is God's throne, nor by earth, for it is his footstool, not by Jerusalem, for it is the city of the great King, nor by your own head, because you cannot turn one hair of it white or black. Plain "Yes" or "No" is all you need to say; anything beyond that comes from the devil.

'You have learned that they were told, "An eye for an eye, and a tooth for a tooth." But what I tell you is this: Do not set yourself against the man who wrongs you. If someone slaps you on the right cheek, turn and offer him your left. If a man wants to sue you for your shirt, let him have your coat as well. If a man in authority makes you go one mile, go with him two. Give when you are asked to give; and do not turn your back on a man who wants to borrow.

'You have learned that they were told, "Love your neighbour, hate your enemy." But what I tell you is this: Love your enemies and pray for your persecutors; only so can you be children of your heavenly Father, who makes his sun rise on good and bad alike, and sends the rain on the honest and the dishonest. If you love only those who love you, what reward can you expect? Surely the tax-gatherers do as much as that. And if you greet only your brothers, what is there extraordinary about that? Even the heathen do as much. You must therefore be all goodness, just as your heavenly Father is all good.

'Be careful not to make a show of your religion before men; if you do, no reward awaits you in your Father's house in heaven.

'Thus, when you do some act of charity, do not announce it with a flourish of trumpets, as the hypocrites do in synagogue and in the streets to win admiration from men. I tell you this: they have their reward already. No; when you do some act of charity, do not let your left hand know what your right is doing; your good deed must be secret, and your Father who sees what is done in secret will reward you.

'Again, when you pray, do not be like the hypocrites; they love to say their prayers standing up in synagogue and at the streetcorners, for everyone to see them. I tell you this: they have their reward already. But when you pray, go into a room by yourself, shut the door, and pray to your Father who is there in the secret place; and your Father who sees what is secret will reward you.

'In your prayers do not go babbling on like the heathen, who imagine that the more they say the more likely they are to be heard. Do not imitate them. Your Father knows what your needs are before you ask him.

'This is how you should pray:

"Our Father in heaven,
Thy name be hallowed;
They kingdom come,
Thy will be done,
On earth as in heaven,
Give us today our daily bread,
Forgive us the wrong we have done,
As we have forgiven those who have
wronged us.
And do not bring us to the test,
But save us from the evil one."

For if you forgive others the wrongs they have done, your heavenly Father will also forgive you; but if you do not forgive others, then the wrongs you have done will not be forgiven by your Father.

'So too when you fast, do not look gloomy like the hypocrites: they make their faces unsightly so that other people may see that they are fasting. I tell you this: they have their reward already. But when you fast, anoint your head and wash your face, so that men may not see that you are fasting, but only your Father who is in the secret place; and your Father who sees what is secret will give you your reward.

'Do not store up for yourselves treasure on earth, where it grows rusty and moth-eaten, and thieves break in to steal it. Store up treasure in heaven, where there is no moth and no rust to spoil it, no thieves to break in and steal. For where your wealth is, there will your heart be also.

'The lamp of the body is the eye. If your eyes are sound, you will have light for your whole body; if the eyes are bad, your whole body will be in darkness. If then the only light you have is darkness, the darkness is doubly dark.

'No servant can be slave to two masters; for either he will hate the first and love the second, or he will be devoted to the first and think nothing of the second. You cannot serve God and Money.

'Therefore I bid you put away anxious thoughts about food and drink to keep you alive, and clothes to cover your body. Surely life is more than food, the body more than clothes. Look at the birds of the air; they do not sow and reap and store in barns, yet your heavenly Father feeds them. You are worth more than the birds! Is there a man of you who by anxious thought can add a foot to his height? And why be anxious about clothes? Consider how the lilies grow in the fields; they do not work, they do not spin; and yet, I tell you, even Solomon in all his splendour was not attired like one of these. But if that is how God clothes the grass in the fields, which is there today, and tomorrow is thrown on the stove, will he not all the more clothe you? How little faith you have! No, do not ask anxiously, "What are we to eat? What are we to drink? What shall we wear?" All these are things for the heathen to run after, not for you, because your heavenly Father knows that you need them all. Set your mind on God's kingdom and his justice before everything else, and all the rest will come to you as well. So do not be anxious about tomorrow; tomorrow will look after itself. Each day has troubles enough of its own.

'Pass no judgment, and you will not be judged. For as you judge others, so you will yourselves be judged, and whatever measure you deal out to others will be dealt back to you. Why do you look at the speck of sawdust in your brother's eye, with never a thought for the great plank in your own? Or how can you say to your brother, "Let me take the speck out of your eye", when all the time there is that plank in your own? Hypocrite! First take the plank out of your own eye, and then you will see clearly to take the speck out of your brother's.

'Do not give dogs what is holy; do not feed your pearls to pigs: they will only trample on them, and turn and tear you to pieces.

'Ask, and you will receive; seek, and you will find; knock, and the door will be opened. For everyone who asks receives, he who seeks finds, and to him who knocks, the door will be opened.

'Is there a man among you who will offer his son a stone when he asks for bread, or a snake when he asks for fish? If you, then, bad as you are, know how to give your children what is good for them, how much more will your heavenly Father give good things to those who ask him!

'Always treat others as you would like them to treat you: that is the Law and the prophets.

'Enter by the narrow gate. The gate is wide that leads to perdition, there is plenty of room on the road, and many go that way; but the gate that leads to life is small and the road is narrow, and those who find it are few.

'Beware of false prophets, men who come to you dressed up as sheep while underneath they are savage wolves. You will recognize them by the fruits they bear. Can grapes be picked from briars, or figs from thistles? In the same way, a good tree always yields good fruit, and a poor tree bad fruit. A good tree cannot bear bad fruit, or a poor tree good fruit. And when a tree does not yield good fruit it is cut down and burnt. That is why I say you will recognize them by their fruits.

'Not everyone who calls me "Lord, Lord" will enter the kingdom of Heaven, but only those who do the will of my heavenly Father. When that day comes, many will say to me, "Lord, Lord, did we not prophesy in your name, cast out devils in your name, and in your name perform many miracles?" Then I will tell them to their face, "I never knew you: out of my sight, you and your wicked ways!"

'What then of the man who hears these words of mine and acts upon them? He is like a man who had the sense to build his house on rock. The rain came down, the floods rose, the wind blew, and beat upon that house; but it did not fall, because its foundations were on rock. But what of the man who hears these words of mine and does not act upon them? He is like a man who was foolish enough to build his house on sand. The rain came down, the floods rose, the wind blew, and beat upon that house; down it fell with a great crash.'

When Jesus had finished this discourse the people were astounded at his teaching; unlike their own teachers he taught with a note of authority.

Ethics 2

Practical Christianity: James 1

Probably this is an early account of what following Jesus means in practice. It does not explicitly state the doctrines and faith underlying the exhortation, but it chimes in with the more explicitly Christ-related ethics of Paul.

From James, a servant of God and the Lord Jesus Christ. Greetings to the Twelve Tribes[1] dispersed throughout the world.

My brothers, whenever you have to face trials of many kinds, count yourselves supremely happy, in the knowledge that such testing of your faith breeds fortitude, and if you give fortitude full play you will go on to complete a balanced character that will fall short in nothing. If any of you falls short in wisdom, he should ask God for it and it will be given him, for God is a generous giver who neither refuses nor reproaches anyone. But he must ask in faith, without a doubt in his mind; for the doubter is like a heaving sea ruffled by the wind. A man of that kind must not expect the Lord to give him anything; he is double-minded, and never can keep a steady course.

The brother in humble circumstances may well be proud that God lifts him up; and the wealthy brother must find his pride in being brought low. For the rich man will disappear like the flower of the field; once the sun is up with its scorching heat the flower withers, its petals fall, and what was lovely to look at is lost for ever. So shall the rich man wither away as he goes about his business.

Happy the man who remains steadfast under trial, for having passed that test he will receive for his prize the gift of life promised to those who love God. No one under trial or temptation should say, 'I am being tempted by God'; for God is untouched by evil, and does not himself tempt anyone. Temptation arises when a man is enticed and lured away by his own lust; then lust conceives, and gives birth to sin; and sin fully-grown breeds death.

Do not deceive yourselves, my friends. All good giving and every perfect gift comes from above, from the Father of the lights of heaven. With him there is no variation, no play of passing shadows. Of his set purpose, by declaring the truth, he gave us birth to be a kind of first fruits of his creatures.

Of that you may be certain, my friends. But each of you must be quick to listen, slow to speak, and slow to be angry. For a man's anger cannot promote the justice of God. Away then with all that is sordid, and the malice that hurries to excess, and quietly accept the message planted in your hearts, which can bring you salvation.

Only be sure that you act on the message and do not merely listen; for that would be to mislead yourselves. A man who listens to the message but never acts upon it is like one who looks in a mirror at the face nature gave him. He glances at himself and goes away, and at once forgets what he looked like. But the man who looks closely into the perfect law, the law that makes us free, and who lives in its company, does not forget what he

[1] i.e. Israel, namely the New Israel.

hears, but acts upon it; and that is the man who by acting will find happiness.

A man may think he is religious, but if he has no control over his tongue, he is deceiving himself; that man's religion is futile. The kind of religion which is without stain or fault in the sight of God our Father is this: to go to the help of orphans and widows in their distress and keep oneself untarnished by the world.

Ethics 3

A Hymn to Love: I Corinthians 13

Perhaps this is an interpolation into the epistle, but there is little doubt it was composed as a kind of hymn by Paul. Love is seen as the supreme gift which the Spirit bestows upon the Church, and it is through love that the Christian manifests in himself the true nature of God.

I may speak in tongues of men or of angels, but if I am without love, I am a sounding gong or a clanging cymbal. I may have the gift of prophecy, and know every hidden truth; I may have faith strong enough to move mountains; but if I have no love, I am nothing. I may dole out all I possess, or even give my body to be burnt, but if I have no love, I am none the better.

Love is patient; love is kind and envies no one. Love is never boastful, nor conceited, nor rude; never selfish, not quick to take offence. Love keeps no score of wrongs; does not gloat over other men's sins, but delights in the truth. There is nothing love cannot face; there is no limit to its faith, its hope, and its endurance.

Love will never come to an end. Are there prophets? their work will be over. Are there tongues of ecstasy? they will cease. Is there knowledge? it will vanish away; for our knowledge and our prophecy alike are partial, and the partial vanishes when wholeness comes. When I was a child, my speech, my outlook, and my thoughts were all childish. When I grew up, I had finished with childish things. Now we see only puzzling reflections in a mirror, but then we shall see face to face. My knowledge now is partial; then it will be whole, like God's knowledge of me. In a word, there are three things that last for ever: faith, hope, and love; but the greatest of them all is love.

Postscript

The Bible was not only authoritative for Christians as a source of knowledge about God and his will: it also, obviously, played a central role in the worship of the Church. Since Christian worship incorporated basically two elements, the synagogue service common to Jews and the celebration of the Lord's Supper, it included readings from the Old Testament. By the 2nd century there were incorporated readings from the New Testament. Eventually both in East and West, the Old Testament readings mainly dropped out, and the concentration was on a reading from an Epistle and one from a Gospel. For those who were not educated these were the main occasions for contact with the scripture. The Reformation brought back the Old Testament and at the same time caused the scriptures to be translated into the vernacular and to be widely disseminated through printing. Thus, increasingly, the Bible came to be not merely a liturgical and doctrinal phenomenon, but a source of personal piety and inspiration.

Among highly influential translations of the Bible have been: Jerome's Latin Bible (known as the Vulgate, or Common Version, early 5th century); Wycliffe's English Bible (14th century and banned by the clergy); the King James Authorized Version (published in 1611); the German Bible of Martin Luther (1534); the Russian Bible (1860–75); the Douai Bible (Roman Catholic, 1609–10); the Revised Standard Version (1946–57); the New English Bible (1961–70); and the many Bibles in the languages of non-literate peoples – often the first book to appear in their languages.

Bibliography

The following are the best-known versions of the Christian Bible in English:

King James Version (Authorized Version of 1611)
A New Translation of the Bible (Moffat)
Revised Standard Version (1971)
The New English Bible (1970)
The Jerusalem Bible (1975)

A Greek Orthodox priest holds the Gospels at a Holy Week ceremony at Mount Athos. The reading from the Gospels is a presentation of Christ as the Word, and thus the liturgy repeats the original revelation in a living form.

Boys are instructed in the Qur'ān at a mosque in Oman. Learning the Qur'an by heart imprints it in the mind of the young Muslim.

Islam

Introduction

It is often said that the Qur'ān is the Muslim's Bible. Certainly, it is the sacred book of Islam, but one must be very careful in pushing its affinities with the Bible, either the Hebrew Bible or the New Testament. For Muslims, the Qur'ān is a single book, a complete and perfect manifestation of the Qur'ān preserved in heaven. It contains all the decrees of God and is the most perfect form of wisdom. Literally, the Qur'ān is the word of God dictated to the Prophet Muḥammad by the angel Gabriel. The Qur'ān is the record of this singular prophet's experience of the transcendent, his teachings and activities. These very simple facts suggest that the Qur'ān is different from the Bible, which is a collection of texts and books assembled over a long period of time. The Bible, unlike the Qur'ān, arises from the experiences of numerous individuals, although the traditions of Judaism and Christianity have consistently maintained that there is a continuity of divine revelation among the various individuals throughout this long period. Perhaps it would be more accurate to say that the Qur'ān is to Islam what the Torah is to Judaism or what Jesus is to Christianity.

Muḥammad ibn 'Abdallāh ibn 'Abd al-Muṭallib was born in the Arabian city of Mecca in the year 570 CE. He was from the Hashemite clan of the tribe of Quraysh which then controlled the city of his birth. By the age of six he was orphaned and taken into the homes of relatives. The Mecca of the young Muḥammad was quickly becoming a major political centre, situated on the caravan trail linking Yemen in the south with Byzantine Egypt and Syria-Palestine to the north-west, and the Sassanian Empire to the north-east. Mecca also contained a diverse religious population made up of followers of indigenous Arab traditions, often referred to in the literature as Arab paganism, Jews and Christians. Muḥammad may have had some contact with Jews and Christians through his family's mercantile affairs. In addition, the city was home to other religious figures called *ḥanīfs*, freelance religious seekers, *kāhins*, soothsayers, and *shā'irs*, poets, who drew their inspiration from local jinn or spirits. Later, the population of Mecca and other places would confuse Muḥammad with these figures, and the Qur'ān itself reveals Muḥammad's efforts to distinguish himself from them; the source of his authority and the reality of his message was greater than the authority of the lowly jinn and the transitory, confused revelations of *ḥanīfs* and *kāhins*. Around the age of forty, in approximately 610, after he had married his first wife Khadīja, Muḥammad began to have visions of a nameless apparition only later identified as the angel Gabriel. These experiences continued until his death and became the foundation of his prophetic mission, although shortly after the initial revelations they became limited to acoustic experiences.

After preaching his message of the single Creator and Judge with relative success for some years, Muḥammad's position with the ruling Meccans became increasingly difficult. In 622 he was forced to migrate north to the city of Medina. The date of this migration or *hijra* marks the beginning of the Muslim era and calendar so that one always dates events and individuals 'after the *hijra*' (or simply AH). In Medina, his following grew quickly so that by the year 627, after several successful battles with surrounding cities and tribes, he had established hegemony over a relatively large area, although the ruling aristocracy of Mecca, the Banū Umayya, did not yield to him until 630. There are two very important aspects of Muḥammad's experience in Medina. First, the migration forced upon Muḥammad and his followers the consciousness that they were a distinct religious community or *umma*, separate both from the community they had just left behind in Mecca and from other communities in Medina, particularly the Jews and Christians. With the Prophet's successes, the *umma* expanded and increased in numbers, and naturally became a unified religious and political community. Second, the expansion of the *umma* drew it into tension with the Jewish and Christian communities in Medina and its environs. Muḥammad had learned much from both the Jews and Christians in his youth, and their monotheism had undoubtedly prepared the ground for his own message in Medina. He had hoped that both communities would recognize him as the fulfilment of their revelations, and when this did not occur the differences between the communities were heightened. For example, early in his career Muḥammad had ordered his community to direct its prayers toward Jerusalem, but tension with the Jews of Medina forced him to reorient prayer toward Mecca, and change a number of other details in the ritual life of the community which he had inherited from the Jews. Ultimately, these communities were subjugated to the *umma*.

Yet Muḥammad remained impressed with the prophets who had arisen among the Jews and Christians. In his understanding, both Jews and Christians had failed to listen to these prophets, and had even falsified their messages. Hence he referred to himself as 'the seal (*khatm*) of the prophets' or the last of the prophets. He often recast the narrative of these prophets so that a figure like Abraham becomes the very first Muslim in Muḥammad's sacred narrative, and constructs the Ka'ba in Mecca. Jesus is recognized as a 'spirit from God', who was neither killed nor crucified, but 'lifted up' by God and was thus no different from any other prophet. Indeed, the long chain of prophets who had not been listened to was regarded by Muḥammad as a positive proof of God's compassion and mercy. This does not mean that Muḥammad found himself in agreement with the theological structures of Judaism and Christianity. His own perception of the radical transcendence and oneness of God put him on a collision course with the Christian doctrines of the Trinity and Incarnation. He directly rejects these theological formulations when he indicates in the Qur'ān that 'they surely are infidels who say "Allah is the third of three"' and 'far be it from Him that He should have a son'.

At the moment when the *umma* was expanding Muḥammad was taken sick, and died after a short illness in the year 632. It should be emphasized that Muḥammad had no unusual, intrinsic quality or special authority: he was only the vehicle for transmitting the word of God. It is therefore inappropriate to call his followers Muḥammadans or the religion he founded Muḥammadanism; these terms would suggest that the Prophet had some special quality which overshadowed his message. This does not mean that Muḥammad has not been the subject of countless sacred biographies nor that he is not the moral or ethical ideal within his tradition. But the paradigm for religion, as he is presented in the Qur'ān, is Abraham, because in his great test, which required that he sacrifice his son, he surrendered (*aslama*) to the will of God. Hence, Muḥammad was prompted to call his community of believers Islam, those who submit or surrender to the will of God. A *Muslim* therefore is not simply a follower of the Prophet, but more importantly, one who surrenders himself to the will of God.

The word Qur'ān is derived from a pan-Semitic root which means both 'to recite' and 'to read'. It is made up of 114 chapters or Sūras of varying lengths. These Sūras reflect the Prophet's life in Mecca and Medina, and both tradition and scholarship often divide the chapters according to whether they are from the Mecca or Medina period. The Sūras from the Mecca period are among the shortest, some no more than ten lines in length. As time went on the Sūras become longer and more developed, but the organizational principle behind the canon of the Qur'ān is to put the longest Sūras first, moving to the shortest. The second Sūra, titled 'The Cow', contains 288 lines, while the last Sūra, titled 'Men', has only five lines. The reader of the Qur'ān familiar with the chronological narrative of the biblical text will have some difficulty with the Qur'ān's non-chronological style. One of the only Sūras which presents itself in a style like the biblical text is Sūra 12, titled 'Joseph', which reinterprets the biblical narrative of Joseph and his brothers. While the narrative seems familiar, its reinterpretation should not be overlooked. Muḥammad is not interested in the Joseph who fulfills the promise given by God to Abraham, 'I will bless those who bless you, and him who curses you I will curse; and by you all the families of the earth shall bless themselves' (Genesis 12:3), but with the Joseph who is a prophet. The real climax of the Qur'ānic presentation is when Joseph meets his father and mother upon their arrival in Egypt (Sūra 12:100–103):

'See, father,' he said, 'this is the interpretation of my vision of long ago;
  my Lord had made it true.
He was good to me when He brought me forth from the prison,
  and again when He brought you out of the desert,
  after that Satan set at variance me and my brethren.
My Lord is gentle to what He will;
  He is the All-knowing, the All-wise.
O my Lord, Thou hast given me to rule
    and Thou hast taught me the interpretation of tales.
O Thou, the Originator of the heavens and earth,
  Thou art my Protector in this world and the next.
O receive me to Thee in true submission,
  and join me with the righteous.'

Thus the biblical figure of Joseph is recast so as to become another prophet in the long chain of messengers leading to Muḥammad.

From the very beginning of Islamic history, revelation has been understood as flowing from the concept of *sharīʿa*. Literally, this term means a 'road' or 'path', but within the tradition it takes the meaning of the divinely ordained pattern of human life and conduct. It is the sacred law which the new Prophet brings or makes accessible as part of revelation. Certainly, the Qur'ān is the most important form of revelation, but it is supplemented by the *sunna*. *Sunna* also has the literal sense of a 'well-trodden path' or a 'clear-cut way' and is composed of Prophetic traditions or some act or saying of the Prophet not recorded in the Qur'ān. These Prophetic traditions are supplemented by traditions going back to the *aṣḥāb* or the face-to-face companions of the Prophet, the *al-tābi'ūn* or the followers of the Prophet, and the Prophet's wives. The traditions or *ḥadīth*, as they are called, make up the *sunna*, and go back to an eyewitness who was present at the time and whose exact words are carefully reported, together with the words uttered by Muḥammad. Every *ḥadīth* is made up of two components. First, the *isnād* or the 'chain of guarantors' and, second, the *matn* or the actual deed or saying of the Prophet. The further removed from the Prophet, the longer the *isnād* becomes, so that in a typical *ḥadīth* we may read that A heard from B, who heard C say that D told him that he was one day in the presence of the Prophet when he said . . . The *sunna* and the Qur'ān then make up the totality of sacred literature in Islam and are understood to be the fullest manifestation of *sharī'a*. Yet this distinction between the Qur'ān and the *sunna* lies at the heart of the sectarian division within Islam from the 7th century between the orthodox Sunni and the Shī'a sect. Sunnite Islam relies on the *sharī'a* (the Qur'ān and *sunna*) to ensure the continuity within Islam. The Shī'a does not impugn the finality of the Qur'ān nor the legitimacy of the *sunna*, but adds to them a sequence of Imāms who stand in lineal relation to the Prophet. Here, the Imām is not simply the prayer-leader of the Sunnite tradition, but a continuation of the prophetic office of Muḥammad. This does not mean that every Imām is another prophet; this would contradict the self-consciousness of the Qur'ān itself. Rather, the Imām renews the original manifestation of the Qur'ān and the 'light of Muḥammad'.

In this chapter we have sought to include representative *ḥadīth* materials alongside Qur'ānic passages reflecting the six dimensions of our study. The Qur'ān is almost anti-mythological, and the dimension of sacred narrative is illustrated by materials concerning the Prophet, the Qur'ān and preceding revelations and prophets. The materials selected on the Prophet reflect both the Meccan period and years in Medina. The *ḥadīth* expand upon the Prophet's call and elaborate the Sūra passages. The materials selected for the Qur'ān illustrate its internal sense of being a heavenly book sent down to man. The *ḥadīth* describe the process by which this sacred text was assembled and outline its miraculous nature. The preceding revelations and prophets are illustrated by a series of passages on Adam, Abraham, Ishmael, Moses, Jesus, and the Torah and Gospel. Here, one clearly sees the climactic nature of the revelation itself and the chain of prophets leading to Muḥammad. Finally, we include a *ḥadīth* describing how Arab soothsayers, Jewish Rabbis and Christian monks spoke about the Messenger of Allah before his time drew near.

The dimension of doctrine is illustrated by four major categories. First we include a number of Sūra passages in which Allah is described, along with a medieval list of the ninety-nine most beautiful names of Allah. All of these names are drawn from the Qur'ān and are the basis of much philosophical and theological reflection on God in Islam. Second, we include a series of Qur'ānic passages describing the role of angels, satans and jinn. Third, we have included one Sūra passage on the Day of Judgment and the rewards or punishments awaiting the believers and unbelievers. The *ḥadīth* describes at some length the paradise that awaits those who have submitted to the will of Allah. Lastly, we illustrate the dimension of doctrine through two passages from the Qur'ān which describe predestination, one of the most problematic issues in the later development of Islam. Here, the *ḥadīth* reflect this central doctrine and underscore how problematic it is to reconcile this doctrine with a compassionate deity.

The dimension of ritual is best illustrated in Islam through the 'Five Pillars' of the tradition, which inform not only specific temporal moments but the entirety of life. Hence, within Islam ritual is totally assimilated into the daily life of the community. We begin with the *kalima* or creed and include a *ḥadīth* which demonstrates the excellence of the ritual formula 'There is no God but Allah and Muḥammad is his Messenger'. Second, we have included a number of Qur'ānic passages which speak of prayer as an essential duty of the Muslim. Here, the *ḥadīth* concerns the virtue of the Friday or 'Day of Congregation' prayer. Third, we reprint two Sūra passages on almsgiving which interlock this act with prayer. The *ḥadīth* describes the sinfulness of withholding *zakāt*, one of the two forms of alms or tithing. The Fourth Pillar is fasting, and here the reader will find one Sūra passage enjoining the act of fasting and a *ḥadīth* which describes the merits of the fast. The Fifth Pillar, pilgrimage, is illustrated by a Sūra passage which comes from Muḥammad's time in Medina and reflects the reorientation of the tradition toward Mecca. The *ḥadīth* describes the origin of the Ka'ba and effectively makes the Mosque in Mecca the very centre of the world.

The dimension of institutional expression is illustrated by three topics. First, the community is described in a Sūra passage and a *ḥadīth*. Second, we include a passage on 'the People of the Book'. These people, or *dhimmī*, where those with whom a covenant or bond had been made. They were tolerated monotheists, Jews, Christians, Ṣābians and Zoroastrians, who lived within the community of Islam, paid tribute and observed sumptuary laws as a token of inferior status and self-abasement. Third, we include two Sūra passages describing *jihād* or the 'struggle' for Islam. This word has been understood as 'Holy War', but this is only one of its meanings. The *ḥadīth* suggests that the *jihād* also carries with it the meanings of complete self-sacrifice in the submission of the human will to the will of God and martyrdom.

The dimension of experience is illustrated first by two Qur'ānic passages which describe Muḥammad's experience of the transcendence and immanence of God. These passages, along with many others from the Qur'ān, serve as the models for similar experience within the Islamic mystical schools. Second, we have included a full Sūra, a very short one, which describes the Prophet's certainty about his relationship with God, a certainty generated from his experience. Third, in a very brief Qur'ānic passage the Prophet alludes to the Night Journey in which he was taken from Mecca to Jerusalem. The *ḥadīth* expand upon this experience and we glimpse how the Prophet was taken on his heavenly ascension into the presence of God by the angel Gabriel.

The dimension of ethics is first illustrated by a Sūra passage which is very much akin to a code of personal behaviour. Second, we have included two passages from the Qur'ān which describe true piety for the Muslim. Lastly, a collection of *ḥadīth* demonstrate how Muḥammad is understood as the moral ideal within the tradition. The Prophet exhibits all the perfections and virtues in his dealing with the companions, and so his life becomes the guide for human excellence.

Sacred Narrative 1

Muḥammad: The Seal of the Prophets and the Messenger of Allah: Sūra 53, Sūra 52, Sūra 7, Sūra 33 and Ḥadīth

Each of these passages reflects Muḥammad's role as the 'Seal of the Prophets' and the Messenger of Allah. Sūra 53 is traditionally understood as coming from the early Meccan period and here it is the angel Gabriel, described as 'one terrible in power, very strong' who approaches the Prophet. The Prophet describes two occasions when he began to have visions, once in the open where Gabriel appeared on the horizon and approached him, and the second when he was in a garden in Mecca. In Sūra 52, the Prophet indicates that he has not been inspired by anything less than Allah himself. Sūra 7 probably comes from the period when Muḥammad had moved to Medina and here he speaks of himself as the messenger and prophet 'written down with them in the Torah and the Gospel'. In Sūra 33, Allah describes in succinct fashion Muḥammad's mission as the prophet of God. Lastly, a *ḥadīth* from al-Ṭabarī describes the call of Muḥammad and the first appearance of the angel Gabriel.

Sūra 53:1–18

By the Star when it plunges,
your comrade is not astray, neither errs,
nor speaks he out of caprice.
This is naught but a revelation revealed,
taught him by one terrible in power,
very strong; he stood poised,
being on the higher horizon,
then drew near and suspended hung,
two bows'-length away, or nearer,
then revealed to his servant that he revealed.
His heart lies not of what he saw;
what, will you dispute with him what he sees?

Indeed, he saw him another time
by the Lote-Tree of the Boundary
nigh which is the Garden of the Refuge,
when there covered the Lote-Tree that which covered;
his eye swerved not, nor swept astray.
Indeed, he saw one of the greatest signs of his Lord.

Sūra 52:29–34

So warn, for thou art not, by the grace of thy Lord, a sooth-sayer, nor one jinn-possessed.

Or are they saying: 'A poet, for whom we may wait expectantly the uncertainties of fate'?

Say: 'Wait! for I am with you among those who wait expectantly.'

Is it that their minds bid them to this? Or are they an iniquitous folk?

Or are they saying, 'He has forged it'? Nay, they will not believe.

So let them bring a discourse like it, if they are those who speak the truth.

Sūra 7:155–8

And prescribe for us in this world good, and in the world to come; we have repented unto Thee.

Said He, 'My chastisement – I smite with it whom I will; and My mercy embraces all things, and I shall prescribe it for those who are godfearing and pay the alms, and those who indeed believe in Our signs, those who follow the Messenger, the Prophet of the common folk, whom they find written down with them in the Torah and the Gospel, bidding them to honour, and forbidding them dishonour, making lawful for them the good things and making unlawful for them the corrupt things, and relieving them of their loads, and the fetters that were upon them. Those who believe in him and succour him and help him, and follow the light that has been sent down with him – they are the prosperers.'

Say: 'O mankind, I am the Messenger of God to you all, of Him to whom belongs the kingdom of the heavens and of the earth. There is no god but He. He gives life, and makes to die. Believe then in God, and in His Messenger, the Prophet of the common folk, who believes in God and His words, and follow him; haply so you will be guided.'

Sūra 33:44–6

O Prophet, We have sent thee as a witness, and good tidings to bear and warning, calling unto God by His leave, and as a light-giving lamp. Give good tidings to the believers that there awaits them with God great bounty.

And obey not the unbelievers and the hypocrites; heed not their hurt, and put thy trust in God; God suffices as a guardian.

A ḥadīth

Ibn Humayd has related to me on the authority of Salma, from Muḥammad b. Isḥaq, who said: Wahb b. Kaysān, client of the Zubayr family, has related to me that he heard 'Abdallāh b. al-Zubayr say to 'Ubayd b. 'Umayr b. Qatāda al-Laythī: Relate to us, O 'Ubayd, how it was when the Apostle of Allah – upon whom be Allah's blessing and peace – first began his prophetic career, when Gabriel – upon whom be peace – came to him. 'Ubayd replied – and I was there when he began relating to 'Abdallāh b. al-Zubayr and the folk who were with him: The Apostle of Allah – upon whom be Allah's blessing and peace – used to retreat to Ḥirā' one month every year. That was part of the *taḥannuth*[1] the Quraysh[2] used to practise in the pre-Islamic period. *Taḥannuth* means *tabarrur* [i.e., to practise exercises of piety]. Abū Ṭālib[3] said: He was an ascender, going up to Ḥirā', and descending again.

Now the Apostle of Allah – upon whom be Allah's blessing and peace – used to retreat there annually for that one month and feed such needy persons as came to him. Then when the Apostle of Allah – upon whom be Allah's blessing and peace – had finished this month's retreat, the first place he would visit on his return from his retreat, before he even entered his house, was the Ka'ba,[4] which he would circumambulate seven times, or as often as Allah willed, and then would return to his house. This went on until it was the month in which Allah – mighty and majestic is He – desired to show him the favour He had willed for him, that year in which He sent him forth [as a prophet]. It was the month of Ramaḍān, and the Apostle of Allah – upon whom be Allah's blessing and peace – went out to Ḥirā', as he had been wont to do, for his retreat, taking his family with him. Now when it was the night on which Allah was going to honour him with a call to apostleship, and thereby show mercy to mortals, Gabriel, by Allah's command, came to him.

Said the Apostle of Allah – upon whom be Allah's blessing and peace: 'He came to me while I was asleep, bringing a silken cloth (*namaṭ min dībāj*) on which was some writing. He said: "Recite"; but I answered: "What shall I recite?" Then he so grievously treated me that I thought I should die, but he pushed me off and said: "Recite". I answered: "But what shall I recite?"; saying this only to guard myself against doing again to me the like of what he had done to me. He said: "Recite, 'in the name of thy Lord who has created,' and so on as far as 'taught man what he did not know.'" (Sūra 96:1–5). So I recited it, and that ended the matter, for he departed from me. Thereupon I awoke from my sleep, and it was as though he had written it on my heart.

'Now it so happened that [at that time] no creature of Allah was more loathsome to me than a poet or a man possessed by jinn,[5] the sight of neither of whom could I bear. So I said: "That one – meaning himself – has become either a poet or a man jinn-possessed. The Quraysh will never

[1] Prayers.
[2] The Quraysh were the tribe in power during Muhammad's early career.
[3] Muhammad's uncle who cared for him after the death of his parents.
[4] The shrine in the city of Mecca and the centre of the pilgrimage.
[5] A familiar or unfamiliar spirit.

say this about me. I shall go to some high mountain cliff and cast myself down therefrom so that I may kill myself and be at rest." I went off with this in mind, but when I was in the midst of the mountains I heard a voice from heaven saying: "O Muḥammad, thou art Allah's Apostle, and I am Gabriel." At that I raised my head to the skies, and there was Gabriel in clear human form, with his feet on the edges of the skies, saying: "O Muḥammad, thou art Allah's Apostle, and I am Gabriel." I stood there gazing at him, and that kept me from what I had intended doing. I neither advanced nor retreated, but I began to turn my face from him to the whole expanse of the skies, but no matter in what direction I looked there I saw him. So I stood there, neither advancing forward nor retreating backward, while Khadīja [who had accompanied him to Ḥirā'] sent her messengers to look for me. They even reached Mecca and returned to her while I was still standing in my place.'

Sacred Narrative 2

Qur'ān as Sacred Book: Sūra 3, Sūra 29, Sūra 43, Sūra 10 and Ḥadīth

In Sūra 3:1–7, the sending down of the Qur'ān confirms the truth of earlier revelations in the Torah and the Gospel. 'Torah' and 'Gospel' appear as terms describing the scriptures belonging to both Jews and Christians. Sūra 29 indicates that the Qur'ān is truly miraculous and sacred, for the Prophet did not read or write before the Qur'ān was revealed to him. According to Sūra 43, the Arabic Qur'ān is created so that Muḥammad and other believers will understand the will of God, but the celestial archetype of the book remains with Allah. As the Qur'ān is an exact copy of the celestial book, Sūra 10 indicates that it cannot be forged or altered, despite the carpings of the evil-doers. A *ḥadīth* preserved in al-Bukhārī's *Ṣaḥiḥ* describes the process by which the first codex or recension of the Qur'ān was compiled by the Caliph 'Uthmān. Finally, a *ḥadīth* by Al-Bāqillānī indicates that the Qur'ān itself is the paradigm miracle confirming Muḥammad's prophetic office.

Sūra 3:1–7

Alif Lam Mim[1]
God
there is no god but He, the
Living, the Everlasting.

He has sent down upon thee the Book with the truth, confirming what was before it, and He sent down the Torah and the Gospel aforetime, as guidance to the people, and He sent down the Salvation.

As for those who disbelieve in God's signs, for them awaits a terrible chastisement; God is All-mighty, Vengeful.

From God nothing whatever is hidden in heaven and earth. It is He who forms you in the womb as He will. There is no god but He, the All-mighty, the All-wise.

It is He who sent down upon thee the Book, wherein are verses clear that are the Essence of the Book, and others ambiguous. As for those in whose hearts is swerving, they follow the ambiguous part, desiring dissension, and desiring

[1] A number of the Sūras of the Qur'ān begin with mysterious letters of the Arabic alphabet whose meaning is known only to Allah.

its interpretation; and none knows its interpretation, save only God. And those firmly rooted in knowledge say, 'We believe in it; all is from our Lord'; yet none remembers, but men possessed of minds.

Sūra 29:46–50

Even so We have sent down to thee the Book. Those to whom We have given the Book believe in it; and some of these believe in it; and none denies Our signs but the unbelievers.

Not before this didst thou recite any Book, or inscribe it with thy right hand, for then those who follow falsehood would have doubted.

Nay; rather it is signs, clear signs in the breasts of those who have been given knowledge; and none denies Our signs but the evildoers.

They say, 'Why have signs not been sent down upon him from his Lord?' Say: 'The signs are only with God, and I am only a plain warner.'

What, is it not sufficient for them that We have sent down upon thee the Book that is recited to them? Surely in that is a mercy, and a reminder to a people who believe.

Sūra 43:1–4

Ha Mim

By the Clear Book,
  behold, We have made it an Arabic Qur'ān;
  haply you will understand;
  and behold, it is in the Essence of the Book;
  with Us;
  sublime indeed, wise.
Shall We turn away the Remembrance from you,
    for that you are a prodigal people?

Sūra 10:38–41

This Qur'ān could not have been forged apart from God; but it is a confirmation of what is before it, and a distinguishing of the Book, wherein is no doubt, from the Lord of all Being.

Or do they say, 'Why, he has forged it'?

Say: 'Then produce a sūra like it, and call on whom you can, apart from God if you speak truly.'

No; but they have cried lies to that whereof they comprehended not the knowledge, and whose interpretation has not yet come to them. Even so those that were before them cried lies; then behold how was the end of the evildoers!

And some of them believe in it, and some believe not in it. Thy Lord knows very well those who do corruption.

A ḥadīth

Zayd ibn Thābit said: Abū Bakr sent for me at the time of the battle of al-Yamāma, and 'Umar ibn al-Khaṭṭāb was with him. Abū Bakr said: 'Umar has come to me and said, 'Death raged at the battle of al-Yamāma and took many of the reciters of the Qur'ān. I fear lest death in battle overtake the reciters of the Qur'ān in the provinces and a large part of the Qur'ān be lost. I think you should give orders to collect the Qur'ān.'

'What?' I asked 'Umar, 'Will you do something which the Prophet of God himself did not do?'

'By God,' replied 'Umar, 'it would be a good deed.'

'Umar did not cease to urge me until God opened my heart to this and I thought as 'Umar did.

Zayd continued: Abū Bakr said to me, 'You are a young man, intelligent, and we see no fault in you, and you have already written down the revelation for the Prophet of God, may God bless and save him. Therefore go and seek the Qur'ān and assemble it.'

By God, if he had ordered me to move a mountain it would not have been harder for me than his order to collect the Qur'ān. 'What?' I asked, 'Will you do something which the Prophet of God himself, may God bless and save him, did not do?'

'By God,' replied Abū Bakr, 'it would be a good deed.'

And he did not cease to urge me until God opened my heart to this as he had opened the hearts of Abū Bakr and 'Umar.

Then I sought out and collected the parts of the Qur'ān, whether written on palm leaves or flat stones or in the hearts of men. Thus I found the end of the Sūra of Repentence, which I had been unable to find anywhere else, with Abu'l-Khuzayma al-Anṣārī. These were the verses: 'There came to you a Prophet from among yourselves. It grieves him that you sin . . .' to the end (Sūra 9:129–30).

The leaves were with Abū Bakr until his death,

then with 'Umar as long as he lived, and then with Ḥafṣa, the daughter of 'Umar.

Anas ibn Mālik said: Ḥudhayfa ibn al-Yamān went with 'Uthmān when he was preparing the army of Syria to conquer Armenia and Ādharbayjān, together with the army of Iraq. Ḥudhayfa was shocked by the differences in their reading of the Qur'ān, and said to 'Uthmān, 'O Commander of the Faithful, catch this community before they differ about their book as do the Jews and Christians.'

'Uthmān sent to Ḥafṣa to say, 'Send us the leaves. We shall copy them in codices and return them to you.'

Ḥafṣa sent them to 'Uthmān, who ordered Zayd ibn Thābit, 'Abdallāh ibn al-Zubayr, Sa'īd ibn al-'Āṣ, and 'Abd al-Raḥmān ibn al-Ḥārith ibn Hishām to copy them into codices. 'Uthmān said to the three of them who were of the tribe of Quraysh, 'If you differ from Zayd ibn Thābit on anything in the Qur'ān, write it according to the language of Quraysh, for it is in their language that the Qur'ān was revealed.'

They did this, and when they had copied the leaves into codices, 'Uthmān returned the leaves to Ḥafṣa. He sent copies of the codex which they made in all directions and gave orders to burn every leaf or codex which differed from it.

A ḥadīth

What makes it necessary to pay quite particular attention to that [branch of Qur'ānic] science [known as] *I'jāz al-Qur'ān* is that the prophetic office of the Prophet – upon whom be peace – is built upon this miracle. Even though later on he was given the support of many miracles, yet those miracles all belonged to special times, special circumstances, and concerned special individuals. [The accounts about] some of these have been transmitted by many lines of tradition, testifying to knowledge of their occurrence. Others have been transmitted by a particular line of tradition, yet [that unique line] relates the evidence of a great many who testify that they witnessed [the miracle], so that were the matter other than what has been related these would deny it, or at least some would deny it, so that this group occupies essentially the position of the former, even though the original account is not from many lines of tradition. Some, however, depend on a single line of tradition and happened in the presence of only a single person. [As against all this] the evidence of the Qur'ān is to a miracle of a general kind [witnessed] in common by men and *jinn*, and which has remained a miracle throughout the ages. . . .

Not only our own friends but others have mentioned three particular aspects of the miraculous nature (*i'jāz*) of the Qur'ān.

One of them is that it contains information about the unseen, and that is something beyond the powers of humans, for they have no way to attain it. One example is the promise Allah, Most High, made to His Prophet – upon whom be peace – that his religion would triumph over the [other] religions. Thus He – mighty and exalted is He – said: 'He it is who has sent His messenger with guidance and the religion of truth, that He might make it victorious over all religion, even though the polytheists dislike it,' and this He did. Abū Bakr, the trusty one – with whom may Allah be pleased – when he sent out his troops raiding, used to remind them of Allah's promise to make His religion victorious, so that they should be hopeful of victory and feel certain of success. 'Umar b. al-Khaṭṭāb – with whom may Allah be pleased – also used to do likewise in his day, so that his army commanders were aware of it. So Sa'd b. Abī Waqqāṣ – on whom may Allah have mercy – and other army leaders like him, used to remind their companions of that, urging them on by it and making them hopeful. And they used to meet with success in their ventures, such that in the latter days of 'Umar – with whom may Allah be pleased – they had captured all [the lands] as far as Balkh and to the land of India. [Then he goes on with lists of the various places they had conquered, where other monarchs had ruled and other religions had been practised.]

Allah – mighty and majestic is He – also said: 'Say to those who disbelieve: "Ye will be overcome and will be gathered into Gehenna[2] – how evil a bed."': and this came true. Also He said with reference to those [who fought] at Badr: 'And when Allah was promising you one of the two parties that they should be yours,' He fulfilled to them what He had promised. It would be far too much [to set out] all the verses of the Qur'ān which contain information about the

[2] The place where the unbelievers will be punished on the Day of Judgment.

unseen. All we wanted was to draw attention to some which might stand for all.

The second aspect is that it is well known that the Prophet – upon whom be Allah's blessing and peace – was an *ummi*[3] who could not write, and who could not read very well. Likewise it was generally recognized that he had no knowledge whatever of the books of the earlier peoples, nor of their records, their histories, their biographies. Yet he produced summaries of what had happened [in history], told about mighty matters [of past days], and gave the important life histories from the creation of the Adam – on whom be peace – up to his own mission. He makes mention in the Book, which he brought as his miracle, of the story of Adam – upon whom be peace – how he was created, what brought about his being turned out of the garden, then somewhat about his progeny and his condition, and his repentance. He also makes mention of the story of Noah – on whom be peace – what happened between him and his people, and how his affair turned out in the end. Likewise [he told] about Abraham – upon whom be peace – and about all the other prophets mentioned in the Qur'ān, and the kings and Pharaohs who lived in the days of the prophets – on whom be Allah's blessings.

Now we know for sure that he had no way to [obtain knowledge of all] this save that of being taught, and since it is known that he had no intimacy with antiquarians or those who stored up information [about such matters], and did not go frequently to get teaching from them, and that he was not one who could read, so that he might have taken this from some book that could possibly have come to him, then the conclusion is that he did not obtain this knowledge save by aid from revelation. This is what Allah – mighty and majestic is He – has said: 'Thou wast not reciting any book before it, nor writing it with thy right hand, otherwise those who consider it worthless would have been suspicious.' He also said: 'And thus do We change about the signs, and [We do so] that they may say: "Thou hast been studying."' We have already made clear that one who was accustomed to go repeatedly to receive instruction and busy himself at becoming intimate with those who had skill [in these matters] would not have been able to hide this from the people, nor would there have been any disagreement among them as to the way he was acting. It was well known among them who [those were who] had knowledge of these matters, even though such persons were seldom to be met, who was in the habit of going to such for instruction. It was no secret who was the man most learned in each of these matters and who was being instructed [by him] in them, so if [Muḥammad] had been among the latter this would have been no secret.

The third aspect is that [the Qur'ān] is wonderfully arranged, and marvellously composed, and so exalted in its literary elegance as to be beyond what any mere creature could attain. This is in substance the opinion expressed by the learned theologians.

Sacred Narrative 3

The Preceding Prophets and Revelations: Sūra 2, Sūra 6, Sūra 28, Sūra 3, Sūra 5, and Ḥadīth

The Qur'ān gives much attention to the figures of the Hebrew Bible and the New Testament. Indeed, they become critical in the unfolding of Revelation and, as we have seen above, the sacred literature of the Jews and Christians becomes a proof for the truth of the Qur'ān itself. In Sūra 2, Muḥammad narrates the creation of Adam and how only one angel, Iblīs, refuses

[3] An unlettered man.

to bow before Adam; he becomes a fallen angel and synonymous with Satan. The passages that follow describe how Abraham became a believer, how the covenant was established between Allah and Abraham, how Abraham and Ishmael built the Ka'ba in Mecca, Moses' confrontation with God at the burning bush, how Pharaoh is the paradigmatic unbeliever, how Allah calls Mary and educates Jesus, and how the early revelations have been rejected. The rejection of the earlier revelations makes Muḥammad's task more urgent. Lastly, a *ḥadīth* from Ishaq (*Sīrat Rasūl Allāh*) indicates that Arabs, Jews and Christians had begun to speak about Muḥammad as the Messenger of God before his time drew near.

Sūra 2:27–37

And when thy Lord said to the angels,
'I am setting in the earth a viceroy,'
They said, 'What, wilt Thou set therein one who will do corruption there, and shed blood,
while We proclaim Thy praise and call Thee Holy?'
He said, 'Assuredly I know that you know not.'
And He taught Adam the names, all of them;
then He presented them unto the angels and said,
'Now tell Me the names of these, if you speak truly.'
They said, 'Glory be to Thee! We know not save what Thou hast taught us.
Surely Thou art the All-knowing, the All-wise.'
He said, 'Adam, tell them their names.'
And when he had told them their names He said,
'Did I not tell you I know the unseen things of the heavens and earth?
And I know what things you reveal, and what you were hiding.'
And when We said to the angels,
'Bow yourselves to Adam'; so they bowed themselves, save Iblis;
he refused, and waxed proud, and so he became one of the unbelievers.
And We said, 'Adam, dwell thou, and thy wife, in the Garden,
and eat thereof easefully where you desire;
but draw not night this tree, lest you be evildoers.'
Then Satan caused them to slip therefrom
and brought them out of that they were in;
and We said, 'Get you all down, each of you an enemy of each;
and in the earth a sojourn shall be yours, and enjoyment for a time.'
Thereafter Adam received certain words from his Lord, and He turned towards him;
truly He turns, and is All-compassionate.
We said, 'Get you down out of it, all together;
yet there shall come to you guidance from Me,
and whosoever follows My guidance,
no fear shall be on them, neither shall they sorrow.
As for the unbelievers who cry lies to Our signs,
those shall be the inhabitants of the Fire,
therein dwelling forever.'

Sūra 6:74–82

And when Abraham said to his Father Azar,
'Takest thou idols for gods? I see thee,
and thy people, in manifest error,'
So We were showing Abraham the kingdom of the heavens and earth, that he might be of those having sure faith.
When night outspread over him he saw a star
and said, 'This is my Lord.'
But when it set he said, 'I love not the setters.'
When he saw the moon rising, he said,
'This is my Lord.'
But when it set he said,
'If my Lord does not guide me
I shall surely be of the people gone astray.'
When he saw the sun rising, he said,
'This is my Lord; this is greater!'
But when it set he said, 'O my people,
surely I am quit of that you associate.
I have turned my face to Him who originated the heavens and the earth, a man of pure faith;
I am not of the idolators.'
His people disputed with him. He said,
'Do you dispute with me concerning God,
and He has guided me?
I fear not what you associate with Him, except

my Lord will aught.
My Lord embraces all things in His knowledge;
will you not remember?
How should I fear what you have associated,
seeing you fear not that you have associated
with God that whereon He has not sent
down on you any authority?'

Sūra 2:117–28

And when his Lord tested Abraham with certain words, and he fulfilled them, He said, 'Behold, I make you a leader for the people.' Said he, 'And of my seed?' He said 'My covenant shall not reach the evildoers.'

And when We appointed the House[1] to be a place of visitation for the people, and a sanctuary, and: 'Take to yourselves Abraham's station for a place of prayer'. And We made covenant with Abraham and Ishmael: 'Purify My House for those that shall go about it and those that cleave to it, to those who bow and prostrate themselves.'

And when Abraham said, 'My Lord, make this a land secure, and provide its people with fruits, such of them as believe in God and the Last Day.' He said, 'And whoso disbelieves, to him I shall give enjoyment a little, then I shall compel him to the chastisement of the Fire – how evil a homecoming!'

And when Abraham, and Ishmael with him, raised up the foundations of the House: 'Our Lord, receive this from us; Thou art the All-hearing, the All-knowing; and, our Lord, make us submissive to Thee, and of our seed a nation submissive to Thee; and show us our holy rites, and turn towards us; surely Thou turnest, and art All-compassionate; and, our Lord, do Thou send among them a Messenger, one of them, who shall recite to them Thy signs, and teach them the Book and the Wisdom, and purify them; Thou art the All-mighty, the All-wise.'

Who therefore shrinks from the religion of Abraham, except he be foolish-minded? Indeed, We chose him in the present world, and in the world to come he shall be among the righteous.

When his Lord said to him, 'Surrender,' he said, 'I have surrendered me to the Lord of all Being.'

And Abraham charged his sons with this and Jacob likewise: 'My sons, God has chosen for you the religion; see that you die not save in surrender.'

Why, were you witnesses, when death came to Jacob? When he said to his sons, 'What will you serve after me?' They said, 'We will serve thy God and the God of thy fathers Abraham, Ishmael and Isaac, One God; to Him we surrender.'

That is a nation that has passed away; there awaits them that they have earned, and there awaits you that you have earned; you shall not be questioned concerning the things they did.

Sūra 28:29–49

So when Moses had accomplished the term and departed with his household, he observed on the side of the Mount a fire. He said to his household, 'Tarry you here; I observe a fire. Perhaps I shall bring you news of it, or a faggot from the fire, that haply you shall warm yourselves.'

When he came to it, a voice cried from the right bank of the watercourse, in the sacred hollow, coming from the tree: 'Moses, I am God, the Lord of all Being. Cast down thy staff.' And when he saw it quivering like a serpent, he turned about retreating, and turned not back. 'Moses, come forward, and fear not; for surely thou art in security. Insert thy hand into thy bosom, and it will come forth white without evil; and press to thee thy arm, that thou be not afraid. So these shall be two proofs from thy Lord to Pharaoh and his Council; for surely they are an ungodly people.'

Said he, 'My Lord, I have indeed slain a living soul among them, and I fear that they will slay me. Moreover my brother Aaron is more eloquent than I. Send him with me as a helper and to confirm I speak truly, for I fear they will cry me lies.'

Said He, 'We will strengthen thy arm by means of thy brother, and We shall appoint to you an authority, so they they shall not reach you because of Our signs; you, and whoso follows you, shall be the victors.'

So when Moses came to them with Our signs, clear signs, they said, 'This is nothing but a forged sorcery. We never heard of this among our fathers, the ancients.'

But Moses said, 'My Lord knows very well who comes with the guidance from Him, and shall possess the Ultimate Abode; surely the evildoers

[1] Ka'ba.

will not prosper.'

And Pharaoh said, 'Council, I know not that you have any god but me. Kindle me, Haman, a fire upon the clay, and make me a tower, that I may mount up to Moses' god; for I think that he is one of the liars.'

And he waxed proud in the land, he had his hosts, wrongfully; and they thought they should not be returned to Us.

Therefore We seized him and his hosts, and cast them into the sea; so behold how was the end of the evildoers!

And We appointed them leaders, calling to the Fire; and on the Day of Resurrection they shall not be helped; and We pursued them in this world with a curse, and on the Day of Resurrection they shall be among the spurned.

And We gave Moses the Book, after that We had destroyed the former generations, to be examples and a guidance and a mercy, that haply so they might remember.

Thou wast not upon the western side when We decreed to Moses the commandment, nor wast thou of those witnessing; but We raised up generations, and long their lives continued. Neither wast thou a dweller among the Midianites, reciting to them Our signs; but We were sending Messengers.

Thou wast not upon the side of the Mount when We called; but for a mercy from thy Lord, that thou mayest warn a people to whom no warner came before thee, and that haply they may remember. Else, did an affliction visit them for that their own hands have forwarded then they might say, 'Our Lord, why didst Thou not send a Messenger to us that we might follow Thy signs and so be among the believers?'

Yet when the truth came to them from Ourselves, they said, 'Why has he not been given the like of that Moses was given?' But they, did they not disbelieve also in what Moses was given aforetime? They said, 'A pair of sorceries mutually supporting each other.' They said, 'We disbelieve both.'

Sūra 3:38–64

And when the angels said, 'Mary, God has chosen thee, and purified thee; He has chosen thee above all women. Mary, be obedient to thy Lord, prostrating and bowing before Him.' (That is of the tidings of the Unseen, that We reveal to thee; for thou wast not with them, when they were casting quills which of them should have charge of Mary; thou wast not with them, when they were disputing.)

When the angels said, 'Mary, God gives thee good tidings of a Word from Him whose name is Messiah, Jesus, son of Mary; high honoured shall he be in this world and the next, near stationed to God. He shall speak to men in the cradle, and of age, and righteous he shall be.'

'Lord,' said Mary, 'how shall I have a son seeing no mortal has touched me?'

'Even so,' God said, 'God creates what He will. When He decrees a thing He does but say to it "Be", and it is. And he will touch him the Book, the Wisdom, the Torah, the Gospel, to be a Messenger to the Children of Israel saying, "I have come to you with a sign from your Lord. I will create for you out of clay as the likeness of a bird; then I will breathe into it, and it will be a bird, by the leave of God. I will also heal the blind and the leper, and bring to life the dead, by the leave of God. I will inform you too of what things you eat, and what you treasure up in your houses. Surely in that is a sign for you, if you are believers. Likewise confirming the truth of the Torah that is before me, and to make lawful to you certain things that before were forbidden unto you. I have come to you with a sign from your Lord; so fear you God, and obey you me. Surely God is my Lord and your Lord; so serve Him. This is a straight path."'

And when Jesus perceived their unbelief, he said, 'Who will be my helpers unto God?' The Apostles said, 'We will be helpers of God; we believe in God; witness thou our submission. Lord, we believe in that Thou hast sent down, and we follow the Messenger. Inscribe us therefore with those who bear witness.' And they devised, and God devised, and God is the best of devisers.

When God said, 'Jesus, I will take thee to Me and will raise thee to Me, and I will purify thee of those who believe not. I will set thy followers above the unbelievers till the Resurrection Day. Then unto Me shall you return, and I will decide between you, as to what you were at variance on. As for the unbelievers, I will chastise them with a terrible chastisement in this world and the next; they shall have no helpers.'

But as for the believers, who do deeds of righteousness, He will pay them in full their wages: And God loves not the evildoers.

This We recite to thee of signs and wise remembrance. Truly, the likeness of Jesus, in God's sight, is as Adam's likeness; He created him of dust, then said He unto him, 'Be', and he was. The truth is of God; be not of the doubters.

And whoso disputes with thee concerning him, after the knowledge that has come to thee, say: 'Come now, let us call our sons and your sons, our wives and your wives, our selves and your selves, then let us humbly pray and so lay God's curse upon the ones who lie.' This is the true story. There is no god but God, and assuredly God is the All-mighty, the All-wise. And if they turn their backs, assuredly God knows the workers of corruption.

Say: 'People of the Book! Come now to a word common between us and you, that we serve none but God, and that we associate not aught with Him, and do not some of us take others as Lords, apart from God.' And if they turn their backs, say: 'Bear witness that we are Muslims.'

People of the Book! Why do you dispute concerning Abraham? The Torah was not sent down, neither the Gospel, but after him. What, have you no reason?

Ha, you are the ones who dispute on what you know; why then dispute you touching a matter of which you know not anything? God knows, and you know not.

No; Abraham in truth was not a Jew, neither a Christian; but he was a Muslim and one of pure faith; certainly he was never of the idolators.

Surely the people standing closest to Abraham are those who followed him, and this Prophet, and those who believe; and God is the Protector of the believers.

There is a party of the People of the Book yearn to make you go stray; yet none they make to stray, except themselves, but they are not aware.

People of the Book! Why do you disbelieve in God's signs, which you yourselves witness? People of the Book! Why do you confound the truth with vanity, and conceal the truth and that wittingly?

Sūra 5:48–55

Surely We sent down the Torah, wherein is guidance and light; thereby the Prophets who had surrendered themselves gave judgment for those of Jewry, as did the masters and the rabbis, following such portion of God's Book as they were given to keep and were witnesses to. So fear not men, but fear you Me; and sell not My signs for a little price. Whoso judges not according to what God has sent down – they are the unbelievers.

And therein We prescribed for them: 'A life for a life, an eye for an eye, a nose for a nose, an ear for an ear, a tooth for a tooth, and for wounds retaliation'; but whosoever forgoes it as a freewill offering, that shall be for him an expiation. Whoso judges not according to what God has sent down – they are the evildoers.

And We sent, following in their footsteps, Jesus, son of Mary, confirming the Torah before him; and We gave to him the Gospel, wherein is guidance and light, and confirming the Torah before it, as a guidance and an admonition unto the godfearing.

So let the People of the Gospel judge according to what God has sent down therein. Whosoever judges not according to what God has sent down – they are the ungodly.

And We have sent down to thee the Book with the truth, confirming the Book that was before it, and assuring it. So judge between them according to what God has sent down, and do not follow their caprices, to forsake the truth that has come to thee. To every one of you We have appointed a right way and an open road.

If God had willed, He would have made you one nation; but that He may try you in what has come to you. So be you forward in good works; unto God shall you return, all together; and He will tell you of that whereon you were at variance. And judge between them according to what God has sent down, and do not follow their caprices, and beware of them lest they tempt thee away from any of what God has sent down to thee. But if they turn their backs, know that God desires only to smite them for some sin they have committed; surely, many men are ungodly. Is it the judgment of pagandom then that they are seeking? Yet who is fairer in judgment than God', for a people having sure faith?

A ḥadīth

Jewish rabbis, Christian monks, and Arab soothsayers had spoken about the apostle of God before his mission when his time drew near. As to the rabbis and monks, it was about his description and the description of his time which they found in their scriptures and what their prophets had enjoined upon them. As to the Arab soothsayers, they had been visited by satans from the jinn with reports which they had secretly overheard before they were prevented from hearing by being pelted with stars. Male and female soothsayers continued to let fall mention of some of these matters to which the Arabs paid no attention until God sent him and these things which had been mentioned happened and they recognized them. When the prophet's mission came the satans were prevented from listening and they could not occupy the seats in which they used to sit and steal the heavenly tidings for they were pelted with stars, and the jinn knew that that was due to an order which God had commanded concerning mankind. God said to His prophet Muḥammad when He sent him as he was telling him about the jinn when they were prevented from listening and knew what they knew and did not deny what they say: 'Say it has been revealed to me that a number of the jinn listened and said "We have heard a wonderful Qur'ān which guides to the right path, and we believe in it and we will not associate anyone with our Lord and that He (exalted be the glory of our Lord) hath not chosen a wife or a son. A foolish one among us used to speak lies against God, and we had thought men and jinn would not speak a lie against God and that when men took refuge with the jinn, they increased them in revolt," ending with the words: "We used to sit on places therein to listen; he who listens now finds a flame waiting for him. We do not know whether evil is intended against those that are on earth or whether their lord wishes to guide them in the right path."' When the jinn heard the Qur'ān they knew that they had been prevented from listening before that so that revelation should not be mingled with news from heaven so that men would be confused with the tidings which came from God about it when the proof came and doubt was removed; so they believed and acknowledged the truth. Then 'They returned to their people warning them, saying, O our people have heard a book which was revealed after Moses confirming what went before it, guiding to the truth and to the upright path.'

In reference to the saying of the jinn, 'that men took refuge with them and they increased them in revolt,' Arabs of the Quraysh and others when they were journeying and stopped at the bottom of a vale to pass a night therein used to say, 'I take refuge in the lord of this valley of the jinn tonight from the evil that is therein.'

Ya'qūb b. 'Utna b. al-Mughīra b. al-Akhnas told me that he was informed that the first Arabs to be afraid of falling stars when they were pelted with them were this clan of Thaqīf, and that they came to one of their tribesmen called 'Amr b. Umayya, one of the Banū 'Ilāj who was a most astute and shrewd man, and asked him if he had noticed this pelting with stars. He said: 'Yes, but wait, for if they are the well-known stars which guide travellers by land and sea, by which the seasons of summer and winter are known to help men in their daily life, which are being thrown, then by God! it means the end of the world and the destruction of all that is in it. But if they remain constant and other stars are being thrown, then it is for some purpose which God intends towards mankind.'

Muḥammad b. Muslim b. Shihāb al-Zuhrī on the authority of 'Alī b. al-Ḥusayn b. 'Alī b. Abū Ṭālib from 'Abdallāh b. al-'Abbās from a number of the Anṣār mentioned that the apostle of God said to them, 'What were you saying about this shooting star?' They replied, 'We were saying, a king is dead, a king has been appointed, a child is born, a child has died.' He replied, 'It is not so, but when God has decreed something concerning His creation the bearers of the throne hear it and praise Him, and those below them praise Him, and those lower still praise Him because they have praised, and this goes on until the praise descends to the lowest heaven where they praise. Then they ask each other why, and are told that it is because those above them have done so and they say, "Why don't you ask those above you the reason?" and so it goes on until they reach the bearers of the throne who say that God has decreed so-and-so concerning His creation and the news descends from heaven to heaven to the lowest heaven where they discuss it, and the satans steal it by listening, mingling it with conjecture and false intelligence. Then they convey it to the soothsayers and tell them of it, sometimes being wrong and sometimes right, and so the soothsayers are sometimes right and sometimes wrong. Then God shut off the satans by these stars with which they were pelted, so soothsaying has been cut off today and no longer exists.'

'Amr b. Abū Ja'far from Muḥammad b. 'Abd al-Rahmān b. 'Abū Labība from 'Alī b. al-Ḥusayn b. 'Alī told me that same tradition as that of Ibn Shihāb.

A learned person told me that a woman of the Banū Sahm called al-Ghayṭala who was a soothsayer in the time of ignorance was visited by her familiar spirit one night. He chirped beneath her, then he said,

'I know what I know,
The day of wounding and slaughter.'

When the Quraysh heard of this they asked what he meant. The spirit came to her another night and chirped beneath her saying,

'Death, what is death?
In it bones are thrown here and there.'

When the Quraysh heard of this they could not understand it and decided to wait until the future should reveal its meaning. When the battle of Badr and Uhud took place in a glen, they knew that this was the meaning of the spirit's message.

'Alī b. Nafī' al-Jurashī told me that the Janb, a tribe from the Yaman, had a soothsayer in the time of ignorance, and when the news of the apostle of God was blazed abroad among the Arabs, they said to him, 'Look into the matter of this man for us,' and they gathered at the bottom of the mountain where he lived. He came down to them when the sun rose and stood leaning on his bow. He raised his head toward heaven for a long time and began to leap about and say:

'O men, God has honoured and chosen Muḥammad,
Purified his heart and bowels.
His stay among you, O men, will be short.'

Then he turned and climbed up the mountain whence he had come.

A person beyond suspicion told me on the authority of 'Abdallāh b. Ka'b a freedman of 'Uthmān b. 'Affān that he was told that when 'Umar b. al-Khaṭṭāb was sitting with the people in the apostle's mosque, an Arab came in to visit him. When 'Umar saw him he said, 'This fellow is still a polytheist, he has not given up his old religion yet, [or, he said] he was a soothsayer in the time of ignorance.' The man greeted him and sat down and 'Umar asked him if he was a Muslim; he said that he was. He said, 'But were you a soothsayer in the time of ignorance?' The man replied, 'Good God, commander of the faithful, you have thought ill of me and have greeted me in a way that I never heard you speak to anyone of your subjects since you came into power.' 'Umar said, 'I ask God's pardon. In the time of ignorance we did worse than this; we worshipped idols and images until God honoured us with his apostle and with Islam.' The man replied, 'Yes, by God, I was a soothsayer.' 'Umar said, 'Then tell me what [was the most amazing thing] your familiar spirit communicated to you.' He said, 'He came to me a month or so before Islam and said:

"Have you considered the jinn and their confusion,
Their religion a despair and delusion,
Clinging to their camels' saddle cloths in profusion?"'

'Abdallāh b. Ka'b said, Thereupon 'Umar said, 'I was standing by an idol with a number of the Quraysh in the time of ignorance when an Arab sacrificed a calf. We were standing by expecting to get a part of it, when I heard a voice more penetrating than I have ever heard coming out of the belly of the calf (this was a month or so before Islam), saying:

'O blood red one,
The deed is done,
A man will cry
Beside God none.'

Such is what I have been told about soothsayers among the Arabs.

Doctrine 1

Allah: Sūra 2, Sūra 13 and the Ninety-nine Most Beautiful Names of Allah

The most important doctrine in the whole of Islam is the concept of Allah. Muḥammad gives emphasis throughout the Qur'ān to Allah's transcendence and uniqueness, and this has been taken by orthodox Islam to mean that the greatest sin is *shirk* or 'association', in which one gives someone or something a share in Allah's transcendence or sovereignty. Theological reflection on Sūras 2 and 13, along with many others, has underscored the 'oneness' or *tawḥīd* of Allah. Hence, true Muslims are *al-muwaḥḥidūn*, 'those who maintain the Oneness'. We also include here Muḥammad al-Madanī's 'Ninety-nine Most Beautiful Names of Allah', which is drawn from the epithets of Allah in the Qur'ān. These names have become the foundation of theological and philosophical reflections on the attributes of Allah, which include life, knowledge, power, will, sensibility, speech and activity.

Sūra 2:256–7

God
there is no god but He, the
Living, the Everlasting.
Slumber seizes Him not, neither sleep;
to Him belongs all that is in the heavens and
the earth.
Who is there that shall intercede with Him
save by His leave?
He knows what lies before them
and what is after them,
and they comprehend not anything of His
knowledge save such as He wills.
His Throne comprises the heavens and earth;
the preserving of them oppresses Him not;
He is the All-high, the All-glorious.

Sūra 13:2–4

God is He who raised up the heavens without
pillars you can see,
then He sat Himself upon the Throne.
He subjected the sun and the moon,
each one running to a term stated.
He directs the affair; He distinguishes the signs;
haply you will have faith in the encounter with
your Lord.

The Ninety-nine Most Beautiful Names of Allah

1. Allah, the Name that is above every name.
2. al-Awwal, the First, who was before the beginning.
3. al-Ākhir, the Last, who will still be after all has ended.
4. al-Badī', the Contriver, who contrived the whole art of creation.
5. al-Bāri', the Maker, from whose hand we all come.
6. al-Barr, the Beneficent, whose liberality appears in all His works.
7. al-Baṣīr, the Observant, who sees and hears all things.
8. al-Bāsiṭ, the Spreader, who extends His mercy to whom He wills.
9. al-Bāṭin, the Inner, who is immanent within all things.
10. al-Bā'ith, the Raiser, who will raise up a witness from each community.
11. al-Bāqī, the Enduring, who is better and more enduring.
12. al-Tawwāb, the Relenting, who relented toward Adam and relents to all his descendants.
13. al-Jabbār, the Mighty One, whose might and power are absolute.
14. al-Jalīl, the Majestic, mighty and majestic is He.
15. al-Jāmi', the Gatherer, who gathers all men to an appointed Day.
16. al-Ḥasīb, the Accounter, who is sufficient as a reckoner.
17. al-Ḥafīẓ, the Guardian, who keeps watch

over everything.

18. al-Ḥaqq, the Truth.
19. al-Ḥākim, the Judge, who gives judgment among His servants.
20. al-Ḥakīm, the Wise, who is both wise and well informed.
21. al-Ḥalīm, the Kindly, who is both forgiving and kindly disposed.
22. al-Ḥamīd, the Praiseworthy, to whom all praise is due.
23. al-Ḥayy, the Living, who is the source of all life.
24. al-Khabir, the Well-Informed, who is both wise and well informed.
25. al-Khafīḍ, the Humbler, who humbles some while He exalts others.
26. al-Khāliq, the Creator, who has created all things that are.
27. Dhū'l-Jalāl wa'l-Ikrām, Lord of Majesty and Honour.
28. al-Ra'ūf, the Gentle, who is compassionate toward His people.
29. al-Raḥmān, the Merciful, the most merciful of those who show mercy.
30. al Raḥīm, the Compassionate, who is gentle and full of compassion.
31. al-Razzāq, the Provider, who provides but asks no provision.
32. al-Rashīd, the Guide, who leads believers in the rightminded way.
33. al-Rāfi', the Exalter, who exalts some while He humbles others.
34. al-Raqīb, the Watcher, who keeps watch over His creation.
35. al-Salām, the Peace-Maker, whose name is Peace.
36. al-Samī', the Hearer, who sees and hears all things.
37. al-Shakūr, the Grateful, who graciously accepts the service of His people.
38. al-Shahīd, the Witness, who is witness to all things.
39. al-Ṣabūr, the Forbearing, who has great patience with His people.
40. al-Ṣamad, the Eternal, who begets not and is not begotten.
41. al-Ḍārr, the Afflicter, who sends affliction as well as blessings.
42. al-Ẓāhir, the Outer, who is without as well as within.
43. al-'Adl, the Just, whose word is perfect in veracity and justice.
44. al-'Aziz, the Sublime, mighty in His sublime sovereignty.
45. al-'Aẓīm, the Mighty, He who above all is high and mighty.
46. al-'Afuw, the Pardoner, ever ready to forgive His servants.
47. al-'Alīm, the Knowing One, who is well aware of everything.
48. al-'Alī, the High One, He who is high and mighty.
49. al-Ghafūr, the Forgiving, who is both forgiving and well disposed.
50. al-Ghaffār, the Pardoning, ever ready to pardon and forgive.
51. al-Ghanī, the Rich, since it is He who possesses all things.
52. al-Fattāḥ, the Opener, who clears and opens up the Way.
53. al-Qābiḍ, the Seizer, who both holds tight and is open-handed.
54. al-Qādir, the Able, who has the power to do what He pleases.
55. al-Quddūs, the Most Holy One, to Whom all in heaven and on earth ascribe holiness.
56. al-Qahhār, the All-Victorious, who overcomes all.
57. al-Qawī, the Strong, sublime in His strength and His power.
58. al-Qayyūm, the Self-Subsistent, eternally existing in and for Himself alone.
59. al-Kabīr, the Great One, who is both high and great.
60. al-Karīm, the Munificent, who is not only rich but generous.
61. al-Laṭīf, the Gracious, whose grace extends to all His servants.
62. al-Muta'akhkhir, the Deferrer, who when He wills defers punishment.
63. al-Mu'min, the Faithful, who grants security to all.
64. al-Muta'ālī, the Self-Exalted, who has set Himself high above all.
65. al-Mutakabbir, the Proud, whose pride is in His works.
66. al-Matīn, the Firm, firm in His possession of strength.
67. al-Mubdi', the Originator, who both originates and restores.
68. al-Mujīb, the Answerer, who responds when His servants call.
69. al-Majīd, the Glorious, praiseworthy and glorious is He.

70. al-Muḥṣī, the Computer, who has counted and numbered all things.
71. al-Muḥyī, the Quickener, who quickens and brings to life the dead.
72. al-Mudhill, the Abaser, who raises to honour or abases whom He will.
73. al-Muzīl, the Separator, who will separate men from the false gods they vainly worship.
74. al-Muṣawwir, the Fashioner, who fashions His creatures how He pleases.
75. al-Mu'īd, the Restorer, who both originates and restores.
76. al-Mu'izz, the Honourer, who honours or abases whom he will.
77. al-Mu'ṭī, the Giver, from whose hand come all good things.
78. al-Mughnī, the Enricher, who enriches men from His bounty.
79. al-Muqīt, the Well-Furnished, provided with power over all things.
80. al-Muqtadir, He who prevails having evil men in His powerful grip.
81. al-Muqaddim, the Bringer-Forward, who sends His promises on ahead.
82. al-Muqsiṭ, the Observer of Justice, who will set up the balances with justice.
83. al-Malik, the King, who is king of kings.
84. Mālik al-Mulk, Possessor of the Kingdom, who grants sovereignty to whom He will.
85. al-Mumīt, He who causes to die, just as He causes to live.
86. al-Muntaqim, the Avenger, who wreaks vengeance on sinners and succours the believers.
87. al-Muhaymin, the Preserver, whose watchful care is over all.
88. al-Naṣīr, the Helper, and sufficient as a helper is He.
89. al-Nūr, the Light, illuminating both earth and heaven.
90. al-Hādī, the Guide, who leads believers in the straight path.
91. al-Wāḥid, the One, unique in His Divine sovereignty.
92. al-Waḥīd, the Unique, who alone has created.
93. al-Wadūd, the Loving, compassionate and loving to His servants.
94. al-Wārith, the Inheritor, unto whom all things will return.
95. al-Wāsi', the Wide-Reaching, whose bounty reaches all.
96. al-Wakīl, the Administrator, who has charge of everything.
97. al-Waliy, the Patron, and a sufficient patron is He.
98. al-Wālī, the Safeguard, other than whom men have no sure guard.
99. al-Wahhāb, the Liberal Giver, who gives freely of His bounty.

Doctrine 2

Angels, Satans and Jinn: Sūra 2 and Sūra 72

The Qur'ān speaks of at least four groups of semi-divine beings who are all subordinate to Allah. First, the highest order of the angelic host is made up of Gabriel, the angel of revelation, Michael, the angel of providence, Isrāfīl, the angel of the trumpet of doom, and 'Azrā'īl, the angel of death. The second order is made up of ministering angels including Ridwān, the Grand Chamberlain of Paradise, Mālik, the Grand Chamberlain of Hell, the recording angels, and Munkar and Nakīr, who question the dead. The fallen angels are presided over by Iblīs or Satan, and include the angels Hārūt and Mārūt. The jinn represent a large class of beings who are much nearer to humans. They can inspire humans as well as take possession of them. In Sūra 2, the rejection of Gabriel and Michael, perhaps because of their closeness to revelation, makes one an unbeliever. Iblīs' revolt against Allah is narrated and he swears to pervert the ways of man. Sūra 72 suggests that it is easier for men to believe in the works inspired by the jinn than in Qur'ān, although some of the jinn recognize the true revelation.

Sūra: 2:91–7

Say: 'Whosoever is an enemy to Gabriel – he it was that brought it down upon thy heart by the leave of God, confirming what was before it, and for a guidance and good tidings to the believers. Whosoever is an enemy to God and His angels and His Messengers, and Gabriel, and Michael – surely God is an enemy to the unbelievers.' And We have sent down unto thee signs, clear signs, and none disbelieve in them except the ungodly.

Why, whensoever they have made a covenant, does a party of them reject it? Nay, but the most of them are unbelievers. When there has come to them a Messenger from God confirming what was with them, a party of them that were given the Book reject the Book of God behind their backs, as though they knew not, and they follow what the Satans recited over Solomon's kingdom. Solomon disbelieved not, but the Satans disbelieved, teaching the people sorcery, and that which was sent down upon Babylon's two angels, Harut and Marut; they taught not any man, without they said, 'We are but a temptation; do not disbelieve.' From them they learned how they might divide a man and his wife, yet they did not hurt any man thereby, save by the leave of God, and they learned what hurt them, and did not profit them, knowing well that whoso buys it shall have no share in the world to come; evil then was that they sold themselves for, if they had but known.

Yet had they believed, and been godfearing, a recompense from God had been better, if they had but known.

Sūra 15:28–43

Surely We created man of a clay
of mud moulded,
and the jinn created We before
of fire flaming.
And when thy Lord said to the angels,
'See, I am creating a mortal of a clay
of mud moulded.
When I have shaped him, and breathed My spirit
in him,
fall you down, bowing before him!'
Then the angels bowed themselves all together
save Iblis;
he refused to be among those bowing.
Said He, 'What ails thee, Iblis,
that thou art not among those bowing?'
Said he, 'I would never bow myself before a
mortal whom Thou hast created of a clay
of mud moulded.'
Said He, 'Then go thou forth hence;
thou art accursed.
Upon thee shall rest the curse,
till the Day of Doom.'
Said he, 'My Lord, respite me till the day they
shall be raised.'
Said He, 'Thou art among the ones
that are respited unto the day
of a known time.'
Said he, 'My Lord, for Thy perverting me
I shall deck all fair to them in the earth,
and I shall pervert them, all together,
excepting those Thy servants among them
that are devoted.'
Said He, 'This is for Me a straight path:
over My servants
thou shalt have no authority, except those
that follow thee, being perverse;
Gehenna shall be their promised land
all together.'

Sūra 72:1–13

Say: It has been revealed to me that a company of
the jinn gave ear, then they said,
'We have indeed heard a Qur'ān wonderful,
guiding to rectitude.
We believe in it,
and we will not associate with our Lord
anyone.
He – exalted be our Lord's majesty! – has not
taken to Himself either consort or a son.
The fool among us spoke against God outrage,
and we had thought that men and jinn would

never speak against God a lie.
But there were certain men of mankind who
would take refuge with certain men of the
jinn, and they increased them in vileness,
and they thought, even as you also thought,
that God would never raise up anyone.
And we stretched towards heaven, but we found
it filled with terrible guards and meteors.
We would sit there on seats to hear;
but any listening now finds a meteor in wait
for him.
And so we know not whether evil is intended for
those in the earth,
or whether their Lord intends for them
rectitude.
And some of us are the righteous, and some of us
are otherwise;
we are sects differing.
Indeed, we thought that we should never be able
to frustrate God in the earth, neither be
able to frustrate Him by flight.'

Doctrine 3

The Day of Judgment: Sūra 56 and Ḥadīth

In Sūra 56, the Prophet describes the final judgment where a division is made between the 'Companions of the Right' and the 'Companions of the Left'. The former are those who will enjoy paradise while the latter are those who have rejected the idea of resurrection and their destiny is Hell. We also include a *ḥadīth* from ibn Makhlūf describing Paradise in great detail; like all *ḥadīths*, it develops from a close reading of the Qur'ān.

Sūra: 56:1–55

When the Terror descends
(and none denies its descending)
abasing, exalting,
when the earth shall be rocked and the
mountains crumbled and become a dust
scattered,
and you shall be three bands –

Companions of the Right (O Companions of the
Right!)
Companions of the Left (O Companions of the
Left!)
and the Outstrippers: the Outstrippers
those are they brought nigh the Throne, in
the Gardens of Delight
(a throng of the ancients and how few of the
later folk)
upon close-wrought couches
reclining upon them, set face to face,
immortal youths going round about them
with goblets, and ewers, and a cup from a
spring
(no brows throbbing, no intoxication)
and such fruits as they shall choose,
and such flesh of fowl as they desire,
and wide-eyed houris as the likeness of hidden
pearls,
a recompense for that they laboured.
Therein they shall hear no idle talk, no cause of
sin,
only the saying 'Peace, Peace!'

The Companions of the Right (O Companions of
the Right!)
mid thornless lote-trees and serried acacias,
and spreading shade and outpoured waters,
and fruits abounding
unfailing, unforbidden,
and upraised couches.
Perfectly We formed them, perfect,

and We made them spotless virgins,
chastely amorous, like of age
for the Companions of the Right.
A throng of the ancients
and a throng of the later folk.

The Companions of the Left (O Companions of the Left!)
mid burning winds and boiling waters,
and the shadow of a smoking blaze
neither cool, neither goodly;
and before that they lived at ease,
and persisted in the Great Sin,
ever saying,
'What, when we are dead and become dust and bones,
shall we indeed be raised up?
What, and our fathers, the ancients?'

Say: 'The ancients, and the later folk shall be gathered to the appointed time of a known day.
Then you erring ones, you that cried lies,
you shall eat of a tree called Zakkoum,
and you shall fill therewith your bellies
and drink on top of that boiling water
lapping it down like thirsty camels.'
This shall be their hospitality on the Day of Doom.

A ḥadīth

Said Ḥammād b. Sulaymān: When the Blessed have entered Paradise and have established themselves there in pleasure and delight, in a magnificent kingdom, a noble residence where they are in security and tranquillity, they quite forget there what they were promised in this world of how they would [one day] see Allah and go to visit Him, so occupied are they with the blessings and the pleasures they are enjoying there. So while they are thus, behold, an angel from before Allah – mighty and majestic is He – looks down upon them from one of the mighty walls of Paradise, from an eminence so high that not a thing in Paradise is hidden from him. [It is a wall] made of glistening pearl whose light shines over against the Throne and shines to the highest point of heaven. This angel will call out at the top of his voice: 'O people of Paradise, greeting of peace to you,' yet with a voice so full of compassion that, though it is so loud, all ears incline to it and all faces turn toward it, all souls being moved by it, rejoicing at it, and responding eagerly to it. All of them hear the voice and take cognizance that this is a herald from before Allah – mighty and majestic is He. It will evoke no doubt in them, so they will respond: 'Labbayka! Labbayka![1] O summoner from Allah, our Lord. We have heard and we respond.' Then he will say: 'Welcome to you, O ye saints of Allah! Welcome! Most welcome! Allah – mighty and majestic is He – sends you greeting of peace, saying that He is well pleased with you [and asking] are ye well pleased with him.' They will reply: 'Praise be to Allah who has guided us to this, for we were not such as would have been guided had not Allah guided us. Praise be to Him, since He is well pleased with us and has made us well satisfied. To Him be praise and thanksgiving, since He has been bountiful to us and given us [all this].' Then [the angel] will say: 'O saints of Allah, Allah – glory be to Him – sends you greeting of peace and says: "Have I fulfilled the promises I made to you in the world, or have I come short of them in any way?"' They will answer: 'Praise be to Allah, His are the gifts and the favours. He has indeed fulfilled His promises and bestowed on us bounty from Himself, this Paradise in which we go about wherever we wish.' Then [the angel] will say to them: 'Allah – glory be to Him – gives you greeting of peace, and reminds you that in the world He promised you that in Paradise you would visit Him, approach Him, and look upon Him. Now He would fulfill what He promised you, so He gives you here and now permission to prepare yourselves to have your happiness made complete in His presence.'

When they hear that, everything they have been enjoying there and all they have so far attained in Paradise will seem to them a little thing compared with that exceeding great happiness. Indeed, all that Paradise contains will seem insignificant over against the fact that Allah is well pleased with them and [is allowing them] to visit Him and look upon Him. So they will get themselves ready for a visit to their Lord in their finest estate and their most beautiful attire. They will clothe themselves with the most

[1] This ancient cry was used by those who approached the Ka'ba.

precious robes and the choicest ornaments they have, perfume themselves with the most fragrant perfumes, and mount the finest of horses and the most nobly born steeds, the most precious that they have, and putting crowns upon their heads they will come forth, each man from his palace and his garden, till he reaches the farthest end of his property and moves out into the paths of Paradise, his *wildān* [youths] preceding him and guiding him on the way to the visitation of the most illustrious King. Meanwhile they raise their voices in expressions of remembrance and encomium and hallelujahs (*tahlīl*), and whenever any man among them comes out into the paths of Paradise he meets his brother [Muslim] who has come out for the same purpose that he has.

Thus they will journey along till they come to a broad open space at the borders of Paradise, where the ground is unencumbered, vacant, white, and camphored, its soil being of camphor mixed with musk and ambergris, and its stones of pearl and jacinth. There they will assemble, preceded by the angel who had summoned them and who has travelled on ahead of them till he has brought them to this Garden of Eden. Allah will have given a call to this Garden, [saying]: 'Adorn yourself, for I have called My saints to visit Me within you,' so the Garden will have adorned itself with the most exquisite and beautiful adornment, and its attendants and *wildān* will likewise have got themselves ready. So when the saints arrive at the gate of the Garden, the angel will precede them, having with him the people of Paradise, and all of them will cry: 'Greeting to you, O ye angels of our Lord.' Then there will be opened for them a gate between whose leaves is the distance between the East and the West here on earth. This gate is of green emerald and over it are curtains of light of such brightness as almost to destroy the sight. They will enter and pour out into a valley-bed there whose enormous size, both in length and breadth, is known only to Him who created it by His power and fashioned it in His wisdom. Its soil is of finest musk and saffron and ambergris, its stones of jacinths and jewels, its little pebbles and rubble are of gold, while on its banks are trees whose limbs hang down, whose branches are low, whose fruits are within easy reach, whose birds sing sweetly, whose colours shine brightly, whose flowers blossom in splendour, and from which comes a breeze [so delightful] as to reduce to insignificance all other delights, one needle's-eye full of which, were it sent to this world, would cure all the sick.

Beneath these trees are chairs and benches of light that gleam, chairs and benches of jacinth and of jewels, and the like of red gold, of green emerald, of musk and ambergris, set there for the prophets, the messengers, then for the saints and the pious, then for the martyrs and the just, then for the Blessed from among all the rest of the people. Over [those seats] are cloths of brocade and satin and green silk, very precious, the silk woven and hemmed with jacinths and with jewels, and [on them] also are cushions of red brocade. On these they will be given permission to seat themselves in accordance with the honourable rank each has. They will be met by cries of welcome and applause, with ascriptions of honour and merit. So each man of them will take his station according to the measure of honour he has with his Lord, and his position of nearness to Him and in His favour, while the angels and the *wildān* show them great respect in seating them. Then, when every man has taken his place and settled himself according to his rank, orders will be given that they be served with the finest food. So they will eat it and enjoy it with such pleasure that they forget any food they have eaten hitherto, and everything they have ever known before seems insignificant to them. [It will be served to them] on platters the like of which they have never seen before and on tables whose like they have never beheld. Then orders will be given that they be served the finest varieties of drinks such as they never yet have drunk, [served to them] in vessels of pearl and jacinth which shine brilliantly, giving out lights the like of whose splendour and loveliness they have hitherto never beheld. So they will drink and enjoy it, and then orders will be given for them to be [perfumed] with perfumes such as they have never before enjoyed. Then orders will be given for them to be clothed with garments [of honour] the like of which they have not seen in Paradise, and of such splendour and beauty as they have never before had for their delight.

This will be their state, so ask not about their happiness and their joy there, for all that they have had before now seems to them of no account. Then Allah – glory be to Him – will say: 'O My saints, O My servants, have I fulfilled to you what I promised you in the world? Have I amply fulfilled My promise?' They will answer: 'Yes, O our Lord, by Thy might, Thou hast fulfilled to us Thy promise and hast amply fulfilled what Thou didst promise us.' Then He – glory be to Him – will say: 'Nay, by My might, there still remains for you one thing which you covet yet more and which has a still higher place in your estimation. What is there after you have come to Me but that you should look upon Me, that thereby your blessedness may be complete?' Then He – glory be to Him – will give command to the veils of light so they will be raised, and to the dread awfulness so that it is set aside. Then He – glory be to Him – will reveal Himself to them and they will look upon Him. Thus will they see Him without suffering any injury or any harm, and no joy can equal their joy in that, nor can any happiness or delight stand beside their happiness in that. So they will fall down before their Lord in prostration and deep humility, saying: 'Glory be to Thee, O our Lord. In Thy praise Thou art blessed and exalted, and blessed is Thy name.'

Doctrine 4

Predestination: Sūra 9, Sūra 36 and Ḥadīth

The Qur'ān has a strong bent for predestination. Hence, Sūra 9 suggests that everything which happens to humans is prescribed. Traditional reflection on this passage and others has taken the position that all human thoughts, words and deeds are foreseen, predetermined and decreed from all eternity. Sūra 36 underscores the ambivalence of such expressions which conflict with divine justice and mercy. Even though the Prophet and Qur'ān have been sent down, there are those whose necks are in fetters, for everything that happens takes place according to what has been written for it. Two *ḥadīth*, the first on the distance from Paradise to Hell from Muslim's *Ṣaḥīḥ*, the second on the works of the Blessed and the Damned from al-Bukhārī's *Ṣaḥīḥ*, underscore this predetermination; even if the distance between Paradise and Hell is only an arm's length, the individual's destiny can be radically altered when he is overtaken by what is decreed.

Sūra 9:49–54

Some of them there are that say, 'Give me leave and do not tempt me.' Have not such men fallen into temptation? And surely Gehenna encompasses the unbelievers.

If good fortune befalls thee, it vexes them; but if thou art visited by an affliction, they say, 'We took our dispositions before,' and turn away, rejoicing.

Say: 'Naught shall visit us but what God has prescribed for us; He is our Protector; in God let the believers put all their trust.'

Say: 'Are you awaiting for aught to come to us but one of the two rewards most fair? We are awaiting in your case too, for God to visit you with chastisement from Him, or at our hands; so await; we are awaiting with you.'

Say: 'Expend willinging, or unwillingly, it shall not be accepted from you; you are surely a people ungodly.'

And naught prevents that their expendings should be accepted from them, but that they believe not in God and His Messenger, and perform not the prayer save lazily, and that they expend not without they are averse.

Sūra 36:1–11

By the Wise Qur'ān, thou art truly among the Envoys on a straight path; the sending down of the All-mighty, the All-wise, that thou mayest warn a people whose fathers were never warned, so they are heedless.

The Word has been realized against most of them, yet they do not believe.

Surely We have put on their necks fetters up to the chin, so their heads are raised; and We have put up before them a barrier and behind them a barrier; and We have covered them, so they do not see.

Alike it is to them whether thou hast warned them or thou hast not warned them, they do not believe. Thou only warnest him who follows the Remembrance and who fears the All-merciful in the Unseen; so give him the good tidings of forgiveness and a generous wage.

Surely it is We who bring the dead to life and write down what they have forwarded and what they have left behind; everything We have numbered in a clear register.

A ḥadīth

It may be that one of you will be performing the works of the people of Paradise, so that between him and Paradise there is the distance of only an arm's length, but then what is written for him overtakes him, and he begins to perform the works of the people of Hell, into which he will go. Or maybe one of you will be performing the works of the people of Hell, so that between him and Hell there is the distance of only an arm's length, but then what is written for him will overtake him, and he will begin to perform the works of the people of Paradise, into which he will go.

A ḥadīth

'Alī said: We were one day at a funeral in the Baqī' al-Gharqad, when the Prophet – upon whom be Allah's blessing and peace – came and sat, and we sat around him. He had with him a staff and he bowed his head and began to make marks with his staff on the ground. Then he said: 'There is no one of you, no soul that has been born, but has his place in Paradise or in Hell already decreed for him, or, to put it otherwise, his unhappy or his happy fate has been decreed for him.' A man spoke up: 'O Apostle of Allah, shall we not then just entrust ourselves to what is written for us, and renounce works of the Blessed, and he amongst us who belongs to the Damned will inevitably be led to the works of the Damned?' He answered: 'As for those [who are to be among the] Blessed, the works of the Blessed will be made easy for them, and as for those [who are to be among the] Damned, the works of the Damned will be made easy for them.' Then he recited: 'So as for him who gives [generously] and shows piety, and gives credence to what is best, We shall ease the way for him to that which is easy, but as for him who is miserly and takes pride in [his] wealth, and treats what is best as false, for him We shall ease the way to that which is hard, nor will his wealth avail him when he is perishing. It is Ours to give guidance, and to Us belong both the first and the last.'

Ritual 1

The Kalima or Creed of Islam: Ḥadīth

The ritual dimension of Islam is most fully expressed in the 'Five Pillars' of the tradition, the *Kalima*, prayer, almsgiving, fasting and pilgrimage. The first pillar, the *Kalima*, functions as the watchword or creed for all Islam. The normal formulation of the *Kalima* is *lā ilāha ill'Allāh, Muḥammad Rasūl Allāh*, 'There is no god but Allah: Muḥammad is the Messenger of Allah.' As the creed of Islam, its ritual and non-ritual recitation has been invested with tremendous symbolic power. The power of the *Kalima* is suggested by the following *ḥadīth* from Muḥammad Ḥaqqī al-Nāzilī's *Khazīnat al-Asrār.*

Muslim has reported from 'Ubāda b. al-Ṣāmit – with whom may Allah be pleased – that the Messenger of Allah – upon whom be Allah's blessing and peace – said: 'Allah will forbid the Fire [from touching] anyone who has testified: "There is no God save Allah and Muḥammad is the Messenger of Allah."' Al-Ṭabarānī and Abū Nu'aym have quoted from 'Ubāda b. al-Ṣāmit how he told that the Messenger of Allah – upon whom be Allah's blessing and peace – said: 'The faith that has most virtue is that you should recognize that Allah is with you wherever you may be.' Al-Ṭabarānī has reported from Abu'l-Dardā – with whom may Allah be pleased – that the Messenger of Allah – upon whom be Allah's blessing and peace – said: 'There is no person who says a hundred times: "There is no God save Allah, and Muḥammad is the Messenger of Allah," but will be raised up by Allah on the Day of Resurrection with a face shining like the moon on the night of its fullness. No one on that Day will hand up [for assessment] works superior to his works save those who have said the like of what he has said or have increased [the number of times].' Muslim has reported from al-Muṭṭalib b. Ḥinṭab – with whom may Allah be pleased – that the Prophet – upon whom be Allah's blessing and peace – said: 'The finest thing I have ever said, and that the Prophets who were before me have ever said, is to bear witness that there is no God save Allah.'

Muslim has reported from 'Uthmān – with whom may Allah be pleased – that the Prophet – upon whom be Allah's blessing and peace – said: 'He who dies while acknowledging that there is no God save Allah, and holds fast to his belief in it, will enter Paradise.' That he should have said 'Allah will forbid the Fire [from touching] him' is seen by the divines to be in contradiction with other texts which indicate that some disobedient believers will be tormented therein. Some seek to reconcile them by saying that this promise can be claimed only by him who repents of his wickedness before dying, others by saying that the promise was made before the incumbent duties had been ordained. Al-Ḥasan al-Baṣrī said that the meaning was: 'Whosoever says this *kalima* and fulfills all that it connotes and all the incumbent duties.' The preferred explanation is that it means that confession of the Divine Unity (*tawḥīd*) will prevent one from being kept eternally in the Fire.

Ritual 2

Prayer: Sūra 107, Sūra 4, Sūra 2, Sūra 62 and Ḥadīth

Prayer forms the second pillar in the ritual life of Islam and it is to be performed five times: at dawn, midday, afternoon, evening and night. Prayer may be performed in private or in congregation, but if it is recited in congregation it is presided over by a prayer-leader or *imām*. At the five times set for prayer, the *muezzin* calls the faithful together from the court or minaret of the mosque. The importance of prayer is such that the Qur'ān indicates that it must be performed properly; Sūra 107 indicates that one should not be 'heedless' of prayer. The tradition developed at least eight fundamentals for proper prayer, among them facing the *qibla*, the sacred shrine at Mecca, bending the body so that the palms touch the knees, and the demonstration of obeisance by prostration in which the forehead touches the floor or ground of the place of prayer. Sūra 4 underscores the importance of prayer even when among the unbelievers. The direction of prayer, to the *qibla*, was toward Jerusalem in early Islam, but when Muḥammad broke with the Jews the direction of prayer was re-oriented toward the sacred shrine in Mecca. Sūra 2 reflects this change in sacred geography. The most important congregational prayer is for what Sūra 62 calls the 'Day of Congregation' or Friday. While there are affinities between the Friday prayer and the Jewish and Christian Sabbath, it never become a 'day of rest' in Islamic countries. The *ḥadīth* from the *Sunan* of Abū 'Abd al-Raḥmān Aḥmad al-Nasā'ī develops the distinction between the Friday prayer and the Sabbath of Jews and Christians.

Sūra 107:1–7

Hast thou seen him who cries to the Doom?
That is he who repulses the orphan
and urges not the feeding of the needy.

So woe to those that pray
and are heedless of their prayers,
to those who make display and refuse charity.

Sūra 4:101–4

Whoso emigrates in the way of God will find in the earth many refuges and plenty; whoso goes forth from his house an emigrant to God and His Messenger, and then death overtakes him, his wage shall have fallen on God; surely God is All-forgiving, All-compassionate. And when you are journeying in the land there is no fault in you that you shorten the prayer, if you fear the unbelievers may afflict you; the unbelievers are for you a manifest foe.

When thou art amongst them, and performest for them the prayer, let a party of them stand with thee, and let them take their weapons. When they bow themselves, let them be behind you; and let another party who have not prayed come and pray with thee, taking their precautions and their weapons. The unbelievers wish that you should be heedless of your weapons and your baggage, then they would wheel on you all at once. There is no fault in you, if rain molests you, or you are sick, to lay aside your weapons; but take your precautions. God has prepared for the unbelievers a humbling chastisement.

When you have performed the prayer, remember God, standing and sitting and on your sides. Then, when you are secure, perform the prayer; surely the prayer is a timed prescription for the believers.

Sūra 2:138–45

'To God belong the East and the West;
He guides whomsoever He will
to a straight path.'

Thus We appointed you a midmost nation that you might be witnesses to the people, and that the Messenger might be a witness to you; We did not appoint the direction thou wast facing, except that We might know who followed the Messenger from him who turned on his heels – though it were a grave thing save for those whom God has guided; but God would never leave your faith to waste – truly, God is All-gentle with the people, All-compassionate.

We have seen thee turning thy face about in the heaven; now We will surely turn thee to a direction that shall satisfy thee. Turn thy face towards the Holy Mosque; and wherever you are, turn your faces towards it. Those who have been given the Book know it is the truth from their Lord; God is not heedless of the things they do.

Yet if thou shouldst bring to those that have been given the Book every sign, they will not follow thy direction; thou art not a follower of their direction, neither are they followers of one another's direction. If thou followest their caprices, after the knowledge that has come to thee, then thou wilt surely be among the evildoers whom We have given the Book, and they recognize it as they recognize their sons, even though there is a party of them conceal the truth and that wittingly.

The truth comes from thy Lord; then be not

among the doubters.

Every man has his direction to which he turns; so be you forward in good works. Wherever you may be, God will bring you all together; surely God is powerful over everything. From whatever place thou issuest, turn thy face towards the Holy Mosque; and wherever you may be, turn your faces towards it, that the people may not have any argument against you, excepting the evildoers of them; and fear you them not, but fear you me; and that I may perfect My blessing upon you, and that haply so you may be guided.

Sūra 62:9–11

O believers, when proclamation is made for prayer on the Day of Congregation, hasten to God's remembrance and leave trafficking aside; that is better for you, did you but know. Then, when the prayer is finished, scatter in the land and seek God's bounty, and remember God frequently; haply you will prosper.

But when they see merchandise or diversion they scatter off to it, and they leave thee standing. Say: 'What is with God is better than diversion and merchandise, God is the best of providers.'

A ḥadīth

That the Assembling [on Friday] is a Duty

Sa'īd b. 'Abd al-Raḥmān al-Makhzūmī has informed us on the authority of Sufyān, from Abū'l-Zinād, from al-A'raj, from Abū Hurayra, as also Abū Ṭā'ūs, from his father, from Abū Hurayra, that the Apostle of Allah – upon whom be Allah's blessing and peace – said: 'We are the last and yet the first. [We Muslims are] last since they [i.e., the Jews and Christians] were given scripture before us, we being given it later than they were, and [they were given] also this day which Allah – mighty and majestic is He – ordained for them, but they differed about it [i.e., about Friday], so Allah guided us to it so that other communities follow us [i.e., come after us] in this, the Jews tomorrow and the Christians the day after tomorrow.'

Wāṣil b. 'Abd al-A'lā has informed us on the authority of Ibn Fuḍayl, from Abū Mālik al-Ashja'ī, from Abū Ḥāzim, from Abū Hurayra, and from Rab'ī b. Ḥirash from Ḥudhayfa, both of whom reported that the Apostle of Allah – upon whom be Allah's blessing and peace – said: 'Allah – mighty and majestic is He – led astray from Friday those who came before us, so that the Jews have Saturday and the Christians Sunday; then Allah brought us along and guided us to Friday. [The order of days as] He has appointed them is Friday, Saturday, Sunday, so on the Last Day [when peoples are called in their communities] they will be following after us. Thus in this world we are the last people [to be formed into a religious community] but on the Day we shall be the first, those who receive their judgment before [other] creatures.'

Ritual 3

Almsgiving: Sūra 2 and Ḥadīth

Sūra 2:172–3 offers a short code of true piety in which the giving of alms to kinsmen, orphans, the needy, the traveller, beggars and to ransom the slave is equivalent in importance to prayer. The Qur'ān uses two terms for almsgiving, *zakāt* and *ṣadaqa*. In later traditions, as witnessed by the *ḥadīth* we produce here, a distinction is drawn between these forms of almsgiving. *Zakāt* is taken to be the obligatory tithing which every Muslim must observe, and *ṣadaqa* to be charitable giving beyond what is legally required. This meaning of *ṣadaqa* is presented in Sūra 2:263–75.

Sūra 2:172–3

It is not piety, that you turn your faces
to the East and to the West,
True piety is this:
to believe in God, and the Last Day,
the angels, the Book, and the Prophets,
to give of one's substance, however cherished,
to kinsmen, and orphans,
the needy, the traveller, beggars,
and to ransom the slave,
to perform the prayer, to pay the alms.
And they who fulfil their covenant
when they have engaged in a covenant,
and endure with fortitude
misfortune, hardship and peril,
these are they who are true in their faith,
these are the truly godfearing.

Sūra: 2:263–75

The likeness of those who expend their wealth in the way of God is as the likeness of a grain of corn that sprouts seven ears, in every ear a hundred grains. So God multiplies unto whom He will; God is All-embracing, All-knowing.

Those who expend their wealth in the way of God then follow not up what they have expended with reproach and injury, their wage is with their Lord, and no fear shall be on them, neither shall they sorrow. Honourable words, and forgiveness, are better than a freewill offering followed by injury; and God is All-sufficient, All-clement.

O believers, void not your freewill offerings with reproach and injury, as one who expends of his substance to show off to men and believes not in God and the Last Day. The likeness of him is as the likeness of a smooth rock on which is soil, and a torrent smites it, and leaves it barren. They have no power over anything that they have earned. God guides not the people of the unbelievers.

But the likeness of those who expend their wealth, seeking God's good pleasure, and to confirm themselves, is as the likeness of a garden upon a hill; a torrent smites it and it yields its produce twofold; if no torrent smites it, yet dew; and God sees the things you do.

Would any of you wish to have a garden of palms and vines, with rivers flowing beneath it, and all manner of fruit there for him, then old age smites him, and he has seed, but weaklings, then a whirlwind with fire smites it, and it is consumed? So God makes clear the signs to you; haply you will reflect.

O believers, expend of the good things you have earned, and of that We have produced for you from the earth, and intend not the corrupt of it for your expending; for you would never take it yourselves, except you closed an eye on it; and know that God is All-sufficient, All-knowing.

He gives the Wisdom to whomsoever He will, and whoso is given the Wisdom, has been given much good; yet none remembers but men possessed of minds.

And whatever expenditure you expend, and whatever vow you vow, surely God knows it. No helpers have the evildoers. If you publish your freewill offerings, it is excellent; but if you conceal them, and give them to the poor, that is better for you, and will acquit you of your evil deeds; God is aware of the things you do.

Thou art not responsible for guiding them; but God guides whomsoever he will.

And whatever good you expend is for yourselves, for then you are expending, being desirous only of God's Face; and whatever good you expend shall be repaid to you in full, and you will not be wronged, it being for the poor who are restrained in the way of God, and are unable to journey in the land; the ignorant man supposes them rich because of their abstinence, but thou shalt know them by their mark – they do not beg of men importunately. And whatever good you expend, surely God has knowledge of it.

Those who expend their wealth night and day, secretly and in public, their wage awaits them with their Lord, and no fear shall be on them, neither shall they sorrow.

A ḥadīth

Suwayd b. Sa'īd has related to us, on the authority of Ḥafṣ, i.e., Ibn Maysara al-Ṣan'ānī, from Zayd b. Aslam, that Abū Ṣāliḥ Dhakwān informed him that he had heard Abū Hurayra say that the Apostle of Allah – upon whom be Allah's blessing and peace – said: 'There is no one in possession of gold or silver who does not pay what is due thereon but will find himself on the Day of Resurrection plated with plates of fire and roasted upon them in the fire of Gehenna, so that his sides, his forehead, his back are scorched, and as soon as they have cooled off they are returned to him, during "a Day whose length is fifty thousand years", until the judgment among men is finished and he is shown his path, either to Paradise or to Hell.' Someone said: 'O Apostle of Allah, what about camels?' He answered: 'There is no owner of camels who does not pay what is due thereon, and what is due on their milk on the day they come down to water, but on the Day will be cast down before them on a level spot, and however numerous they may be not a single young weaned camel will be missing, and they will trample him under their feet and bite him with their mouths, and whenever the last has finished with him the first will begin again, during a Day whose length is fifty thousand years, till the judgment among men is finished, and he is shown his path either to Paradise or to Hell.' Someone asked: 'O Apostle of Allah, what about cattle and sheep?' He replied: 'There is no owner of cattle or sheep who does not pay what is due thereon, but on the Day he will be cast down before them on a level spot, and not one of them will be missing, whether horned, or hornless, or broken-horned, and they will gore him with their horns and trample him with their hooves, and whenever the last have finished with him the first will begin again, during a Day whose length is fifty thousand years, until the judgment among men is finished, and he shown his path either to Paradise or to Hell.'

Ritual 4

Fasting: Sūra 2 and Ḥadīth

The fourth pillar of Islam is fasting. Pious Muslims will practise fasting at various times in conjunction with expiating and rectifying various breaches in the observance of religion, but the major annual fast is the month of Ramaḍān. Sūra 2:179–83 states the institution of this fast, setting forth the stipulation that those who are sick are exempted from the strenuousness of the fast. During the month of Ramaḍān, Muslims will abstain from food, drink and sex during the daylight hours, or from the time one can distinguish a white thread from a black thread in the morning until they can no longer be distinguished in the evening. The *ḥadīth* that follows this Qur'ānic passage stresses that fasting is done for Allah, and that he alone will reward it on the Day of Resurrection.

Sūra 2:179–83

O believers, prescribed for you is the Fast, even as it was prescribed for those that were before you – haply you will be godfearing – for days numbered; and if any of you be sick, or if he be on a journey, then a number of other days; and for those who are unable to fast, a redemption by feeding a poor man. Yet better it is for him who volunteers good, and that you should fast is better for you, if you but know; the month of Ramaḍan, wherein the Qur'ān was sent down to the people, and as clear signs of the Guidance and the Salvation. So let those of you, who are present at the month, fast it; and if any of you be sick, or if he be on a journey, then a number of other days; God desires ease for you, and desires not hardship for you; and that you fulfil the number, and magnify God that He has guided you, and haply you will be thankful.

And when My servants question thee concerning Me – I am near to answer the call of the caller, when he calls to Me; so let them respond to Me, and let them believe in Me; haply so they will go aright.

Permitted to you, upon the night of the Fast, is

to go in to your wives; they are a vestment for you, and you are a vestment for them. God knows that you have been betraying yourselves and has turned to you and pardoned you. So now lie with them, and seek what God has prescribed for you. And eat and drink, until the white thread shows clearly to you from the black thread at the dawn; then complete the Fast unto the night, and do not lie with them while you cleave to the mosques. Those are God's bounds; keep well within them. So God makes clear His signs to men; haply they will be godfearing.

A ḥadīth

Muḥammad b. Rāfi' has related to me, on the authority of 'Abd al-Razzāq, on the authority of Ibn Jurayj, from 'Aṭā', from Abū Ṣāliḥ al-Zayyāt, that he heard Abū Hurayra – with whom may Allah be pleased – say: Said the Apostle of Allah – on whom be Allah's blessing and peace: 'Allah – mighty and majestic is He – has declared: "Every good work a man does is done for himself save fasting, which [is done] for Me, wherefore I Myself shall reward him for it.' Fasting is a protection, so when it is a fast day for any one of you let him use no unseemly language on that day, nor raise any clamour. Should anyone abuse him or pick a fight with him, let him say: "I am a man who is fasting." By Him in whose hand is Muḥammad's soul, the bad breath from the mouth of one who is fasting will smell sweeter to Allah on the Day of Resurrection than the perfume of musk. He who fasts has two occasions for rejoicing. When he finishes his fast he rejoices at its finishing, and when he meets his Lord he will have joy because of his fasting.'

Abū Bakr b. Abī Shayba has related to us, on the authority of Abū Mu'āwiya and of Wakī', from al-A'mash; and Zuhayr b. Ḥarb has related to us, on the authority of Jarīr, from al-A'mash; and Abū Sa'īd al-Ashajj, whose wording we give, has related to us, on the authority of Wakī', from al-A'mash, from Abū Ṣāliḥ, from Abū Hurayra – with whom may Allah be pleased – that the Apostle of Allah – upon whom be Allah's blessing and peace – said: 'Allah – mighty and majestic is He – has declared: "For every good work a man does, merit tenfold to seven hundredfold will be reckoned, save [in the case of] fasting, for it [is done] for Me, and I Myself will reward it, since it is for My sake that he gives up his sex indulgence and his food." He who fasts has two occasions for rejoicing. There is a rejoicing when he has finished his fast, and there is a rejoicing when he meets His Lord, for the bad breath of his mouth will smell sweeter to Allah than the perfume of musk.'

Ritual 5

Pilgrimage: Sūra 22 and Hadīth

Pilgrimage or the *ḥajj* is the fifth pillar of Islam and is perhaps the most arduous aspect of ritual life within the tradition. The Mosque of Mecca is the major object of the pilgrimage, but it also involves visits to other sites in the neighbourhood. Almost every aspect of the *ḥajj* is a re-enactment of sacred events, so that *sa'y* or running seven times through one of the principal streets of Mecca, for example, is a ritual repetition of Hagar's search to find water for Ishmael. Sūra 22:26–38 is a major statement on the *ḥajj*, and the *ḥadīth* following indicates something of the cosmic importance given to the Ka'ba itself.

Sūra 22:26–38

And when We settled for Abraham the place of the House: 'Thou shalt not associate with Me anything. And do thou purify My House for those that shall go about it and those that stand, for those that bow and prostrate themselves; and proclaim among men the Pilgrimage, and they shall come unto thee on foot and upon every lean beast, they shall come from every deep ravine that they may witness things profitable to them and mention God's Name on days well-known over such beasts of the flocks as He has provided them: "So eat thereof, and feed the wretched poor." Let them then finish with their self neglect and let them fulfil their vows, and go about the Ancient House.'

All that; and whosoever venerates the sacred things of God, it shall be better for him with his Lord. And permitted to you are the flocks, except that which is recited to you. And eschew the abomination of idols, and eschew the speaking of falsehood, being men pure of faith unto God, not associating with God anything, it is as though he has fallen from heaven and the birds snatch him away, or the wind sweeps him headlong into a place far away.

All that; and whosoever venerates God's waymarks, that is of the godliness of the hearts. There are things therein profitable to you unto a stated term; thereafter their lawful place of sacrifice is by the Ancient House.

We have appointed for every nation a holy rite, that they may mention God's Name over such beasts of the flocks as He has provided them. Your God is One God, so to him surrender. And give thou good tidings unto the humble who, when God is mentioned, their hearts quake, and such as endure patiently whatever visits them, and who perform the prayer, and expend of what We have provided them.

And the beasts of sacrifice – We have appointed them for you as among God's waymarks; therein is good for you. So mention God's Name over them, standing in tanks; then, when their flanks collapse, eat of them and feed the beggar and the suppliant. So We have subjected them to you; haply you will be thankful. The flesh of them shall not reach God, neither their blood, but godliness from you shall reach Him.

A ḥadīth

Muḥammad b. 'Alī b. al-Ḥusayn has related, saying: I was with my father 'Alī b. al-Ḥusayn (i.e., the great-grandson of the Prophet) at Mecca, and while he was circumambulating the House, and I was following behind him, there came to him a tall man who put his hand on my father's back. My father turned to him, whereat the man said: 'Greetings to you, O child of the daughter of the Apostle of Allah. I want to question you.' My father kept silent, so I and the man remained behind him till he had finished his seven circuits and had entered the Ḥijr and stood beneath the *mīzāb*.[1] The man and I stood behind him while he prayer the two *rak'as* pertaining to his sevenfold circuit. Then he settled himself in a sitting posture and turned to me, whereat I went and sat beside him. He said: 'O Muḥammad, where is this questioner?' I beckoned to the man, whereat he came and sat before my father. My father said: 'About what is it you wish to ask?' 'I want to ask you,' he replied, 'about how the circumambulation of this House began, why and where and how it came to be.' 'Yes,' said my father, 'but from where do you come?' 'I am,' he answered, 'of the people of Shām.' 'And where do you dwell?' he asked. 'In Jerusalem,' answered the man. 'And have you read the two Books?' he asked, meaning the Torah and the Gospel. 'Surely,' replied the man. 'O brother from the people of Shām,' said my father, 'take careful note of what I say and do not transmit from me anything but the truth. As for the beginning of the circumambulation of this House, it goes back to when Allah – blessed and exalted is He – said to the angels: "I am going to appoint a viceregent on the earth." The angels said: "O Lord, a viceregent other than us? One of those who will cause corruption therein and shed blood, those who will be envious of one another, hate each other, tyrannize over one another? O Lord, why not appoint that viceregent from among us? We would not cause corruption therein nor shed blood, and we would not be hating, nor envying, nor tyrannizing over one another. It is we who sing Thy praises with glory and hallow Thee, so we should be obedient to Thee and would not disobey Thee." Allah answered: "I know something ye do not know." Thereat the angels

[1] The waterspout carrying water from the roof on the Ka'ba.

thought that what they had said was a rejecting of what their Lord wanted and so He was wroth with them because of what they had said. So they took refuge at the Throne and raised their heads, making a sign of humility with their fingers and weeping because of their anxiety at His wrath. They went in circuit around the Throne for three hours. Then Allah looked at them and mercy descended on them. Then Allah established beneath the Throne a House on four columns of emerald encrusted with rubies and called that House al-Ḍurāḥ. Then He said to the angels: "Circumambulate this House and leave the Throne." So the angels, leaving the Throne, circumambulated that House, which was much easier for them. That is the Frequented Fane (*al-Bait al-Ma'mūr*) of which Allah has made mention, into which every day and night seventy thousand angels enter never to return to it again. Then Allah sent the angels forth, saying: "Build for me a House on earth the shape and size of this." [When that was done] Allah – glory be to Him – bade all His creatures of earth circumambulate that house precisely as the inhabitants of the Heavens circumambulate the Frequented Fane.'

Said the man: 'You have spoken truly, O child of the daughter of the Apostle of Allah, that indeed was how it was.'

Institutional Expression 1

The Community: Sūra 49 and a Ḥadīth on the Farewell Pilgrimage

The community envisioned in the Qur'ān and created by the Prophet was a radical one in that it substituted religious bonds for ancient tribal bonds. Here, in Sūra 49, the Prophet points to the equality of this new community of believers, united not only by belief but by submission or surrender to God. In the *ḥadīth* from Ibn Hishām's *Life of Muḥammad*, the Prophet delivers one of his noblest sermons after completing the annual pilgrimage to Mecca, a short time before his death.

Sūra 49:6–18

O believers, if an ungodly man comes to you with a tiding, make clear, lest you afflict a people unwittingly, and then repent of what you have done.

And you know that the Messenger of God is among you. If he obeyed you in much of the affair, you would suffer; but God has endeared to you belief, decking it fair in your hearts, and He has made detestable to you unbelief and ungodliness and disobedience. Those – they are the right-minded, by God's favour and blessing; God is All-knowing, All wise.

If two parties of the believers fight, put things right between them; then if one of them is insolent against the other, fight the insolent one till it reverts to God's commandment. If it reverts, set things right between them equitably, and be just, Surely God loves the just.

The believers indeed are brothers; so set things right between your two brothers, and fear God; haply so you will find mercy.

O believers, let not any people scoff at another people who may be better than they; neither let women scoff at women who may be better than themselves. And find no fault with one another, neither revile one another by nicknames. An evil name is ungodliness after belief. And whoso repents not, those – they are the evildoers.

O believers, eschew much suspicion; some suspicion is a sin. And do not spy, neither backbite one another; would any of you like to eat the flesh of his brother dead? You would abominate it. And fear you God; assuredly God turns, and He is All-compassionate.

O mankind, We have created you male and female, and appointed you races and tribes, that you may know one another. Surely the noblest among you in the sight of God is the most god-fearing of you. God is All-knowing, All-aware.

The Bedouins say, 'We believe.' Say: 'You do not believe; rather say, "We surrender"; for belief has not yet entered your hearts. If you obey God and His Messenger, He will not diminish you anything of your works. God is All-forgiving, All-compassionate.'

The believers are those who believe in God and His Messenger, then have not doubted, and have struggled with their possessions and their selves in the way of God; those – they are the truthful ones.

Say: 'What, would you teach God what your religion is, and God knows what is in the heavens and what is in the earth? And God has knowledge of everything.'

They count it as a favour to thee that they have surrendered! Say: 'Do not count your surrendering as a favour to me; nay, but rather God confers a favour upon you, in that He has guided you in belief, if it be that you are truthful. God knows the Unseen of the heavens and of the earth; and God sees the things you do.'

A ḥadīth

Then, the apostle continued his pilgrimage and showed the men the rites and taught them the customs of their *ḥajj*. He made a speech in which he made things clear. He praised and glorified God, then he said: 'O men, listen to my words. I do not know whether I shall ever meet you in this place again after this year. Your blood and your property are sacrosanct until you meet your Lord, as this day and this month are holy. You will surely meet your Lord and He will ask you of your works. I have told you. He who has a pledge let him return it to him who entrusted him with it; all usury is abolished, but you have your capital. Wrong not and you shall not be wronged. God has decreed that there is to be no usury and the usury of 'Abbās b. 'Abd al-Muṭṭalib is abolished, all of it. All blood shed in the pagan period is to be left unavenged. The first claim on blood I abolish is that of b. Rabī'a b. al-Hārith b. 'Abd al-Muṭṭalib (who was fostered among the Banū Layth and whom Hudhayl killed). It is the first blood shed in the pagan period which I deal with. Satan despairs of ever being worshipped in your land, but if he can be obeyed in anything short of worship he will be pleased in matters you may be disposed to think of little account, so beware of him in your religion. "Postponement of a sacred month is only an excess of disbelief whereby those who disbelieve are misled; they allow it one year and forbid it another year that they make make up the number of months which God has hallowed, so that they permit what God has forbidden, and forbid what God has allowed" (Sūra 9:37). Time has completed its cycle and is as it was on the day that God created the heavens and the earth. The number of months with God is twelve; four of them are sacred, three consecutive and the Rajab of Mudar which is between Jumādā and the Sha'bān.

You have rights over your wives and they have rights over you. You have the right that they should not defile your bed and that they should not behave with open unseemliness. If they do, God allows you to put them in separate rooms and to beat them but not with severity. If they refrain from these things they have the right to their food and clothing with kindness. Lay injunctions on women kindly, for they are prisoners with you having no control of their persons. You have taken them only as a trust from God, and you have the enjoyment of their persons by the words of God, so understand my words, O men, for I have told you. I have left with you something which if you will hold fast to it you will never fall into error – a plain indication, the book of God and the practice of His prophet, so give good heed to what I say.

Know that every Muslim is a Muslim's brother, and that the Muslims are brethren. It is only lawful to take from a brother what he gives you willingly, so wrong not yourselves. O God, have I not told you?

Institutional Expression 2

The People of the Book: Sūra 5 and Ḥadīth

It was inevitable that as the Muslim community expanded and grew, it would encounter other religious traditions. The Qur'ān uses the phrase 'the People of the Book' to describe those religious traditions which the Prophet believed had been given revelations in the form of a book. Sūra 5:64–75 is only one of the many descriptions of 'the People of the Book' from the Qur'ān indicating the Prophet's understanding of them. Ultimately, these people became *dhimmīs* within the *umma* or religious community; they were those with whom a covenant or bond (*dhimma*) had been made. The *ḥadīth* from Ibn Hishām's *Life of Muḥammad* describes one of the earliest covenants made between the *umma* of Muḥammad and the non-Muslims and Jews of Medina. In later juridical contexts, a *dhimmī* was taken to be a tolerated monotheist (Jew, Christian, Ṣābian or Zoroastrian) who was allowed to live within the *umma*, paying tribute and observing certain sumptuary laws as a token of inferior status.

Sūra 5:64–75

Say: 'People of the Book, do you blame us for any other cause than that we believe in God, and what has been sent down to us, and what was sent down before, and that most of you are ungodly?'

Say: 'Shall I tell you of a recompense with God, worse than that? Whomsoever God has cursed, and with whom He is wroth, and made some of them apes and swine, and worshippers of idols – they are worse situated, and have gone further astray from the right way.' When they come to you, they say, 'We believe'; but they have entered in unbelief, and so they have departed in it; God knows very well what they are hiding. Thou seest many of them vying in sin and enmity, and how they consume the unlawful; evil is the thing they have been doing. Why do the masters and the rabbis not forbid them to utter sin, and consume the unlawful? Evil is the thing they have been working.

The Jews have said, 'God's hand is fettered. Fettered are their hands, and they are cursed for what they have said. Nay, but His hands are outspread; He expends how He will. And what has been sent down to thee from thy Lord will surely increase many of them in insolence and unbelief; and We have cast between them enmity and hatred, till the Day of Resurrection. As often as they light a fire of war, God will extinguish it. They hasten about the earth, to do corruption there; and God loves not the workers of corruption.

But had the People of the Book believed and been godfearing, We would have acquitted them of their evil deeds, and admitted them to Gardens of Bliss. Had they performed the Torah and the Gospel, and what was sent down to them from their Lord, they would have eaten both what was above them, and what was beneath their feet. Some of them are a just nation; but many of them – evil are the things they do.

O Messenger, deliver that which has been sent down to thee from thy Lord; for if thou dost not, thou wilt not have delivered His message. God will protect thee from men. God guides not the people of the unbelievers.

Say: 'People of the Book, you do not stand on anything, until you perform the Torah and the Gospel, and what was sent down to you from your Lord.' And what has been sent down to thee from thy Lord will surely increase many of them in insolence and unbelief; so grieve not for the people of the unbelievers. Surely they that believe, and those of Jewry, and the Ṣābians, and those Christians, whosoever believes in God and the Last Day, and works righteousness – no fear shall be on them, neither shall they sorrow.

And We took compact with the Children of Israel, and We sent Messengers to them.

Whensoever there came to them a Messenger with that their souls had not desire for, some they cried lies to, and some they slew. And they supposed there should be no trial; but blind they were, and deaf. Then God turned towards them; then again blind they were, many of them, and deaf; and God sees the things they do.

A ḥadīth

The believers shall not leave anyone destitute among them by not paying his redemption money or bloodwit in kindness.

A believer shall not take as an ally the freedman of another Muslim against him. The God-fearing believers shall be against the rebellious or him who seeks to spread injustice, or sin or enmity, or corruption between believers; the hand of every man shall be against him even if he be a son of one of them. A believer shall not slay a believer for the sake of an unbeliever, nor shall he aid an unbeliever against a believer. God's protection is one, the least of them may give protection to a stranger on their behalf. Believers are friend one to the other to the exclusion of outsiders. To the Jew who follows us belong help and equality. He shall not be wronged nor shall his enemies be aided. The peace of the believers is indivisible. No separate peace shall be made when believers are fighting in the way of God. Conditions must be fair and equitable to all. In every foray a rider must take another behind him. The believers must avenge the blood of one another shed in the way of God. The God-fearing believers enjoy the best and most upright guidance. No polytheist shall take the property or person of Quraysh under his protection nor shall be he intervene against a believer. Whosoever is convicted of killing a believer without good reason shall be subject to retaliation unless the next of kin is satisfied (with blood-money), and the believers shall be against him as one man, and they are bound to take action against him.

It shall not be lawful to a believer who holds by what is in this document and believes in God and the last day to help an evil-doer or to shelter him. The curse of God and His anger on the day of resurrection will be upon him if he does, and neither repentance nor ransom will be received from him. Whenever you differ about a matter it must be referred to God and to Muḥammad.

The Jews shall contribute to the cost of war so long as they are fighting alongside the believers. The Jews of the Banū 'Auf are one community with the believers (the Jews have their religion and the Muslims have theirs), their freedmen and their persons except those who behave unjustly and sinfully, for they hurt but themselves and their families. The same applies to the Jews of the Banū al-Najjār, the Banū al-Ḥārith, the Banū Sā'ida, the Banū Jusham, the Banū al-Aus, the Banū Tha'laba, and the Jafna, a clan of the Tha'laba and the Banū al-Shuṭyaba. Loyalty is a protection against treachery. The freedmen of Tha'laba are as themselves. The close friends of the Jews are as themselves. None of them shall go out to war save with the permission of Muḥammad, but he shall not be prevented from taking revenge for a wound. He who slays a man without warning slays himself and his household, unless it be one who has wronged him, for God will accept that. The Jews must bear their expenses and the Muslims their expenses. Each must help the other against anyone who attacks the people of this document. They must seek mutual advice and consultation, and loyalty is a protection against treachery. A man is not liable for his ally's misdeeds. The wronged must be helped. The Jews must pay with the believers so long as the war lasts. Medina shall be sanctuary for the people of this document. A stranger under protection shall be as his host doing no harm and committing no crime. A woman shall only be given protection with the consent of her family. If any dispute or controversy likely to cause trouble should arise it must be referred to God and to Muḥammad the apostle of God. God accepts what is nearest to piety and goodness in this document. The Quraysh and their helpers shall not be given protection. The contracting parties are bound to help one another against any attack on Medina. If they are called to make peace and maintain it they must do so; and if they make a similar demand on the Muslims it must be carried out except in the case of a holy war. Every one shall have his portion from the side to which he belongs; the Jews of al-Aus, their freedmen and themselves have the same standing with the people of this document in pure loyalty from the people of this document.

Loyalty is a protection against treachery: He who acquires aught acquires it for himself. God approves of this document. This deed will not protect the unjust and the sinner. The man who goes forth to fight and the man who stays at home in the city is safe unless he has been unjust and sinned. God is the protector of the good and God-fearing man and Muḥammad is the apostle of God.

Institutional Expression 3

Struggle (Jihād): Sūra 29, Sūra 25 and Ḥadīth

The Arabic word *jihād* is one of the most misunderstood terms of Islam. Literally, it means exerting oneself or struggling. The following Qur'ānic passages suggest that it is a struggle for Allah, but not always with a sword as a Holy War. Here, it has the sense of mission to establish Islam. We have already seen in the famous passage from Sūra 2:256 (Doctrine 1, page 142) that 'there is no compulsion in religion', a doctrine which underscores the peaceful aspect of *jihād*. However, there is the defensive struggle with arms when Islam is endangered. The following *ḥadīth* from Muḥammad Ali's *Manual of Ḥadīth* link the *jihād* to the missionary activities of Islam and to martyrdom, understood from time to time as one of the 'Five Pillars' of Islam. Historically, the passages in the Qur'ān have been interpreted to sanction expansionism as well as the peaceful missionary process.

Sūra 29:65–9

When they embark in the ships, they call on
God,
making their religion sincerely His;
but when He has delivered them to the land,
they associate others with Him,
that they may be ungrateful for what We have
given them, and take their enjoyment;
they will soon know!

Have they not seen that We have appointed a
sanctuary secure,
while all about them the people are snatched
away?
What, do they believe in vanity, and do they
disbelieve in God's blessing?
And who does greater evil than he who forges
against God a lie,
or cries lies to the truth when it comes to him?
What, is there not in Gehenna a lodging for the
unbelievers?

But those who struggle in Our cause,
surely We shall guide them in Our ways;
and God is with the good-doers.

Sūra 25:50–9

And it is He who has loosed the winds,
bearing good tidings before His mercy;
and We sent down from heaven pure water
so that We might revive a dead land,
and give to drink of it, of that We created,
cattle and men a many.

We have indeed turned it about amongst them, so
that they may remember;
yet most men refuse all but unbelief.

If We had willed, We would have raised up in
every city a warner.
So obey not the unbelievers, but struggle with
them thereby mightily.

And it is He who let forth the two seas,
this one sweet, grateful to taste,
and this salt, bitter to the tongue,

and He set between them a barrier, and a ban
forbidden.
And it is He who created of water a mortal,
and made him kindred of blood and marriage;
thy Lord is All-powerful.

And they serve, apart from God, what neither
profits them nor hurts them;
and the unbeliever is ever a partisan against his
Lord.
We have sent thee not, except good tidings to
bear, and warning.
Say: 'I do not ask of you a wage for this,
except for him who wishes to take to his Lord
a way.'

A collection of ḥadīth on jihād

Abū Sa'īd al-Khudrī said, It was said, O Messenger of Allah! Who is the most excellent of men? The Messenger of Allah, said, 'The believer who strives hard in the way of Allah with his person and his property.'

'Imrān ibn Ḥuṣayn said, The Messenger of Allah, said: 'A party of my community shall not cease fighting for the Truth – they shall be triumphant over their opponents.'

Abū Hurayra reported, the Messenger of Allah, said: 'Surely Allah will raise for this community at the beginning of every century one who shall revive for it its faith.'

Abū Hurayra said, The Messenger of Allah, said: 'How would you feel when the son of Mary makes his appearance among you, and he is your imām from among yourselves.'

Sahl reported, He heard the Messenger of Allah, say: '. . . Then invite them to Islam, and inform them of what is incumbent on them; for, by Allah, if a single man is guided aright through thee, it is better for thee than red camels.'

Ibn 'Abbās reported, the Messenger of Allah, wrote to the Caesar inviting him to Islam, and sent his letter to him with Diḥya al-Kalbī, and the Messenger of Allah, ordered him to make it over to the Chief of Buṣrā that he might send it to the Caesar.

Ibn 'Abbās reported, . . . and this (letter) ran as follows:

'In the name of Allah, the Beneficent, the Merciful. From Muḥammad, the servant of Allah and His Messenger, to Heraclius, the Chief of the Roman Empire. Peace be with him who follows the guidance. After this, I invite thee with invitation to Islam. Become a Muslim and thou wilt be in peace – Allah will give thee a double reward; but if thou turnest away, on thee will be the sin of thy subjects. And, O followers of the Book! Come to an equitable proposition between us and you that we shall not serve any but Allah, and that we shall not associate aught with Him, and that some of us shall not take others for lords besides Allah; but if they turn back, then say: Bear witness that we are Muslims.'

Salama said, I swore allegiance to the Prophet, then I turned to the shade of a tree. When the crowd diminished, he (the Prophet) said, 'O Ibn al-Akwa'! Will thou not swear allegiance?' He said; I said, I have already sworn allegiance, O Messenger of Allah!' He said, 'And do it again.' So I swore allegiance to him a second time. I (the reporter) said to him, O Abū Muslim! For what did you swear allegiance (to him) then? He said, For death.

'Abdallah b. Abī Aufā reported, The Messenger of Allah said: 'And know that paradise is beneath the protection of the swords.'

Abū Hurayra said, I heard the Prophet say: 'By Him in Whose hand is my soul, were it not that there are men among the believers who cannot bear to remain behind me – and I do not find that on which to carry them – I would not remain behind an army that fights in the way of Allah; and by Him in Whose hand is my soul, I love that I should be killed in the way of Allah then brought to life, then killed again then brought to life, then killed again then brought to life, then killed again then brought to life, then killed again.'

Abū Hurayra said, The Messenger of Allah, said: Whom do you count to be a martyr among you? They said, O Messenger of Allah! Whoever is killed in the way of Allah is a martyr. He said: 'In that case the martyrs of my community shall be very few – he who is killed in the way of Allah is a martyr; he who dies a natural death in the way of Allah is a martyr; he who dies of the plague (in the way of Allah) is a martyr; he who dies of cholera (in the way of Allah) is a martyr.'

Anas said, On the day that battle was fought at Uḥud, (some) people fled away from the Prophet, He said, And I saw 'Ā'isha, daughter of Abū Bakr and Umm Sulaym, and they had both tucked up their garments, so that I could see the anklets on their shanks, and they were carrying skins (full of water) on their backs, and they poured water into the mouths of the people; then they went back and filled them again, then came and poured them into the mouths of the people.

Experience 1

The Transcendence and Immanence of God: Sūra 24 and Sūra 50

These passages from Sūras 24 and 50 present two different experiences of God. In both passages, the Prophet likens God to the overpowering 'Light of the heavens and the earth' and the one who stretched forth the earth. Yet Allah is also like the lamp enclosed within the niche, and nearer to man than the jugular vein. Here, we see two classic descriptions of man's encounter with the divine, the numinous and totally other alongside the near and familiar. The mystical tradition within Islam has repeatedly seen in these passages the paradigm for the experience of God as both transcendent and immanent.

Sūra 24:35–44

God is the Light of the heavens and earth;
the likeness of His Light is a niche
wherein is a lamp
(the lamp in a glass,
the glass as it were a glittering star)
kindled from a Blessed Tree,
an olive that is neither of the East nor of the West,
Whose oil wellnigh would shine, even if no fire touched it;
Light upon light;
(God guides to His Light whom He will.)
(And God strikes similitudes for men,
and God has knowledge of everything.)
In temples God has allowed to be raised up,
and His Name to be commemorated therein;
therein glorifying Him, in the mornings and the evenings,
are men whom neither commerce nor trafficking diverts from the remembrance of God and to perform the prayer, and to pay the alms,
fearing a day when hearts and eyes shall be turned about,
that God may recompense them for their fairest works and give them increase of His bounty;
and God provides whomsoever He will, without reckoning.

And as for the unbelievers,
their works are as a mirage in a spacious plain
which the man athirst supposes to be water,
till, when he comes to it, he finds it is nothing;
there indeed he finds God,
and He pays him his account in full;
(and God is swift at the reckoning)
or they are as shadows upon a sea obscure
covered by a billow
above which is a billow
above which are clouds,
shadows piled one upon another;
when he puts forth his hand, wellnigh he cannot see it.
And to whomsoever God assigns no light,
no light has he.

Hast thou not seen how that whatsoever is in the heavens and in the earth extols God,
and the birds spreading their wings?
Each – He knows its prayer and its extolling;
and God knows the things they do.

To God belongs the Kingdom of the heavens and
the earth,
and to Him is the homecoming.
Hast thou not seen how God drives the clouds,
then composes them,
then converts them into a mass,
then thou seest the rain issuing out of the
midst of them?
And He sends down out of heaven mountains,
wherein is hail,
so that He smites whom He will with it, and
turns it aside from whom He will;
wellnight the gleam of His lightning snatches
away the sight.
God turns about the day and the night;
Surely in that is a lesson for those who have
eyes.
God has created every beast of water,
and some of them go upon their bellies,
and some of them go upon two feet,
and some of them go upon four;
God creates whatever He will;
God is powerful over everything.

Sūra 50:1–15

Nay, but they marvel that a warner has come to
them from among them; and the
unbelievers say,
'This is a marvellous thing!
What, when we are dead and become dust? That
is a far returning!'
We know what the earth diminishes of them;
with Us is a book recording.
Nay, but they cried lies to the truth when it came
to them,
and so they are in a case confused.
What, have they not beheld the heaven above
them,
how We have built it, and decked it out fair,
and it has no cracks?
And the earth – We stretched it forth, and cast on
it firm mountains,
and We caused to grow therein of every
joyous kind for an insight and a reminder to
every penitent servant.
And We sent down out of heaven water blessed,
and caused to grow thereby gardens and grain
of harvest
and tall palm-trees with spathes compact,
a provision for the servants,
and thereby We revived a land that was dead.
Even so is the coming forth.
Cried lies before them the people of Noah and
the men of Er-Rass, and Thamood, and Ad
and Pharaoh, the brothers of Lot, the men
of the Thicket, the people of Tubba',
Every one cried lies to the Messengers,
and My threat came true.
What, were We wearied by the first creation?
No indeed; but they are in uncertainty as to the
new creation.
We indeed created man; and We know what his
soul whispers within him,
and We are nearer to him than the jugular vein.

Experience 2

Certainty: Sūra 9

Here, the Prophet articulates the certainty that arises from the numinous experience of Sūra 24. The Prophet again uses the imagery of light for the experience of his absolute certitude that God shelters him, guides him and supplies all of his needs.

Sūra 9:1–10

By the white forenoon
and the brooding night!
Thy Lord has neither forsaken thee nor hates
thee and the Last shall be better for thee
than the First.
Thy Lord shall give thee, and thou shalt be
satisfied.

Did He not find thee an orphan, and shelter thee?
Did He not find thee erring, and guide thee?
Did He not find thee needy, and suffice thee?

As for the orphan, do not oppress him,
and as for the beggar, scold him not;
and as for thy Lord's blessing, declare it.

Experience 3

The Night Journey: Sūra 17

At the very beginning of Sūra 17, Muḥammad makes reference to God having carried him 'from the Holy Mosque to the Further Mosque'. This ascension experience is greatly elaborated upon in the *ḥadīth*, and is related to Muḥammad's reception of the Qur'ān. The 'Further Mosque' is understood as the Temple Mount in Jerusalem.

Sūra 17:1–10

Glory be to Him, who carried His servant by
night
from the Holy Mosque to the Further Mosque
the precincts of which We have blessed,
that We might show him some of Our signs.
He is the All-hearing, the All-seeing.

And We gave Moses the Book, and made it a
guidance to the Children of Israel:
'Take not unto yourselves any guardian apart
from Me.'
The seed of those We bore with Noah; he was a
thankful servant.
And We decreed for the Children of Israel in the
Book:
'You shall do corruption in the earth twice,
and you shall ascend exceeding high.'
So, when the promise of the first of these came to
pass,
We sent against you servants of Ours, men of
great might,
and they went through the habitations,
and it was a promise performed.
Then We gave back to you the turn to prevail
over them,
and We succoured you with wealth and
children,
and We made you a greater host.
'If you do good, it is your own souls you do
good to, and if you do evil it is to them
likewise.'
Then, when the promise of the second came to
pass,
We sent against you Our servants to
discountenance you,
and to enter the Temple, as they entered it the
first time,
and to destroy utterly that which they
ascended to.
Perchance your Lord will have mercy upon you;
but if you return, We shall return;
and We have made Gehenna a prison for the
unbelievers.

Surely this Qur'ān guides to the way that is
straightest

and gives good tidings to the believers who
do deeds of righteousness,
that theirs shall be a great wage,

and that those who do not believe in the world
to come – we have prepared for them a
painful chastisement.

Experience 4

The Night Journey: Ḥadīth

This collection of *ḥadīth*, from al-Baghawī's *Maṣābīḥ al-Sunna*, elaborates with great detail upon the Prophet's ascension alluded to in Sūra 17. Here, the Prophet encounters all these important figures of the past, so that his ascension is a passage through the sacred narrative of Islam.

[It is related] from Qatāda, quoting from Anas b. Mālik – with whom may Allah be pleased – from Mālik b. Ṣa'ṣa'a, who said that the Prophet of Allah – on whom be Allah's blessing and peace – related to them [the story of] the night on which he was taken on his heavenly journey, saying: While I was in al-Ḥaṭīm – or maybe he said, While I was in al-Ḥijr – lying at rest, one came to me, split all between here and here – i.e., from the hollow of his throat to his pubic hair – and drew out my heart. Then there was brought a golden basin filled with faith in which he washed my heart and my bowels and then they were returned [to their place]. According to another line of transmission [the Prophet] said: Then he washed my stomach with water of Zamzam,[1] and filled it with faith and wisdom. Then a white riding beast was brought, somewhat smaller than a mule yet bigger than an ass, whose every bound carried him as far as his eye could reach. Him I mounted and Gabriel set off with me till we came to the lowest heaven, which he asked should be opened. 'Who is this?' he was asked. 'Gabriel,' he replied. 'And who is that with you?' 'Muḥammad,' said he. 'And has he had revelation sent him?' 'Assuredly,' said he. 'Then welcome to him. How blessed a coming.' Thereat [the gate] was opened, and when I had cleared it, lo! there was Adam. [Gabriel] said: 'This is your father Adam, greet him.' So I gave him greeting, which he returned, saying, 'Welcome to you, O righteous son, righteous prophet.' Then Gabriel mounted up with me till we came to the second heaven, which he asked should be opened. 'Who is this?' he was asked. 'Gabriel,' he replied. 'And who is that with you?' 'Muhammad,' said he. 'And has he had revelation sent him?' 'Assuredly,' said he. 'Then welcome to him. How blessed a coming.' Thereat [the gate] was opened, and when I had cleared it, lo! there were John [the Baptist] and Jesus, who were cousins on their mothers' side. Said [Gabriel]: 'These are John and Jesus, give them greeting.' So I greeted them and they returned it, saying: 'Welcome to the righteous brother, the righteous prophet.' Then he ascended with me to the third heaven, which he asked should be opened. 'Who is this?' he was asked. 'Gabriel,' he replied. 'And who is that with you?' 'Muḥammad,' said he. 'And has he had revelation sent him?' 'Assuredly,' said he. 'Then welcome to him. How blessed a coming.' Thereat [the gate] was opened, and when I had cleared it, lo! there was Joseph. [Gabriel] said: 'This is Joseph, greet him.' So I gave him greeting, which he returned, saying: 'Welcome to the righteous brother, the righteous prophet.' Then he ascended with me till we came to the

[1] The sacred well in the precincts of the shrine at Mecca.

fourth heaven, which he asked should be opened. 'Who is this?' he was asked. 'Gabriel,' he replied. 'And who is that with you?' 'Muhammad,' said he. 'And has he had revelation sent him?' 'Assuredly,' said he. 'Then welcome to him. How blessed a coming.' Thereat [the gate] was opened, and when I had cleared it, lo! there was Idrīs [Enoch]. Said [Gabriel]: 'This is Idrīs, give him greeting.' So I greeted him, and he returned it, saying: 'Welcome to the righteous brother, the righteous prophet.' Then he ascended with me to the fifth heaven, which he asked should be opened. 'Who is this?' he was asked. 'Gabriel,' he replied. 'And who is that with you?' 'Muḥammad,' said he. 'And has he had revelation sent him?' 'Assuredly,' said he. 'Then welcome to him. How blessed a coming.' When I had cleared [the gate], lo! there was Aaron. Said [Gabriel]: 'This is Aaron, give him greeting.' So I greeted him, and he returned it, saying: 'Welcome to the righteous brother, the righteous prophet.' Then he ascended with me to the sixth heaven, which he asked should be opened. 'Who is this?' he was asked. 'Gabriel,' he replied. 'And who is that with you?' 'Muḥammad,' said he. 'And has he had revelation sent him?' 'Assuredly,' said he. 'Then welcome to him. How blessed a coming.' When I had cleared [the gate], lo! there was Moses. Said [Gabriel]: 'This is Moses, give him greeting.' So I greeted him, and he returned it, saying: 'Welcome to the righteous brother, the righteous prophet.' When I passed on he wept, and one asked him why he wept. 'I weep,' said he, 'because of a youth who has been sent [as an Apostle] after me, more of whose community will enter Paradise than of my community.' Then [Gabriel] ascended with me to the seventh heaven, which he asked should be opened. 'Who is this?' he was asked. 'Gabriel,' he replied. 'And who is that with you?' 'Muḥammad,' said he. 'And has he had revelation sent him?' 'Assuredly,' said he. 'Then welcome to him. How blessed a coming.' When I had cleared [the gate], lo! there was Abraham. Said [Gabriel]: 'This is your father Abraham, so greet him.' I gave him greeting, which he returned, saying: 'Welcome to the righteous son, the righteous prophet.'

Then I ascended to the Sidrat al-Muntahā, whose fruits were the size of Hajar waterpots and its leaves like elephants' ears. Said [Gabriel]: 'This is the Sidrat al-Muntahā.' There I beheld four streams, two within and two without, so I asked: 'What are these, O Gabriel?' 'The two within,' he answered, 'are the two rivers of Paradise, but the two without are the Nile and the Euphrates.' Then I was taken up to the Frequented Fane, where a vessel of wine, a vessel of milk, and a vessel of honey were brought to me. I took the milk, whereat he said: 'This is the *fiṭra*[2] of you and your community.' Then there was laid on me the religious duty of performing fifty prayer services daily, and I departed. As I passed by Moses he asked: 'With what have you been commanded?' 'With fifty prayer services each day,' I replied. 'But your community,' said he, 'will never be able to perform fifty prayers a day. By Allah, I have had experience with people before you, and I had to strive hard with the Children of Israel. Return to your Lord and ask Him to lighten it for your community.' So I went back and He remitted ten. Then I returned to Moses, but he said the like [of what he had said before], so I went back and He remitted ten more. When, however, I got back to Moses he said the like again, so I returned and He remitted another ten. When I returned to Moses he again said the like, so I went back and was commanded ten prayer services each day and night. When I got back to Moses he said as he had said before, so I went back and was bidden perform five prayer services daily. When I got back to Moses, he said: 'And with what are you commanded now?' 'I am bidden,' I replied, 'to perform five prayer services day and night.' 'Your community,' said he, 'will never be able to perform five prayer services daily. I have had experience with people before you, and have have to strive hard with the Children of Israel. Go back to your Lord and ask Him to lighten it for your community.' 'I have been asking of my Lord,' I replied, 'till I am ashamed. I am content and I submit.' Then as I passed on a Crier cried: 'I have settled My ordinance, and have made things easy for My servants.'

Thābit has related on the authority of Anas – with whom may Allah be pleased – quoting the Prophet – on whom be Allah's blessing and peace – who said: Burāq was brought to me. He was a riding beast, white and standing higher than an ass but not so high as a mule, who at each bound placed his hoof at a point as far as his eye could see.

[2] A natural or inborn disposition.

On him I rode till I came to the Bait al-Maqdis,[3] where I tied him to the ring at which the Prophets used to tie him. Then I entered the shrine and prayed a prayer of two *rak'as*. As I went out Gabriel came to me with a vessel of wine and a vessel of milk. I took the milk, whereat Gabriel said: 'You have chosen the *fiṭra*.' Then we ascended up to the heavens. In the third heaven I saw Joseph, to whom had been given one half of all beauty, and he welcomed me and wished me every good thing. In the seventh heaven I saw Abraham with his back propped against the Frequented Fane which every day is entered by seventy thousand angels who never return to it. Then I was taken to the Sidrat al Muntahā, whose leaves are like elephants' ears and its fruits like waterpots, and which is changed when by Allah's command there covers it what covers it, and whose beauty none of Allah's creatures is capable of describing. There Allah revealed to me what He revealed, laying on me the religious duty of performing fifty prayer services each day and night. Then I went down to Moses. Said he [i.e., Muḥammad]: I ceased not going to and fro between Moses and my Lord, till finally He said: 'O Muḥammad, it shall be five prayers each day and night, but each prayer service I will count as ten, so that will make it fifty prayer services. The fact is that when a man intends a good deed but does not perform it I write it to his account as a good deed, but if he performs it I write it as ten good deeds. Also when a man intends an evil deed but does not perform it I write to his account nothing, but if he performs it I write it as one evil deed in his account.'

[It is related] from Ibn Shihāb, relating from Anas – with whom may Allah be pleased – who records that Abū Dharr used to relate that the Apostle of Allah – upon whom be Allah's blessing and peace – said: 'When I was in Mecca [one night] the roof was split asunder above me and Gabriel descended. He slit open my breast which he washed out with Zamzam water. Then he brought a golden basin filled with wisdom and faith which he emptied into my breast and then closed it up. Then, taking me by the hand, he mounted up with me to the heavens. When we came to the lowest heaven Gabriel said to the chamberlain of that heaven: "Open!" When he had opened we went up into the lowest heaven and there was a man sitting with a lot of black specks to his right and a similar lot of black specks to his left. Whenever he looked to his right he laughed, but whenever he looked to his left he wept. He said [to men]: "Welcome to the righteous son, the righteous prophet." I asked Gabriel who this was, and he answered, "This is Adam, and those black specks to his right and his left are the souls of his progeny. Those to the right of him will go to Paradise and those on his left to Hell. So when he looks to his right he laughs and when he looks to his left he weeps."'

Said Ibn Shihāb – with whom may Allah be pleased: Ibn Ḥazm has informed me that Ibn 'Abbās and Abū Ḥayya the Anṣārī used to tell how the Apostle of Allah – on whom be Allah's blessing and peace – said: 'Then he ascended with me till I came forth at a level place where I could hear the scratching of the pens.' Ibn Ḥazm and Anas have reported that the Prophet – upon whom be Allah's blessing and peace – said: Then Allah laid as a religious duty on my community the performance of fifty prayer services. I made my way back till I passed Moses, who kept me going to and fro to get them reduced till finally I went back to Him and He said: 'They are five, but they are fifty, for with Me no sentence changes.' I returned to Moses, who said: 'Go back to your Lord,' but I replied: 'I am ashamed before my Lord.' Then I was taken off to the Sidrat al-Muntahā, which was covered with such colours as I know not [how to describe], and I was let in to Paradise where there were pomegranate blossoms of pearl and whose soil was of musk.

[It is related] that 'Abdallāh [b. Mas'ūd] said that when the Apostle of Allah – upon whom be Allah's blessing and peace – was taken by night he was brought finally to the Sidrat al-Muntahā, which is in the seventh heaven, and is the farthest limit to be reached by anything that ascends from earth, for it catches such, and also the limit reached by anything that falls from above, for that also it catches. He said that the verse 'when there covered the sidra tree what covered it' (Sūra 53:16) means golden moths. He also said that it was there that the Apostle of Allah – upon whom be Allah's blessing and peace – was given three things, viz., the five daily prayers, the concluding verses of Sūra 2, and pardon for anyone of his community who refrains from giving Allah a partner.

[3] The Temple at Jerusalem.

Abū Hurayra has related that the Prophet – upon whom be Allah's blessing and peace – said: You saw me in al-Ḥijr where the Quraysh were asking me about my night journey, questioning me about things at the Jerusalem temple which I could not tell for certain, so that I was distressed as I had never been before, when Allah – exalted be He – raised it up [before my eyes] so that I could look at it, and they could no longer ask me anything but I could inform them about it. Also you saw me in a group of Prophets, and there was Moses standing praying. There also was a man, thin and curly-haired as though he were one of the men of Shanū'a. This was Jesus who was standing praying, and the one who most resembles him is 'Urwa b. Mas'ūd al-Thaqafī. There also was Abraham standing praying, and the one who resembles him most is your companion – meaning himself. Then the time for prayers came and I acted as Imām for them. When we had finished prayers a voice said to me: 'O Muḥammad, this is Mālik, the Chamberlain of Hell, so greet him.' I turned to him and he offered me greeting.

Experience 5

The Prophet is Taken into the Presence of God: Ḥadīth

Here, in this *ḥadīth* from al-Suyūṭī's *al-La'ālī al-maṣnū'a*, the Prophet is taken into the presence of Allah by Gabriel. This narrative forms a part of the extensive traditions arising from Sūra 17:1–10 and underscores the closeness of the Prophet to God. He is drawn into a relationship with God equal to that of the prophets of the past.

Now when I was brought on my Night Journey to the [place of the] Throne and drew near to it, a green *rafraf* [1] was let down to me, a thing too beautiful for me to describe to you, whereat Gabriel advanced and seated me on it. Then he had to withdraw from me, placing his hands over his eyes, fearing lest his sight be destroyed by the scintillating light of the Throne, and he began to weep aloud, uttering *tasbīḥ*, *taḥmīd* and *tathniya*[2] to Allah. By Allah's leave, as a sign of His mercy toward me and the perfection of His favour to me, that *rafraf* floated me into the [presence of the] Lord of the Throne, a thing too stupendous for the tongue to tell of or the imagination to picture. My sight was so dazzled by it that I feared blindness. Therefore I shut my eyes, which was by Allah's good favour. When I thus veiled my sight Allah shifted my sight [from my eyes] to my heart, so with my heart I began to look at what I had been looking at with my eyes. It was a light so bright in its scintillation that I despair of ever describing to you what I saw of His majesty. Then I besought my Lord to complete His favour to me by granting me the boon of having a steadfast vision of Him with my heart. This my Lord did, giving me that favour, so I gazed at Him with my heart till it was steady and I had a steady vision of Him.

There He was, when the veil had been lifted from Him, seated on His Throne, in His dignity, His might, His glory, His exaltedness, but beyond that it is not permitted me to describe Him to you. Glory be to Him! How majestic is He! How bountiful are His works! How exalted is His position! How brilliant is His light! Then He lowered somewhat for me His dignity and drew me near to Him, which is as He has said in His book, informing you of how He would deal with me and honour me: 'One possessed of strength. He stood erect when He was at the highest point of the horizon. Then He drew near and descended, so that He was two bows' lengths off,

[1] A narrow piece of silk brocade.

[2] *Tasbīḥ*, *taḥmīd* and *tathniya* are forms of praising Allah.

or even nearer' (Sūra 53:6–9). This means that when He inclined to me He drew me as near to Him as the distance between the two ends of a bow, nay, rather, nearer than the distance between the crotch of the bow and its curved ends. 'Then He revealed to His servant what he revealed' (Sūra 5:10), i.e., what matters He had decided to enjoin upon me. 'His heart did not falsify what it saw' (Sūra 5:11), i.e., my vision of Him with my heart. 'Indeed he was seeing one of the greatest signs of his Lord' (Sūra 5:181).

Now when He – glory be to Him – lowered His dignity for me He placed one of His hands between my shoulders and I felt the coldness of His fingertips for a while on my heart, whereat I experienced such a sweetness, so pleasant a perfume, so delightful a coolness, such a sense of honour in [being granted this] vision of Him, that all my terrors melted away and my fears departed from me, so my heart became tranquil. Then was I filled with joy, my eyes were refreshed, and such delight and happiness took hold of me that I began to bend and sway to right and left like one overtaken by slumber. Indeed, it seemed to me as though everyone in heaven and earth had died, for I heard no voices of angels, nor during the vision of my Lord did I see any dark bodies. My Lord left me there such time as He willed, then brought me back to my senses, and it was as though I had been asleep and had awakened. My mind returned to me and I was tranquil, realizing where I was and how I was enjoying surpassing favour and being shown manifest preference.

Then my Lord, glorified and praised be He, spoke to me, saying: 'O Muḥammad, do you know about what the Highest Council is disputing?' I answered: 'O Lord, Thou knowest best about that, as about all things, for Thou art the One who knows the unseen.' 'They are disputing,' he said, 'about the degrees and the excellences. Do you know, O Muḥammad, what the degrees and the excellences are?' 'Thou, O Lord,' I answered, 'knowest better and art more wise.' Then He said: 'The degrees are concerned with performing one's ablutions at times when that is disagreeable, walking on foot to religious assemblies, watching expectantly for the next hour of prayer when one time of prayer is over. As for the excellences, they consist of feeding the hungry, spreading peace, and performing the *Tahajjud* prayer at night when other folk are sleeping.' Never have I heard anything sweeter or more pleasant than the melodious sound of His voice.

Such was the sweetness of His melodious voice that it gave me confidence, and so I spoke to Him of my need. I said: 'O Lord, Thou didst take Abraham as a friend, Thou didst speak with Moses face to face, Thou didst raise Enoch to a high place, Thou didst give Solomon a kingdom such as none after him might attain, and didst give to David the Psalter. What then is there for me, O Lord?' He replied: 'O Muḥammad, I take you as a friend just as I took Abraham as a friend. I am speaking to you just as I spoke face to face with Moses. I am giving you the *Fātiḥa* (Sūra 1) and the closing verses of *al-Baqara* (Sūra 2:284–6), both of which are from the treasuries of My Throne and which I have given to no prophet before you. I am sending you as a prophet to the white folk of the earth and the black folk and the red folk, to jinn and to men thereon, though never before you have I sent a prophet to the whole of them. I am appointing the earth, its dry land and its sea, for you and for your community as a place for purification and for worship. I am giving your community the right to booty which I have given as provision to no community before them. I shall aid you with such terrors as will make your enemies flee before you while you are still a month's journey away. I shall send down to you the Master of all Books and the guardian of them, a Qur'ān which We Ourselves have parcelled out. I shall exalt your name for you, even to the extent of conjoining it with My name, so that none of the regulations of My religion will ever be mentioned without you being mentioned along with me.'

Then after this He communicated to me matters which I am not permitted to tell you, and when He had made His covenant with me and had left me there such time as He willed, He took His seat again upon His Throne. Glory be to Him in His majesty, His dignity, His might. Then I looked, and behold, something passed between us and a veil of light was drawn in front of Him, blazing ardently to a distance that none knows save Allah, and so intense that were it to be rent at any point it would burn up all Allah's creation, Then the green *rafraf* on which I was descended with me, gently rising and falling with me in 'Illiyūn . . . till it brought me back to Gabriel, who took me from it. Then the *rafraf* mounted up till it disappeared from my sight.

Ethics 1

A Code of Personal Behaviour: Sūra 17

In Sūra 17 the Qur'ān presents a single code intended to structure human behaviour. This code, in both injunction and prohibition, summarizes or reviews all the major concerns in the ethical dimension of Islam's sacred writings. It bears a close resemblance to the Decalogue of the Hebrew Bible, beginning with a prohibition against idolatry and then moving to the proper care and honour of parents, the prohibition of infanticide and the prohibition of murder outside legitimate vengeance, the prohibition of adultery, and enjoins integrity in matters concerning property and trade and the rights of orphans. These positive and negative commands are interspersed with directives about attitudes and character, especially kindliness, integrity and humility.

Sūra 17:22–39

Set not up with God another god, or thou wilt sit condemned and forsaken.

Thy Lord has decreed you shall not serve any but Him, and to be good to parents, whether one or both of them attains old age with thee; say not to them 'Fie' neither chide them, but speak unto them words respectful, and lower to them the wing of humbleness out of mercy and say, 'My Lord, have mercy upon them as they raised me up when I was little.'

Your Lord knows very well what is in your hearts if you are righteous, for He is All-forgiving to those who are penitent.

And give the kinsman his right, and the needy, and the traveller; and never squander; the squanderers are brothers of Satan, and Satan is unthankful to his Lord. But if thou turnest from them, seeking mercy from thy Lord that thou hopest for, then speak unto them gentle words.

And keep not thy hand chained to thy neck, nor outspread it widespread altogether, or thou wilt sit reproached and denuded.

Surely thy Lord outspreads and straitens His provision unto whom He will; surely He is aware of and sees His servants.

And slay not your children for fear of poverty; We will provide for you and them; surely the slaying of them is a grievous sin.

And approach not fornication; surely it is an indecency, and evil as a way.

And slay not the soul God has forbidden, We have appointed to his next-of-kin authority; but let him not exceed in slaying; he shall be helped.

And do not approach the property of the orphan save in the fairest manner, until he is of age.

And fulfil the covenant; surely the covenant shall be questioned of.

And fill up the measure when you measure, and weigh with the straight balance; that is better and fairer in the issue.

And pursue not that thou hast no knowledge of; the hearing, the sight, the heart – all of those shall be questioned of.

And walk not in the earth exultantly; certainly thou wilt never tear the earth open, nor attain the mountains in height.

All of that – the wickedness of it is hateful in the sight of thy Lord.

Ethics 2

True Piety: Sūra 70 and Sūra 25

The Qur'ān acknowledges the frailty of the human condition in Sūra 70 which describes man as being created 'fretful'; when evil strikes, man is impatient, and when he is touched by the good he grudges. The remedy for this fretfulness is simply piety in attending to prayer, to one's obligations to the needy, and to the Day of Judgment. In Sūra 25 this simple and true piety is extended: one should go in life humbly and address others with '*Salām*', 'Peace'. This text reiterates other ethical themes such as the power of repentance to affect God.

Sūra 70:19–35

Surely man was created fretful,
when evil visits him, impatient,
when good visits him, grudging,
save those that pray and continue at their prayers,
those in whose wealth is a right known for the beggar and the outcast,
who confirm the Day of Doom
and go in fear of the chastisement of their Lord
(from their Lord's chastisement none feels secure)
and guard their private parts save from their wives and what their right hands own,
then not being blameworthy
(but whoso seeks after more than that,
they are the transgressors),
and who preserve their trusts and their covenant,
and perform their witnessings,
and who observe their prayers.
Those shall be in Gardens, high-honoured.

What ails the unbelievers, running with outstretched necks towards thee on the right hand and on the left hand in knots?
What, is every man of them eager to be admitted to a Garden of Bliss?

Sūra 25:64–76

The servants of the All-merciful are those who walk in the earth modestly and who, when the ignorant address them, say, 'Peace'; who pass the night prostrate to their Lord and standing; who say, 'Our Lord, turn Thou from us the chastisement of Gehenna; surely its chastisement is torment most terrible; evil it is as a lodging-place and an abode; who, when they expend, are neither prodigal nor parsimonious, but between that is a just stand; who call not upon another god with God, nor slay the soul God has forbidden except by right, neither fornicate, for whosoever does that shall meet the price of sin – doubled shall be the chastisement for him on the Resurrection Day, and he shall dwell therein humbled, save him who repents, and believes, and does righteous work – those, God will change their evil deeds into good deeds, for God is ever All-forgiving, All-compassionate; and whosoever repents, and does righteousness, he truly turns to God in repentance.

And those who bear not false witness and, when they pass by idle talk, pass by with dignity; who, when they are reminded of the signs of their Lord, fall not down thereat deaf and blind; who say, 'Our Lord, give us refreshment of our wives and seed, and make us a model to the godfearing.' Those shall be recompensed with the highest heaven, for that they endured patiently, and they shall receive therein a greeting and – 'Peace!' Therein they shall dwell forever; fair it is as a lodging-place and an abode.

Say: 'My Lord esteems you not at all were it not for your prayer, for you have cried lies, and it shall surely be fastened.'

Ethics 3

Muḥammad as the Moral Ideal: Ḥadīth

The character of Muḥammad himself is understood as the moral ideal for Muslims. Certainly, the Prophet fully embodied the ethical concerns of the Qur'ān itself and his character is to be emulated by all believers. In this selection from Abū Muḥammad al-Husayn's *Mishkāt al-Maṣābīh*, a late-medieval collection of *ḥadīth*, we see how the Prophet's natural disposition becomes the paradigm for the ethical life.

Anas said: I served the Prophet for ten years and he never said to me, 'Shame!' or 'Why did you do such and such?' or 'Why did you not do such and such?'

He said: God's messenger was one of the best men in character. One day he sent me to do something, and I said, 'I swear by God that I will not go.' But in my heart I felt I should go to do what God's messenger had commanded me, so I went out and came upon some boys who were playing in the street. All of a sudden God's messenger who had come up behind caught me by the back of the neck, and when I looked at him he was laughing. He said, 'Did you go where I ordered you, little Anas?' and I replied, 'Yes, I am on my way, messenger of God.'

He said: When I was walking with God's messenger who was wearing a Najrānī cloak with a coarse fringe, a nomadic Arab caught up on him, and gave his cloak a violent tug, pulling God's Prophet back against his chest, and I saw that the side of God's messenger's shoulder was marked by the fringe of the cloak because of the violence of the man's tug. He said, 'Command that I be given some of God's property which you have, Muḥammad,' and God's messenger turned round to him and laughed, then ordered that he be given something.

He said: God's messenger was the best of men, the most generous of men, the bravest of men. One night when the people of Medina were startled and went in the direction of the sound they were met by the Prophet who had gone in the direction of the sound before them, and he was saying, 'You have nothing to fear, you have nothing to fear.' He was on a barebacked horse with no saddle belonging to Abū Ṭalḥa and had a sword slung on his neck. He said, 'I found it could run like a great river.'

Jābir said that when God's messenger was asked anything he never said, 'No.'

Anas told that when a man had asked the Prophet for enough sheep to fill the valley between two mountains and had been given them he went to his people and said, 'Accept Islam, my people, for I swear by God that Muḥammad gives gifts to such an extent that there is no fear of poverty.'

Jubayr b. Mut'im told that while he was travelling along with God's messenger returning from Ḥunayn the nomadic Arabs persisted in making requests of him till they forced him up against an acacia tree and his cloak was snatched away. The Prophet stopped and said, 'Give me my cloak. If I had as many camels and sheep as these thorny trees I would divide them among you, then you would not find me niggardly, or untruthful, or cowardly.'

Anas told that when God's messenger prayed the dawn prayer the servants in Medina brought their vessels containing water and they would not bring a vessel into which he did not dip his hand. They would often bring them on a cold morning and he would dip his hand into them.

He told that one of the maidservants belonging to the people of Medina would hold God's messenger by the hand and take him where she wished.

He told that a woman whose mind was affected said, 'Messenger of God, I want something from you.' He replied, 'Mother of so and so, consider which of the streets you wish so that I may accomplish what you want.' He then went alone with her into a road till she got all she wanted.

He said that God's messenger was not unseemly in his language, or given to cursing or reviling. All he said when reproaching someone was, 'What is the matter with him? May his forehead cleave to the dust!'

Abū Hurayra told that when God's messenger was asked to invoke a curse on the polytheists he replied, 'I was not sent as one given to cursing; I was sent only as a mercy.'

Abū Sa'īd al-Khudrī said: The Prophet was more modest than a virgin in her apartment, and when he saw anything of which he disapproved we could recognize the fact in his face.

'Ā'isha said she never saw the Prophet laughing so immoderately that she could see his uvula, for he used only to smile.

She said: God's messenger did not go on talking rapidly as you do, but would talk in such a way that anyone who wished to count his words would be able to do so.

Al-Aswad told that he asked 'Ā'isha what the Prophet used to do in his house, and she replied that he used to engage in the *mihna*, i.e., the service, of his family, and when the time for prayer came he went out to prayer.

'Ā'isha said God's messenger was never given his choice between two things without taking the lesser of them provided it involved no sin, for if it did, no one kept further away from it than he. And God's messenger never took revenge on his own behalf for anything unless something God had forbidden had been transgressed, in which event he took revenge for it for God's sake.

She said God's messenger never struck anyone with his hand, neither a woman nor a servant, unless he was striving in God's path; and nothing was ever done to him for which he took revenge on the perpetrator unless things God had forbidden were transgressed, in which event he took revenge for God's sake.

Anas said: I served God's messenger for ten years from the time I was eight years old and he never blamed me for anything which was destroyed at my hand. If any member of his family blamed me he said, 'Leave him alone, for if anything were decreed it would happen.'

'Ā'isha said God's messenger was not unseemly or lewd in his language, nor was he loud-voiced in the streets, nor did he return evil for evil, but he would forgive and pardon.

Anas used to tell of the Prophet that he would visit the sick, attend funerals, accept a slave's invitation, and ride on a donkey. He said he had seen him on a donkey at the battle for Khaybar using a rein of palm-fibres.

'Ā'isha said: God's messenger used to patch his sandals, sew his garment and conduct himself at home as anyone of you does in his house. He was a human being, searching his garment for lice, milking his sheep, and doing his own chores.

Khārija b. Zayd b. Thābit told that some people visited Zayd b. Thābit and asked him to tell them some stories about God's messenger. He replied: I was his neighbour, and when the inspiration descended on him he sent for me and I went to him and wrote it down for him. When we talked about this world he did so along with us, when we talked about the next world he did so along with us, and when we talked about food he did so along with us. All this I tell you about God's messenger.

Anas told that when God's messenger shook hands with a man he did not withdraw his hand till the other did so, he did not turn his face away till the other did so, and he was not seen to put forward his knees in front of one with whom he was sitting. Tiurmidhī transmitted it.

He said that God's messenger did not store up anything for the next day.

Jābir b. Samura said God's messenger was far from talkative.

Jābir said God's messenger spoke in a distinct and leisurely manner.

'Ā'isha said: God's messenger did not go on talking rapidly as you do, but spaced out his words so that those who sat with him could remember them.

'Abdallāh b. al-Hārith b. Jaz' said he had seen no one more given to smiling than God's messenger.

'Abdallāh b. Salām said that when God's messenger sat talking he would often raise his eyes to the sky.

'Amr b. Sa'īd quoted Anas as saying: I never saw anyone more kindly towards children than God's messenger. His son Ibrāhīm was being suckled in the 'Awālī of Medina, and he would go accompanied by us and enter the house which was full of smoke, the boy's foster-father being a blacksmith. He would take him and kiss him, and then go back. 'Amr told that when Ibrāhīm died God's messenger said, 'Ibrāhīm is my son who has died while being suckled, but he has two foster-mothers who will complete his suckling in paradise.

'Abdallāh b. Abī Aufā said: God's messenger

was often given to making mention of God, seldom given to idle talk, he would pray at length, deliver short sermons, not disdain to walk with a widow or a humble person, and he would accomplish for him what he needed.

'Alī told that Abū Jahl said to the Prophet, 'We do not call you a liar, but we say that what you have brought is false.' God most high then sent down concerning them, 'They do not call you a liar, but the evildoers deny God's signs.'

'Ā'isha reported God's messenger as saying, 'If I wished, 'Ā'isha, mountains of gold would go with me. An angel whose waist was as high as the Ka'ba came to me and told me that my Lord sent me a greeting and said that if I wished I could be a prophet and a servant, or if I wished I could be a prophet and a king. I looked at Gabriel and he gave me a sign to humble myself. (In the version by Ibn 'Abbās it says that God's messenger turned to Gabriel as one asking his advice and Gabriel made a gesture with his hand indicating that he should be humble.) I then said that I would be a prophet and a servant.' 'Ā'isha said that after that God's messenger did not eat reclining, saying he would eat like a slave and sit like a slave.

Postscript

After the Prophet's death and the battle of Yamāma (633 CE), in which a great number of those who had mastered the oral and written tradition of the Qur'ān from the Prophet were killed, there was an immediate need to collect these traditions and produce an authoritative text. This task fell to Zayd ibn Thābit, one of the companions of the Prophet, and he began to collect versions of the Qur'ān amongst the other followers of Muḥammad. These versions were temporarily given for safe-keeping to the daughter of the Caliph 'Umar, and were ultimately compiled during the reign of the Caliph 'Uthmān (644–56). This compilation is the canonical version of the Qur'ān, and is often referred to by scholars as the 'Uthmānic recension. Technically, orthodox Muslims understand that a translation of the Qur'ān is impossible. Allah gave an Arabic Qur'ān to his messenger. Arabic is the most perfect of languages and the Arabic of the Qur'ān is the most perfect of all written Arabic. That which is expressed in the Qur'ān cannot be expressed in any other way or language except in the Arabic. Translations produced under Muslim supervision, for example the Urdu and English translations, are not technically translations, and are consistently referred to as paraphrases. Despite this internal understanding of the untranslatable quality of the Qur'ān, a number of important translations are available for the general reader.

Bibliography

Edward R. Palmer completed an English translation of the Qur'ān as volumes 6 and 9 of F. Max Müller's *Sacred Books of the East* (1880). Many European translations have sought to rearrange the sūras of the Qur'ān according to their chronological order instead of the traditional order of the 'Uthmānic recension. This style of translation is illustrated by Richard Bell, *The Qur'ān, Translated, with a Critical Rearrangement of the Surahs* (1933–9), in two volumes. M.M. Pickthall, *The Meaning of the Glorious Koran: An Explanatory Translation* (1930–1, reprinted 1953), presents the modern orthodox interpretation of the Qur'ān by an English convert to Islam. A.J. Arberry, *The Koran Interpreted* (1955) is perhaps the best English translation, attempting to maintain the poetic and artistic qualities of the original text.

An 18th-century illuminated manuscript of the Bhagavad-Gītā. *Here, Rāma, one of the ten avatars or incarnations of Viṣṇu, accompanied by his brother Lakṣmaṇa, confronts the many-headed demon king of Lanka, who had abducted his wife.*

Hinduism

Introduction

The religious tradition of Hinduism is exceedingly lengthy, extending as far back as the beginning of the Indus River civilizations of Mohenjo Daro and Harappā in the 3rd millennium BCE. Certainly, the coming of the Aryans, those pastoral nomads of the Indo-European tribes, altered the indigenous life and religion of the proto-historical peoples of India. But, more importantly, the Aryans provided the cultural spark that nourished the entire history of Hinduism. Historians, philologists, anthropologists and sociologists may point to many transformations and radical departures in this history of almost five thousand years, but for the Hindu, religious history is a matter of continuity. This continuity is in great part the result of specific ideas about authoritative sacred texts.

At the heart of Hinduism, and also from its earliest historical strata, are the Vedas, extensive collections of Aryan hymns. The word Veda comes from the Sanskrit verb *vid*, 'to know', and means 'knowledge' or 'body of knowledge'. There are traditionally four Vedas, arranged in collections or *saṃhitās*; the first three occupy a place of supreme ritual importance and are earlier than the fourth. The first three Vedas, often called *trayī-vidyā*, 'the threefold knowledge', are the *Rgveda*, comprising lyric hymns to various deities, the *Sāmaveda*, comprising hymns from the *Ṛgveda* arranged in reference to the Soma sacrifice, and the *Yajurveda*, comprising sacrificial prayers for a number of domestic and public rituals. The fourth Veda, the *Atharvaveda*, is made up almost exclusively of magical spells and incantations. The Vedas are amplified by later texts, reflecting the developed priestly hierarchy of this early period, called *Brāhmaṇas*, which might be rendered as 'books concerned with ritual and prayer'. These texts sought to relate the hymns of the Vedas to the actual ritual processes and practices and in so doing, also offered explanations and commentary on the ritual itself. Unlike the Vedas, the *Brāhmaṇas* are written predominantly in prose. A second body of literature, also understood to amplify the Vedas, is made up of more philosophical and intellectual speculation. Originally, these texts were considered to be part of the *Brāhmaṇas*, although freed of their ritual context. These texts were called *āraṇyakas* or 'forest books'. Because of their philosophical and speculative nature, these later became identified with the *Upaniṣads*. *Upanisad* means 'sitting near' and we find that they contain a unified theme, the nature of the world-soul in the conception of Brahman and ātman; Brahman representing an abstract principle pervading the entire cosmos and ātman a psychological principle in all human beings. These texts make up *śruti* or 'that which is heard' or what was revealed to the sages from the very beginning of time.

The Vedas, *Brāhmaṇas* and *Upaniṣads* make up the category of revealed sacred literature, comparable to revealed documents in other religious traditions. But these writings are supplemented by other documents of almost equal authority called *smṛti*, 'that which is remembered', representing the tradition of sacred knowledge extending back in time throughout all the generations of sages. This body of writings includes all the collections of *dharma*, duty or law as it applies to all members of society in all situations, the sciences of grammar, the epics and *Purāṇas*. The epic literature, which in India is mastered by memory even to this day, especially the *Mahābhārata* and the *Rāmāyaṇa*, is referred to as *itihāsa*, 'this is how it was' or what we would call 'real' history. These documents assume the reality of all those things related in the *śruti* and other parts of the *smṛti* texts, and have become one of the major vehicles by which Hindus relate the past to the present. Indeed, books from the *smṛti* have often been reinvested with sacred meaning. So, for example, the *Bhagavad-Gītā*, a relatively small section of the immense *Mahābhārata*, has been understood both within the tradition itself and outside it as the one text more illustrative than any other of the main concerns of Hinduism.

We begin the dimension of sacred narrative with a series of texts illustrating creation in *śruti* and *smṛti* traditions. Second, we include a narrative describing how at the very beginning of time Prajāpati, the creator god of the *Brāhmaṇas*, creates the deity Agni and sacrifice. The gods Viṣṇu and Siva, who become important divine figures in classical Hinduism, are presented in traditions narrating their relationship to creation and sacrifice, and their ongoing presence in history. Lastly, we include a narrative concerning the Devī, the supremely powerful goddess, and how she triumphs over the Asuras, the demons who have usurped the position of the Devas or gods.

The dimension of doctrine is illustrated first by a text from the *Bṛhadāraṇyaka Upaniṣad* on rebirth and the doctrine of *karma*. Second, we include Chapter 7 of the *Bhagavad-Gītā* in which Kṛṣṇa, an *avatār* or incarnation of Viṣṇu, describes the importance of *bhakti* or devotion in making god available to all humans. Third, we include two texts from the *Upaniṣads* which describe the nature and practice of *yoga* or discipline. Fourth, we include another Upaniṣadic passage on the one god and the phenomenal world. The one god creates this world as *māyā* or creative illusion in order to manifest himself, and this is illustrated by a text from the *Śvetāśvatara Upaniṣad*. Yet the philosophical reflections upon the relationship of Brahman and ātman in the *Upaniṣads* are also authoritative reformulations of doctrinal concerns. We have therefore included as a sixth selection two passages from Śankara, the first on the superimposition of qualities or characteristics, and the second on the proper knowledge of the essential identity of Brahman and ātman. The seventh text is drawn from Rāmānuja's commentary on the *Bhagavad-Gītā* in which he speaks about the eternality of ātman, not as identical with Brahman, but as a part of the cosmic principle.

We begin illustrating the dimension of ritual with a text describing the Soma sacrifice and the ritual preparations of the sacrificer. Here we also include a hymn from the *Ṛgveda* describing the nature of Soma, the symbolic plant used in almost all Vedic and Brahmanic ritual. We continue with the texts used in the three great kingship rituals of ancient India, the Rājasūya, the Vajāpeya, and the Aśvamedha. Each of these rituals was intended to re-enact events which took place at the very beginning of time. By re-enacting these events, the king became a true master of *dharma* and a universal monarch. Lastly, we have included a Purānic text describing the merits of *pūjā*, the more common act of ritual devotion which ultimately came to replace much of the Vedic and Brahmanic ritual.

The institutional dimension is illustrated first by the *Puruṣa-ṣūkta* of the *Ṛgveda*. Here, the cosmic man is divided into the four social classes or *varnas* of India. This narrative gives reality to the contours of social life. Second, we include two short texts taken from the

Laws of Manu which set forth some of the specific laws in regard to the *āśramas* of the householder and the *sannyāsin*, the one who has severed all ties with society. Third, we include under institutional expression something on the nature of death and the specific laws regarding the experience of death.

The fifth dimension, experience, is illustrated first by the ninth chapter of the *Bhagavad-Gītā* in which the notion of *bhakti* is pushed still further so that not only do all have access to god, but they have access through every means. Second, we have included the eleventh chapter of the *Bhagavad-Gītā* in which Kṛṣṇa reveals his real form to Arjuna. Through this awesome experience Arjuna learns that Kṛṣṇa, the incarnation of Viṣṇu, is the absolute foundation of all things. Third, we have included the *Māndūkya Upaniṣad*'s interpretation of the syllable *Oṃ* and its description of the fourth stage of consciousness, in which all subject-object distinctions are overcome. This is the experience of true egolessness; one is absorbed into Brahman. Fourth, we have a selection from *Nammāḷvār*, 'Sacred Words', in which Kṛṣṇa and the adoring *gopīs* or cowherd girls become the paradigm for the relationship between human beings and god. Last, we have included a very short selection from the *Gospel of Rāmakrishna* describing this 19th-century thinker's experience of enlightenment and *samādhi*.

We have chosen to illustrate the dimension of ethics first by a Purānic text describing the merits of building a temple. The ethical dimension permeates much of Hindu thinking and could easily be illustrated by the *dharma* texts found under institutional expression. However, this Purānic text suggests very concretely that certain ethical acts, building and furnishing a temple, really go beyond this life and affect the past and the future. Second, we include a passage from the *Bṛhadāraṇyaka Upaniṣad* which sets forth the ethical acts of restraint, giving and compassion. Lastly, we illustrate the dimension of ethics with a short passage from Gandhi's autobiography in which he speaks of *ahiṃsā*, non-injury or non-violence, as the single path to truth and god.

Sacred Narrative 1

Creation: Ṛgveda, Manu-Smṛti, Bṛhadāraṇyaka Upaniṣad and Chāndogya Upaniṣad

The sacred texts of Hinduism present a number of narratives relating the process of creation. Here, we have selected four accounts which reflect the diverse currents of thought in Hinduism in which creation is spoken of in the most concrete terms as well as the most abstract terms. In the *Ṛgveda* and the *Chāndogya Upaniṣad*, creation begins to take place through the negation of non-being. In the *Manu-Smṛti*, the creator god Brahmā creates the world from the egg. In the *Bṛhadāranyaka Upanisad*, Prajāpati, one of the most important deities for the ancient Vedic and Brahmanic cult, creates the world for sacrifice.

Here, he is identified with the great horse sacrifice and creates the world as the means to offer himself in this sacrifice. Note that in all the texts there is an overarching concern for unity. Creation is the breaking of that primordial unity.

Ṛgveda 10:129

Then was not non-existent nor existent: there was no realm of air, no sky beyond it.

What covered in, and where? and what gave shelter? Was water there, unfathomed depth of water?

Death was not then, nor was there aught immortal: no sign was there, the day's and night's divider.

That One Thing, breathless, breathed by its own nature: apart from it was nothing whatsoever.

Darkness there was: at first concealed in darkness this All was indiscriminated chaos.

All that existed then was void and formless: by the great power of Warmth was born that Unit.

Thereafter rose Desire in the beginning, Desire, the primal seed and germ of Spirit.

Sages who searched with their heart's thought discovered the existent kinship in the non-existent.

Transversely was their severing line extended: what was above it then, and what below it?

There were begetters, there were mighty forces, free action here and energy up yonder.

Who verily knows and who can here declare it, whence it was born and whence comes this creation?

The Gods are later than this world's production. Who knows then whence it first came into being?

He, the first origin of this creation, whether he formed it all or did not form it, whose eye controls this world in highest heaven, he verily knows it, or perhaps he knows not.

Manu-Smṛti 1:5–16

This (universe) existed in the shape of Darkness, unperceived, destitute of distinctive marks, unattainable by reasoning, unknowable, wholly immersed, as it were, in deep sleep.

Then the divine Self-existent (himself) indiscernible, (but) making (all) this, the great elements and the rest, discernible, appeared with irresistable (creative) power, dispelling the darkness.

He who can be perceived by the internal organ (alone), who is subtile, indiscernible, and eternal, who contains all created beings and is inconceivable shone forth of his own (will).

He, desiring to produce beings of many kinds from his own body, first with a thought created the waters, and place his seed in them.

That (seed) became a golden egg, in brilliancy equal to the sun; in that (egg) he himself was born as Brahmā, the progenitor of the whole world.

The waters are called *nārāh*, (for) the waters are, indeed, the offspring of Nara; as they were his first residence (*ayana*), he thence is named Nārāyaṇa.[1]

From that (first) cause, which is indiscernible, eternal, and both real and unreal, was produced that male (Puruṣa), who is famed in this world (under the apellation of) Brahmā. n.

The divine one resided in that egg during a whole year, then he himself by his thought (alone) divided it into two halves;

And out of those two halves he formed heaven and earth, between them the middle sphere, the eight points of the horizon, and the eternal abode of the waters.

From himself he also drew forth the mind, which is both real and unreal, likewise from the mind egoism, which possesses the function of self-consciousness (and is) lordly;

Moreover, the great one, the soul, and all (products) affected by the three qualities, and, in their order, the five organs which perceive the objects of sensation.

But, joining minute particles even those six,[2] which possess measureless power, with particles of himself, he created all beings.

[1] Nārāyaṇa is another name for Brahmā and hence a pun is used to explain this name.

[2] The traditional commentators suggest that the six are the five organs of sensation and the mind.

Bṛhadāraṇyaka Upaniṣad 1:2.1–7

In the beginning nothing whatsoever was here. This world was covered with death, with hunger – for hunger is death.

Then he made up his mind: 'Would that I had a self!'

So he went on praising. From him, while he was praising, water was produced. 'Verily, while I was praising, I had pleasure!' thought he. This, indeed, is the praising-nature of what pertains to brightness. Verily, there is pleasure for him who knows thus that praising-nature of what pertains to brightness.

The water, verily, was brightness.

That which was the froth of the water became solidified. That became the earth.

On it he tortured himself. When he had tortured himself and practised austerity, his heat and essence turned into fire.

He divided himself threefold: fire (*agni*) one third, the sun (*āditya*) one third, wind (*vāyu*) one third. He also is Life divided threefold.

The eastern direction is his head. Yonder one and yonder one are the fore quarters. Likewise the western direction is his tail. Yonder one and yonder one are the hind quarters. South and north are the flanks. The sky is the back. The atmosphere is the belly. This earth is the chest. He stands firm in the waters. He who knows this, stands firm wherever he goes.

He desired: 'Would that a second self of me were produced!' He – death, hunger – by mind copulated with speech (*vāc*). That which was the semen, became the year. Previous to that there was no year. He bore him for a time as long as a year. After that long time he brought him forth. When he was born, Death opened his mouth on him. He cried *bhān*!' That, indeed, became speech.

He bethought himself: 'Verily, if I shall intend against him I shall make less food for myself.' With that speech, with that self he brought forth this whole world, whatsoever exists here: the Hymns, the Formulas, the Chants,[1] metres, sacrifices, men, cattle.

Whatever he brought forth, that he began to eat. Verily, he eats everything: that is the *aditi*-nature of Aditi (the Infinite). He who knows thus the *aditi*-nature of Aditi becomes an eater of everything here; everything becomes food for him.

He desired: 'Let me sacrifice further with a greater sacrifice!' He tortured himself. He practised austerity. When he had tortured himself and practised austerity, glory and vigour went forth. The glory and vigour, verily, are the vital breaths. So when the vital breaths departed, his body began to swell. His mind, indeed, was in his body.

He desired: 'Would that this body of mine were fit for sacrifice! Woud that by it I had a self!' Thereupon it became a horse, because it swelled. 'It has become fit for sacrifice!' thought he. Therefore the horse-sacrifice is called Aśvamedha.[2] He, verily, knows the Aśvamedha, who knows it thus.

He kept the horse in mind without confining him. After a year he sacrificed him for himself. Other animals he delivered over to the divinities. Therefore men sacrifice the victim which is consecrated to Prajāpati as though offered unto all the gods.

Chāndogya Upaniṣad 6:2.1–4

'In the beginning, my dear, this world was just Being, one only, without a second. To be sure, some people say: "In the beginning this world was just Non-being, one only, without a second; from that Non-being Being was produced."

'But verily, my dear, whence could this be?' said he. 'How from Non-being could Being be produced? On the contrary, my dear, in the beginning this world was just Being, one only, without a second.

'It bethought itself: "Would that I were many! Let me procreate myself!" It emitted heat. The heat bethought itself: "Would that I were many! Let me procreate myself." It emitted water. Therefore whenever a person grieves or perspires from the heat, then water is produced.

'That water bethought itself: "Would that I were many! Let me procreate myself." It emitted food. Therefore whenever it rains, then there is abundant food. So food for eating is produced just from water.'

[1] Here, the Hymns, Formulas and Chants refer to the three Vedas, the *Ṛgveda*, the *Yajurveda* and the *Sāmaveda*.

[2] The etymology of the horse sacrifice is derived from the verb *aśvat*, 'to swell'.

Sacred Narrative 2

Prajāpati Creates Agni: Śatapatha-Brāhmaṇa

Here is another sacred narrative concerning the Vedic and Brahmanic deity Prajāpati. In this narrative, Prajāpati first creates the sacrificial fire, Agni, and then in order to escape being devoured by this fire he creates the offerings of the sacrifice. This text shows how the sacred narrative was integrated into the ritual life, for the *Śatapatha-Brāhmaṇa* is a detailed commentary on the *Yajurveda*. Note also that great importance is given to knowing the origin of the Vedic gods and their rituals. Hence, anyone who knows the origin of the ritual is able to accomplish what the gods did at the beginning of time.

Prajāpati alone, indeed, existed here in the beginning. He considered, 'How may I be reproduced? He toiled and performed acts of penance. He generated Agni from his mouth; and because he generated him from his mouth, therefore Agni is a consumer of food: and verily, he who thus knows Agni to be a consumer of food, becomes himself a consumer of food.

He thus generated him first of the gods; and therefore (he is called) Agni, for *agni* (they say) is the same as *agri*.[1] He, being generated, went forth as the first; for him who goes first, they say that he goes at the head. Such, then, is the origin and nature of that Agni.

Prajāpati then considered, 'In that Agni I have generated a food-eater for myself; but, indeed, there is no other food here by myself, whom, surely, he would not eat.' At that time this earth had, indeed, been rendered quite bald; there were neither plants nor trees. This, then, weighed on his mind.

Thereupon Agni turned towards him with open mouth; and he (Prajāpati) being terrified, his own greatness departed from him. Now his own greatness is his speech: that speech departed from him. He desired an offering in his own self, and rubbed (his hands); and because he rubbed (his hands), therefore both this and this (palm) are hairless. He then obtained either a butter-offering or a milk-offering; but, indeed, they are both milk.

This (offering), however, did not satisfy him, because it had hairs mixed with it. He poured it away (into the fire), saying, 'Drink, while burning (*osham dhaya*)!' From its plants sprang: hence their name 'plants' (*oshadhyayah*). He rubbed (his hands) a second time, and thereby obtained another offering, either a butter-offering or a milk-offering; but, indeed, they are both milk.

This (offering) then satisfied him. He hesitated: 'Shall I offer it up? shall I not offer it up?' he thought. His own greatness said to him, 'Offer it up!' Prajāpati was aware that it was his own (*sva*) greatness that had spoken (*āha*) to him; and offered it up with 'Svāhā!' This is why offerings are made with 'Svāhā!' Thereupon that burning one (i.e., the sun) rose; and then that blowing one (i.e., the wind) sprang up; whereupon, indeed Agni turned away.

And Prajāpati, having performed offering, reproduced himself, and saved himself from Agni, Death, as he was about to devour him. And, verily, whosoever, knowing this, offers the Agnihotra[2] reproduces himself by offspring even as Prajāpati reproduced himself; and saves himself from Agni, Death, when he is about to devour him.

And when he dies, and when they place him on the fire, then he is born (again) out of the fire, and the fire only consumes his body. Even as he is born from his father and mother, so is he born from the fire. But he who offers not the Agnihotra, verily, he does not come into life at all: therefore, the Agnihotra should by all means be offered.

---

[1] Here, the text offers an etymology of the name Agni based on the Sanskrit word *agre*, meaning 'first'.

[2] The Agnihotra is one of the central Vedic and Brahmanic sacrifices which accompanies both domestic and public rituals.

Sacred Narrative 3

Viṣṇu Traditions: Ṛgveda and Śatapatha-Brāhmaṇa

Viṣṇu, while being one of the most important gods in classical Hinduism, already appears in the Vedic and Brahmanic literature as a solar deity. In the *Ṛgveda* text, he is the sky-god who traverses the world in three steps. In the *Śatapatha-Brāhmaṇa* we see something of later developments in the history of the this god, who is associated with a series of *avatars* or incarnations. The *avatārs* are usually numbered at ten and include several animal incarnations, the fish, boar, turtle and lion, along with Rāma and Kṛṣṇa. Some orthodox Hindus understand the Buddha to be an *avatār* of Viṣṇu. It should also be indicated that in later Hindu tradition Viṣṇu is associated with the eagle, Garuḍa, and he is often rendered with his four symbols: the mace, the sea-shell, a disc and a lotus. He is one of the most popular deities of later Hindu tradition, being petitioned as the preserver and restorer.

Ṛgveda 1:154, 1–6

I will declare the mighty deeds of Viṣṇu,
of him who measured out the earthly regions,
Who propped the highest place of congregation,
thrice setting down his footstep, widely striding.
For this his mighty deed is Viṣṇu lauded,
like some wild beast, dread, prowling, mountain-roaming;
He within whose three wide-extended paces all living creatures have their habitation.
Let the hymn lift itself as strength to Viṣṇu, the Bull far-striding, dwelling on the mountains,
Him who alone with triple step hath measured this common dwelling-place, long, far extended.
Him whose three places that are filled with sweetness,
imperishable, joy as it may list them,
Who verily alone upholds the threefold, the earth, the heaven, and all living creatures.
May I attain to that his well-loved mansion where men devoted to the Gods are happy.
For there springs, close akin to the Wide-Strider, the well of meath[1] in Viṣṇu's highest footstep.
Fain would we go unto your dwelling-places where there are many horned and nimble oxen,
For mightily, there, shineth down upon us the widely-striding Bull's sublimest mansion.

Śatapatha-Brāhmaṇa 1:2.5.1–9

The gods and the Asuras,[2] both of them sprung from Prajāpati, were contending for superiority. Then the gods were worsted, and the Asuras thought: 'To us alone assuredly belongs this world!'

They thereupon said: 'Well then, let us divide this world between us; and having divided it, let us subsist thereon!' They accordingly set about dividing it with ox-hides from west to east.

The gods then heard of this, and said: 'The Asuras are actually dividing this earth: come, let us go to where the Asuras are dividing it. For what woud become of us, if we were to get no share in it?' Placing Viṣṇu, (in the shape of) this very sacrifice, at their head, they went (to the Asuras).

They then said: 'Let us share in this earth along with yourselves! Let a part of it be ours!' The Asuras replied rather grudgingly: 'As much as this Viṣṇu lies upon, and no more, we give you!'

[1] Nectar or honey meaning the celestial drink of immortality, Soma.
[2] Demons.

Now Viṣṇu was a dwarf.[1] The gods, however, were not offended at this, but said: 'Much indeed they gave us, who gave us what is equal in size to the sacrifice.'

Having then laid him down eastwards, they enclosed him on all (three) sides with the metres, saying, on the south side, 'With the Gāyatrī metre I enclose thee!', on the west side: 'With the Trishṭubh metre I enclose thee!', on the north side: 'With the Gagatī metre I enclose thee!'[2]

Having thus enclosed him on all (three) sides, and having placed Agni (the fire) on the east side, they went on worshipping and toiling with it (or him, i.e., Viṣṇu, the sacrifice). By it they obtained this entire earth; and because they obtained by it this entire (earth), therefore it (the sacrificial ground) is called *vedi* (the altar). For this reason they say, 'As great as the altar is, so great is the earth'; for by it (the altar) they obtained this entire (earth). And, verily, he who so understands this, wrests likewise this entire (earth) from his rivals, excludes his rivals from sharing in it.

Thereupon this Viṣṇu became tired; but being enclosed on all (three) sides by the metres, with fire on the east, there was no (means of) escaping: he then hid himself among the roots of plants.

The gods said: 'What has become of Viṣṇu? What has become of the sacrifice?' They said: 'On all (three) sides he is enclosed by the metres, with Agni to the east, there is no (way of) escaping: search for him in this very place!' By slightly digging they accordingly searched for him. They discovered him at a depth of three inches (or thumb's breadths): therefore the altar should be three inches deep; and therefore also Pāṇki made the altar for the Soma-sacrifice three inches deep.[3]

[1] The dwarf is understood as the fifth *avatar* of Viṣṇu.

[2] The respective texts of the Veda are recited by these three metres.

[3] Pāṇki is one of the teachers mentioned in the *Śatapatha-Brāhmana* and here he has deduced a specific ritual detail from the sacred narrative.

Sacred Narrative 4

Śiva Traditions: Mahābhārata and Rāmāyaṇa

Like Viṣṇu, Śiva is a god who appears in the Vedic and Brahmanic writings (usually associated with Rudra), but in later Hinduism he becomes both the great unborn creator of the universe and the personal god living in the Himalayas with his wife Pārvatī. He is the paradigmatic yogin, granting boons to those who honour him with their own rigorous practices. Śiva is often represented in the form of the Naṭarāja, the King of Dancing.

In this form, he symbolizes the source of all movement in the cosmos, from life to death and their continual interchange. We have included two texts from the epics, the *Mahābhārata* and the *Rāmāyaṇa*, which describes his role as the Lord of Creatures, but also demonstrate how he assumes many of the functions associated with earlier divine figures. So, in the *Mahābhārata*, he is directly related to sacrifice and in the *Rāmāyaṇa* he functions as the king of the gods, who rescues both the divine beings and humans from the poison churned up from the bottom of the sea.

Mahābhārata 12.274, 2–58

(The listener, Yudhisthira, asked) You have told me that Vṛtra was deluded by Fever and slain by Vāsava with a thunderbolt. How did this Fever appear, and from whence? I would like to hear in detail the origin of Fever.

(The narrator, Bhīṣma, replied) Hear the birth of Fever, as it is famed throughout the world. I will tell you about it at length.

There was once a peak of Mount Meru famed throughout the triple world. This peak was descended from the sun and was named 'Luminary'; it was adorned with all gems, immeasurable, unapproachable by all people. There on the mountain slope adorned with gold and minerals and the god Śiva sat as if on a couch, shining intensely, while Pārvatī, the daughter of the king of the mountains, stayed at his side constantly. The noble gods; the Vasus of great vitality; the two noble Aśvins, the best of physicians; King Kubera Vaiśravana, the overlord of Yakṣas, the prosperous lord who lives on Kailāsa surrounded by the Guhyakas; the divine sages, with Angiras at their head; the Gandharva, Vaśvāvasu; Nārada and Parvata; the massed bands of celestial nymphs – they all came there together. A clear and pleasant wind blew, wafting various perfumes; the great trees were in blossom, bearing flowers of all season. The Vidyādharas, Siddhas and ascetics all came to serve the great god, lord of cattle. The ghosts of diverse forms, the hideous Rākṣasas and the powerful Piśācas of many forms of various weapons – all the servants of the god stood there like fires, rejoicing. The lord Nandin stood there with the god's consent, holding the blazing trident that glowed with its own energy. The Ganges, best of rivers, born of all sacred waters, incarnate served the god. Thus the lord, the great god, was worshipped there by the divine sages and by the gods of good fortune.

Then, after some time, a Prajāpati named Dakṣa began a sacrifice according to the Vedic rites ordained in former times. All the gods, with Śakra at their head, assembled and decided to go to his sacrifice. Shining like fires, the noble gods in their blazing celestial chariots went to the Door of the Ganges with the permission of the god; so the tradition goes. Then the virtuous daughter of the king of the mountains saw the gods setting out, and she said to the god her husband, the lord of cattle, 'My lord, where are all the gods going, with Śakra at their head? Tell me truly, for you know the truth. A great misgiving has come over me.' The great lord replied, 'Blessed lady, the supreme Prajāpati, named Dakṣa, is performing a horse sacrifice, and all the heaven-dwellers are going there.' 'Illustrious one, why are you not going to this sacrifice?' asked Uma.[1] 'What could prevent you from going?' The great lord answered, 'All of this was decided by the gods themselves: in all sacrifices, no share is designated for me. Illustrious lady with a superb complexion, by the course sanctioned by this former agreement, in keeping with *dharma*, properly, the gods do not offer me a share of the sacrifice.' Umā said, 'Lord, among all beings you are supreme in power because of your qualities. You are invincible, unapproachable because of your energy, fame and glory. Illustrious one, sinless one, great sorrow and trembling have come upon me because you have been denied a share.'

When the goddess had said this to the god her husband, the lord of cattle, she fell silent and with a burning heart, and he knew what the goddess thought and longed for in her heart. 'Stay here,' he said to Nandin, and then the lord of all lords of yoga gathered his powers of yoga, and the god of gods whose energy is great, took the Pināka bow and attacked that sacrifice by force with his terrifying servants. Some of them emitted roars; some laughed; others sprinkled the fire with blood. Some with deformed faces uprooted the sacrificial stakes and whirled them about; some swallowed up in their great mouths the priests performing the sacrifice. Then the sacrifice, attacked on all sides, took the form of a deer and flew up into the sky; but the Lord, seeing the sacrifice fleeing in that form, took up his bow and an arrow and followed it.

As the lord of gods, whose energy is infinite, became angry, a terrible drop of sweat came out of his forehead; and as soon as that drop of sweat had fallen on the earth, an enormous fire like the fire of doomsday appeared. In it was born a short man with extraordinarily red eyes and a tawny beard; he was gruesome and his hair stood on end; his body was extremely hairy like that of a hawk or an

[1] Umā is another name for Śiva's wife Pārvatī.

owl. He had a gaping mouth with monstrous teeth; he was hideous, dark-complexioned, and wore red garments. That creature of great essence burnt the sacrifice as a fire burns dry wood, and all the terrified gods fled in all directions. As that man strode about, the earth trembled violently and a moan of woe arose, terrifying everyone. The Grandfather appeared before the great god and said, 'All the gods will give you too a share, O lord. Lord of all gods, Heater of Enemies, great god, withdraw this destruction. All the gods and sages can find no respite from your anger. Supreme god, Knower of *Dharma*, if this man named Fever born of your sweat wanders among people, the whole earth will not be able to bear his energy in one piece; let him be divided into many.' When the god had been addressed in this way by Brahmā, and when he had also been given a share, he accepted the command of the lord Brahmā whose vitality is infinite. Bhava, holding the Pināka bow, was well pleased and began to smile, and he accepted the share that Brahmā had mentioned.

Then who who knows all *dharma* divided Fever into many parts, for the sake of the peace of all beings; hear how he did this. The headaches of elephants, hot exudations of mountains, moss in waters, slough of serpents, shore hooves of bulls, barren saline patches on the surface of the earth, blindness of cattle, constipation of horses, moulting of the crests of peacocks, eye-diseases of cuckoos – each was called Fever by the noble Śiva. And disturbances in all sheep's livers, and hiccups of all parrots, and fatigue among tigers are known as Fever; so we have heard. But among men, the name of Fever is indeed famous; it enters a man at death, at birth, and in the midst of life. This awful energy of the great god is called Fever, and the lord is to be bowed to and honoured by all creatures that breathe.

When Vṛtra, the best of those who uphold *dharma*, was pervaded by this Fever he yawned, and then Śakra hurled the thunderbolt at him. The thunderbolt entered Vṛtra and split him, and when the great demon and great yogi had been split by the thunderbolt he went to the highest place of Viṣṇu, whose energy is infinite. It was because of his devotion to Viṣṇu that he had formerly pervaded the universe, and therefore when he was slain in battle he reached the place of Viṣṇu.

Rāmāyaṇa 1:45, 15–44

In the early days, in the golden age,
There were the strong sons of Diti[1] and the sons of Aditi;[2]
They were very illustrious and most virtuous and they followed the right course of life.
Now the thought occurred to these great beings:
'How can we be immortal and free from old age and disease?'
And it occured to those wise while they were thus engaged in thought:
'When the milky ocean is churned,
Then we shall get hold of the essential juice.'
So they decided to churn, and, being of immeasurable energy,
They used Vāsuki[3] as a rope in their churning equipment,
The mountain Mandara (gigantic and holy) as churn staff, and they began to churn.
A thousand years passed. Then the heads of the serpent, which was used as churning cord, began to strike out at the mountains.
While they struck out with their fangs they were vomiting an incredibly potent poison.
Out came Hālāhala, the mighty poison.
It was like fire.
The whole world of the gods and demons and men was set ablaze by it.
Then the gods were eager for protection by the Great God Śiva.
So they went to him singing his praises and saying:
'Save us! Save us!'
Thus the Lord, the great god of gods was addressed by them.
At that moment Viṣṇu appeared at that place bearing his conch and his discus.
With a smile Viṣṇu spoke to the trident-wielder Śiva:
'That which first of all turned up in the god's churning, o best of gods,
That is thine, since thou, Lord,
Art the foremost of the gods.

[1] The mythical mother of the Daityas, demonic enemies of the gods.
[2] The mythical mother of the gods.
[3] The prince of the serpents.

Stay here and receive the first offering, the poison, O Lord!'
Then and there, having said this,
Viṣṇu the supreme of gods vanished.
But Śiva had seen the fear of the gods and heard the words of the great archer Viṣṇu.
He swallowed up Hālāhala, the terrible poison,
As if it were Immortality itself.
Lord Śiva, the supreme one, left the gods;
And gods and demons together began to churn again.
Then the churn staff, that most glorious mountain Mandara,
Slipped into the underworld,
And gods and the heavenly hosts began to call on Viṣṇu with songs of adoration.
'Thou art the goal of all beings, and especially of the celestials!
Thou with thy strong arms, protect us,
Thou art able to raise up the mountain!'
Viṣṇu heard them. He took the form of a tortoise,
Put the mountain on his back and lay down in the ocean.
And then Viṣṇu himself, the soul of the world, the supreme Puruṣa[1],
Reached out and held the top of the mountain with his hand
And began to churn in the midst of the gods.
After a thousand years of churning
The man of Medical Science arose with his staff and gourd;
He is wholly virtuous, following the right course of life.
Thus he, Dhanvantari by name, arose, and then the heavenly nymphs.
By the churning in the waters
The exquisite damsels came out of that essential fluid.
Therefore they became heavenly nymphs.
Six hundred millions of these exquisite heavenly nymphs sprang forth.
And the servant girls whom they had with them were innumerable.
But neither the gods nor the demons accepted them [as wives].
Since they were not accepted they came to be known as belonging to all.
Then Vāruṇī the illustrious daughter of Varuṇa emerged.
She was seeking acceptance.
The sons of Diti did not receive that daughter of Varuṇa.
But the sons of Aditi did receive that blameless maiden.
Therefore the sons of Diti are demons (*asuras*)
And the sons of Aditi gods (*suras*) –
And the gods were overjoyed because they had received Vāruṇī,
The noble king of heroes, Uccaihśravas, came from the ocean too.
Likewise Kaustubha, the most precious jewel [ornament of Viṣṇu].
And also the supreme juice of Immortality.
Then because of this juice the fall of the house was catastrophic.
The sons of Aditi fought Diti's sons.
Together with the ogres all demons united
And the fight was terrifying
And overwhelmed the whole threefold world.
When all had been destroyed,
The powerful Viṣṇu took on his form of deluding magic
And quickly took away the juice of Immortality.
Those who turned to Viṣṇu, the imperishable, the supreme Puruṣa,
Were destroyed in the fight by Viṣṇu the Lord.
After the defeat of the demons,
Indra, the king of gods, ascended the throne and happily began his dominion
Over the worlds with their seers and angelic singers.

---

[1] 'Soul', 'spirit', and the sacrificial victim of Rgveda 10:90 (see Institutional Expression 1, page 212).

Sacred Narrative 5

The Power of the Goddess: Devī-Māhātmyam

The *Devī-Māhātmyam* is chanted in its entirety on sacred occasions in India, especially during the Durgā-Pūjā. In the narrative, the supremacy and power of the Devī or goddess is stressed. She is the entirety of the sacrificial process; she both protects and destroys; she is armed 'with sword, spear, club, discuss, conch, bow, arrows, slings and iron mace' (1:78); she is terrible to look upon while at the same time 'more pleasing than all the pleasing things and exceedingly beautiful' (1:81). Her narrative is set within a frame-story in which a king who has lost his empire and a merchant who has been thrown out of his family for a number of business failures meet in a temple. There, they seek her intercession by recounting her marvellous deeds. In the end, the king and merchant offer sacrifices to the Devī, the goddess grants the king's wish to be given back his kingdom in this life and the next, and the merchant is given nirvāṇa. In this selection, we read how the Asuras vanquished the Devas. The Devas respond by creating the goddess and giving her their weapons. She is created from the light of the three major deities of Hinduism, Brahmā, Viṣṇu and Śiva. Created and armed by the gods, the Devī enters into battle with the Asuras.

The Ṛṣi said: Of yore when Mahiṣāsura was the lord of the Asuras and Indra the lord of the Devas, there was a war between the Devas and Asuras for a full hundred years. And that army of the Devas was vanquished by the valorous Asuras. After conquering all the Devas, Mahiṣāsura became the lord of heaven (Indra).

Then the vanquished Devas headed by Brahmā, the lord of beings, went to the place where Śiva and Viṣṇu were. The Devas decribed to them in detail, as it had happened, the story of Mahiṣāsura.

'He (Mahiṣāsura) himself has assumed the jurisdictions of Surya, Indra, Agni, Vāyu, Candra, Yama and Varuṇa and other (Devas). Thrown out from heaven by that evil-natured Mahisa, the hosts of Devas wander on the earth like mortals. All that has been done by the enemy of the Devas, has been related to you both, and we have sought shelter under you both. May both of you be pleased to think out the means of his destruction.'

Having thus heard the words of the Devas, Viṣṇu was angry and Śiva, too, and their faces became fierce with frowns.

Then issued forth a great light from the face of Viṣṇu who was full of intense anger, and from that of Brahmā and of Śiva too. From the bodies of Indra and other Devas also sprang forth a very great light. And (all) this light united together.

The Devas saw there a concentration of light like a mountain blazing excessively, pervading all the quarters with its flames. Then that unique light, produced from the bodies of all the Devas, pervading the three worlds with its lustre, combined into one and became a female form.

By that which was Śiva's light, her face came into being; by Yama's (light) her hair, by Viṣṇu's light her arms; and by Candra's (light) her two breasts. By Indra's light her waist, by Varuna's (light) her shanks and thighs and by earth's light her lips.

By Brahmā's light her feet came into being; by Sūrya's light her toes, by Vasus' (light) her fingers, by Kubera's (light) her nose; by Prajāpati's her teeth came into being and similarly by Agni's light her three eyes were formed. The light of the two sandhyas became her eyebrows, the light of Vāyu, her ears; the manifestation of the lights of other Devas too (contributed to the being of the) auspicious Devī.

Then looking at her, who had come into being from the assembled lights of all the Devas, the immortals who were oppressed by Mahiṣāsura experienced joy.

The bearer of Pināka (Śiva) drawing forth a

trident from his own trident presented it to her; and Viṣṇu bringing forth a discus out of his own discus gave it to her. Varuṇa gave her a conch, Agni a spear; and Māruta gave a bow as well as two quivers full of arrows.

Indra, lord of Devas, brang forth a thunderbolt out of (his own) thunderbolt and a bell from that of his elephant Airāvata, gave them to her. Yama gave a staff from his own staff of Death, and Varuṇa, the lord of waters, a noose and Brahmā, the lord of beings, gave a string of beads and a water-pot.

Sūrya bestowed his own rays on all the pores of her skin and Kāla (Time) gave a sword and a spotless shield.

The milk-ocean gave a pure necklace, a pair of undecaying garments, a divine crest-jewel, a pair of earrings, bracelets, a brilliant half-moon (ornament), armlets on all arms, a pair of shining anklets, a unique necklace and excellent rings on all the fingers. Visvakarma gave her a very brilliant axe, weapons of various forms and also an impenetrable armour. The ocean gave her a garland of unfading lotuses for her head and another for her breast, besides a very beautiful lotus in her hand. The (mountain) Hamavat gave her a lion to ride on, and various jewels.

The lord of wealth (Kubera) gave her a drinking cup, ever full of wine. Śeṣa, the lord of all serpents, who supports this earth, gave her a serpent-necklace bedecked with the best jewels. Honoured likewise by other Devas also with ornaments and weapons, she (the Devī) gave out a loud roar with a defying laugh again and again. With her unending, exceedingly great, terrible roar the entire sky was filled, and there was great reverberation. All the worlds shook, the seas trembled.

The earth quaked and all the mountains rocked. 'Victory to you,' exclaimed the Devas in joy in her, the lion-rider. The sages, who bowed their bodies in devotion, extolled her. Seeing the three worlds agitated, the foes of Devas mobilized all their armies and rose together with uplifted weapons. Mahiṣāsura, exclaiming in wrath, 'Ha! What is this?' rushed toward that roar, surrounded by innumerable Asuras. Then he saw the Devī pervading the three worlds with her lustre. Making the earth bend with her footstep, scraping the sky with her diadem, shaking the nether worlds with the twang of her bowstring, and standing there pervading all the quarters around with her thousand arms. Then began a battle between the Devī and the enemies of the Devas, in which the quarters of the sky were illumined by the weapons and arms hurled diversely. Mahiṣāsura's general, a great Asura named Cikṣura, and Cāmara, attended by other Asuras and forces comprising four parts[1] fought. A great Asura named Udagra with sixty thousand chariots, and Mahāhanu with ten million (chariots) gave battle. Asiloman, another great Asura, with fifty millions (of chariots), and Bāṣkala with six millions fought in that battle. An Asura named Biḍāla fought in that battle surrounded with five hundred crores of chariots. And other great Asuras, thousands in number, surrounded with chariots, elephants and horses fought with the Devī in that battle.

Mahiṣāsura was surrounded in that battle with thousands of crores of horses, elephants and chariots. Others (Asuras) fought in the battle against the Devī with iron maces and javelins, with spears and clubs, with swords, axes and halberds. Some hurled spears and others nooses.

They began to strike her with swords in order to kill her. Showering her own weapons and arms, that Devī Caṇḍikā very easily cut to pieces all those weapons and arms. Without any strain on her face, and with the gods and sages extolling her, the Īsvarī threw her weapons and arms at the bodies of the Asuras. And the lion which carried the Devī, shaking its mane in rage, also stalked among the hosts of the Asuras like a conflagration amidst the forests. The sighs which Ambikā, engaged in the battle, heaved became at once her battalions by hundreds and thousands. Energized by the power of the Devī, these (battalions) fought with axes, javelins, swords and halberds, and destroyed the Asuras. Of these battalions, some beat drums, some blew conches and others played on tabors in that great martial festival. Then the Devī killed hundreds of Asuras with her trident, club, showers of spears, swords and the like, and threw down others who were stupefied by the noise of her bell; and binding others with her noose, she dragged them on the ground. Some were split into two by the sharp slashes of her sword, and others, smashed by the blows of her mace, lay down on the ground; and some severely

[1] The four parts of the ancient Indian army were cavalry, charioteers, elephant-soldiers and foot-soldiers.

hammered by her club, vomited forth blood.

Pierced in the breast by her trident, some fell on the ground. Pierced all over by her arrows, and resembling porcupines, some of the enemies of Devas gave up their lives on that field of battle. Some had their arms cut off, some their necks broken; the heads of others rolled down; some others were torn asunder in the middle of their trunks, and some great Asuras fell on the ground with their legs severed.

Some, rendered one-armed, one-eyed, and one-legged, were again cloven in twain by the Devī. The others, though rendered headless, fell and rose again.

Headless trunks fought with the Devī with the best weapons in their hands. Some of these headless trunks danced there in the battle to the rhythm of the musical instruments.

The trunks of some great Asuras, with their swords, spears and lances still in their hands, shouted at the Devī with their heads just severed, 'Stop, stop.' That part of the earth where the battle was fought became impassable with Asuras, elephants, horses and chariots that had been felled.

The profuse blood from the Asuras, elephants and horses flowed immediately like large rivers amidst that army of the Asuras. As fire consumes a huge heap of straw and wood, so did Ambikā destroy that vast army of Asuras in no time.

And her carrier-lion, thundering aloud, with quivering mane, prowled about in the battlefield, appearing to search out the vital breaths from the bodies of the enemies of Devas. In that battlefield the battlions of the Devī fought in such a manner with the Asuras that the Devas in heaven, showering flowers, extolled them.

Doctrine 1

Rebirth and the Doctrine of Karma: Bṛhadāraṇyaka Upaniṣad

The technical term *karma* (action) in Vedic and Brahmanic literature is confined to ritual process and actions. Further, the Vedas and *Brahmaṇas* seem to understand death as a final transition in which the person moved from this world to the world of the fathers or to the world of the gods without the hindrance of the mortal body. The sage Yājñavalkya in the *Bṛhadāraṇyaka Upaniṣad* began a movement of reinterpretation, in which *karma* means more than ritual action. He identifies the self as Brahman, but at the moment of death this self is taken hold of by actions performed during the individual's life. These actions condition what that person will be in his next life. He states in this extract that 'one becomes virtuous by virtuous action, bad by bad action.' The solution for the endless cycle of rebirth and embodiment in which the essential self is trapped is the cessation of desire. This allows the self to go beyond all the natural and cosmic processes which condition each life. However, while Yājñavalkya expands the meaning of *karma*, he does not negate the more restricted sense of ritual actions.

When this self comes to weakness and to confusedness of mind, as it were, then the breaths gather around him. He takes to himself those particles of energy and descends into the heart. When the person in the eye turns away, back (to the sun), then one becomes non-knowing of forms.

'He is becoming one,' they say; 'he does not

see.' 'He is becoming one,' they say; 'he does not smell.' 'He is becoming one,' they say, 'he does not speak.' 'He is becoming one,' they say; 'he does not hear.' 'He is becoming one,' they say; 'he does not think.' 'He is becoming one,' they say; 'he does not touch.' 'He is becoming one,' they say; 'he does not know.' The point of his heart becomes lighted up. By that light the self departs, either by the eye, or by the head, or by other bodily parts. After him, as he goes out, the life (*prāṇa*) goes out. After the life, as it goes out, the life (*prāṇa*) go out. He becomes one with intelligence. What has intelligence departs with him. His knowledge and his works and his former intelligence (i.e., instinct) lay hold of him.

Now as a caterpillar, when it has come to the end of a blade of grass, in taking the next step draws itself together towards it, just so this soul in taking the text step strikes down this body, dispels its ignorance, and draws itself together (for making this transition).

As a goldsmith, taking a piece of gold, reduces it to another newer and more beautiful form, just so this soul, striking down this body and dispelling its ignorance, makes for itself another newer and more beautiful form like that either of the fathers, or of the Gandharvas, or of the gods, or of Prajāpati, or of Brahmā, or of other beings.

rebirth?

Verily, this soul is Brahmā, made of knowledge of mind, of breath, of seeing, of hearing, of earth, of water, of wind, of space, of energy and of non-energy, of desire and of non-desire, of anger and of non-anger, of virtuousness and of non-virtuousness. It is made of everything. This is what is meant by the saying 'made of this, made of that'.

According as one acts, according as one conducts himself, so does he become. The doer of god becomes good. The doer of evil becomes evil. One becomes virtuous by virtuous action, bad by bad action.

But people say: 'A person is made (not of acts, but) of desires only.' (In reply to this I say:) As is his desire, such is his resolve; as is his resolve, such the action he performs; what action (*karma*) he performs, that he procures for himself.

On this point there is this verse:

Where one's mind is attached – the inner self
  Goes thereto with action, being attached to it
    alone.
Obtaining the end of his action,
  Whatever he does in this world,
  He comes again from that world
  To this world of action.
So the man who desires.

Doctrine 2

Bhakti and the Availability of God: Bhagavad-Gītā

The *Bhagavad-Gītā* forms a small section of the great Indian epic, the *Mahābhārata*. This epic describes the conflict between the five Pāṇḍava brothers and their cousins, the Kauravas. The *Gītā* opens with Arjuna, the third oldest of the Pāṇḍavas, and his charioteer Kṛṣṇa on the battlefield with all the troops prepared to fight for possessions of the family kingdom. Unknown to Arjuna, Kṛṣṇa is not simply the princely warrior who has volunteered to aid him, but an incarnation of the god Viṣṇu. Arjuna is overcome by doubt and confusion: should he enter into battle and slay his own kinsmen, or flee the field and become a world-renouncing mendicant? Gradually, Arjuna begins to realize that Kṛṣṇa is something more than a simple volunteer. In their dialogue, the god Kṛṣṇa indicates that there are other ways to look at Arjuna's problem. Kṛṣṇa teaches Arjuna that 'the discipline of knowledge' (*jñāna-yoga*) and 'the discipline of action' (*karma-yoga*) will begin to resolve his confusion. The discipline of knowledge will teach him that the real self cannot be injured and hence he should fight. The discipline of action will teach him that right actions or those done in accord with *dharma* should be performed without regard for their fruits. However, the highest form of discipline is *bhakti*, which is usually translated as 'devotion'. While it is the highest form of *yoga* or discipline, in this passage it is also the means by which God becomes available to all. The word *bhakti* comes from the root *bhaj* which means 'to share' and the Lord Kṛṣṇa states that very few people ever 'come to know Me as I really am'. Yet single-minded devotion will reveal the mysterious presence of God in all things.

The Blessed Lord said:

Attach thy mind to Me; engaged in Yogic exercise, put thy trust in Me; [this doing] listen how thou mayest come to know Me in my entirety, all doubt dispelled.

This wisdom derived from sacred writ and the wisdom of experience I shall proclaim to thee, leaving nothing unsaid.

This knowing, never again will any other thing that needs to be known remain.

Among thousands of men but one, maybe, will strive for self-perfection; and even among these [athletes] who have won perfection['s crown] But one, maybe, will come to know Me as I really am.

Eightfold divided is my Nature – thus: Earth, water, fire and air, space, mind, and also soul [*buddhi*], the ego [last].

This is the lower: but other than this I have a higher Nature; this too must thou know.

(And this is) Nature seen as life by which this universe [*jagat*] is kept in being.

From these [two Natures] all beings take their origin; be very sure of this.

Of the whole [wide] universe the origin of the dissolution too am I.

Higher than I there's nothing whatsoever:

On Me the universe (*sarvam*) is strung like clustered pearls upon a thread.

In water I am the flavour, in sun and moon the light, in all the Vedas *Oṃ* [the sacred syllable], in space I'm sound: in man [his] manliness am I.

Pure fragrance in the earth am I, flame's onset in the fire; [and] life [am I] in all contingent beings, in ascetics [their] fierce austerity.

Know that I am the eternal seed of all contingent beings: reason in the rational, glory in the glorious am I.

Power in the powerful I – [such power] as knows nor passion nor desire: desire am I in contingent beings, [but such desire as is] not at war with right [*dharma*].

Know too that all states of being, whether they be of [Nature's constituent] Goodness, Passion or Darkness, proceed from Me; but I am not in them, they are in Me.

By these three states of being inhering in the 'constituents' this whole universe is led astray, and does not understand that I am far beyond them: I neither change nor pass away.

For [all] this is my creative powder [*māyā*], divine, hard to transcend.

Whoso shall put his trust in Me alone, shall pass beyond this [my] uncanny power [*māyā*].

Doers of evil, deluded, base, put not their trust in Me; their minds seduced by this uncanny power, they cleave to a devilish form of life [*bhāva*].

Fourfold are the doers of good who love and worship [*bhaj*] Me – the afflicted, the man who seeks for wisdom, the man who strives for gain, and the man who wisdom knows.

Of these the man of wisdom, ever integrated, who loves and worships [*bhakti*] One alone, excels: to such a man I am exceeding dear, and he is dear to Me.

All these are noble and exalted, but the man of wisdom is my very self, so must I hold. His self [already] integrated, he puts his trust in Me, the [one] All-Highest Way. At the end of many a birth the man of wisdom resigns himself to Me, [knowing tht Kṛṣna,] Vasudeva's son, is All: a man so great of soul [mahātman] is exceeding hard to find.

[All] wisdom swept away by manifold desires, men put their trust in other gods, relying on diverse rules and precepts: for their own nature forces them thereto.

Whatever form, [whatever god] a devotee with faith desires to honour, that very faith do I confirm in him, making it unswerving and secure.

Firm established [*yukta*] in that faith, he seeks to reverence that [god], and thence he gains all he desires, though it is I who am the true dispenser.

But finite is the reward [*phala*] of such men of little wit: whoso worships the gods, to the gods will [surely] go, [but] whoso loves and worships [*bhakta*] Me, to Me will come indeed.

Fools think I am the Unmanifest in manifest form displayed: they know nothing of my higher state, the Unchangeable, All-Highest.

Because my creative power [*yoga-māyā*] conceals Me, I am not revealed to all: this world, deluded, knows Me not – [Me] the Unborn and Changeless.

All beings past and present, and yet to come I know: but none there is that knoweth Me.

By dualities [*dvandva*] are men confused, and these arise from desire and hate; thereby are all contingent beings bewildered the moment they are born.

But some there are for whom [all] ill is ended – doers of what is good and pure: released [at last] from the confusion of duality, steadfast in their vows, they love and worship [*bhaj*] Me.

Whoso shall strive to win release from age and death, putting his trust in Me, will come to know That Brahman in Its wholeness, what appertains to self and the whole [mystery] of works.

Whoso shall know Me and all that appertains to contingent being, to the divine and to the sacrifice, will come to know Me at the time of passing on, for integrated their thought will be.

Doctrine 3

Yoga: Śvetāśvatara Upaniṣad and Maitrī Upaniṣad

We have seen the usage of the term *yoga* as discipline in the preceding passage from the *Bhagavad-Gītā*. Here, in this selection from the *Śvetāśvatara Upaniṣad*, we find the basic characteristics of later formal yoga: proper sitting posture (*āsana*), withdrawal of the senses from external contact (*pratyāhāra*) and the reduction of breathing (*prāṇāyāma*). The *Maitrī Upaniṣad* adds the further stages of meditation (*dhyāna*), concentration (*dhāraṇā*) and absorption (*samādhi*) in which thought merges with non-thought. In both cases, *yoga* is the discipline of the mind, the senses and the intellect in order to overcome the human limitations that make us what we are and to identify the individual self with the undifferentiated, eternal self.

Śvetāṣvatara Upanisad 2:8–17

Holding his body steady with the three upper
parts erect,
And causing the senses with the mind to enter
into the heart,
A wise man with the Brahma-boat should
cross over
All the fear-bringing streams.
Having repressed his breathings here in the body,
and having his movements checked,
One should breathe through his nostrils with

diminished breath.
Like that chariot yoked with vicious horses,
His mind the wise man should restrain undistractedly.
In a clean level spot, free from pebbles, fire and gravel,
By the sound of water and other propinquities favourable to thought, not offensive to the eye,
In a hidden retreat protected from the wind, one should practise Yoga.
Fog, smoke, sun, fire, wind,
Fire-flies, lightning, a crystal, a moon –
These are the preliminary appearances,
Which produce the manifestation of Brahma in Yoga.
When the fivefold quality of Yoga has been produced,
Arising from earth, water, fire, air, and space,
No sickness, no old age, no death has he
Who has obtained a body made out of the fire of Yoga.
Lightness, healthiness, steadiness,
Clearness of countenance and pleasantness of voice,
Sweetness of odour, and scanty excretions –
These, they say, are the first stage in the progress of Yoga.
Even as a mirror stained by dust
Shines brilliantly when it has been cleansed,
So the embodied one, on seeing the nature of the Soul [*ātman*],
Becomes unitary, his end attained, from sorrow freed.
When with the nature of the self, as with a lamp,
A practiser of Yoga beholds here the nature of Brahma,
Unborn, steadfast, from every nature free –
By knowing God [*deva*] one is released from all fetters!
That God faces all the quarters of heaven.
Aforetime was he born, and he it is within the womb,
He has been born forth. He will be born.
He stands opposite creatures, having his face in all directions.
The God who is in fire, who is in water, who has entered into the whole world, who is in plants, who is in trees – to that God be adoration! – yea, be adoration!

Maitrī Upaniṣad 6:18–19

The precept for effecting this [unity] is this: restraint of the breath [*prāṇāyāma*], withdrawal of the senses [*pratyāhāra*], meditation [*dhyāna*], concentration [*dhāraṇā*], contemplation [*tarka*], absorption [*samādhi*]. Such is said to be the sixfold Yoga. By this means

When a seer see the brilliant
Maker, Lord, Person, the Brahma-source,
Then, being a knower, shaking off good and evil,
He reduces everything to unity in the supreme Imperishable.

For thus has it been said:

As to a mountain that's enflamed
Deer and birds do not resort –
So, with the Brahma-knowers, faults
Do never any shelter find.

Now, it has elsewhere been said: 'Verily, when a knower has restrained his mind from the external, and the breathing spirit [*prāṇa*] has put to rest objects of sense, there upon let him continue void of conceptions. Since the living individual [*jīva*] who is named "breathing spirit" has arisen here from what is not breathing spirit therefore, verily, let the breathing spirit restrain his breathing spirit in what is called the fourth condition [*turya*].'[1] For thus it has been said:

That which is non-thought, [yet] which stands in the midst of thought,
The unthinkable, supreme mystery! –
Thereon let one concentrate his thought
And the subtile body [*liṅga*], too, without support.

---

[1] This fourth condition *turya* (or *turīya*) is a transcendental consciousness. See Experience 3, page 223, and the inward consciousness of the *Māṇḍūkya Upaniṣad*.

Doctrine 4

The One God and the Phenomenal World: Śvetāśvatara Upaniṣad

In the later Upaniṣads there is already a move to identify Brahman as the one, transcendent god, who creates and sustains the phenomenal world in all its diversity. Here, in this passage from the *Śvetāśvatara Upaniṣad*, Brahman is described as the 'One' who is 'the source of all'. Yet it is possible through knowledge to go beyond the phenomenal world created by Brahman and in so doing transcend the world, or in the words of the text, leave 'the body behind'.

In the imperishable, infinite, supreme Brahman
are two things;
For therein are knowledge and ignorance
placed hidden.
Now ignorance is a thing perishable, but
knowledge is a thing immortal.
And He who rules the ignorance and the
knowledge is another,
[Even] the One who rules over every single
source,
All forms and all sources;
Who bears in his thoughts, and beholds when
born,
That red [*kapila*] seer who was engendered in
the beginning.
That Gods spreads out each single net [of
illusion] manifoldly,
And draws it together here in the world.
Thus again, having created his Yatis,[1] the Lord
[*īśa*],
The Great Soul [*mahātman*], exercises
universal overlordship.
As the illumining sun shines upon
All regions, above, below, and across,
So that One God, glorious, adorable,
Rules over whatever creatures are born from a
womb.
The source of all, who develops his own nature,
Who brings to maturity whatever can be
ripened,
And who distributes all qualities [*guna*] –
Over this whole world rules the One.
That which is hidden in the secret of the Vedas,
even the Mystic Doctrines [*upaniṣad*] –
Brahmā knows That as the source of the
sacred word [*brahman*].
The gods and seers of old who knew That,
They, [coming to be] of Its nature, verily,
have become immortal.
Whoever has qualities [*guṇa*, distinctions] is the
doer of deeds that bring recompense;
And of such action surely he experiences the
consequence.
Undergoing all forms, characterized by the three
Qualities,[2] treading the three paths,[3]
The individual self roams about according to
its deeds [*karman*].
He is the measure of a thumb, of sun-like
appearance,
When coupled with conception [*saṃkalpa*]
and egoism [*ahaṃkāra*].
But with only the qualities of intellect and of self,
The lower [self] appears of the size of the
point of an awl.
This living self is to be known as a part
Of the hundredth part of the point of a hair
Subdivided a hundredfold;
And yet it partakes of infinity.
Not female, nor yet male is it;
Nor yet is this neuter.
Whatever body he takes to himself,
With that he becomes connected.

[1] Yatis, according to the Ṛgveda, are lower deities who assisted in the creation of the world.

[2] The three qualities are pureness, passion, and darkness.

[3] The three paths are religiousness, irreligiousness, and knowledge.

By the delusions [*moha*] of imagination, touch, and sight,
And by eating, drinking, and impregnation there is a birth and development of the self [*ātman*].
According unto his deeds [*karman*] the embodied one successively assumes forms in various conditions.
Coarse and fine, many in number,
The embodied one chooses forms according to his own qualities.
[Each] subsequent cause of his union with them is seen to be
Because of the quality of his acts and of himself.

Him who is without beginning and without end, in the midst of confusion,
The Creator of all, of manifold form,
The One embracer of the universe –
By knowing God [*deva*] one is released from all fetters.
Him who is to be apprehended in existence, who is called 'incorporeal',
The maker of existence [*bhāva*] and non-existence, the kindly one [*śiva*].
God [*deva*], the maker of the creation and its parts –
They who know Him, have left the body behind.

Doctrine 5

Māyā: Śvetāśvatara Upaniṣad

The preceding passage stresses the impersonal dimension of the one, transcendent god, but the *Śvetāśvatara Upaniṣad*, also contains the idea of a personal god. The personal god resides in the individual's self. Once this knowledge is gained, constant and persistent meditation allows the individual to turn away from the illusory quality of reality. The world has the characteristic of *māyā*, the creative power of the Lord, which fascinates and beguiles the self, but it is only ephemeral. It is constant change and flux; true permanence and peace can only be gained by turning from this *māyā* to the Lord, who is both impersonal and personal.

This has been sung as the supreme Brahman.

In it there is a triad.[1] It is the firm support, the Imperishable.

By knowing what is therein, Brahman-knowers become merged in Brahman, intent thereon, liberated from the womb [i.e. from rebirth].

That which is joined together as perishable and imperishable, as manifest and unmanifest – the Lord [*īśa*, Potentate] supports it all.

Now, without the Lord the soul [*ātman*] is bound, because of being an enjoyer; by knowing God [*deva*] one is released from all fetters.

There are two unborn ones: the knowing [Lord] and the unknowing [individual soul], the Omnipotent and the impotent.

She [i.e. Nature, Prakṛiti], too, is unborn, who is connected with the enjoyer and objects of enjoyment.

Now, the soul [*ātman*] is infinite, universal, inactive.

When one finds out this triad, that is Brahman.

What is perishable, is Primary Matter [*pradhāna*]. What is immortal and imperishable, is

[1] The triad is made up of the world, the individual soul, and the cosmic soul.

Hara [the 'Bearer', the soul].

Over both the perishable and the soul the One God [*deva*] rules.

By meditating upon Him, by union with Him, and by entering into His being more and more, there is finally cessation from every illusion [*māyā-nivṛtti*].

By knowing God [*deva*] there is a falling off of all fetters; with distresses destroyed, there is cessation of birth and death.

By meditating upon Him there is a third stage at the dissolution of the body, even universal lordship; being absolute [*kevala*], the desire is satisfied.

That Eternal should be known as present in the self [*ātmasaṃstha*].

Truly there is nothing higher than that to be known. When one recognizes the enjoyer, the object of enjoyment, and the universal Actuator, all has been said. This the threefold Brahman.

Doctrine 6

Śaṅkara's Advaita Vedānta: Commentary on the Brahmasūtras and Upadeśa-Sahāsrī

Knowledge (*jñana*), as we have seen in the Vedic, Brahmanic and Upaniṣadic texts, has a critical role in Hinduism. Hence, philosophical reflections and schools in India are understood to be authoritative reformulations of the Vedic, Brahmanic and Upaniṣadic knowledge of Brahman and ātman (self). Perhaps the greatest of all Indian philosophers of Hinduism was Śaṅkara (*c*788–820 CE). His philosophical system is set forth in a series of commentaries on the major *Upaniṣads*, the *Bhagavad-Gītā*, the *Brahmasūtras* of Bādarāyana (a collection of brief aphorisms that summarize the main content of the *Upaniṣads*), and in a philosophical manual entitled *Upadeśa-Śahāsrī*. Throughout all these works, he maintains a strict *advaita* or non-dualistic philosophy, in which there is no substantial difference between the Brahman and the individual self. In the first selection from his commentary on the *Brahmasūtras* he argues that the impersonal Brahman is devoid of all qualities, which he calls *nirguṇa*. These qualities are the result of superimposition upon the unified Brahman, and are the result of ignorance or *avidyā* which results from *māyā*. Here, Śaṅkara gives the Upanisadic *māyā* a very negative meaning, taking it for illusion. The second selection from the *Upadeśa-Sahāsrī*, although quite short, presents us with what he thought was the essence of proper knowledge. Note that for Śaṅkara and other philosophers of India and Hinduism, their doctrines of 'knowing' or Vedānta are understood to be the essential teaching or message of the entire sacred writings of the tradition.

Commentary on the Brahmasūtras 1:1

It is a matter not requiring any proof that the object and the subject whose respective spheres are the notion of the 'Thou' (the Non-Ego) and the 'Ego', and which are opposed to each other as much as darkness and light are, cannot be identified. All the less can their respective attributes be identified. Hence it follows that it is wrong to superimpose upon the subject – whose Self is intelligence, and which has for its sphere the notion of the Ego – the object whose sphere is the notion of the Non-Ego, and the attributes of the object, and vice versa to superimpose the subject and the attributes of the subject on the object. In spite of this it is on the part of man a natural procedure – which has its cause in wrong knowledge – not to distinguish the two entities (object and subject) and their respective attributes, although they are absolutely distinct, but to superimpose upon each the characteristic nature and the attributes of the other, and thus, coupling the Real and the Unreal, to make use of expressions such as 'That am I', 'That is mine'. But what have we to understand by the term 'superimposition'? The apparent presentation, in the form of remembrance, to consciousness of something previously observed, in some other thing.

Some indeed define the term 'superimposition' as the superimposition of the attributes of one thing on another thing. Others, again, define superimposition as the error founded on the non-apprehension of the difference of that which is superimposed from that on which it is superimposed. Others, again, define it as the fictitious assumption of attributes contrary to the nature of that thing on which something else is superimposed. But all these definitions agree in so far as they represent superimposition as the apparent presentation of the attributes of one thing in another thing. And therewith agrees also the popular view which is exemplified by expressions such as the following: 'Mother-of-pearl appears like silver,' 'The moon although only one appears as if she were double.' But how is it possible that on the interior Self which itself is not an object there should be superimposed objects and their attributes? For everyone superimposes an object only on such other objects as are placed before him (i.e. in contact with his sense-organs), and you have said before that the interior Self which is entirely disconnected from the idea of the Thou (the Non-Ego) is never an object. It is not, we reply, non-object in the absolute sense. For it is the object of the notion of the Ego, and the interior Self is well known to exist on account of its immediate (intuitive) presentation. Nor is it an exceptionless rule that objects can be superimposed only on such other objects as are before us, i.e. in contact with our sense-organs; for non-discerning men superimpose on the ether, which is not the object of sensuous perception, dark-blue colour.

Hence it follows that the assumption of Non-Self being superimposed on the interior Self is not unreasonable.

This superimposition thus defined, learned men consider to be nescience (*avidyā*), and the ascertainment of the true nature of that which is (the Self) by means of the discrimination of that (which is superimposed on the Self), they call knowledge (*vidyā*). There being such knowledge (neither the Self nor the Non-Self) are affected in the least by any blemish or (good) quality produced by their mutual superimposition. The mutual superimposition of the Self and the Non-Self, which is termed Nescience, is the presupposition on which they base all the practical distinctions – those made in ordinary life as well as those laid down by the Veda – between means of knowledge, objects of knowledge (and knowing persons), and all scriptural texts, whether they are concerned with injunctions and prohibitions (of meritorious and non-meritorious actions), or with final release.

But how can the means of right knowledge such as perception, inference, etc., and scriptural texts have for their object that which is dependent on Nescience? Because, we reply, the means of right knowledge cannot operate unless there be a knowing personality, and because the existence of the latter depends on the erroneous notion that the body, the senses, and so on, are identical with, or belong to, the Self of the knowing person. For without the employment of the senses, perception and the other means of right knowledge cannot operate. And without a basis (i.e. the body) the senses cannot act. Nor does anybody act by means of a body on which the nature of the Self is not superimposed. Nor can, in the absence of all that, the Self which, in its own nature is free from all contact, become a knowing agent. And if there is no knowing agent, the means of right knowledge cannot operate (as said above). Hence perception and the other means of right knowledge, and the Vedic texts have for their object that which is dependent on nescience. (That human cognitional activity has for its presupposition the superimposition described above) follows also from the non-difference in that respect of men from animals. Animals, when sounds or other sensible qualities affect their sense of hearing or other sensible qualities affect their sense of hearing or other senses, recede or advance according as the idea derived from the sensation is a comforting or disquieting one. A cow, for instance, when she sees a man approaching with a raised stick in his hand, thinks that he wants to beat her, and therefore moves away; while she walks up to a man who advances with some fresh grass in his hand. Thus men also – who possess a higher intelligence – run away when they see strong fierce-looking fellows drawing near with shouts and brandishing swords; while they confidently approach persons of contrary appearance and behaviour. We thus see that men and animals follow the same course of procedure with reference to the means and objects of knowledge. Now it is well known that the procedure of animals bases on the non-distinction (of Self and Non-Self); we therefore conclude that, as they present the same appearances, men also – although distinguished by superior intelligence – proceed with regard to perception and so on, in the same way as animals do; as long, that is to say, as the mutual superimposition of Self and Non-Self lasts. With reference again to that kind of activity which is founded on the Veda (sacrifices and the like), it is true indeed that the reflecting man who is qualified to enter on it, does so not without knowing that the Self has a relation to another world; yet the qualification does not depend on the knowledge, derivable from the Vedānta texts, of the true nature of the Self as free from all wants, raised above the distinctions of the Brāhmaṇa and Kṣatriya classes and so on, transcending transmigratory existence. For such knowledge is useless and even contradictory to the claim (on the part of sacrificers, etc. to perform certain actions and enjoy their fruits). And before such knowledge of the Self has arisen, the Vedic texts continue in their operation, to have for their object that which is dependent on nescience. For such texts as the following, 'A Brāhmana is to sacrifice', are operative only on the supposition that on the Self are superimposed particular conditions such as caste, stage of life, age, outward circumstances and so on. That by superimposition we have to understand the notion of something in some other thing we have already explained. (The superimposition of the Non-Self will be understood more definitely from the following examples.) Extra-personal attributes are superimposed on the Self, if a man considers himself sound and entire, or the contrary, as long as his wife, children, and so on are sound and entire or not. Attributes of the body are superimposed on the Self, if a man thinks of himself (his Self) as stout, lean, fair, as standing, walking, or jumping. Attributes of the sense-organs, if he thinks 'I am mute, or deaf, or one-eyed, or blind.' Attributes of the internal organ when he considers himself subject to desire, intention, doubt, determination, and so on. Thus the produce of the notion of Ego (i.e. the internal organ) is superimposed on the interior Self, which, in reality, is the witness of all the modifications of the internal organ, and vice versa the interior Self, which is the witness of everything, is superimposed on the internal organ, the senses, and so on. In this way there goes on this natural beginning – and endless superimposition, which appears in the form of wrong conception, is the cause of individual souls appearing as agents and enjoyers (of the results of their actions), and is observed by every one.

With a view of freeing one's self from that wrong notion which is the cause of all evil and attaining thereby the knowledge of the absolute unity of the Self the study of the Vedānta texts is begun. That all the Vedānta texts have the mentioned purport we shall show in this so-called *Sārīraka-mīmāṃsā.*[1]

Upadeśa-Sahāsrī 4:1–5

How can those actions of which the root is egoism,[2] and which are accumulated in the mind, produce results when they are burnt by the fire of non-egoism (i.e. the right knowledge that the Self is neither the doer of actions nor the experiencer of their results)?

(*The objector:*) Actions burnt by the fire of knowledge may produce results like the seen ones (of the actions of the man of knowledge). (*Reply:*) No. They are due to another cause. (*The objector:*) I ask you how there can be actions when egoism is destroyed? Please answer.

(*Reply:*) Such actions produce their results by overpowering the knowledge of Brahman in you, because they have the power of producing the

[1] The philosophical enquiry whose aim is the demonstration that the ātman of the individual is identical with Brahman.

[2] Identification of the self with the body.

body, etc. Knowledge, however, becomes manifest when the results of these actions come to an end.

As knowledge and the experiencing (of pain and pleasure) are both results of actions that have given rise to the present body and have begun to produce results it is reasonable that they are not incompatible with each other. But other kinds of actions are different in nature.

The knowledge of one's identity with the pure Self, that negates the (wrong) notion of the identity of the body and the Self, sets a man free even against his will when it becomes as firm as the belief of the man that he is a human being.

All this, therefore, is established. And reasons have been already given by us.

Doctrine 7

Rāmānuja on the Ātman and Body: Commentary to the Bhagavad-Gītā

Rāmānuja (?d.1137 CE) argued directly against the position of Śaṅkara, which by his own time had become a dominant philosophical and religious position. However, Rāmānuja was strongly influenced by devotional traditions surrounding Viṣṇu, and his philosophical position attempted to secure the primacy of these traditions. Like Śaṅkara, he wrote commentaries on the *Bhagavad-Gītā* and the *Brahmasūtras*. As consistently as Śaṅkara argued for monism, Rāmānuja argued that the phenomenal world was real, being the product of the Lord's creative power. Indeed, the world is *not* illusory, but the result of Brahman's intention to become manifold. Individual selves are real and related to the one Brahman as a part is related to a whole. Yet the embodied selves are trapped as the result of karma, and do not recognize their identity. They can be released from bondage not by knowledge exclusively. Knowledge is very important, but karma arises from action in the world and their must be a counter-action, the devotion to Viṣṇu, which breaks this karma. In this passage, Rāmānuja comments on the relationships between the individual ātman and the body.

The ātmans can give no reason for grief, for they are immortal. One does not mourn over the embodied ātman when it passes from one stage to another. But these immortal ātmans are subject to beginningless karma, and are, for this reason, created conjointly with bodies that are determined by their various karma. By means of these bodies the ātmans perform acts which are prescribed by the *śāstras* to each station and stage of life, not for the sake of the results of their acts but to be released from their bondage to these bodies. So the ātmans have inevitably contacts with objects through the senses of their bodies and these contacts cause sensations of pain and pleasure. These contacts with objects should be suffered until the acts have been performed. If one is persistent, one will be able to endure them, for they are transient by nature, i.e. the transitory and the transitoriness will cease to exist as such, as soon as the evil which has caused the ātmans' bondage has been annihilated. Therefore one should persist in performing acts and one should consider the pain, which inevitably accompanies the performance of acts, as pleasure. If one performs acts, not for the sake of their results but because they are means of attaining immortality,

then one will attain immortality. One is capable of doing so precisely because the ātmans are immortal.

[Returning to the topic that the immortality of the ātmans and the mortality of the bodies can cause no grief, it is further demonstrated that the body, being a perishable entity, cannot be imperishable and that the ātman, being an imperishable entity, cannot be perishable.] If one positively apprehends both entities, body and ātman, and consequently perceives what they are, one will at the same time perceive this conclusion that the body, being a perishable entity, is essentially perishable and that the ātman, being an imperishable entity, is essentially imperishable. The terms *sattva* and *asattva* in the text have the sense of perishableness and imperishableness. This verse cannot refer to Asatkāryavāda as it has nothing to do with it. Only the difference between the natures of body and ātman, viz. their perishableness and imperishableness respectively, is under discussion here.

The entity ātman, which is a spiritual being, pervades the non-spiritual entity which is different from the ātman. Hence it follows that the ātman is subtler than all other beings which necessarily must be grosser if the ātman is to pervade them. Now, the thing that destroys must be subtler than the thing it destroys, for it can only destroy by pervading a thing and thereby decomposing it. Nothing, however, is subtle enough to pervade the ātman; so the ātman is indestructible.

The body, however, is perishable. The word *deha* proves that a body is a quantity that can be increased. Now things that are characterized by their liability to increase or decrease, e.g. jugs, are finite. Thus bodies are finite. Those bodies, which are conglomerated elements, serve to enable their innate ātmans to undergo their previous karma. If, therefore, that karma is consumed, then the bodies will perish.

Further, the ātman is eternal because it is not the object but the subject of knowledge. Therefore the ātman, forming a unity by itself, cannot be understood to exist in a plurality of forms or to be liable to increase and decrease: in the propositon: 'In all the various parts of my body I know this or that,' something different from the body is understood to be the knower; and this knower exists as a unity because it is not experienced as being different in different members of the body it knows.

Summing up, the ātman is eternal because (1) being a unit it is not liable to increase or decrease; (2) it is the subject of knowledge; (3) it pervades all that is different from itself. The body is perishable because (1) being liable to increase or decrease it exists in a plurality of forms; (2) it serves to enable its innate ātman to undergo its karman; (3) it can be pervaded.

Therefore, nobody can kill the ātman; the verb 'to kill' means nothing but 'to separate the ātman from the body'. The ātman is not subject to developments because it is eternal. So it is not born when the body is born and does not die when the body dies, whether in individual life or in cosmic life. It does not suffer developments like the *prakṛti* does; so nothing has preceded it. All these arguments prove that grief for the ātman results from a misconception. The innate ātman cannot be destroyed, even if its body be destroyed. This nature is common to all embodied ātmans, so they are essentially equal and eternal; inequality and perishableness are brought about by the body.

Nothing whatever can have hold on the ātman, for the ātman will always be subtler than any other entity, and so it is eternal. It escapes the *pramāṇas* by which all other entities are verified, so it is of an entirely different order. Consequently, it cannot be thought of in the terms of these entities; therefore it is not subjected to transformations. This is why positive knowledge of the ātman is so difficult to obtain and why any information one gathers about the ātman will rarely be true.

Ritual 1

The Soma Sacrifice and the Preparation of the Sacrificer: Ṛgveda and Yajurveda (Taittirīya Saṃhitā)

Ritual in the Vedic and Brahmanic texts is an exceedingly complex matter involving long periods of time and a highly differentiated priesthood. Certain rituals were to be performed in the house and others were official public rituals to be performed by kings and princes. However, the important domestic and public rituals always involved a sacrificial ritual of Soma called the *Agniṣṭoma*, 'the praise of Agni'. Soma was understood to be a divine plant whose ingestion rendered the drinker immortal. The immense power of this plant is indicated by the hymn from the *Ṛgveda*, while the text from the *Yajurveda* is recited for the sacrificer as he prepares to press the Soma plant in order to withdraw its sacred juices.

Ṛgveda 8:48.1–15

I have tasted the sweet drink of life, knowing that it inspires good thoughts and joyous expansiveness to the extreme, that all the gods and mortals seek it together, calling it honey.

When you penetrate inside, you will know no limits, and you will avert the wrath of the gods. Enjoying Indra's friendship, O drop of Soma, bring riches as a docile cow brings the yoke.

We have drunk the Soma; we have become immortal; we have gone to the light; we have found the gods. What can hatred and the malice of a mortal do to us now, O immortal one?

When we have drunk you, O drop of Soma, be good to our heart, kind as a father to his son, thoughtful as a friend to a friend. Far-famed Soma, stretch out our life-span so that we may live.

The glorious drops that I have drunk set me free in wide space. You have bound me together in my limbs as thongs bind a chariot. Let the drops protect me from the foot that stumbles and keep lameness away from me. Inflame me like a fire kindled by friction; make us see far; make us richer, better. For when I am intoxicated with you, Soma, I think myself rich. Draw near and make us thrive.

We would enjoy you, pressed with a fervent heart, like riches from a father. King Soma, stretch out our life-spans as the sun stretches the spring days.

King Soma, have mercy on us for our well-being. Know that we are devoted to your laws. Passion and fury are stirred up. O drop of Soma, do not hand us over to the pleasure of the enemy.

For you, Soma, are the guardian of our body; watching over men, you have settled down in every limb. If we break your laws, O god, have mercy on us like a good friend, to make us better.

Let me join closely with my compassionate friend so that he will not injure me when I have drunk him. O lord of bay horses, for the Soma that is lodged in us I approach Indra to stretch out our life-span.

Weaknesses and diseases have gone; the forces of darkness have fled in terror. Soma has climbed up in us, expanding. We have come to the place where they stretch out life-spans. That drop that we have drunk has entered our hearts, an immortal inside mortals. O fathers, let us serve that Soma with the oblations and abide in his mercy and kindness.

Uniting in agreement with the fathers, O drop of Soma, you have extended yourself through sky and earth. Let us serve him with an oblation; let us be masters of riches. You protecting gods, speak out for us. Do not let sleep or harmful speech seize us. Let us, always dear to Soma, speak as men of power in the sacrificial gathering. Soma, you give us the force of life on every side. Enter into us, finding the sunlight, watching over men. O drop of Soma, summon your helpers and protect us before and after.

Yajurveda (Taittirīya Saṃhitā) 2:1

May the waters wet [thee] for life,
For length of days, for glory.
O plant, protect him.
Axe, hurt him not.
Obedient to the gods I shear these.[1]
With success may I reach further days.
Let the waters, the mothers, purify us,
With ghee let those that purify our ghee purify us,
Let them bear from us all pollution,
Forth from these waters do I come bright, in purity.
Thou art the body of Soma, guard my body.
Thou art the milk of the great ones, thou art the giver of splendour;
splendour place in me.
Thou art the pupil in Vṛtra's eye, thou art the guardian of the eye;
guard my eye.
Let the lord of thought purify thee,
let the lord of speech purify thee,
let the god Savitṛ purify thee
with the flawless purifier,
with the rays of the bright sun.
O lord of the purifier, with thy purifier for whatsoever I purify myself,
that may I have strength to accomplish.
We approach you, O gods,
Ye that have true ordinances at the sacrifice;
What O gods ye can assent to,
For that we ask you, O holy ones.
Indra and Agni, heaven and earth, waters and plants.
Thou art the lord of consecrations, guard me that am here.
To the purpose, to the impulse, to Agni, hail!
To wisdom, to thought, to Agni, hail!
To consecration, to penance, to Agni, hail!
To Sarasvatī, to Pūṣan, to Agni, hail!
O ye divine, vast, all-soothing waters!
Heaven and earth, wide atmosphere!
May Bṛhaspati rejoice in our oblation, hail!
Let every man choose the companionship
Of the god who leadeth.
Every man prayeth for wealth;
Let him choose glory that he may prosper, hail!
Ye are images of the Ṛc and the Sāman. I grasp you two; do ye two protect me until the completion of this sacrifice.
O god, Varuṇa, do thou sharpen this prayer to him who implores thee,
Sharpen his strength, his insight;
May we mount that safe ship
Whereby we may pass over all our difficulties.
Thou art the strength of the Angirases, soft as wool; grant me strength, guard me, harm me not.
Thou art the protection of Viṣṇu, the protection of the sacrificer, grant me protection.
Guard me from the lustre of the Nakṣatras.
Thou art the birthplace of Indra; harm me not.
For ploughing thee, for good crops,
For the plants with good berries thee!
Thou art of easy access, divine tree.
Being erect, guard me until the completion [of the sacrifice].
Hail! with my mind the sacrifice [I grasp]; hail! from heaven and earth, hail! from the broad atmosphere, hail! from the wind the sacrifice I grasp.
The thought divine we meditate,
Merciful, for our help,
That giveth glory, and carrieth the sacrifice.
May it guide us safely according as we will.
The gods, mind-born, mind-using,
The wise, the sons of wisdom,
May they guard us, may they protect us,
To them honour! to them, hail!
O Agni, be thou wakeful;
Let us be glad;
Guard us to prosperity;
Grant to us to wake again.
Thou, O Agni, art the guardian of vows,
Among the gods and men.
Thou art to be invoked at our sacrifices.
All the gods have surrounded me,
Pūṣan with grain, Soma with a gift,
The god Savitṛ, the giver of brightness.
O Soma, give so much, and bear more hither.
May he that filleth never miss of fullness.
Let me not be parted with life.
Thou art gold; be for my enjoyment.
Thou art raiment; be for my enjoyment.
Thou art a cow; be for my enjoyment.
Thou art a horse; be for my enjoyment.

[1] The preparation of the sacrificer involves his purification through shaving, bathing, putting on his garment, anointing himself with butter, and anointing himself with salve.

Thou art a goat; be for my enjoyment.
Thou art a ram; be for my enjoyment.
To Vāyu thee; to Varuṇa thee; to Nirṛti thee; to
Rudra thee!
Fit for oblation, mighty, most exhilarating,
That stream of yours may I not step upon.
Along an unbroken web of earth may I go.
From good to better do thou advance.
May Bṛhaspati be thy leader;
Then set him free on the chosen spot of earth;
Drive afar the foes with all thy strength.
We have come to the place on earth for sacrifice
to the gods,
Wherein aforetime all the gods rejoiced.
Accomplishing [the rite] with Ṛc, Sāman and
Yajus,
Let us rejoice in fullness of wealth, in sustenance.

Ritual 2

The Vājapeya: Yarjurveda (Taittirīya Saṃhitā)

The *Vājapeya*, 'the drink of victory', was the first of the three kingship rituals of ancient India, and was associated, as its name would suggest, with the rituals of the Soma. The ritual involved a race with 17 chariots, which the king always won, on a race course marked by 17 arrows. A Brahman perched on a chariot wheel on a pole in the centre of the race course supervised the ritual. At the conclusion of the race, the sacrificer or king and his wife ascended this pole toward a wheel made of dough affixed to the top of the pole. The ritual lasted 17 days. In the following selection from the *Yajurveda*, the sacrificer makes oblation to the horses and drivers of the chariots.

O god Savitṛ, instigate the sacrifice, instigate the
lord of the sacrifice for good luck;
May the divine Gandharva who purifieth
thoughts purify our thought;
May the lord of speech today make sweet our
utterance.
Thou art the thunderbolt of Indra, slaying
obstructions,
with thee may this one smite Vṛtra.
On the instigation of strength, the mother, the
mighty one,
We shall proclaim with our speech, Aditi, by
name,
Into whom all this world hath entered;
In her may the god Savitṛ instigate right for us.
In the waters is ambrosia, in the waters is
medicine;
Through the guidance of the waters
Be ye steeds, O ye that are strong.
Or Vāyu, or Manu thee,
The seven and twenty Gandharvas;
They first yoked the steed;
They placed swiftness in it.
Child of the waters, swift one, the towering
onrushing wave most fain to win the prize,
With it may he win the prize.
Thou art the stepping of Viṣṇu, thou art the step
of Viṣṇu, thou art the stride of Viṣṇu.
May the two Añkas, the two Nyañkas, which are
on either side of the chariot,
Speeding on with the rushing wind,
The far-darting, powerful one, the winged
one,
The fires which are furtherers, further us.
On the instigation of the god Savitṛ, through
Bṛhaspati, winner of the prize, may I win
the prize.
On the instigation of the god Savitṛ, through

Bṛhaspati, winner of the prize, may I
mount the highest vault.
To Indra utter our voices, make Indra win the
prize, Indra hath won the prize.
O whip, strong, having strength for the prizes,
Do thou in the contests strengthen the steeds.
The swift art thou, the runner, the strong.
O steeds, haster for the prize; conquer on the
instigation of the Maruts; measure ye the
leagues; establish the ways; attain the goal.
For each prize aid us, O ye steeds,
For the rewards, O ye wise, immortal,
righteous ones;
Drink of this mead, rejoice in it;
Delighted go by paths on which the gods go.
May the swift couriers, who hear the call,
All hearken to our cry.
Strong limbed, winning a thousand,
Eager to gain in the gaining of praise,
The steeds, which have won in the contests
great prizes,
May they be propitious to us when we call.
Among the gods, strong limbed, good praisers,
Destroying the serpent, the wolf, the
Rakṣases,
For ever may they remove from us evil.
This steed speedeth his swift course,
Bound at the neck, the shoulder, and the
mouth;
Displaying his strength Dadhikrā springeth
along the bends of the ways.
After him as he hasteneth in triumphant speed
Bloweth the wind as after the wing of the bird,
Of the impetuous eagle,
(after him) Dadhikrāvan,
As in his might he crosseth the winding ways.
May there come to me the instigation of strength;
May there come sky and earth with all healing;
Come to me father and mother;
May Soma come to me for immortality.
O ye steeds, prize winning, about to run for the
prize, about to win the prize, do ye touch
Bṛhaspati's portion.
O ye steeds, prize winning, that have run for the
prize, that have won the prize, do ye be
pure in Bṛhaspati's portion.
True hath been the compact
That ye did make with Indra.
Ye have made Indra win the prize, O trees;
now be ye loosed.
Thou art the caul of the kingly class, thou art the
womb of the kingly class.
O wife, come hither to the heaven; let us two
mount! Yes, let us two mount the heaven;
I will mount the heaven for us both.
Strength, instigation, the later born, inspiration,
heaven, the head, the Vyaśniya, the
offspring of the last, the last, the offspring
of being, being, the overlord.
May life accord with the sacrifice, may expiration
accord with the sacrifice, may inspiration
accord with the sacrifice, may cross-
breathing accord with the sacrifice, may eye
accord with the sacrifice, may ear accord
with the sacrifice, may mind accord with
the sacrifice, may the body accord with the
sacrifice, may the sacrifice accord with the
sacrifice.
We have come to the heaven, to the gods; we
have become immortal; we have become
the offspring of Prajāpati.
May I be united with offspring, offspring with
me; may I be united with increase of
wealth, increase of wealth with me.
For food thee! For proper food thee!
For strength thee! For the conquering of
strength thee!
Thou art ambrosia, thou art prospering, thou art
begetting.

Ritual 3

The Rājasūya: Śatapatha-Brāhmaṇa

The second kingship sacrifice, the *Rājasūya*, 'the royal consecration', was intended to establish or re-establish the king's power and allow him to master time. Its central ritual was the sprinkling of the king with various liquids by the priests, and a ritual cattle raid. The ritual also included a game of dice (the stake being a cow and, as in all kingship rituals, the king never lost) and an extensive series of oblations involving ten participants drinking from ten cups. This text from the *Śatapatha-Brāhmaṇa* describes the *pūrṇāhuti* or libation of ghee in the Soma sacrifice. The *Brāhmaṇas*, unlike the Vedas, not only preserve the liturgical texts and hymns, but also describe the ritual process. In this sense, the *Brāhmaṇas* are the priests' manuals, even describing what is to be done in the event of a ritual error at any point in the process.

He offers a full-offering; for the full means the All: 'May I be consecrated after encompassing the All!' thus he thinks. At this (offering) he bestows a boon; for a boon means all: 'Having encompassed the All (the universe), may I be consecrated!' thus he thinks. He may perform this offering, if he chooses; or, if he chooses, he may disregard it.

And on the following day he prepares a cake on eight potsherds, as sacrificial food for the Anumati.[1] And whatever portion of (the grains) being ground, either flour or rice-grains, falls down behind the pin, that he throws together into the dipping-spoon (*sruva*). They take a firebrand from the Anvāhāryapakana or (southern) fire, and therewith go southward. And where he finds a self-produced hollow or cleft, having there made up a fire, he offers with, 'This O Nirṛiti, is thy portion: accept it graciously, hail! For Nirṛiti is this (Earth); whomsoever she seizes upon with evil, him she seizes upon with destruction (*nirṛiti*): hence whatever part of this (Earth) is of the Nirṛiti nature, that he thereby propitiates; and thus Nirṛiti does not seize upon him, while being consecrated. And the reason why he offers in a self-produced hollow or cleft is that that much of this (earth) is possessed with Nirṛiti.

They then return (to the sacrificial ground) without looking backward. He now proceeds with the cake on eight potsherds for Anumati. For Anumati is this (Earth); and whosoever knows to do that work which he intends to do, for him indeed she approves (*anu-man*) thereof; hence it is her he thereby pleases, thinking 'May I be consecrated, approved by that (genius of) approval!'

And as to why it is a (cake) on eight potsherds – the Gāyatrī consists of eight syllables, and this earth is Gāyatrī. And as to why he offers of the same sacrificial food both (oblations): thereby, indeed, both of it come to be this latter one (viz. Anumati, or approval). A garment is the sacrificial fee for this (offering): for even as one clad in a garment does not venture into the forest, but having deposited that garment (somewhere) escapes (robbers), in like manner no assault befalls him while being consecrated.

And on the following day he prepares a cake on eleven postsherds for Agni and Viṣṇu, and offers it in the same way as the (regular) *iṣṭi*[1]: this indeed is just what that approved initiation offering to Agni and Viṣṇu is there. Now Agni is all the deities, since in Agni one offers to all deities, and Agni forsooth is the lower end, and Viṣṇu is the upper end: 'May I be consecrated, after thus encompassing all the deities, and after encompassing the whole sacrifice!' thus he thinks, and hence there is a cake of eleven potsherds to Agni and Viṣṇu. Gold is the sacrificial fee for this (offering); for to Agni belongs the sacrifice, and gold is Agni's seed. As to Visnu, he is the sacrifice,

[1] Anumati is the favour or approval of the deities personified.
[2] *Iṣṭi* means a vegetable sacrifice.

and Agni forsooth is the sacrifice: nevertheless this is Agni's alone, therefore gold is the fee.

And on the following day he prepares a cake on eleven potsherds for Agni and Soma, and offers it in the same way as an (ordinary) *iṣṭi*, for it was thereby Indra slew Vitṛa, and thereby he gained that universal conquest which now is his. And in like manner does this (king, the Sacrificer) thereby slay his wicked, hateful enemy, and in like manner does he gain victory. 'May I be consecrated, when safety and security from evil-doers have been gained!' thus he thinks: hence there is a cake on eleven potsherds for Agni and Soma. For this (offering) a bull set at liberty is the sacrificial fee; for yonder moon they slay while setting him at liberty: to wit, by the full-moon offering they slay him, and by the new-moon offering they set him at liberty; therefore a bull set at liberty is the fee.

And on the following day he prepares a cake on twelve potsherds for Indra and Agni, and offers it in the same way as an (ordinary) *iṣṭi*. Now when Indra slew Vṛtra, that vigour and energy of his went out of him, being frightened: by this offering he again possessed himself of that vigour and energy. And in like manner does this (Sacrificer) by this offering possess himself of vigour and energy; for Agni is fiery spirit, and Indra is vigour and energy: 'May I be consecrated, having embraced both these energies!' thus he thinks: hence there is a cake on twelve potsherds for Indra and Agni. A bull is the fee for this (offering), by his shoulder he is of Agni's nature, and by his testicles he is of Indra's nature: therefore a bull is the fee for it.

Thereupon he performs the offering of first-fruits; for verily he who performs the Rājasūya secures for himself (the benefits of) all sacrificial rites, all *iṣṭis*, even the spoon-offerings; and instituted by the gods, in truth, that is *iṣṭi*, that *Āgrayaṇeṣṭi*: 'May this also be offered by me!' thus he thinks, and therefore he performs the offering of first-fruits. Moreover, it is for the plants that he who is consecrated, is consecrated; therefore he now makes the plants healthy and faultless, thinking, 'May I be consecrated for (the obtainment of) healthy, faultless plants (crops)!' A cow is the fee for this (offering).

Thereupon he performs the Seasonal offerings; for verily he who performs the Rājasūya secures for himself (the benefits of) all sacrificial rites, all *iṣṭis*, even the spoon-offerings; and instituted by the gods, in truth, is that sacrificial rite, the Seasonal offering: 'May these also be offered by me! May I be consecrated by these offerings also!' thus he thinks and therefore he performs the Seasonal offerings.

Ritual 4

The Aśvamedha: Śatapatha-Brāhmaṇa

The third and most elaborate of the kingship rituals of ancient India was the *Aśvamedha* or horse sacrifice. This sacrifice involved releasing a horse to range free for an entire year. After that year, the horse was returned to the sacrificial ground where, amidst elaborate ritual actions, it was smothered. The purpose of this sacrifice was to make the king a true universal monarch. This passage describes a portion of the preliminary ritual, prior to the horse's release, in which the horse was taken a pond adjacent to the sacrificial ground. A four-eyed dog accompanied the horse and at the pond it was clubbed to death. The dog symbolized the enemies of the king, and in its death the enemies of the king were rendered powerless to injure the sacrifice or to capture the horse as it roamed free. While this sacrifice is a repetition of the mythic acts of Prajāpati, Indra and Vāyu are also participants in the sacrifice.

He (the Adhvaryu) cooks the priests' mess of rice: it is seed he thereby produces. Having greased a rope with the ghee which is left over, he takes it; for ghee is (a type of) fiery spirit, and the horse is sacred to Prajāpati: he thus endows Prajāpati with fiery spirit. Impure, and unfit for sacrifice, indeed, is that animal, to wit, the horse.

The rope consists of darbha grass; for darbha stalks are a means of purification: he thus purifies that (horse), and immolates it as one purified and meet for sacrifice.

Now, when the horse was immolated, its seed went from it and became gold: thus when he gives gold (to the priests) he supplies the horse with seed.

Prajāpati produced the sacrifice. His greatness departed from him, and entered the great sacrificial priests. Together with the great priests he went in search of it, and together with the great priests he found it: when the great priests eat the priests' mess of rice, the Sacrificer thereby secures for himself the greatness of the sacrifice. Along with the priests' mess of rice he presents gold (to the priests); for the mess of rice is seed, and gold is seed: by means of seed he thus lays seed into that (horse, and Sacrificer). It (the gold) weighs a hundred (grains); for man has a life of a hundred (years), and a hundred energies: it is life, and energy, vigour, he lays into his own self. At midday he takes Vasatīvarī[1] water of four kinds; it is brought together from the four quarters, for food is in (all) the four quarters, and water is food: by means of food he thus secures food for him.

Now, unsuccessful in the sacrifice, assuredly, is what is performed without a formula. 'This rope did they take, at the first age of the truth (the sages, at the rites: it had been with us at this Soma-sacrifice, declaring the course in the gaining of the truth).' He takes the halter of the horse in order to supply a formula for the success of the sacrifice. It (the rope) is twelve cubits long – twelve months make a year: it is the year, the sacrifice, he secures.

Concerning this they say, 'Is the rope to be made twelve cubits long, or thirteen cubits long?' Well, that year is the bull among the seasons, and the thirteenth (or intercalary) month is an excrescence of the year; and this Aśvamedha is the bull among sacrifices; and inasmuch as the bull has an excrescence (hump), one may add on a thirteenth cubit to the rope as an excrescence of this (Aśvamedha): even as the bull's hump is attached (to his back), suchlike would this be.

(He puts the halter on the horse), 'Encompassing thou art' – therefore the offerer of the Aśvamedha conquers all the quarters; 'the world thou art' – the world he thus conquers; 'a ruler thou art, an upholder,' he thus makes him a ruler and upholder; 'go thou into Agni Vaiśvānara' – he thus makes him go to Agni Vaiśvānara (the friend of all men); 'of wide extent' – he thus causes him to extend in offspring and cattle; 'consecrated by Svāhā (hail!)' – this is the *Vaṣaṭ*-call[2] for it – 'good speed (to) thee for the gods!' – he thus makes it of good speed for the gods; 'for Prajāpati' – the horse is sacred to Prajāpati: he thus supplies it with his own deity.

But, verily, he who fetters the horse without announcing it to the Brahman and the gods is liable to incur injury. He addresses the Brahman (the superintending priest) by saying, 'O Brahman, I will fetter the horse for the gods, for Prajāpati: may I prosper therewith!' and having made the announcement to the Brahman, he ties up the horse, and thus incurs no injury. 'Fetter it for the gods, for Prajāpati: prosper thou therewith!' thus the Brahman urges him, and supplies it (the horse) with its own deity. He then sprinkles it (with water): the (symbolic) meaning of this is the same as before.

He sprinkles it, with 'I sprinkle thee (so as to be) acceptable to Prajāpati' – for Prajāpati is the most vigorous of the gods: it is vigour he bestows on it, whence the horse is the most vigorous of animals.

'I sprinkle thee, acceptable to Indra and Agni' – for Indra and Agni are the most powerful of the gods: it is power he bestows on it, whence the horse is the most powerful of animals.

'I sprinkle thee, acceptable to Vāyu' – for Vāyu is the swiftest of gods: it is speed he bestows on it, whence the horse is the swiftest of animals.

'I sprinkle thee, acceptable to the All-gods' – for the All-gods are the most famous of gods: it is fame he bestows on it, whence the horse is the most famous of animals. 'I sprinkle thee, acceptable to all the gods.'

Concerning this they say, 'Seeing that the horse is sacred to Prajāpati, wherefore (does he say) "I

[1] The water used for the Soma sacrifice.
[2] This is one of the sacrificial calls used by the priests.

sprinkle thee" for other deities also?' Well, all the gods are concerned in the horse-sacrifice; when he says, 'I sprinkle thee for all the gods,' he makes all the gods take a concern in the horse-sacrifice; whence all the gods are concerned in the horse-sacrifice. But his wicked enemy seeks to lay hold of him who performs the horse-sacrifice, and the horse is a thunderbolt; having killed the four eyed dog, he – with 'Undone is the man! undone is the dog!' – plunges it under the horse's feet: it is by means of the thunderbolt he thus stamps him down; and the wicked enemy does not lay hold of him.

Ritual 5

Pūjā: Agni Purāṇa

Pūjā, which might be translated as worship or adoration, gradually replaced the Vedic structure of *Yajña* or sacrifice, and by the 9th and 10th centuries of the Common Era it was the norm in both temples and homes. *Pūjā* normally includes invocation of the deity, offering water for the deity to wash his feet and hands, bathing the image of the deity, offering a new garment, offering a sacred thread, anointing the image with various unguents, offering incense, offering foods and gifts, making obeisance to the deity, *pradakṣiṇa* or circumambulation, and praising the deity. The image of the deity is treated as if it were the god himself, for the image is the *mūrti* or form of the deity made manifest to his worshippers. The *pūjā* ritual underscores the personal nature of Puranic religious texts as distinct from the more impersonal nature of ritual in the Vedic and Brahmanic texts. This selection from the *Agni Purāṇa* describes the *pūjā* to Viṣṇu and other gods.

Nārada said: I will now describe the mode of (offering) *pūjā* by performing which *vipras*[1] attain all objects of life. Washing his head, rinsing his mouth and controlling his speech one should well protected sit in *svastika*, *padma*[2] or any other posture, with his face directed towards the east. He should then meditate in the middle of his navel on the mantram *Yam*, smoke coloured and identical with the terrific wind, and purify all the impurities of the body. Then meditating on the mantram *Kshoum*, the ocean of light, situate in the lotus heart, he should, with flames going up, down and in contrary directions, burn down all impurities. He should then meditate on the mantram *Van* of the shape of the moon situate in the sky. And then the intelligent worshipper should sprinkle his own body extending from the lotus heart with nectarine drops, through the tubular organ Susumnā passing through the generative organ and other tubes.

Having purified the *tattvas* (ingredients of worship) he should assign them. He should then purify his hand and the implements. First, he should assign, beginning with the thumb of the right hand, the fingers of the two hands to the principal limbs. Then with sixty-two mantrams he should assign the twelve limbs to the body namely heart, head, tuft of hair on head, skin, two eyes, belly, back, arms, thighs, knee-joints and feet. Then having offered *Mudrā* and recited his name one hundred and eight times he should meditate on and adore Viṣṇu. Having placed a water-jar on

[1] Sages.
[2] These are the various *āsanas* or sitting postures used in yoga.

his left and articles of worship on his right he should wash them with implements and then place flowers and scents. Having recited eight times the adorable light of Omnipresence and consciousness he should take up water in his palm with the mantram *phat* and then meditate on Hari [Viṣṇu-Kṛṣṇa]. With his face directed towards the south-east direction presided over by Agni he should pray for virtue, knowledge, disassociation from worldly objects and lordly powers; he should cast off his sins and physical impurities in the Yoga postures beginning with the East. In the *kūrma* [tortoise] posture he should adore Ananta [Viṣṇu], Yama, the sun and other luminous bodies. Having first meditated on them in his heart, invoked them and adored them in the circle he should again place offerings, water for washing feet, water for rinsing mouth, and *madhuparka*. Then by means of the knowledge of the art of worshipping the lotus-eyed deity [Viṣṇu] he should place water for bathing, cloth, sacred thread, ornaments, scents, flowers, incense, lamps and edibles.

He should first adore the limbs at the gate in the east and then Brahmā. He should then assign the discus and club to the southern quarter and the conch-shell and bow to the corner presided over by the moon. He should then assign arrows and the quiver to the left and right side of the deity. He should assign leathern fence and prosperity to the left and nourishment to the right. With mantrams he should worship the garland of wild-flowers, the mystic mark *Śrīvasta* [Viṣṇu] and the *kaustava* gem and all the deities of the quarters in the outside – all these paraphernalia and attendants of Viṣṇu. Either partially or wholly he should recite the mantrams for adoring limbs, and adore them, circumambulate them and then offer offerings. He should meditate in his mind 'I am Brahmā, Hari' and should utter the world 'come' in the ceremony of *āhvāna*[3] and the words 'forgive me' in the rite of *visarjana*.[4] Those who seek salvation should thus perform *pūjā* with the mantram of eight letters. I have described the worship of one form. Hear, I will now describe that of nine *vyūhas*.[5]

He should assign Vāsudeva, Bala and others, first to his two thumbs and then severally to his head, forehead, mouth, heart, navel, buttocks, knees, head and afterwards worship them. He should then worship one *pītha* (the seat of a deity) and nine *vyūhas* or parts of the body. He should as before worship in nine lotuses the nine forms and the nine parts of the body. In the midst thereof he should adore Vāsudeva.

Institutional Expression 1

The Order of Human Life: Ṛgveda

Perhaps one of the most famous hymns of the *Ṛgveda* is the Puruṣa-sūkta in which the gods create the world by dismembering the giant man, Puruṣa. From the body of the sacrificial victim, the four social classes or *varṇas* come forth: the Brahmins (the priestly class), the Kṣatriyas (the warrior class), the Vaiśyas (the artisans, merchants and farmers) and the Śūdras (the servants or serfs). Hence, the Puruṣa is a sacred narrative setting the proper order of the social world.

---

[3] The invocation in which the deity is installed in the image.
[4] The concluding ritual in which the image is discarded.
[5] The parts of the body.

The Man has a thousand heads, a thousand eyes, a thousand feet. He pervaded the earth on all sides and extended beyond it as far as ten fingers.

It is the Man who is all this, whatever has been and whatever is to be. He is the ruler of immortality, when he grows beyond everything through food.

Such is his greatness, and the Man is yet more than this.

All creatures are a quarter of him; three quarters are what is immortal in heaven.

With three quarters the Man rose upwards, and one quarter of him still remains here. From this he spread out in all directions, into that which eats and that which does not eat.

From him Virāj[1] was born, and from Virāj came the Man. When he was born, he ranged beyond the earth behind and before.

When the gods spread the sacrifice with the Man as the offering, spring was the clarified butter, summer the fuel, autumn the oblation.

They anointed the Man, the sacrifices born at the beginning, upon the sacred grass. With him the gods, Sādhyas, and sages sacrificed.

From the sacrifice in which everything was offered, the melted fat was collected, and he made it into those beasts who live in the air, in the forest, and in villages.

From that sacrifice in which everything was offered, the verses and chants were born, the metres were born from it, and from it the formulas were born. Horses were born from it, and those other animals that have two rows of teeth; cows were born from it, and from it goats and sheep were born.

When they divided the Man, into how many parts did they apportion him? What do they call his mouth, his two arms and thighs and feet?

His mouth became the Brahmin; his arms were made into the Warrior, his thighs the People, and from his feet the Servants were born.

The moon was born from his mind; from his eye the sun was born. Indra and Agni came from his mouth, and from his vital breath the Wind was born.

From his navel the middle realm of space arose; from his head the sky evolved. From his two feet came the earth, and the quarters of the sky from his ear. Thus they set the worlds in order.

There were seven enclosing-sticks for him, and thrice seven fuel-sticks, when the gods, spreading the sacrifice, bound the Man as the sacrificial beast.

With the sacrifice the gods sacrificed to the sacrifice. These were the first ritual laws. These very powers reached the dome of the sky where dwell the Sādhyas, the ancient gods.

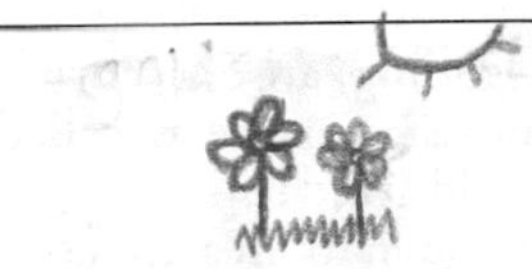

Institutional Expression 2

The Householder and the Sannyāsin: Mānava-dharma-śāstra (The Laws of Manu)

Hindu social and institutional life is regulated at all level amd stages by the concept of *dharma*, which is often rendered as 'law' or 'duty'. However, *dharma* is much more than law, although law is one very important manifestation of this concept. *Dharma* pervades the entire cosmos. Each social class or *varṇa* has its own *dharma*, but in the twice-born *varṇas* (the Brahmin, Kṣatriya and Vaiśya) there are levels of duty, correlated to one's stage in life or *āśrama*. Traditional systems of *dharma* understand that there are four such stages: the student (*brahmacārin*), householder (*gṛhastha*), forest-dweller (*vānaprastha*), and the one

[1] The active female creative principle.

who has renounced all ties to society (*sannyāsin*). Here, in this text from 'The Laws of Manu' we see some of the specific legal injunctions and ideals set forth for the householder and the *sannyāsin*).

Mānava-dharma-śāstra 4:1–18

Having dwelt with a teacher during the fourth part of (a man's) life, a Brahmin shall live during the second quarter (of his existence) in his house, after he has wedded a wife. A Brahmin must seek a means of subsistence which either causes no, or at least little pain (to others), and live (by that) except in times of distress.

For the purpose of gaining bare subsistence, let him accumulate property by (following those) irreproachable occupations (which are prescribed for) his (caste), without (unduly) fatiguing his body.

He may subsist by Rita (truth), and Amrita (ambrosia), or by Mrita (death) and by Pramrita (what causes many deaths); or even by (the mode) called Satyānrita (a mixture of truth and falsehood), but never by Svavritti (a dog's mode of life).

By Rita shall be understood the gleaning of corn; by Amrita, what is given unasked; by Mrita, food obtained by begging, and agriculture is declared to be Pramrita.

But trade and (money-lending) are Satyānrita, even by that one may subsist. Service is called Svavritti; therefore one should avoid it.

He may either possess enough to fill a granary, or a store filling a grain-jar; or he may collect what suffices for three days, or make no provision for the morrow.

Moreover, among these four Brahmin householders, each later-(named) must be considered more distinguished and through his virtue to have conquered the world more completely.

One of these follows six occupations, another subsists by three, one by two, but the fourth lives by the Brahmassattra.

He who maintains himself by picking up grains and ears of corn, must be always intent on (the performance of) the Agnihotra, and constantly offer those *iṣṭis* only, which are prescribed for the days of the conjunction and opposition (of the moon), and for the solstices.

Let him never, for the sake of subsistence, follow the ways of the world; let him live the pure straightforward, honest life of a Brahmin.

He who desires happiness must strive after a perfectly contented disposition and control himself; for happiness has contentment for its root, the root of unhappiness is the contrary disposition.

A Brahmin, who is a Snātaka and subsists by one of the (above-mentioned) modes of life, must discharge the (following) duties which secure heavenly bliss, long life, and fame.

Let him, untired, perform daily the rites prescribed for him in the Veda; he who performs those according to his ability, attains to the highest state.

Whether he be rich or even in distress, let him not seek wealth through pursuits to which men cleave, nor by forbidden occupations, or (let him accept presents) from any (giver whosoever he may be).

Let him not, out of desire (for enjoyments), attach himself to any sensual pleasures, and let him carefully obviate an excessive attachment to them, by (reflecting on the worthlessness in) his heart.

Let him avoid all (means of acquiring) wealth which impede the study of the Veda; (let him maintain himself) anyhow, but study, because that (devotion to the Veda-study secures) the realization of of his aims.

Let him walk here (on earth), bringing his dress, speech, and thoughts to a conformity with his age, his occupation, his wealth, his sacred learning, and his race.

Mānava-dharma-śāstra 6:33–60

But having pased the third part of (a man's natural term of) life in the forest, he may live as an ascetic during the fourth part of his existence, after abandoning all attachment to worldly objects.

He who after passing from order to order, after offering sacrifices and subduing his senses, becomes, tired with (giving) alms and offering of food, an ascetic, gains bliss after death.

When he has paid the three debts, let him apply

his mind to (the attainment of) final liberation; he who seeks it without having paid (his debts) sinks downwards.

Having studied the Vedas in accordance with the rule, having begat sons according to the sacred law, and having offered sacrifices according to his ability, he may direct his mind to (the attainment of) final liberation.

A twice-born man who seeks final liberation, without having studied the Vedas, without having begotten sons, and without having offered sacrifices, sinks downwards.

Having performed the *iṣṭi*, sacred to the Lord of creatures (Prajāpati), where (he gives) all his property as the sacrificial fee, having reposited the three sacred fires in himself, a Brahmin may depart from his house (as an ascetic).

Worlds, radiant in brilliancy, become (the portion) of him who recites (the texts regarding) Brahman and departs from his house (as an ascetic), after giving a promise of safety to all created beings.

For that twice-born man, by whom not the smallest danger even is caused to created beings, there will be no danger from any (quarter), after he is freed from his body.

Departing from his house fully provided with the means of purification (Pavitra), let him wander about absolutely silent, and caring nothing for enjoyments that may be offered to him.

Let him always wander alone, without any companion, in order to attain (final liberation), fully understanding that the solitary man, who neither forsakes nor is forsaken, gains his end.

He shall neither possess a fire, nor a dwelling, he may go to a village for his food, (he shall be) indifferent to everything, firm of purpose, meditating (and) concentrating his mind on Brahman.

A potsherd (instead of an alms-bowl), the roots of trees (for a dwelling), coarse worn-out garments, life in solitude and indifference towards everything, are the marks of one who has attained liberation.

Let him not desire to die, let him not desire to live; let him wait for (his appointed) time, as a servant (waits) for the payment of his wages.

Let him put down his foot purified by his sight, let him drink water purified by (straining with) a cloth, let him utter speech purified by truth, let him keep his heart pure.

Let him patiently bear hard words, let him not insult anybody, and let him not become anybody's enemy for the sake of this (perishable) body.

Against an angry man let him not in return show anger, let him bless when he is cursed, and let him not utter speech, devoid of truth, scattered at the seven gates.

Delighted in what refers to the Soul, sitting (in postures prescribed by the Yoga), independent (of external help), entirely abstaining from sensual enjoyments, with himself for his only companion, he shall live in this world, desiring the bliss (of final liberation).

Neither by (explaining) prodigies and omens, nor by skill in astrology and palmistry, nor by giving advice and by the exposition (of the śāstras), let him ever seek to obtain alms.

Let him not (in order to Beg) go near a house filled with hermits, Brahmins, birds, dogs, and other mendicants.

His hair, nails, and beard being clipped, carrying an alms-bowl, a staff, and a water-pot, let him continually wander about, controlling himself and not hurting any creature.

His vessels shall not be made of metal, they shall be free from fractures; it is ordained that they shall be cleansed with water, like (the cups called) Kamasa, at a sacrifice.

A gourd, a wooden bowl, an earthen (dish), or one made of split cane, Manu, the son of Svayambhu, has declared (to be) vessels (suitable) for an ascetic.

Let him go to beg once (a day), let him not be eager to obtain a large quantity (of alms); for an ascetic who eagerly seeks alms, attaches himself also to sensual enjoyments.

When no smoke ascends from (the kitchen), when the pestle lies motionless, when the embers have been extinguished, when the people have finished their meal, when the remnants in the dishes have been removed, let the ascetic always go to beg.

Let him not be sorry when he obtain nothing, nor rejoice when he obtains (something), let him (accept) so much only as will sustain life, let him not care about the (quality of his) utensils.

Let him disdain all (food) obtained in consequence of humble salutations, (for) even an ascetic who has attained final liberation, is bound (with the fetters of the saṃsāra) by accepting (food given) in consequence of humble situations.

By eating little, and by standing and sitting in

solitude, let him restrain his sense, if they are attracted by sensual objects.

By the restraint of his senses, by the destruction of love and hatred, and by the abstention from injuring the creatures, he becomes fit for immortality.

Institutional Expression 3

Death: Ṛgveda and Vaiṣṇava-dharma-śāstra

The burial hymn from the *Ṛgveda* contains a number of symbolic gestures that may have accompanied the ritual of burial in the early Vedic period. For example, the text states 'when you have gone, wiping away the footprint of death', which may reflect the ritual of wiping away the footprints of the mourners after they leave the burial site. The text from the *Vaiṣṇava-dharma-śāstra* captures some of the attitudes of the individual as death draws near and conveys the idea of saṃsāra or passage into a new body.

Ṛgveda 10: 18.1–14

Go away, death, by another path that is your own, different from the road of the gods. I say to you who have eyes, who have ears: do not injure our children or our men.

When you have gone, wiping away the footprint of death, stretching farther your own lengthening span of life, become pure and clean and worthy of sacrifice, swollen with offspring and wealth.

These who are alive have now parted from those who are dead.

Our invitation to the gods has become auspicious today.

We have gone forward to dance and laugh, stretching farther our own lengthening span of life.

I set up this wall for the living, so that no one else among them will reach this point. Let them live a hundred full autumns and bury death in this hill.

As days follow days in regular succession, as seasons come after seasons in proper order, in the same way order their life spans, O Arranger, so that the young do not abandon the old.

Climb on to old age, choosing a long life-span, and follow in regular succession, as many as you are. May Tvaṣṭṛ who presides over good births be persuaded to give you a long life-span to live.

These women who are not widows, who have good husbands – let them take their places, using butter to anoint their eyes. Without tears, without sickness, well dressed, let them first climb into the marriage bed.

Rise up, woman, into the world of the living. Come here; you are lying beside a man whose life's breath has gone. You were the wife of this man who took your hand and desired to have you.

I take the bow from the hand of the dead man, to be our supremacy and glory and power, and I say, 'You are there, we are here. Let us as great heroes conquer all envious attacks.'

Creep away to this broad, vast earth, the mother that is kind and gentle. She is a young girl, soft as wool to anyone who makes offerings; let her guard you from the lap of Destruction.

Open up, earth; do not crush him. Be easy for him to enter and to burrow in. Earth, wrap him up as a mother wraps a son in the edge of her skirt.

Let the earth as she opens up stay firm, for a thousand pillars must be set up. Let them be houses dripping with butter for him, and let them be a refuge for him here for all his days.

I shore up the earth all around you; let me not injure you as I lay down this clod of earth. Let the fathers hold up this pillar for you; let Yama build a house for you here.

On a day that will come, they will lay me in the earth, like the feather of an arrow. I hold back speech that goes against the grain, as one would restrain a horse with a bridle.

Vaiṣṇava-dharma-śāstra 20:39–53

Till the *Sapiṇḍkaraṇa* has been performed the dead man remains a disembodied spirit (and is afflicted with hunger and thirst). Give rice and a jar with water to the man who has passed into the abode of disembodied spirits.

Having passed into the abode of the manes (after the performance of the *Sapiṇḍīkaraṇa*) he enjoys in the shape of celestial food his portion of the Srāddha (funeral oblation); offer the Śrādda, therefore, to him who has passed into the abode of the manes.

Whether he has become a god, or stays in hell, or has entered the body of an animal, or of a human being, he will receive the Śrāddha offered to him by his relatives.

The dead person and the performer of the Śrāddha are sure to be benefited by its performance. Perform the Śrāddha always, therefore, abandoning bootless grief.

This is the duty which should be constantly discharged towards a dead person by his kinsmen; by mourning a man will neither benefit the dead nor himself.

Having seen that no help is to be had from this world, and that his relations are dying (one after the other), you must choose virtue for your only associate, O ye men.

Even were he to die with him, a kinsman is unable to follow his dead relative: all excepting his wife are forbidden to follow him on the path of Yama.

Virtue alone will follow him, wherever he may go; therefore do your duty unflinchingly in this wretched world.

Tomorrow's business should be done today, and the afternoon's business in the forenoon; for death will not wait, whether a person has done it or not.

While his mind is fixed upon his field, or traffic, or his house, or while his thoughts are engrossed by some other (beloved) object, death suddenly carries him away as his prey, as a she-wolf catches a lamb.

Kāla (time) is no one's friend and no one's enemy: when the effect of his acts in a former existence, by which his present existence is caused, has expired, he snatches a man away forcibly.

He will not die before his time has come, even though he has been pierced by a thousand shafts; he will not live after his time is out, even though he has only been touched by the point of a blade of kusa grass.

Neither drugs, nor magical formulas, nor burnt-offerings, nor prayers will save a man who is in the bonds of death or old age.

An impending evil cannot be averted even by a hundred precautions; what reason then for you to complain?

Even as a calf finds his mother among a thousand cows, an act formerly done is sure to find the perpetrator.

Of existing beings the beginning is unknown, the middle (of their career) is known, and the end again unknown; what reason then for you to complain?

As the body of a mortal undergoes (successively the vicissitudes of) infancy, youth, and old age, even so will it be transformed into another body (hereafter); a sensible man is not mistaken about that.

As a man put on new clothes in this world, throwing aside those which he formerly wore, even so the self of man puts on new bodies, which are in accordance with his acts (in a former life).

No weapons will hurt the self of man, no fire burn it, no waters moisten it, and no wind dry it up.

It is not to be hurt, not to be burnt, not to be moistened, and not to be dried up; it is imperishable, perpetual, unchanging, immovable, without beginning.

It is further said to be immaterial, passing all thought, and immutable. Knowing the self of man to be such, you must not grieve (for the destruction of his body).

Experience 1

'Everything is a Sacrifice to Me': Bhagavad-Gītā

In this passage, Chapter 9 of the *Bhagavad-Gītā*, the availability of God is pushed beyond the doctrine we have seen in Chapter 7 (Doctrine 2, page 193), so that all individuals in society have equal access to God through all acts. This is a radical departure from earlier traditions, in which women and Śūdras in particular were denied access to salvation by traditional Vedic and Brahmanic means. The openness of God to all and through every means became the fundamental experience for the development of Hinduism during the period of the Epics and Purāṇas.

The Lord:
You are a man of good will, and I shall tell you the most secret wisdom,
And explain how it can be attained.
Then nothing will stand in your way.
It is the supreme purifier, the master science, the sovereign mystery.
It is right and perfectly obvious, easy to do, and everlasting.
Men who do not trust in this which is right, O Conqueror,
Do not reach me, and return to the endless round of deaths.
My shape is unmanifest, but I pervade the world.
All beings have their being in me,
but I do not rest in them.
See my sovereign technique:
creatures both in me and not in me.
Supporting beings, my person brings beings to life, without living in them.
I am omnipresent as the stormwind which resides in space.
All beings exist in me.
Remember that.
All creatures enter into my nature at the end of an aeon.
In another beginning I send them forth again.
Establishing my own nature, time after time I send them forth,
This host of beings, without their will, by dint of that nature.
This activity does not imprison me, O Fighter for Wealth!
I appear as an onlooker, detached in the midst of this work.
Nature gives birth to all moving and unmoving things. I supervise.
That is how the world keeps turning, Son of Kuntī!
Fools misjudge me when I take a human form,
Because they do not know my supreme state as Lord of Beings.
Unconscious, they fall prey to beguiling nature such as belongs to ogres and demons,
For their hopes are vain, and so are their rituals and their search for wisdom.
But great men resort to me, to divine nature.
Thinking of no one else, they worship me,
for they know me as the changeless source of existence.
Making my name great as always, firm, not straying from their vow,
Revering me in their devotion, constant in discipline, in reverence they know me.
Others know me in reverence, when thirsting for wisdom they bring their sacrifices,
Know my unique form, my many and successive forms, my face turned toward everyone.
I am the rite, I am the sacrifice, the libation for the ancestors and the juice for the gods,
The priest's verse and the sacrificial butter.
I take the offering, I am the offering.
I am father and mother of the world.
In ancient days I established it.
I am what need be known, what purifies,
the sacred syllable *Oṃ*,
The verse of the sacred books,
Your way and goal, upholder, friend, witness, dwelling, refuge, friend,
The world's origin, continuance and dissolution, abiding essence, changeless seed.
I scorch. I stop and send the rain.

I am deathlessness and death.
O Arjuna, I am the entire world.
Cleansed of evil knowers of the holy Scriptures,
Drinkers of sacred libations,
Make sacrifice to me and seek to attain heaven.
They reach the blessed world of the Lord of the gods,
And in the divine world taste the gods' divine enjoyments.
But after they have enjoyed the wide expanse of heaven,
Their merit exhausted, they return to mortal life.
Thus they follow the practice of the Scriptures,
They lust and desire and get what comes and goes.
Those who think on me with reverence,
and think of nothing else,
When their zeal is constant – I grant them a sure prize.
And when devotees have other gods and full of trust bring sacrifices outside the established liturgy,
they sacrifice to none but me.
For I receive and I command all sacrifices.
But not all sacrificers recognize me as I am.
Hence they fail.
The gods' devotees go to the gods.
Who vow to ancestral spirits go to those.
Sacrificers to demons go to the demons.
Who sacrifices to me come to me.
When you offer with love a leaf, a flower, or water to me,
I accept that offer of love from the giver who gives himself.
Whatever you do, or eat, or sacrifice, or offer,
Whatever you do in self-restraint,
do as an offering to me.
Thus you will be freed from the prison of deeds and their results, good and evil.
Wholly trained in renunciation, released, you will come to me.
I am equal-minded toward all beings.
They neither enrapture me nor enrage me.
But if they worship me lovingly,
they are in me and I in them.
Even if a very wicked man worships,
loving none but me –
That man should be considered wise and good.
He knows what he is about.
He soon becomes completely righteous.
He is bound for everlasting peace.
I am speaking to *you*. *Understand*:
No devotee of mine gets lost.
For all who rely on me, no matter how vile their birth – women, artisans, labourers –
go to the highest goal.
How much more my devotees who have merit by birth or are rulers with vision!
You have entered this fleeting, joyless world.
Worship and love me!
Think of me, be devoted to me.
Revere me while sacrificing to me.
Thus disciplining yourself, wholly intent on me,
you will come to me.

Experience 2

'The Absolute Foundation of All Things': Bhagavad-Gītā

Arjuna has now learned that his princely charioteer is god and that all have access to him through many means. But Arjuna wants to see Kṛṣṇa in his form as god. In this chapter of the *Bhagavad-Gītā*, the Lord reveals all his hundreds and thousands of forms to the questioning Arjuna. It is an awesome and terrifying experience of which the narrator of the *Mahābhārata*, Saṃjaya, states 'If the light of a thousand suns should effulge all at once, it would resemble the radiance of that god of overpowering reality.' Arjuna is shown in his experience on the battlefield that God is 'the absolute foundation of all things'.

Arjuna:
You have favoured me by disclosing the highest secret, concerning the self.
Your words have cleared away the darkness of my mind,
For you have taught me at length the origin and end of creatures,
And also about your glory, which is endless.
O highest Lord, I wish I could see you,
your form as Lord,
Just as you yourself say you are,
Supreme Divine Being.
O Lord, if you think it is possible that I might see you –
Then, Lord of Mystic power, show to me your changeless self.

The Lord:
Open your eyes and see
my hundreds, my thousands of forms,
In all their variety, heavenly splendour,
in all their colours and semblances.
Look upon the Gods of Heaven, the Radiant Gods,
the terrifying Gods, the Kind Celestial Twins.
See Arjuna, countless marvels never seen before.
Here in my body, in one place, now the whole world –
All that moves and does not move –
and whatever else you want to see.
Of course, with the ordinary eye you cannot see me.
I give you divine vision.
Behold my absolute power!

Saṃjaya:
With these words, Viṣṇu, the great Lord of mystic power,
Gave Arjuna the vision of his highest, absolute form –
His form with many mouths and eyes,
appearing in many miraculous ways,
With many divine ornaments
and divine, unsheathed weapons.
He wore garlands and robes and ointments of divine fragrance.
He was a wholly wonderful god,
infinite, facing in every direction.
If the light of a thousand suns should effulge all at once,
It would resemble the radiance of that god of overpowering reality.
Then and there, Arjuna saw the entire world unified,
Yet divided manifold,
embodied in the God of gods.
Bewildered and enraptured,
Arjuna, the Pursuer of Wealth,
bowed his head to the god,
joined his palms, and said:

Arjuna:
Master! Within you I see the gods,
and all classes of beings,
the Creator on his lotus seat,
and all seers and divine serpents.
Far and near, I see you without limit,
Reaching, containing everything, and with innumerable mouths and eyes.
I see no end to you, no middle,
And no beginning –
O universal Lord and form of all!
You, Wearer of Crown, Mace and Discus,
You are a deluge of brilliant light all around.
I see you,
Who can hardly be seen,
With the splendour of radiant fires and suns,
Immeasurable.
You are the one imperishable
Paramount necessary core of knowledge,
The world's ultimate foundation;
You never cease to guard the eternal tradition.
You are the everlasting Divine Being.
There is no telling what is beginning, middle or end in you.
Your power is infinite.
Your arms reach infinitely far.
Sun and moon are your eyes.
This is how I see you.
Your mouth is a flaming sacrificial fire.
You burn up the world with your radiance.
For you alone fill the quarters of heaven
And the space between heaven and earth.
The world above, man's world,
And the world in between
Are frightened at the awesome sight of you,
O mighty being!
There I see throngs of gods entering you.
Some are afraid,
They join their palms and call upon your name.
Throngs of great seers and perfect sages hail you with magnificent hymns,
The Terrifying Gods,

The Gods of Heaven, the Radiant Gods,
Also the Celestial Spirits,
The All-Gods, the Celestial Twins,
The Storm-Gods and the Ancestors;
Multitudes of heavenly musicians,
Good sprites, demons and perfect sages
All look upon you in wonder.
When the worlds see your form
Of many mouths and eyes,
Of many arms, legs and feet,
Many torsos, many terrible tusks,
They tremble, as do I.
For seeing you ablaze with all the colours of the rainbow,
Touching the sky,
With gaping mouths and wide, flaming eyes,
My heart in me is shaken.
O God, I have lost all certainty, all peace.
Your mouths and their terrible tusks evoke
The world in conflagration.
Looking at them I can no longer orient myself.
There is no refuge.
O Lord of gods, dwelling place of the world,
Give me your grace.
And there the sons of Dhṛtarāṣṭra enter you,
All of them,
Together with a host of kings, Bhīṣma, Droṇa,
And also the charioteer's son, Karṇa –
And our own commanders,
Even they are with them!
They rush into your awful mouths
With those terrible rusks.
Some can be seen stuck between your teeth,
Their heads crushed.
As the many river torrents rush toward one sea,
Those worldly heroes enter your flaming mouths.
As moths hasten frantically into the fire
To meet their end,
So men enter your jaws.
Devouring all with the flames of your mouths
Lapping and licking all around,
You fill the world with effulgence,
And your awesome splendour is scorching, O God!
I bow before you, supreme God. Be gracious.
You, who are so awesome to see,
Tell me, who are you?
I want to know you, the very first Lord,
For I do not understand what it is you are doing.

The Lord:
I am Time who destroys man's world.
I am the time that is now ripe
To gather in the people here;
That is what I am doing.
Even without you, all these warriors
Drawn up for battle in opposing ranks
Will cease to exist.
Therefore rise up! Win glory!
When you conquer your enemies,
Your kingship will be fulfilled.
Enjoy it.
Be just an instrument,
You, who can draw the bow
with the left as well as the right hand!
I myself have slain your enemies long ago.
Do not waver.
Conquer the enemies whom I have already slain –
Droṇa and Bhīṣma and Jayadratha,
And Karṇa also, and the other heroes at arms.
Fight! You are about to defeat your rivals in war.

Saṃjaya:
After these words of Kṛṣṇa,
The wearer of the crown was overwhelmed.
Joining his palms he honoured Kṛṣṇa.
He bowed down, then spoke again,
Stammering, overcome by fear:

Arjuna:
It is right, Kṛṣṇa, that the world
Revels in your glory,
That demons are frightened
And flee in all directions,
And all the host of perfect sages honour your.
Why should they not bow to you, O mighty one!
For you are most worthy of honour;
You impelled even the creator.
O infinite Lord of the gods and abode of the world,
You are the imperishable beginning,
You are what exists and what does not exist,
And you are beyond both.
You are the very first god,
The primal Divine Being,
The absolute foundation of all things,
Knower and known,
And the highest estate.
You of infinite form stretched out the world.
You who are Wind, Death, Fire,
The God of Streams, the Moon,
The Lord of living beings, of creation,

You should receive honour
A thousandfold – Time and again,
Honour, honour to you!
Let honour be given to you
Before you and behind
And on all sides.
You who are all,
Your might is boundless,
Your strength unmeasured.
You are all, for you fulfill all.
Whatever I blurted out, carelessly or out of affection –
Kṛṣṇa! Son of Yadhu! My Friend! –
Thinking of you as my companion,
And unaware of this, of your greatness,
And whatever I did improperly to you, jokingly,
In playing, resting, sitting, or eating,
Either by myself or in public –
O imperishable Lord, I ask your pardon for it.
You are immeasurable.
You are the father of the world
With all its moving and unmoving things.
You are its spiritual guide,
Most venerable and worthy of worship.
There is none like you.
How could there be anyone higher
In the world above, in man's world,
And in the realm between the two,
O paramount Lord!
Therefore, I bow,
I prostrate myself,
I beg your grace,
For your are the Lord to be worshipped.
Please, God, be patient with me
As a father with his son, a friend with his friend
A lover with his beloved.
I have seen what no one saw before,
And I rejoice.
But my heart is stricken with fear.
Show me that one usual form of yours, O God,
Be gracious, Lord of gods,
Refuge of the world.
I would like to see you just like that
With your crown and club and the discus in your hand.
O you with thousand arms and of all forms,
Appear again in that four-armed shape of yours.

The Lord:
I am pleased with you, Arjuna,
And by my own will I have shown you my supreme form.
This is the form of my majesty,
It is my universal form, primordial and endless.
No one but you has ever seen it.
No one but you, foremost of the Kurus,
In the world of men can see me in this form,
Whether by knowledge of Sacred Texts,
Or by sacrifices, study, or acts of generosity,
Or rituals, or grim austerities.
Having no fear, no anxieties,
When you see this shape of mine,
However terrifying it is.
See, here is my usual form again.
Your fear is dispelled, your heart at ease.

Saṃjaya:
Thus Kṛṣṇa spoke to Arjuna
And showed his own form again.
The mighty being took on his agreeable form,
And he comforted that frightened man.

Arjuna:
Now that I see this pleasant, human shape of yours, Kṛṣṇa,
I regain my senses and become normal again.

The Lord:
Even the gods long to see this form of mine
That is very difficult to see and that you have seen.
The way you have seen me I cannot be seen
By knowing sacred texts, by austerity, generosity, or sacrifice,
But I can be known and seen in this way, as I really am;
I am accessible through devotion directed to me alone.
Who does his rites for me and is intent on me,
Who loves me without other desires,
And has no ill will toward any creatures at all,
He comes to me.

Experience 3

The Symbolism of *Oṃ* and the Transcendental Consciousness: Māṇḍūkya Upaniṣad

The *Māṇḍūkya Upaniṣad* is among the shortest of the major Upaniṣads. Yet it offers a powerful interpretation of the word *Oṃ*, in which four stages of consciousness are described. The first three are described as wakefulness, dream, and dreamless sleep. The fourth stage of consciousness (*turīya*) is that of transcental consciousness, in which all subject-object distinctions are overcome. The self becomes truly egoless and impersonal. In short, this Upaniṣad describes the process of union outlined in other Upaniṣadic texts and in the philosophical reflections of Śaṅkara.

Oṃ! – this syllable is this whole world.

Its further explanation is:

The past, the present, the future – everything is just the word *Oṃ*.

And whatever else that transcends threefold time – that, too, is just the word *Oṃ*.

For truly, everything here is Brahman; this self (*ātman*) is Brahman. This same self has four fourths.

The waking state (*jāgarita-sthāna*), outwardly cognitive, having seven limbs, having nineteen mouths, enjoying the gross (*sthūla-bhuj*), the Common-to-all-men (*vaiśvānara*), is the first fourth.

The dreaming state (*svapna-sthāna*), inwardly cognitive, having seven limbs, having nineteen mouths, enjoying the exquisite (*pravivikta-bhuj*), the Brilliant (*taijasa*), is the second fourth.

If one asleep desires no desire whatsoever, sees no dream whatsoever, that is deep sleep (*suṣupta*).

The deep-sleep state (*suṣupta-sthāna*), unified (*ekī-bhūta*), just (*eva*) a cognition-mass (*prajñāna-ghana*), consisting of bliss (*ānanda-maya*), enjoying bliss (*ānanda-bhuj*), whose mouth is thought (*cetas-*), the Cognitional (*prājña*), is the third fourth.

This is the lord of all (*sarveśvara*). This is the all-knowing (*sarva-jña*). This is the inner controller (*antar-yāmin*). This is the source (*yoni*) of all, for this is the origin and the end (*prabhavāpyayau*) of beings.

Not inwardly cognitive (*antahg-prajña*), not outwardly cognitive (*bahiḥ-prajña*), not bothwise cognitive (*ubhayataḥ-prajña*), not a cognition-mass (*prajñāna-ghana*), unseen (*a-dṛṣṭa*), with which there can be no dealing (*a-vyavahārya*), ungraspable (*a-grāhya*), having no distinctive mark (*a-lakṣaṇa*), non-thinkable (*a-cintya*), that cannot be designated (*a-vyapadeśya*), the essence of the assurance of which is the state of being with the Self (*ekātmya-pratyaya-sara*), the cessation of development (*prapañcopaśama*), tranquil (*śanta*), benign (*śiva*), without a second (*a-dvaita*) – (such) they think is the fourth. He is the Self (*ātman*). He should be discerned.

This is the Self with regard to the word *Oṃ*, with regard to its elements. The elements (*mātra*) are the fourths; the fourths, the elements: the letter *a*, the letter *u*, the letter *m*.[1]

The waking state, the Common-to-all-men, is the letter *a*, the first element, from *āpti* ('obtaining') or from *ādimatvā* ('being first').

He obtains, verily, indeed, all desires, he becomes first – he who knows this.

The sleeping state, the Brilliant, is the letter *u*, the second element, from *utkarṣa* ('exaltation') or from *ubhayatvā* ('intermediateness').

He exalts, verily, indeed, the continuity of knowledge; and he becomes equal (*samāna*); no one ignorant of Brahman is born in the family of him who knows this.

The deep-sleep state, the Cognitional, is the letter *m*, the third element, from *miti* ('erecting') or from *apīti* ('emerging').

He, verily, indeed, erects (*minoti*) this whole world, and he becomes its emerging – he who knows this.

The fourth is without an element, with which

[1] *Oṃ* in Sanskrit is made up of a diphthong *a* + *u* + *m*.

there can be no dealing, the cessation of development, benign, without a second.

Thus *Oṃ* is the Self (*ātman*) indeed.

He who knows this, with his self enters the Self – yea, he who knows this!

Experience 4

Longing for Kṛṣṇa: Nammāḷvār's Tiruviruttam

During the 6th century of the Common Era there developed in South India a new devotionalism for the gods Viṣṇu and Śiva. Such devotionalism already had predecessors in the Epic and Puranic literature, and perhaps even before these bodies of literature developed. However, this devotionalism was new in that it was the product of great Śaivite and Vaiṣṇavite poet-saints: the devotees of Śiva were called Nāyanārs, 'leaders', and those of Viṣṇu Aḷvārs, 'divers' into the sacred. The Āḷvārs utilized the imagery of love to articulate the relationship between humans and god, developing their religious poetry around Kṛṣṇa Gopāla, the divine cowherd. Kṛṣṇa, as cowherd, is surrounded by the adoring *gopīs* or cowherd girls. The *gopīs*' relationship to Kṛṣṇa becomes the model for the devotees' relation to god. The following selection comes from Nammāḷvār (*c* late 7th–8th century), who wrote the *Tiruviruttam*, 'Sacred Words', describing the Āḷvār and the cowherd girls' longing for Viṣṇu's *avatār* Kṛṣṇa.

[Invocation: the Āḷvār prays to be delivered from rebirth]

Be gracious, Lord of all the heavenly ones,
Born in all births to save all lives,
And hear thy servant's plea.
Grant, not again may I such nature win as this – my body foul,
Wisdom unsound, and character defiled.

[The maid speaks, seeing the state of her mistress, unable to endure separation from her lord, who has left her. Here the maid stands for the Āḷvār's disciples, the mistress for the Āḷvār, the lord for Viṣṇu.]

Long may she love, this girl with luring looks,
Who loves the feet that heavenly ones adore,
The feet of Kaṇṇan,[1] dark as rainy clouds:
Her red eyes all abrim with tears of grief,
Like darting Kayal fish in a deep pool.

[The mistress to her maid]

Will't stay or come again, my lonely heart
Which has pursued the bird flame-angry,
Driven by the lord of tulasī,[2] arm'd with fatal wheel,
Whom gods adore! – the piping cowherds' girl,
Bhūdevī, Śrī, his shadows, it perceives!

[Plaint of the mistress]

Wind that art tulasī-poisoned, blowing thoughts
Of him who drain'd the traitress demon's breast,
Oh, shame to come and with trembling me,
Me, whom his bird ere now of her one heart
Has reft! No heart for tulasī remains.

[1] Kṛṣṇa.

[2] The holy basil, a plant dedicated to Viṣṇu.

[The pity of the maid on seeing her mistress' loss of colour through grief]

Hot in this village now doth blow the breeze
Whose nature coolness is.
Hath he, this once,
The rain-cloud hued, his sceptre turned aside
To steal the love-glow from my lady, lorn
For tulasi, with wide eyes raining tears?

[The mistress is troubled at the coming of the rainy season, which should have brought her lord back to her]

Is this sky in which the strong dark bulls
Pawing the ground till earth shakes, sweat and fight?
Is this the cool fair time that takes the form
Of Viṣṇu, and sounds his harshness who
Is gone? Sinful, I know not what I see.

[The lord – here the Āḻvār's devotees – speaks of the difficulty of parting from his mistress]

Ah, who can leave her, like a creeper hung
With glorious flowers, like unto Viṣṇu's heaven?
Are these but eyes? Nay, lotus, lilies red,
Wide petals, lined in black, and all abrim with pearls of white – wide, like a shy deer's eyes.

[The words of the lord on seeing his mistress' eyes fill with tears]

Oh rare the vision of today! Thou maid
That givest bliss like Kaṇṇan's heaven, I say
'He that seeks wealth must needs go far' – and lo!
Thy fish-like eyes, large as a hand, with pearls
Ashine, and gold, a ransom for the world!

[Lamentation of the mistress]

Love's glow is paling, and instead, a dark and sickly yellow spreading: – and the night becomes an age!
This is the matchless wealth my good heart gave me when it yearned and sought
Keen discus-wielding Kaṇṇan's tulasī cool!

Experience 5

Rāmakrishna's Enlightenment: The Gospel of Rāmakrishna

For Hinduism, the vitality of mystical experience is by no means confined to the past, and one finds no better example of its continued importance than in the life of Rāmakrishna (1836–86). He was for a period of time a priest at a Kālī temple near Calcutta; there he meditated on the goddess, speaking of her as Mother, until he reached the state of *samādhi*. Throughout the remainder of his life he continued to cultivate *samādhi* under Tantric and, later, Advaita Vedānta teachers. Yet the focus of his religious life remained Kālī, and here we have selected a short section from his own description of his experience.

What a state it was! The slightest cause aroused in me the thought of the Divine Ideal. One day I went to the Zoological Garden in Calcutta. I desired especially to see the lion, but when I beheld him, I lost all sense-consciousness and went into *samādhi*. Those who were with me wished to show me the other animals, but I repled: 'I saw everything when I saw the king of beasts. Take me home.' The strength of the lion had aroused in me the consciousness of the omnipotence of God and had lifted me above the world of phenomena.

Another day I went to the parade ground to see the ascension of a balloon. Suddenly my eyes fell upon a young English boy leaning against a tree. The very posture of his body brought before me the vision of the form of Kṛṣṇa and I went into *samādhi*.

Again I saw a woman wearing a blue garment under a tree. She was a harlot. As I looked at her, instantly the ideal of Sītā[1] appeared before me! I forgot the existence of the harlot, but saw before me pure and spotless Sītā, approached Rāma, the Incarnation of Divinity, and for a long time I remained motionless. I worshipped all women as representatives of the Divine Mother. I realized the Mother of the universe in every woman's form.

Mathua Bābu, the son-in-law of Rāshmoni, invited me to stay in his house for a few days. At that time I felt so strongly that I was the maidservant of my Divine Mother that I thought of myself as a woman. The ladies of the house had the same feeling; they did not look upon me as a man. As women are free before a young girl, so were they before me. My mind was above the consciousness of sex.

What a Divine state it was! I could not eat here in the Temple. I would walk from place to place and enter into the house of strangers after their meal hour. I would sit there quietly, without uttering a word. When questioned, I would say: 'I wish to eat here.' Immediately they would feed me with the best things they had.

Ethics 1

The Merit of Building a Temple: Agni-Purāṇa

We have already seen that *dharma* extends to all aspects of life; no sector or dimension of real human action is free of duty and law. *Dharma* also has particular actualizations in the *āśramas* or stages of life (Institutional Expression, page 2/213). Here, in this text from the *Agni-Purāṇa*, building and fitting out a temple for a god or gods becomes the paradigmatic ethical act. Building a temple, among other things, frees one from all sin, is equivalent to offering sacrifices, and makes one truly pious.

Agni said: I will now describe the fruits of making temples for the residence of Vāsudeva and other deities. He who attempts to erect temples for gods is freed from the sins of a thousand births. Those who think of building a temple in their minds are freed from the sins of a hundred births. Those who approve of a man's building as temple for Kṛṣṇa, freed from sins, repair to the region of Achyuta. Having desired to build a temple for Hari a man immediately takes a million of his generations, past and future, to the region of Viṣṇu. The departed manes of the person who builds a temple for Kṛṣṇa, freed from the sufferings of hell and well adorned, live in the region of Viṣṇu. The construction of a temple for a deity dissipates even the sin of Brahmancide. By building a temple one reaps the fruit which he does not even by celebrating a sacrifice. By building a temple one acquires the fruits of bathing at all the sacred shrines. The construction of a temple, which gives heaven, by a religious or an irreligious man, yields the fruit reaped by persons slain in a battle undertaken on behalf of the celestials. By making one temple one goes to heaven; by making three one goes to the region of Brahmā; by making five one goes to the region of Hari. By making sixteen one attains all objects of enjoyment and emancipation. By making the biggest, middling

[1] The consort of Rāma.

and smallest temples of Hari one in order acquires heaven, the region of Viṣṇu and emancipation. A poor man, by building a smallest temple, reaps the same benefit which a rich man does by building a biggest temple for Viṣṇu. Having acquired riches and built a temple with a small portion of it a person acquires piety and gets boons from Hari. By making a temple with a lakh of rupees, or a thousand, or a hundred and fifty a man goes where the Garuḍa-emblemed deity resides. He who, in his childhood, even sportively makes a temple of Vāsudeva with sand, repairs to his region. He who builds temples of Viṣṇu at sacred places, shrines and hermitages, reaps threefold fruits. Those who decorate the temple of Viṣṇu with scents, flowers and sacred mud, repair to the city of the Lord. Having erected a temple for Hari, a man either fallen, about to fall, or half-fallen, reaps twofold fruits. He who brings about the fall of a man is the protector of one fallen. By making a temple for Viṣṇu one attains to his region. As long as the collection of bricks of Hari's temple exists the founder of his family lives gloriously in the region of Viṣṇu. He becomes pious and adorable both in this world and in the next.

He who builds a temple for Kṛṣṇa, the son of Vāsudeva, is born as a man of good deeds and his family is purified. He who builds temples for Viṣṇu, Rudra, the sun-god and other deities, acquires fame. What is the use of wealth unto him which is hoarded up by ignorant men? Useless is the acquisition of his riches, who, with hard-earned money, does not have a temple built for Kṛṣṇa, whose wealth is not enjoyed by the Pitris, Brahmanas, the celestials and friends. As death is certain unto men so is his destruction. The man who does not spend his money for his enjoyments or in charities and keeps it hoarded up, is stupid and is fettered even when alive. What is his merit who, obtaining riches either by an accident or by manliness, does not spend it for a glorious work or for religion. (What is his merit) who having given away his wealth unto the leading twice-born, makes his gift circulated or who speaks more than he gives away in charities? Therefore a wise man should have temples built for Viṣṇu and other deities. Having entered the region of Hari he acquires reverential faith in Narottama. He pervades all the three worlds containing the mobile and immobile, the past, future and present, gross, subtle and all the inferior objects. From Brahmā to a pillar everything has originated from Viṣṇu. Having obtained entrance into the region of the Great Soul, Viṣṇu, the omnipresent God and gods, a man is not born again on earth.

By building temples for other gods a man reaps the same fruit which he does by building one for Viṣṇu. By building temples for Śiva, Brahmā, the sun, Chaṇḍī and Lakṣmi one acquires religious merit. Greater merit is acquired by installing images. In the sacrifice attendant upon the setting up of an image there is no end of fruits. One made of wood gives greater merit than what is made of clay; one made of bricks yields greater than a wooden one. One made of stone yields greater than what is made of bricks. Images made of gold and other metals yield the greater religious merit. Sins accumulated in seven births are dissipated even at the very commencement. One building a temple goes to heaven; he never goes to hell. Having saved one hundreds of his family he takes them to the region of Viṣṇu. Yama said to his emissaries: 'Do not bring to hell persons who have built temples and adored images. Bring those to my view who have not built temples. Range thus rightly and follow my commands.

'Persons can never disregard your commands except those who are under the protection of the endless Father of the universe. You should always pass over those persons who have their minds fixed on the Lord. They are not to live here. You should avoid them from a distance who adore Viṣṇu. These, who sing the glories of Govinda, those, who worship Janārddana with daily and occasional rites, should be shunned by you from a distance. They, who attain to that station, should not be even looked at by you. The persons who adore Him with flowers, incense, raiments and favourite ornaments, should not be marked by you. They go to the region of Kṛṣṇa. Those who besmear the body of Viṣṇu with unguents, who sprinkle his body, should be left in the abode of Kṛṣṇa. Even a son of any other member, born in the family of one who has built a temple of Viṣṇu, should not be touched by you. Hundreds of persons, who have built temples of Viṣṇu with wood or stone, should not be looked at by you with an evil mind.'

By building a golden temple one is freed from all sins. He, who has got a temple built for Viṣṇu, reaps the great fruit which one does by celebrating sacrifices every day. By building a temple for the Lord he takes his family, a hundred generations past and a hundred to come, to the region of

Achyuta. Viṣṇu is identical with the seven worlds. He, who builds a temple for him, saves the endless worlds and himself attains to immortality. As long as the bricks will last, the maker of the temple will live for so many thousand years in heaven. The maker of the image attains to the region of Viṣṇu, and he who consecrates the installation of the same is immersed in Hari. The person who builds a temple and an image as well as he who consecrates them come before him.

This rite of *pratiṣṭha* (installation) of Hari was related by Yama. For creating temples and images of the deities Hayaśīrṣa described it to Brahmā.

Ethics 2

The Three Da's: Bṛhadāraṇyaka Upaniṣad

The three cardinal virtues of Hinduism are often referred to as the three *da*'s: *damyata*, restraint or self-control, *datta*, giving, and *dayadhvam*, compassion. These, according to this text, were spoken and enacted at the very beginning to time. They are the foundation of all Hindu ethical thought and reflection.

The threefold offspring of Prajāpati – gods, men, and demons (*asuras*) – dwelt with their father Prajāpati as students of sacred knowledge (*brahmacarya*).

Having lived the life of a student of sacred knowledge, the gods said: 'Speak to us, sir.' To them then he spoke this syllable, '*Da*.' 'Did you understand?' 'We did understand,' said they. 'You said to us, "Restrain yourselves (*damyata*)."' 'Yes (*Oṃ*)!' said he. 'You did understand.'

So then the men said to him: 'Speak to us, sir.' To them then he spoke this syllable, '*Da*.' 'Did you understand?' 'We did understand,' said they. 'You said to us, "Give (*datta*)."' 'Yes (*Oṃ*)!' said he. 'You did understand.'

So then the demons said to him: 'Speak to us, sir.' To them, then he spoke this syllable, '*Da*.' 'Did you understand?' 'We did understand,' said they. 'You said to us, "Be compassionate (*dayadhvam*)."' 'Yes (*Oṃ*)!' said he. 'You did understand.'

This same thing does the divine voice here, thunder, repeat: *Da*! *Da*! *Da*! that is, restrain yourselves, give, be compassionate. One should practise this same triad: self-restraint, giving, compassion.

Ethics 3

Ahimsā: Mohandas Gandhi, An Autobiography

Mohandas K. Gandhi (1869–1948) utilized much of the Hindu tradition in the formulation of Indian nationalism. For example, he understood the *Bhagavad-Gītā*'s *karma-yoga* as the active involvement in the political world, but an involvement characterized by selflessness and dispassion. Central to this thinking was ahiṃsā, non-injury or non-violence, which already had a long history in Hinduism. As early as the *Laws of Manu*, ahiṃsā carried with it the sense of doing what was beneficial for a fellow-being in a non-violent manner. Here, in this short selection from his autobiography, Gandhi indicates how ahiṃsā is the path to God.

My uniform experience has convinced me that there is no other God than Truth. And if every page of these chapters does not proclaim to the reader that the only means for the realization of Truth is non-violence, I shall deem all my labour in writing to have been in vain. And, even though my efforts in this behalf may prove fruitless, let the readers know that the vehicle, not the great principle, is at fault. After all, however sincere my striving after ahiṃsāmay have been, they have still been imperfect and inadequate. The little fleeting glimpses, therefore, that I have been able to have of Truth can hardly convey an idea of the indescribable lustre of Truth, a million times more intense than that of the sun we daily see with our eyes. In fact what I have caught is only the faintest glimmer of that mighty effulgence. But this much I can say with assurance, as a result of all my experiments, that a perfect vision of Truth can only follow a complete realization of ahiṃsā.

To see that universal and all-pervading Spirit of Truth face to face one must be able to love the meanest of creation as oneself. And a man who aspires after that cannot aford to keep out of any field in life. That is why my devotion to Truth has drawn me into the field of politics; and I can say without the slightest hesitation, and yet in all humility, that those who say that religion has nothing to do with politics do not know what religion means.

Identification with everything that lives is impossible without self-purification; without self-purification the observance of the law of ahiṃsā must remain an empty dream; God can never be realized by one who is not pure of heart. Self-purification therefore must mean purification in all the walks of life. And purification being highly infectious, purification of oneself necessarily leads to the purification of one's surroundings.

But the path of self-purification is hard and steep. To attain to perfect purity one has to become absolutely passion-free in thought, speech and action; to rise above the opposing currents of love and hatred, attachment and repulsion. I know that I have not in me as yet that triple purity, in spite of constant ceaseless striving for it. That is why the world's praise fails to move me, indeed it very often stings me. To conquer the subtle passions seems to me to be harder far than the physical conquest of the world by the force of arms. Ever since my return to India I have had experiences of the dormant passions lying hidden within me. The knowledge of them has made me feel humiliated though not defeated. The experiences and experiments have sustained me and given me a great joy. But I know that I have still before me a difficult path of traverse. I must reduce myself to zero. So long as a man does not of his own free will put himself last among his fellow creatures, there is no salvation for him. Ahiṃsā is the farthest limit of humility.

In bidding farewell to the reader, for the time being at any rate, I ask him to join with me in prayer to the God of Truth that He may grant me the boon of ahiṃsā in mind, word, and deed.

Postscript

The British conquest of India, completed in the 19th century, stimulated a new Hindu self-consciousness, and the work of orientalists made the ancient texts more readily available. Whereas the scriptures had once been largely the preserve of the Brahmin class, they now helped to inspire a wider Hindu renaissance. Modern Indian writers such as Vivekananda (1863–1902) and Radhakrishnan (1888–1975), together with Westerners such as Aldous Huxley (1894–1963), have thus reinterpreted the past and seen in the tradition the resources for a new statement of Vedānta available for the whole of mankind.

In the 19th century, great advances were made in the translation of Sanskrit texts. F. Max Müller (1823–1900) initiated the first English translation of many Sanskrit texts in his 50-volume *Sacred Books of the East*. Some of these translations have become outdated through new advances in scholarship, but in their own time they sparked considerable interest in Hinduism. In the 20th century the process of editing and translating Hindu religious writings has continued, though less attention has been paid to the ritual texts than to the more accessible philosophical and mythological material.

Bibliography

Some of the better translations of the sacred texts of Hinduism include:

F. Max Müller, ed. and trans., *Vedic Hymns*, in *Sacred Books of the East*, vol. 32 (1891)
Hermann Oldenberg, trans., *Vedic Hymns*, in *Sacred Books of the East*, ed. F. Max Müller, vol. 46 (1897)
Wendy Doniger O'Flaherty, trans., *The Rig Veda: an Anthology* (1981)
Sarvepalli Radhakrishnan, trans., *The Principal Upanishads* (1963, repr. 1969)
Robert E. Hume, trans., *The Thirteen Principal Upanishads* (1921, revised 1931)
Manmatha Nath Dutt, ed., *A Prose Translation of the Mahabharata*, 8 vols. (1895–1905, repr. 1960)
Kees W. Bolle, trans., *The Bhagavadgītā: a New Translation* (1979)

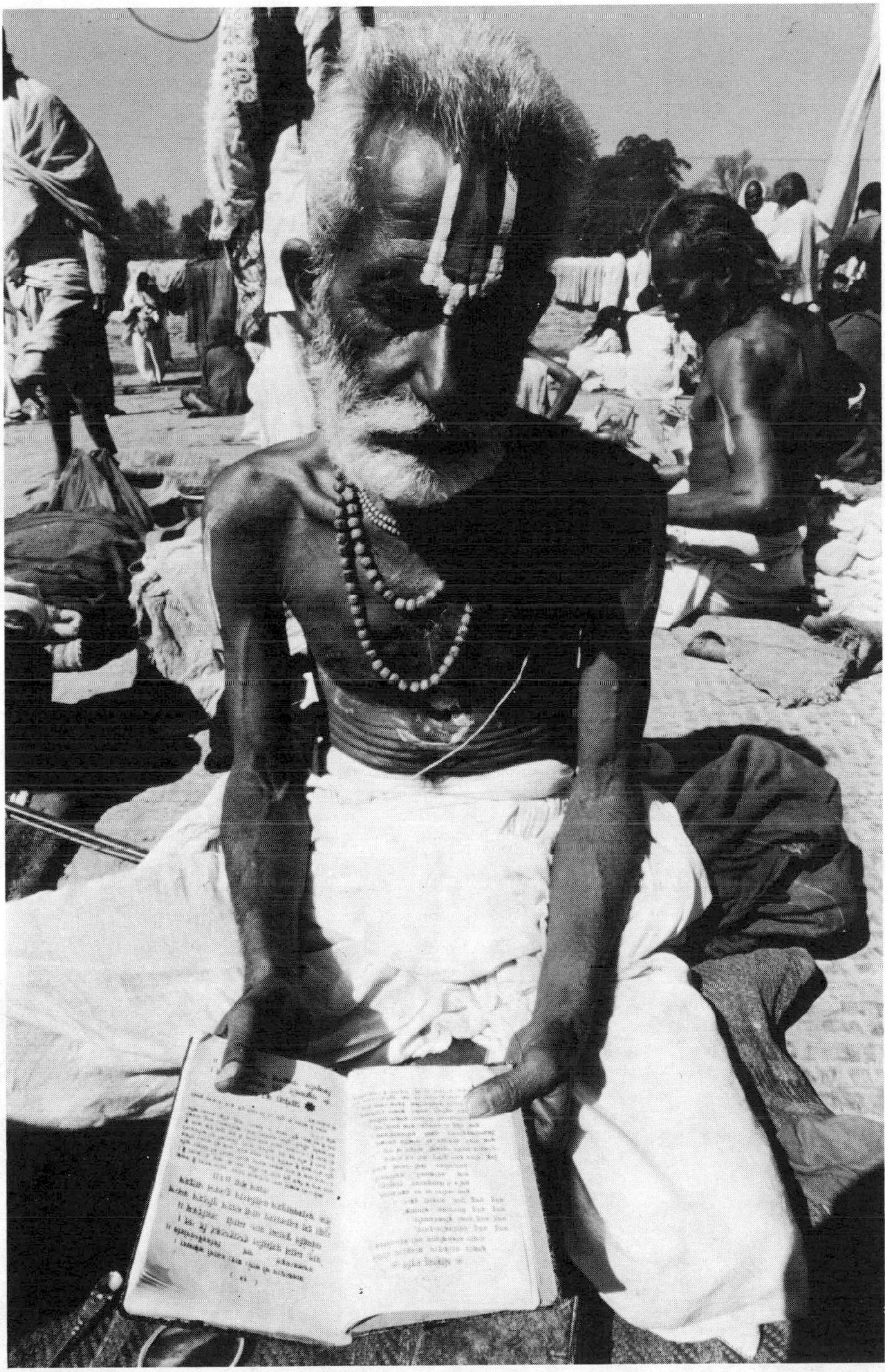

At a centre of pilgrimage in Nepal a follower of Visnu, bearing the traditional ash marks on his forehead, reads from a sacred text. In modern times, the printed word has often replaced memory as the source of knowledge of the divine.

Theravādin monks, robed in saffron and with shaven heads, attend an ordination ceremony. In the early centuries, the Sangha or Order was responsible for arranging the scriptures, and the transmission of the Dharma or Teaching of Buddha remains a major aspect of the life of the monks.

Buddhism

Introduction

The Buddhist scriptures and other esteemed works are awesome in length and complexity. There is the Pāli Canon, written in the language known as Pāli, which is normative for Theravāda Buddhism (in Sri Lanka, Burma and much of South-East Asia), which in the Thai edition comprises 45 substantial volumes. There remain still portions of other parallel collections from other schools of the Lesser Vehicle. There are the Greater Vehicle or Mahāyāna collections, including notably the Chinese *Tripiṭaka* and the Japanese version; these are of even greater size. Many of the works are also extant in Sanskrit, or hybrid (mixed) Sanskrit, the language of the major early Greater Vehicle scriptures as they were composed in India. In addition there are the Tibetan and Mongolian collections. Not all of these works have been fully edited and translated, and it is only over the last hundred years or so that the task of making this great literature available to the West and to a wider world has been in train.

The writings, many of which, notably in the Pāli Canon, were handed down initially by word of mouth, were in early centuries divided into three groups or baskets. *Tripitaka* means 'three baskets', namely: Sutta or Sūtra, Discourses of the Buddha; Vinaya or Discipline, primarily of the Sangha or Order which carried on the Buddha's teaching (Dhamma or Dharma in Pāli or Sanskrit); and the Abhidhamma or Abhidharma, that is, Analysis of the Teaching.

The Pāli Canon includes in the *Suttapitaka* or Sūtra Basket a number of kinds of writings other than discourses and dialogues of the Buddha, for instance verse collections, mixed prose and verse works, tales about future punishments in the various purgatories, lives of the Buddha in previous existences and lives of previous Buddhas. The Mahāyāna collections include some major new sutras of which the most famous is the Lotus Sūtra, and the vast collection known as the Avatamsaka Sūtra, the Wisdom Literature known as the *Prajñapāramitā,* philosophical texts of the Madhyamika school and others, devotional literature such as the Pure Land Sūtra and various edifying collections. The Tibetan scriptures also incorporate Tantric writings which expound, often rather mysteriously, the ideas and practices of Tantric or sacramental Buddhism which had developed in north India in the second half of the 2nd millennium CE and was further elaborated in Tibet.

In the Mahāyāna no firm line can be drawn between what is canonical and what is not. What is important is that different schools came to pay special attention to certain texts and to those who gave expositions of them. It is not possible to give more than a taste of the variety in the selections which follow. But clearly certain motifs are important: the role of the Buddha as teacher, the idea of the emptiness and insubstantiality of the phenomenal world, the inner experience of liberation, the growth of devotion to celestial Buddhas and Bodhisattvas, the ideal of compassion and the various means which are used to take people along the path of liberation.

In the section on Sacred Narrative some main events of the Buddha's career are depicted – enlightenment, first sermon, decease. A later *Jātaka* tale indicates that the historical Buddha is also traditionally conceived as having an enormous and fruitful series of previous lives as the Bodhisattva or Buddha-to-be. By using the famous so-called 'Buddhist parable of the Prodigal Son' from the Lotus Sūtra we point to the theory of the continuance of the work of the Buddha through skill in means, beyond the more immediate historical anchorage of Gautama's life.

In Doctrine 1 there is an exposition of the areas which cannot meaningfully be expounded; the sense of the limitation of ordinary words and concepts surrounds Buddhist doctrine, and is the basis of the distinction between ordinary and transcendental truth, seen in Doctrine 5. The other passages from the Theravādin scriptures relate to no-self, rebirth and the chain of dependence or causation – all central to the Buddha's analysis of our condition. By including a philosophical passage from Nagārjunā we see something of didactic literature, while in Doctrine 6 there is expounded the essence of the Wisdom Literature of Buddhism. The notions of truth-levels and emptiness were given fresh interpretation in China, and the Platform Sūtra exhibits the style of Ch'ān; later, under the dimension of Experience, a short Zen poem is included.

The gentleness of Buddhism connects with the rejection of animal sacrifice as practised by Brahmins (here seen in a *Jātaka* tale), which introduces the selections on the ritual dimension of Buddhism, centring on the growing cult of relics, whose origin is seen in the *Buddhacarita*, on the importance of giving offerings to acquire merit, and the self-discipline of the order through the practice of confession. A taste of later esoteric ritual which came to be important in Tibetan Buddhism is given in the passage from the *Hevajra Tantra* (Ritual 5).

The primary institutional expression of Buddhism is the Sangha or Order, here seen in three passages marking the ordination, the details of the discipline and the problems of the decay of the rules.

Regarding experience, there is a passage from the Pāli Canon on the experience of Emptiness, through the ascending stages of meditation, which links with Mahāyāna teaching. By contrast, Brahmin teaching about the gods is rejected because it is not based on immediate experience (Doctrine 2): Buddhism is here conceived as *ehipassiko*, a 'come-and-see-ish' teaching. More autobiographical expression is found in the poetry of the *Theragāthā* which, with the corresponding anthology of nuns' writings, forms a remarkable corpus of experiential literature. Liberation or nirvāna is to be realized existentially and a feeling for its joys is found in a passage from the *Milindapañha*, the most famous non-canonical writing in Pāli. A Zen poem shows us something beyond the inner-mystical type of experience of Buddhism, namely the sense of unity with the flow of nature. Another contrast is devotional or *bhakti* Buddhism, directed towards celestial Buddhas such as Amitābha and culminating in the visionary expectation of paradise. The sense of reliance on grace is found in Shinran (Experience 6) and the perception of paradise in the Pure Land Sūtra (Experience 7).

The ethical dimension of Buddhism is expressed through a number of Pāli passages including an instance of the extensive commentarial literature (in this case something by the Theravāda's most famous systematizer, Buddhaghoṣa). But the more expansive ideal of the

Bodhisattva became a main motif of Greater Vehicle ethics, here seen in the early *Mahāvastu* and in the lay life as depicted in the influential (especially in the Far East) Vimalakirti.

Sacred Narrative 1

The Enlightenment of the Buddha: Buddhacarita

The *Buddhacarita* is a work of Aśvaghoṣa of the 2nd century CE. It relates poetically the career of the Buddha, as the title states. It seems to draw on various mainstream sources. Here the central event of the Buddha's life is described. Just prior to the events recounted the Buddha had decided to give up severe self-mortification, which he had been practising in accord with one strand of Indian religion down to this day, because it proved to be counter-productive.

Because the great Sage, the scion of a line of royal seers, had made his vow to win emancipation, and had seated himself in the effort to carry it out, the whole world rejoiced – but Māra[1], the inveterate foe of the true Dharma, shook with fright. People address him gladly as the God of Love, the one who shoots with flower-arrows, and yet they dread this Māra as the one who rules events connected with a life of passion, as one who hates the very thought of freedom. He had with him his three sons – Flurry, Gaiety and Sullen Pride – and his three daughters – Discontent, Delight and Thirst. These asked him why he was so disconcerted in his mind. And he replied to them with these words: 'Look over there at that sage, clad in the armour of determination, with truth and spiritual virtue as his weapons, the arrows of his intellect drawn ready to shoot! He has sat down with the firm intention of conquering my realm. No wonder that my mind is plunged in deep despondency! If he should succeed in overcoming me, and could proclaim to the world the way to final beautitude, then my realm would be empty today, like that of the king of Videha of whom we hear in the Epics that he lost his kingdom because he misconducted himself by carrying off a Brahmin's daughter. But so far he has not yet won the eye of full knowledge. He is still within my sphere of influence. While there is time I therefore will attempt to break his solemn purpose, and throw myself against him like the rush of a swollen river breaking against the embankment!'

But Māra could achieve nothing against the Bodhisattva[2], and he and his army were defeated, and fled in all directions – their elation gone, their toil rendered fruitless, their rocks, logs and trees scattered everywhere. They behaved like a hostile army whose commander had been slain in battle. So Māra, defeated, ran away together with his followers. The great seer, free from the dust of passion, victorious over darkness's gloom, had vanquished him. And the moon, like a maiden's gentle smile, lit up the heavens, while a rain of sweet-scented flowers, filled with moisture, fell down on the earth from above.

Now that he had defeated Māra's violence by his firmness and calm, the Bodhisattva, possessed of great skill in Transic meditation[3], put himself into trance, intent of discerning both the ultimate

[1] Māra or 'Death-dealer' is the Buddhist Evil One or Satan.

[2] Bodhisattva (i.e. a Being destined for Enlightenment): until his Enlightenment the Buddha has the title of Bodhisattva.

[3] Transic meditation: the relevant term is *dhyāna* or *jhāna* (Pāli).

reality of things and the final goal of existence. After he had gained complete mastery over all the degrees and kinds of trance:

1. In the first watch of the night he recollected the successive series of his former births. 'There was I so and so; that was my name; deceased from there I came here' – in this way he remembered thousands of births, as though living them over again. When he had recalled his own births and deaths in all these various lives of his, the Sage, full of pity, turned his compassionate mind towards other living beings, and he thought to himself: 'Again and again they must leave the people they regard as their own, and must go on elsewhere, and that without ever stopping. Surely this world is unprotected and helpless, and like a wheel it turns round and round.' As he continued steadily to recollect the past thus, he came to the definite conviction that this world of saṃsāra is as unsubstantial as the pith of a plantain tree.

2. Second to none in valour, he then, in the second watch of the night, acquired the supreme heavenly eye, for he himself was the best of all those who have sight. Thereupon with the perfectly pure heavenly eye he looked upon the entire world, which appeared to him as though reflected in a spotless mirror. He saw that the decease and rebirth of beings depend on whether they have done superior or inferior deeds. And his compassionateness grew still further. It became clear to him that no security can be found in this flood of saṃsāric existence, and that the threat of death is ever-present. Beset on all sides, creatures can find no resting place. In this way he surveyed the five places of rebirth with his heavenly eye. And he found nothing substantial in the world of becoming, just as no core of heartwood is found in a plantain tree when its layers are peeled off one by one.

3. Then, as the third watch of that night drew on, the supreme master of trance turned his meditation to the real and essential nature of this world: 'Alas, living beings wear themselves out in vain! Over and over again they are born, they age, die, pass on to a new life, and are reborn! What is more, greed and dark delusion obscure their sight, and they are blind from birth. Greatly apprehensive, they yet do not know how to get out of this great mass of ill.' He then surveyed the twelve links of conditioned co-production[4], and saw that, beginning with ignorance, they lead to old age and death, and, beginning with the cessation of ignorance, they lead to the cessation of birth, old age, death and all kinds of ill.

When the great seer had comprehended that where there is no ignorance whatever, there also the karma-formations are stopped – then he had achieved a correct knowledge of all there is to be known, and he stood out in the world as a Buddha. He passed through the eight stages of Transic Insight, and quickly reached their highest point. From the summit of the world downwards he could detect no self anywhere. Like the fire, when its fuel is burnt up, he became tranquil. He had reached perfection, and he thought to himself: 'This is the authentic Way on which in the past so many great seers, who also knew all higher and all lower things, have travelled on to ultimate and real truth. And now I have obtained it!'

4. At that moment, in the fourth watch of the night, when dawn broke and all the ghosts that move and those that move not went to rest, the great seer took up the position which knows no more alteration, and the leader of all reached the state of all-knowledge. When, through his Buddhahood, he had cognized this fact, the earth swayed like a woman drunken with wine, the sky shone bright with the Siddhas[5] who appeared in crowds in all the directions, and the mighty drums of thunder resounded through the air. Pleasant breezes blew softly, rain fell from a cloudless sky, flowers and fruits dropped from the trees out of season – in an effort, as it were, to show reverence for him. Mandarava flowers and lotus blossoms, and also water lilies made of gold and beryl, fell from the sky on to the ground near the Shakya sage, so that it looked like a place in the world of the gods. At that moment no one anywhere was angry, ill, or sad; no one did evil, none was proud; the world became quite quiet, as though it had reached full perfection. Joy spread through the ranks of those gods who longed for salvation; joy also spread among those who lived in the regions below. Everywhere the virtuous were strengthened, the influence of Dharma increased, and the world rose from the dirt of the passions and the darkness of ignorance. Filled with joy and wonder at the Sage's work, the seers of the solar

[4] These are described on p. 236–7

[5] Siddhas are men who have obtained perfection.

race who had been protectors of men, who had been royal seers, who had been great seers, stood in their mansions in the heavens and showed him their reverence. The great seers among the hosts of invisible beings could be heard widely proclaiming his fame. All living things rejoiced and sensed that things went well. Māra alone felt deep displeasure, as though subjected to a sudden fall.

For seven days he dwelt there – his body gave him no trouble, his eyes never closed, and he looked into his own mind. He thought: 'Here I have found freedom', and he knew that the longings of his heart had at last come to fulfilment. Now that he had understood the principle of causation and had become certain of the lack of self in all that is, he roused himself again from his deep trance, and in his great compassion he surveyed the world with his Buddha-eye, intent on giving it peace. When, however, he saw on the one side of the world lost in low views and confused efforts, thickly covered with the dirt of the passions, and saw on the other side the exceeding subtlety of the Dharma of emancipation, he felt inclined to take no action. But when he weighed up the significance of the pledge to enlighten all beings he had taken in the past, he became again more favourable to the idea of proclaiming the path to Peace. Reflecting in his mind on this question, he also considered that, while some people have a great deal of passion, others have but little. As soon as Indra and Brahmā, the two chiefs of those who dwell in the heavens, had grasped the Sugata's[6] intention to proclaim the path to Peace, they shone brightly and came up to him, the weal of the world their concern. He remained there on his seat, free from all evil and successful in his aim. The most excellent Dharma which he had seen was his most excellent companion. His two visitors gently and reverently spoke to him these words, which were meant for the weal of the world: 'Please do not condemn all those that live as unworthy of such treasure! Oh, please engender pity in your heart for beings in this world! So varied is their endowment, and while some have much passion, others have only very little. Now that you, O Sage, have yourself crossed the ocean of the world of becoming, please rescue also the other living beings who have sunk so deep into suffering! As a generous lord shares his wealth, so may also you bestow your own virtues on others! Most of those who know what for them is good in this world and the next, act only for their own advantage. In the world of men and in heaven it is hard to find anyone who is impelled by concern for the weal of the world.' Having made this request to the great seer, the two gods returned to their celestial abode by the way they had come. And the sage pondered over their words. In consequence he was confirmed in his decision to set the world free.

Then came the time for the alms-round, and the World Guardians of the four quarters presented the seer with begging-bowls. Gautama accepted the four, but for the sake of his Dharma he turned them into one. At that time two merchants of a passing caravan came that way. Instigated by a friendly deity, they joyfully saluted the seer, and, elated in their hearts, gave him alms. They were the first to do so. . . . His mind thereupon turned to the five mendicants. In order to proclaim the path to Peace, thereby dispelling the darkness of ignorance, just as the rising sun conquers the darkness of night, Gautama betook himself to the blessed city of Kashi[7] . . . which is adorned with the Vārāṇasī river and with many splendid forests. Then, before he carried out his wish to go into the region of Kashi, the Sage, whose eyes were like those of a bull, and whose gait like that of an elephant in rut, once more fixed his steady gaze on the root of the Bodhi-tree, after he had turned his entire body like an elephant.

---

6 Sugata: another title of the Buddha, 'One who has gone well'.
7 Kashi: the ancient name of Benares or Vārāṇasī. Outside the city at Sarnath he delivered the First Sermon.

Sacred Narrative 2

The First Sermon: Vinaya, Mahāvagga

This is the Pāli version of the Buddha's First Sermon delivered to five recluses who had earlier been his companions in the pursuit of the spiritual life. The translation makes use of the word 'Ill' to translate *dukkha* which is often in English rendered 'suffering'. Since it is the opposite of *sukha* or welfare, perhaps 'illfare' would also be a satisfactory translation.

Thus have I heard: once the Exalted One was dwelling near Benares at Isipatana, in the Deer Park.

Then the Exalted One thus spake unto the company of five monks. 'Monks, these two extremes should not be followed by one who has gone forth as a wanderer. What two?

'Devotion to the pleasures of sense, a low practice of villagers, a practice unworthy, unprofitable, the way of the world [on the one hand]; and [on the other] devotion to self-mortification, which is painful, unworthy and unprofitable.

'By avoiding these two extremes the Tathāgata[1] has gained knowledge of that middle path which giveth vision, which giveth knowledge, which causeth calm, special knowledge, enlightenment, Nibbāna[2].

'And what, monks, is that middle path which giveth vision . . . Nibbāna?

'Verily it is this noble eightfold way, to wit: Right view, right aim, right speech, right action, right living, right effort, right mindfulness, right concentration. This, monks, is that middle path which giveth vision, which giveth knowledge, which causeth calm, special knowledge, enlightenment, Nibbāna.

'Now this, monks, is the noble truth about Ill:

'Birth is Ill, decay is Ill, sickness is Ill, death is Ill: likewise sorrow and grief, woe, lamentation and despair. To be conjoined with things which we dislike: to be separated from things which we like – that also is Ill. Not to get what one wants – that also is Ill. In a word, this body, this fivefold mass which is based on grasping – that is Ill.

'Now this, monks, is the noble truth about the arising of Ill:

'It is that craving that leads back to birth, along with the lure and the lust that lingers longingly now here, now there: namely, the craving for sensual pleasure, the craving to be born again, the craving for existence to end. Such, monks, is the noble truth about the arising of Ill.

'And this, monks, is the noble truth about the ceasing of Ill:

'Verily it is the utter passionless cessation of, the giving up, the forsaking, the release from the absence of longing for this craving.

'Now this, monks, is the noble truth about the practice that leads to the ceasing of Ill:

'Verily it is this noble eightfold way, to wit: Right view, right aim, right speech, right action, right living, right effort, right mindfulness, right concentration.

'Monks, at the thought of this noble truth of Ill, concerning things unlearnt before, there arose in me vision, insight, understanding: there arose in me wisdom, there arose in me light.

'Monks, at the thought: This noble truth about Ill is to be understood – concerning things unlearnt before, there arose in me vision, insight, understanding: there arose in me wisdom, there arose in me light.

'Again, monks, at the thought of this noble truth about the arising of Ill, concerning things unlearnt before, there arose in me vision, insight, understanding: there arose in me wisdom, there arose in me light.

'At the thought: This arising of Ill is to be put away – concerning things unlearnt before . . . there arose in me light.

'Again, monks, at the thought of this noble

[1] Tathāgata: a major title of the Buddha, meaning (probably) 'Thus-gone', i.e. one whose way can only be pointed to or indicated by the word 'thus'.
[2] This is the Pāli spelling of the more familiar 'nirvāna'.

truth about the ceasing of Ill, concerning things unlearnt before . . . there arose in me light.

'At the thought: This ceasing of Ill must be realized – concerning things unlearnt before . . . there arose in me light.

'At the thought: This noble truth about the ceasing of Ill has been realized – concerning things unlearnt before . . . there arose in me light.

'Again, monks, at the thought of this noble truth about the practice leading to the ceasing of Ill, concerning things unlearnt before . . . there arose in me light.

'At the thought: This noble truth about the practice leading to the ceasing of Ill has been cultivated – concerning things unlearnt before there arose in me vision, insight, understanding: there arose in me wisdom, there arose in me light.

'Now, monks, so long as my knowledge and insight of these thrice-resolved twelvefold noble truths, in their essential nature, was not quite purified – so long was I not sure that in this world there was one enlightenment with supreme enlightenment.

'But, monks, so soon as my knowledge and insight of these thrice-resolved twelvefold noble truths, in their essential nature, was quite purified, then, monks, was I assured what it is to be enlightened with supreme enlightenment. Now knowledge and insight have arisen in me so that I know. Sure is my heart's release. This is my last birth. There is no more becoming for me.'

Sacred Narrative 3

The Death of the Buddha: Mahāparinibbāna Suttanta

At the time of his death the Buddha is here seen as affirming that the Dharma and the discipline of the Order are to be the Teacher once he has gone. He is also represented as ascending at his death through the various levels of meditation (*jhāna*, *dhyāna*). In a later selection (*see* p. 251) we note how his cremated remains form the focus of the cult which developed into that of the *stūpa* or pagoda.

Then the Blessed One addressed the venerable Ānanda:

'It may be, Ānanda, that some of you will think, "The word of the Teacher is a thing of the past; we have now no Teacher." But that, Ānanda, is not the correct view. The Doctrine and Discipline, Ānanda, which I have taught and enjoined upon you is to be your teacher when I am gone. But whereas now, Ānanda, all the monks address each other with the title of "brother", not so must they address each other after I am gone. A senior monk, Ānanda, is to address a junior monk either by his given name, or by his family, or by the title of "brother"; a junior monk is to address a senior monk with the title "reverend sir", or "venerable". If the Order, Ānanda, wish to do so, after I am gone they may abrogate all the lesser and minor precepts. On Channa, Ānanda, after I am gone, the higher penalty is to be inflicted.'

'Reverend Sir, what is this higher penalty?'

'Let Channa, Ānanda, say what he likes, he is not to be spoken to nor admonished nor instructed by the monks.'

Then the Blessed One addressed the monks:

'It may be, O monks, that some monk has a doubt or perplexity respecting either the Buddha or the Doctrine or the Order or the Path or the course of conduct. Ask any questions, O monks, and suffer not that afterwards ye feel remorse, saying "Our Teacher was present with us, but we failed to ask him all our questions".'

When he had so spoken, the monks remained

silent.

And a second time the Blessed One, and a third time the Blessed One addressed the monks:

'It may be, O monks, that some monk has a doubt or perplexity respecting either the Buddha or the Doctrine or the Order or the Path or the course of conduct. Ask any questions, O monks, and suffer not that afterwards ye feel remorse, saying, "Our Teacher was present with us, but we failed to ask him all our questions."

And a third time the monks remained silent.

Then the Blessed One addressed the monks:

'It may be, O monks, that it is out of respect to the Teacher that ye ask no questions. Then let each one speak to his friend.'

And when he had thus spoken, the monks remained silent.

Then the venerable Ānanda spoke to the Blessed One as follows:

'It is wonderful, Reverend Sir! It is marvellous, Reverend Sir! Reverend Sir, I have faith to believe that in this congregation of monks not a single monk has a doubt or perplexity respecting either the Buddha or the Doctrine or the Order or the Path or the course of conduct.'

'With you, Ānanda, it is a matter of faith, when you say that; but with the Tathāgata, Ānanda, it is a matter of knowledge that in this congregation of monks not a single monk has a doubt or perplexity respecting either the Buddha or the Doctrine or the Order or the Path or the course of conduct. For of all these five hundred monks, Ānanda, the most backward one has become converted, and is not liable to pass into a lower state of existence, but is destined necessarily to attain supreme wisdom.'

Then the Blessed One addressed the monks:

'And now, O monks, I take my leave of you; all the constituents of being are transitory; work out your salvation with diligence.'

And this was the last word of the Tathāgata.

Thereupon the Blessed One entered the first trance; and rising from the first trance, he entered the second trance; and rising from the second trance, he entered the third trance; and rising from the third trance, he entered the fourth trance; and rising from the fourth trance, he entered the realm of the infinity of space; and rising from the realm of the infinity of space, he entered the realm of the infinity of consciousness; and rising from the realm of the infinity of consciousness, he entered the realm of nothingness; and rising from the realm of nothingness, he entered the realm of neither perception nor yet non-perception; and rising from the realm of neither perception nor yet non-perception, he arrived at the cessation of perception and sensation.

Thereupon the venerable Ānanda spoke to the venerable Anuruddha as follows:

'Reverend Anuruddha, the Blessed One has passed into nirvāna.'

'Nay, brother Ānanda, the Blessed One has not passed into nirvāna; he has arrived at the cessation of perception and sensation.'

Thereupon the Blessed One rising from the cessation of his perception and sensation, entered the realm of neither perception nor yet non-perception; and rising from the realm of neither perception nor yet non-perception, he entered the realm of nothingness; and rising from the realm of nothingness, he entered the realm of the infinity of consciousness; and rising from the realm of the infinity of consciousness, he entered the realm of the infinity of space; and rising from the realm of the infinity of space, he entered the fourth trance; and rising from the fourth trance, he entered the third trance; and rising from the third trance, he entered the second trance; and rising from the second trance, he entered the first trance; and rising from the first trance, he entered the second trance; and rising from the second trance, he entered the third trance; and rising from the third trance, he entered the fourth trance; and rising from the fourth trance, immediately the Blessed One passed into nirvāna.

Sacred Narrative 4

The Transcendental Initiative: The Lotus Sūtra

This is the most famous allegory of all the Mahāyāna writings, and shows how the Buddha (conceived as a transcendental and not just an earthly being) uses skill in means (*upāyakauśalya*) in teaching his message, which goes beyond what is here seen as the narrower, but provisionally useful, Lesser Vehicle. Sometimes this story is called the Buddhist Parable of the Prodigal Son, though the messages of the relevant Christian story are rather different.

It is like a youth who, on attaining manhood, leaves his father and runs away. For long he dwells in some other country, ten, twenty, or fifty years. The older he grows, the more needy he becomes. Roaming about in all directions to seek clothing and food, he gradually wanders along till he unexpectedly approaches his native country. From the first the father searched for his son, but in vain, and meanwhile has settled in a certain city. His home becomes very rich; his goods and treasures are incalculable; gold, silver, lapis lazuli, corals, amber, crystal, and other gems so increase that his treasuries overflow; many youths and slaves has he, retainers and attendants, and countless elephants, horses, carriages, animals to ride, and kine and sheep. His revenues and investments spread to other countries, and his traders and customers are many in the extreme.

At this time, the poor son, wandering through village after village, and passing through countries and cities, at last reaches the city where his father has settled. Always has the father been thinking of his son, yet, though he has been parted from him over fifty years, he has never spoken of the matter to anyone, only pondering over it within himself and cherishing regret in his heart, as he reflects: Old and worn, I own much wealth; gold, silver, and jewels, granaries and treasuries overflowing; but I have no son. Some day my end will come and my wealth be scattered and lost, for there is no one to whom I can leave it. Thus does he often think of his son, and earnestly repeats this reflection: If I could only get back my son and commit my wealth to him, how contented and happy should I be, with never a further anxiety!

World-honoured One! Meanwhile the poor son, hired for wages here and there, unexpectedly arrives at his father's house. Standing by the gate, he sees from afar his father seated on a lion-couch, his feet on a jewelled footstool, revered and surrounded by brāhmanas, kshatriyas, and citizens, and with strings of pearls, worth thousands and myriads, adorning his body; attendants and young slaves with white chowries wait upon him right and left; he is covered by a rich canopy from which hang streamers of flowers; perfume is sprinkled on the earth, all kinds of famous flowers are scattered around, and precious things are placed in rows for his acceptance or rejection. Such is his glory, and the honour of his dignity. The poor son, seeing his father possessed of such greater power, is seized with fear, regretting that he has come to this place, and secretly reflects thus: This must be a king, or someone of royal rank; it is no place for me to obtain anything for the hire of my labour. I had better go to some poor hamlet, where there is a place for letting out my labour, and food and clothing are easier to get. If I tarry here long, I may suffer oppression and forced service.

Having reflected thus, he hastens away. Meanwhile the rich elder on his lion-seat has recognized his son at first sight, and with great joy in his heart has also reflected: Now I have someone to whom my treasuries of wealth are to be made over. Always have I been thinking of this my son, with no means of seeing him; but suddenly he himself has come and my longing is satisfied. Though worn with years, I yearn for him as of old.

Instantly he dispatches his attendants to pursue him quickly and fetch him back. Thereupon the messengers hasten forth to seize him. The poor son, surprised and scared, loudly cries his complaint: 'I have committed no offence against you; why should I be arrested?' The messengers all the more hasten to lay hold of him and compel him to go back. Thereupon the poor son, thinking within himself that though he is innocent yet he will be imprisoned, and that now he will surely die, is all the more terrified, faints away and falls prostrate on the ground. The father, seeing this from afar, sends word to the messengers. 'I have no need for this man. Do not bring him by force. Sprinkle cold water on his face to restore him to consciousness and do not speak to him any further.' Wherefore? The father, knowing that his son's disposition is inferior, knowing that his own lordly position has caused distress to his son, yet convinced that he is his son, tactfully does not say to others: 'This is my son.'

A messenger says to the son: 'I now set you free; go wherever you will.' The poor son is delighted, thus obtaining the unexpected. He rises from the ground and goes to a poor hamlet in search of food and clothing. Then the elder, desiring to attract his son, sets up a device. Secretly he sends two men, doleful and shabby in appearance, saying: 'You go and visit that place and gently say to the poor man, there is a place for you to work here; you will be given double wages. If the poor man agrees, bring him back and give him work. If he asks what work you wish him to do, then you may say to him, we will hire you for scavenging, and we both also will work along with you.' Then the two messengers go in search of the poor son and having found him, place before him the above proposal. Thereupon the poor son, having received his wages beforehand, joins with them in removing a dirt heap.

His father, beholding the son, is struck with compassion for, and wonder at, him. Another day he sees at a distance, through a window, his son's figure, gaunt, lean, and doleful, filthy and unclean with dirt and dust; thereupon he takes off his strings of jewels, his soft attire, and ornaments, and puts on a coarse, torn and dirty garment, smears his body with dust, takes a dust hod in his right hand, and with an appearance fear-inspiring says to the labourers: 'Get on with your work, don't be lazy.' By such a device he gets near to his son, to whom he afterward says: 'Aye, my man, you stay and work here, do not go again elsewhere; I will increase your wages; give whatever you need, bowls, utensils, rice, wheat, flour, salt, vinegar and so on; have no hesitation; besides there is an old and worn-out servant whom you shall be given if you need him. Be at ease in your mind; I am, as it were, your father; do not be worried again. Wherefore? I am old and advanced in years, but you are young and vigorous; all the time you have been working, you have never been deceitful, lazy, angry or grumbling; I have never seen you, like the other labourers, with such vices as these. From this time forth you shall be as my own begotten son.'

Thereupon the elder gives him a new name and calls him a son. The poor son, though he rejoices at this happening, still thinks of himself as a humble hireling. For this reason, during twenty years he continues to be employed in scavenging. After this period, there grows mutual confidence between them, and he goes in and out and is at his ease, though his abode is still the original place.

World-honoured One! Then the elder becomes ill and, knowing that he will die before long, says to the poor son: 'Now I possess abundance of gold, silver, and precious things, and my granaries and treasuries are full to overflowing. The quantities of these things, and the amounts which should be received and given, I want you to understand in detail. Such is my mind, and you must agree to this my wish. Wherefore? Because, now, I and you are of the same mind. Be increasingly careful so that there be no waste.'

The poor son accepts his instruction and commands, and becomes acquainted with all the goods, gold, silver, and precious things, as well as all the granaries and treasuries, but has no idea of expecting to inherit so much as a meal, while his abode is still the original place and he is yet unable to abandon his sense of inferiority.

After a short time has again passed, the father, knowing that his son's ideas have gradually been enlarged, his aspirations developed, and that he despises his previous state of mind, on seeing that his own end is approaching, commands his son to come, and gathers together his relatives, and the kings, ministers, kshatriyas, and citizens. When they are all assembled, he thereupon addresses them saying: 'Now, gentlemen, this is my son, begotten by me. It is over fifty years since, from a certain city, he left me and ran away to endure loneliness and misery. His former name was so-and-so and my name was so-and-so. At that time in that city I sought him sorrowfully. Suddenly in this place I met and regained him. This is really my son and I am really his father. Now all the wealth which I possess entirely belongs to my son, and all my previous disbursements and receipts are known by this son.'

World-honoured One! When the poor son heard these words of his father, great was his joy at such unexpected news, and thus he thought: Without any mind for, or effort on my part, these treasures now come of themselves to me.

World-honoured One! The very rich elder is the Tathāgata, and we are all as the Buddha's sons. The Tathāgata has always declared that we are his sons. World-honoured One! Because of the three sufferings, in the midst of births and deaths we have borne all kinds of torments, being deluded and ignorant and enjoying our attachment to trifles. Today the World-honoured One has caused us to ponder over and remove the dirt of all diverting discussions of inferior things. In these we have hitherto been diligent to make progress and have got, as it were, a day's pay for our effort to reach nirvāna. Obtaining this, we greatly rejoiced and were contented, saying to ourselves: For our diligence and progress in the Buddha-law what we have received is ample. But the World-honoured One, knowing beforehand that our minds were attached to low desires and took delight in inferior things, let us go our own way and did not discriminate for us, saying: You shall yet have possession of the treasury of Tathāgata-knowledge. The World-honoured One, in his tactfulness, told of the Tathāgata-wisdom; but we, though following the Buddha and receiving a day's wage of nirvāna, deemed this a sufficient gain, never having a mind to seek after the Great Vehicle. We also have declared and expounded the Tathāgata-wisdom to Bodhisattvas, but in regard to this Great Vehicle we have never had a longing for it. Wherefore? The Buddha, knowing that our minds delighted in inferior things, by his tactfulness taught according to our capacity, but still we did not perceive that we were really Buddha-sons.

Now we have just realized that the World-honoured One does not grudge even the Buddha-wisdom. Wherefore? From of old we are really sons of Buddha, but have only taken pleasure in minor matters; if we had had a mind to take pleasure in the Great, the Buddha would have preached the Great Vehicle Law to us. At length, in this sutra, he preaches only the One Vehicle; and though formerly, in the presence of bodhisattvas, he spoke disparagingly of śrāvakas[1] who were pleased with minor matters, yet the Buddha had in reality been instructing them in the Great Vehicle. Therefore we say that though we had no mind to hope or expect it, yet now the Great Treasure of the King of the Law has of itself come to us, and such things as Buddha-sons should obtain we have all obtained.

Doctrine 1

Doctrinal Limits: Majjhima Nikāya, Lesser Māluṅkyāputta Sutta

In the Theravādin tradition various metaphysical questions are seen as unanswerable, as to whether or not the liberated saint who has gained nirvāna exists or not after death, whether the universe is finite or not, etc. In the Greater Vehicle the principle that doctrinal truths cannot be formulated is generalized, as in the philosophical teaching of Nāgārjuna (*see* p. 245), so that the higher truth cannot be stated but only pointed at or experienced, and all lower truths of ordinary life, including the teachings of the Buddha, are provisional or conventional.

[1] Disciples or 'hearers'.

'Accordingly, Māluṅkyāputta, bear always in mind what it is that I have not elucidated, and what it is that I have elucidated. And what, Māluṅkyāputta, have I not elucidated? I have not elucidated, Māluṅkyāputta, that the world is not eternal; I have not elucidated that the world is eternal; I have not elucidated that the world is finite; I have not elucidated that the world is infinite; I have not elucidated that the soul and the body are identical; I have not elucidated that the soul is one thing and the body another; I have not elucidated that the saint exists after death; I have not elucidated that the saint does not exist after death; I have not elucidated that the saint both exists and does not exist after death; I have not elucidated that the saint neither exists nor does not exist after death. And why, Māluṅkyāputta, have I not elucidated this? Because, Māluṅkyāputta, this profits not, nor has to do with the fundamentals of religion, nor tends to aversion, absence of passion, cessation, quiescence, the supernatural faculties, supreme wisdom, and nirvāna; therefore have I not elucidated it.

'And what, Māluṅkyāputta, have I elucidated? Misery, Māluṅkyāputta, have I elucidated; the origin of misery have I elucidated; the cessation of misery have I elucidated; and the path leading to the cessation of misery have I elucidated. And why, Māluṅkyāputta, have I elucidated this? Because, Māluṅkyāputta, this does profit, has to do with the fundamentals of religion, and tends to aversion, absence of passion, cessation, quiescence, knowledge, supreme wisdom, and nirvāna; therefore have I elucidated it. Accordingly, Māluṅkyāputta, bear always in mind what it is that I have not elucidated, and what it is that I have elucidated.'

Thus spake the Blessed One; and, delighted, the venerable Māluṅkyāputta applauded the speech of the Blessed One.

Doctrine 2

No Self: Saṃyutta Nikāya

The idea of a permanent self or soul is repudiated in Buddhism. Chiefly the denial is aimed at theories of an individual permanent self, which is seen as having no role to play in a world which is impermanent. Instead Buddhism offers a permanent liberation (nirvāna). But the denial of the self or soul is considered compatible with belief in rebirth.

The body, monks, is soulless. If the body, monks, were the soul, this body would not be subject to sickness, and it would be possible in the case of the body to say, 'Let my body be thus, let my body not be thus.' Now, because the body is soulless, monks, therefore the body is subject to sickness, and it is not possible in the case of the body to say, 'Let my body be thus, let my body not be thus'.

Feeling is soulless . . . perception is soulless . . . the dispositions are soulless . . .

Consciousness is soulless. For if consciousness were the soul, this consciousness would not be subject to sickness, and it would be possible in the case of consciousness to say, 'Let my consciousness be thus, let my consciousness not be thus.'

Now, because consciousness is soulless, therefore consciousness is subject to sickness, and it is not possible in the case of consciousness to say, 'Let my consciousness be thus, let my consciousness not be thus.'

What think you, monks, is the body permanent or impermanent?

Impermanent, Lord.

But is the impermanent painful or pleasant?

Painful, Lord.

But is it fitting to consider what is impermanent, painful, and subject to change as, 'this is mine, this am I, this is my soul'?

No indeed, Lord.

[And so of feeling, perception, the dispositions, and consciousness.] Therefore in truth, monks, whatever body, past, future, or present, internal or external, gross or subtle, low or eminent, near or far, is to be looked on by him who duly and rightly understands, as, 'all this body is not mine, not this am I, not mine is the soul.' [And so of feeling, etc]

Thus perceiving, monks, the learned noble disciple feels loathing for the body, for feeling, for perception, for the dispositions, for consciousness. Feeling disgust he becomes free from passion, through freedom from passion he is emancipated, and in the emancipated one arises the knowledge of his emancipation. He understands that destroyed is rebirth, the religious life has been led, done is what was to be done, there is nought [for him] beyond this world.

Doctrine 3

The Simile of the Blind Turtle: Majjhima Nikāya, Bālapaṇḍitasutta

Though the doctrine of rebirth might cause people to relax their efforts (is there always not another chance?), the Buddha preaches here on the urgency of liberation. Reference is made in this passage to Niraya Hell: or strictly a purgatory. In Buddhist cosmology, heavens and hells are rewards and punishments, but are not everlasting, so that even the murderer will at last leave a hell, having worked off the bad karmic effects of his action.

'Monks, it is like a man who might throw a yoke with one hole into the sea. An easterly wind might take it westwards, a westerly wind might take it eastwards, a northerly wind might take it southwards, a southerly wind might take it northwards. There might be a blind turtle there who came to the surface once in a hundred years. What do you think about this, monks? Could that blind turtle push his neck through that one hole in the yoke?'

'If at all, reverend sir, then only once in a very long while.'

'Sooner or later, monks, could the blind turtle push his neck through the one hole in the yoke; more difficult than that, do I say, monks, is human status once again for the fool who has gone to the Purgatory. What is the cause of that? Monks, there is no Dhamma-faring there, no even-faring, no doing of what is skilled, no doing of what is good. Monks, there is devouring of one another there and feeding on the weak. Monks, if some time or other once in a very long while that fool came to human status (again), he would be born into those families that are low: a family of low caste or a family of hunters or a family of bamboo-plaiters or a family of cartwrights or a family of refuse-scavengers, in such a family as is needy, without enough to drink or to eat, where a covering for the back is with difficulty obtained. Moreover, he would be ill-favoured, ugly, dwarfish, sickly, blind or deformed or lame or paralysed; he would be unable to get food, drink, clothes, vehicles, garlands, scents and perfumes, bed, dwelling and lights; he would fare wrongly in body, wrongly in speech, wrongly in thought. Because he had fared wrongly in body, speech and thought, at the breaking up of the body after dying he would arise in the sorrowful ways, a bad bourn, Niraya Hell.

Doctrine 4

Dependence and the Middle Path: Saṃyutta Nikāya

In this passage the Buddha expounds how his teaching is a middle one between being and non-being (i.e. because everything is reduced to complex processes). He also spells out the doctrine of dependent origination which explains how it is that by the removal of ignorance the rest of the chain of causation is destroyed and liberation achieved.

The world, for the most part, O Kaccāna, holds either to a belief in being or to a belief in non-being. But for one who in the light of the highest knowledge, O Kaccāna, considers how the world arises, belief in the non-being of the world passes away. And for one who in the light of the highest knowledge, O Kaccāna, considers how the world ceases, belief in the being of the world passes away. The world, O Kaccāna, is for the most part bound up in a seeking, attachment, and proclivity [for the groups[1]], but a monk does not sympathize with this seeking and attachment, nor with the mental affirmation, proclivity and prejudice which affirms an Ego. He does not doubt or question that it is only evil that springs into existence, and only evil that ceases from existence, and his conviction of this fact is dependent on no one besides himself. This, O Kaccāna, is what constitutes Right Belief.

That things have being, O Kaccāna, constitutes one extreme of doctrine; that things have no being is the other extreme. These extremes, O Kaccāna, have been avoided by the Tathāgata, and it is a middle doctrine he teaches:

On ignorance depends karma;
On karma depends consciousness;
On consciousness depend name and form;
On name and form depend the six organs of sense;
On the six organs of sense depends contact;
On contact depends sensation;
On sensation depends desire;
On desire depends attachment;
On attachment depends existence;
On existence depends birth;
On birth depend old age and death, sorrow, lamentation, misery, grief, and despair. Thus does this entire aggregation of misery arise.

But on the complete fading out and cessation of ignorance ceases karma;
On the cessation of karma ceases consciousness;
On the cessation of consciousness cease name and form;
On the cessation of name and form cease the six organs of sense;
On the cessation of the six organs of sense ceases contact;
On the cessation of contact ceases sensation;
On the cessation of sensation ceases desire;
On the cessation of desire ceases attachment;
On the cessation of attachment ceases existence;
On the cessation of existence ceases birth;
On the cessation of birth cease old age and death, sorrow, lamentation, misery, grief, and despair. Thus does this entire aggregation of misery cease.

---

[1] 'Groups' or *khandhas* (*skandhas* in Sanskrit), referring to the constituent classes of events which go to make up the individual person (states of consciousness, dispositions, feelings, perceptions and bodily processes).

Doctrine 5

Two Levels of Truth: Nāgārjuna's Mādhkyamikaśāstra

In this philosophical work Nāgārjuna (the most influential of Mahāyāna thinkers and chief exponent of the Mādhyamika or Middle School) propounds the teaching of *śūnyatā* or emptiness. Everything is empty precisely because it is devoid of self-existence (*svabhāva*). Thus the Buddha's teaching of universal causation (*pratītyasamutpāda*) (*see* p. 236) means that each thing or event depends on another and is relative. Likewise truths about them are relative or provisional. The higher truth of Suchness or Emptiness is to be experienced, and is beyond description. By a paradox in the higher truth even the lower truths taught by the Buddha disappear, as well as birth and death and even the distinction between nirvāna and empirical existence (saṃsāra).

The Buddha's teaching rests on the discrimination of two kinds of truth (*satya*): absolute and relative. Those who do not have any adequate knowledge of them are unable to grasp the deep and subtle meaning of Buddhism. [The essence of being, Dharmatā, is beyond verbal definition or intellectual comprehension, for there is neither birth nor death in it, and it is even like unto nirvāna. The nature of Suchness, *tattva*, is fundamentally free from conditionality, it is tranquil, it distances all phenomenal frivolities, it discriminates not, nor is it particularized.]

But if not for relative truth, absolute truth is unattainable, and when absolute truth is not attained, nirvāna is not to be gained.

The dull-headed who do not perceive the truth rightfully go to self-destruction, for they are like an awkward magician whose trick entangles himself, or like an unskilled snakecatcher who gets himself hurt. The World-honoured One knew well the abstruseness of the Doctrine which is beyond the mental capacity of the multitudes and was inclined not to disclose it before them.

The objection that Buddhism onesidedly adheres to emptiness and thereby exposes itself to grave errors, entirely misses the mark; for there are no errors in emptiness. Why? Because it is on account of emptiness that all things are at all possible, and without emptiness all things will come to naught. Those who deny emptiness and find fault with it, are like a horseman who forgets that he is on horseback.

If they think that things exist because of their self-essence (*svabhāva*) [and not because of their emptiness], they thereby make things come out of causelessness, they destroy those relations that exist between the acting and the act and the acted; and they also destroy the conditions that make up the law of birth and death.

All is declared empty because there is nothing that is not a product of universal causation. This law of causation, however, is merely provisional, though herein lies the middle path.

As thus there is not an object (Dharma) which is not conditioned (*pratītya*), so there is nothing that is not empty.

If all is not empty, then there is no death nor birth, and withal disappears the Fourfold Noble Truth.

Therefore, it is taught by the Buddha that those who recognize the law of universal causation, recognize the Buddha as well as Suffering, Accumulation, Cessation and the Path.

Doctrine 6

The Essence of Insight: The Heart Sūtra

Possibly of the 4th century CE the Heart Sūtra is, with the Diamond Sūtra, one of the texts regarded as containing quintessentially the central teaching of Buddhism: it is an expression of *prajñā* or insight. It also introduces as its source Avalokiteśvara or Avalokita, the Lord who looks down with compassion (as his name implies), one of the great Bodhisattva figures of the Great Vehicle.

I. The invocation

Homage to the Perfection of Wisdom, the lovely, the holy!

II. The prologue

Avalokita, the holy Lord and Bodhisattva, was moving in the deep course of the wisdom which has gone beyond. He looked down from on high, he beheld but five heaps, and he saw that in their own-being they were empty.

III. The dialectics of emptiness. First stage

Here, O Sariputra, form is emptiness, and the very emptiness is form; emptiness does not differ from form, form does not differ from emptiness; whatever is form, that is emptiness, whatever is emptiness, that is form. The same is true of feelings, perceptions, impulses, and consciousness.[1]

IV. The dialectics of emptiness. Second stage

Here, O Sariputra, all Dharmas are marked with emptiness; they are not produced or stopped, not defiled or immaculate, not deficient or complete.

V. The dialectics of emptiness. Third stage

Therefore, O Sariputra, in emptiness there is no form, nor feeling, nor perception, nor impulse, nor consciousness; no eye, ear, nose, tongue, body, mind; no forms, sounds, smells, tastes, touchables or objects of mind; no sight-organ-element, and so forth, until we come to: no mind-consciousness-element; there is no ignorance, no extinction of ignorance, and so forth, until we come to: there is no decay and death, no extinction of decay and death; there is no suffering, no origination, no stopping, no path; there is no cognition, no attainment, and no non-attainment.

VI. The concrete embodiment and practical basis of emptiness

Therefore, O Sariputra, it is because of his indifference to any kind of personal attainment that a Bodhisattva, through having relied on the perfection of wisdom, dwells without thought-coverings. In the absence of thought-coverings he has not been made to tremble, he has overcome what can upset, and in the end he attains to nirvāna.

VII. Full emptiness is the basis also of Buddhahood

All those who appear as Buddhas in the three periods of time fully awake to the utmost, right and perfect enlightenment because they have relief on the perfection of wisdom.

VIII. The teaching brought within reach of the comparatively unenlightened

Therefore one should know the Prajñaparamita

[1] Here the emptiness of the cycle of dependent origination is affirmed.

as the great spell,[2] the spell of great knowledge, the utmost spell, the unequalled spell, allayer of all suffering, in truth – for what could go wrong? By the Prajñaparamita has this spell been delivered. It runs like this: Gone, Gone, Gone beyond, Gone altogether beyond, O what an awakening, All Hail!

This completes the Heart of Perfect Wisdom.

Doctrine 7

Beyond Words: The Platform Sūtra

Meditation Buddhism (Chinese Ch'ān, Japanese Zen) theoretically depends on direct transmission, and not upon scriptures. It thus traces its source back to the Buddha. However, it developed its own writings, the most esteemed of which is the Platform Sūtra – the only Chinese work to attain this title of Sūtra or Classic – which goes back to the records of the teaching of the Sixth Patriarch Hui-neng. With Meditation Buddhism the Buddhist trend towards direct experience rather than verbal truth is extended in an interesting and creative way.

Monk Hung-jen asked Hui-neng: 'Whence have you come to pay homage to me? What do you want from me?'

Hui-neng answered: 'Your discipline is from Lingnan [south of the Mountain Ranges, in the region of the present Canton]. A citizen of Hsin-chou, I have come a great distance to pay homage, without seeking anything except the Law of the Buddha.'

The Great Master reproved him, saying: 'You are from Lingnan and, furthermore, you are a barbarian. How can you become a Buddha?'

Hui-neng answered: 'Although people are distinguished as northerners and southerners, there is neither north nor south in Buddha-nature. In physical body, the barbarian and the monk are different. But what is the difference in their Buddha-nature?'

The Great Master intended to argue with him further, but, seeing people around, said nothing. Hui-neng was ordered to attend to duties among the rest. It happened that one monk went away to travel. Thereupon Hui-neng was ordered to pound rice, which he did for eight months.

One day the Fifth Patriarch [Hung-jen] suddenly called all his pupils to come to him. As they assembled, he said: 'Let me say this to you. Life and death are serious matters. You people are engaged all day in making offerings [to the Buddha], going after blessings and rewards only, and you make no effort to achieve freedom from the bitter sea of life and death. Your self-nature seems to be obscured. How can blessings save you? Go to your rooms and examine yourselves. He who is enlightened use his perfect vision of self-nature and write me a verse. When I look at his verse, if it reveals deep understanding, I shall give him the robe and the Law and make him the Sixth Patriarch. Hurry, hurry!'

At midnight Shen-hsiu, holding a candle, wrote a verse on the wall of the south corridor, without anyone knowing about it, which said:

Our body is the tree of Perfect Wisdom,
And our mind is a bright mirror.
At all times diligently wipe them,
So that they will be free from dust.

[2] The word for spell is *mantra* or 'sacred formula', and points to the use of diagrams and formulae to transmit power: in this case, the Heart Sūtra itself becomes a spell transmitting what it refers to and what it is about – namely enlightenment.

The Fifth Patriarch said: 'The verse you wrote shows some but not all understanding. You have arrived at the front of the door but you have not yet entered it. Ordinary people, by practising in accordance with your verse, will not degenerate. But it will be futile to seek the Supreme Perfect Wisdom while holding to such a view. One must enter the door and see his self-nature. Go away and come back after one or two days of thought. If you have entered the door and seen your self-nature, I shall give you the robe and the Law.'

Shen-hsiu went away and for several days could not produce another verse.

Hui-neng also wrote a verse . . . which says:

The tree of Perfect Wisdom is originally no tree.
Nor has the bright mirror any frame.
Buddha-nature is forever clear and pure.
Where is there any dust?

Another verse:

The mind is the tree of Perfect Wisdom.
The body is the clear mirror.
The clear mirror is originally clear and pure.
Where has it been affected by any dust?

Monks in the hall were all surprised at these verses. Hui-neng, however, went back to the rice-pounding room. The Fifth Patriarch suddenly realized that Hui-neng was the one of good knowledge but was afraid lest the rest learn it. He therefore told them: 'This will not do.' The Fifth Patriarch waited till midnight, called Hui-neng to come to the hall, and expounded the Diamond Sutra. As soon as Hui-neng heard this, he understood. That night the Law was imparted to him without anyone knowing it, and thus the Law and the robe [emblematic] of Sudden Enlightenment were transmitted to him. 'You are now the Sixth Patriarch.' said the Fifth Patriarch to Hui-neng. 'The robe is the testimony of transmission from generation to generation. As to the Law, it is to be transmitted from mind to mind. Let people achieve understanding through their own effort.'

The Fifth Patriarch told Hui-neng: 'From the very beginning, the transmission of the Law has been as delicate as a hanging thread of silk. If you remain here, some one might harm you. You had better leave quickly.'

Hui-neng [having returned South] said: 'I came and stayed in this place [Canton] and have not been free from persecution by government officials, Taoists, and common folk. The doctrine has been transmitted down from past sages; it is not my own idea. Those who wish to hear the teachings of the past sages should purify their hearts. Having heard them, they should first free themselves from their delusions and then attain enlightenment.'

Great Master Hui-neng declared: 'Good friends, perfection is inherent in all people. it is only because of the delusions of the mind that they cannot attain enlightenment by themselves. They must ask the help of the enlightened and be shown the way to see their own nature. Good friends, as soon as one is enlightened, he will achieve Perfect Wisdom.

'Good friends, in my system, meditation and wisdom are the bases. First of all, do not be deceived that the two are different. They are one reality and not two. Meditation is the substance (*t'i*) of wisdom and wisdom is the function (*yung*) of meditation. As soon as wisdom is achieved, meditation is included in it, and as soon as meditation is attained, wisdom is included in it. Good friends, the meaning here is that meditation and wisdom are identified. A follower after the Way should not think wisdom follows meditation or vice versa or that the two are different. To hold such a view would imply that the Dharmas possess two different characters. To those whose words are good but whose hearts are not good, meditation and wisdom are not identified. But to those whose hearts and words are both good and for whom the internal and external are one, meditation and wisdom are identified. Self-enlightenment and practice do not consist in argument. If one concerns himself about whether [meditation or wisdom] comes first, he is deluded. Unless one is freed from the consideration of victory or defeat, he will produce the [imagining of] Dharmas and the self, and cannot be free from the characters [of birth, stagnation, deterioration, and extinction].

'Good friends, there is no distinction between sudden enlightenment and gradual enlightenment in the Law, except that some people are intelligent and others stupid. Those who are ignorant realize the truth gradually, while the enlightened ones attain it suddenly. But if they know their own minds and see their own nature, then there will be no difference in their enlightenment. Without enlightenment, they will be forever bound in transmigration.

'Good friends, in my system, from the very beginning, whether in the sudden enlightenment or gradual enlightenment tradition, absence of thought has been instituted as the main doctrine, absence of phenomena as the substance, and nonattachment as the foundation. What is meant by absence of phenomena? Absence of phenomena means to be free from phenomena when in contact with them. Absence of thought means not to be carried away by thought in the process of thought. Nonattachment is man's original nature. [In its ordinary process] thought moves forward without a halt; past, present, and future thoughts continue as an unbroken stream. But if we can cut off this stream by an instant of thought, the Dharma-body will be separated from the physical body, and at no time will a single thought be attached to any Dharma. If one single instant of thought is attached to anything, then every thought will be attached. That will be bondage. But if in regard to all Dharmas, no thought is attached to anything, that means freedom. This is the reason why nonattachment is taken as the foundation.

'Good friends, to be free from all phenomena means absence of phenomena. Only if we can be free from phenomena will the reality of nature be pure. This is the reason why absence of phenomena is taken as the substance.

'Absence of thought means not to be defiled by external objects. It is to free our thoughts from external objects and not to allow Dharmas to cause our thoughts to rise. If one stops thinking about things and wipes out all thought, then as thought is terminated once and for all, there will be no more rebirth. Take this seriously, followers of the Path. It is bad enough for a man to be deceived himself through not knowing the meaning of the Law. How much worse is it to encourage others to be deceived! Not only does he fail to realize that he is deceived, but he also blasphemes against the scripture and the Law. This is the reason why absence of thought is instituted as the doctrine.

'All this is because people who are deceived have thoughts about sense-objects. With such thoughts, pervasive views arise, and all sorts of defilements and erroneous thoughts are produced from them.

'However, the school instituted absence of thought as the doctrine. When people are free from [erroneous] views, no thought will arise. If there are no thoughts, there will not even be "absence of thought". Absence means absence of what? Thought means thought of what? Absence means freedom from duality and all defilements. Thought means thought of Thusness and self-nature. True Thusness is the substance of thought and thought is the function of True Thusness. It is the self-nature that gives rise to thought. [Therefore] in spite of the funtioning of seeing, hearing, sensing, and knowing, the self-nature is not defiled by the many sense-objects and always remains as it truly is. As the Vimalakīrti Scripture says: "Externally it skillfully differentiates the various Dharma-characters and internally it abides firmly in the First Principle".

'Good friends, in this system sitting in meditation is at bottom neither attached to the mind nor attached to purity, and there is neither speech nor motion. Suppose it should be attached to the mind. The mind is at bottom an imagination. Since imagination is the same as illusion, there is nothing to be attached to. Suppose it were attached to purity, man's nature is originally pure. It is only because of erroneous thought that True Thusness is obscured. Our original nature is pure as long as it is free from erroneous thought. If one does not realize that his own nature is originally pure and makes up his mind to attach himself to purity, he is creating an imaginary purity. Such purity does not exist. Hence we know that what is to be attached to is imaginary.

'This being the case, in this system, what is meant by sitting in meditation? To sit means to obtain absolute freedom and not to allow any thought to be caused by external objects. To meditate means to realize the imperturbability of one's original nature. What is meant by meditation and calmness? Meditation means to be free from all phenomena and calmness means to be internally unperturbed. If one is externally attached to phenomena, the inner mind will at once be disturbed, but if one is externally free from phenomena, the inner nature will not be perturbed. The original nature is by itself pure and calm. It is only because of causal conditions that it comes into contact with external objects, and the contact leads to perturbation. There will be calmness when one is free from external objects and is not perturbed. Meditation is achieved when one is externally free from phenomena and calmness is achieved when one is internally unperturbed. Meditation and calmness mean that externally meditation is attained and internally calmness is achieved.'

'All scriptures and writings of the Mahāyāna and Hīnayāna schools as well as the twelve sections of the Canon were provided for man. It is because man possesses the nature of wisdom that these were instituted. If there were no man, there would not have been any Dharmas. We know, therefore, that Dharmas exist because of man and there are all these scriptures because there are people to preach them.

'Among men some are wise and others stupid. The stupid are inferior people, whereas the wise ones are superior. The ignorant consult the wise and the wise explain the Law to them and enable them to understand. When the ignorant understand, they will no longer be different from the wise. Hence we know that without enlightenment, a Buddha is no different from all living beings, and with enlightenment, all living beings are the same as a Buddha. Hence we know that all Dharmas are immanent in one's person. Why not seek in one's mind the sudden realization of the original nature of True Thusness?'

The Great Master said to Chi-ch'eng [pupil of Shen-hsiu]: 'I hear that your teacher in his teaching transmits only the doctrine of discipline, calmness, and wisdom. Please tell me his explanation of these teachings.'

Chi-ch'eng said: 'The Reverend Shen-hsiu said that discipline is to refrain from all evil actions, wisdom is to practise all good deeds, and calmness is to purify one's own mind. These are called discipline, calmness, and wisdom. This is his explanation. I wonder what your views are.'

Patriarch Hui-neng answered: 'His theory is wonderful, but my views are different.'

Chi-ch'eng asked: 'How different?'

Hui-neng answered: 'Some people realize [the Law] more quickly and others more slowly.'

Chi-ch'eng then asked the Patriarch to explain his views on discipline, calmness, and wisdom. The Great Master said: 'Please listen to me. In my view, freeing the mind from all wrong is the discipline of our original nature. Freeing the mind from all disturbances is the calmness of our original nature. And freeing the mind from all delusions is the wisdom of our original nature.'

Master Hui-neng continued: 'Your teacher's teaching of discipline, calmness, and wisdom is to help wise men of the inferior type but mine is to help superior people. When one realizes his original nature, then discipline, calmness, and wisdom need not be instituted.'

Chi-ch'eng said: 'Great Master, please explain why they need not be instituted.'

The Great Master said: 'The original nature has no wrong, no disturbance, no delusion. If in every instant of thought we introspect our minds with Perfect Wisdom, and if it is always free from Dharmas and their appearances, what is the need of instituting these things? The original nature is realized suddenly, not gradually step by step. Therefore there is no need of instituting them.'

Chi-ch'eng bowed, decided not to leave Ts'ao-li Mountain, but immediately became a pupil and always stayed close by the Master.

Ritual 1

The Rejection of Brahmin Sacrifice: Jātakas

The birth narrative describes the Buddha as the Bodhisatta (the Pāli version of Bodhisattva) combatting the teachings of Arittha, who was his brother in a previous life. The Bodhisatta in this narrative is a Nāga or serpent, conceived in the Indian tradition as being a sacred or propitious kind of being.

Thus Ariṭṭha described the Brahmins and their sacrifices and Vedas.

When they heard his words, many Nāgas came to visit the Bodhisatta's sick-bed, and they said to one another, 'He is telling a legend of the past', and they seemed to be in danger of accepting false doctrine. Now the Bodhisatta heard it all as he lay in his bed, and the Nāgas told him about it; then the Bodhisatta reflected, 'Ariṭṭha is telling a false legend, I will interrupt his discourse, and put true views into the assembly. So he rose and bathed, and put on all his ornaments, and sat down in the pulpit and gathered all the Nāga multitude together. Then he sent for Ariṭṭha and said to him, 'Ariṭṭha, you have spoken falsely when you describe the Brahmins and the Vedas, for the sacrifice of victims by all these ceremonies of the Vedas is not held to be desirable and it does not lead to heaven – see what unreality there is in your words'; so he repeated these verses describing the various kinds of sacrifice:

'These Veda studies are the wise man's toils,
The lure which tempts the victims whom he
spoils;
A mirage formed to catch the careless eye,
But which the prudent passes safely by.

The Vedas have no hidden power to save
The traitor or the coward or the knave;
The fire, though tended well for long years
past,
Leaves his base master without hope at last.

Though all earth's trees in one vast heap
were piled
To satisfy the fire's insatiate child,
Still would it crave for more, insatiate still –
How could a Nāga hope that maw to fill?

Milk ever changes – thus where milk has
been
Butter and curds in natural course are seen;
And the same thirst for change pervades the
fire,
Once stirred to life it mounts still higher and
higher.

Fire bursts not forth in wood that's dry or
new,
Fire needs an effort ere it leaps to view;
If dry fresh timber of itself could burn,
Spontaneous would each forest blaze in turn.

If he wins merit who to feed the flame
Piles wood and straw, the merit is the same
When cooks light fires or blacksmiths at
their trade
Or those who burn the corpses of the dead.

But none, however, zealously he prays
Or heaps the fuel round to feed the blaze,
Gains any merit by his mummeries –
The fire for all its crest of smoke soon dies.

Ritual 2

Relics and Liberation: Buddhacarita

Here is described how the cult of the relics of the Buddha originated after his decease, and also the custom of reciting the teachings. The later ceremonial of the *stūpa* (pagoda) originates from this pious veneration of the remains of Buddhas or others who have attained the liberated state. Such piety helps the individual psychologically and in terms of karma towards his own liberation.

Those who had not yet got rid of their passions shed tears. Most of the monks lost their composure and felt grief. Those only who had completed the cycle were not shaken out of their composure, for they knew well that it is the nature of things to pass away. In due course the Mallas[1] heard the news. Like cranes pursued by a hawk they quickly streamed forth under the impact of this calamity, and cried in their distress, 'Alas, the Saviour!' In due course the weeping Mallas, with their powerful arms, placed the Seer on a priceless bier of ivory inlaid with gold. They then performed the ceremonies which befitted the occasion, and honoured Him with many kinds of charming garlands and with the finest perfumes. After that, with zeal and devotion they all took hold of the bier. Slender maidens, with tinkling anklets and copper-stained fingernails, held a priceless canopy over it, which was like a cloud white with flashes of lightning. Some of the men held up parasols with white garlands, while others waved white yaks' tails set in gold. To the accompaniment of music the Mallas slowly bore along the bier, their eyes reddened like those of bulls. They left the city through the Naga Gulf, crossed the Hiranyavati river, and then moved on to the Mukuta shrine, at the foot of which they raised a pyre. Sweet scented barks and leaves, aloewood, sandalwood, and cassia they heaped on the pyre, sighing with grief all the time. Finally they placed the Sage's body on it. Three times they tried to light the pyre with a torch, but it refused to burn. This was due to Kashyapa the Great[2] coming along the road, Kashyapa whose mind was meditating pure thoughts. He longed to see the remains of the holy body of the departed Hero, and it was his magical power which prevented the fire from flaring up. But now the monk approached with rapid steps, eager to see his Teacher once more, and immediately he had paid his homage to the Best of Sages the fire blazed up of its own. Soon it had burnt up the Sage's skin, flesh, hair and limbs. But although there were plenty of ghee, fuel, and wind, it could not consume His bones. These were in due time purified with the finest water, and placed in golden pitchers in the city of the Mallas. And the Mallas chanted hymns of praise over them: 'These jars now hold the relics great in virtue, as mountains hold their jewelled ore. No fire harms these relics great in virtue; like Brahma's realm when all else is burned up. These bones, His friendliness pervades their tissue; the fire of passion has no strength to burn them; the power of devotion has preserved them; cold though they are, how much they warm our hearts!'

For some days they worshipped the relics in due form and with the utmost devotion. Then, however, one by one, ambassadors from the seven neighbouring kings arrived in the town, asking for a share of the relics. But the Mallas, a proud people and also motivated by their esteem for the relics, refused to surrender any of them. Instead, they were willing to fight. The seven kings, like the seven winds, then came up with great violence against Kusinagara, and their forces were like the current of the flooded Ganges.

Wiser counsels prevailed, and the Mallas devotedly divided into eight parts the relics of Him who had understood Life. One part they kept for themselves. The seven others were handed over to the seven kings, one to each. And these rulers, thus honoured by the Mallas, returned to their own kingdoms, joyful at having achieved their purpose. There, with the appropriate ceremonies, they erected in their capital cities *stūpas* for the relics of the Seer.

In due course the five hundred Arhats assembled in Rajagriha, on the slope of one of its five mountains, and there and then they collected the sayings of the Great Sage, so that his Dharma might abide. Since it was Ananda who had heard Him speak more often than anyone else. they decided, with the agreement of the wider Buddhist community, to ask him to recite His utterances. The sage from Vaideha then sat down in their midst, and repeated the sermons as they had been spoken by the Best of All speakers. And each one he began with, 'Thus have I heard', and with a statement of the time, the place, the occasion, and the person addressed. It is in this way that he established in conjunction with the Arhats the Scriptures which contain the Dharma of the great Sage. They have in the past led to nirvāna those who have made the effort fully to master them. They still today help them to nirvāna, and they will continue to do so in the future.

[1] A nearby tribal people, represented in the texts as having a republican form of polity.
[2] A leading disciple of the Buddha.

Ritual 3

Offerings: Majjhima Nikāya

In these verses there is an anlysis of what is gained by offerings. *Dāna* or 'giving', whether charitably or in piety to the monastic Order, is one of the three ingredients of the holy life, together with virtue or *sīla* and *samādhi* or the practice of meditation.

Whoever, moral in habit, gives to the poor in moral habit
A gift rightfully acquired, the mind well inspired,
Firmly believing in the rich fruit of kamma –
This is an offering purified by the river.

Whoever, poor in moral habit, gives to those of moral habit
A gift unrightfully acquired, the mind not inspired,
Not believing in the rich fruit of kamma –
This is an offering purified by the recipient.

Whoever, poor in moral habit, gives to the poor in moral habit
A gift unrightfully acquired, the mind not inspired,
Not believing in the rich fruit of kamma –
This is an offering purified by neither.

Whoever, moral in habit, gives to those of moral habit
A gift rightfully acquired, the mind well inspired,
Firmly believing in the rich fruit of kamma –
I assert this gift to be of abundant fruit.

Whoever, without attachment, gives to those without attachment
A gift rightfully acquired, the mind well inspired,
Firmly believing in the rich fruit of kamma –
I assert this gift to be a gift abundant in gain.

Ritual 4

Confession of Faults: Mahāvagga

The Vinaya section of the canon defines the duties of the Buddha's followers. In this account the Buddha adapts the customs prevalent among other non-Brahminical groups of his day by setting a twice-a-month fast period, during which among other things the monks recite their faults and are given thereby a kind of absolution.

Now it happened to the Blessed One, being in seclusion and plunged in meditation, that a consideration presented itself to his mind, as follows:

'What if now I prescribe that the monks recite a confession of all those precepts which have been laid down by me; and this shall be for them a fast-day duty?'

Then the Blessed One, in the evening of the day, rose from his meditation, and on this occasion and in this connection, after he had delivered a doctrinal discourse, addressed the monks.

'O monks, it happened to me, as I was just now seated in seclusion and plunged in meditation, that a consideration presented itself to my mind, as follows: "What if now I prescribe that the monks recite a confession of all those precepts which have been laid down by me; and this shall be for them a fast-day duty?" I prescribe, O monks, that ye recite a confession. And after this manner, O monks, is it to be recited.

'Let a learned and competent monk make announcement to the congregation, saying, "Let the reverend congregation hear me. Today is the fast-day of the fifteenth day of the half-month. If the congregation be ready, let the congregation keep fast-day, and recite the confession. What is the first business before the congregation? Venerable sirs, the proclaiming of your innocency. I will recite the confession, and let as many of us as are here present listen carefully and pay strict attention. If any one have sinned, let him reveal the fact; if he have not sinned, let him remain silent; by your silence I shall know that your reverences are innocent. But now, in assemblages like this, proclamation is made up to the third time, and each one must make confession as if individually asked. But if, when proclamation up to the third time has been made, any monk shall remember a sin and not reveal it, it will be a conscious falsehood. But a conscious falsehood, reverend sirs, has been declared by the Blessed One to be a deadly sin. Therefore, if a monk remember having committed a sin, and desire again to be pure, let him reveal the sin he committed, and when it has been revealed, it shall be well for him." '

Ritual 5

Tantric Means: Hevajra Tantra

Tibetan Buddhism among other things helped to synthesize various tendencies in later Indian Buddhism, and among these was the practice of Tantra, or sacramental and orgiastic means of self-training and enlightenment. The following passage indicates how Tantra owed part of its dynamic to the way the male-female relationship symbolized the mystical quest. The male corresponds to *upāya* or the 'skill in means' of the adept, while the female stood for *prajña* or transcendental insight. Themes from shamanism and cultic worship of the gods are blended into this new complex of ritual ways of pursuing the Buddhist path.

Now we shall further tell of the practice so excellent and supreme, the cause of perfection by means of which one gains the finality of this perfection in Hevajra.

The yogin must wear the sacred earrings, and the circlet on his head; on his wrists the bracelets, and the girdle round his waist, rings round his ankles, bangles round his arms; he wears the bone-necklace and for his dress a tiger-skin, and his food must be the five ambrosias. He who practises the yoga of Heruka should frequent the five classes. These five classes that are associated together, he conceives of as one, for by him no distinction is made as between one class or many.

Meditation is good if performed at night beneath a lonely tree or in a cemetery, or in the mother's house, or in some unfrequented spot.

When some heat[1] has been developed, if one wishes to perform this practice and to gain perfection, then upon this course one should proceed. Take a girl of the Vajra[2] family, fair-featured and large-eyed and endowed with youth and beauty, who has been consecrated by oneself and is possessed of a compassionate disposition, and with her the practice should be performed. In the absence of one from the Vajra family, it should be performed with a girl from the family of one's special divinity, or (if this fails) from some other. Take her then who is now consecrated with the depositing of the seed of enlightenment.

If in joy songs are sung, then let them be the excellent Vajra-songs, and if one dances when joy has arisen, let it be done with the release as its object. Then the yogin, self-collected, performs the dance in the place of Hevajra . . .

He should abandon desire and folly, fear and anger, and any sense of shame. He should forgo sleep and uproot the notion of a self, and then the practice may be performed, there is no doubt. Only when he has made an offering of his own body, should he commence the practice. Nor should he make this gift with the consideration of who is worthy and who is not. Enjoying food and drink he should take it as it comes, making no distinction between that which is liked or disliked, eatable or uneatable, drinkable or undrinkable. Nor should he ever wonder whether a thing is suitable or unsuitable.

Even when he has attained to *siddhi*[3] and is resplendent in his perfect knowledge, a disciple respectfully greets his master, if he wishes to avoid the Avīci Hell.

Free from learning and ceremony and any cause of shame, the yogin wanders, filled with great compassion in his possession of a nature that is common to all beings. He has passed beyond oblations, renunciation, and austerities, and is freed from *mantra* and meditation. Released from all the conventions of meditation, the yogin performs the practice.

Whatever demon should appear before him, even though it be the peer of Indra, he would have no fear, for he wanders like a lion.

For the good of all beings, his drink is always compassion, for the yogin who delights in the drink of yoga, becomes drunk with no other drink.

Institutional Expression 1

Ordination into the Order: Vinaya, Mahāvagga

The primary institution or the transmission of Buddhism was the Order of monks (and nuns), the Sangha, considered with the Buddha and the Dhamma to be one of the three refuges or three jewels.

At that time the monks brought to the Buddha from different regions and different countries, persons who desired to leave the world and be ordained, thinking: the Blessed One will confer on them the one and the other ordination. But the monks became tired, and those also who desired to obtain the ordination. Now when the Blessed One was alone and had retired into solitude, the

[1] *Tapas* – heat supposedly generated by asceticism according to the Indian yogic tradition.
[2] That is, affiliated to those practising the Vajrayāna or 'Diamond Vehicle', a name for the sacramental Buddhist movement found chiefly in Tibet.
[3] Supernormal powers such as clairvoyance and levitation which throughout Buddhism were held to accrue upon higher contemplative achievements.

following consideration presented itself to his mind: the monks now bring to me from different regions and different countries persons who desire to obtain ordination, thinking: the Blessed One will confer on them the ordination. Now both the monks become tired, and those also who desire to obtain ordination. What if I were to grant permission to the monks, saying: 'Confer henceforth, monks, in the different regions and in different countries both modes of ordination yourselves'.

And the Blessed One, having left his solitude in the evening, in consequence of that, and on this occasion, after having delivered a religious discourse, thus addressed the monks: 'When I was alone, monks, and had retired into solitude, the following consideration presented itself to me: what if I were to permit . . .

'I grant you, monks, this permission: Confer henceforth in the different regions and in the different countries both modes of ordination yourselves on those who desire to receive them. And you ought, monks, to confer them in this way: Let him who desires to receive ordination first have his hair and beard cut off, let him put on yellow robes, adjust his upper robe so as to cover one shoulder, salute the feet of the monks with his head, and sit down squatting; then let him raise his joined hands and tell him to say:

' "I take my refuge in the Buddha, I take my refuge in the Dhamma, I take my refuge in the Sangha. And for the second time I take my refuge in the Buddha, I take my refuge in the Dhamma, I take my refuge in the Sangha. And for the third time I take my refuge in the Buddha, and for the third time I take my refuge in the Dhamma, and for the third time I take my refuge in the Sangha!"

'I prescribe, O monks, that the world be left and ordination given by the three times repeated declaration of taking refuge.'

Institutional Expression 2

Women and the Order: Vinaya, Cullavagga

Supposedly the Buddha was reluctant to admit women to the Order, but hedged admission round with right rules here mentioned – that a nun was to regard herself however long ordained as junior to the newest monk, that nuns should not congregate in the same areas as monks etc. There is also here a prediction of the decline of the Buddha's religion, in line with a general theory of the downward path of history. It was in view of such a theory that Pure Land and other forms of devotional Buddhism came to substitute other-help for self-help, and so develop a doctrine of salvation by grace rather than effort.

Then the venerable Ānanda drew near to where the Blessed One was; and having drawn near and greeted the Blessed One, he sat down respectfully at one side. And seated respectfully at one side, the venerable Ānanda spoke to the Blessed One as follows:

'Mahā-Pajāpatī of the Gautama clan, Reverend Sir, has accepted the eight weighty regulations; the sister of the mother of the Blessed One has become ordained.'

'If, Ānanda, women had not retired from household life to the houseless one, under the Doctrine and Discipline announced by the Tathāgata, religion, Ānanda, would long endure; a thousand years would the Good Doctrine abide. But since, Ānanda, women have now retired from household life to the houseless one, under the Doctrine and Discipline announced by the Tathāgata, not long, Ānanda, will religion endure; but five hundred years, Ānanda, will the Good Doctrine abide. Just as, Ānanda, those families which consist of many women and few men are easily overcome by burglars, in exactly the same way, Ānanda, when women retire from household life to the houseless one, under a doctrine and discipline, that religion does not long endure. Just as, Ānanda, when the disease called mildew falls upon a flourishing field of rice, that field of rice does not long endure, in exactly the same way, Ānanda, when women retire from household life to the houseless one, under a doctrine and discipline, that religion does not long endure. Even as, Ānanda, when the disease called rust falls upon a flourishing field of sugarcane, that field of sugarcane does not long endure in exactly the same way, Ānanda, when women retire from household life to the houseless one, under a doctrine and discipline, that religion does not long endure. And just as, Ānanda, to a large pond a man would prudently build a dyke, in order that the water might not transgress its bounds, in exactly the same way, Ānanda, have I prudently laid down eight weighty regulations, not to be transgressed as long as life shall last.'

Institutional Expression 3

The Rules of the Order: Sarvāstivāda, Prātimokṣa Sūtra

This passage is from the *Sarvāstivāda* canon of the 'Realist' school which was a major branch of the traditional parallel to the Theravāda. It indicates the discipline which came to shape the community.

Here, Venerable Gentlemen, are the four rules about the offences which deserve expulsion. They should be recited every fortnight:

1. If a monk should have sexual intercourse with anyone, down to an animal, this monk has fallen into an offence which deserves expulsion, and he should no longer live in the community. This holds good for any monk who has entered on a life based on a monk's training, unless he has thereafter repudiated the training, and declared his weakness.

2. If a monk, whether he dwells in a village or in solitude, should take anything not given, he should no longer live in the community. This, however, only applies to thefts for which a king or his police would seize a thief, and kill, imprison, banish, fine, or reprove him.

3. If a monk should intentionally take the life of a human being or of one like a human being, with his own hand, or with a knife, or by having him assassinated, then he has fallen into an offence which deserves expulsion. And this applies also to a monk who incites others to self-destruction, and who speaks to them in praise of death, with such words as, 'O man, what is the use to you of this miserable life? It is better for you to die than be alive!'

4. Unless a monk be actuated by excessive self-conceit, he commits an offence which deserves expulsion if, vainly and without basis in fact, he falsely claims to have realized and perceived superhuman states or the fullness of the insight of the Saints; and if later on, whether questioned or not, in his desire to get rid of his fault and regain his purity, he admits that he had claimed to have realized, without having done so, that he had claimed to have perceived, without having done so, and that he had told a falsehood and lie.

Venerable Gentlemen, the four offences leading to expulsion have been recited. A monk who has committed any of them should no longer live in the community. Now, I ask you, Venerable Ones, 'Are you quite pure in this matter?' A second and a third time I ask, 'Are you quite pure in this matter?' The Venerable Ones keep silence. They are therefore quite pure in this matter. So I do take it to be.

Here, Venerable Gentlemen, are the thirteen offences which deserve suspension, and which should every fortnight be recited in the

Prāṭimokṣa Sūtra. These forbid a monk:

1. Intentionally to emit his semen, except in a dream.

2. With a mind excited and perverted by passion to come into bodily contact with a woman; he must not hold her hand or arm, touch her hair or any other part of her body, above or below, or rub or caress it.

3. With a mind excited and perverted by passion to persuade a woman to sexual intercourse, speaking wicked, evil, and vulgar words, as young men use to their girls.

4. With a mind excited and perverted by passion, in the presence of a woman to speak highly of the merit of the gift of her own body, saying: 'That is the supreme service or gift, dear sister, to offer intercourse to monks like us, who have been observing strict morality, have abstained from intercourse and lived lonely lives!'

5. To act as a go-between between women and men, arranging marriage, adultery, or even a brief meeting.

6. To build for himself, without the help of a layman, a temporary hut on a site which involves the destruction of living beings and has no open space round it, and that without showing the site to other monks, and without limiting its size to the prescribed measurements.

7. To build for himself, with the help of a layman, a more permanent living place in a dangerous and inaccessible site, which involves the destruction of living beings and has no open space round it, and that without showing the site to other monks.

8. From anger, malice, and dislike to accuse falsely a pure and faultless monk of an offence which deserves expulsion, intent on driving him out of the religious life. That becomes an offence which deserves suspension if on a later occasion he withdraws his accusation, and admits to having spoken from hatred; and likewise if

9. He tries to base his false accusation on some trifling matter or other which is really quite irrelevant.

10. To persist, in spite of repeated admonitions, in trying to cause divisions in a community which lives in harmony, and in emphasizing those points which are calculated to cause division.

11. To side with a monk who strives to split the community.

12. To refuse to move into another district when reproved by the other monks for habitually doing evil deeds in a city or village where he resides, deeds which are seen, heard, and known, and which harm the families of the faithful. This becomes an offence deserving suspension when the erring monk persistently answers back, and says: 'You, Venerable Monks, are capricious, spiteful, deluded, and over-anxious. For you now want to send me away, though you did not send away other monks who have committed exactly the same offence.'

13. To refuse to be admonished by others about the non-observance of the *Prāṭimokṣa* rules.

These, Venerable Gentlemen, are the thirteen offences which deserve suspension. The first nine become offences at once, the remaining four only after the third admonition. The offending monk will first be put on probation, then for six days and nights he must do penance, and thereafter he must undergo a special ceremony before he can be rehabilitated. But he can be reinstated only by a community which numbers at least twenty monks, not one less.

Now, three times I ask the Venerable Ones, 'Are you quite pure in this matter?' The Venerable Ones keep silent. They are therefore quite pure in this matter. And so I take it to be.

Experience 1

Meditation and Emptiness: Majjhima Nikāya

The practice of the stages of meditation (the *jhānas*; the Sanskrit equivalent of the Pāli *jhāna* is *dhyāna*, equals Chinese *ch'ān* and Japanese *zen*) relates to the way the mind is systematically emptied. This experience found strong expression in the Great Vehicle notion of the Void or *śūnyatā*. Experientially the Theravāda and the Mahāyāna do not here seem at all far apart. The passage is the 'Lesser Discourse on Emptiness'.

This have I heard: At one time the Lord was staying near Sávatthī in the eastern monastery in the palace of Migāra's mother. Then the venerable Ānanda, emerging from solitary meditation towards evening, approached the Lord; having approached and greeted the Lord, he sat down at a respectful distance. As he was sitting down at a respectful distance, the venerable Ānanda spoke thus to the Lord:

'At one time, revered sir, the Lord was staying among the Sakyans. Nagaraka is the name of a market town of the Sakyans. And while I was there, revered sir, face to face with the Lord I heard, face to face I learnt: "I, Ānanda, through abiding in emptiness, am now abiding in the fullness thereof." I hope that I heard this properly, revered sir, learnt it properly, attended to it properly and understood it properly?'

'Certainly, Ānanda, you heard this properly, learnt it properly, attended to it properly and understood it properly. Formerly I, Ananda, as well as now, through abiding in emptiness, abide in the fullness thereof. As this palace of Migāra's mother is empty of elephants, cows, horses and mares, empty of gold and silver, empty of assemblages of men and women, and there is only this that is not emptiness, that is to say the unity grounded on the Order of monks; even so, Ananda, a monk, not attending to the perception of village, not attending to the perception of human beings, attends to unity grounded on the perception of forest. His mind is satisfied with, pleased with, set on and freed in the perception of forest. He comprehends thus: "The disturbances there might be resulting from the perception of human beings do not exist here. There is only this degree of disturbance, that is to say, unity grounded on the perception of forest." He comprehends, "This perceiving is empty of the perception of village." He comprehends, "This perceiving is empty of the perception of human beings. And there is only this that is not emptiness, that is to say unity grounded on the perception of forest." He regards that which is not there as empty of it. But in regard to what remains there he comprehends, "That being, this is." Thus, Ānanda, this comes to be for him a true, not a mistaken, utterly purified realization of emptiness.

'And again, Ānanda, a monk not attending to the perception of human beings, not attending to the perception of forest, attends to unity grounded on the perception of earth. Ānanda, it is like a bull's hide well stretched on a hundred pegs, its virtue gone. Even so, Ānanda, a monk, not attending to anything on this earth: dry land and swamps, rivers and marshes, plants bearing stakes and thorns, hills and plains, attends to unity grounded on the perception of earth. His mind is satisfied with, pleased with, set on and freed in the perception of earth. He comprehends thus: "The disturbances there might be resulting from the perception of forest do not exist here. There is only this degree of disturbance, that is to say unity grounded on the perception of earth." He comprehends, "This perceiving is empty of the perception of human beings; this perceiving is empty of the perception of forest. And there is only this that is not emptiness, that is to say unity grounded on the perception of earth." He regards that which is not there as empty of it. But in regard to what remains there he comprehends, "That being, this is." Thus, Ānanda, this too comes to be for him a true, not mistaken, and utterly purified realization of [the concept of] emptiness.

'And again, Ānanda, a monk, not attending to the perception of forest, not attending to the perception of earth, attends to unity grounded on the perception of the plane of infinite space. His mind is satisfied with, pleased with, set on and freed in the perception of the plane of infinite space. He comprehends thus: "The disturbances there might be resulting from the perception of forest do not exist here; the disturbances there might be resulting from the perception of earth do not exist here. There is only this degree of disturbance, that is to say unity grounded on the plane of infinite space." He comprehends, "This perceiving is empty of the perception of forest." He comprehends, "This perceiving is empty of the perception of earth. And there is only this that is not emptiness, that is to say the unity grounded on the perception of the plane of infinite space." He regards that which is not there as empty of it. But in regard to what remains there he comprehends, "That being, this is." Thus, Ananda, this too comes to be for him a true . . . realization of emptiness.

'And again, Ānanda, a monk, not attending to the perception of earth, not attending to the perception of the plane of infinite space attends to unity grounded on the plane of infinite consciousness. His mind is satisfied with . . . and freed in the perception of the plane of infinite consciousness. He comprehends thus: "The disturbances there might be resulting from the perception of earth . . . from the perception of the plane of infinite space do not exist here. There is only this degree of disturbance, that is to say unity grounded on the perception of the plane of infinite consciousness." He comprehends, "This perceiving is empty of the perception of earth . . . empty of the perception of the plane of infinite space. And there is only this that is not emptiness, that is to say unity grounded on the perception of the plane of infinite consciousness." He regards that which is not there as empty of it. But in regard to what remains he comprehends, "That being, this is." Thus, Ānanda, this too comes to be for him a true . . . realization of emptiness.

'And again, Ānanda, a monk, not attending to the perception of the plane of infinite space, not attending to the perception of the plane of infinite consciousness, attends to unity grounded on the perception of the plane of no-thing. His mind is satisfied with . . . and freed in the perception of the plane of no-thing. He comprehends thus: "The disturbances there might be resulting from the perception of the plane of infinite space . . . from the perception of the plane of infinite consciousness do not exist here. There is only this degree of disturbance, that is to say unity grounded on the perception of the plane of no-thing." He comprehends, "This perceiving is empty of the perception of the plane of infinite space." He comprehends, "This perceiving is empty of the perception of the plane of infinite consciousness. And there is only this that is not emptiness, that is to say unity grounded on the perception of the plane of no-thing." He regards that which is not there as empty of it. But in regard to what remains there he comprehends, "That being, this is." Thus, Ānanda, this too comes to be for him a true . . . realization of emptiness.

'And again, Ānanda, a monk, not attending to the perception of the plane of infinite consciousness, not attending to the perception of the plane of no-thing, attends to unity grounded on the perception of the plane of neither-perception-nor-non-perception. His mind is pleased with . . . and freed in the perception of the plane of neither-perception-nor-non-perception. He comprehends thus: "The disturbances there might be resulting from the perception of the plane of infinite consciousness . . . resulting from the perception of the plane of no-thing do not exist here. There is only this degree of disturbance, that is to say unity grounded on the perception of the plane of neither-perception-nor-non-perception." He comprehends, "This perceiving is empty of the perception of the plane of infinite consciousness . . . of the perception of the plane of no-thing. And there is only this that is emptiness, that is to say unity grounded on the perception of the plane of neither-perception-nor-non-perception." He regards that which is not there as empty of it. But in regard to what remains there he comprehends, "That being, this is." Thus, Ānanda, this too comes to be for him a true . . . realization of emptiness.

'And again, Ānanda, a monk, not attending to the perception of the plane of no-thing, not attending to the perception of the plane of neither-perception-nor-non-perception, attends to unity grounded on the concentration of mind that is signless. His mind is satisfied with . . . and freed in the concentration of mind that is signless. He comprehends thus: "The disturbances there might be resulting from the perception of the plane of no-thing . . . from the perception of the plane of neither-perception-nor-non-perception do not exist here. There is only this degree of disturbance, that is to say the six sensory fields that, conditioned by life, are grounded on this body itself." He comprehends: "This perceiving is empty of the plane of no-thing . . . empty of the perception of the plane of neither-perception-nor-non-perception. And there is only this that is not emptiness, that is to say the six sensory fields that, conditioned by life, are grounded on this body itself." He regards that which is not there as empty of it. But in regard to what remains there he comprehends, "That being, this is." Thus, Ānanda, this too comes to be for him a true, not mistaken, utterly purified realization of emptiness.

'And again, Ānanda, a monk, not attending to the perception of the plane of no-thing, not attending to the perception of the plane of neither-perception-nor-non-perception, attends to unity grounded on the concentration of mind that is signless. His mind is satisfied with, pleased with, set on and freed in the concentration of mind that is signless. He comprehends thus, "This concentration of mind that is signless is effected and thought out. But whatever is effected and thought out, that is impermanent, it is liable to stopping." When he knows this thus, sees this thus, his mind is freed from the canker of sense-pleasures and his mind is freed from the canker of becoming and his mind is freed from the canker of ignorance. In freedom is the knowledge that he is freed and he comprehends: "Destroyed is birth, brought to close the Brahma-faring, done is what was to be done, there is no more of being such or so." He comprehends thus: "The disturbances there might be resulting from the canker of sense-pleasures do not exist here; the disturbances there might be resulting from the canker of becoming do not exist here; the disturbances there might be resulting from the canker of ignorance do not exist here. And there is only this degree of disturbance, that is to say the six sensory fields that, conditioned by life, are grounded on this body itself." He comprehends: "This perceiving is empty of the canker of sense-pleasures." He comprehends: "This perceiving is empty of the canker of ignorance. And there is only this that is not emptiness, that is to say the six sensory fields that, conditioned by life, are grounded on this body itself." He regards that which is not there as empty of it. But in regard to what remains he comprehends: "That being, this is." Thus, Ānanda, this comes to be for him a true, not mistaken, utterly purified and incomparably highest realization of emptiness.

'And those recluses or brahmans, Ānanda, who in the distant past, entering on the utterly purified and incomparably highest emptiness, abided therein – all these, entering on precisely this utterly purified and incomparably highest emptiness, abided therein. And those recluses or brahmans, Ānanda, who in the distant future, entering on the utterly purified and incomparably highest emptiness, will abide therein – all these, entering on precisely this utterly purified and incomparably highest emptiness, will abide therein. And those recluses or brahmans, Ānanda, who at present, entering on the utterly purified and incomparably highest emptiness, are abiding in it – all these, entering on precisely this utterly purified and incomparably highest emptiness, are abiding therein. Wherefore, Ānanda, thinking: "Entering on the utterly purified and incomparably highest emptiness, I will abide therein" – this is how you must train yourself, Ānanda.'

Thus spoke the Lord. Delighted, the venerable Ānanda rejoiced in what the Lord had said.

Experience 2

The Appeal to Experience: Majjhima Nikāya, Tevijja Sutta

In this discourse the Buddha deals with the claims of the Brahmins that the three Vedas are revelatory and authoritative. The reference to three rather than the four recognized in Hindu tradition reflects the way that the Rg, Yajur and Sāma Vedas only later had the Atharva added to them. The passage indicates how in theory the Vedas were heard and transmitted by the ancient Rishis.

And while they were thus seated the young Brahmin Vasettha said to the Exalted One:

'As we, Gautama, were taking exercise and walking up and down, there sprang up a conversation between us on which was the true path and which the false. Regarding this matter, Gautama, there is a strife, a dispute, a difference of opinion between us.'

'Wherein, then, O Vasettha, is there a strife, a dispute, a difference of opinion between you?'

'Concerning the true path and the false, Gautama. Various Brahmins, Gautama, teach various paths. Are all those saving paths? Are they all paths which will lead him, who acts according to them, into a state of union with Brahmā?'

'Vasettha, is there a single one of the Brahmins versed in the three Vedas who has ever seen Brahmā face to face?'

'No, indeed, Gautama.'

'Well, then, Vasettha, those ancient Rishis of the Brahmins versed in the three Vedas, the authors of the verses, the utterers of the verses, whose ancient form of words so chanted, uttered, or composed, the Brahmins of today chant over again or repeat; intoning or reciting exactly as has been intoned or recited; did even they speak thus, saying: "We know it, we have seen it, where Brahmā is, whence Brahmā is, whither Brahmā is"?'

'Not so, Gautama!'

'Then you say, Vasettha, that none of the Brahmins, or of their teachers, or of their pupils, even up to the seventh generation, has even seen Brahmā face to face. And that even the Rishis of old, the authors and utterers of the verses, of the ancient form of words which the Brahmins of today so carefully intone and recite precisely as they have been handed down – even they did not pretend to know or to have seen where or whence or whither Brahmā is. So that the Brahmins versed in the three Vedas have forsooth said thus: "What we know not, what we have not seen, to a state of union with that we can show the way, and can say: 'This is the straight path, this is the direct way which makes for salvation, and leads him, who acts according to it, into a state of union with Brahmā!'"

'Now what think you, Vasettha? Does it not follow, this being so, that the talk of the Brahmins, versed though they be in the three Vedas, turns out to be foolish talk?'

'In truth, Gautama, that being so, it follows that the talk of the Brahmins versed in the three Vedas is foolish talk!'

Experience 3

Early Poetical Expression: Theragāthā

These three poems are drawn from the 'Elders' Verses' or *Theragāthā*, anthologies of sometimes autobiographical poems compiled over about three centuries from the earliest times. In the first there is mention of the impact of the hearing of the Dharma (hearing was how revelation was often described, words somehow conveying a transcendental message). In the second the life of meditation reaches its climax as the peacocks herald the rainy season. In the third, Māra the Tempter is turned back because the dancing girl is suddenly seen as a suffering not an alluring being.

In the woodland thickets beyond Ambātaka
park
His craving pulled up by the root lucky
Bhaddiya lives in meditation.
Though some like the music of drums
or of cymbals and mandolins,
My delight as I sit by a tree
is the sound of the Buddha's message.
And if the Buddha would grant me a wish and the
wish were mine,
I would choose that the whole world might
constantly be alert to the transcience of all
physical things.

The peacocks shriek. Ah, the lovely crests and
tails and the sweet sound of the blue-
throated peacocks!
The great grassy plain now runs with water
beneath the thunder-clouded sky.

Your body's fresh, you are vigorous now and
fit to test the Teaching:
Reach now for that saintly rapture,
So bright, so pure, so subtle, so hard to
fathom,
The highest, the eternal place.

Got up with flowers and perfumes
Dressed in alluring clothes,
The dancing-girl in the main-street
Swayed to the sound of a band.
I'd gone down into the city
To beg, and had seen her there,
In all her finery, dancing,
A snare that the Tempter had laid.

Then the basic truth of the matter
And the misery of it all
Became suddenly transparent,
And so produced distaste.

Experience 4

The Qualities of Nirvāna: Milindapañha

The Questions of King Milinda (or Menander, a Greek king ruling over the far northwest of India in the mid-part of the 2nd century BCE) is a great literary work in Pali; though not canonical, its lucidity and charm have earned it wide influence. In the passage quoted, the qualities of nirvāna are described, the supposition being that nirvāna is something to be experienced in this life: one who realizes nirvāna thus is a saint or *arhant* and has absolute assurance of final release upon death (this is nirvāna without substrate, while the saint has gained nirvāna with substrate, that is while continuing to exist in bodily form).

King Milinda said: 'I will grant you, Nagasena, that nirvāna is absolute ease, and that nevertheless one cannot point to its form or shape, its duration or size, either by simile or explanation, by reason or by argument. But is there perhaps some quality of nirvāna which it shares with other things, and which lends itself to a metaphorical explanation?' 'Its form, O king, cannot be elucidated by similes, but its qualities can.' 'How good to hear that, Nagasena! Speak then, quickly, so that I may have an explanation of even one of the aspects of nirvāna! Appease the fever of my heart! Allay it with the cool sweet breezes of your words!'

'Nirvāna shares one quality with the lotus, two with water, three with medicine, ten with space, three with the wishing jewel, and five with a mountain peak. As the lotus is unstained by water, so is nirvāna unstained by all the defilements. As cool water allays feverish heat, so also nirvāna is cool and allays the fever of all the passions. Moreover, as water removes the thirst of men and beasts who are exhausted, parched, thirsty, and overpowered by heat, so also nirvāna removes the craving for sensuous enjoyments, the craving for further becoming, the craving for the cessation of becoming. As medicine protects from the torments of poison, so nirvāna from the torments of the poisonous passions. Moreover, as medicine puts an end to sickness so nirvāna to all sufferings. Finally, nirvāna and medicine both give security. And these are the ten qualities which nirvāna shares with space. Neither is born, grows old, dies, passes away, or is reborn; both are unconquerable, cannot be stolen, are unsupported, are roads respectively for bids and *arhants* to all one can desire, brings joy, and sheds light. As a mountain peak is lofty and exalted, so is nirvāna. As a mountain peak is unshakeable, so is nirvāna. As a mountain peak is inaccessible, so is nirvāna inaccessible to all the passions. As no seeds can grow on a mountain peak, so the seeds of all the passions cannot grow in nirvāna. And finally, as a mountain peak is free from all desire to please or displease, so is nirvāna.'

'Well said, Nagasena! So it is, and as such I accept it.'

Experience 5

Zen Enlightenment: A poem by Hakugai

This 14th-century poem reflects the Rinzai account of satori as being 'sudden' rather than the gradual increase in insight favoured by the Soto school. Zen is pervaded by a strong sense of nature and some satori experiences appear to be what has been called 'panenhenic' ('all in one' experiences of a sense of the unity of oneself and nature).

Satori poem

Defying the power of speech, the Law
    Commission on Mount Vulture!
Kasyapa's smile told the beyond-telling.
What's up there to reveal in that perfect all-
    suchness?
Look up! the moon-mind glows unsmirched.

Myoyu (1333–93, Soto)

Satori poem

Last year in a lovely temple in Hirosawa,
  This year among the rocks of Nikko,
  All's the same to me:
  Clapping hands, the peaks roar at the blue!

Hakugai (1343–1414, Rinzai)

Experience 6

The Sense of Dependence: A poem by Shinran

Shinran (1173–1262) took Buddhist *bhakti* or devotional religion to its ultimate conclusion through a sense of dependence upon the Buddha Amitābha (Amida in Japanese) to deliver human beings who in these latter days have lost the power to help themselves. By appealing to the name of Amida in faith one may be assured of rebirth in the paradise of the Pure Land. No longer is there emphasis upon inner contemplation as the means to nirvāna, so Shinran's *bhakti* contrasts notably with the spirit of some of the previous passages.

Though I seek my refuge in the true faith of the Pure Land,
Yet hath not mine heart been truly sincere.
Deceit and untruth are in my flesh,
And in my soul is no clear shining.

In their outward seeming are all men diligent and truth speaking,
But in their souls are greed and anger and unjust deceitfulness,
And in their flesh do lying and cunning triumph.

Too strong for me is the evil of my heart. I cannot overcome it.
Therefore is my soul like unto the poison of serpents;
Even my righteous deeds, being mingled with this poison,
Must be named the deeds of deceitfulness.

Shameless though I be and having no truth in my soul,
Yet the virtue of the Holy Name, the gift of Him that is enlightened,
Is spread throughout the world through my words,
Although I am as I am.

There is no mercy in my soul. The good of my fellow man is not dear in mine eyes.
If it were not for the Ark of Mercy,
The divine promise of the Infinite Wisdom,
How should I cross the Ocean of Misery?

I, whose mind is filled with cunning and deceit as the poison of reptiles,
Am impotent to practice righteous deeds.
If I sought not refuge in the gift of our Father,
I should die the death of the shameless.

Experience 7

A Vision of Paradise: Sukhāvatīvyūha Sūtra

This scripture describing the Pure Land of the great Buddha Amitābha gives a wonderful account of the visionary expectations of those who have faith. Increasingly such Buddhas wear the aspect of a gracious and loving God, and the feeling of such devotional Buddhism is reminiscent of similar motifs of religious sentiment in *bhakti* Hinduism and evangelical Christianity.

This world Subhavati, Ānanda, which is the world system of the Lord Amitābha, is rich and prosperous, comfortable, fertile, delightful and crowded with many Gods and men. And in this world system, Ānanda, there are no hells, no animals, no ghosts, no Asuras[1] and none of the

[1] Antigods, opposed to the Devas.

inauspicious places of rebirth. And in this our world no jewels make their appearance like those which exist in the world system Sukhāvatī.

And that world system Sukhāvatī, Ānanda, emits many fragrant odours, it is rich in a great variety of flowers and fruits, adorned with jewel trees, which are frequented by flocks of various birds with sweet voices, which the Tathāgata's miraculous power has conjured up. And these jewel trees, Ānanda, have various colours, many colours, many hundreds of thousands of colours. They are variously composed of the seven precious things, in varying combinations, that is, of gold, silver, beryl, crystal, coral, red pearls or emerald. Such jewel trees, and clusters of banana trees and rows of palm trees, all made of precious things, grow everywhere in this Buddha-field. On all sides it is surrounded with golden nets, and all round covered with lotus flowers made of all the precious things. Some of the lotus flowers are half a mile in circumference, others up to ten miles. And from each jewel lotus issue thirty-six hundred thousand billions of rays. And at the end of each ray there issue thirty-six hundred thousand billions of Buddhas, with golden-coloured bodies, who bear the thirty-two marks of the supermen, and who, in all the ten directions, go into the countless world systems, and there demonstrate Dharma.

And further, Ānanda, in this Buddha-field there are nowhere any mountains – black mountains, jewel mountains, Sumerus, kings of mountains, circular mountains and great circular mountains. But the Buddha-field is everywhere even, delightful like the palm of the hand, and in all its parts the ground contains a great variety of jewels and gems.

And many kinds of rivers flow along in this world system Sukhāvatī. There are great rivers there, one mile broad, and up to fifty miles broad and twelve miles deep. And all these rivers flow along calmly, their water is fragrant with manifold agreeable odours, in them there are bunches of flowers to which various jewels adhere, and they resound with various sweet sounds. And the sound which issues from these great rivers is as pleasant as that of a musical instrument, which consists of hundreds of thousands of billions of parts, and which, skilfully played, emits a heavenly music. It is deep, commanding, distinct, clear, pleasant to the ear, touching the heart, delightful, sweet, pleasant, and one never tires of hearing it, it always agrees with one and one likes to hear it, like the words 'Impermanent, peaceful, calm, and not-self'. Such is the sound that reaches the ears of those beings.

And, Ānanda, both the banks of those great rivers are lined with variously scented jewel trees, and from them bunches of flowers, leaves, and branches of all kinds hang down. And if those beings wish to indulge in sports full of heavenly delights on those river-banks, then, after they have stepped into the water, the water in each case rises as high as they wish it to – up to the ankles, or the knees, or the hips, or their sides, or their ears. And heavenly delights arise. Again, if beings wish the water to be cold, for them it becomes cold; if they wish it to be hot, for them it becomes hot and cold, to suit their pleasure. And those rivers flow along, full of waters scented with the finest odours and covered with beautiful flowers, resounding with the sounds of many birds, easy to ford, free from mud, and with golden sand at the bottom. And all the wishes those beings may think of, they all will be fulfilled, as long as they are rightful.

Ethics 1

The Way to Nirvāna: Khuddaka Nikāya, Itivuttaka

This passage indicates the style of life which the monk or nun should follow if he or she is to gain nirvāna. Two aspects of nirvāna are distinguished – one in this life, the other at decease.

This was said by the Exalted One, said by the *Arhant*, so I have heard:

Monks, I am your surety for not returning to birth. Do ye give up lust, ill-will, delusion, wrath, spite, pride. I am your surety for not returning.

Monks, the man who does not understand and comprehend the all, who has not detached his mind therefrom, who has not abandoned the all, can make no growth in extinguishing ill. But, monks, he who does understand and comprehend the all, who has detached his mind therefrom, who has abandoned the all, he makes growth in extinguishing ill.

Monks, for the monk who is a learner not yet come to mastery of mind, but who dwells aspiring for peace from the bond, making it a matter concerning what is outside the self, I see no other single factor so helpful as friendship with the lovely. Monks, one who is a friend of the lovely abandons the unprofitable and makes the profitable to become.

Here, monks, I discern a certain person with mind at peace to be such because I compass his thoughts with my mind; and, if at this moment this person were to make an end, he would be put just so into the heaven-world according to his deserts. What is the reason for that? His mind at peace. Indeed it is because of a mind at peace, monks, that in this way certain beings, when the body breaks up, after death arise again in the happy bourn, in the heaven-world.

Monks, if beings knew, as I know, the ripening of sharing gifts, they would not enjoy their use without sharing them, nor would the taint of stinginess obsess the heart and stay there. Even if it were their last bit, their last morsel of food, they would not enjoy its use without sharing it, if there were any one to receive it. But inasmuch, monks, as beings do not know, as I know, the ripening of sharing gifts, therefore they enjoy their use without sharing them, and the taint of stinginess obsesses their heart and stays there.

Monks, whatsoever grounds there be for good works undertaken with a view to rebirth, all of them are not worth one sixteenth part of that goodwill which is the heart's release; goodwill alone, which is the heart's release, shines and burns and flashes forth in surpassing them. Just as, monks, the radiance of all the starry bodies is not worth one sixteenth part of the moon's radiance, but the moon's radiance shines and burns and flashes forth in surpassing them, even so, monks, goodwill . . . flashes forth in surpassing good works undertaken with a view to rebirth.

Monks, two Dhamma-teachings of the wayfarer *arhant*, a rightly awakened one, take place one after the other. What two? 'Look at evil as evil' is the first Dhamma-teaching. 'Seeing evil as evil, be disgusted therewith, be cleansed of it, be freed of it' is the second Dhamma-teaching.

Monks, ignorance leads the way to the attainment of unprofitable things; shamelessness and disregard to blame follow after. But, monks, knowledge leads the way to the attainment of profitable things, shrinking and fear of blame follow after.

Monks, there are these two conditions of nirvāna. What two? The condition of nirvāna with the basis still remaining and that without basis. Of what sort, monks, is the condition of nirvāna which has the basis still remaining? Herein, monks, a monk is *arhant*, one who has destroyed the cankers, who has lived the life, done what has to be done, laid down the burden, won the goal, worn out the fetter of becoming, one released by perfect knowledge. In him the five sense-faculties still remain, through which, as they have not yet departed, he experiences sensations pleasant and unpleasant, undergoes pleasure and pain. In him the end of lust, malice and delusion, monks, is called 'the condition of nirvāna with the basis still remaining'.

And of what sort, monks, is the condition of nirvāna that is without basis?

Herein a monk is . . . released by perfect knowledge, but in him in this very life all things that are sensed have no delight for him, they have become cool. This is called 'the condition of nirvāna without basis'. So, monks, these are the two conditions of nirvāna.

Monks, do ye delight in solitary communing; delighted by solitary communing, given to mental calm in the inner self, not neglecting musing, possessed of insight, do ye foster resort to empty places? One of two fruits is to be looked for in those who do these things, namely, gnosis in this very life or, if there be still a basis, not-return to this world.[1]

[1] One who does not return goes to a heaven and there attains nirvāna.

Ethics 2

Wisdom and Foolishness in Action: The Dhammapada

The *Dhammapada* is the most famous collection of wise sayings, many on ethical themes from early Buddhism. The two passages stress the importance of right attitudes and the danger of false values.

Moral attitudes: Dhammapada, 1: The Twin Verses

All that we are is the result of what we have thought: it is founded on our thoughts, it is made up of our thoughts. If a man speaks or acts with an evil thought, pain follows him, as the wheel follows the foot of the ox that draws the carriage.

All that we are is the result of what we have thought: it is founded on our thoughts, it is made up of our thoughts. If a man speaks or acts with a pure thought, happiness follows him, like a shadow that never leaves him.

'He abused me, he beat me, he defeated me, he robbed me' – in those who harbour such thoughts hatred will never cease.

'He abused me, he beat me, he defeated me, he robbed me' – in those who do not harbour such thoughts hatred will cease.

For hatred does not cease by hatred at any time; hatred ceases by love – this is an old rule.

The world does not know that we must all come to an end here; but those who know it, their quarrels cease at once.

He who lives looking for pleasures only, his senses uncontrolled, immoderate in his food, idle, and weak, Māra [the tempter] will certainly overthrow him, as the wind throws down a weak tree.

He who lives without looking for pleasures, his sense well-controlled, moderate in his food, faithful, and strong, him Māra will certainly not overthrow, any more than the wind throws down a rocky mountain.

He who wishes to put on the yellow dress without having cleansed himself from sin, who disregards also temperance and truth, is unworthy of the yellow dress.

But he who has cleansed himself from sin, is well grounded in all virtues, and endowed also with temperance and truth: he is indeed worthy of the yellow dress.

They who imagine truth in untruth, and see untruth in truth, never arrive at truth but follow vain desires.

They who know truth in truth, and untruth in untruth, arrive at truth and follow true desires.

As rain breaks through an ill-thatched house, passion will break through an unreflecting mind.

As rain does not break through a well-thatched house, passion will not break through a well-reflecting mind.

The evildoer mourns in this world, and he mourns in the next; he mourns in both. He mourns and suffers when he sees the evil result of his own work.

The virtuous man delights in this world, and he delights in the next; he delights in both. He delights and rejoices, when he sees the purity of his own work.

The evildoer suffers in this world, and he suffers in the next; he suffers in both. He suffers when he thinks of the evil he has done; he suffers more when going on the evil path.

The virtuous man is happy in this world, and he is happy in the next; he is happy in both. He is happy when he thinks of the good he has done; he is still more happy when going on the good path.

The thoughtless man, even if he can recite a large portion of the law, but is not a doer of it, has no share in the priesthood, but is like a cowherd counting the cows of others.

The follower of the law, even if he can recite only a small portion of the law, but, having forsaken passion and hatred and foolishness, possesses true knowledge and serenity of mind, he, caring for nothing in this world or that to come, has indeed a share in the holy life.

Karma: Dhammapada, 5: The Fool

Long is the night to him who is awake; long is a

mile to him who is tired; long is life to the foolish who do not know the true law.

If a traveller does not meet with one who is his better, or his equal, let him firmly keep to his solitary journey; there is no companionship with a fool.

'These sons belong to me, and this wealth belongs to me' – with such thoughts a fool is tormented. He himself does not belong to himself; how much less sons and wealth?

The fool who knows his foolishness is wise at least so far. But a fool who thinks himself wise, he is called a fool indeed.

If a fool be associated with a wise man even all his life, he will perceive the truth as little as a spoon perceives the taste of soup.

If an intelligent man be associated for one minute only with a wise man, he will soon perceive the truth, as the tongue perceives the taste of soup.

Fools of poor understanding have themselves for their greatest enemies, for they do evil deeds which bear bitter fruits.

That deed is not well done of which a man must repent, and the reward of which he receives crying and with a tearful face.

No, that deed is well done of which a man does not repent, and the reward of which he receives gladly and cheerfully.

As long as the evil deed done does not bear fruit, the fool thinks it is like honey; but when it ripens, then the fool suffers grief.

Let a fool month after month eat his food [like an ascetic] with the tip of a blade of kusa-grass, yet is he not worth the sixteenth particle of those who have well weighed the law.

An evil deed, like newly-drawn milk, does not turn suddenly; smouldering, like fire covered by ashes, it follows the fool.

And when the evil deed, after it has become known, turns to sorrow for the fool, then it destroys his bright lot, nay, it cleaves his head.

Let the fool wish for a false reputation, for precedence among the monks, for lordship in the convents, for worship among other people!

'May both the layman and he who has left the world think that this is done by me; may they be subject to me in everything which is to be done or is not to be done' – thus is the mind of the fool, and his desire and pride increase.

'One is the road that leads to wealth, another the road that leads to nirvāna' – if the monk, the disciple of Buddha, has learned this, he will not yearn for honour, he will strive after separation from the world.

Ethics 3

The Five Precepts and their Meaning: Buddhaghoṣa's Commentary: Papanasudani

The five precepts or virtues (*sīlāni*) are the basic rules for lay and monastic Buddhists; monks and nuns had to obey a further five precepts as well. Buddhaghoṣa's commentary shows how Theravādin understanding of the applications of the rules had advanced by about 400 CE. Buddhaghoṣa was a prolific writer whose most influential systematic work was the *Visuddhimagga* or 'Path of Purity', which summarizes the holy life and the teachings of the Theravāda.

'I undertake to observe the rule
to abstain from taking life;
to abstain from taking what is not given;
to abstain from sensuous misconduct;
to abstain from false speech;
to abstain from intoxicants as tending to cloud the mind.'

The first four precepts are explained by Buddhaghoṣa as follows:

1. 'Taking life' means to murder anything that lives. It refers to the striking and killing of living beings. 'Anything that lives' – ordinary people speak here of a 'living being', but more philosophically we speak of 'anything that has the life-force'. 'Taking life' is then the will to kill anything that one perceives as having life, to act so as to terminate the life-force in it, insofar as the will finds expression in bodily action or in speech. With regard to animals it is worse to kill large ones than small, because a more extensive effort is involved. Even where the effort is the same, the difference in substance must be considered. In the case of humans the killing is the more blameworthy the more virtuous they are. Apart from that, the extent of the offence is proportionate to the intensity of the wish to kill. Five factors are involved: a living being, the perception of a living being, a thought of murder, the action of carrying it out, and death as a result of it. And six are the ways in which the offence may be carried out: with one's own hand, by instigation, by missiles, by slow poisoning, by sorcery, by psychic power.

2. 'To take what is not given' means the appropriation of what is not given. It refers to the removing of someone else's property, to the stealing of it, to theft. 'What is not given' means that which belongs to someone else. 'Taking what is not given' is then the will to steal anything that one perceives as belonging to someone else, and to act so as to appropriate it. Its blameworthiness depends partly on the value of the property stolen, partly on the worth of its owner. Five factors are involved: someone else's belongings, the awareness that they are someone else's, the thought of theft, the action of carrying it out, the taking away as a result of it. This sin, too, may be carried out in six ways. One may also distinguish unlawful acquisition by way of theft, robbery, underhand dealings, stratagems, and the casting of lots.

3. 'Sensuous misconduct' – here 'sensuous' means 'sexual' and 'misconduct' is extremely blameworthy bad behaviour. 'Sensuous misconduct' is the will to transgress against those whom one should not go into, and the carrying out of this intention by unlawful physical action. By 'those one should not go into', first of all men are meant. And then also twenty kinds of women. Ten of them are under some form of protection, by their mother, father, parents, brother, sister, family, clan, co-religionists, by having been claimed from birth onwards, or by the king's law. The other ten kinds are: women bought with money, concubines for the fun of it, kept women, women bought by the gift of a garment, concubines who have been acquired by the ceremony which consists in dipping their hands into water, concubines who once carried burdens on their heads, slave girls who are also concubines, servants who are also concubines, girls captured in war, temporary wives. The offence is the more serious, the more moral and virtuous the person transgressed against. Four factors are involved: someone who should not be gone into, the thought of cohabitating with that one, the actions which lead to such cohabitation, and its actual performance. There is only one way of carrying it out: with one's own body.

4. 'False' – this refers to actions of the voice, or actions of the body, which aim at decieving others by obscuring the action facts. 'False speech' is the will to deceive others by words or deeds. One can also explain: 'False' means something which is not real, not true. 'Speech' is the intimation that that is real or true. 'False speech' is then the volition which leads to the deliberate intimation to someone else that something is so when it is not so. The seriousness of the offence depends on the circumstances. If a householder, unwilling to give something says that he has not got it, that is a small offence; but to represent something one has seen with one's own eyes as other than one has seen it, that is a serious offence. If a mendicant has on his rounds got very little oil or ghee, and if he then exclaims, 'What a magnificent river flows along here, my friends!' that is only a rather stale joke, and the offence is small; but to say that one has seen what one has not seen, that is a serious offence. Four factors are involved: something which is not so, the thought of deception, an effort to carry it out, the communication of the falsehood to someone else. There is only one way of doing it: with one's own body.

'To abstain from' – one crushes or forsakes sin. It means an abstention which is associated with wholesome thoughts. And it is threefold: I. one feels obliged to abstain; II. one formally undertakes to do so; III. one has lost all temptation not to do so.

I. Even those who have not formally

undertaken to observe the precepts may have the conviction that it is not right to offend against them. So it was with Cakkana, a Ceylonese boy. His mother was ill, and the doctor prescribed fresh rabbit meat for her. His brother sent him into the field to catch a rabbit, and he went as he was bidden. Now a rabbit had run into a field to eat of the corn, but in its eagerness to get there had got entangled in a snare, and gave forth cries of distress. Cakkana followed the sound, and thought: 'This rabbit has got caught there, and it will make a fine medicine for my mother!' But then he thought again: 'It is not suitable for me that, in order to preserve my mother's life, I should deprive someone else of his life.' And so he released the rabbit, and said to it: 'Run off, play with the other rabbits in the wood, eat grass and drink water!' On his return he told the story to his brother, who scolded him. He then went to his mother and said to her: 'Even without having been told, I know quite clearly that I should not deliberately deprive any living being of life.' He then fervently resolved that these truthful words of his might make his mother well again, and so it actually happened.

II. The second kind of abstention refers to those who not only have formally undertaken not to offend against the precepts, but who in addition are willing to sacrifice their lives for that. This can be illustrated by a layman who lived near Uttaravarddhamana. He had received the precepts from Buddharakkhita, the Elder. He then went to plough his field, but found that his ox had got lost. In his search for the ox he climbed up the mountain, where a huge snake took hold of him. He thought of cutting off the snake's head with his sharp knife, but on further reflection he thought to himself: 'It is not suitable that I, who have received the Precepts from the venerable Guru, should break them again.' Three times he thought, 'My life I will give up, but not the precepts!' and then he threw his knife away. Thereafter the huge viper let him go, and went somewhere else.

III. The last kind of abstention is association with the holy Path. It does not even occur to the Holy Persons to kill any living being.

Ethics 4

The Ethics of the Eightfold Path: Majjhima Nikāya

In this 'discourse on the analysis of truth' (as its title is) the moral path is seen as an integral part of the eightfold way which leads to liberation, as recounted by Sariputra, one of the Buddha's main disciples.

And what, your reverences, is the noble truth of the course leading to the stopping of anguish? It is this noble Eightfold Way itself, that is to say: right view, right aspiration, right speech, right action, right mode of livelihood, right endeavour, right mindfulness, right concentration.

And what, your reverences, is right view? Whatever, your reverences, is knowledge of anguish, knowledge of the arising of anguish, knowledge of the stopping of anguish, knowledge of the course leading to the stopping of anguish – this, your reverences, is called right view.

And what, your reverences, is right aspiration? Aspiration for renunciation, aspiration for non-malevolence, aspiration for harmlessness – this, your reverences, is called right aspiration.

And what, your reverences, is right speech? Refraining from lying speech, refraining from slanderous speech, refraining from harsh speech, refraining from gossip, this, your reverences, is called right speech.

And what, your reverences, is right action? Refraining from onslaught on creatures, refraining from taking what has not been given, refraining from going wrongly among the sense-pleasures, this, your reverences, is called right action.

And what, your reverences, is right mode of

livelihood? As to this, your reverences, a disciple of the noble ones, getting rid of a wrong mode of livelihood, makes his living by a right mode of livelihood. This, your reverences, is called right mode of livelihood.

And what, your reverences, is right endeavour? As to this, your reverences, a monk generates desire, endeavours, stirs up energy, exerts his mind and strives for the non-arising of evil unskilled states that have not arisen . . . for the getting rid of evil unskilled states that have arisen . . . for the arising of skilled states that have not arisen . . . for the maintenance, preservation, increase, maturity, development and completion of skilled states that have arisen. This, your reverences, is called right endeavour.

And what, your reverences, is rightmindfulness? As to this, your reverences, a monk fares along contemplating the body in the body . . . the feelings in the feelings . . . the mind in the mind . . . the mental states in the mental states, ardent, clearly conscious [of them], mindful [of them] so as to control the covetousness and dejection in the world. This, your reverences, is called right mindfulness.

And what, your reverences, is right concentration? As to this, your reverences, a monk, aloof from pleasures of the sense, aloof from unskilled states of mind, enters on and abides in the first meditation which is accompanied by initial thought and discursive thought, is born of aloofness, and is rapturous and joyful. By allaying initial thought and discursive thought, with the mind subjectively tranquillised and fixed on one point, he enters on and abides in the second meditation which is devoid of initial thought and discursive thought, is born of concentration, and is rapturous and joyful. By the fading out of rapture . . . he enters on and abides in the third meditation . . . the fourth meditation. This, your reverences, is called right concentration.

This, your reverences, is called the noble truth of the course leading to the stopping of anguish.

Your reverences, the matchless Wheel of Dhamma set rolling by the Tathāgata, perfected one, fully Self-Awakened One in the deer-park at Isipatana near Benares cannot be rolled back by a recluse or brahman or deva[1] or Māra or Brahmā or by anyone in the world. That is to say, it was a proclamation, a teaching, laying down, establishing, opening up, analysing, and making plain of these four noble truths.

Thus spake the venerable Sariputra.

Ethics 5

The Bodhisattva Ideal: Mahavāstu

In this transitional work, in which early Mahāyāna trends are foreshadowed, there is depicted the ideal of the Buddha-to-be or Bodhisattva, who embodies compassion and was to play such a crucial role in the moral inspiration of the Greater Vehicle.

They are Bodhisattvas who live on from life to life in the possession of manifold good qualities. They are Bodhisattvas who have won the mastery over karma, and made their deeds renowned through their accumulation of merit. They are resolute and valiant, intent on endurance, trustworthy, upright and sincere. They are generous, firm, gentle, tender, patient, whole and tranquil of heart, difficult to overcome and defeat, intent on what is real, charitable, and faithful to their promises. They are intelligent, brilliantly intelligent, gifted with insight, and not given to gratification of sensual desires. They are devoted to the highest good. They win converts by the

[1] deva: 'god' or 'spirit'.

means of sympathetic appeal. They are pure in conduct and clean of heart, full of exceeding great veneration, full of civility to elder and noble. They are resourceful, in all matters using conciliatory and agreeable methods, and in affairs of government they are adept in persuasive speech. They are men whose voice is not checked in the assembly, men who pour forth their eloquence in a mighty stream. With knowledge as their banner they are skilled in drawing the multitude to them. They are endowed with equanimity, and their means of living is beyond reproach. They are men of successful achievements, and are ready to come to the assistance of others and help those in distress. They do not become enervated by prosperity, and do not lose composure in adversity. They are skilled in uprooting the vices of mean men. They are unwearying in clothing the nakedness of others. They are anxious not to blight the maturing of their karma, and they acquire the roots of virtue by keeping themselves aloof from passion, hatred and folly. They are skilled in bringing solace to those in trouble and misfortune. They do no hesitate to render all kinds of service. In all matters they are untiring in their purpose. They are endowed here in this world with the profound attributes of a Buddha. In their progress towards their goal they are undefiled in acts of body, speech and thought. Through the uprightness of their lives in former existences they are untarnished and pure in conduct. Possessing perfect knowledge they are men of undimmed understanding. They are eager to win the sphere of power of a Buddha – so far are they from refusing it. With knowledge as their banner they are untiring in speech and skilled in teaching. Being of irreproachable character they are immune from disaster. They are free from sin. They shun the threefold distractions. Leaving vain babblers alone, they love their enemies. They do not indulge in sexual pleasures. They know how to win the affection of all creatures. When they enter the world they have become endowed with powers that are in accordance with the vow they have made. In all matters they are skilled in the knowledge of correct and faulty conclusions. They are rich in goodness and blessed with good qualities. Eminent, wise in their illimitable virtue, they are serene among their fellows. On this matter it is said:

As it is not possible for any bird to reach the confines of the sky, so it is not possible for any man to comprehend the good qualities of the self-becoming Buddhas.

Ethics 6

The Lay Ideal: Vimalakīrtinirdesa Sūtra

This work, composed in Sanskrit and translated by Kumārajīva into Chinese in the early 4th century CE, was influential in China and even more so in Japan, as it gives a practical application to the idea that nirvāna and saṃsāra (the round of rebirth) are one: freedom from ill is to be found in a re-evaluation of the world, not by leaving it through the path of withdrawal and asceticism. Here then there is depicted the ideal lay person, Vimalakīrti.

At that time, there dwelt in the great city of Vaiśāli[1] a wealthy householder named Vimalakīrti. Having done homage to the countless Buddhas of the Past, doing many good works, attaining to aquiescence in the Eternal Law, he was a man of wonderful eloquence.

Exercising supernatural powers, obtaining all of the powers of meditation, arriving at the state of fearlessness,

Repressing all evil enmities, reaching the gate

[1] A city of North India.

of profound truth, walking in the way of wisdom,

Acquainted with the necessary means, fulfilling the Great Vows,[2] comprehending the past and the future of the intentions of all beings, understanding also both their strength and weakness of mind,

Ever pure and excellent in the way of the Buddha, remaining loyal to the Mahāyāna,

Praised by all the Buddhas, revered by all the disciples and all the gods such as a Śakra[3] or Brahmā, the lord of this world,

Residing in Vaiśāli only for the sake of the necessary means for saving creatures, abundantly rich, ever careful of the poor, pure in self-discipline, obedient to all precepts,

Removing all anger by the practice of patience, removing all sloth by the practice of diligence, removing all distraction of mind by intent meditation, removing all ignorance by fullness of wisdom;

Though he is but a simple layman, yet observing the pure monastic discipline;

Though living at home, yet never desirous of anything;

Though possessing a wife and children, always exercising pure virtues;

Though surrounded by his family, holding aloof from worldly pleasures;

Though using the jewelled ornaments of the world, yet adorned with spiritual splendour;

Though eating and drinking, yet enjoying the flavour of the rapture of meditation;

Though frequenting the gambling house, yet leading the gamblers into the right path;

Though coming in contact with heresy, yet never letting his true faith be impaired;

Though having a profound knowledge of worldly learning, yet ever finding pleasure in things of the spirit as taught by Buddha;

Revered by all as the first among those who were worthy of reverence;

Governing both the old and young as a righteous judge;

Though profiting by all the professions, yet far above being absorbed by them;

Benefiting all beings, going wheresoever he pleases, protecting all beings as a judge with righteousness;

Leading all with the Doctrine of the Mahāyāna when in the seat of discussion;

Ever teaching the young and ignorant when entering the hall of learning;

Manifesting to all the error of passion when in the house of debauchery; persuading all to seek the higher things when at the shop of the wine dealer;

Preaching the Law when among wealthy people as the most honourable of their kind;

Dissuading the rich householders from covetousness when among them as the most honourable of their kind;

Teaching kshatriyas [i.e. warriors] patience when among them . . .

Removing arrogance when among brāhmans . . .

Teaching justice to the great ministers . . .

Teaching loyalty and filial piety to the princes . . .

Teaching honesty to the ladies of the court when among them . . .

Persuading the masses to cherish the virtue of merits . . .

Instructing in highest wisdom the Brahman gods . . .

Showing the transient nature of the world to the Śakra gods . . .

Protecting all beings when among the guardians as the most honourable of their kind;

– Thus by such countless means Vimalakīrti, the wealthy householder, rendered benefit to all beings.

---

[2] That is, the Great Vows of the Bodhisattva, which set the saintly person on the conscious path to serving others.

[3] Another name for Indra, the Aryan warrior god.

Postscript

Over much of the history of Buddhism the most important use of the Buddhist texts, which came to be reduced to writing several centuries after the Buddha's decease, or which came to be elaborated or composed in written form, was for study. The doctrinal dimension of Buddhism was always central, together with the experiential, since it was through analysis and the purification of consciousness that higher insight was generally thought to be attained.

However, some parts of the Pāli Canon, for instance the *Sumangala Sutta*, came to be chanted for more popularly practical purposes – the warding off of evil and sickness – and in connection with ceremonies related to the cult of relics etc.

Likewise Greater Vehicle texts sometimes were viewed as having sacramental significance (as in the Heart Sūtra, *see* p. 246), so that the utterance of the words themselves was thought to be spiritually efficacious. Likewise in later Mahāyāna Buddhism the veneration of the Lotus Sūtra assigned to it something of the saving power also ascribed to Amitābha (Amida).

The effects of the scriptures on Buddhist art were great. Thus scenes from the *Jātaka* stories are most frequently represented in paintings and bas reliefs. Similarly the rise of Pure Land Buddhism generated many iconic representations of the Buddhist Paradise. In the Tantric phase of Buddhism the distinction between scripture and icon breaks down in the sense that the doctrines and experiences of the Path are expressed and elucidated through mandalas and other diagrams and pictures.

The modern period has seen the work of Western and Asian scholars in recovering and re-presenting the vast materials of the Buddhist heritage. Especially important was the work of those who came to edit such series as the Pāli Text Society editions and translations. But there is still much work to be done as Buddhism enters on a new phase of being a religion with global outreach through the dispersal of Buddhist monks and teachers through much of the Western world because of missionary endeavours and exile from oppression, and through the growth of the modern study of Buddhism in universities and elsewhere.

Bibliography

A number of the major texts are to be found in F. Max Müller (ed.), *Sacred Books of the East* (1880–1910, reprinted 1962). The bulk of the relevant Pāli literature is in the Pāli Text Society Translation Series (1909 onwards) and *Sacred Books of the Buddhists* (1899 onwards). Useful anthologies are Edward Conze, *Buddhist Texts through the Ages* (1953) and Clarence H. Hamilton, *Buddhism, a Religion of Infinite Compassion: Selections from Buddhist Literature* (1952).

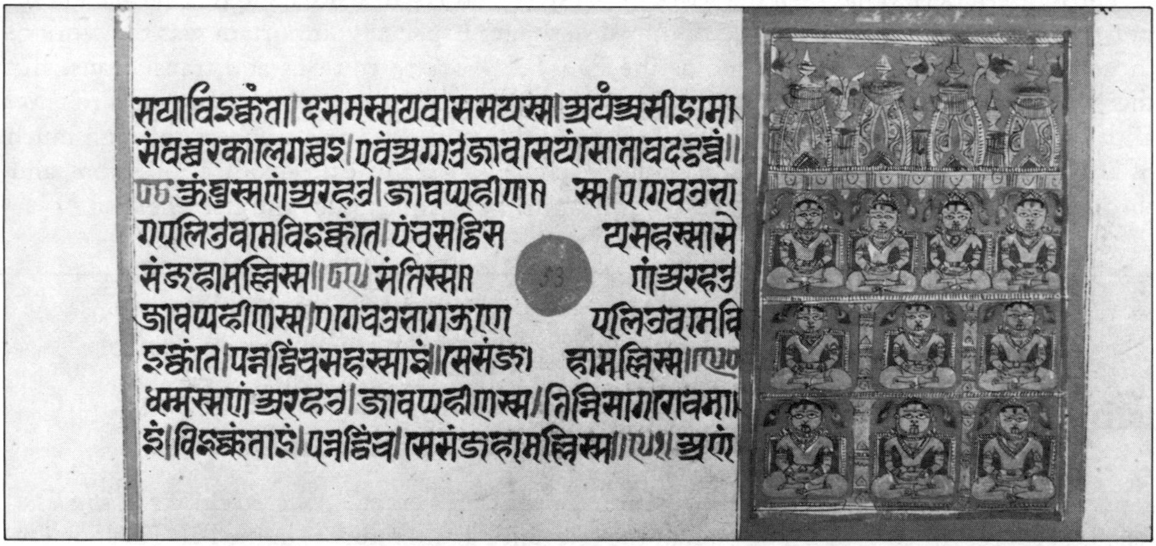

Part of the Kalpasūtra, *the text describing the succession of Jain heroes and leaders, the last of whom was Mahāvirā. The red dots mark the place where a hole would have been made for the string which secured the palm-leaf pages together.*

Jainism

Introduction

Jainism had its historical origins in the same region of northern India as Buddhism and Mahāvīra, the Jina or Victor, leader of the movement, was a contemporary of the Buddha. Jain teachings were transmitted orally. However, the two sects of Jainism, into which the movement split (probably) during the 3rd century BCE, have differing attitudes to the scriptures. The Digambaras or 'Sky-clad', whose monks practise nudity as a sign of complete renunciation of possessions, are more conservative than the Śvetāmbaras or 'White-clad', and they think that the transmission of the original teachings has been hopelessly corrupt. Thus, they do not recognize the canonical writings which the Śvetāmbaras revere. In fact their only canonical material, known as *Siddhānta*, is somewhat difficult, attracting large commentarial treatments. The Śvetāmbaras, though they lost some of the early sources, did retain various works called *Aṅgas* or limbs, plus a subsidiary canon (the *Aṅgabāhya*). This includes various commentaries and hagiographical works in praise of Jain leaders and saints. Jainism also developed an extensive philosophical literature.

Despite the split between the two sects, Jain doctrine (except on the matter of nudity, the consequent position of nuns, and one or two other matters) remained remarkably uniform. The conservatism was reinforced by the Jain theory of history which suggests that things have been running downhill since the time of Mahāvīra; this means that as religion declines it is all the more important to hang on to the memories and practices of the past.

The following extracts deal with the mythic career of Mahāvīra (Sacred Narrative 1) and indicate the content of his teaching towards his final decease (Sacred Narrative 2). Though Jain philosophical doctrine is rich and subtle, the main shape of Jain cosmology is plain and is seen in the two extracts on doctrine. We have included in Ritual 1 a non-canonical ritual formula which shows something of lay reverence to monks and the need to confess sins, and in Ritual 2 we have a prayer, well-known throughout the Jain community, which sums up its ascetic aspirations. Ritual 3 is a passage which foreshadows later devotional literature in praise of the Tīrthāṅkaras, or saving heroes of the Jain tradition, to whom, in the rich days of medieval Jain influence in Mysore, Gujarat and elsewhere, well-endowed temples were dedicated. Institutional Expression 1 indicates something of the early evolution of the Jain monastic movement. In Experience 1 we see a reflection of the 'cloud of unknowing' as described by Mahāvīra himself, and in Experience 2 and Experience 3 we have a taste of some of the Jain inner quest, both monastic and lay. Finally, we have included two famous aspects of Jain ethics: its rigorous emphasis on non-injury to all living beings including the most minute forms of life lodged in the environment, in Ethics 1, and the great vows which the Jain recluse undertakes, in Ethics 2.

Sacred Narrative 1

Mahāvīra as Liberator: Kalpasūtra

These passages describe the Great Renunciation and Enlightenment of Mahāvīra. As the 24th great leader of the present world cycle, he is not so much founder as restorer of the teaching. The present account follows the Śvetāmbara tradition, and modifies Mahāvīra's commitment to the tradition of nudity as the fitting condition of being a monk and one who renounces the world.

Then the Venerable ascetic Mahāvīra – gazed on by a circle of thousands of eyes, praised by a circle of thousands of mouths, extolled by a circle of thousands of hearts, being the object of many thousands of wishes, desired because of his splendour, beauty, and virtues, pointed out by a circle of thousands of forefingers, answering with [a salaam] of his right hand a circle of thousands of joined hands of thousands of men and women, passing along a row of thousands of palaces, greeted by sweet and delightful music . . . in which joined shouts of victory, and the low and pleasing murmur of the people; accompanied by all his pomp, all his splendour, all his army, all his train, by all his retinue, by all his magnificence, by all his grandeur, by all his ornaments, by all the tumult, by all the throng, by all subjects, by all actors, by all time-beaters, by the whole household; adorned with flowers, scented robes, garlands, and ornaments . . . which were accompanied at the same time by trumpets – went right through Kundapuna to a park called the Shaṇdavana of the Jñātris and proceeded to the excellent Ashoka tree. There under the excellent Ashoka tree he caused his palanquin to stop, descended from his palanquin, took off his ornaments, garlands and finery with his own hands, and with his own hands plucked out his hair in five handfuls. When the moon was in conjunction with the asterism Uttaraphalgunī, he, after fasting two-and-a-half days without drinking water, put on a holy robe, and quite alone, nobody else being present, he tore out his hair and leaving the house entered the state of houselessness.

The venerable ascetic Mahāvīra for a year and a month wore clothes; after that time he walked about naked, and accepted alms in the hollow of his hand.[1] For more than twelve years the venerable ascetic Mahāvīra neglected his body and abandoned the care of it; he with equanimity bore, underwent and suffered all pleasant or unpleasant occurrences arising from divine powers, men or animals.

Henceforth the venerable ascetic Mahāvīra was houseless, circumspect in his walking, circumspect in his speaking, circumspect in his begging, circumspect in his accepting anything, in the carrying of his outfit and drinking vessel; circumspect in evacuating excrements, urine, saliva, mucus and uncleanliness of the body; circumspect in his thoughts, circumspect in his works, circumspect in his acts; guarding his thoughts, guarding his words, guarding his acts, guarding his senses, guarding his chastity; without wrath, without pride, without deceit, without greed; calm, tranquil, composed, liberated, free from temptations, without egoism, without property; he had cut off all earthly ties, and was not stained by any worldliness: as water does not adhere to a copper vessel, or collyrium to mother-of-pearl so sins found no place in him; like the firmament he needed no support; like the wind he knew no obstacles; his heart was pure like water in autumn; nothing could soil him like the leaf of a lotus; his senses were well protected like those of a tortoise; he was single and alone like the horn of a rhinoceros; he was free like a bird; he was always waking like the fabulous bird

[1] This reflects Digambara Jain practice, without even clothes or an alms bowl.

Bharuṇḍa,[2] valorous like an elephant, strong like a bull, difficult to attack like a lion, steady and firm like Mount Mandara, deep like the ocean, mild like the moon, refulgent like the sun, pure like excellent gold, like the earth he patiently bore everything; like a well-kindled fire he shone in his splendour.

These words have been summarised in two verses:

A vessel, mother of pearl, life, firmament, wind, water in autumn, leaf of lotus, a tortoise, a bird, a rhinoceros, and Baharuṇḍa;

An elephant, a bull, a lion, the king of the mountains, and the ocean unshaken – the moon, the sun, gold, the earth, well-kindled fire.

The Venerable One lived, except in the rainy season, all the eight months of summer and winter, in villages only a single night, in towns only five nights; he was indifferent alike to the smell of ordure and of sandal, to straw and jewels, dirt and gold, pleasure and pain, attached neither to this world nor to that beyond, desiring neither life nor death, arrived at the shore of the saṃsāra, and he exerted himself for the suppression of the defilement of karma.

With supreme knowledge, with supreme intuition, with supreme conduct, in blameless lodgings, in blameless wandering, with supreme valour, with supreme uprightness, with supreme mildness, with supreme dexterity, with supreme patience, with supreme freedom from passions, with supreme control, with supreme contentment, with supreme understanding, on the supreme path to final liberation, which is the fruit of veracity, control, penance, and good conduct, the Venerable One meditated on himself for twelve years.

During the thirteenth year, in the second month of summer, in the fourth fortnight, the light [fortnight] of the month Vaisākha, on its tenth day, when the shadow had turned towards the east and the first wake was over, on the day called Suvrata . . . outside of the town Gṛmbhagrāma on the bank of the river Rjupālika, not far from an old temple, in the field of the householder Sāmāga under a Sal tree, when the moon was in conjunction with the asterism Uttaraphalgunī, in a squatting position with joined heels, exposing himself to the heat of the sun, after fasting two-and-a-half days without drinking water, being engaged in deep meditation, he reached the highest knowledge and intuition, called 'wholeness',[3] which is infinite, supreme, unobstructed, unimpeded, complete and full.

When the venerable ascetic Mahāvīra had become a Jina and Saint, he was a Liberated One, omniscient and comprehending all objects; he knew and saw all conditions of the world, of gods, men and demons: whence they come, whither they go, whether they are born as men or animals or become gods or beings in purgatory, the ideas, the thoughts of their minds, the food, doings, desires, the open and secret deeds of all the living beings in the whole world; he the Saint, for whom there is no secret, knew and saw all conditions of all living beings in the world, what they thought, spoke, or did at any moment.

In that period, in that age the venerable ascetic Mahāvīra stayed the first rainy season in Asthikagrāma, three rainy seasons in Champā, twelve in Vaiṣālī and Vāṇijagrama, fourteen in Rājagṛha and the suburb of Nālandā, six in Mithilā, two in Bhadrikā, one in Alabhikā, one in Paṇitabhūmi, one in Śrāvasti, one in the town of Pāpā in King Hastipāla's office of the writers: that was his very last rainy season.

In the fourth month of that rainy season, in the seventh fortnight, in the dark of Kārtika, on its fifteenth day, in the last night, in the town of Pāpā, in King Hastipāla's office of the writers, the venerable ascetic Mahavira died, went off, quitted the world, cut asunder the ties of birth, old age and death; became a Perfect One, a Buddha, a Free One, a maker of the end, finally liberated, freed from all pains.

---

[2] This bird was supposed to have three legs and two heads.

[3] The term is *Kevala*, meaning an isolated perfection cut off from the realm of rebirth.

Sacred Narrative 2

The Simile of the Leaf: Uttarādhyāyana

Indrabhūti Gautama was one of the two chief disciples of Mahāvīra, who is supposed to have uttered the following words on the day of his death to encourage Indrabhūti, who still was too fond of his master, to be utterly detached. It is a favourite passage of Jain devotion.

As the fallow leaf of the tree falls to the ground, when its days are gone, even so the life of men; Gautama, be careful all the while!

As the dew-drop dangling on the top of a blade of grass lasts but a short time, even so the life of men; Gautama, be careful all the while!

As life is so fleet and existence so precarious, wipe off the sins you ever committed; Gautama, be careful all the while!

A rare chance, in the long course of time, is human birth for a living being; hard are the consequences of actions; Gautama, be careful all the while!

When the soul has once got into an earth-body,[1] it may remain in the same state as long as an aeon; Gautama, be careful all the while!

When the soul has once got into a water-particle, it may remain in the same state as long as an aeon; Gautama, be careful all the while!

When a soul has once got into a fire-particle, it may remain in the same state as long as an aeon; Gautama, be careful all the while!

When the soul has once got into a wind-particle, it may remain in the same state as long as an aeon; Gautama, be careful all the while!

When the soul has once got into a vegetable-body, it remains long in that state, for an endless time, after which its lot is not much bettered; Gautama, be careful all the while!

When the soul has once got into a body of a being possessing two organs of sense it may remain in the same state for millennia; Gautama, be careful all the while!

When the soul has once got into a body of a being possessing three organs of sense it may remain in the same state for millenia; Gautama, be careful all the while!

When the soul has once got into a body of a being possessing four organs of sense it may remain in the same state for millennia; Gautama, be careful all the while!

When the soul has once got into a body of a being possessing five organs of sense it may remain in the same state as long as seven or eight births; Gautama, be careful all the while!

When the soul has once got into the body of a god or of a denizen it may remain in that state one whole life; Gautama, be careful all the while!

Thus the soul which suffers for its carelessness, is driven about in the round of rebirth by its good and bad karma; Gautama, be careful all the while!

Though one be born as a man, it is a rare chance to become an Aryan; for many are the Dasyus[2] and barbarians; Gautama, be careful all the while!

Though one be born as an Aryan,it is a rare chance to possess all five organs of sense; for we see many who lack one organ or other; Gautama, be careful all the while!

Though he may possess all five organs of sense, still it is a rare chance to be instructed in the best Law; for people follow heretical teachers; Gautama, be careful all the while!

Though he may have been instructed in the right Law, still it is a rare chance to believe in it; for many people are heretics; Gautama, be careful all the while!

Though one believe in the Law, he will rarely practise it; for people are engrossed by pleasures; Gautama, be careful all the while!

When your body grows old, and your hair turns white, the power of your ears decreases; Gautama, be careful all the while!

[1] An earth-particle: here earth particles are seen as containing a primitive form of life. This and the following beings are those which have only one sense,namely touch.

[2] Dasyus – one conquered by the Aryans, the Indo-European speakers who invaded India and dominated the indigenous population.

When your body grows old, and your hair turns white, the power of your eyes decreases; Gautama, be careful all the while!

When your body grows old, and your hair turns white, the power of your nose decreases; Gautama, be careful all the while!

When your body grows old, and your hair turns white, the power of your tongue decreases; Gautama, be careful all the while!

When your body grows old, and your hair turns white, the power of your touch decreases; Gautama, be careful all the while!

When your body grows old, and your hair turns white, all your powers decrease; Gautama, be careful all the while!

Despondency, the king's evil, cholera, mortal diseases of many kinds befall you; your body wastes and decays; Gautama, be careful all the while!

Cast aside from you all attachments, as the lotus lets drop off the pure monsoon water, exempt from every attachment; Gautama, be careful all the while!

Give up your wealth and your wife; you have entered the state of the houseless; do not, as it were, return to your vomit; Gautama, be careful all the while!

Leave your friends and relations, the large fortune you have amassed; do not desire them a second time; Gautama, be careful all the while!

There is now no Jina, but there is a highly esteemed guide to show the way; now being on the right path, Gautama, be careful all the while!

Now you have entered on the path from which the thorns have been cleared, the great path; walk in the right path; Gautama, be careful all the while!

Do not get into an uneven road like a weak burden-bearer; for you will repent of it afterwards; Gautama, be careful all the while!

You have crossed the great ocean; why do you halt so near the shore? Make haste to get on the other side; Gautama, be careful all the while!

Going through the same religious practices as perfected saints, you will reach the world of perfection, Gautama, where there is safety and perfect happiness; Gautama, be careful all the while!

The enlightened and liberated monk should control himself, whether he be in a village or a town, and he should preach to all the road of peace; Gautama, be careful all the while!

Having heard the Buddha's[3] well-delivered sermon, adorned by illustrations, Gautama cut off love and hatred and reached perfection.

Thus I say.

[3] Note that this title ('Enlightened One') is applied too to Mahāvīra, just as 'Jina' was used of the Buddha in the Buddhist scriptures. Both traditions took up existing themes and a common terminology from preceding religious movements.

Doctrine 1

Living Beings and the Round of Rebirth: Uttarādhyāyana

This gives in brief compass a sketch of the Jain picture of life: innumerable living beings in the process of rebirth, with some through the Teaching gaining liberation. The cosmos is seen as like a cylinder on end, the upper part being a series of ascending heavens, and beyond them at the summit of the universe the motionless realm of ultimate liberation whither the heroic freed souls arise.

Four things of paramount value are difficult to obtain here by a living being: human birth, instruction in the Law, belief in it, and energy in self-control.

I. The universe is peopled by manifold creatures who are, in this round of rebirth, born in different families and castes for having done various actions.

Sometimes they go to the world of the gods, sometimes to the hells, sometimes they become Asuras in accordance with their actions.

Sometimes they become nobles or outcastes and untouchables, or worms and moths, or . . . ants.

Thus living beings of sinful actions, who are born again and again in ever-recurring births, are not disgusted with the round of rebirth, but they are like warriors, never tired of the battle of life.

Living beings bewildered through the influence of their actions, distressed and suffering pains, undergo misery in non-human births.

But by the cessation of karma, perchance, living beings will reach in due time a pure state and be born as men.

II. And, though they be born with a human body, it will be difficult for them to hear the Law, having heard which they will do penances, combat their passions and abstain from killing living beings.

III. And though, by chance, they may hear the Law, it will be difficult for them to believe in it; many who are shown the right way, stray from it.

IV. And though they have heard the Law and believe in it, it is difficult for them to fulfill it strenuously; many who approve of the religion, do not adopt it.

Having been born as a man, having heard the Law, believing in it, and fulfilling it strenuously, an ascetic should restrain himself and shake off sinfulness.

The pious obtain purity, and the pure stand firmly in the Law: the soul afterwards reaches the highest Nirvāna, being like unto a fire fed with ghee.

Leave off the causes of sin, acquire fame through patience! You will rise to the upper regions after having left this body of clay.

The spirits who are gifted with various virtues, live one above the other, shining forth like the great luminaries, and hoping never to descend thence.

Intent on enjoying divine pleasures and changing their form at will, they live in the upper heavens many centuries of aeons.

The spirits having remained there according to their merit, descend thence at the expiration of their life and are born as men.

Doctrine 2

Suffering and Freedom: Actions and Reward: Ācārānga Sūtra

This passage also mentions some of the key ideas of Jainism: the existence of innumerable *jīvas* or souls, the reality of the world, the operation of karma, the necessity for taking responsibility for one's own actions, the possibility of liberation.

Similarly, some do not know whether their soul is born again and again or not; not what they were formerly, nor what they will become after having died and left this world. Now this is what one should know, either by one's own knowledge or through the instruction of the highest, or having heard it from others: that he descended in an eastern direction, or in any other direction. Similarly, some know that their soul is born again and again, that it arrives in this or that direction, whatever direction that may be. He believes in soul, believes in the world, believes in reward, believes in actions, acknowledged to be our own doing in such judgments as these: 'I did it'; 'I shall cause another to do it'; 'I shall allow another to do it'. In the world, these are all the causes of sin, which must be comprehended and renounced. A man that does not comprehend and renounce the causes of sin, descends in a cardinal or intermediate direction, wanders to all cardinal or intermediate directions, is born again and again in manifold births, experiences all painful feelings. About this the Revered One has taught the truth. For the sake of the splendour, honour and glory of this life, for the sake of birth, death and final liberation, for the removal of pain, all these causes of sin are at work, which are to be comprehended and renounced in this world. He who, in the world, comprehends and renounces these causes of sin, is called a sage. Thus I say.

Ritual 1

Reverence for the Order: Vandana Formula

This formula of reverence is an indication of the attitude of the laity to members of the Jain order, who represent the ideal of those who, in attaining a higher stage of asceticism and insight, have an effect in raising the state of others and so helping them further along the path to ultimate purification.

I wish to reverence you, ascetic who suffers with equanimity, with intense concentration.

Response: So be it.

You will have passed the day auspiciously with little disturbance.

Response: Yes.

You make spiritual progress.

Response: And you also.

I wish to ask pardon for transgressions.

Response: I ask for it too.

I must confess, ascetic who suffers with equanimity, for lack of respect and day-to-day transgressions of the mind, speech or body, through anger, pride, deceit or greed, false behaviour and neglect of the Teaching, and whatever offence I have committed I here confess, repudiate and repent of it and set aside my past deeds.

Ritual 2

Cessation: Nityanaimittika-pāthāvalī

This short formula is a Jain prayer summing up the faith. It is used by lay persons to express their ultimate aspiration to give up everything and enter the holy state of monk or nun.

Ceasing of illfare,
Ceasing of karmic effects,
Death in contemplative trance,
Gaining enlightenment:

Let these be mine, friend of
the whole universe,
Conqueror, for I have come for refuge
In your path.

Ritual 3

Praise of the Great Hero: Sūtrakṛtāṅga

The cult of the Tīrthāṅkaras and notably Mahāvīra developed richly in the evolution of Jainism. Though strictly the Jina has ascended to the summit of the universe and lives disembodied and motionless there forever, so that transactions with people here below are ruled out, nevertheless the Jina is also an object of supreme reverence as an ideal being. This passage reveals something of the intensity of this reverence.

Recluses and Brahmins, householders and heretics, have asked me: Who is he that proclaimed this unrivalled truly wholesome Law, which was proclaimed with true knowledge?

What was the knowledge, what the faith, and what the conduct of the Jñāntiputra? If you know it truly, O monk, tell us as you have heard it, as it was told you!

This wise and clever great sage possessed infinite knowledge and infinite faith. Learn and think about the Law and the piety of the glorious man who lived before our eyes!

This wise man had explored all beings, whether they move or not, on high, below, and on earth, as well as the eternal and transient things. Like a lamp he put the Law in a true light.

He sees everything; his knowledge is transcendental; he has no impurity; he is virtuous, of a fixed mind, the highest, the wisest in the whole world; he has broken from all ties; he is above danger and the necessity to continue life.

Omniscient, wandering about without a home, crossing the flood, wise, and of an unlimited perception, without an equal, he shines forth like the sun, and he illumines the darkness like a brilliant fire.

The omniscient sage has proclaimed this highest law of the Jinas; he, the illustrious one, is prominent among humans like the thousand-eyed Indra among the gods of heaven.

His knowledge is inexhaustible like the sea; he has no limits and is pure like the great ocean; he is free from passion, unfettered, and brilliant like Indra, the lord of the gods.

By his vigour he is the most vigorous; as Meru is the best of all mountains, or as heaven is a very mine of delight, he shines forth endowed with many virtues.

He bears everything like the earth; he annihilates karma; he is free from greed; he, the Omniscient, does not keep store of anything; he has crossed the ocean of life like the sea; he, the Hero, who grants protection to all, and whose perception is infinite.

Having conquered the passions which defile the soul: wrath, pride, deceit and greed, the Liberated Saint, the great sage, does not commit any wrong, nor does he cause it to be committed.

He understood the doctrines of other sects . . . he had mastered all philosophical systems, and he practised control as long as he lived.

He abstained from women, and from eating at night, he practised austerities for the removal of pain, he knew this world and that beyond; the lord renounced everything at every time.

Having heard and believing in the Law, which has been proclaimed and taught by the Saint, and has been demonstrated with arguments, people will either make an end of their mundane existence, or they will become like Indra, the king of gods.

Institutional Expression

The Order of Monks and Nuns: Kalpasūtra, Sāmākāri

As with Buddhism, an important factor in the unification of the early Order was the need to spend part of each year – in or around the rainy season – in retreat together. Some of the details of the life style of the Order are given in this discourse by Mahāvīra.

During the annual season of retreat monks or nuns should not use harsh words after the commencement of the retreat; if they do, they should be warned: 'Reverend brother [or sister], you speak unmannerly'. One who [nevertheless] uses harsh words after the commencement of the retreat should be excluded from the community.

If, during the retreat, among monks or nuns occurs a quarrel or dispute or dissension, the young monk should ask forgiveness of the superior, and the superior of the young monk. They should forgive and ask forgiveness, appease and be appeased, and converse without restraint. For him who is appeased, there will be success in control; for him who is not appeased, there will be no success; therefore one should appease one's self. 'Why has this been said, Sir?' 'Peace is the essence of monachism.'

During the retreat monks or nuns should have three lodging-places; two for occasional use, which must be inspected; one for constant use, which must be swept.[1]

During the retreat monks or nuns should give notice of the direction or intermediate direction in which they intend to go forth for the sake of begging alms. 'Why has this been said, Sir?' 'During the retreat the reverend monks frequently undertake austerities; and ascetic becoming weak and exhausted might swoon or fall down. In case of such an accident the remaining reverend monks will undertake their search in that direction or intermediate direction which the ascetic had named.'

During the retreat monks or nuns are not allowed to travel further than four or five leagues and then to return. They are allowed to stay in some intermediate place, but not to pass there the night.

[1] The inspection and gentle sweeping are to prevent the inadvertent killing of insect life.

Experience 1

The Consciousness of Liberation: Ācārānga Sūtra

This passage is possibly a reflection of Mahāvira's own experience, and it runs parallel to reports of the higher contemplative states in other religious traditions.

The liberated is not long nor small nor round nor triangular nor quadrangular nor circular; he is not black nor blue nor red nor green nor white; neither of good nor bad smell; nor bitter nor pungent nor astringent nor sweet; neither rough nor soft; neither heavy nor light; neither cold nor hot; neither harsh nor smooth; he is without body, without resurrection, without contact of matter, he is not feminine nor masculine nor neuter; he perceives, he knows, but there is no analogy whereby to know the transcendent; its essence is without form; there is no condition of the unconditioned. There is no sound, no colour, no smell, no taste, no touch – nothing of that kind. Thus I say.

Experience 2

Higher Meditation: Uttarādhyāyana

The practice of interior meditation is an important adjunct to the austerities prescribed for the Jain yogi. Here the stage of 'pure meditation' is described, as being the achievement of the person who has become a *kevalin* or liberated one. It is the prelude to final decease, when the soul ascends to the summit of the cosmos.

Then . . . he discontinues to act, and enters upon the third degree of pure meditation, from which there is no relapse, and which requires the most subtle functions only, of his organs; he first stops the functions of his mind, then the functions of speech, then those of the body, at last he ceases to breathe. During the time required for pronouncing five short syllables, he is engaged in the final pure meditation, in which all functions of his organs have ceased, and he simultaneously annihilates the four remnants of karma, that is those determining pain and pleasure, life span, destiny and environment.

Then having, by all methods, got rid of his bodies, the soul takes the form of a straight line, goes in one moment, without touching anything and taking up no space upwards to the cosmic summit, and there develops into its natural form, obtains perfection, enlightenment, deliverance, and final beatitude, and puts an end to all misery.

This indeed is the subject of the discourse, called exertion in righteousness, which the venerable ascetic Mahāvira has told, declared, explained, demonstrated.

Experience 3

The Lay Person's Inner Voyage: Nityanaimittika-pāthāvalī

Here is expressed the lay person's meditative practice, which foreshadows a more complete renunciation of the world.

As long as I am seated in this meditation,
I shall patiently suffer all calamities
that may befall me, be they caused
by an animal, a human being, or a god.
I renounce, for the duration [of this meditation],
my body, all food, and all passions.
Attachment, aversion, fear, sorrow, joy,
anxiety, self-pity . . . all these
I abandon with body, mind, and speech.
I further renounce all delight and all repulsion
of a sexual nature.
Whether it is life or death, whether gain or loss,
Whether defeat or victory, whether meeting
or separation,
Whether friend or enemy, whether pleasure
or pain,
I have equanimity towards all
In [the attainment of] knowledge, insight,
and proper conduct,
[the cause] is invariably nothing but my
own soul.
Similarly, my soul [is the primary cause] for both
the influx of karmas and the stopping of that
influx.
One and eternal is my soul,
Characterized by intuition and knowledge;
All other states that I undergo are external
to me,
for they are formed by associations.
Because of these associations
my soul has suffered the chains of misery;
Therefore I renounce with body, mind,
and speech,
all relationships based on such associations.
Thus have I attained to equanimity
and to my own self-nature.
May this state of equanimity be with me
until I attain to salvation.

Ethics 1

Non-Injury and the Path: Sūtrakṛtāṅga

Ahiṃsā or non-injury to all living beings, including minute forms of life found in the earth etc, is the central Jain ethical value, which has left its imprint on the Indian tradition, for example in the thinking of Gandhi.

This is the quintessence of wisdom: not to kill anything. Know this to be the legitimate conclusion from the principle of the reciprocity with regard to non-killing.

He should cease to injure living beings whether they move or not, on high, below and on earth. For this has been called the Nirvāna, which consists in peace.

Master of his senses and avoiding wrong, he should do no harm to anybody, neither by thoughts, nor words, nor acts.

A wise man who restrains his senses and possesses great knowledge, should accept such things as are freely given him, being always circumspect with regard to the accepting of alms, and abstaining from what he is forbidden to accept.

A true monk should not accept such food and drink as has been especially prepared for him involving the slaughter of living beings.

He should not partake of a meal which contains but a particle of forbidden food: this is the Law of him who is rich in control. Whatever [food a monk] suspects, he may not eat.

A man who guards his soul and subdues his senses, should never assent to anybody killing living beings . . .

Hearing the talk of people, one should not say 'This is a good action' nor 'This is a bad action'. For there is an objection to either answer.

He should not say that it is meritorious, because he ought to save those beings, whether they move or not, which are killed there for the sake of making a gift.

Nor should he say that it is not meritorious, because he would then prevent those for whose sake the food and drink in question is prepared, to get their due.

Those who praise the fit, are accessory to the killing of beings; those who forbid it, deprive others of the means of subsistence.

Those, however, who give neither answer, viz. that it is meritorious, or is not so, do not expose themselves to guilt, and will reach blessedness.

Knowing that blessedness is the best thing as the moon is among the stars, a sage always restrained and subduing his sense brings it about.

A pious man shows an island to the beings which are carried away by the flood of existence and suffer for their deeds. This place of safety has been proclaimed.

He who guards his soul, subdues his senses, puts a stop to the current, and is free from defiling influences, is entitled to expound the pure, complete, unparalleled Law.

Those who do not know this Law are not awakened, though they fancy themselves awakened; believing themselves awakened, they are beyond the boundary of right faith.

Eating seeds and drinking cold water[1] and what has been especially prepared for them, they enter upon meditation, but are ignorant of the truth, and do not possess carefulness.

As herons, ospreys, and cormorants meditate upon capturing fish, [which is] a sinful and very low meditation, so some heretical, unworthy recluses contemplate the pursuit of pleasures; they are sinful and very low like herons.

Here some weak-minded persons, abusing the pure path,„enter upon a wrong path. They thereby will go to misery and destruction.

As a blind-born man getting into a leaky boat wants to reach the shore, but is drowned during the passage; so some unworthy, heretical recluses having got into the full current will incur great danger.

But knowing this Law which has been proclaimed by the Conqueror, a monk crosses the dreadful current, and wanders about intent on the benefit of his soul.

Indifferent to worldly objects, a man should wander about treating all creatures in the world so as he himself would be treated.

A wise man knowing the nature of excessive pride and deceit, giving them up all, brings about his Liberation.

He acquires good qualities, and leaves off bad qualities; a monk, who vigorously practises austerities, avoids anger and pride.

The Buddhas[2] that were, and the Buddhas that will be, they have Peace as their foundation, even as all things have the earth for their foundation.

And if any accidents whatever befall him who has gained that [foundation], he will not be overpowered by them as a mountain by the storm.

A restrained, very learned, and wise [monk] should accept such alms as are freely given him, being free from passions and waiting for his end. This is the doctrine of the Kevalin.

Thus I say.

---

[1] This is an attack on other traditions such as the Buddhists whose recluses eat living things unknowingly or unthinkingly – e.g. minute forms of life in water.

[2] 'Buddha' here is a title for a Jain Enlightened One.

Ethics 2

Five Great Vows: Ācārānga Sūtra

These vows laid down by Mahāvīra prescribe the life-style of the monk or nun; they also represent an ideal for the lay person to aspire to.

The first great vow, Sir, runs thus:

I renounce all killing of living beings, whether subtle or gross, whether movable or immovable. Nor shall I myself kill living beings (nor cause others to do it, nor consent to it). As long as I live, I confess and blame, repent and exempt myself of these sins, in the thrice threefold way, in mind, speech, and body.

The second great vow runs thus:

I renounce all vices of lying speech arising from anger or greed or fear or mirth. I shall neither myself speak lies, nor cause others to speak lies, nor consent to the speaking of lies by others. I confess and blame, repent and exempt myself of these sins in the thrice threefold way, in mind, speech, and body.

The third great vow runs thus:

I renounce all taking of anything not given, either in a village or a town or a wood, either of little or much, of small or great, of living or lifeless things. I shall neither take myself what is not given, nor cause others to take it, nor consent to their taking it. As long as I live, I confess and blame, repent and exempt myself of these sins in the thrice threefold way, in mind, speech and body.

The fourth great vow runs thus:

I renounce all sexual pleasures, either with gods or men or animals. I shall not give way to sensuality, nor cause others to give way to it, nor consent to their giving way to it. As long as I live, I confess and blame, repent and exempt myself.

The fifth great vow runs thus:

I renounce all attachments, whether little or much, small or great, living or lifeless; neither shall I myself form such attachments, nor cause others to so, nor consent to their doing so. As long as I live, I confess and blame, repent and exempt myself.

He who is well provided with these great vows and their twenty-five clauses is really homeless, if he, according to the sacred teaching, the precepts and the way correctly practises, follows, executes, explains, establishes and, according to the precept, effects them.

Postscript

Jain writings multiplied in the period from about the 3rd to the 13th centuries of the Common Era, with much in the way of apologetic and polemical writing defending such doctrines as the omniscience of Mahāvīra, and placing his teachings on a par with the Vedas of the orthodox Hindu tradition, which became more and more the major cultural environment of the Jainas. There were compiled philosophical works of considerable subtlety, also, expounding Jainism's distinctive notion of 'pluralism' or 'contextualism' (*anekāntavāda*), according to which statements have to be seen in context as expressing differing *nayas* or perspectives. The last 100 years have seen the revival of Jain studies and the editing and publishing in modern form of the bulk of traditional Jain literature.

Bibliography

Many major texts are found in *Sacred Books of the Jainas* (1914–40) and some in F. Max Müller (ed.), *Sacred Books of the East* (1880–1910, reprinted 1962). See also Padmanabh Jaini, *The Jain Path of Purification* (1979).

One of the great Jain sacred monuments is the huge statue of Gommatesvara at Sravan Belgola in southern India. The saint stands nude with creepers growing up his body, signifying his detachment from the world. Every twelve years, the Digambara sect holds an elaborate ceremony, anointing the statue with milk, clarified butter and other pure foods.

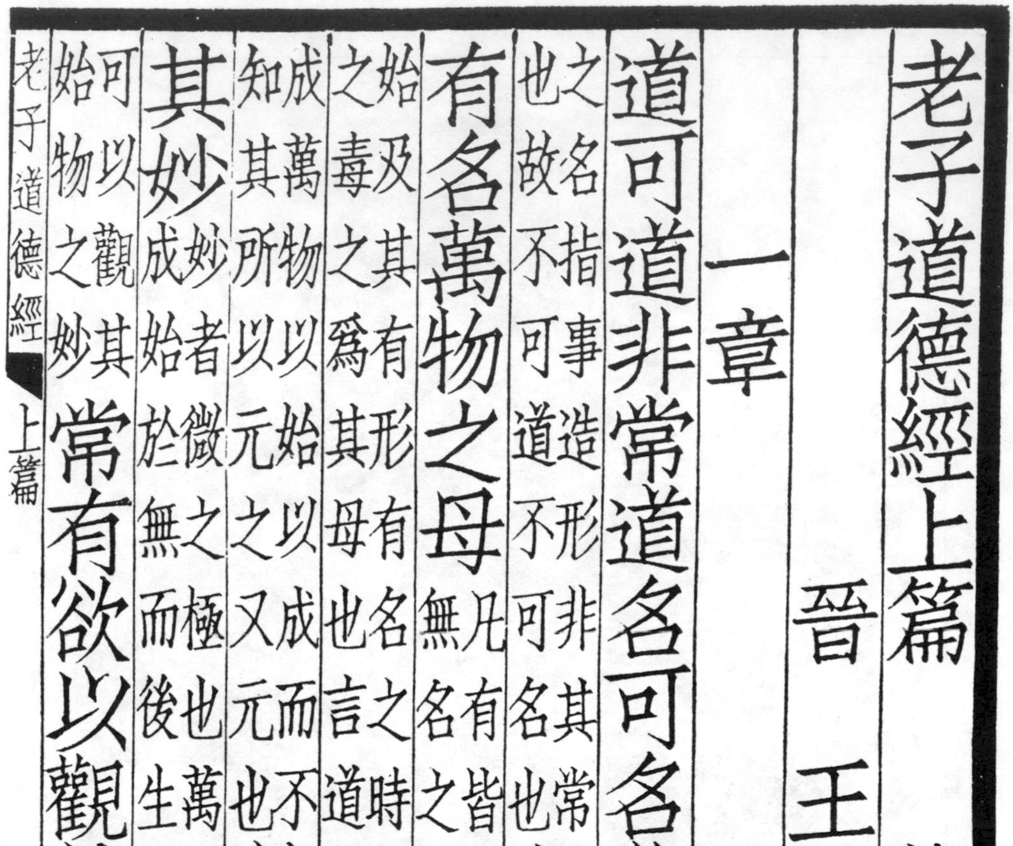
老子道德經上篇　華亭張氏原本

晉　王弼　注

一章

道可道非常道名可名非常名可道之道可名之名指事造形非其常也故不可道不可名也無名天地之始有名萬物之母凡有皆始於無故未形無名之時則為萬物之始及其有形有名之時則長之育之亭之毒之為其母也言道以無形無名始成萬物以始以成而不知其所以元之又元也故常無欲以觀其妙妙者微之極也萬物始於微而後成始於無而後生故常無欲空虛可以觀其始物之妙常有欲以觀其徼徼歸終也凡有之為

老子道德經　上篇　中華書局聚

A modern printed version of the opening lines of the Tao Te Ching, *with an exigesis of the meaning in smaller characters. The mysterious quality of these lines has attracted a wide variety of interpretations* (see page 292).

Taoism

Introduction

Taoism as a philosophy and a religion (for the Chinese make roughly this distinction between early and later organized Taoism) is a vital thread running through Chinese civilization. The early book, an anthology called the *Lao Tzu* or *Tao Te Ching*, has not only attracted vast respect within official Taoism, but has left its stamp both upon Chinese and more recently Western thinking; it also helped to mould Ch'ān (Japanese Zen) Buddhism. Lao Tzu, a legendary master, was later deified, to become a member of the supreme triad of divinities. Though he was supposed to be an elder contemporary of Confucius (6th to 5th centuries BCE), the book named after him seems somewhat later. Similarly the next great classic of Taoist thought, the *Chuang Tzu*, is supposed to reflect the thinking of a shadowy master of that name. Its ideas seem to date it to the 4th or 3rd century BCE. Another important and somewhat similar compilation is from the 3rd century CE, the *Lieh Tzu*. But in due course various religious and magical elements came to surround 'philosophical Taoism'. These influences arose from two sources: alchemy, which developed in the south of China after the collapse of the Han Empire in 220 CE, which is represented scripturally by the *Pao-p'u-tzu* ('He who keeps to simplicity'), and revolutionary messianism, which goes back to the inspiration of the *T'ai P'ing Ching* ('Great Peace Classic') of the 1st century BCE and the organized priestly Taoism instituted by Chang Tao-ling following a revelation which he experienced in 142 BCE. Gradually the disparate elements coalesced into a general movement in Chinese philosophical and popular religion, and acquired an immense canon.

The following selections are intended to bring out some of the different motifs in Taoism. Thus we begin with that mysterious and dramatic opening of the *Tao Te Ching* ('The Classic of the Way and its Power'), the book of Lao Tzu. This is followed by Chapter 25 of that book, which puts the beginning of things in a form which hints at both poise and movement. We then turn to an influential Taoist text describing the creation of the universe which was also incorporated into the Confucian tradition. The early Taoist view of the world was practical too, and we see in the next passage how a mythic theme is treated with gentle irony, and expresses the sage person's capacity to let things be. Also included is the famous little story about Chuang Chou (Master Chuang Tzu).

For the doctrinal aspect we have selected some further chapters of the *Tao Te Ching*, and an account from the *Pao-p'u Tzu* emphasizing the relationship of Taoist teaching to the Confucian and Buddhist traditions. This is a key text in understanding how Taoism has a key role in the symbiosis of the 'three religions of China', which made up the traditional fabric of Chinese values and religiosity. The first of the next two selections reflects the Chinese interest in divination and the meaning of the ancient hexagrams of the *I Ching*, which served a magico-ritual function; the second reflects the institutional expression of the religion through its adepts and priestly families, whose knowledge of the secret meaning of the tradition helps to confer on them the power to facilitate rituals which help the people in their day-to-day life.

The experiential side of Taoism is evident in the early classics. In the first passage about the experiential dimension included here, the *Chuang Tzu* reflects a typically empty, and yet full, mystical experience. Similar passages from the *Lieh Tzu* and the *Tao Te Ching* follow, together with another that emphasizes the proper Taoist way of looking at death.

On the ethical side, Taoism stresses quietism and gentleness above all, and a kind of anarchism in politics. Hence it has often appealed to revolutionaries, whose methods however were by no means as peaceful as early Taoism would have wanted. The first passage we reproduce here is from the *Tao Te Ching*, and expresses early Taoism's dissatisfaction with formalized morality and its opposition to the Confucian ethic. From later Taoism we also see how belief in the afterlife and the notion of rewards for merit came to infuse a popular morality of considerable power.

Sacred Narrative 1

The Ineffable Tao: Tao Te Ching

This amazing and mysterious passage sets the scene for viewing the universe, variously called in the book 'the ten thousand things', 'heaven and earth', and that which is 'beneath heaven'. There have been numerous attempts to translate Tao: here 'Way' is used; 'Principle', 'Logos', 'Reason' and other terms have been offered, but Way is the least inaccurate.

The way that can be followed
Is not the eternal way;
The name that can be named
Is not the eternal name.
That which is without name is of heaven and earth the beginning;
That which is nameable is of the ten thousand things the mother.
He who is eternally without desire
Perceives the spiritual side of it;
He who is permanently with desire
Perceives the limit of it.
These two things
Are the same in origin
but different in name;
Calling them the same is a mystery;
Indeed it is the mystery of mysteries;
Of all spirituality it is the gate.

Sacred Narrative 2

The Universe Flows from the Tao: Tao Te Ching

Here a mysterious account of creation is given. The character rendered 'oh!' signifies an expression of awe at the deep and ungraspable nature of the Tao. There is reference to the Tao as having an aspect of the mysterious female – the womb, as it were, out of which the universe emerges. In Doctrine 1 (pages 294–5) it is referred to also as the 'valley spirit'.

There was something containing all,
Before heaven and earth it exists:
Tranquil, oh! Incorporeal, oh!
Alone it stands and does not change.
It goes everywhere and is not hindered.
It can thereby become the universe's mother.

I know not its name;
I characterize it by calling it the Way.
Forced to make a name for it I call it the Great.
Great I call the elusive.
The elusive I call the far.
The far I call the returning.

Sacred Narrative 3

The Creation of the Universe: Huai-nan Tzu

This Taoist account of creation amplifies earlier ones. It is of special interest because it was taken over by Confucianists and incorporated into the Japanese Shinto scripture, the *Nihongi*. It makes reference to three ideas important in Chinese thinking – the theme of the yin and the yang, the female and male principles which in alternation express and govern the rhythm of things and events in the universe, and *ch'i*, here translated 'material-force', but signifying the dynamic spirit or breath of life in living beings and in the cosmos.

Before heaven and earth had taken form all was vague and amorphous. Therefore it was called the Great Beginning. The Great Beginning produced emptiness and emptiness produced the universe. The universe produced material-force which had limits. That which was clear and light drifted up to become heaven, while that which was heavy and turbid solidified to become earth. It was very easy for the pure, fine material to come together but extremely difficult for the heavy, turbid material to solidify. Therefore heaven was completed first and earth assumed shape after. The combined essences of heaven and earth became the yin and yang, the concentrated essences of the yin and yang became the four seasons, and the scattered essences of the four seasons became the myriad creatures of the world. After a long time the hot force of the accumulated yang produced fire and the essence of the fire force became the sun; the cold force of the accumulated yin became water and the essence of the water force became the moon. The essence of the excess force of the sun and moon became the stars and planets. Heaven received the sun, moon and stars while earth received water and soil.

Sacred Narrative 4

The Great and the Small: Chuang Tzu

In the book of Chuang Tzu there are references to mythic monsters, and here they are treated with a certain humour and disdain: the quail can laugh at them as the wise man also may laugh at those with pretensions to power and greatness. The early Taoists regarded the fact that distinctions vanish in the Tao and beyond death as subversive of both speculative thinking and social discriminations. We append also the famous story of Chuang Tzu's dream; the relativity of supposed knowledge is the lesson to be drawn: true insight is intuitive and experiential.

In the question put by T'ang to Chi, there was a similar statement: 'In the barren north, there is a sea, the Celestial Lake. In it there is a fish, several thousand li in breadth, and no one knows how many li in length. Its name is the kun. There is also a bird, named the p'eng, with a back like Mount T'ai, and wings like clouds across the sky. Upon a whirlwind it soars up to a height of ninety thousand leagues. Beyond the clouds and atmosphere, with the blue sky above it, it then directs its flight to the south, and thus proceeds to the ocean there.

'A quail laughs at it, saying: "Where is that bird going? I spring up with a bound, and when I have reached not more than a few yards I come down again. I just fly about among the brushwood and the bushes. This is also the perfection of flying. Where is that bird going?"' This is the difference between the great and the small.

There are some men whose knowledge is sufficient for the duties of some office. There are some men whose conduct will secure unity in some district. There are some men whose virtue befits him for a ruler. There are some men whose ability wins credit in the country. In their opinion of themselves, they are just like what is mentioned above.

Once upon a time, Chuang Chou dreamed that he was a butterfly, a butterfly flying about, enjoying itself. It did not know that it was Chuang Chou. Suddenly he awoke, and veritably was Chuang Chou again. We do not know whether it was Chuang Chou dreaming that he was a butterfly, or whether it was the butterfly dreaming that is was Chuang Chou. Between Chuang Chou and the butterfly there must be some distinction. This is a case of what is called the transformation of things.

Doctrine 1

The Meaning of Taoist Emptiness: Tao Te Ching

The main lines of the teaching of the Lao Tzu are sketched in these mysterious passages. The Tao is unseen, empty, yet also profound and the originator of all that is. It is like a mother and the eternal spirit of the valley; no doubt here the author or authors draw on a mythological notion of a water god animating a valley, but here the idea seems to be used symbolically. The valley which is the empty space between mountains signifies the creative power of emptiness, and echoes the emptiness of the fecund female's womb. The attitudes implied by these doctrines are also drawn out in these passages.

When in the world all know beauty as
beauty in action
Then only is there ugliness.
When in the world all know goodness as
goodness in action
Then only is there ungoodness.
Existence and non-existence are mutually
produced;
The hard and the easy are mutually
accomplished;
The long and the short are mutually measured;
The high and the low are mutually made.
Pitch and sound make harmony together;
The before and after mutually follow.
Therefore the holy man lives by making non-
action his business;
He practises non-speech as his teaching.
The ten thousand things, behold, arise
And he does not reject them.
He produces but does not own,
He acts and makes no claim.
He achieves merit and does not dwell in it.
In that he does not dwell in it
It does not depart.

Not exalting the worthy means the people do not
envy;
No prizing hard-to-get valuables means the
people do not steal.
Not looking at that which creates desire makes
the heart undisturbed.
Therefore the holy man's government empties
their hearts and fills their stomachs.
He weakens their desire, but strengthens their
bones.
He gets people not to know and not to desire,
Which means that those knowing ones do not
dare to act indeed.
He acts by not acting, thus there is nothing not
governed.

The Way is empty and yet its use
Does not seem to exhaust it.
Profound oh! It is like the ancestor of the ten
thousand things.
It blunts its sharpness;
It looses it bonds;
It dims its light;
It blends its dust.
Tranquil oh! It seems like to remain forever.
I do not know whose child it is:
It seems to be God's elder.

Heaven and earth are not humane:
They treat the ten thousand creatures like
straw dogs!
The holy man is not humane:
He looks on the hundred clans as straw dogs.
The space between heaven and earth
Is like a bellows.
When empty it does not collapse:
When moved more and more comes forth.
Gossip is often exhausted:
Not like keeping the middle path.

The valley spirit does not die:
It is called the mysterious woman.
The gate of the mysterious woman
Is called the root of the universe.
Continually, perpetually it seems to remain:
It functions with no effort.

Doctrine 2

The Relationship of Taoism to other Schools: Pao-p'u Tzu

In the early 4th century one of the most important and encyclopedic writers of the Taoist tradition composed the *Pao-p'u Tzu.* The following passages relate Taoism to some of the other movements in China including Confucianism, Moism, stressing attitudes of love, and founded by Mo Tzu (5th century BCE), Legalism, stressing legal positivism and the cult of power dominant in the 3rd century BCE, and logical or dialectical enquiries, concerned with the application of names to reality (4th century BCE).

Someone asked: Which is first and which is last, Confucianism or Taoism?

Pao-p'u Tzu answered: Taoism is the essence of Confucianism and Confucianism is an appendage to Taoism. First of all, there was the teaching of the yin-yang school which had many taboos that made people constrained and afraid. The Confucianists had extensive learning but little that was essential; they worked hard but achieved little. Moism emphasized thrift but was difficult to follow, and could not be practised exclusively. The Legalists were severe and showed little kindness; they destroyed humanity and righteousness. The teachings of the Taoist school alone enable men's spirits to be concentrated and united and their action to be in harmony with the formless. . . . Taoism embraces the good points of both Confucianism and Moism and combines the essentials of the Legalists and Logicians. It changes with the times and responds to the transformations of things. . . . Its precepts are simple and easy to understand; its works are few but its achievements many. It is devoted to the simplicity that preserves the Great Heritage and adheres to the true and correct source.

Ritual

Divination and the Tao: Chou-i lüeh-li

This work by Wang Pi represents a later Taoist interpretation of the hexagrams described by the *I Ching*, a central and ancient book on divination. It makes use of the concepts of the alternating principles so vital in Chinese cosmology, the yin (female, yielding) and the yang (male, dynamic). Wang Pi (3rd century CE) belonged to the 'mysterious learning' movement, a title which echoes the *Tao Te Ching's* reference to the Tao as 'mystery of mysteries'. The thinkers of this school saw no contradiction between Confucianism and Taoism, but worked out ways of seeing the former as relevant to public service and the latter as related to the tranquil effortless life of the recluse. The ritual and magical side of the Chinese tradition placed a central value on divination.

What is an explanation of a hexagram as a whole? It discusses generally the substance of a hexagram and makes clear the controlling principle out of which it is developed. Now, the many cannot be regulated by the many. They are regulated by the smallest in number (the one). Activity cannot be controlled by activity. They are controlled by that which is firmly rooted in the one. The reason why the many can exist is that their ruling principle returns always to the one and all activities can function because they have all come from the same source. Things never err; they always follow their principle. There is the chief to unite them, and there is the leader to group them together. Therefore, though complex, they are not chaotic, and though many, they are not confused. Hence the intermingling of the six lines in a hexagram can be understood by taking up one [of them, for one is always the ruling factor of the six] and the interaction of weakness (yin) and strength (yang) can be determined by having the basic controlling principle well established. Therefore, 'for gathering things together, enumerating qualities, and distinguishing right and wrong, there would be insufficiency if there were not one line among [the six as the ruling factor].' Therefore if we investigate things by approaching them as a united system, although they are many, we know we can handle them by adhering to the one, and if we view them from the point of view of the fundamental, although their concepts are broad, we know we can cover all of them under a single name. If we view the great heavenly movements through an astronomical instrument, we shall not wonder at the movements of heaven and earth, and if we occupy the central point to view whatever may come, then all things coming in from the six directions will not be beyond control. Therefore when the name of the hexagram is mentioned, we have the ruling factor of all its concepts, and as soon as we read the explanation of a hexagram, we understand more than half of the ideas involved.

Although past and present are not the same and armies and states appear different, we must not neglect the application of the central principle [in considering them]. Differences vary in a thousand ways, but the leading, ruling principle remains. This is the thing most highly valued in the explanation of a hexagram.

The little is valued by the plentiful, and the few are the leaders of the many. If there are five yang (undivided lines) and one yin (divided), the yin is the ruling factor. If there are five yin and one yang, the one yang is the ruling factor. For yin seeks after yang and yang seeks after yin. If yang is one and unified, how can all the five yin help returning to it? If yin is singular, how can all the five yang help following it? Thus although the yin is lowly, yet it is the controlling principle of the hexagram because it occupies the position of the least. Some people discard the lines and split the substance of a hexagram, but does the substance of the hexagram not depend on the lines? Although things are complex, there is no worry about their becoming chaotic, and although they change, there is no worry about their being confused. That which broadens is preserved by that which restricts, and the many is helped by the simple. The explanation of hexagrams alone can [show this]. Unless the explanation represents the most subtle and profound [principle] in the world, how can it avoid confusion in chaos and alteration in the process of change? If we view an explanation of a hexagram in this way, its concepts will become readily clear.

Institutional Expression

The Role of the Priest: The Teachings of Master Chuang

The following ritual invocation helps to bring out the role of the Taoist priest who, ideally, has mastered the esoteric teachings of the tradition and is conversant with the canon. In traditional society, the various rites of renewal, repentance and other matters over which the priest presides give the Taoist church a function to play in keeping the community in correct contact with the unseen world. Some of the longer rites were special to the monasteries, where the adepts hoped to achieve immortality through union with the Tao.

Man's body (microcosm) is noble.
Therefore the Tao opened a path,
Bequeathing chieh rules, ching canons and wen scripts,[1]
Whereby the bodily state could be transcended

[1] The chieh rules teach the disciple the right attitude in performing ritual for the benefit of the people, for sacred power is so great that there is the fearsome prospect of its being turned into 'black magic' harmful to others. The rules are summed up in three commandments: not to leave the roots to seek the branches, not to benefit oneself to the harm of others, and not to get involved in things and lose sight of the Tao. The ching are the classic Taoist canonical scriptures. The wen scripts are esoteric writings resembling Sanskrit devised as a secret counterweight to the prestige of Buddhist Sanskrit formulae used in ritual and teaching.

By a higher state of union with the Tao.
By preserving life essences,
Through performing the rituals,
And promising to fulfil the moral commandments,
The heart is quiet and contemplates darkness (yin);
The will is fixed on undivided brightness (yang);
All thought is reduced to the one.
The six fu administrative centres of the microcosm
By centring (in the Yellow Court)[2] are without sensation,
Inside and outside, pure and empty,
Joined as one with all of nature.
Then one offers incense, and pronounces the vows,
Causing the heart to ascend to the heavens,
And all the heavenly spirits to come down to earth,
To hear the music of the sacred liturgy, and
To answer the prayers of all men,
According to how they have kept the moral precepts,
And followed the way of the eternal Tao.

Experience 1

The Domain of Nothingness: Chuang Tzu

Here the central Taoist experience of emptiness, matching themes in Buddhism too, is alluded to. Complete identity or harmony with the Tao means seeing the world as it is without distinctions. Thus the true sage does not even have a name.

T'ien Ken was travelling to the south of Yin Mountain. He had reached the river Liao when he met a nameless sage, to whom he said, 'I beg to ask about governing the world.'

'Go away,' said the nameless man, 'you are a low fellow. How unpleasant is your question! I would be in companionship with the Maker of things. When wearied, I would mount on the bird of ease and emptiness, proceed beyond the world, wander in the land of nowhere, and live in the domain of nothingness. Why do you come to worry me with the problem of setting the world in order?'

T'ien Ken again asked his question, and the nameless man replied: 'Make excursion in pure simplicity. Identify yourself with nondistinction. Follow the nature of things and admit no personal bias, then the world will be in peace.'

[2] The ritual referred to reflects the conception that just as heaven is patterned after the bureaucratic structure of the Empire, so the body contains a like structure. The ritual referred to involves bringing forth the spirits of the six aspects of the body's function and thus centring the spirit on the inmost region, the Yellow Court. The language is different, but the ideas are similar to those of tantric yoga.

Experience 2

Blankness of Mind: Lieh Tzu

Lieh Tzu and his disciples had been to see a rival teacher, Nan-kuo Tzu, who seemed totally withdrawn and was rather horrid in appearance. He failed to recognize Lieh Tzu, but suddenly talked quite pleasantly to some of the disciples in the back row.

The disciples were astonished at this, and when they got home again, all wore a puzzled expression. Their Master Lieh Tzu said to them: 'He who has reached the stage of thought is silent. He who has attained to perfect knowledge is also silent. He who uses silence in lieu of speech really does speak. He who for knowledge substitutes blankness of mind really does know. Without words and speaking not, without knowledge and knowing not, he really speaks and really knows. Saying nothing and knowing nothing, there is in reality nothing that he does not say, nothing that he does not know. This is how the matter stands, and there is nothing further to be said. Why are you thus astonished without cause?'

Experience 3

The Self-Training of the Sage: Tao Te Ching

Here again the theme of shutting out the stimuli of the outer world, which was the basis of Taoist as other yoga, is alluded to.

He who knows does not speak.
He who speaks does not know.
He closes his apertures, shuts his gates.
He blunts his sharpness,
  Unwinds his tangles,
  Dims his brightness, unites with dust.
This is called deep union.

He cannot be got and loved;
He cannot be got and discarded;
He cannot be got and benefited;
He cannot be got and harmed;
He cannot be got and honoured;
He cannot be got and humbled;
Therefore there arises the world's honour.

Experience 4

Sadness Must Be Transcended: Lieh Tzu

Here the Taoist attitude to suffering appears stoical, and somewhat different at first sight to the Buddhist reaction to death, but a similar equanimity is encouraged.

Duke Ching of Ch'i was travelling across the northern flank of the Ox-mountain in the direction of the capital. Gazing at the view before him, he burst into a flood of tears, exclaiming: 'What a lovely scene! How verdant and luxuriantly wooded! To think that some day I must die and leave my kingdom, passing away like running water! If only there were no such thing as death, nothing should induce me to stir from this spot.' Two of the Ministers in attendance on the Duke, taking their cue from him, also began to weep, saying: 'We, who are dependent on your Highness's bounty, whose food is of an inferior sort, who have to ride on unbroken horses or in jolting carts – even we do not want to die. How much less our sovereign liege!'

Yen Tzu, meanwhile, was standing by, with a broad smile on his face. The Duke wiped away his tears and, looking at him, said 'Today I am stricken with grief on my journey, and both K'ung and Chu mingle their tears with mine. How is it that you alone can smile?' Yen Tzu replied: 'If the worthy ruler were to remain in perpetual possession of his realm, Duke T'ai and Duke Huan would still be exercising their sway. If the bold ruler were to remain in perpetual possession, Duke Chuang and Duke Ling would still be ruling the land. But if all these rulers were now in possession, where would your Highness be? Why, standing in the furrowed fields, clad in coir cape and hat! Condemned to a hard life on earth, you would have had not time, I warrant, for brooding over death. Again, how did you yourself come to occupy this throne? By a series of successive reigns and removals, until at last your turn came. And are you alone going to weep and lament over this order of things? That is unmanly. It was the sight of these two objects – an unmanly prince and his fawning attendants – that was affording me food for laughter just now.'

Duke Ching felt much ashamed and, raising his goblet, fined himself and his obsequious courtiers two cups of wine apiece.

Ethics 1

The True Virtue of the Way: Tao Te Ching

The paradoxical message of these lines is that insistence on Confucian virtues such as humanity (*jen*) and filial piety, and striving to produce good behaviour through education, are appropriate only when there is already a problem. Thus in any case good behaviour has to be imposed by force, and this creates resentment and more bad behaviour. The plea of the Taoist sage is for naturalness and gentleness; thus goodness will arise spontaneously.

The great Way declines:
We have humanity and justice:
Prudence and wisdom appear;
There is cultivation of behaviour.
When the six family relationships
Are out of accord, there is filial piety, and parental affection.
When state and dynasty are disordered
There is loyal trust.

Abandon saintliness, relinquish prudence.
The people will gain ten thousand per cent;
The people will be back to filial piety, parental affection.
Abandon cleverness, relinquish profit,
Thieves and robbers there will not be.
These are three ways in which active culture is insufficient:
Therefore hold to the things which are reliable.
Look to simplicity; embrace purity;
Lessen the self; diminish desire.

Ethics 2

The Reward for Deeds: P'ao-p'u Tzu

The notion that there is a net of heaven which catches the evil-doers in its meshes is an ancient one, and here Taoism also makes use of the notion of a divine Arbiter who creates a system of reward and punishment. Note that the responsibility is collective, so that descendants of an evil-doer have to cope with the problem.

Furthermore, as Heaven and earth are the greatest of things, it is natural, from the point of view of universal principles, that they have spiritual power. Having spiritual power it is proper that they reward good and punish evil. Nevertheless their expanse is great and their net is wide-meshed. There is not necessarily an immediate response as soon as this net is set in operation. As we glance over the Taoist books of discipline, however, all are unanimous in saying that those who seek immortality must set their minds to the accumulation of merits and the accomplishment of good work. Their hearts must be kind to all things. They must treat others as they treat themselves, and extend their humaneness (*jen*) even to insects. They must rejoice in the fortune of men and pity their suffering, relieve the destitute and save the poor. Their hands must never injure life, and their mouths must never encourage evil. They must consider the success and failure of others as their own. They must not regard themselves highly, nor praise themselves. They must not envy those superior to them, nor flatter dangerous and evil-minded people. In this way they may become virtuous and blessed by Heaven; they may be successful in whatever they do, and may hope to become immortal.

If, on the other hand, they hate good and love evil; if their words do not agree with their thoughts; if they say one thing in people's presence and the opposite behind their backs; if they twist the truth; if they are cruel to subordinates or deceive their superiors; if they betray their task and are ungrateful for kindness received; if they manipulate the law and accept bribes; if they tolerate injustice but suppress justice; if they destroy the public good for their selfish ends; if they punish the innocent, wreck people's homes, pocket their treasures, injure their bodies, or seize their positions; if they overthrow virtuous rulers or massacre those who have surrendered to them; if they slander saints and sages or hurt Taoist priests; if they shoot birds in flight or kill the unborn in womb or egg; if in spring or summer hunts they burn the forests or drive out the game; if they curse spiritual beings; if they teach others to do evil or conceal their good deeds or endanger others for their own security; if they claim the work of others as their own; if they spoil people's happy affairs or take away what others love; if they cause division in people's families or disgrace others in order to win; if they overcharge or underpay; if they set fire or inundate; if they injure people with trickery or coerce the weak; if they repay good with evil; if they take things by force or accumulate wealth through robbery and plunder; if they are unfair or unjust, licentious, indulgent or perverted; if they oppress orphans or mistreat widows; if they squander inheritance and accept charity; if they cheat or deceive; if they love to gossip about people's private affairs or criticize them for their defects; if they drag Heaven and earth into their affairs and rail at people in order to seek vindication; if they fail to repay debts or play fair in the exchange of goods; if they seek to gratify their desires without end; if they hate and resist the faithful and sincere; if they disobey orders from above or do not respect their teachers; if they ridicule others for doing good; if they destroy people's crops or harm their tools so as to nullify their utility, and do not feed people with clean food; if they cheat in weights or measures; if they mix spurious articles with genuine; if they take dishonourable advantage; if they tempt others to steal; if they meddle in the affairs of others or go beyond their position in life: if they leap over wells or hearths (which provide water and fire for food); if they sing in the last day of the month (when the end should be sent off with sorrow) or cry in the first day of the month (when the beginning should be welcomed with joy); if they commit any of these evil deeds; it is a sin.

The Arbiter of Human Destiny will reduce their terms of life by units of three days or three hundred days in proportion to the gravity of the evil. When all days are deducted they will die. Those who have the intention to do evil but have not carried it out will have three-day units taken just as if they had acted with injury to others. If they die before all their evil deeds are punished, their posterity will suffer for them.

Postscript

As Taoism grew from a religio-philosophical movement stressing inner harmony and non-action, through to more elaborate speculations within the general ambit of Chinese reflection about the cosmos, and beyond that to a fully elaborated priestly system for coping with the quest for immortality and with the concerns of daily living, so its texts multiplied into a vast canon. Part of the function of these scriptures was to provide a body of texts for use in ceremonial and to embody esoteric teachings conferring expertise and prestige upon the adept who has mastered them. Much of this material remains unexplored by Western scholars. The most easily available systematic account in English of the evolution and nature of the scriptures is found in Michael Saso's book, from which we have quoted above, *The Teachings of the Buddhist Master Chuang*.

Bibilography

Among numerous translations of the *Tao Te Ching* are:

J. Legge, *The Texts of Taoism* (1881)
A. Waley, *The Way and its Power* (1934)

Other collections are:

W.T. de Bary and others, *Sources of Chinese Tradition* (1960)
A.C. Graham, *The Book of Lieh-tzu* (1961)
D.C. Lau, *Lao Tzu* (1963)
Wing-tsi Chan, *A Source Book in Chinese Philosophy* (1963)
B Watson, *The Complete Works of Chuang Tzu* (1968).

A 17th-century bronze representing the legendary figure Lao Tzu mounted on the water buffalo on which he left China to travel to the west. The Tao Te Ching *is ascribed to Lao Tzu, although it is more likely that it is an anthology.*

Confucianism

Introduction

Confucianism as a system of belief has traditionally been interwoven with education and with aspects of popular religion. It has formed the philosophy of how to conduct oneself humanely and decorously in society, and so has done much to shape Chinese interpersonal relationships. It has aspects of a religion, and yet at the same time can also been seen as a system of scholarship. The reason for all this is that over a long period, until 1905, the Confucian classical writings were used as a basis for education; education was used as the means of recruiting an administrative class; and the administration was the fabric of an imperial system which on the whole (with periods when Taoism and Buddhism were also competitors for official recognition) rested on Confucianism as its ideology. Both at local and imperial level the ideology also incorporated the cult of ancestors, so that society was seen as a living past as well as a living present, and Confucius was regarded as holding a primary place among official ancestors: his cult was made official by the Emperor Ming in 59 CE, and in due course each of China's more than two thousand counties had its own temple to Confucius.

The basic writings of the Confucian tradition are the Five Classics (Wu Ching) and the Four Books (Ssu Shu). They formed the substance of the civil service examinations. The three major figures of Confucian philosophy were K'ung himself (Confucius is a Latinized version of Kung-fu-tzu, 'Master K'ung'), who lived from 551 to 479 BCE, Mencius or Meng-tzu (c.371–289) and Hsün-tzu (c.298–c.230). But also of great importance was the Neo-Confucian revival, which was in part a reaction to Buddhism, and was an attempt to systematize Confucian teachings in a way that would express a reaffirmation of orthodoxy. Chun Hsi (1130–1200 CE) was not only a prolific and well-organized writer, but his commentaries on the Classical writings came to be incorporated into the State syllabus. Wang Yang-ming (1472–1529), a statesman and military leader as well as a thinker with a contemplative bent, was a major source of inspiration for those who saw official Confucianism as too formal.

Various lists of Classics are recognized in Chinese history, but the most traditional and accepted canon, which served as the basis of education and represented the heart of the tradition and of Confucius' teachings, are the Five Classics and the Four Books, with Chu Hsi's commentary. In the ensuing selection we only venture outside this official canon to use two passages from Wang Yang-ming.

The Five Classics were edited by K'ung, and one, the *Ch'un Ch'iu*, was ascribed to his authorship. The 'Book of Changes' or *I Ching* is perhaps the most ancient. It was used for divination, and included 64 hexagrams for use in divining; and it also incorporated the theory of the yin and the yang as cosmic principles, which came to be so deeply entrenched in Chinese thinking and cosmology. The *Shu Ching* (Classic of History) and the *Ch'un Ch'iu* (Spring and Autumn Annals) are chronicles. The *Shih Ching* (Classic of Poetry) is an anthology: poetry and music are interwoven in the Confucian tradition, and the sage set great store by music as creating the right emotions to underlie the rules of formal conduct. The *Li Chi* (Classic of Ritual) is the fundamental text of traditional ceremonial. The Four Books comprise *Lun yü* (the Analects), *Meng-tzu* (Book of Mencius), the *Ta hsüeh* (Great Learning) and the *Chung Yung* (Doctrine of the Mean). The last two are actually chapters from the *Li Chi*, edited separately and commented by Chu Hsi. Certain other works are sometimes listed as classics, the most important being the *Hsiao Ching* (Classic of Filial Piety) sometimes ascribed to Confucius himself.

In the selections that follow we start with an account of history as Confucius saw it, beginning with the period of Great Harmony in primordial times, and continue with two excerpts from the Analects which tell us something of Confucius the man, whose life was of course a paradigm for later generations. Two passages illustrate Confucian doctrines: one from the Classic of Poetry looks to the concept of the Mandate of Heaven, and the second deals with Chu Hsi's conception of the Great Ultimate, at the root of the universe. As for ritual, we have a passage in which Hsün-tzu expounds the centrality of that crucial Confucian concept *li* (ceremonial, ritual, right behaviour). There is also an excerpt from the Doctrine of the Mean about the service due to ancestors, whose cult has played so great a role in weaving together the fabric of Chinese society. These passages are a prelude to an account of how Confucian practices are institutionalized in society. For although Confucianism has its specialists (notably the *ju* or scholars), it is essentially a religion of society as a whole: society is its 'church'. But the outer forms only work if they conform to inner experience. We turn next to a passage from the Great Learning with Chu Hsi's Introduction, which stresses inner sincerity and the other attitudes residing at the root of good social practice, and then to a more direct passage from the Great Learning on experiencing sincerity. In the next passage we see the experiential character of the 'investigation of things' as Wang Yang-ming interpreted it – namely that exploration which lies at the heart of the teachings of the Great Learning (though Wang saw it as something akin to Buddhist meditation and was too individualistic for some later Confucianists). Finally, to illustrate further Confucian ethics, we look to two famous passages in which Confucius expounds reciprocity, and another in which Mencius expounds on how the virtue of *jen* (humaneness) and other virtues are innate. It will be seen, however, that the interwoven themes of good conduct and right ritual run through the whole Confucian teaching, which thus expounds perhaps more clearly than any other religious tradition the civilizing and compassionate character of the use of the right code of ritual and courtesy.

Sacred Narrative 1

The Mythic Past: Li Chi (Classic of Ritual), Li yün

Confucius modelled his teachings on the past, and so his hope, in an age of disorder, was to restore some of the virtues exemplified by such legendary figures as the Duke of Chou (11th century BCE), and such sage kings as Yao and Shun farther back.

Confucius said: 'The practice of the Great Tao and the eminent men of the Three Dynasties – this I have never seen in person, and yet I have a mind to follow them. When the Great Tao prevailed, the world was a commonwealth; men of talent and virtue were selected, mutual confidence was emphasized, and brotherhood was cultivated. Therefore, men did not regard as parents only their own parents, nor did they treat as sons only their own sons. Old people were able to enjoy their old age; young men were able to employ their talents; juniors respected their elders; helpless widows, orphans and cripples were well cared for. Men had their respective occupations, and women their homes. They hated to see wealth lying about in waste, and they did not hoard it for their own use. They hated not to use their energies, and they used their energies not for their own benefit. Thus evil schemings were repressed, and robbers, thieves and traitors no longer appeared, so that the front door remained open. This was called *Ta-tung* [Grand Unity].

'Now the Great Tao has fallen into obscurity, and the world is in the possession of families. Each regards as parents only his own parents and treats as sons only his own sons; wealth and labour are employed for selfish purpose. The sovereigns take it as the proper *li* that their states should be hereditary; they endeavour to make their cities and suburbs strong, their ditches and moats secure. *Li* and *i* are used as the norms to regulate the relationship between ruler and subject, to ensure affection between father and son, harmony between brothers, and concord between husband and wife; to set up institutions, organize farms and hamlets, honour the brave and the wise, and bring merit to the individual. Hence schemes and plottings come about and men take up arms.

'It was in this way that Emperor Yü, Kings T'ang, Wen, Wu, Ch'eng, and the Duke of Chou achieved eminence: all these six noble men paid attention to *li*, and made manifest their *i* and acted in good faith. They exposed their errors, made *jen* their law and prudence their practice, thus showing the people wherein they should constantly abide. If there were any who did not follow these principles, he would lose power and position and be regarded by the multitude as dangerous. This is called *Hsiao-K'ang* [Minor Peace].'

Sacred Narrative 2

Confucius in Brief: Analects

This is a thumbnail sketch of Confucius. It contains some of the primary themes of his thought – his concern with good government, his love of the ancient classics and poetry as a way of shaping character, his emphasis on *li* or propriety (or 'educated behaviour' as it might be translated).

K'ung said, 'The ruler who governs the state through virtue is like the pole star, which stays put while the other stars revolve round it.'

K'ung said, 'All of the three hundred odes in the Classic of Poetry can be summed up in one of its lines, "Have no wrong thoughts."'

K'ung said, 'If you control the people by government acts and keep them in line with law and order, they will refrain from doing wrong, but they will not have a sense of honour or shame. But if you lead them through virtue and regulate them by the laws of propriety, then they will have a sense of shame and will attain goodness.'

K'ung said, 'At fifteen my mind was fixed on learning. By thirty my character had been formed. At forty I had no more confusions. At fifty I understood the Mandate of Heaven. At sixty it was easy for me to hear the truth. At seventy I could follow my desires without transgressing what was right.'

Sacred Narrative 3

Confucius' Conversation and Manners: Analects

Confucius saw himself as scholar and teacher. But teaching involved personal example as well as precept, and his figure thus became the prototype for the superior person of the Confucian tradition.

K'ung said, 'With rough rice to eat and water to drink and one's bent arm to be a pillow, there is still happiness. Riches and reputation if gained dishonourably are just floating clouds.'

K'ung said, 'Give me a few more years and I will complete half a century of study of the *I Ching*: I may then be free of major errors.'

K'ung often spoke about the following things – poetry, history and performing the rules of proper behaviour. All these were frequent topics for him.

The Duke of She asked a disciple, Tzu-lu, about K'ung, and Tzu-lu did not reply. K'ung said 'Why did you not tell him that I am a person who forgets to eat when concentrating on some pursuit, am so happy that I forget any worries and do not realize that old age is approaching?'

K'ung said, 'I was not born endowed with knowledge, but I love traditional teaching and earnestly pursue it.'

K'ung never discussed abnormal phenomena, physical exploits, disorderly conduct, or spiritual beings.

K'ung fished with a line but not with a net. While shooting he would not shoot a bird at rest.

K'ung said, 'There are those who act without knowledge. But I am not like that. Apart from innate knowledge there is another kind: to hear a lot, select what is excellent, follow it, to see a lot and remember it.'

Doctrine 1

The Mandate of Heaven: Classic of Poetry, Ode

When this poem about the founder of the Chou Dynasty was written, Heaven was thought of as a divine being with personal characteristics, but by the time of developed Confucianism and particularly in the thought of Chu Hsi, the Mandate of Heaven was conceived of as the moral law woven into the fabric of the universe. For many Chinese, 'the Mandate of Heaven' has something of the semi-personal flavour of 'the decree of providence'. The theory of the Mandate of Heaven was vital in Chinese traditional political theory; the ruler who flouted the moral law had heaven's mandate withdrawn, a prelude to disaster.

The Mandate of Heaven,
How lovely and permanent,
Ah how glorious
Was the clarity of King Wen's virtue.
He inundates us with blessings:
We shall receive the blessings.
They are a great favour from King Wen,
May his successors keep firmly to them.

Doctrine 2

Chu Hsi on the Great Ultimate: Chu tzu ch'üan-shu

In developed Confucian philosophy the interplay of the forces of nature – the yin and the yang – and of the 'myriad' things, i.e. the things which make up the universe, is traced back to a single Great Ultimate or ground of being.

Question: You said, 'Principle is a single, concrete entity, and the myriad things partake of it as their reality. Hence each of the myriad things possesses in it a Great Ultimate.' Acording to this theory, does the Great Ultimate not split up into parts?

Answer: Fundamentally there is only one Great Ultimate, yet each of the myriad things has been endowed with it and each in itself possesses the Great Ultimate in its entirety. This is similar to the fact that there is only one moon in the sky but when its light is scattered upon rivers and lakes, it can be seen everywhere. It cannot be said that the moon has been split.

The Great Ultimate is not spatially conditioned; it has neither corporeal form nor body. There is no spot where it may be placed. When it is considered in the state before activity begins, this state is nothing but tranquillity. Now activity, tranquillity, yin and yang are all within the realm of corporeality. However, activity is after all the activity of the Great Ultimate and tranquillity is also its tranquillity, although activity and tranquillity themselves are not the Great Ultimate. This is why Master Chou Tun'i[1] spoke only of that state as Non-ultimate. While the state before activity begins cannot be spoken of as the Great Ultimate, nevertheless the principles of pleasure, anger, sorrow and joy are already inherent in it. Pleasure and joy belong to yang, and anger and sorrow belong to yin. In the initial state the four are not manifested, but their principles are already there. As contrasted with the state after activity begins, it may be called the Great Ultimate. But still it is difficult to say. All this is but a vague description. The truth must be genuinely and earnestly realized by each individual himself.

Ritual 1

The Centrality of Li: Hsün-tzu

Hsün-tzu (3rd century BCE) wrote extensively on the practical aspects of the Confucian ethos, and was especially interested in music as well as *li* or ceremonial propriety. Music had prominence in the Confucian outlook because it was a way of arousing the right emotions, for throughout the tradition mere propriety was not enough – it had to flow from the heart.

In general, the rules of proper conduct begin with primitive practices, attain refinement, and finally achieve beauty and felicity. When *li* is at its best, man's emotion and sense of beauty are both fully expressed. When *li* is at the next level, either the emotion or the sense of beauty overlaps the other. When *li* is at the lowest level, the emotion reverts to the state of simplicity.

[1] Chou Tun-i was a pioneer of the Neo-Confucian school, and lived in the 11th century CE.

Indeed it is through *li* that Heaven and earth are in harmony, that the sun and moon are splendid, that the four seasons succeed each other, that the stars follow their movements, that the rivers and streams maintain their flow, that all things and creatures enjoy prosperity, that love and hatred are tempered, and joy and anger are controlled. *Li* causes the lower orders of society to be obedient, and the higher orders to be illustrious. One who abides by *li* never goes astray amid the multifarious changes; one who deviates from *li* is lost. Is not *li* the greatest of all principles?

When *li* is established with all the proper solemnity, it becomes the guiding principle of all, and nothing in the world can enhance or lessen its value. Its source and aim are in accord with each other; its end and beginning are mutually related. *Li* attains refinement, for it maintains the distinctions; it achieves its comprehensiveness, for it embraces all. When the world follows it, there is good government; when it departs from it, there is anarchy. One who follows it is safe; one who deviates from it is in danger. One who follows it endures; one who deviates from it perishes. But the *hsiao-jen* [the ignorant] cannot comprehend this.

Deep indeed is the principle of *li*: it penetrates and permeates 'hardness and whiteness' or 'likeness and unlikeness'. Great indeed is the principle of *li*: it penetrates and eradicates unauthorized laws and depraved doctrines. High indeed is the principle of *li*: it penetrates and overcomes tyranny, insolence, cynicism, and self-importance. Hence, when the plumb-line is truly laid out, one cannot be deceived as to crookedness or straightness; when the balances are truly placed, one cannot be deceived of the weight; when the compass and square are truly applied, one cannot be deceived as to squareness or roundness. Similarly, when the 'superior individual' is well versed in *li*, he cannot be deceived of what is false. For the plumb-line is the measure of straightness; the balances are the measure of equilibrium; the compass and square are the measure of squareness and roundness; so *li* is the measure of human Tao. Moreover, one who neither follows *li* nor maintains *li* is a man without the Tao: one who follows *li* and maintains *li* is a man with the Tao. To be able to meditate on *li* is to be able to reflect; to be able to persist in keeping *li* is to be firm. One who is able to reflect and to be firm, with a love of *li*, is a sage. Just as Heaven is the extreme of height, earth is the extreme of depth; as the boundless is the extreme of breadth, so the sage is the extreme of Tao. Hence one who persists in learning *li* becomes a sage; one who fails to learn *li* is a person without the Tao.

Li provides wealth and things for its use, the noble and low for its adornment, the many and the new for its distinction, and the embellishment and simplification for its occasion. *Li* is embellished when its refinement is elaborate but sparing in its emotion. *Li* is simplified when it is sparing in its refinement but generous in emotion. *Li* secures the mean when its refinement and emotion are related as its external conduct and internal sentiment, which go together and are interrelated to each other. Hence the 'superior individual' in major ceremonials reaches the embellishment of *li* and in minor ceremonials its simplification; as to ceremonials at large, he secures the mean. While walking and running, riding, and charioteering, he will not depart from *li* – this is the 'superior individual's' terrace and his palace. If a man keeps within its boundary, he is a scholar or a 'superior individual'; if he goes beyond it, he is but an unlearned man. Then, he who conducts himself within the scope of *li* and conforms to its order is a sage. He is honoured because he accumulates *li*; he is great because he broadens *li*; he is exalted because he embellishes *li*; he is illustrious because he perfects *li*. The *Shih* says:

> As *li* and *i* are followed,
> Smiles and words are proper.

This expresses what I mean.

Li requires that life and death be carefully treated. Life is the beginning of man; death is the end of man. When man's end and beginning are both well treated, the Tao of humanity is fulfilled. Hence the 'superior individual' respects the beginning and attends to the end. To treat them alike is the Tao of the 'superior individual' and the refinement of *li* and *i*. To exhalt the living and belittle the dead is to respect one who has consciousness and neglect one who has lost it – this is the way of the evil man, with a rebellious heart. The noble man would consider it shameful to treat a lowly slave with a rebellious heart. How much better he will treat those whom he honours or loves.

Ritual 2

The Reverence for Ancestors: Doctrine of the Mean

Here K'ung deals with the cult which was to become a pervasive feature of Chinese life. As usual, he appeals to model figures of the past (Wu and the Duke of Chou), and though he was not explicit in his religious teachings he saw service to God as an integral part of the good social life.

Confucius said, 'King Wu and Duke Chou were indeed eminently filial. Men of filial piety are those who skillfully carry out the wishes of their forefathers and skillfully carry forward their undertakings. In spring and autumn they repaired their ancestral temple, displayed their ancestral vessels and exhibited the ancestral robes, and presented the appropriate offerings of the season. The ritual of the ancestral temple is in order to place the kindred on the left or on the right according to the order of descent. This order in rank meant to distinguish the more honourable or humbler stations. Services in the temple are arranged in order so as to give distinction to the worthy [according to their ability for those services]. In the pledging rite the inferiors present their cups to their superiors, so that people of humble stations may have something to do. In the concluding feast, honoured places were given people with white hair, so as to follow the order of seniority. To occupy places of their forefathers, to practise their rites, to perform their music, to reverence those whom they honoured, to love those who were dear to them, to serve the dead as they were served while alive, and to serve the departed as they were served while still with us: this is the height of filial piety.

'The ceremonies of sacrifices to Heaven and Earth are meant for the service of the Lord on High, and the ceremonies performed in the ancestral temple are meant for the service of ancestors. If one understands the ceremonies of the sacrifices to Heaven and Earth and the meaning of the grand sacrifice and the autumn sacrifice to ancestors, it would be as easy to govern a kingdom as to look at one's palm.'

Institutional Expression

The Well-Ordered Society: Doctrine of the Mean

Confucian philosophy is a mode of expressing a type of harmonious ethos which finds its true expression not in any given institution, but rather in society as a whole. It is also manifested through the superior individual, who by his wisdom and conduct can influence others in the path of rectitude and courtesy.

Duke Ai[1] asked about government. Confucius said, 'The governmental measures of King Wen and King Wu are spread out in the records. With their kind of men, government will flourish. When their kind of men are gone, their government will come to an end. When the right principles of man operate, the growth of good government is rapid, and when the right principles of soil operate, the growth of vegetables is rapid. Indeed, government is comparable to a fast-growing plant. Therefore the conduct of government depends upon the men. The right men are obtained by the ruler's personal character. The cultivation of the person is to be done through the Way, and the cultivation of the Way is to be done through humanity. Humanity (*jen*) is [the distinguishing characteristic of] man, and the greatest application of it is in being affectionate toward relatives. Righteousness (*i*) is the principle of setting things right and proper, and the greatest application of it is in honouring the worthy. The relative degree of affection we ought to feel for our relatives and the relative grades in the honouring of the worthy give rise to the rules of propriety. [If those in inferior positions do not have the confidence of their superiors, they will not be able to govern the people.]

'Therefore, the ruler must not fail to cultivate his personal life. Wishing to cultivate his personal life, he must not fail to serve his parents. Wishing to serve his parents, he must not fail to know man. Wishing to know man, he must not fail to know Heaven.

'There are five universal ways [in human relations], and the way by which they are practised is three. The five are those governing the relationship between ruler and minister, between father and son, between husband and wife, between elder and younger brothers, and those in the intercourse between friends. These five are universal paths in the world. Wisdom, humanity and courage, these three are the universal virtues. The way by which they are practised is one.

'Some are born with the knowledge [of these virtues]. Some learn it through study. Some learn it through hard work. But when the knowledge is acquired, it comes to the same thing. Some practise them naturally and easily. Some practise them for their advantage. Some practise them with effort and difficulty. But when the achievement is made, it comes to the same thing.'

Confucius said, 'Love of learning is akin to wisdom. To practise with vigour is akin to humanity. To know to be shameful is akin to courage. He who knows these three things knows how to cultivate his personal life. Knowing how to cultivate his personal life, he knows how to govern other men. And knowing how to govern other men, he knows how to govern the empire, its states, and the families.

'There are nine standards by which to administer the empire, its states, and the families. They are: cultivating the personal life, honouring the worthy, being affectionate to relatives, being respectful toward the great ministers, identifying oneself with the welfare of the whole body of officers, treating the common people as one's own children, attracting the various artisans, showing tenderness to strangers from far countries, and extending kindly and awesome influence on the feudal lords. If the ruler cultivates his personal life, the Way will be established. If he honours the worthy, he will not be perplexed. If he is affectionate to his relatives, there will be no grumbling among his uncles and brothers. If he respects the great ministers, he will not be deceived. If he identifies himself with the welfare of the whole body of officers, then the officers will repay him heavily for his courtesies. If he treats the common people as his own children, then the masses will exhort one another [to do good]. If he attracts the various artisans, there will be sufficiency of wealth and resources in the country. If he shows tenderness to strangers from far countries, people from all quarters of the world will flock to him. And if he extends kindly and awesome influence over the feudal lords, then the world will stand in awe of him.'

---

[1] Ruler of Lu, 494–465 BCE.

Experience 1

Moral and Social Programmes: The Great Learning

Here is the beginning of the Great Learning with Chu Hsi's commentary (following that of Ch'eng I of the 11th century CE). It indicates how important in Confucianism is the cultivation of the emotions.

Master Ch'eng I said: 'The Great Learning is a surviving work of the Confucian school and is the gate through which the beginning student enters into virtue. It is only due to the preservation of this work that the order in which the ancients pursued their learning may be seen at this time. The Analects and the Book of Mencius are next to it. The student should by all means follow this work in his effort to learn, and then he will probably be free from mistakes.

The Text:

The Way of learning to be great (adult education) consists in manifesting the clear character, loving the people, and abiding (*chih*) in the highest good.

Only after knowing what to abide in can one be calm. Only after having been calm can one be tranquil. Only after having achieved tranquillity can one have peaceful repose. Only after having peaceful repose can one begin to deliberate. Only after deliberation can the end be attained. Things have their roots and branches. Affairs have their beginnings and their ends. To know what is first and what is last will lead one near the Way.

The ancients who wished to manifest their clear character to the world would first bring order to their states. Those who wished to bring order to their states would first regulate their families. Those who wished to regulate their families would first cultivate their personal lives. Those who wished to cultivate their personal lives would first rectify their minds. Those who wished to rectify their minds would first make their wills sincere. Those who wished to make their wills sincere would first extend their knowledge. The extension of knowledge consists in the investigation of things. When things are investigated, knowledge is extended; when knowledge is extended, the will becomes sincere; when the will is sincere, the mind is rectified; when the mind is rectified, the personal life is cultivated; when the personal life is cultivated, the family will be regulated; when the family is regulated, the state will be in order; and when the state is in order, there will be peace throughout the world. From the Son of Heaven down to the common people, all must regard cultivation of the personal life as the root or foundation. There is never a case when the root is in disorder and yet the branches are in order. There has never been a case when what is treated with great importance becomes a matter of slight importance or what is treated with slight importance becomes a matter of great importance.

Chu Hsi's Remark. The above is the text in one chapter. It is the words of Confucius, handed down by Tseng Tzu.

Experience 2

The Investigation of the Mind: Wang Yang-ming's Conversations with Huang I-fang

In these passages, Wang explains how ultimately the truth must be seen within. There are affinities with Buddhist practice (especially Zen). The second chapter describes how during a period of banishment to Kuei-chou 'among the barbarians' during the first decade of the 16th century CE Wang realized the primacy of investigating the mind.

The Teacher said, 'Former scholars interpreted the investigation of things as investigating all the things in the world. How can all things in the world be investigated? [Ch'eng I] even said "Every blade of grass and every tree possess principle." How can we investigate? Even if we could succeed in investigating every blade of grass and every tree, how can we return to ourselves and make the will sincere? I interpret the word *ko* to mean rectifying and *wu* to mean affairs or events. By personal life the Great Learning means the ears, the eyes, the mouth, the nose and the four limbs. To cultivate the personal life means for the eyes not to see what is contrary to propriety, the ears not to hear what is contrary to propriety, the mouth not to say what is contrary to propriety, and the four limbs not to do what is contrary to propriety. But if we want to cultivate the personal life, how can we do so by applying the effort to the body? The mind is the master of the body. Although the eye sees, what makes it see is the mind. Although the ear hears, what makes it hear is the mind. And although the mouth and the four limbs speak and move, what makes them speak and move is the mind. Therefore to cultivate the personal life lies in realizing through personal experience the true substance of one's mind and always making it broad and extremely impartial without the slightest incorrectness. Once the master is correct, then, as it operates through the channel of the eye, it will naturally see nothing which is contrary to propriety. As it operates through the channel of the ear, it will naturally hear nothing which is contrary to propriety. And as it operates through the channels of the mouth and the four limbs, it will naturally say or do nothing which is contrary to propriety. This means that the cultivation of the personal life consists in rectifying the mind.

'But the original substance of the mind is characterized by the highest good. Is there anything in the original substance of the mind that is not good? Now that we want to rectify the mind, where in this original substance must we direct out effort? We must direct it where the mind operates and then the effort can be earnest and concrete. In the mind's operation, it is impossible for it to be entirely free from evil. Therefore it must be here that we make earnest and concrete effort. This means to make the will sincere. For instance, when a thought to love the good arises, right then and there make an earnest and concrete effort to love the good. When a thought to hate evil arises, right then and there make an earnest and concrete effort to hate evil. If whenever the will operates it is sincere, how can the original substance of the mind help being correct? Therefore if one wishes to rectify the mind, he must first make his will sincere. Only when the effort reaches this point of sincerity of the will, will it find a solution.

'However, the foundation of the sincerity of the will lies in the extension of knowledge. What has been described as "what people do not know but I alone know" is exactly the innate knowledge in our mind. If one knows what good is but does not do it right then and there according to this innate knowledge, or knows what evil is but does not get rid of it according to this innate knowledge, this innate knowledge will be obscured. This means that knowledge cannot be extended. If the innate knowledge of our mind cannot be extended to the utmost, then although we know that we should love the good, we cannot earnestly and concretely love it and although we know that we should hate evil, we cannot earnestly and concretely hate it. How can the will be sincere? Therefore the extension of knowledge is the foundation of the sincerity of the will. But this extension of knowledge is not something to be done in a vacuum. It is to rectify [what is wrong in the mind] in whatever actual things one is doing. For instance, if one has the will to do good, then he should do it right in the things he happens to be doing. If one has the will to get rid of evil, he should resist evil right in the things he is doing. Getting rid of evil is, of course, to rectify what is incorrect in the mind and return to the original state of correctness. When good is done, evil is corrected. Hence, doing good is also to rectify what is incorrect in the mind and return to the original state of correctness. In this way the innate knowledge of our mind will not be obscured by selfish desires and can then be extended to the utmost, and whenever the will operates, its desire to love good and to get rid of evil will always be sincere. Thus the concrete starting point of the effort to make the will sincere lies in the investigation of things. If the investigation of things is to be done in this way, everyone can do it. This is why "Every man can become Yao and Shun."'

The Teacher said, 'People merely say that in the investigation of things we must follow Chu Hsi, but when have they carried it out in practice? I have carried it out earnestly and definitely. In my earlier years my friend Ch'ien and I discussed the idea that to become a sage or a worthy one must investigate all the things in the world. But how can a person have such tremendous energy? I therefore pointed to the bamboos in front of the pavilion and told him to investigate them and see. Day and night Mr Ch'ien went ahead trying to investigate to the utmost the principles in the bamboos. He exhausted his mind and thoughts and on the third day he was tired out and took sick. At first I said that it was because his energy and strength were insufficient. Therefore I myself went to try to investigate to the utmost. From morning till night, I was unable to find the principles of the bamboos. On the seventh day I also became sick because I thought too hard. In consequence we sighed to each other and said that it was impossible to be a sage or a worthy, for we do not have the tremendous energy to investigate things that they have. After I had lived among the barbarians for [almost] three years, I understood what all this meant and realized that there is really nothing in the things in the world to investigate, that the effort to investigate things is only to be carried out in and with reference to one's body and mind, and that if one firmly believes that everyone can become a sage, one will naturally be able to take up the task of investigating things. This idea, gentlemen, I must convey to you.'

Ethics 1

Reciprocity: Analects

In these passages, Confucius expresses versions of the Golden Rule.

Chung-Kung asked about humaneness (*jen*), and the Master said: 'When going about, behave to each person as if you were meeting an esteemed guest; employ people as if you were assisting at a great ceremony. Do not do to others what you would want them to do to you. Then there will be no resentment against you in the country or in your family.' Chung-Kung replied 'Though I am no genius, I'll try and put your teaching into practice.'

Tzu-kung asked 'Is there one word which can express the essence of right conduct in life?' K'ung replied: 'It is the word *shu* – reciprocity: Do not do to others what you do not want them to do to you.'

Ethics 2

The Innateness of the Four Great Virtues: Mencius

The four virtues here referred to – humaneness, righteousness (or justice), propriety and wisdom – sum up the Confucian ethic. Mencius argues here that their roots are in human nature. Thus virtue is human nature properly expressed.

Meng said: 'All men are such that they cannot bear seeing others suffer. The kings of old had this kind of compassion and it governed their policy. One could easily rule the whole world with attitudes like that: it would be like turning it round in the palm of the hand.

'I say that men are like that because anyone seeing a child fall into a well would have a feeling of horror and distress. They don't feel this out of sympathy for the parents, or to gain a reputation among friends and neighbours, or for fear of being considered unfeeling. Not to feel the distress would be against human nature. Similarly not to feel shame and disgrace and not to feel respect for others and not to have a sense of right and wrong are contrary to human nature. The feeling of distress is the beginning of humaneness; the feeling of shame is the beginning of righteousness; the feeling of respect is the beginning of propriety; the feeling of right and wrong is the beginning of wisdom. People have these four sentiments as they have four limbs. To have these four beginnings and to say they can't be developed is to injure oneself; to say that the ruler has them but cannot develop them is to injure him. Since all have them all should be able to develop them and fulfil them. They are like embers ready to burst into flame, or a spring ready to gush forth from the earth. If in fact they can be realized, they will protect the whole world. If they are not then they will not be enough even to protect one's parents.'

Postscript

The Confucian ideology and the examination system centred upon the Classics were the cement for the remarkably stable imperial system which, however, finally crumbled in the face of Western incursions in the 19th and 20th centuries. Signalling the new era was the abolition of the old examination system in 1905. The Classics continued to have influence, but their domination of the cultivated Chinese mind was over. Sun Yat-sen incorporated elements of Confucianism into his Kuomintang ideology in the 1920s. The victory of the Communists in 1949 finally set the seal on the Classical tradition. But Confucian scholarship has flourished outside China in the second half of the 20th century.

Bibliography

Most of the main classics were translated in J. Legge's five–volume series *The Chinese Classics* (repr. 1960). Also useful are:

E.R. Hughes, *The Great Learning and the Mean in Action* (1942); D.C. Lau, *Mencius* (1970) and Wing-tsit Chan, *A Source Book in Chinese Philosophy* (1963)

The Emperor Wu Wang, founder of the Chou dynasty and one of the ideal figures of the Confucian past, presides over a contest between alternative methods of divinations: hexagrams (left) and tortoise shells. The hexagrams found favour; expounded in the I Ching, *they became an important source of speculation in China.*

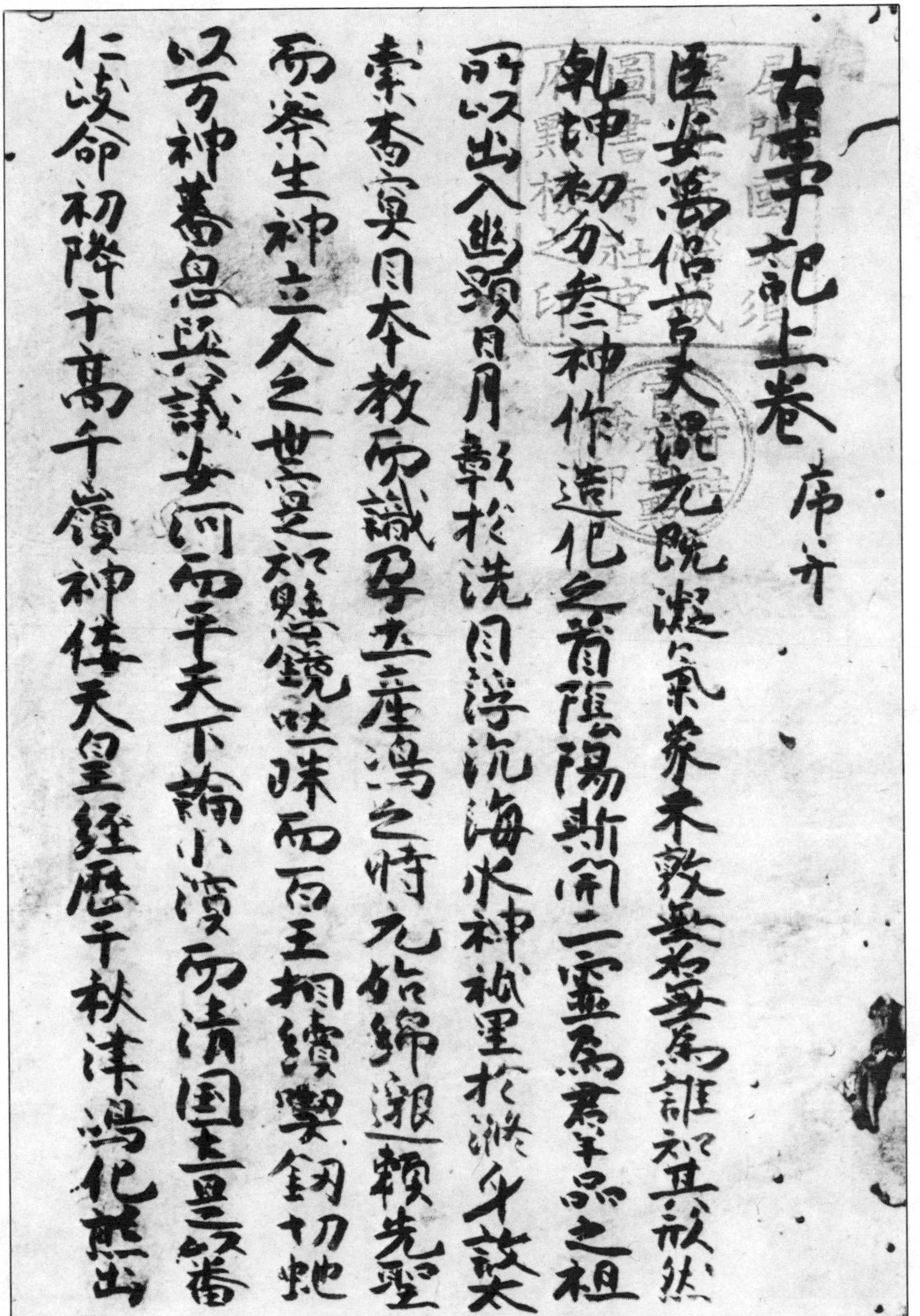
古事記上巻　序并
臣安萬侶言夫混元既凝氣象未效無名無爲誰知其形然
乾坤初分參神作造化之首陰陽斯開二靈爲群品之祖
所以出入幽顯日月彰於洗目浮沈海水神祇呈於滌身故太
素杳冥因本教而識孕土産嶋之時元始綿邈頼先聖
而察生神立人之世寔知懸鏡吐珠而百王相續喫劍切蛇
以萬神蕃息與議安河而平天下論小濱而清國土是以番
仁岐命初降于高千嶺神倭天皇經歴于秋津嶋化熊出

Shinto's historic and mythical traditions are to be found in the scriptures, notably the Kojiki. *This is part of the oldest extant copy of that work, penned by a monk in the 14th century and now lodged in the National Diet Library in Tokyo.*

The rule of the Emperor Meiji saw the creation of modern Japan, and each July a religious ceremony marks the anniversary of his death in 1912. Here, on the third day of the ceremonies, a Shinto priest is purified before he takes part in the final rituals at the shrine.

Shintoism

Introduction

Shinto is the traditional 'way of the gods' and forms an important element in Japanese religious life. It has not been displaced by the ethic of Confucianism nor by Buddhism, although both have proved profoundly influential in Japanese culture. All three strands have been interwoven in Japanese history.

Shinto derives from the most ancient mythic and ritual patterns of the Japanese, and is directed towards the innumerable *kami* or spirits which permeate the past and the present environment of Japan. Its practice is centred in the shrines, where Shinto priests preside over ritual relations with the gods. The original mythology and the early history of Japan and of its imperial house are to be found in the two main compilations which have come to be regarded as the primary sacred texts of Shinto, the *Kojiki* or Records of Ancient Matters and the *Nihongi* or Chronicles of Japan. Both texts were put into written form in the 8th century CE, but were based on a prior oral tradition. The scriptures provided an ideology for the ruling imperial house down the ages, and likewise the innumerable *kami* served as local points of divine contact for particular communities.

In modern times, Shinto was used as the basis for the national awakening of Japan during the Meiji era (from 1868). The Imperial Rescript on Education of 1890 attempted to inject a national traditional sentiment, partly Confucian in tone but Shinto in content, into the new centralized educational system. Its aim was to balance the absorption of Western techniques and ideas, necessary for the modernization of Japan, by a reaffirmation of older ethical and religious values. This more nationalistic Shinto was summed up in the *Kokutai no Hongi* or Cardinal Principles of the National Entity of Japan, the official policy document laying down the ideological line and defining some of the principles of State Shinto. At the end of the Second World War, under the control of the American military authorities, official Shinto was abolished, but Shinto worship has nevertheless continued; shrine worship remains an important ingredient in the religious life of Japan, and some of the new religious movements of Japan reflect Shinto forms.

We have here selected some key passages from the *Nihongi* and *Kojiki*, together with three relatively modern documents – the Imperial Rescript on Education, the *Kokutai ni Hongi* and Hirohito's Rescript of New Year's Day 1946. The first passage is a summary of the mythic beginnings of the world and the events preceding the foundation of the imperial dynasty. The second and the third relate to Amaterasu the Sun Goddess, the most important of the *kami* in the Land of the Rising Sun, and her ancestral relationship with the royal family. Although Shinto is largely without formal doctrines the next passage, from the *Kokutai*, deals with the idea of the harmony between gods, nature and humankind which underlies the Shinto view of the world. Regarding ritual, we reproduce a mythic account of the foundation of Shinto's most ancient shrine. The next passage shows the change brought about by the postwar revolution, affirming Shinto's institutional severance from the State and its transformation into a cultic tradition for private or family observance. Next, a brief excerpt from the *Kokutai* expresses something of the experiences associated with the reverence of the *kami* at the shrines. Finally, an illustration of the Shinto ethic, influenced by Confucianism, will be found in the Imperial Rescript on Education.

Sacred Narrative 1

The Origins: Kojiki, Preface

This preface was written by the compiler of the records, and shows off the Chinese written style. It summarizes the early sections of the *Kojiki*.

I, Yasumaro, say:

Now when chaos had begun to condense, but force and form were not yet manifest, and there was nought named, nought done, who could know its shape? Nevertheless Heaven and Earth first parted, and the Three Deities performed the commencement of creation; the Passive and Active Essences then developed, and the Two Spirits became the ancestors of all things.[1] Therefore did he enter obscurity and emerge into light, and the Sun and Moon were revealed by the washing of his eyes; he floated on and on plunged into the sea-water, and Heavenly and Earthly Deities appeared through the ablutions of his person. So in the dimness of the great commencement, we, by relying on the original teaching, learn the time of the conception of the earth and of the birth of islands; in the remoteness of the original beginning, we, by trusting the former sages, perceive the era of the genesis of Deities and of the establishment of men.

[1] The three deities are the first gods to emerge, who typically of the *kami* have complex names: Master-of-the-August-Centre-of-Heaven, High-August-Wondrous-Producing, Divine-Producing-Wondrous. More important are the active and passive beings, Izanami and Izanagi (literally the Female-Who-Invites and the Male-Who-Invites).

Sacred Narrative 2

Birth of Amaterasu: Nihongi

This myth describes the birth of the Sun Goddess, and though she is not depicted as Creator, she is the central focus of attention in the elaborate scheme of descent by which the imperial family and the whole of Japan claimed a divine essence.

Izanagi no Mikoto and Izanami no Mikoto consulted together, saying: 'We have now produced the Great-eight-island country, with the mountains, rivers, herbs and trees. Why should we not produce someone who shall be lord of the universe?' They then together produced the Sun Goddess, who was called Ō-hiru-me no muchi.[1]

(Called in one writing Amaterasu no Ō kami.)

(In one writing she is called Amaterasu-ō-hiru-me no Mikoto.)

The resplendent lustre of this child shone throughout all the six quarters.

Therefore the two Deities rejoiced, saying: 'We have had many children, but none of them have been equal to this wondrous infant. She ought not to be kept long in this land, but we ought of our own accord to send her at once to Heaven, and entrust to her the affairs of Heaven.'

At this time Heaven and Earth were still not far separated, and therefore they sent her up to Heaven by the ladder of Heaven.

They next produced the Moon-god.

(Called in one writing Tsuki-yumi no Mikoto, or Tsuki-yomi no Mikoto.)

His radiance was next to that of the Sun in splendour. This God was to be the consort of the Sun Goddess, and to share in her government. They therefore sent him also to Heaven.

Next they produced the leech-child, which even at the age of three years could not stand upright. They therefore placed it in the rock-camphor-wood boat of Heaven, and abandoned it to the winds.

Their next child was Susa-no-o.

(Called in one writing Kami Sosa-no-o no Mikoto or Haya Sosa-no-o no Mikoto.)

This God had a fierce temper and was given to cruel acts. Moreover he made a practice of continually weeping and wailing. So he brought many of the people of the land to an untimely end. Again he caused green mountains to become withered. Therefore the two Gods, his parents, addressed Sosa-no-o no Mikoto, saying: 'Thou art exceedingly wicked, and it is not meet that thou shouldst reign over the world. Certainly thou must depart far away to the Netherland.' So they at length expelled him.

Sacred Narrative 3

The Creation of the Divine Ancestors: Kojiki

The ancestors of the imperial line are here produced by Amaterasu and her wild brother, the stormy Susa-no-o, through the agency of her divine ornaments, which are prototypes of the imperial regalia, handed on at each succession.

---

[1] This name means Great-Female-Noon-of-Possessor. The more usual name is Amaterasu or Heaven-Shining [Deity].

So thereupon His-Swift-Impetuous-Male-Augustness said: 'If that be so, I will take leave of Amaterasu, and depart.' He forthwith went up to Heaven, whereupon all the mountains and rivers shook, and every land and country quaked. So the Heaven-Shining-Deity, alarmed at the noise, said: 'The reason of the ascent hither of His Augustness my elder brother is surely no good intent. It is only that he wishes to wrest my land from me.' And she forthwith, unbinding her august hair, twisted it into august bunches; and both into the left and into the right august bunch, as likewise into her august head-dress and likewise on to her left and her right august arm, she twisted an augustly complete string of curved jewels eight feet long of five hundred jewels; and, slinging on her back a quiver holding a thousand arrows, and adding thereto a quiver holding five hundred arrows, she likewise took and slung at her side a mighty and high-sounding elbow-pad, and brandished and stuck her bow upright so that the top shook; and she stamped her feet into the hard ground up to her opposing thighs, kicking away the earth like rotten snow, and stood valiantly like unto a mighty man, and waiting, asked: 'Wherefore ascendest thou hither?' Then Susa-no-o replied, saying, 'I have no evil intent. It is only that when the Great-August-Deity our father spoke, deigning to enquire the cause of my wailing and weeping, I said: "I wail because I wish to go to my deceased mother's land;" whereupon the Great-August-Deity said: "Thou shalt not dwell in this land," and deigned to expel me with a divine expulsion. It is therefore, solely with the thought of taking leave of thee and departing, that I have ascended hither. I have no strange intentions.' Then the Heaven-Shining-Deity said: 'If that be so, whereby shall I know the sincerity of thine intentions?' Thereupon Susa-no-o replied, saying 'Let each of us swear, and produce children.' So as they then swore to each other from the opposite banks of the Tranquil River of Heaven, the august names of the Deities that were born from the mist of her breath when, having first begged Susa-no-o to hand her the ten-grasp sabre which was girded on him and broken it into three fragments, and with the jewels making a jingling sound, having brandished and washed them in the True-Pool-Well of Heaven, and having crunchingly crunched them, the Heaven-Shining-Deity blew them away, were Her Augustness Torrent-Mist-Princess, another august name for whom is Her Augustness Princess-of-the-Island-of-the-Offing; next Her Augustness Lovely-Island-Princess, another august name for whom is Her Augustness Good-Princess; next Her Augustness Princess-of-the-Torrent. The august name of the Deity that was born from the mist of his breath when, having begged the Heaven-Shining-Deity to hand him the augustly complete string of curved jewels eight feet long of five hundred jewels that was twisted in the left august bunch of her hair, and with the jewels making a jingling sound having brandished and washed them in the True-Pool-Well of Heaven, and having crunchingly crunched them, Susa-no-o blew them away, was His Augustness Truly - Conqueror - I - Conquer - Conquering - Swift - Heavenly - Great - Great - Ears. The august name of the Deity that was born from the mist of his breath when again, having begged her to hand him the jewels that were twisted in the right august bunch of her hair, and having crunchingly crunched them, he blew them away, was His Augustness Ame-no-hohi. The august name of the Deity that was born from the mist of his breath when again, having begged her to hand him the jewels that were twisted in her august head-dress, and having crunchingly crunched them, he blew them away, was His Augustness Prince-Lord-of-Heaven. The august name of the Deity that was born from the mist of his breath when again, having begged her to hand him the jewels that were twisted on her left august arm, and having crunchingly crunched them, he blew them away, was His Augustness Prince-Lord-of-Life. The august name of the Deity that was born from the jewels that were twisted on her right august arm, and having crunchingly crunched them, he blew them away, was His-Wondrous-Augustness-of-Kumanu. Five Deities in all.

Doctrine

Harmony between Humankind and Nature: Kokutai ni Hongi

Here the Western alienation between God and humanity and between humanity and nature is contrasted with the Shinto consciousness of national harmony.

Furthermore, in our country one finds harmony between God and man. When we compare this with the relationship between God and man in Western countries, we notice a great difference. Such things as the expulsion and punishment by God and His severe chastisement, which appear in Occidental mythology, differ widely from our nation's stories handed down since of old; and here we find a great difference between the relationship between God and man as of our nation and that as of Western nations. This is a thing clearly seen also in our nation's religious rites and Shinto prayers; and in our country, God is not a terrible being, but One that extends divine help and is fondly esteemed and toward whom gratitude is felt. And the relationship between God and man is extremely intimate.

Again, this harmony is also seen in the most intimate relationship between man and nature. Our country is surrounded by the sea, excels in mountains, is blessed with limpid waters and with happy changes in the four seasons, and has natural features not found in other countries. These beautiful natural features were brought to birth by the heavenly deities together with the many deities; and though they be things on which one may set one's affection they are certainly not objects of fear. It is here that our national trait to love nature is begotten and the harmony between man and nature is established. India, for instance, is overpowered by her natural features, and in the Occident one senses the subjugation of nature by man, and there is not found a deep harmony between man and nature as in our country. On the contrary, our people are in constant harmony with nature. In literature, too, many are the poems that sing of this harmonious mind toward nature, and deep love toward nature forms the principal theme of our poetry. This is not confined to the world of literature; but in our daily lives, too, nature and human existence harmonize. If we look at the events of the year according to the four seasons mentioned in *Kuji Kongen* and others, we see the exquisite harmony since of old between human existence and nature. The New Year's functions, needless to say, and the Dolls' Festival in March are functions that befit the natural beauties of spring, and the Chrysanthemum Festival also befits the greeting of autumn. In our country, where the transitions between the seasons are clearly marked, this harmony of nature and human existence is especially and beautifully vivid. Besides, in family crests zoological and botanical designs are much used, and in attire, architectural objects, and gardens, too, natural beauty is effectively used. This intimate, single relationship between nature and man, also, finds its source in our original, national ideology in which man and nature enjoy coalescent intimacy.

Ritual

The Most Ancient Shrine: Nihongi

This myth delineates the establishment of the shrine in Izumo which is regarded as the most ancient of all Japan's ritual centres. A visit there is efficacious for those who wish to marry and for promoting concord within families.

After this Princess Yamato became the wife of Prince Plenty. This God, however, was never seen in the day-time, but came at night. Princess Yamato said to her husband: 'As my Lord is never seen in the day-time, I am unable to view his august countenance distinctly; I beseech him therefore to delay a while, that in the morning I may look upon the majesty of his beauty.' The Great God answered and said: 'What thou sayest is clearly right. Tomorrow morning I will enter thy toilet-case and stay there. I pray thee be not alarmed at my form.' Princess Yamato wondered secretly in her heart at this. Waiting until daybreak, she looked into her toilet-case. There was there a beautiful little snake, of the length and thickness of the cord of a garment. Thereupon she was frightened, and uttered an exclamation. The Great God was ashamed, and changing suddenly into human form, spake to his wife, and said 'Thou didst not contain thyself, but hast caused me shame: I will in my turn put thee to shame.' So treading the Great Void, he ascended to Mount Mimoro. Hereupon Princess Yamato looked up and had remorse. She flopped down on a seat and with a chopstick stabbed herself in the pudenda so that she died. She was buried at O-chi. Therefore the men of that time called her tomb the Chopstick Tomb. This tomb was made by men in the day-time, and by Gods at night. It was built of stones carried from Mount O-saka. Now the people standing close to each other passed the stones from hand to hand, and thus transported them from the mountain to the tomb. The men of that time made a song about this, saying:

If one passed from hand to hand
  The rocks
  Built up
  On Ō-saka,
How hard 'twould be to send them!

Institutional Expression

Separation of Shinto and State: Imperial Rescript, January 1, 1946

The Emperor Hirohito here affirms plainly the separation of Shinto and State, by rejecting the more extravagant claims of the *Kokutai ni Hongi*; yet at the same time the solidarity of people and emperor in feeling is maintained.

In greeting the new year we recall to mind that the Emperor Meiji proclaimed as the basis of our national policy the five clauses of the charter at the beginning of the Meiji era. The charter oath signified:

(1) Deliberate assemblies shall be established and all measures of government decided in accordance with public opinion.

(2) All classes high and low shall unite in vigorously carrying on the affairs of State.

(3) All common people, no less than the civil and military officials, shall be allowed to fulfil their just desires so that there may not be any discontent among them.

(4) All the absurd usages of old shall be broken through and equity and justice to be found in the workings of nature shall serve as the basis of action.

(5) Wisdom and knowledge shall be sought throughout the world for the purpose of promoting the welfare of the Empire.

The proclamation is evident in its significance and high in its ideals. We wish to make this oath anew and restore the country to stand on its own feet again. We have to reaffirm the principles embodied in the charter and proceed unflinchingly toward elimination of misguided practices of the past; and, keeping in close touch with the desires of the people, we will construct a new Japan through thoroughly being pacific, the officials and the people alike obtaining rich culture and advancing the standard of living of the people.

The devastation of the war inflicted on our cities the miseries of the destitute, the stagnation of trade, shortage of food and the great and growing number of the unemployed are indeed heartrending; but if the nation is firmly united in its resolve to face the present ordeal and to see civilization consistently in peace, a bright future will undoubtedly be ours, not only for our country but for the whole of humanity.

Love of the family and love of country are especially strong in this country. With more of this devotion should we now work toward love of mankind.

We feel deeply concerned to note that consequent upon the protracted war ending in our defeat our people are liable to grow restless and to fall into the slough of despond. Radical tendencies in excess are gradually spreading and the sense of morality tends to lose its hold on the people with the result that there are signs of confusion of thought.

We stand by the people and we wish always to share with them in their moment of joys and sorrows. The ties between us and our people have always stood upon mutual trust and affection. They do not depend upon mere legends and myths. They are not predicated on the false conception that the Emperor is divine and that the Japanese people are superior to other races and fated to rule the world.

Our Government should make every effort to alleviate their trials and tribulations. At the same time, we trust that the people will rise to the occasion and will strive courageously for the solution of their outstanding difficulties and for the development of industry and culture. Acting upon a consciousness of solidarity and of mutual aid and broad tolerance in their civic life, they will prove themselves worthy of their best tradition. By their supreme endeavours in that direction they will be able to render their substantial contribution to the welfare and advancement of mankind.

The resolution for the year should be made at the beginning of the year. We expect our people to join us in all exertions looking to accomplishment of this great undertaking with an indomitable spirit.

Experience

Purity and Awe: Kokutai ni Hongi

Though this document is partly nationalistic in spirit, it also delineates the sense of purification which a visit to a shrine may bring, and the sense of quiet awe before the *kami*.

At festivals we serve the deities by purifying ourselves, with sincerity revere the dignity of the deities, return thanks for their benefits, and offer earnest prayers. (The sentiment in coming before the deities springs in our country from the most fundamental element seen in the relationship between parents and children. In effect, it is found in drawing near to our ancestors by purifying ourselves of our sins and stains, in leaving self behind to unite with the public, and in 'dying to self' to become one with the State.)

And as a natural expression of a devout heart which has been purified we find an example in a poem by Saigyō Hōshi [A.D. 1118–90] which reads:

What is enshrined I do not know,
But the awe of a sense of gratitude
Brings tears to my eyes.

Ethics

The Japanese Ethos: Imperial Rescript on Education, October 30, 1890

Know ye, Our Subjects:

Our Imperial Ancestors have founded Our empire on a basis broad and everlasting and have deeply and firmly implanted virtue; Our subjects ever united in loyalty and filial piety have from generation to generation illustrated the beauty thereof. This is the glory of the fundamental character of Our Empire, and herein also lies the source of Our education. Ye, Our subjects, be filial to your parents, affectionate to your brothers and sisters; as husbands and wives be harmonious, as friends true; bear yourselves in modesty and moderation; extend your benevolence to all; pursue learning and cultivate arts, and thereby develop intellectual faculties and perfect moral powers; furthermore, advance public good and promote common interests; always respect the Constitution and observe the laws; should emergency arise, offer yourselves courageously to the State; and thus guard and maintain the prosperity of Our Imperial Throne coeval with heaven and earth. So shall ye not only be Our good and faithful subjects, but render illustrious the best traditions of your forefathers.

The Way here set forth is indeed the teaching bequeathed by Our Imperial Ancestors, to be observed alike by Their Descendants and the subjects, infallible for all ages and true in all places. It is Our wish to lay it to heart in all reverence, in common with you, Our subjects, that We may all thus attain to the same virtue.

Postscript

In addition to traditional shrine Shinto, during the Meiji and modern period a variety of revivalist Shinto movements, or Sect Shinto, have developed, the most important being Tenrikyō, founded by Nakayama Miki (1798–1887). These movements often blend Shinto with other religious motifs. Since World War II, there has been a renewal of interest in Shinto as a philosophy exhibiting an open-ended and non-dogmatic naturalism. Thus some of the teachings of the *Kokutai* remain influential even though its military ideology has been transcended.

Bibliography

Kojiki, tr. B. H. Chamberlain (1932)
Nihongi, tr. W. G. Aston (1896)
Kokutai ni Hongi, tr. J.O. Gauntlett (1949): this includes the Imperial Rescripts of 1890 and 1946 as appendices.

Also useful is Ryusaku Tsunoda, W. Theodore de Bary and Donald Keene (eds.), *Sources of Japanese Tradition*, vol. 1 (1958).

ਜਪੁ ਜੀ ਸਾਹਿਬ

ੴ ਸਤਿਨਾਮੁ ਕਰਤਾ ਪੁਰਖੁ
ਨਿਰਭਉ ਨਿਰਵੈਰੁ ਅਕਾਲ ਮੂਰਤਿ
ਅਜੂਨੀ ਸੈਭੰ ਗੁਰ ਪ੍ਰਸਾਦਿ ॥

॥ ਜਪੁ ॥

ਆਦਿ ਸਚੁ ਜੁਗਾਦਿ ਸਚੁ ॥
ਹੈ ਭੀ ਸਚੁ ਨਾਨਕ ਹੋਸੀ ਭੀ ਸਚੁ ॥੧॥
ਸੋਚੈ ਸੋਚਿ ਨ ਹੋਵਈ ਜੇ ਸੋਚੀ ਲਖ
ਵਾਰ ॥ ਚੁਪੈ ਚੁਪ ਨ ਹੋਵਈ
ਜੇ ਲਾਇ ਰਹਾ ਲਿਵ ਤਾਰ ॥ ਭੁਖਿਆ
ਭੁਖ ਨ ਉਤਰੀ ਜੇ ਬੰਨਾ ਪੁਰੀਆ ਭਾਰ ॥
ਸਹਸ ਸਿਆਣਪਾ ਲਖ ਹੋਹਿ
ਤ ਇਕ ਨ ਚਲੈ ਨਾਲਿ ॥

The mūl mantra, *and the opening lines of the* Japjī, *which constitute the central formulation of Sikh belief* (see page 330)*, printed in a prayer book for private use.*

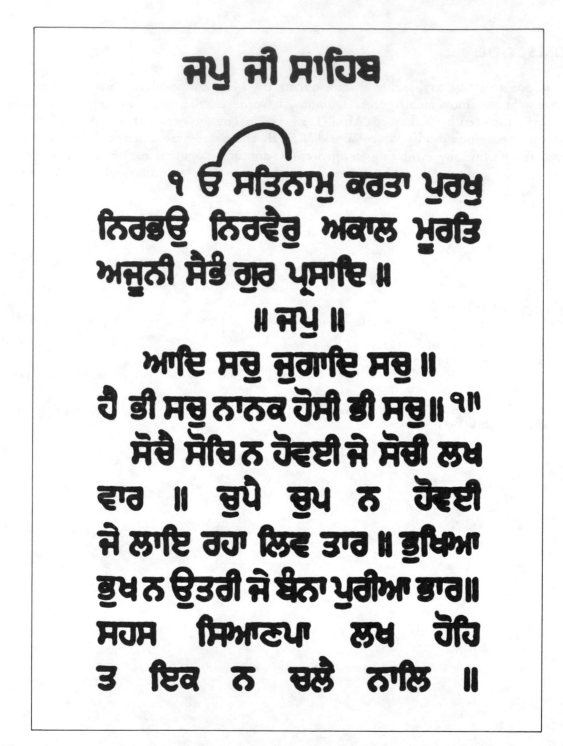

Sikhism

Introduction

Sikhism derives from the 15th century in India, and reflects in its origins a desire to cut through the external differences which separated Muslims and Hindus and caste from caste. The life and thought of Kabīr (1440–1518) had already linked Hindu devotionalism and Muslim mysticism; but the chief leader of the new movement and first of a line of leaders and teachers, the ten Sikh Gurūs, was Nānak (1469–1539), around whose life grew many stories of his experiences, travels and teachings. Such life stories, known as *Janamsākhī*, are not canonical, but reflect traditional piety towards the founder. We reproduce here a famous passage from these writings, recounting a major visionary experience of Nānak's life and the occasion of his prophetic calling. Other Gurūs maintained Nānak's fervent and peaceable teachings during periods of persecution. The fifth compiled the *Adi Granth*, which became the central scripture of the Sikhs, and held a crucial place in the life of the community after the passing of the tenth Gurū, Gurū Gobind, for the text was now treated as the Gurū. It is thus commonly spoken of as the Gurū Granth, and occupies the sacred central position in a Sikh place of worship. It is the essential focus of divine presence, as was the living human Gurū in the earlier tradition.

With the tenth Gurū, the Sikhs became a military community, and were ready to fight to preserve their existence, mainly in the area of the Punjab. The community was defined as the pure, the Khālsā, and came to be culturally different from both Hindus and Muslims through the use of external badges such as unshorn hair and the wearing of a steel bangle on the right arm. Thus paradoxically Sikhism, starting from the desire to cut through externals, has developed its own particular forms and separate scriptural traditions. But the sense of the central importance of the right inner spiritual attitudes to the One God pervades the *Ādi Granth*. The work is an anthology of hymns, chiefly of the first five Gurūs. A separate volume contains works ascribed to the last Gurū, some of which of disputed authenticity.

The first of the passages we reproduce is from a *Janamsākhī*. The second is the opening part of the Gurū Nānak's *Japjī*, and expresses the central creed of Sikhism. The third passage illustrates the central emphasis of Sikh ritual from early times: fervent worship of the Divine Being and the repetition and remembrance of the Divine Name. This passage too comes from the *Japjī*, which is the chief prayer of the faith. The following text is the primary Sikh congregational prayer, and recalls in brief compass the heritage of the community as institutionally organized by Gobind Singh, who composed the first part of the prayer. To illustrate the dimension of experience, we reproduce a hymn which in origin expresses the progressive union of the soul with God, and thus blends themes from devotion (*bhakti*) and the contemplative mysticism of the Indian tradition. Finally, there is a hymn showing how truth in conduct is the mainspring of ethics.

Sacred Narrative

Nānak's Call: A Janamsākhī

In this extract from a *Janamsākhī*, a life story of Nānak, the Gurū has a profound visionary experience which changes his life. He is supposed to have gone out by night to swim in the river, and disappeared for a while. The servant who accompanied him heard a mysterious voice in the darkness saying 'Do not lose patience'. While the river was being dredged on the supposition that Nānak had drowned, he ascended to God. Three days later he emerged from the river, and thereafter was a changed man.

Nānak made his obeisance. The Almighty gave him a bowl of milk. 'Nānak! Drink this bowl,' He commanded. 'It is not milk as it may seem; this is nectar (*amrit*). It will give thee power of prayer, love of worship, truth and contentment.'

Nānak drank the nectar and was overcome. He made another obeisance. The Almighty then blessed him. 'I release thee from the cycle of birth, death and rebirth; he that sets his eyes on you with faith will be saved. He that hears your words with conviction will be saved; he that calls on you for succour will be helped by Me; he that you forgive will be forgiven by Me. I grant thee salvation. Nānak, go back to the evil world and teach men and women to pray (*nām*), to give in charity (*dān*) and live cleanly (*iśnān*). Do good to the world and redeem it in the age of sin (*Kaliyuga*).'

Three days later, in the early hours of the dawn following the 15th of Bhadon Sambat 1564, Nānak re-emerged from the Bein. Nānak was then 36 years, 6 months and 15 days old.

Doctrine

God as Truth: Gurū Nanak's Japjī

The Gurū Nanak's *Japjī* is understood by Sikhs to be the most important articulation of their religious tradition. It is repeated silently in the morning, and every Sikh must know it by heart. It opens with the *mūl maṅtra*, or root mantra, which stresses the uniqueness, omnipotence and immortality of God, and concludes with a statement suggesting that knowledge of God is only obtained through the Gurū. The Gurū Nānak wrote this composition towards the end of his life, and it has become enshrined in the *Adi Granth* as its opening formulation on God and truth.

There is but one God whose name is true, the Creator, devoid of fear and enmity, immortal, unborn, self-existent; by the favour of the Gurū.

The True One was in the beginning;
the True One was in the primal age.
The True One is now also, O Nanak;
the True One also shall be.

By thinking I cannot obtain a conception of
Him, even though I think hundreds of
thousands of times.

Even though I be silent and keep my attention
firmly fixed on Him, I cannot preserve
silence.
The hunger of the hungry for God subsideth not
though they obtain the load of the worlds.
If man should have thousands and hundreds of
thousands of devices, even one would not
assist him in obtaining God.
How shall man become true before God?
How shall the veil of falsehood be rent?
By walking, O Nānak, according to the will of
the Commander as preordained.

By His order bodies are produced; His order
cannot be described.
By His order souls are infused into them; by His
order greatness is obtained.
By His order men are high or low; by His order
they obtain preordained pain or pleasure.
By His order some obtain their reward; by His
order others must ever wander in
transmigration.
All are subject to His order; none is exempt
from it.
He who understandeth God's order, O Nānak,
is never guilty of egoism.

Who can sing His power? Who hath power to
sing it?
Who can sing His gifts or know his signs?
Who can sing His attributes, His greatness
and His deeds?
Who can sing His knowledge whose study is
arduous?
Who can sing Him, who fashioneth the body
and again destroyeth it?
Who can sing Him, who taketh away life and
again restoreth it?
Who can sing Him, who appeareth to be far, but
is known to be near?
Who can sing Him, who is all-seeing and
omnipresent?
In describing Him there would be never an end.
Millions of men give millions upon millions of
descriptions of Him, but they fail to
describe Him.
The Giver giveth; the receiver groweth weary of
receiving.
In every age man subsisteth by His bounty.
The Commander by His order hath laid out the
way of the world.
Nānak, God the unconcerned is happy.
True is the Lord, true is His name; it is uttered
with endless love.
People pray and beg, 'Give us, give us'; the
Giver giveth His gifts.
Then what can we offer Him whereby his court
may be seen?
What words shall we utter with our lips, on
hearing which He may love us?
At the ambrosial hour of morning meditate on
the true Name and God's greatness.
The Kind One will give us a robe of honour, and
by His favour we shall reach the gate of
salvation.
Nānak, we shall thus know that God is
altogether true.

He is not established, nor is He created.
The pure one existeth by Himself.
They who worshipped Him have obtained
honour.
Nānak, sing His praises who is the Treasury of
excellences.
Sing and hear and put His love into your hearts.
Thus shall your sorrows be removed, and you
shall be absorbed in Him who is the abode
of happiness.
Under the Gurū's instruction God's word is
heard;
under the Gurū's instruction knowledge is
acquired;
under the Gurū's instruction man learns that
God is everywhere contained.
The Gurū is Śiv; the Gurū is Viṣṇu and Brahmā;
the Gurū is Parvatı, Lakṣmı and Saraswatī.
If I knew Him, should I not describe Him? He
cannot be described by words.
My Gurū hath explained one thing to me –
That there is but one Bestower on all living
beings; may I not forget Him!

Ritual

The Repetition of the Divine Name: The Japjī

The emphasis in this passage from the *Japjī* upon devotion to God and the name reflects the purified sense of ritual in the Sikh tradition; although the scriptures themselves came to be afforded veneration, there was a rejection of external images and the richness of typical Hindu temple cults. Pure and truthful worship concentrates on the name of God as an efficacious symbol of the ultimate truth.

By hearing the Name man obtaineth a knowledge
of the continents, the worlds, and the
nether regions.
By hearing the Name death doth not affect one.
Nanak, the saints are ever happy.
By hearing the Name sorrow and sin are no
more.

By hearing the Name man becometh as Śiv,
Brahmā, and Indar.
By hearing the Name even the low become
highly lauded.
By hearing the Name the way of Yoga and the
secrets of the body are obtained.
By hearing the Name man understandeth the real
nature of the Śāstras, the Smrtis, and the
Vedas.
Nānak, the saints are ever happy.
By hearing the Name sorrow and sin are no
more.

By hearing the Name truth, contentment, and
divine knowledge are obtained.
Hearing the Name is equal to bathing at the
sixty-eight places of pilgrimage.
By hearing the Name and reading it man
obtaineth honour.
By hearing the Name the mind is composed and
fixed on God.
Nānak, the saints are very happy.
By hearing the Name sorrow and sin are no
more.

By hearing the Name, the depth of the sea of
virtue is sounded.
By hearing the Name men become Sheikhs,
Pīrs,[1] and Emperors.
By hearing the Name a blind man findeth his
way.
By hearing the Name the unfathomable becomes
fathomable.
Nānak, the saints are ever happy.
By hearing the Name sorrow and sin are no
more.

The condition of him who obeyeth God cannot
be described.
Whoever trieth to describe it, shall afterward
repent.
There is no paper, or pen, or writer
To describe the condition of him who
obeyeth God.
So pure is His name –
Whoever obeyeth God knoweth the pleasure
of it in his own heart.

By obeying Him wisdom and understanding
enter the mind;
By obeying Him man knoweth all worlds;
By obeying Him man suffereth not
punishment;
By obeying Him man shall not depart with
Yama[2] –
So pure is God's name –
Whoever obeyeth God knoweth the pleasure
of it in his own heart.

By obeying Him man's path is not obstructed;
By obeying Him man departeth with honour
and distinction;

[1] Spiritual leaders and saints in the Islamic tradition.

[2] The Hindu Yama is King of the Dead; this verse means that man shall not die again, but will be absorbed into God.

By obeying Him man proceedeth in ecstasy on his way;
By obeying Him man formeth an alliance with virtue –
So pure is God's name –
Whoever obeyeth God knoweth the pleasure of it in his own heart.

By obeying Him man attaineth the gate of salvation;
By obeying Him man is saved with his family;
By obeying Him the Gurū is saved, and saveth his disciples;
By obeying him, O Nānak, man wandereth not in quest of alms –
So pure is God's name –
Whoever obeyeth God knoweth the pleasure of it in his own heart.

The elect are acceptable, the elect are distinguished;
The elect obtain honour in God's court;
The elect shed lustre on the courts of the kings;
The attention of the elect is bestowed on the one Gurū.
If any one say he can form an idea of God, he may say so,
But the Creator's works cannot be numbered.
The bull that is spoken of is righteousness, the offspring of mercy,
Which supported by patience maintaineth the order of nature.
Whoever understandeth this is a true man.
What a load there is upon the bull!
Beyond this earth there are more worlds, more and more.
What power can support their weight?
The names of living things, their species, and colours
Have all been written with a flowing pen.
Doth any one know how to write an account of them?
If the account were written, how great it would be!
What power and beautiful form are Thine, O God!
Who hath power to know how great Thy gifts are?
By one word Thou didst effect the expansion of the world,
Whereby hundreds of thousands of rivers were produced.
What power have I to describe Thee?
So powerless am I, that I cannot even once be a sacrifice unto Thee.
Whatever pleaseth Thee is good.
Thou, O Formless One, are ever secure.

Numberless Thy worshippers, and numberless Thy lovers;
Numberless Thine adorers, and numberless they who perform austerities for Thee;
Numberless the reciters of sacred books and Veds;
Numberless Thy Yogis whose hearts are indifferent to the world;
Numberless the saints who ponder on Thine attributes and divine knowledge;
Numberless Thy true men; numberless Thine almsgivers;
Numberless Thy heroes who face the steel of their enemies;
Numberless Thy silent worshippers who lovingly fix their thoughts upon Thee.
What power have I to describe Thee?
So lowly am I, that I cannot even once be a sacrifice unto Thee.
Whatever pleaseth Thee is good.
O Formless One, Thou art ever secure.

Numberless are the fools appallingly blind;
Numberless are the thieves and devourers of others' property;
Numberless those who establish their sovereignty by force;
Numberless the cut-throats and murderers;
Numberless the sinners who pride themselves on committing sin;
Numberless the liars who roam about lying;
Numberless the filthy who enjoy filthy gain;
Numberless the slanderers who carry loads of calumny on their heads;
Nānak thus describeth the degraded.
So lowly am I, I cannot even once be a sacrifice unto Thee.
Whatever pleaseth Thee is good.
O Formless One, Thou art ever secure.

Institutional Expression

The Community and its Past Saints: A Congregational Prayer

This prayer contains lines ascribed to Gurū Gobind Singh, and is used at the conclusion of Sikh worship, both in the temple and at home. It celebrates the pure community, the Khālsā. The first part refers to the line of the ten Gurūs who established the Sikh tradition.

Having first remembered Lord thy God, call on Gurū Nānak
And then on Gurū Angad, Amar Dās and Rām Dās:
May they ever protect us.
Then call on Arjun and Hari Gobind and the holy Hari Rai,
And then on Hari Krishna, who can dispel all one's sorrows.
Then remember Tegh Bahādur, the ninth Gurū, that the nine treasures may hasten to thy home.
O masters be ye ever with us.
May the tenth king Gurū Gobind Singh be ever on our side.
And now turn your thoughts to the Gurū Granth Sahib, the visible embodiment of the Gurūs, and say 'Glory be to God'.
(*Congregation responds:*) 'Wonderful Lord.'

The four sons, the five beloved ones, the forty saved ones,[1] the martyrs, the true disciples, the contemplators of God, and those who remained steadfast in the Path: remember their glorious deeds and say 'Glory be to God'.
(*Response*) 'Wonderful Lord.'

Those who constantly remembered God's Name, shared their earnings, wielded the sword on the battlefield, and shared food in companionship, offered their heads at the altar of the holy Law, were cut up limb from limb, were skinned or boiled or sawn alive but uttered not a sign and did not falter in their faith – remember their glorious deeds and say 'Glory be to God'.
(*Response*) 'Wonderful Lord.'

O great King, save us from the five sins of lust, wrath, greed, attachment and egoism. O God, let us call on Thee alone, yea, Thee alone, and let the remembrance be happiness of all kinds. O God, wherever the members of the holy Khālsā are, extend Thy protection and mercy to them. Let the Way be ever victorious: let the sword be forever our protector: let the war-cry of the Khālsā resound across the world: 'Glory be to God'.
(*Response*) 'Wonderful Lord.'

O God, may Thy Sikhs (disciples) be blessed with faith, discipline, trust, mental awakening and, above all, the contemplation of Thy Name.

May the banners, the staying-places, the choirs of the Khālsā stay whole through the ages, and may true religion be ever victorious.

O God, let our minds be for ever humble, and our intellects exalted, and may Thou be ever protector of our minds.

Say, O Khālsā, 'Glory be to God.
(*Response*) 'Wonderful Lord.'

---

[1] The reference is to the sons of Gobind Singh, who were martyred, the first five disciples initiated into the Khālsā by Gurū Gobind, and others who died in battle.

Experience

Spiritual Marriage: The Bāra Māh

It was a common poetical form to compose verses describing the months of the year. In this late poem by Nānak, the soul's journey through the year is beautifully portrayed. Here we see the last three months, which bring an inner marriage between the saint and God. The atmosphere is one of both devotion and mystical contemplation.

The Month of Pokh (December–January)

As in the month of Pokh
Winter's frost doth freeze
The sap in the tree and bush,
So does the absence of the Lord
Kill the body and the mind.
O Lord, why comest not thou?
I praise through the Gurū's Word
Him that gives life to all the world,
His light shines in all life born
Of egg or womb or sweat or seed.
Merciful God and Master, Thy vision grant
And grant me salvation.
Nānak says, only she mingles with Him
Who loves the Lord, giver of life.

The Month of Māgh (January–February)

In the month of Māgh
I made my ablution,
The Lord entered my being,
I made pilgrimage within myself and was purified.
I met Him.
He found me good
And let me lose myself in Him.
'Beloved! If Thou foundest me fair,
My pilgrimage is made,
My ablution done.
More than the sacred waters,
Of Ganga, Yamuna and Triveni mingled at the Sangam,[1]
More than the seven seas.
All these and charity, almsgiving and prayer,
Are the knowledge of eternity that is the Lord.'
Nānak says, Māgh is the essence of ambrosia
For him who hath worshipped the great giver of life . . .

The Month of Phālgun (February–March)

In the month of Phalgun
She whose heart is full of love
Is ever in full bloom.
Day and night she is in spiritual exaltation:
She is in bliss because she hath no love of self.
Only those that love Thee
Conquer love of self.
Be kind to me
And make my home Thy abode.
Many a lovely garment did I wear.
The Master willed not
And his palace doors were barred to me.
When he wanted me I went with garlands and strings of jewels and raiments of finery.
O Nanak, a bride welcomed in the Master's mansion
Hath found her true Lord and Love.

---

[1] The confluence of the three sacred rivers of north India at Prayāg (now Allahabad).

Ethics

Truth as the Heart of Conduct

Since, for Nānak and the Sikh tradition, God is Truth, authenticity is at the heart of Sikh ethics. Evil comes from being immersed in the illusions of the world, instead of being filled with God's goodness. The person who lets Truth into his soul sheds the evils which come from sin.

He alone is truly truthful
In whose heart is the True One living,
Whose soul within is rinsed of falsehood
And his body without is cleansed by washing.
He alone is truly truthful
Who loves truth with passion,
Whose heart rejoices in the Name
And finds the door to salvation.
He alone is truly truthful
Who knows the art of living,
Who prepares his body like a bed
And plants the seed of the Lord therein.
He alone is truly truthful
Who accepts the true message,
Towards the living shows mercy
Gives something as alms and in charity.
He alone is truly truthful
Whose soul in pilgrimage resides,
Who consults the true Gurū
And by his counsel ever abides.
Truth is the nostrum for all ills.
It exorcises sin,
washes the body clean.
Those that have truth in their aprons
Before them doth Nānak himself demean.

Postscript

Since Gurū Gobind Singh declared that the scriptures were the Teacher, the *Granth* has had a central place in Sikh piety. Its words point to God and art in a sense divine, just as the human Gurūs, without being *avatārs* or incarnations of God, for there is in Sikhism no need for any intermediaries between God and humans, were men who attained union with the True. The notion that a gurū can pass on his experience to the pupil is echoed in the thought that it is through the scriptures that God speaks to the faithful disciple. This has led to the creation of a scripture-cult in which offerings are made to the Granth, as in Hinduism ghee, flowers, money and other gifts are offered to images of the gods.

Bibliography

An early source in English including much material from the *Janamsākhīs* is M.A. Macauliffe, *The Sikh Religion*, 6 vols. (1909). A modern anthology is T. Singh and others, *Selections from the Sacred Writings of the Sikhs* (1960). Under Unesco auspices, *The Hymns of Gurū Nānak*, translated by Khushwant Singh, were published in 1969. Another useful source is Gopal Singh, *The Religion of the Sikhs* (1969).

A granthī *reading the* Ādi Granth *(the* Gurū Granth Sahib*) in a Sikh temple. An attendant stands behind him holding a* chauri *symbolizing respect for the scriptures.*

*Black Elk at the centre of the earth (*see page 359*). This illustration of his visionary experience, drawn by Standing Bear, is from* Black Elk Speaks, being the Life Story of a Holy Man of the Ogalala Sioux, as told to John G. Neihardt (Flaming Rainbow), *published in 1932.*

Small-scale Traditional Religions

Introduction

We have collected in this chapter a series of texts from what we describe as small-scale traditional religions. The religions of small-scale communities are usually described as 'primitive' religions or the religions of 'non-literate' peoples. This terminology almost immediately separates these religious documents from those of the 'world-historical' religions, such as Judaism, Christianity and Buddhism. In many collections of sacred texts they are omitted entirely, contributing to the invisibility of small-scale traditional religions and further removing them to the antechamber of real religious texts. However, it should be remembered that if we reckon that cultural man has been on earth for some 2,000,000 years, then for over 99 per cent of this period he has lived as a member of small-scale traditional societies. The anthropologists estimate that only in the last 10,000 years or so has man begun to domesticate plant life and animals. It was of course the agricultural revolution, as it appeared in various parts of the world at different times, that established the cultural foundations of the religious traditions represented in the other chapters of this volume. Of the estimated 150 billion human beings who have lived on earth, the anthropologists tell us, over 60 per cent have lived in small-scale societies dependent upon hunting and gathering for their food sources; approximately 35 per cent have lived by agriculture, both small-scale and large-scale; and the remaining few per cent of human beings have lived in our familiar industrial-technological societies, characterized by extensive social differentiation. The implication of these simple figures is that the great majority of human religious experience has been within the context of small-scale society. For this reason alone, the religious texts of the 'small-scales' must be included in our effort to understand the diversity of religious experience and its communication in sacred documents.

Almost every text included in this chapter has been recorded by anthropologists and ethnographers in its living context. While the texts were not written down by individuals within the tradition, but were preserved for successive generations in oral tradition, they must nevertheless be understood as authoritative documents and texts. Revelation, in the same way that it functions in determining the authority of other religious texts, is crucial in small-scale traditional religions. The 'sacred book', so important in the religions of our world, is replaced in small-scale traditional religions by authoritative individuals who transmit the text in oral form. Here, the reader will encounter individuals such as Black Elk and Ogotemmêli, who will transmit that which is most important to them and to the construction of their worldviews. Each text is authoritative, in that it is preserved by individuals who are understood to be authoritative and in the degree to which they inform the entire spectrum of traditional life.

Within small-scale traditional religions there is consistently a sharp distinction between 'true' and 'false' narratives and stories. The 'true' narratives are what many scholars describe as myth and what we understand as the dimension of sacred narrative. We have collected a series of texts which are examples of repeated motifs in creation narratives, or narratives which describe not only the creation of the world, but also how the world became liveable for human beings. Many creation narratives begin with the earth in place and human beings, the ancestors, emerging from it. Here, we reproduce a Pueblo narrative which exemplifies the emergence motif. In some creation narratives, the world and the first humans are the result of cosmic parents or twins who existed at the very beginning of time; here we have included two such narratives, one from Polynesia and the second from the Zuñi. In other creation narratives, the world was created from a cosmic egg or shell. This is illustrated by a Polynesian narrative in which the High-God Ta'aroa creates the world from a primordial shell which is surrounded by complete darkness. Another motif found in creation narratives is creation from nothing. This motif is most familiar to us from the opening chapter of the Book of Genesis in the Hebrew Bible, and we have included two narratives to illustrate it, the first from the Australian aborigines, the second another narrative about Ta'aroa. Yet another motif found in these sacred narratives describing the creation of the world is what anthropologists and folklorists describe as the earth-diver motif, which we have illustrated through a Siberian-Altaic myth. Lastly, some creation narratives preserve the motif of creation through a primordial sacrifice, illustrated here by one of the most important myths of small-scale traditional religions, the myth of Hainuwele.

Under the dimension of doctrine, we have included three texts which illustrate reflection upon God among the small-scale traditional religions: a text on the nature and reality of Ngai, the High-God of the Gikuyu, then a traditional Pygmy hymn on God, and lastly a Dakota Indian on wakan beings and Wakan Tanka. Many other realities of the small-scale religions might have been presented here, but the doctrinal issue of the nature of God is most important. Here, the reader will encounter three sophisticated descriptions which may be placed along other such sophisticated reflections upon God.

The ritual dimension is illustrated by three texts. The first two, from the Yahuna of the Amazonian basin and Cahuilla Indians of California, describe the origin of plant life, which is vital to human life. These narratives are similar to the narrative of Hainuwele, in that human life is made possible through the plants generated from the body of the ancestor. Agriculture is thus the ritual extension of the events presented by the creation narrative. Planting, harvesting, and using plant life are not simply understood as a human necessity, but are a ritual repetition of events which took place at the very beginning of time. The third text describes the conditions under which a Teton Sioux would participate in the ritual of the Sun Dance.

We have chosen to illustrate the institutional dimension first by an anthropologist's summary of the sacred narrative of the Ngaju Dayak of Borneo. This narrative indicates that all human institutions are the result of mythic actions at the beginning of time. The institutional life of the village, kinship structures and human relations, indeed every stage of human life from birth to death is given reality and meaning by its relationship to those events. Second, we have included a song from the Gabon pygmies on their experience of exile. This text illustrates the difficulty of real human life in any institutional form when one is cut off from one's place. Last, we have included a Dogon text narrating the descent of the cosmic granary to earth.

The dimension of experience among small-scale traditional religions is perhaps best illustrated by the figure of the shaman. The word 'shaman' is an Ural-Altaic word used to describe a specific technician of the sacred. The shaman is able to ascend to the world of the gods (in some cases he journeys to the bottom of the sea) and return to the world of human beings. His technical knowledge and experience make the shaman a particularly powerful figure within small-scale traditional religions, since he is able to cure the sick, ensure the success of the hunt, and accompany the dead to the world of the ancestors. Here, we include a description of how an individual became a shaman from the Kwakiutl Indians of the Pacific Northwest. The dimension of experience is also illustrated by the Vision Quest among Native American peoples. Here we include two texts from the Sioux. The first describes Brave Buffalo's visionary experience, and the second is Black Elk's detailed record of his experience. Lastly, we have included the testimony of Jack Wilson, who after his experience later reclaimed his Paiute name, Wavoka. Narrated in the form of a letter, his experience was to become central in one of the most influential pan-Native American movements of the 1890's, the Ghost Dance. Here, we include an anthropologist's description of how the experience of Wavoka was acted out in the dance.

Among small-scale traditional religions, the ethical dimension is best illustrated in the instruction given to men and women during the rituals which mark the stages of life or the passage from one stage to another. It is in the context of these rituals that the individual is given the code of conduct and told the manner in which he is to organize his life: the old ways are left behind and one takes on new responsibilities appropriate to the new stage of existence. Here, we include a brief example from the Yamana of ethical instruction given to individuals in the ritual of transition.

Sacred Narrative 1

The Emergence of the Worlds (Pueblo)

The following sacred narrative illustrates the emergence motif common in many small-scale traditional religions. The narrative indicates that at the beginning of time, when the earth was soft, everything could talk and growth was very rapid. The time when these events took place was very different from our time. It should be noted that this narrative represents a composite drawn from various informants.

'Long ago when the earth was soft' all the relations with the Spirits were more intimate. Everything could talk, animals, plants, even wood or stone. The kachina came in person to dance or, as at Acoma, to fight. Coyote was a well-behaved messenger between the underworld and White House. The War Brothers begotten by Sun or Water not only produced order by finding the directions or making mountains and valleys but led the migrant people or borrowed curing societies or freed people from dangerous personages or from monsters the women had borne in the lower world after they quarrelled with the men. Sun became a handsome man to appear on earth to his sons. It was a golden age. Water gushed from rocks [Isleta]. Dew Boy made corn grow for the people of Oraibi in a single day, giving the seeds to the Corn clan. The seeds the

Keresan Mothers obtained from their skin were planted at sunrise, ripened at noon, and were dry at sunset. It was only after the trouble with P'ashaya'ni that corn had to be planted as it is planted today. In those days all growth was miraculously rapid. The War Brothers as well as other children begot by the gods grew up overnight or rather in four days. Even human persons were wonderful. The two girls who played hide-and-seek with Ne'wekwe and perched invisible on his hair plumes were able to do this 'because the world was still new. When the world was raw, people used to be like this. They were very wonderful in those days, the old people tell us.'

The underworld, the four underground wombs or levels, was dark [Zuñi]; Sun sent emissaries to the underworld people to bid them come up into the light. Sun wanted company and prayer-sticks and prayer-meal. In Keresan myth [Acoma excepted] the upper world was dark, the sun was a secondary creation. The 'Mothers' sent out Ma'sewi to look for the sun and, having found it, to place it properly. Tewa emissaries to the upper world seek for the proper 'directions', but they are not aided by Sun. In Tewa, Isleta and Jemez myth, Sun does not figure at all in the Emergence. Hopi make their sun by throwing upward a back tablet or shield covered with buckskin or cotton cloth together with a fox skin and a parrot tail, for the lights of dawn.

Sacred Narrative 2

Rangi and Papa Create the World (Polynesia)

In this narrative we find the myth of cosmic parents, identified with the heaven and earth. However, while they remain united there is no room for human life. Creation, at least of the world of their children, is the result of separation. It is the separation of the cosmic parents which allows real life and the definition of the elements in the cosmos, such as darkness and light.

According to the traditions of our race, Rangi and Papa, or Heaven and Earth, were the source from which, in the beginning, all things originated. Darkness then rested upon the heaven and upon the earth, and they still both clove together, for they had not yet been rent apart; and the children they had begotten were ever thinking amongst themselves what might be the difference between darkness and light; they knew that beings had multiplied and increased, and yet light had never broken upon them, but it ever continued dark.

Sacred Narrative 3

The Cosmic Parents and Twin Brothers (Zuñi)

In this sacred narrative, the cosmic parents are the Sun-father and Foam-cap. They generate the twin brothers who, by using their knives, enter the dark of the underworld where they organize human life and bring all living creatures to the surface of the earth.

Then did the Sun-father take counsel within himself, and casting his glance downward espied, on the great waters, a Foam-cap near to the Earth-mother. With his beam he impregnated and with his heat incubated the Foam-cap, whereupon she gave birth to Úanam Achi Píahkoa, the Beloved Twain who descended; first, Úanam Éhkoma, the Beloved Preceder, then Úanam Yáluna, the Beloved Follower, Twin brothers of Light, yet Elder and Younger, the Right and the Left, like to question and answer in deciding and doing. To them the Sun-father imparted, still retaining, control-thought and his own knowledge-wisdom, even as to the offspring of wise parents their knowingness is imparted and as to his right hand and his left hand a skillful man gives craft freely surrendering not his knowledge. He gave them, of himself and their mother the Foam-cap, the great cloud-bow, and for arrows the thunderbolts of the four quarters (twain to either) and for buckler the fog-making shield, which (spun of the floating clouds and spray and woven, as of cotton we spin and weave) supports as on wind, yet hides (as a shadow hides) its bearer, defending also. And of men and all creatures he gave them the fathership and dominion, also as a man gives over the control of his work to the management of his hands. Well instructed of the Sun-father, they lifted the Sky-father with their great cloud-bow into the vault of the high zenith, that the earth might become warm and thus fitter for their children, men and the creatures. Then along the trail of the sun seeking Póshaiyank'ya, they sped backward swiftly on their floating fog-shield, westward to the Mountain of Generation. With their magic knives of the thunderbolt they spread open the uncleft depths of the mountain, and still on their cloud-shield – even as a spider in her web descendeth – so descended they unerringly, into the dark of the underworld. There they abode with men and the creatures, attending them, coming to know them, and becoming known of them as masters and fathers, thus seeking the ways for leading them forth.

Sacred Narrative 4

Ta'aroa Creates the Cosmos (Polynesia)

The central motif in this sacred narrative is the cosmic egg or shell. Here the High-God, Ta'aroa, creates the world from a shell. All reality reflects the structure of this first shell occupied by Ta'aroa, from the heaven and earth to men and women.

For a long period Ta'aroa dwelt in his shell [crust]. It was round like an egg and revolved in space in continuous darkness.

There was no sun, no moon, no land, no mountain, all was in a confluent state. There was no man, no beast, no fowl, no dog, no living thing, no sea, and no fresh water.

But at last Ta'aroa was filling his shell, as he sat in close confinement, and it cracked, and broke open. Then he slipped out and stood upon the shell, and he cried out, 'Who is above there? Who is below there?' No voice answered! 'Who is in front there? Who is in back there?' No voice answered! Only the echo of his own voice resounded and nothing else.

Then Ta'aroa said, 'O rock, crawl hither!' But there was no rock to crawl to him. And he said, 'O sand, crawl hither!' But there was no sand to crawl to him. Then he got vexed because he was not obeyed.

So he overturned his shell and raised it up to form a dome for the sky and called it Rumia. And he became wearied and after a short period he slipped out of another shell that covered him, which he took for rock and for sand. But his anger was not yet appeased, so he took his spine for a mountain range, his ribs for mountain slopes, his vitals for broad floating clouds, his flare and his flesh for fatness of the earth, his arms and legs for strength for the earth; his fingernails and toenails for scales and shells for the fishes; his feathers for trees, shrubs and creepers, to clothe the earth; and his intestines for lobsters, shrimps and eels for the rivers and the seas; and the blood of Ta'aroa got heated and drifted away for redness for the sky and for rainbows.

But Ta'aroa's head remained sacred to himself, and he still lived, the same head on an indestructible body. He was master of everything. There was expansion and there was growth.

Ta'aroa conjured forth gods, but it was much later that man was conjured, when Tu was with him.

As Ta'aroa had crusts, that is, shells, so has everything a shell.

The sky is a shell, that is, endless space in which the gods placed the sun, the moon, the Sporades and the constellations of the gods.

The earth is a shell to the stones, the water, and plants that spring from it.

Man's shell is woman because it is by her that he comes into the world; and woman's shell is woman because she is born of woman.

One cannot enumerate the shells of all the things that this world produces.

Sacred Narrative 5

Karora Creates the World from Nothing (Australia)

In this sacred narrative Karora, the ancestor and High-God, creates the world from nothing. The narrative indicates that Karora, at the beginning of time, was asleep at the bottom of the dry ground. From his body are created all things. The primordial darkness is shattered when Karora bursts from the dry ground and this begins the creation of real human life.

In the very beginning everything was resting in perpetual darkness: night oppressed all the earth like an impenetrable thicket. The gurra ancestor – his name was Karora – was lying asleep in everlasting night, at the very bottom of the soak of Ilbalintja; as yet there was no water in it, but all was dry ground. Over him the soil was red with flowers and overgrown with many grasses; and a great tnatantja was swaying above him. This tnatantja had sprung from the midst of the bed of purple flowers which grew over the soak of Ilbalintja. At its root rested the head of Karora himself: from thence it mounted up towards the sky as though it would strike the very vault of the heavens. It was a living creature, covered with a smooth skin like the skin of a man.

And Karora's head lay at the root of the great tnatantja: he had rested thus ever from the beginning.

And Karora was thinking, and wishes and desires flashed through his mind. Bandicoots began to come out from his navel and from his armpits. They burst through the sod above, and sprang into life.

And now dawn was beginning to break. From all quarters men saw a new light appearing: the sun itself began to rise at Ilbalintja, and flooded everything with its light. Then the gurra ancestor was minded to rise, now that the sun was mounting higher. He burst through the crust that had covered him: and the gaping hole that he left behind became the Ilbalintja Soak, filled with the sweet dark juice of the honeysuckle buds. The gurra ancestor rose, feeling hungry, since magical powers had gone out from his body.

As yet he feels dazed; slowly his eyelids begin to flutter; then he opens them a little. He gropes about in his dazed state; he feels a moving mass of bandicoots all around him. He is now standing more firmly on his feet. He thinks, he desires. In his great hunger he seizes two young bandicoots; he cooks them some little distance away, close to the spot where the sun is standing, in the white-hot soil heated by the sun; the sun's fingers alone provide him with fire and hot ashes.

His hunger satisfied, his thoughts turn towards a helpmate. But now evening is approaching over the earth; the sun hides his face with a veil of hair-string, covers his body with hair-string pendants, vanishes from the sight of men. And Karora falls asleep, stretching his arms out on both sides.

While he is asleep, something emerges from underneath his armpit in the shape of a bull-roarer. It takes on human form, and grows in one night to a full-grown young man: this is his first-born son. At night Karora wakes up, because he feels that his arm is being oppressed with the weight of something heavy: he sees his first-born son lying at his side, his head resting on his father's shoulder.

Dawn breaks. Karora rises; he sounds the loud vibrating call known as raiankintja. The son is thereby stirred into life. He rises; he dances the ceremonial dance around the father who is sitting adorned with full ceremonial designs worked in blood and feather-down. The son totters and stumbles; he is still only half awake. The father puts his body and chest into a violent quiver; then the son places his hands upon him. The first ceremony has come to an end.

The son is now sent by his father to kill some more of the bandicoots which are playing peacefully about nearby in the shade. The son brings them back to his father who cooks them in the sun-glowing soil as before, and shares the cooked meat with his son. Evening has come again, and soon both are asleep. Two more sons are born that night to the father, from out of his armpits; these he calls into life on the following morning by the raiankintja call as before.

This process is repeated for many days and nights. The sons do the hunting; and the father brings into life an increasing number of sons each night – as many as fifty on some nights. But the end cannot be delayed overlong; soon father and sons have succeeded in devouring all the bandicoots which had originally sprung from Karora's body. In their hunger the father sends his sons away on a three-days' hunt, to scour the great Ilbalintja Plain as far as Ininta and Ekallakuna. For hours they search patiently amongst the tall white grass, in the half-light of the almost limitless expanse of mulga-trees. But the vast mulga thicket is devoid of bandicoots, and they have to return.

It is the third day.

The sons are returning, hungry and tired, through the great stillness. Suddenly a sound comes to their ears, a sound like that of a whirling bull-roarer. They listen; they proceed to search for the man who may be swinging it. They search and search and search. They stab with their tjurunga sticks into all bandicoot nests and resting places. Suddenly something dark and hairy darts up and is gone. A shout goes up – 'There goes a sandhill wallaby.' They hurl their tjurunga sticks after it and break its leg. And then they hear the words of a song coming from the injured animal:

> I, Tjenterama, have now grown lame,
> Yes, lame; and the purple everlastings are
> clinging to me.
> 'I am a man as you are; I am not a bandicoot.'
> With these words the lame Tjenterama limps away.

The astonished gurra brothers continue on their way home to their father. Soon they see him approaching. He leads them back to the soak. They sit on its edge in circles, one circle around the other, ever widening out like ripples in disturbed water. And then the great pmoara flood of sweet honey from the honeysuckle buds comes from the east and engulfs them; it swirls them back into the Ilbalintja Soak.

Here the aged Karora remained; but the sons were carried by the flood under the ground to a spot in the mulga thicket. Here they rejoined the great Tjenterama, whose leg they had unwittingly broken with their tjurunga sticks.

Today, at that new ceremonial ground the natives point out the rocks and stones which represent the undying bodies of the gurra brothers which lie on top of the round stone which is said to be the body of Tjenterama; and this Tjenterama whom they had injured is now their new chief; and in all the present-day bandicoot ceremonies Tjenterama is represented as the great gurra chief of Ilbalintja. Karora, the natives say, remained behind at his original home: he is lying in eternal sleep at the bottom of the Ilbalintja Soak; and men and women who approach the soak to quench their thirst may do so only if they bear in their hands bunches of green inuruna boughs which they lay down on the edge of the soak. For then Karora is pleased with their coming and smiles in his sleep.

Sacred Narrative 6

Ta'aroa Creates the Universe (Polynesia)

While some of the narratives of the High-God Ta'aroa exemplify the motif of the cosmic egg or shell, this creation narrative exemplifies creation from nothing. At the beginning of time there was no earth, no sky, no sea and no human beings. Ta'aroa existed completely alone and created the entire cosmos from nothing. However, while this narrative seems dominated by this motif, the imagery of shells persists in the specific geography; Hawaii is created as the Shell of Ta'aroa.

He existed, Ta'aroa was his name.
In the immensity [space]
There was no earth, there was no sky.
There was no sea, there was no man.
Above, Ta'aroa calls.
Existing alone, he became the universe.
Ta'aroa is the origin, the rocks.
Ta'aroa is the sands,
It is thus that he is named.
Ta'aroa is the light;
Ta'aroa is within;
Ta'aroa is the germ.
Ta'aroa is beneath;
Ta'aroa is firm;
Ta'aroa is wise.
He created the land of Hawaii,
Hawaii the great and sacred,
As a body or shell for Ta'aroa . . .

Sacred Narrative 7

An Earth-Diver Narrative from Siberia (Siberian-Altaic)

This sacred narrative illustrates the motif of creation with the aid of the earth-diver. These narratives are quite extensive, appearing among circumpolar peoples, in eastern Europe and in North America. The standard elements in the narrative are that the gods are situated above a primordial body of water, the creator deity needs earth from below the water but cannot enter the water himself, and must use the services of another figure, the diver. The diver, here the 'First Man', gathers the earth, but always tries to conceal a small amount for himself. These sacred narratives always suggest some tension or dualism between the competing creators, with the diver's creation always turning out flawed. Here, the 'First Man' is forced to spit the earth out and in so doing creates the boggy places on the earth.

In the beginning when there was nothing but water, God and the First Man moved about in the shape of two black geese over the waters of the primordial ocean. The devil, however, could not hide his nature, but endeavoured ever to rise higher, until he finally sank down into the depths. Nearly suffocating, he was forced to call to God for help, and God raised him again into the air with the power of his word. God then spoke: 'Let a stone rise from the bottom of the ocean!' When the stone appeared, 'Man' seated himself upon it, but God asked him to dive under the water and bring land. Man brought earth in his hand and God scattered it on the surface of the water saying, 'Let the world take shape!' Once more God asked Man to fetch earth. But Man then decided to take some for himself and brought a morsel in each hand. One handful he gave to God but the other he hid in his mouth, intending to create a world of his own. God threw the earth which the devil had brought him beside the rest on the water, and the world at once began to expand and grow harder, but with the growing of the world the piece of earth in Man's mouth also swelled until he was about to suffocate, so that he was again compelled to seek God's help. God inquired: 'What was thy intention? Didst thou think thou couldst hide earth from me in thy mouth?' Man now told his secret intentions and at God's request spat the earth out of his mouth. Thus were formed the boggy places upon the earth.

Sacred Narrative 8

Hainuwele, the Maiden of Ceram (West Ceram)

This sacred narrative illustrates the motif of creation through sacrifice. The ancestors described by the narrative are not quite deities, but they are equally not fully human. Consequently, they are consistently described by anthropologists and historians of religions as Dema-deities. Here, we are told of the amazing powers of Hainuwele who gives the original nine families of mankind a series of wonderful gifts. However, the ancestors become jealous of Hainuwele and murder her. From her body come the tuberous plants which have been the major food supply ever since. Her creative sacrifice alters the world and makes it liveable for human beings and it has been suggested that this motif articulates a fundamental notion that life is dependent upon killing.

Nine families of mankind came forth in the beginning from Mount Nunusaku, where the people had emerged from clusters of bananas. And these families stopped in West Ceram, at a place known as the 'Nine Dance Grounds', which is the jungle between Ahiolo and Varoloin.

But there was a man among them whose name was Ameta, meaning 'Dark', 'Black', or 'Night', and neither was he married nor had he children. He went off, one day, hunting with his dog. And after a little, the dog smelt a wild pig, which it traced to a pond into which the animal took flight; but the dog remained on the shore. And the pig, swimming, grew tired and drowned, but the man, who had arrived meanwhile, retrieved it. And he found a coconut on its tusk, though at that time there were no cocopalms in the world.

Returning to his hut, Ameta placed the nut on a stand and covered it with a cloth bearing a snake design, then lay down to sleep. And in the night there appeared to him the figure of a man who said: 'The coconut that you placed upon the stand and covered with a cloth you must plant in the earth; otherwise it won't grow.' So Ameta planted the coconut the next morning, and in three days the palm was tall. Again three days and it was bearing blossoms. He climbed the tree to cut the blossoms, from which he wished to prepare himself a drink, but as he cut he slashed his finger and the blood fell on a leaf. He returned home to bandage his finger and in three days came back to the palm to find that where the blood on the leaf had mingled with the sap of the cut blossom the face of someone had appeared. Three days later, the trunk of the person was there, and when he returned again in three days he found that a little girl had developed from his drop of blood. That night the same figure of a man appeared to him in a dream. 'Take your cloth and snake design,' he said, 'wrap the girl of the cocopalm in the cloth carefully and carry her home.'

So the next morning Ameta went with his cloth to the cocopalm, climbed the tree, and carefully wrapped up the little girl. He descended cautiously, took her home, and named her Hainuwele. She grew quickly and in three days was a nubile maiden. But she was not like an ordinary person; for when she would answer the call of nature her excrement consisted of all sorts of valuable articles, such as Chinese dishes and gongs, so that her father became rich.

And about that time there was to be celebrated in the place of the Nine Dance Grounds a great Maro Dance, which was to last nine full nights, and the nine families of mankind were to participate. Now when the people dance the Maro, the women sit in the centre and from there reach betel nut to the men, who form, in dancing, a large ninefold spiral. Hainuwele stood in the centre at this Maro festival, passing out betel nut to the men. And at dawn, when the performance ended, all went home to sleep.

The second night, the nine families of mankind assembled on the second ground; for when the Maro is celebrated it must be performed each night in a different place. And once again, it was Hainuwele who was placed in the centre to reach betel nut to the dancers; but when they asked for it she gave them coral instead, which they found very nice. The dancers and the others, too, then began pressing in to ask for betel nut and she gave them coral. And so the performance continued until dawn, when they all went home to sleep.

The next night the dance was resumed on a third ground, with Hainuwele again in the centre; but this time she gave beautiful porcelain dishes, and everyone present received such a dish. The fourth night she gave bigger porcelain dishes and the fifth great bush knives; the sixth, beautifully worked betel boxes of copper; the seventh, golden earrings; and the eighth, glorious gongs. The value of the articles increased, that way, from night to night, and the people thought this thing mysterious. They came together and discussed the matter.

They were extremely jealous that Hainuwele could distribute such wealth and decided to kill her. The ninth night, therefore, when the girl was again placed in the centre of the dance ground, to pass out betel nut, the men dug a deep hole in the area. In the innermost circle of the great ninefold spiral the men of the Lesiela family were dancing, and in the course of the slowly cycling movement of their spiral they pressed the maiden Hainuwele toward the hole and threw her in. A loud, three-voiced Maro Song drowned out her cries. They covered her quickly with earth, and the dancers trampled this down firmly with their steps. They danced on till dawn, when the festival ended and the people returned to their huts.

But when the Maro festival ended and Hainuwele failed to return, her father knew that she had been killed. He took nine branches of a certain bushlike plant whose wood is used in the casting of oracles and with these reconstructed in his home the nine circles of the Maro Dancers. Then he knew that Hainuwele had been killed in the Dancing Ground. He took nine fibres of the cocopalm leaf and went with these to the dance place, stuck them one after the other into the earth, and with the ninth came to what had been the innermost circle. When he stuck the ninth fibre into the earth and drew it forth, on it were some of the hairs and blood of Hainuwele. He dug up the corpse and cut it into many pieces, which he buried in the whole area about the Dancing Ground – except for the two arms, which he carried to the maiden Satene: the second of the supreme Dema-virgins of West Ceram. At the time of the coming into being of mankind Satene had emerged from an unripe banana, whereas the rest had come from ripe bananas; and she now was the ruler of them all. But the buried portions of Hainuwele, meanwhile, were already turning into things that up to that time had never existed anywhere on earth – above all, certain tuberous plants that have been the principal food of the people ever since.

Ameta cursed mankind and the maiden Satene was furious at the people for having killed. So she built on one of the dance grounds a great gate, consisting of a ninefold spiral, like the one formed by the men in the dance; and she stood on a great log inside this gate, holding in her two hands the two arms of Hainuwele. Then, summoning the people, she said to them: 'Because you have killed, I refuse to live here any more; today I shall leave. And so now you must all try to come to me through this gate. Those who succeed will remain people, but to those who fail something else will happen.'

They tried to come through the spiral gate, but not all succeeded, and everyone who failed was turned into either an animal or a spirit. That is how it came about that pigs, deer, birds, fish and many spirits inhabit the earth. Before that time there had been only people. Those, however, who came through walked to Satene; some to the right of the log on which she was standing, others to the left; and as each passed she struck him with one of Hainuwele's arms. Those going left had to jump across five sticks of bamboo, those to the right, across nine, and from these two groups, respectively, were derived the tribes known as the Fivers and the Niners. Satene said to them: 'I am departing today and you will see me no more on earth. Only when you die will you again see me. Yet even then you shall have to accomplish a very difficult journey before you attain me.'

And with that, she disappeared from the earth. She now dwells on the mountain of the dead, in the southern part of West Ceram, and whoever desires to go to her must die. But the way to her mountain leads over eight other mountains. And ever since that day there have been not only men but spirits and animals on earth, while the tribes of men have been divided into the Fivers and the Niners.

Doctrine 1

Ngai, the High-God of the Gikuyu (Kenya)

Here, Jomo Kenyatta, the first President of Kenya and also by training an anthropologist, comments on the supreme being of the Gikuyu people. Anthropologists and historians of religions have described this type of supreme being as the 'High-God' and is found in many small-scale traditional religions. The High-God is usually involved in creation in some way, but after creation assumes a transcendent position, relatively removed from everyday human concerns. Hence, Kenyatta notes as part of his 'doctrinal' reflection upon Ngai that the god takes little interest in individuals' daily lives, but is called upon at the most critical moments in the individual's life. He is also the guardian of morality.

He has no father, no mother or companion of any kind. He loves or hates people according to their behaviour. The Creator lives in the sky, but has temporary homes on earth, situated on mountains, where he may rest during his visits. The visits are made with a view to his carrying out a kind of general inspection, *Koroora thi*, and to bring blessings and punishments to the people . . . Ngai cannot be seen by mortal eyes. He is a distant being and takes but little interest in individuals in their daily walks of life. Yet at the crisis of their lives he is called upon. At the birth, initiation, marriage and death of every Gikuyu, communication is established on his belief with Ngai . . . . It is said that lightning is a visible representation of some of God's weapons which he uses on ahead to warn people of his coming and to prepare and clear the way. His approach is foretold only by the sounds of his own preparations. Thunder is cracking of his joints, as a warrior limbering up for action.

Doctrine 2

A Traditional Pygmy Hymn on God

Here, in this traditional pygmy song, is another reflection on a High-God who is understood to be eternal and without physical form. This simple text contradicts many of the erroneous ideas about the deities of small-scale traditional peoples; the High-God cannot be rendered in a totemic or human form. The real being of God is related to word and not form.

In the beginning was God,
Today is God
Tomorrow will be God.
Who can make an image of God?
He has no body.
He is as a word
which comes out of your mouth.
That word! It is no more,
It is past, and still it lives!
So is God.

Doctrine 3

Sword, a Dakota Indian, on Wakan Tanka

In this text, Sword describes wakan as the source of all life. There is a hierarchy of divine beings or wakan beings, extending from the High-God, identified with the sky, to human beings and animals. However, there is solidarity between all life forms, and that is the very meaning of the name Wakan Tanka. This solidarity in the cosmos becomes a central doctrinal principle found in many small-scale traditional religions.

Every object in the world has a spirit and that spirit is wakan. Thus the spirits of the tree or things of that kind, while not like the spirit of man, are also wakan. Wakan comes from the wakan beings. These wakan beings are greater than mankind in the same way that mankind is greater than animals. They are never born and never die. They can do many things that mankind cannot do. Mankind can pray to the wakan beings for help. There are many of these beings but all are of four kinds. The word Wakan Tanka means all of the wakan beings because they are all as if one. Wakan Tanka Kin signifies the chief or leading wakan being which is the Sun. However, the most powerful of the wakan beings is Nagk Tanka, the Great Spirit who is also Taku Skanskan. Taku Skanskan signifies the Blue, in other words, the Sky. . . . Mankind is permitted to pray to the wakan beings. If their prayer is directed to all the good wakan beings, they should pray to Wakan Tanka; but if the prayer is offered to only one of these beings, then the one addressed should be named. . . . Wakan Tanka is like sixteen different persons; but each person is kan. Therefore, they are only the same as one.

Ritual 1

The Yahuna of the Amazonian Basin Narrate the Origin of Manioc

In this narrative from the Yahuna of Brazil and Columbia we see a relationship between agricultural plants and events which took place at the beginning of time. The acts involved in planting, raising and harvesting plants become rituals through which those events are re-experienced. Also, ritual instruments are grounded in the very same events.

From the great Water House, the Land of the Sun, there came, many years ago, a little boy who sang so beautifully that many people flocked from near and far to see and hear him; and the name of this boy was Milomaki. But when those who had heard him returned to their homes and ate fish, they all died. Hence their relatives seized Milomaki, who meanwhile had grown to young manhood, and because he was so dangerous, having killed their brothers, they cremated him on a great pyre. Nevertheless, the youth continued to sing beautifully to the very end, and even while the flames were licking his body he was singing: 'Now I die, now I die, now I die, my Son, now I depart from this world!' And when his body was swelling with the heat, he still was singing in glorious tones: 'Now my body breaks, now I am dead!' And his body burst. He died and was consumed by the flames, but his soul ascended to heaven, while from his ashes there grew, that very day, a long, green blade, which became steadily bigger and bigger, spreading out, until the next day it was already a tall tree – the first paxiuba palm in the world . . .

The people fashioned huge flutes of the wood of this palm and these gave forth the same wonderfully beautiful tones that formerly had been sung by Milomaki himself. Furthermore, the men blow on such flutes to this day when the fruits are ripe, and they dance while doing so, in memory of Milomaki, who is the creator and giver of all fruits. But the women and children must not see these flutes; for if they did, they would die.

Ritual 2

Mukat and the Origin of Plants (Cahuilla Indians of California)

In this narrative from the Cahuilla Indians we learn once again that the most fundamental things of human life are derived from events at the beginning of time. It is from Mukat's body that foodstuffs come into the world. Hence, the simple act of harvesting food becomes a ritual re-experience of those first things, and through ritual one is reminded of the source of all life.

Then in the place where Mukat was burned there began to grow all kinds of strange plants, but no one knew what they were. They were afraid to go near the place for a hot wind always blew there. One Palmitcawut, a great shaman, said 'Why do you not go and ask our father what they are?' No one would go, so he followed the trail of Mukat's spirit although whirlwinds had hidden the trail. In one place were thickets of prickly cactus and clumps of interlaced thorny vines, but at the touch of his ceremonial staff they opened for him to pass. Far away on the horizon he saw a bright glow where the spirit of Mukat was leaning against a rock. The creator's spirit spoke, 'Who are you that follows me and makes me move when I am lying still?' When the creator's spirit spoke Palmitcawut was dumb and could not answer, though Mukat asked him several times. Finally, he was able to speak: 'Yes, I am the one who disturbs you while you rest, but we your creatures do not know what the strange things are that grow where your body was burned.' Mukat's spirit answered him, 'Yes, that was the last thing I wanted to tell you, but you killed me before I could do so.' Then he continued, 'You need not be afraid of those things. They are from my body.' He asked Palmitcawut to describe them and when he had finished the spirit of Mukat said, 'That big tree is tobacco. It is my heart. It can be cleaned with white clay, and smoked in the big house to drive away evil spirits. The vines with the yellow squashes are from my stomach, watermelons are from the pupil of my eye, corn is from my teeth, wheat is my lice eggs, beans are from my semen, and all other vegetables are from other parts of my body.' (Thus when any vegetables are gathered and brought to the big house all of the people must pray to the creator.)

Ritual 3

The Sun Dance as Described by Chased-by-Bears (Teton Sioux)

Here, Chased-by-Bears describes the reasons why an individual participates in one of the most rigorous rituals of the plains Indians of North America, the Sun Dance. This ritual becomes the vehicle by which one offers thanksgiving for the aid of God. In the ritual one literally sacrifices the body in acknowledgment of divine protection.

Later in the same year I went with a party of about twenty warriors. As we approached the enemy some of the men came to me saying that they desired to make Sun-dance vows and asking if I would 'speak the vow' for the party. Each man came to me alone and made some gift with the request. He also stated what gifts he would make at the Sun Dance, but did not always say what part he intended to take in the dance. One man said, 'I will give my whole body to Wakan Tanka.' I did not understand what he meant, nor was it necessary that I should do so, but at the time of the Sun Dance he asked that his body be suspended entirely above the ground.

Just before sunrise I told the warriors to stand side by side facing the East. I stood behind them and told them to raise their right hands. I raised my right hand with them and said: 'Wakan Tanka, these men have requested me to make this vow for them. I pray you, take pity on us and on our families at home. We are now between life and death. For the sake of our families and relatives we desire that you will help us conquer the enemy and capture his horses to take home with us. Because they are thankful for your goodness and will be thankful if you grant this request, these men promise that they will take part in the next Sun Dance. Each man has some offering to give you at the proper time.'

We were successful and returned home victorious. Knowing that these men had vowed to take part in the Sun Dance, I saw that their vows were fulfilled at the next ceremony and personally did the cutting of their arms and the suspension of their bodies.

Institutional Expression 1

The Hornbill, the Watersnake and the Institutions of the Ngaju Dayak (South Borneo)

This text describes the world as seen by the Ngaju Dayak of Southern Borneo. True dwelling-space and all human institutions are real only insofar as they are related to the twin aspects of the Ngaju godhead, represented by Mahatala, the hornbill, and Jata, the watersnake. These represent the upper world and the lower world. Throughout Ngaju social life and institutions these twin aspects of God are represented.

The area inhabited by the sacred people is the sacred land. It was given to them by the godhead, which had shaped it out of the remains of the sun and the moon. It lies among the primeval waters, between Upperworld and Underworld, and rests on the back of the Watersnake. It is bounded by the raised tail and head of the deity of the Underworld. We also find in myths the idea that the world is enclosed in a circle formed by the Watersnake biting its own tail. The world is thus supported and enclosed by the godhead, a man lives under its protection, in divine peace and well-being. Man lives in the sacred, divine land of Mahatala and Jata. The mountains of the sacred land reach up to the Upperworld. The godhead descends on to them and on them he meets men and gives them his sacred gifts. Man lives in the sacred land in communion with the supreme deities. He climbs the sacred mountain and there practises asceticism (*batapa*), and Matahala draws close to him there and regards him. In the still of the night he lets himself drift on a small raft in the river, and the Watersnake emerges and sees him. The godhead is everywhere, and man can appear before it everywhere, for he is in the godhead's land and under its protection, and the godhead has created for him an approach to the Upperworld and the Underworld.

The world described here is the primeval village Batu Nindan Tarong, the origin of which is told in the creation myth, and which is pictured in the sacred designs. The head and tail of the Watersnake are usually represented in these drawings as the Tree of Life, and this representation is meaningful in that the Watersnake and the Tree of Life are identical. The first human beings lived in this primeval village, and their three sons were born to them there, and when this time is spoken of or sung about the sacred legends and songs say: 'At that time, in the beginning, when our ancestors were still living in the mouth of the coiled Watersnake (which lay circled about the village), such-and-such happened,' and in this village the sacred ceremonies were first established.

With the exception of Maharaja Sangen, the three brothers did not stay in Batu Nindan Tarong. They left there and settled in the Upperworld and in our world. But the sacred people did not stay together in this world. The tribal organization collapsed, its members moved to other rivers and settled among strangers, and the idea of the sacred land diminished. Instead of a tribal area there is now the village, with its neighbouring villages upstream and downstream. The world and mankind (*kalunen*), or man as part of this mankind, are synonymous and the same term *kalunen* is employed for both. The world is nothing but the sacred land, and the sacred land is inhabited only by the sacred people. The Ngaju calls his world (today, his village) by various names, e.g. *batu lewu*, home village, *lewu danumku*, my village and my native river. The name always used in myths and chants is *lewu injam tingang*, the village lent by the Watersnake, or it is also described as the village where the hornbill enjoyed the Watersnake. The real native village of mankind is not in this world: it is Batu Nindan Tarong, in the Upperworld. Man dwells only for a time in this world, which is 'lent' to him, and when the time has come and he is old, then he returns for ever to his original home. To die is not to become dead; it is called *buli*, to return home. This idea has nothing to do with any Christian influence; it is an ancient Dayak concept which is understandable in relation to the primeval sacred events and the mode of thought connected with them.

The Dayak loves the world into which he is born and where he grows up. His village is the largest and most beautiful place in the whole world, and he would change it for no other. If he leaves his village he takes with him sacred medicines which will guarantee his safe return, and if he himself never comes back his bones or his ashes are still brought back into the village and thereby he finds his last resting place in the sacred land. The description of the village and the world in myths and priestly chants has poetic force and beauty. There are old people, mostly women, who have never left their own village, not because they have never had a chance to, but because they simply never felt the need to do so. Why should one leave the village? Why roam far among strangers? Peace, safety, happiness, and the good life are to be found only in one's own village, only in one's own world where one is protected by the godhead, surrounded by the primevally maternal Watersnake, where one rests on its body and is enclosed by its head and tail.

The love for one's own world is expressed in the parting song of a dead person who leaves his village for ever to enter the village of the dead. He is fetched away by Tempon Telon and journeys to the Upperworld. His boat stops before the entrance. The dead person looks down once more on the world, and sings to his village and his river and to all those he loved:

'I can still not express my innermost thought
properly,
Nor is it possible for me to speak what fills my
heart.
I have thrown away the village lent by Hornbill,
as one discards a useless plate,
I have pushed away the place where the
hornbills live widely scattered as one rejects
an unusable dish,
And I have myself become like a cast stone,
never to return,
I am like a clod of earth thrown away, never
again to come home.'

This is not hopelessness, it is simply the farewell of the deceased, and with these words the boat travels on towards the true and eternal home to which the dead may return and where he will be joyfully received by the ancestors and by all who have travelled this road before him.

The world which is borne on the back of the Watersnake and enclosed by its body is the good, sacred land. The surroundings of the village, i.e. the area which is not bounded and fenced in by the Watersnake's body, is a strange, horrible and fearsome land where one no longer feels at home, where one will not readily build a house, which one will not enter without taking grave precautions and providing oneself with protective medicines. Persons who have died bad deaths lie outside the village, and this is where criminals are buried, that is, those who are excluded from the sacred people by the community and even by the godhead itself. They do not rest in the midst of the sacred people and in the sacred land, nor are they enclosed in death by the Watersnake, and they are buried in unhallowed ground. God and man have no more to do with them, and they are separated for ever from them, they are thrust out into solitude and homelessness, banished to ominous surroundings. There they live in the company of those who have died bad deaths, i.e. who have lost their lives in an unnatural way, by accident or by a particularly dreaded illness (leprosy, smallpox), as punishment for some known or unknown offence. The godhead has caused them to die an 'unripe death' (*matei manta*), has put a mark upon them and thrust them out for ever from the community of the living and from that of the ancestors. This community of unfortunate and homeless souls continues to live the existence of evil spirits in the bush and forests surrounding the village. As such, they attack people, make them ill, or take their lives . . .

One's own world is the central point of all worlds, the focus of the whole divine cosmic order and harmony. This applies also to the village, which after the collapse of the tribal organization has taken over everything that we said above about the sacred land. The village also represents the social and cosmic totality; the village also possesses the dual division. The upper part of the village (i.e. the upstream, *ngaju*, part) is lived in by the superior group, and the lower part (*ngawa*) belongs to the lower group and to the slaves (if any) . . .

The sacred land is the land of the godhead. It was not only created and maintained by the godhead, it is the godhead itself and represents the totality of Upperworld and Underworld, of Mahatala and Jata. Man lives not only in the divine land, not only in the peace of the godhead, but actually in the godhead, for the sacred land is a part of the Tree of Life, it was created from the sun and the moon, which flank the tree, and which issued from the Gold Mountain and the Jewel Mountain, and thus from the total godhead.

Institutional Expression 2

The Gabon Pygmies on Exile

In this song from the Gabon pygmies one sees the inverse perception of space to that of the Ngaju Dayak. Being separated from one's place as it was created in the beginning is a profound experience of exile. Real life and social institutions are impossible when one is cut off from those sacred realities. Hence, social institutions are what they are only in relationship to those events of the mythic past.

The night is black, the sky is blotted out,
We have left the village of our Fathers,
The Maker is angry with us . . .
The light becomes dark,
the night and again night,
The day with hunger tomorrow –
The Maker is angry with us.

The Old Ones have passed away,
Their homes are far off, below,
Their spirits are wandering –
Where are their spirits wandering?
Perhaps the passing wind knows.
Their bones are far off below.

Are they below, the spirits?
Are they here?
Do they see the offerings set out?
Tomorrow is naked and empty,
For the Maker is no longer with us – there,
He is no longer the host seated with us at our fire.

Institutional Expression 3

Ogotemmêli Narrates the Descent of the Cosmic Granary (Dogon)

The narrator of this text is an elder of the Dogon of West Africa, and he transmits in the narrative a detailed description of how the 'ancestral constructor' created a long series of common but necessary implements used in daily life. The central institution of Dogon life is the granary, and in the narrative all these simple and practical implements refer to that central institution which was created at the beginning of time and descended to earth.

The ancestral constructor had assembled on the flat roof the tools and implements of a forge, for his future task was to teach men the use of iron to enable them to cultivate the land.

The bellows was made out of two vessels of unfired powdered earth and a white sheepskin; the two vessels were joined to one another like two twins, the wide opening being closed by a skin. An earthen duct led from each to the nozzle.

The hammer was in the form of a large iron block with a cone-shaped handle and a square strike. The anvil similarly shaped was fixed in a wooden beam.

The ancestral smith was equipped with an iron bow and spindles for arrows. One of these arrows he aimed at the granary roof at the centre of the circle representing the moon, and he wound a long thread of gossamer round the shank to form a bobbin, so that the whole edifice became a gigantic spindle-whorl. Taking a second arrow, he attached the other end of the thread to it, and shot it into the vault of the sky to give it purchase.

A whole constellation of symbols was now to appear. In the first place there was the miraculous granary itself symbolizing the world-system, set in place and classified into categories of creatures. It was the plaited basket, which its constructor had copied, and which was to serve men as a unit of volume. The unit of length was the tread or the rise of the step in the stairways, or one cubit. The unit of area was provided by the flat roof, whose sides were eight cubits. The two primary geometrical figures were shown in the square of the roof and the circular base, which, in the basket, was in fact the opening. This was the model granary in which men were to store their crops.

As such it was the ideal and ultimate realization of the arrangement of the anthill, which had already served as a model for men in the transformation of their underground dwellings.

It was also the spindle-whorl, the deadhead of the arrow which the smith had shot at the flat roof, and which served as the axis for the winding of the downward thread.

Symbolically it represented the shape of the iron used for ginning cotton, a shuttle, pointed at each end, in outline resembling a smith's hammer.

It was the head of the hammer; and, according to popular belief, it was in his hammer that the smith brought the seeds to men.

It was also the four-sided anvil, which is female, forged in imitation of the hammer, which is male.

It was the webbed hand of the Nummo, of which the hammer was the image; it was the upper half of the Nummo's body, which is also symbolized by the hammer; two opposite surfaces represent his breast and back: the others are his arms.

Lastly, it was the bodily form of the female element of the smith, who like all beings was dual.

All was now ready for departure except that there was no fire in the smithy. The ancestor slipped into the workshop of the great Nummo, who are Heaven's smiths, and stole a piece of the sun in the form of live embers and white-hot iron. He seized it by means of a 'robber's stick' the crook of which ended in a slip, open like a mouth. He dropped some of the embers, came back to pick them up, and fled towards the granary; but his agitation was such that he could no longer find the entrances. He made the round of it several times before he found the steps and climbed to the flat roof, where he hid the stolen goods in one of the skins of the bellows, exclaiming '*Gouyo*!', which is to say, 'Stolen!'.

The word is still part of the language, and means 'granary'. It is a reminder that without the fire of the smithy and the iron of hoes there would be no crops to store.

Without losing a moment the smith flung the truncated pyramid along a rainbow. The edifice stood without turning on itself, and the thread unwound in serpentine coils suggesting the movement of water.

With hammer and bow in his hands, the smith stood ready to defend himself against attack from outer space. But the attack, when it came, was unexpected; to the accompaniment of a clap of thunder a brand flung by the female Nummo hit the flat roof. The smith in self-defence snatched one of the skins of the bellows and brandished it above his head – thus making a buckler of it. The skin, inasmuch as it had been in contact with a piece of the sun, had absorbed the essence of the sun, and the celestial fire could not prevail against it. The ancestor thereupon extinguished with water from his leather bottle the burning brand which was setting the edifice on fire. This brand, whose name was *bazu*, was to become the origin of the worship of the female fire.

A second thunderclap followed the first. It came this time from the male Nummo, but was no more effective than its predecessor. The smith extinguished the second brand, named *anakyé*, which was to become the origin of the worship of the male fire.

The granary then pursued its course along the rainbow, but its speed increased owing to the impetus given by the thunder.

The smith meanwhile resumed his position of defence on the roof, but, tired of holding his hammer clasped in his hand, he laid it across his arms raised slightly in front of him. The anvil he carried in a kind of sling made of a long leather strap round his neck hanging down over his shoulders behind. The wooden beam in which the anvil was fixed knocked against his legs.

During his descent the ancestor still possessed the quality of a water spirit, and his body, though preserving its human appearance, owing to its being that of a regenerated man, was equipped with four flexible limbs like serpents after the pattern of the arms of the Great Nummo.

The ground was rapidly approaching. The ancestor was still standing, his arms in front of him and the hammer and anvil hanging across his limbs. The shock of his final impact on the earth when he came to the end of the rainbow scattered in a cloud of dust the animals, vegetables and men disposed on the steps.

When calm was restored, the smith was still on the roof, standing erect facing towards the north, his tools still in the same position. But in the shock of landing the hammer and the anvil had broken his arms and legs at the level of elbows and knees, which he did not have before. He thus acquired the joints proper to the new human form, which was to spread over the earth and to devote itself to toil.

It was in order to work that his arm was bent, for the flexible limbs were ill-fitted for the labours of forge and field. For hammering red-hot iron or for digging the land the leverage of the forearm was needed.

On making contact with the soil, therefore, the ancestor was ready for his civilizing work. He came down the north stairway, and marked out a square field, ten times eight cubits on each side, oriented in the same way as the flat roof on which he had descended, and on which the unit measurement of landholdings was to be based.

The field was divided into eighty times eighty squares of one cubit a side, which were distributed among the eight families descended from the ancestors whose destiny it was to remain on earth. Along the median line of the square from north to south eight dwelling-houses were built, in which the earth was mixed with mud taken from the granary. The smithy was set up to the north of this line.

'They put celestial mud in the field,' said Ogotemmêli, 'and thus purified the soil; and later, as the land was gradually cleared, the impurity of the earth receded.'

The blind man always insisted on this matter of the impurity of the soil, the cause of the first disturbance of the order of the world.

'Originally, at the creation, the earth was pure. The lump flung by God was of pure clay. But the offence of the jackal defiled the earth and upset the world-order. That is why the Nummo came down to reorganize it. The earth which came down from Heaven was pure earth, and wherever it was put, it imparted its purity to the spot and to all the ground that was cleared. Wherever cultivation spread, impurity receded.'

The renewal of the soil was not the only work to be done. The granary came down full of new foods, intended for the regeneration and renewing of men . . .

Experience 1

The Shaman's Initiation (Kwakiutl Indians)

The dimension of experience in small-scale traditional religions is perhaps best illustrated by the shaman. The shaman is able to perform a variety of functions due to intense experience with the sacred. Here, Lebid is initiated into his role as a shaman among the Kwakiutl by being reborn after his death. This experience allows him to perform the actions which are characteristic of shamans and in the text we are given a detailed description of that experience of initiation.

'Lebid had been sick for a long time,' said the one who told the tale. 'For three winters he had been sick abed and he was just bones. It was real mid-winter and it was very cold. . . .

[After Lebid had died, his body was wrapped in blankets and laid at the far end of the village site. It was too cold to bury him.]

Night came. When all the Gwasila lay down, a wolf began to howl behind Gwekelis. It was not long that one wolf was howling, when many wolves began to howl. They gathered at the place where Lebid was wrapped up on the rock. Then the Gwasila guessed that the wolves were going to eat him. Probably the wolves were sitting around the dead one, for they were all howling together. The Gwasila did not sleep for they were afraid. When it was near daylight the wolves were still howling, many. Then all the Gwasila heard Lebid singing his sacred song among the howling wolves and they knew that Lebid had now become a shaman. When day came in the morning the many howling wolves went back into the woods, and Lebid went also into the woods, singing his sacred song. He kept together with the wolves. Now the sisters of Lebid and his late wife, Maxmaklodalaogwa, were running about in vain, looking at the place where he had been wrapped up on the rocks. They saw the tracks of Lebid who had been walking among the wolves. Now the Gwasila were asked by the shamans of the Nakwaxdax that they should all go and wash, with the women and children in the morning and in the evening, so that they should all purify themselves. Then they did so. Now he had been away for two days, then he was heard singing his sacred song inland from the village of Gwekelis. . . . When day came in the morning the Gwasila went to get firewood. Lebid's wife and daughters and sisters cleared Lebid's house so as to make it clean. . . . All the Gwasila were purified. When it got dark in the evening he came singing his sacred song. They could hardly hear him in the woods. Now at once the Gwasila started a fire in the middle of the house. All the men and the women who were not menstruating and the children went in. Now the shaman of Nakwaxdax told all those who went into the house to carry batons. When they were all holding the batons the shaman of the Nakwaxdax, whose name was Making-Alive (Qwequlagila) told the Gwasila to beat fast time together. They all beat time together. For a long time they were beating time. Then they stopped beating time and the sound of Lebid came nearer as he was singing his sacred song behind the village. Three times the Gwasila beat fast time. Then the sound of the sacred song came to the front of the house. Again they beat fast time; the fourth time Lebid came into the door, really naked, only hemlock was wound around his head and hemlock was wound around his neck. He was really lean. The Gwasila beat fast time. He went around the fire in the middle of the house still singing his sacred song. These are the words of his sacred song:

'I was taken away far inland to the edge of the
world by the magical power of heaven, the
treasure, ha, wo, ho.
Only then was I cured by it, when it was really
thrown into me, the past life bringer of
Naualakume, the treasure, ha, wo, ho.
I come to cure with this means of healing of
Naualakume, the treasure. Therefore I shall
be a life bringer, ha, wo, ho.
I come with the water of life given into my hand
by Naualakume, the means of bringing to
life, the treasures, ha, wo, ho.'

Then Lebid sang his other sacred song:

'He turns to the right side, poor one, this
supernatural one, so as to obtain the
supernatural one, ha, wo, ho.
Let the supernatural one be the life bringer, the
supernatural one, ha, wo, ho.
That the poor one may come to life with the
lifebringer of Naualakume, ha, wo, ho.
The poor one comes, this supernatural one, to
give protection with the means of giving
protection of Naualakume, ha, wo, ho.'

After he had danced, all those went out of the house who were not shamans. Then the real shamans of Gwasila sat down in the house. Lebid sat down on a new mat in the rear of the house. All had their faces blackened, the old shamans, and all had on their heads the shamans' head rings of red cedar bark. All had around their necks shamans' neck rings of red cedar bark. Then they all lay on their backs and there was no talking. Only Lebid, the new shaman who had come back to life, was sitting on his new mat. . . . They were waiting for all the men and women who were not shamans to go to sleep. When they thought they were all asleep they sent four real shamans to go and look into the doors of all the houses of the Gwasila to see whether they were not barred. Then they found that all the doors of the houses were barred. They came into the meeting house of the shamans and they barred the door of the house. Then they sat down. They were sitting quite a while in silence, then arose one of the shamans, whose name was Bringing-Life-out-of-the-Woods (Qulamoltelsila). He spoke and said, 'Indeed, friends, indeed, this is the way it is done, for we came here to this house, that Lebid, who is newly added to us, our friend, may tell us how it was brought right down to this shaman. Now he will tell us why he came to life again. He will keep nothing hidden from his friends.' Thus he said and sat down.

Then Lebid spoke and said, 'Indeed, friends, you fellow-shamans, thus you must do to a new shaman. Now I will tell you, friends. I was very sick, and a man came into the place where I was lying in another house and invited me to follow him. Immediately I arose and followed him. Then I saw that my body was still lying here groaning. We had not gone far into the woods before we arrived at a house and we entered the house. I was asked by the other man to go and sit down in the rear of the house. When I had seated myself, then spoke the man who was sitting on the right hand side of the doorway of the house. He said, "Go on, speak, Naualakume, he who is the great shaman, of what we shall do to him who has come and is sitting among us," said he. Then a man came who had tied around his head a thick ring of red cedar bark and a thin neck ring of cedar bark. He spoke and said, "Our friend will not stay away, for I wish him to go back to his tribe so that he may become a great shaman and that he may cure the sick in his tribe. And he shall have my name for his name. Now he shall have the name Naualakume. And I shall take out the breath from his body so that I may keep it," said he as he went out of the door of the house. It was not long before he came back. He spoke and said, "Now his body is dead on the ground, for I am holding his breath, which is the owner of the soul of our friend. Now I shall give him my shamanistic power," said he and he vomited a quartz crystal. Then all the men beat fast time on the boards. He sang his sacred song as he threw the quartz crystal into the lower part of my sternum, and now I had become a shaman after this as it was getting daylight. Then Naualakume said, "Again we shall beat time for our friend tonight," said he. Then all the wolves who were now men, went to sleep. In the evening they all went into the house, for Lebid was still sitting there. And when the men were all in, Naualakume came singing his sacred song outside the house. Then he came in. There was a wolf carved out of yew wood on the back of his rattle. He went around the fire in the middle of the house. After he had gone around four times he sat down near me and pressed [on top] with his right hand on the top of my head, and he put down his rattle and pressed with his left hand the top of my head; then he sang his sacred song. Then he pressed down with both his hands on both sides of my head, down to the lower end of my trunk. And so he brought his hands together, put his hands flat together, and raised his hands throwing up the sickness of Lebid. After he had done this four times he finished. . . . Then all the men put on their wolf masks and when they were all dressed, they all went out of the door of the house, and also Lebid. As soon as all had come out, all the wolves howled. Lebid walked among them, and also Naualakume kept the breath of the body of Lebid, for only his soul had been taken by the wolves. Now they went to where the body of Lebid was wrapped on the rocks. As soon as they had arrived there, Naualakume asked the other wolves to take off the mat that had been spread over the body and the wrapping of two pairs of blankets. As soon as all had been taken off, Naualakume went there. He called Lebid to sit by his side. He took his breath and drew it into his mouth. Then he blew it into the mouth of Lebid's body. He asked the many wolves that they all should lick the body of the dead one. 'Now my soul was sitting on the ground and was just watching the wolves as they were licking the body. They had not been licking it long when it began to breathe. Then Naualakume pressed both his hands on the head of the soul of Lebid and he pressed down with both his hands on his head. Then the soul began to get small and it was of the size of a large fly. He took it and put it on top of the head of Lebid and blew it in. Immediately Lebid arose and sang his sacred song. Now he was singing among the wolves who were howling and they went back into the woods and went home to their house. Lebid also followed them. Again the wolves beat time at night. And now they really taught Lebid who had now the name Naualakume how to treat the sick. He said that he could not throw [sickness]; and other Gwasila say that he could throw [sickness], he who had now the name

Naualakume. Then said the great shaman of the wolves [i.e. Lebid] that he would always make him dream "about what I should do when curing really sick ones, as he was giving instructions to me". Now I came into this house where we are sitting now.'

Experience 2

The Vision Quest of Brave Buffalo (Teton Sioux)

The vision quest is a common experience among Native American peoples. It is in this quest that the individual is given power which then functions throughout his life. Here, Brave Buffalo describes that experience and how the vision allows him to represent the Buffalo in a more complete way.

When I was ten years old, I dreamed a dream, and in my dream a buffalo appeared to me. I dreamed that I was in the mountains and fell asleep in the shade of a tree. Something shook my blanket. It was a buffalo, who said, 'Rise and follow me.' I obeyed. He took a path, and I followed. The path was above the ground. We did not touch the earth. The path led upward and was smooth like smooth black rock. It was a narrow path, just wide enough for us to travel. We went upward a long distance and came to a tent made of buffalo hide, the door of which faced us. Two buffalo came out of the tent and escorted me in. I found the tent filled with buffalo and was placed in the midst of them.

The chief buffalo told me that I had been selected to represent them in life. He said the buffalo play a larger part in life than men realize, and in order that I might understand the buffalo better day by day they gave me a plain stick (or cane) and told me that when I looked at it I should remember that I had been appointed to represent them. The cane was similar to the one which I now carry and have carried for many years. I would not part with this cane for a fortune.

Experience 3

The Great Vision of Black Elk (Oglala Sioux)

One of the greatest documents from small-scale traditional religions is the vision of Black Elk of the Oglala Sioux. This vision became the unifying force not only in Black Elk's own life, but also in the life of his people, giving meaning to all that would follow. Here, he is taken to the centre of the world and shown the place of his people in the world: it is at once a vision of bitterness and of promise.

It was the summer when I was nine years old, and our people were moving slowly towards the Rocky Mountains. We camped one evening in a valley beside a little creek just before it ran into the Greasy Grass[1], and there was a man by the name of Man Hip who liked me and asked me to eat with him in his tepee.

While I was eating, a voice came and said: 'It is time; now they are calling you.' The voice was so loud and clear that I believed it, and I thought I would just go where it wanted me to go. So I got right up and started. As I came out of the tepee, both my thighs began to hurt me, and suddenly it was like waking from a dream, and there wasn't any voice. So I went back into the tepee, but I didn't want to eat. Man Hip looked at me in a strange way and asked me what was wrong. I told him that my legs were hurting me. . . .

When we had camped again, I was lying in our tepee and my mother and father were sitting beside me. I could see out through the opening, and there two men were coming from the clouds, head-first like arrows slanting down, and I knew they were the same that I had seen before. Each now carried a long spear, and from the points of these a jagged lightning flashed. They came clear down to the ground this time and stood a little way off and looked at me and said: 'Hurry! Come! Your Grandfathers are calling you!'

Then they turned and left the ground like arrows slanting upward from the bow. When I got up to follow, my legs did not hurt me any more and I was very light. I went outside the tepee, and yonder where the men with flaming spears were going, a little cloud was coming very fast. It came and stopped and took me and turned back to where it came from, flying fast. And when I looked down I could see my mother and my father yonder, and I felt sorry to be leaving them.

Then there was nothing but the air and the swiftness of the little cloud that bore me and those two men still leadng up to where white clouds were piled like mountains on a wide blue plain, and in them thunder beings lived and leaped and flashed.

Now suddenly there was nothing but a world of cloud, and we three were there alone in the middle of a great white plain with snowy hills and mountains staring at us; and it was very still; but there were whispers.

Then the two men spoke together and they said: 'Behold him, the being with four legs!'

I looked and saw a bay horse standing there, and he began to speak: 'Behold me!' he said. 'My life-history you shall see.' Then he wheeled about to where the sun goes down, and said: 'Behold them! Their history you shall know.'

I looked, and there were twelve black horses yonder all abreast with necklaces of bison hoofs, and they were beautiful, but I was frightened, because their manes were lightning and there was thunder in their nostrils.

Then the bay horse wheeled to where the great white giant lives [the north] and said: 'Behold!' And yonder there were twelve white horses all abreast. Their manes were flowing like a blizzard wind and from their noses came a roaring, and all about them white geese soared and circled.

Then the bay wheeled round to where the sun shines continually [the east] and bade me look; and there twelve sorrel horses, with necklaces of elk's teeth, stood abreast with eyes that glimmered like the day-break star and manes of morning light.

Then the bay wheeled once again to look upon the place where you are always facing [the south], and yonder stood twelve buckskins all abreast with horns upon their heads and manes that lived and grew like trees and grasses.

And when I had seen all these, the bay horse said: 'Your Grandfathers are having a council. These shall take you; so have courage.'

Then all the horses went into formation, four abreast – the blacks, the whites, the sorrels, and the buckskins – and stood behind the bay, who turned now to the west and neighed; and yonder suddenly the sky was terrible with a storm of plunging horses in all colours that shook the world with thunder, neighing back.

Now turning to the north the bay horse whinnied, and yonder all the sky roared with a mighty wind of running horses in all colours, neighing back.

And when he whinnied to the east, there too the sky was filled with glowing clouds of manes and tails of horses in all colours singing back. Then to the south he called, and it was crowded with many coloured, happy horses, nickering.

Then the bay horse spoke to me again and said: 'See how your horses all come dancing!' I looked,

[1] The Little Big Horn River.

and there were horses, horses everywhere a whole skyful of horses dancing round me.

'Make haste!' the bay horse said; and we walked together side by side, while the blacks, the whites, the sorrels and the buckskins followed, marching four by four.

I looked about me once again, and suddenly the dancing horses without number changed into animals of every kind and into all the fowls that are, and these fled back to the four quarters of the world from whence the horses came, and vanished.

Then as we walked, there was a heaped up cloud ahead that changed into a tepee, and a rainbow was the open door of it; and through the door I saw six old men sitting in a row.

The two men with the spears now stood beside me, one on either hand, and the horses took their places in their quarters, looking inward, four by four. And the oldest of the Grandfathers spoke with a kind voice and said: 'Come right in and do not fear.' And as he spoke, all the horses of the four quarters neighed to cheer me. So I went in and stood before the six, and they looked older than men can ever be – old like hills, like stars.

The oldest spoke again: 'Your Grandfathers all over the world are having a council, and they have called you here to teach you.' His voice was very kind, but I shook all over with fear now, for I knew that these were not old men, but the Powers of the World. And the first was the Power of the West; the second, of the North; the third, of the East; the fourth, of the South; the fifth, of the Sky; the sixth, of the Earth. I knew this, and was afraid, until the first Grandfather spoke again: 'Behold them yonder where the sun goes down, the thunder beings! You shall see, and have from them my power; and they shall take you to the high and lonely centre of the earth that you may see; even to the place where the sun continually shines, they shall take you there to understand.'

And as he spoke of understanding, I looked up and saw the rainbow leap with flames of many colours over me.

Now there was a wooden cup in his hand and it was full of water and in the water was the sky.

'Take this,' he said. 'It is the power to make live, and it is yours.'

Now he had a bow in his hands. 'Take this,' he said. 'It is the power to destroy, and it is yours.'

Then he pointed to himself and said: 'Look close at him who is your spirit now, for you are his body and his name is Eagle Wing Stretches.'

And saying this, he got up very tall and started running toward where the sun goes down; and suddenly he was a black horse that stopped and turned and looked at me, and the horse was very poor and sick; his ribs stood out.

Then the second Grandfather, he of the North, arose with a herb of power in his hand, and said: 'Take this and hurry.' I took and held it toward the black horse yonder. He fattened and was happy and came prancing to his place again and was the first Grandfather sitting there.

The second Grandfather, he of the North, spoke again: 'Take courage, younger brother,' he said; 'on earth a nation you shall make live, for yours shall be the power of the white giant's wing, the cleansing wind.' Then he got up very tall and started running toward the north; and when he turned toward me, it was a white goose wheeling. I looked about me now, and the horses in the west were thunders and the horses of the north were geese. And the second Grandfather sang two songs that were like this:

'They are appearing, may you behold!
They are appearing, may you behold!
The thunder nation is appearing, behold!

They are appearing, may you behold!
They are appearing, may you behold!
The white geese nation is appearing, behold!'

And now it was the third Grandfather who spoke, he of where the sun shines continually. 'Take courage, younger brother,' he said, 'for across the earth they shall take you!' Then he pointed to where the daybreak star was shining, and beneath the star two men were flying. 'From them you shall have power,' he said, 'from them who have awakened all the beings of the earth with roots and legs and wings.' And as he said this, he held in his hand a peace pipe which had a spotted eagle outstretched upon the stem; and this eagle seemed alive, for it was poised there, fluttering, and its eyes were looking at me. 'With this pipe,' the Grandfather said, 'you shall walk upon the earth, and whatever sickens there you shall make well.' Then he pointed to a man who was bright red all over, the colour of good and of plenty, and as he pointed, the red man lay down and rolled and changed into a bison that got up and galloped toward the sorrel horses of the east, and they too turned to bison, fat and many.

And now the fourth Grandfather spoke, he of the place where you are always facing [the south], whence comes the power to grow. 'Younger brother,' he said, 'with the powers of the four quarters you shall walk, a relative. Behold, the living centre of a nation I shall give you, and with it many you shall save.' And I saw that he was holding in his hand a bright red stick that was alive, and as I looked it sprouted at the top and sent forth branches, and on the branches many leaves came out and murmured and in the leaves the birds began to sing. And then for just a little while I thought I saw beneath it in the shade the circled villages of people and every living thing with roots or legs or wings, and all were happy. 'It shall stand in the centre of the nation's circle,' said the Grandfather, 'a cane to walk with and a people's heart; and by your powers you shall make it blossom.'

Then when he had been still a little while to hear the birds sing, he spoke again: 'Behold the earth!' So I looked down and saw it lying yonder like a hoop of peoples, and in the centre bloomed the holy stick that was a tree, and where it stood there crossed two roads, a red one and a black. 'From where the giant lives [the north] to where you always face [the south] the red road goes, the road of good,' the Grandfather said, 'and on it shall your nation walk. The black road goes from where the thunder beings live [the west] to where the sun continually shines [the east], a fearful road, a road of troubles and of war. On this also you shall walk, and from it you shall have the power to destroy a people's foes. In four ascents you shall walk the earth with power.'

I think he meant that I should see four generations, counting me, and now I am seeing the third.

Then he rose very tall and started running toward the south, and was an elk; and as he stood among the buckskins yonder, they too were elks.

Now the fifth Grandfather spoke, the oldest of them all, the Spirit of the Sky. 'My boy,' he said, 'I have sent for you and you have come. My power you shall see!' He stretched his arms and turned into a spotted eagle hovering. 'Behold,' he said, 'all the wings of the air shall come to you, and they and the winds and the stars shall be like relatives. You shall go across the earth with my power.' Then the eagle soared above my head and fluttered there; and suddenly the sky was full of friendly wings all coming toward me.

Now I knew the sixth Grandfather was about to speak, he who was the Spirit of the Earth, and I saw that he was very old, but more as men are old. His hair was long and white, his face was all in wrinkles and his eyes were deep and dim. I stared at him, for it seemed I knew him somehow; and as I stared, he slowly changed, for he was growing backwards into youth, and when he had become a boy, I knew that he was myself with all the years that would be mine at last. When he was old again, he said: 'My boy, have courage, for my power shall be yours, and you shall need it, for your nation on the earth will have great troubles. Come.'

He rose and tottered out through the rainbow door, and as I followed I was riding on the bay horse who had talked to me at first and led me to that place.

Then the bay horse stopped and faced the black horses of the west, and a voice said: 'They have given you the cup of water to make live the greening day, and also the bow and arrow to destroy.' The bay neighed, and the twelve black horses came and stood behind me, four abreast.

The bay faced the sorrels of the east, and I saw that they had morning stars upon their foreheads and they were very bright. And the voice said: 'They have given you the sacred pipe and the power that is peace, and the good red day.' The bay neighed, and the twelve sorrels stood behind me, four abreast.

My horse now faced the buckskins of the south, and a voice said: 'They have given you the sacred stick and your nation's hoop, and the yellow day; and in the centre of the hoop you shall set the stick and make it grow into a shielding tree, and bloom.' The bay neighed, and the twelve buckskins came and stood behind me, four abreast.

Then I knew that there were riders on all the horses there behind me, and a voice said: 'Now you shall walk the black road with these; and as you walk, all the nations that have roots or legs or wings shall fear you.'

So I started, riding toward the east down the fearful road, and behind me came the horsebacks four abreast – the blacks, the whites, the sorrels and the buckskins – and far away above the fearful road the daybreak star was rising very dim.

I looked below me where the earth was silent in a sick green light, and saw the hills look up afraid and the grasses on the hills and all the animals; and everywhere about me were the cries of frightened birds and sounds of fleeing wings. I was the chief of all the heavens riding there, and when I looked behind me, all the twelve black horses reared and plunged and thundered and their manes and tails were whirling hail and their nostrils snorted lightning. And when I looked below again, I saw the slant hail falling, and the long, sharp rain, and where we passed, the trees bowed long and all the hills were dim.

Now the earth was bright again as we rode. I could see the hills and valleys and the creeks and rivers passing under. We came above a place where three streams made a big one – a source of mighty waters[2] – and something terrible was there. Flames were rising from the waters and in the flames a blue man lived. The dust was floating all about him in the air, the grass was short and withered, the trees were wilting, two-legged and four-legged beings lay there thin and panting, and wings too weak to fly.

Then the black horse riders shouted 'Hoka hey!' and charged down upon the blue man, but were driven back. And the white troop shouted, charging, and was beaten; then the red troop and the yellow.

And when each had failed, they all cried together: 'Eagle Wing Stretches, hurry!' And all the world was filled with voices of all kinds that cheered me, so I charged. I had the cup of water in one hand and in the other was the bow that turned into a spear as the bay and I swooped down, and the spear's head was sharp lightning. It stabbed the blue man's heart, and as it struck I could hear the thunder rolling and many voices that cried 'Un-hee!', meaning that I had killed. The flames died. The trees and grasses were not withered any more and murmured happily together, and every living being cried in gladness with whatever voice it had. Then the four troops of horsemen charged down and struck the dead body of the blue man, counting coup; and suddenly it was only a harmless turtle.

You see, I had been riding with the storm clouds, and had come to earth as rain, and it was drouth that I had killed with the power that the Six Grandfathers gave me. So we were riding on the earth now down along the river flowing full from the source of waters, and soon I saw ahead the circled village of a people in the valley. And a Voice said: 'Behold a nation; it is yours. Make haste, Eagle Wing Stretches!'

I entered the village, riding, with the four horse troops behind me – the blacks, the whites, the sorrels and the buckskins; and the place was filled with moaning and with mourning for the dead. The wind was blowing from the south like fever, and when I looked around I saw that in nearly every tepee the women and the children and the men lay dying with the dead.

So I rode around the circle of the village, looking in upon the sick and dead, and I felt like crying as I rode. But when I looked behind me, all the women and the children and the men were getting up and coming forth with happy faces.

And a Voice said: 'Behold, they have given you the centre of the nation's hoop to make it live.'

So I rode to the centre of the village, with the horse troops in their quarters round about me, and there the people gathered. And the Voice said: 'Give them now the flowering stick that they may flourish, and the sacred pipe that they may know the power that is peace, and the wing of the white giant that they may have endurance and face all winds with courage.'

So I took the bright red stick and at the centre of the nation's hoop I thrust it in the earth. As it touched the earth it leaped mightily in my hand and was a waga chun, the rustling tree, very tall and full of leafy branches and of all birds singing. And beneath it all the animals were mingling with the people like relatives and making happy cries. The women raised their tremolo of joy, and the men shouted all together: 'Here we shall raise our children and be as little chickens under the mother sheo's wing.'

Then I heard the white wind blowing gently through the tree and singing there, and from the east the sacred pipe came flying on its eagle wings, and stopped before me there beneath the tree, spreading deep peace around it.

Then the daybreak star was rising, and a Voice said: 'It shall be a relative to them; and who shall see it, shall see much more, for thence comes wisdom; and those who do not see it shall be dark.' And all the people raised their faces to the east, and the star's light fell upon them, and all the dogs barked loudly and the horses whinnied.

Then when the many little voices ceased, the

[2] Black Elk thinks this was the Three Forks of the Missouri.

great Voice said: 'Behold the circle of the nation's hoop, for it is holy, being endless, and thus all powers shall be one power in the people without end. Now they shall break camp and go forth upon the red road, and your Grandfathers shall walk with them.' So the people broke camp and took the good road with the white wing on their faces, and the other of their going was like this:

First, the black horse riders with the cup of water; and the white horse riders with the white wing and the sacred herb; and the sorrel riders with the holy pipe; and the buckskins with the flowering stick. And after these the little children and the youths and maidens followed in a band.

Second, came the tribe's four chieftains, and their band was all young men and women.

Third, the nation's four advisers, leading men and women neither young nor old.

Fourth, the old men hobbling with their canes and looking to the earth.

Fifth, old women hobbling with their canes and looking to the earth.

Sixth, myself all alone upon the bay with the bow and arrows that the First Grandfather gave me. But I was not the last; for when I looked behind me there were ghosts of people like a trailing fog as far as I could see – grandfathers of grandfathers and grandmothers of grandmothers without number. And over these a great Voice – the Voice that was the South – lived, and I could feel it silent.

And as we went the Voice behind me said: 'Behold a good nation walking in a sacred manner in a good land!'

Then I looked up and saw that there were four ascents ahead, and these were the generations I should know. Now we were on the first ascent, and all the land was green. And as the long line climbed, all the old men and women raised their hands, palms forward, to the far sky yonder and began to croon a song together, and the sky ahead was filled with clouds of baby faces.

When we came to the end of the first ascent we camped in the sacred circle as before, and in the centre stood the holy tree, and still the land about us was all green.

Then we started on the second ascent, marching as before, and still the land was green, but it was getting steeper. And as I looked ahead, the people changed into elks and bison and all four-footed beings and even into fowls, all walking in a sacred manner on the good red road together. And I myself was a spotted eagle soaring over them. But just before we stopped to camp at the end of that ascent, all the marching animals grew restless and afraid that they were not what they had been, and began sending forth voices of trouble, calling to their chiefs. And when they camped at the end of that ascent, I looked down and saw that leaves were falling from the holy tree.

And the Voice said: 'Behold your nation, and remember what your Six Grandfathers gave you, for thenceforth your people walk in difficulties.'

Then the people broke camp again, and saw the black road before them towards where the sun goes down, and black clouds coming yonder; and they did not want to go but could not stay. And as they walked the third ascent, all the animals and fowls that were the people ran here and there, for each one seemed to have his own little vision that he followed and his own rules; and all over the universe I could hear the winds at war like wild beasts fighting.

And when we reached the summit of the third ascent and camped, the nation's hoop was broken like a ring of smoke that spreads and scatters and the holy tree seemed dying and all its birds were gone. And when I looked ahead I saw that the fourth ascent would be terrible.

Then when the people were getting ready to begin the fourth ascent, the Voice spoke like someone weeping, and it said: 'Look there upon your nation.' And when I looked down, the people were all changed back to human, and they were thin, their faces sharp, for they were starving. Their ponies were only hide and bones, and the holy tree was gone.

And as I looked and wept, I saw that there stood on the north side of the starving camp a sacred man who was painted red all over his body, and he held a spear as he walked into the centre of the people, and there he lay down and rolled. And when he got up, it was a fat bison standing there, and where the bison stood a sacred herb sprang up right where the tree had been in the centre of the nation's hoop. The herb grew and bore four blossoms on a single stem while I was looking – a blue, a white, a scarlet, and a yellow – and the bright rays of these flashed to the heavens.

I know now what this meant, that the bison were the gift of a good spirit and were our strength, but we should lose them, and from the same good spirit we must find another strength. For the people all seemed better when the herb had grown and bloomed, and the horses raised their tails and neighed and pranced around, and I could see a light breeze going from the north among the people like a ghost; and suddenly the flowering tree was there again at the centre of the nation's hoop where the four-rayed herb had blossomed.

I was still the spotted eagle floating, and I could see that I was already in the fourth ascent and the people were camping yonder at the top of the third long rise. It was dark and terrible about me, for all the winds of the world were fighting. It was like rapid gunfire and like whirling smoke, and like women and children wailing and like horses screaming all over the world.

I could see my people yonder running about, setting the smoke-flap poles and fastening down their tepees against the wind, for the storm cloud was coming on them very fast and black, and there were frightened swallows without number fleeing before the cloud.

Then a song of power came to me and I sang it there in the midst of that terrible place where I was. It went like this:

A good nation I will make live.
This the nation above has said.
They have given me the power to make over.

Experience 4

Wavoka's Letter and an Anthropologist's Description of the Ghost Dance

In the late 1880's, Jack Wilson, a Paiute Indian, fell ill and during his illness received a vision of the world's regeneration. Shortly thereafter he reclaimed his true name, Wavoka, and his vision became the basis of a messianic movement which spread throughout many Native American peoples. This movement, which was called the Ghost Dance, turned around a specific message in which the dead would return, sickness would be overcome and the world would be made anew. Here is one of Wavoka's early letters.

When you get home you must make a dance to continue five days. Dance four successive nights, and the last night keep up the dance until the morning of the fifth day, when all must bathe in the river and then disperse to their homes. You must all do in the same way.

I, Jack Wilson, love you all, and my heart is full of gladness for the gifts you have brought me. When you get home I shall give you a good cloud [rain?] which will make you feel good. I give you a good spirit and give you all good paint. I want you to come again in three months, some from each tribe there [the Indian Territory].

There will be a good deal of snow this year and some rain. In the fall there will be such a rain as I have never given you before.

Grandfather [a universal title of reverence among Indians and here meaning the messiah] says, when your friends die you must not cry. You must not hurt anybody or do harm to anyone. You must not fight. Do right always. It will give you satisfaction in life. This young man has a good father and mother. [Possibly this refers to Casper Edson, the young Arapaho who wrote down this message of Wavoka for the delegation.]

Do not tell the white people about this. Jesus is now upon the earth. He appears like a cloud. The dead are alive all again. I do not know when they will be here; maybe this fall or in the spring. When the time comes there will be no more sickness and everyone will be young again.

Do not refuse to work for the whites and do not

make any trouble with them until you leave them. When the earth shakes [at the coming of the new world] do not be afraid. It will not hurt you.

I want you to dance every six weeks. Make a feast at the dance and have food that everybody may eat. Then bathe in the water. That is all. You will receive good words again from me some time. Do not tell lies.

The American ethnographer, James Mooney, studied the movement just at its peak in 1890 and here he offers a description of the dance as it appeared in various groups. Again, it is to be noted that this dance, which became a pan-Native American ritual is based upon the experience of Wavoka.

The dance commonly begins about the middle of the afternoon or later, after sundown. When it begins in the afternoon, there is always an intermission of an hour or two for supper. The announcement is made by the criers, old men who assume this office apparently by tacit understanding, who go about the camp shouting in a loud voice to the people to prepare for the dance. The preliminary painting and dressing is usually a work of about two hours. When all is ready, the leaders walk out to the dance place, and facing inward, join hands so as to form a small circle. Then, without movement from their places they sing the opening song, according to previous agreement, in a soft undertone. Having sung it through once more they raise their voices to their full strength and repeat it, this time slowly circling around in the dance. The step is different from that of most other Indian dances, but very simple, the dancers moving from right to left, following the course of the sun, advancing the left foot and following it with the right, hardly lifting the feet from the ground. For this reason it is called by the Shoshoni the 'dragging dance'. All the songs are adapted to the simple measure of the dance step. As the song rises and swells the people come singly and in groups from the several tepees, and one after another joins the circle until any number from fifty to five hundred men, women, and children are in the dance. When the circle is small, each song is repeated through a number of circuits. If large, it is repeated only through one circuit, measured by the return of the leaders to the starting point. Each song is started in the same manner, first in an undertone while the singers stand still in their places, and then with full voice as they begin to circle around. At intervals between the songs, more especially after the trances have begun, the dancers unclasp hands and sit down to smoke or talk for a few minutes. At such times the leaders sometimes deliver short addresses or sermons, or relate the recent trance experience of the dancer. In holding each other's hands the dancers usually intertwine the fingers instead of grasping the hand as with us. Only an Indian could keep the blanket in place as they do under such circumstances. Old people hobbling along with sticks, and little children hardly past the toddling period sometimes form a part of the circle, the more vigorous dancers accommodating the movement to their weakness. Frequently a woman will be seen to join the circle with an infant upon her back and dance with the others, but should she show the least sign of approaching excitement watchful friends lead her away that no harm may come to the child. Dogs are driven off from the neighbourhood of the circle lest they should run against any of those who have fallen into a trance and thus awaken them. The dancers themselves are careful not to disturb the trance subjects while their souls are in the spirit world. Full Indian dress is worn, with buckskin, paint and feathers, but among the Sioux the women discarded the belts ornamented with discs of German silver, because the metal had come from the white man. Among the southern tribes, on the contrary, hats are sometimes worn in the dance, although this was not considered in strict accordance with the doctrine.

No drum, rattle, or other musical instrument is used in the dance, excepting sometimes by an individual dancer in imitation of a trance vision. In this respect particularly the Ghost Dance differs from every other Indian dance. Neither are any fires built within the circle, so far as known, with any tribe excepting the Walapai. The northern Cheyenne, however, built four fires in a peculiar fashion outside of the circle, as already described.

With most tribes the dance was performed around a tree or pole planted in the centre and variously decorated. In the southern plains, however, only the Kiowa seem ever to have followed this method, they sometimes dancing around a cedar tree. On breaking the circle at the end of the dance the performers shook their blankets or shawl in the air, with the idea of driving away all evil influences. On later instructions from the messiah all then went down to bathe in the stream, the men in one place and the women in another, before going to their tepees. The idea of washing away evil things, spiritual as well as earthly, by bathing in running water is too natural and universal to need comment . . .

Ethics

Instructions in the Ciexaus Ceremony (Yamana)

The ethical dimension of small-scale religious traditions is best illustrated by the ethical instruction given at initiation rituals. As the individual moves from one stage of life to the next, he must take on new relationships to those around him. Here, members of the Yamana are given a very direct and precise code of behaviour which is to accompany them in their new position in the community.

Do not seek to benefit only yourself, but think of other people also. If you yourself have an abundance, do not say: 'The others do not concern me, I need not bother about them!' If you were lucky in hunting, let others share it. Moreover, show them the favourable spots where there are many sea lions which can be easily slain. Let others have their share occasionally. If you want to amass everything for yourself, other people will stay away from you and no one will want to be with you. If you should one day fall ill, no one will visit you because, for your part, you did not formerly concern yourself about others.

Grant other people something also. The Yamana do not like a person who acts selfishly.

No one likes a perverse, obstinate person: everyone speaks scornfully of him and avoids him.

Postscript

Our understanding of small-scale traditional religions was greatly affected by the Age of Discovery in the 16th and 17th centuries, when for the first time Europeans came in contact with the great civilizations of the New World, Africa, Indonesia, Australia and the Pacific. In the 18th century, the question of similarity and difference was repeatedly asked by those Europeans who, for one reason or another, spent time in these areas. For example, the French Jesuit J.F. Lafitau (1670–1740) had been a missionary among Canadian Indians, and in his book *Moeurs des sauvages américains comparés aux moeurs des premiers temps* (1724) he sought to draw parallels between what he had seen among the Native American peoples and the civilizations of classical antiquity. In the 19th century, ethnological data from small-scale traditional peoples was collected by civil servants and Christian missionaries, both Protestant and Catholic. Knowing the language of the people they worked with was often a prerequisite for their activities, and this allowed them to begin the process of entering the religious worlds of small-scale traditional peoples. In many cases, their pronouncements about 'primitive', 'pagan' and 'heathen' religion were entirely wrong, and issued not from what they actually saw but from their inability to remove the spectacles of European Christianity. However, these officials and missionaries were exceedingly hard-working in collecting data, and more recent scholarship has yet to take full cognizance of the materials they collected. With the development of the academic discipline of anthropology at the end of the 19th century, expeditions were sent out to gather data to prove or disprove one of the theories developed in the various schools of anthropology. Among the most famous of these 'schools' were Leo Frobenius (d. 1938) in Frankfurt, Father Wilhelm Schmidt (1868–1954) in Vienna and Franz Boaz (d. 1942) in North America.

Bibliography

A number of very fine collections of documents about small-scale traditional religions are available to the general reader. These include Joseph Campbell's *The Masks of God: Primitive Mythology* (1959), Charles H. Long's *Alpha: The Myths of Creation* (1963) and Mircea Eliades's *From Primitives to Zen: A Thematic Sourcebook on the History of Religions* (1967). There are many fine specific studies of the religions of small-scale traditional peoples, but one might include at the top of the list Hans Schärer's *Ngaju Religion: The Conception of God among a South Borneo People* (1963), Gregory Bateson's *Naven* (1965), Alphonso Ortiz's *Tewa World: Space, Time, Being and Becoming in a Pueblo Society* (1969) and Jan van Baal's *Dema: Description and Analysis of Marind-anim Culture (South New Guinea)* (1966). The very best general introduction to the religious traditions of small-scale traditional peoples is Sam D. Gill's *Beyond the 'Primitive': The Religions of Non-literate Peoples* (1982).

Initiation ceremonies are often the principal way in which oral traditions are handed down. Here, in Arnhem Land, Australia, a boy is painted with sacred designs before being introduced to the sacred tales and rituals of his clan.

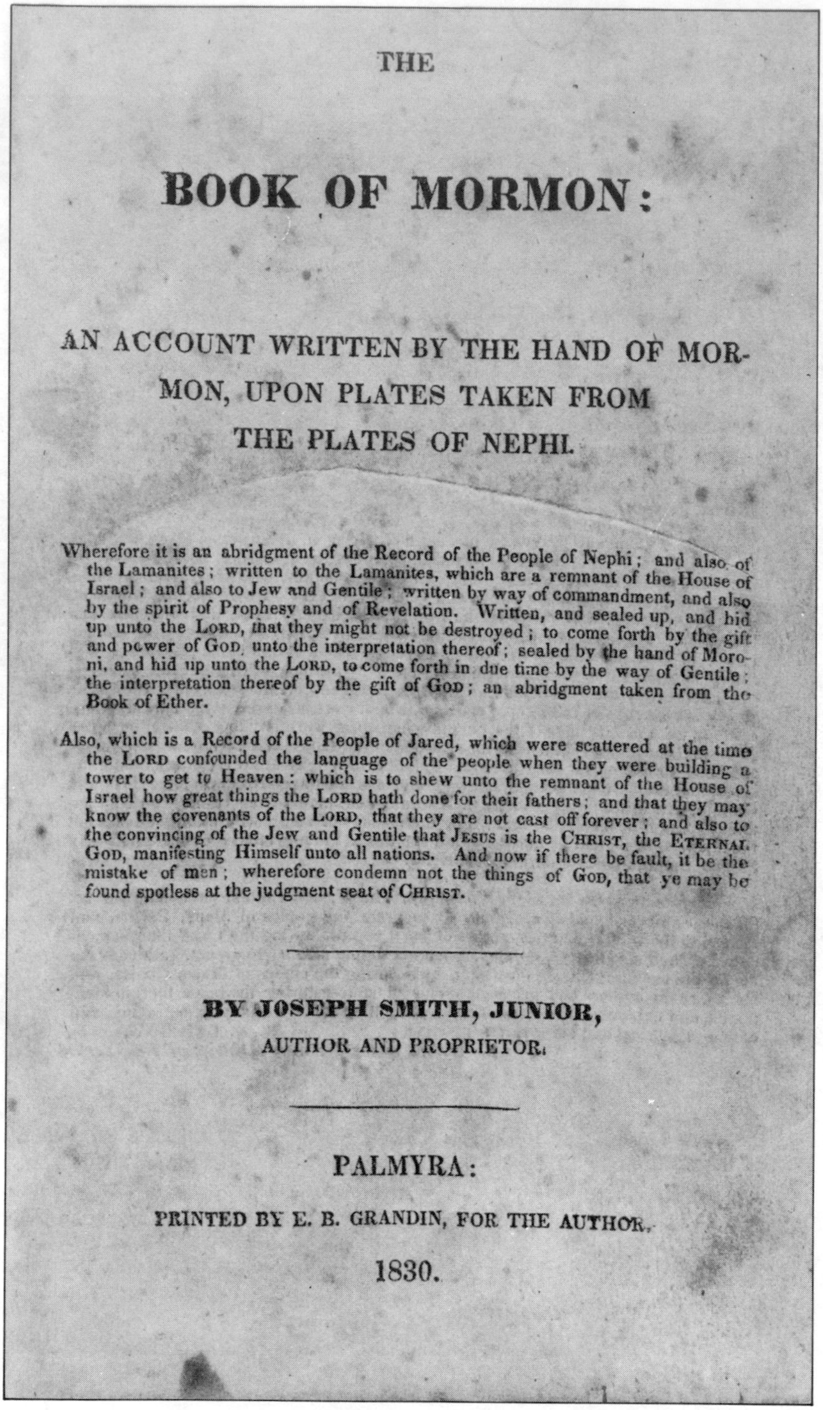

THE

BOOK OF MORMON:

AN ACCOUNT WRITTEN BY THE HAND OF MORMON, UPON PLATES TAKEN FROM THE PLATES OF NEPHI.

Wherefore it is an abridgment of the Record of the People of Nephi; and also of the Lamanites; written to the Lamanites, which are a remnant of the House of Israel; and also to Jew and Gentile; written by way of commandment, and also by the spirit of Prophesy and of Revelation. Written, and sealed up, and hid up unto the LORD, that they might not be destroyed; to come forth by the gift and power of GOD, unto the interpretation thereof; sealed by the hand of Moroni, and hid up unto the LORD, to come forth in due time by the way of Gentile; the interpretation thereof by the gift of GOD; an abridgment taken from the Book of Ether.

Also, which is a Record of the People of Jared, which were scattered at the time the LORD confounded the language of the people when they were building a tower to get to Heaven: which is to shew unto the remnant of the House of Israel how great things the LORD hath done for their fathers; and that they may know the covenants of the LORD, that they are not cast off forever; and also to the convincing of the Jew and Gentile that JESUS is the CHRIST, the ETERNAL GOD, manifesting Himself unto all nations. And now if there be fault, it be the mistake of men; wherefore condemn not the things of GOD, that ye may be found spotless at the judgment seat of CHRIST.

BY JOSEPH SMITH, JUNIOR,

AUTHOR AND PROPRIETOR.

PALMYRA:

PRINTED BY E. B. GRANDIN, FOR THE AUTHOR.

1830.

The title page of the first edition of the Book of Mormon, *published in 1830. In that year, Joseph Smith founded The Church of Jesus Christ of Latter-Day Saints; the* Book of Mormon, *together with the Bible, became its main scripture.*

New Religions

Introduction

Modern history has seen a large number of new religions, as indeed has virtually every period of recorded history. In the following selections we have drawn on some of the main categories of new faiths or movements. Some are more controversial than others. First, there are the new faiths of the New World, notably Christian Science – here represented by an excerpt from *Science and Health* – which has been one of a number of new religions founded by women, and, in a rather different key, the religion of the prophet Joseph Smith II, with its vision of a new Jerusalem in the West. Second, there are new currents of spirituality combining Indian and Western motifs, here represented by an extract from the writings of Aurobindo, the famous guru whose Ashram was one of the pioneers of a cross-cultural synthesis between East and West. Then there are the new religions of Japan, which have arisen in the context of Japan's rapid cultural, political and economic transformations of the last 120 years. We include here the positive and life-affirming ethic of the Perfect Liberty Kyodan. Then, fourthly, there are the many religions of black Africa, here represented by a testimony from the Zulu Zion movement founded through Isaiah Shembe. Much interest has been aroused by those new movements sometimes called 'cults' in the West. We reproduce here a passage from the *Divine Principle* of Sun Myung Moon. Finally we cite a passage expounding some of the values of the Baha'i faith, important as one of the modernizing new religions, pointing towards a new world civilization, and stemming out of the cultural milieu of 19th-century Iranian Islam.

These passages illustrate the variety of styles and substance of these proliferating new religions. Which will survive the test of centuries and retain vitality for the distant future? History itself is a winnowing process. But whatever happens the religions will remain as testimonies to how modern people have coped religiously with the crises and opportunities of modern global change. Christian Science looked at the anxieties of illness and suffering and tried to revive religion's healing mission. The Mormons represent the aspiration to found a new Jerusalem in a newly discovered and settled land. Aurobindo tried to modernize the conception of Yoga and of the Ashram, in the context of Western thought and evolutionary theory. The Perfect Liberty Association and other new religions try to make sense of personal existence in a changed society. Shembe expresses the search for a new spiritual identity in the context of the conquest of peoples in the colonial era. The cults testify to hungers among many of the young for new communities and new ideals.

Sacred Narrative

Sun Myung Moon's Divine Principle

Sun Myung Moon's *Divine Principle* was published in the USA in 1973, and forms the basis for the teachings of the Unification Church. This passage deals with the 'last things' and occurs as part of a Biblical reinterpretation of human history into which are woven Confucian and other elements drawn from Moon's own visionary experience. The usual belief is that he himself is the Lord of the Second Advent. The main departure from orthodox Christian interpretation is the belief that Jesus' death stopped him from completing his task, so that another has to finish the Messianic mission for him.

God's third blessing to men[1] signified Adam and Eve's dominion over the world of creation after they attained perfection. Man's dominion over the world of creation has two aspects – internal and external. We can see that in the present age the two aspects of man's dominion, lost with the human fall, are being restored.

Internal dominion means the dominion of heart-and-zeal. When a man has perfected his individuality he becomes one in heart-and-zeal with God; thus he is able to experience God's own heart-and-zeal. On the day when man, after having perfected himself, comes to love the world of creation with heart-and-zeal identical to God's, and when he receives the beauty returned by the creation, he becomes the dominator in heart-and-zeal over the world of creation. However, due to the fall, man failed to experience God's heart-and-zeal and has not been able to regard the creation with God's heart-and-zeal. Nonetheless, God has been working His providence of restoration by means of religion, philosophy and ethics, constantly elevating by degrees the spiritual standard of fallen men toward God. Thus, man in the present age is restoring his qualification as the dominator in heart-and-zeal over the world of creation.

External dominion means domination through science. If man, having perfected himself, had been able to dominate the world of creation internally with heart-and-zeal identical to that which God had over the world of creation at the time of its creation, man's scientific achievement could have reached its culmination in an extremely short time, because man's spiritual sensibility would have been developed to the highest dimension. Thus, men could have dominated externally all the things of creation. In consequence, man not only could have subdued the world of nature, including the heavenly bodies, at the earliest possible date, but he also could have brought about an extremely comfortable living environment due to the economic development that would have accompanied scientific achievement.

However, man, by losing his spiritual light due to the fall and by thus being deprived of his internal domination over the things of creation, fell to the status of a barbarian with a spiritual sensibility as dull as that of the animals. Thus, he lost the external domination over creation. Man, according to God's providence of restoration, now has restored his spiritual light. Consequently, both his internal and external dominations have, by degrees, been restored. Therefore, scientific development in the present day has also reached its highest degree. So it has come about that modern men have created an extremely comfortable living environment, due to economic developments which followed brilliant scientific achievements.

We see then that God's third blessing to men is being restored, and from this we cannot deny that today we have reached the Last Days.

As we have observed repeatedly, the development of the cultural spheres also shows that a worldwide cultural sphere is now being formed centred on one religion. Nations, too, are moving toward one worldwide structure of sovereignty, starting from the League of Nations,

[1] The other blessings are supposed to be firstly individuality and, secondly, parenthood and social existence.

through the United Nations and reaching today for world government. Regarding economic development, the world is now on the threshold of forming one common market. Extremely well-developed transportation and communication facilities have reduced the limitations of time and space. Men are able to communicate with one another on the earth as easily as if the earth were the garden of a house in which people of all the different races of the East and the West lived as one family. All mankind is crying out for brotherly love.

However, a home is formed around the parents; there alone can true brotherly love occur. Therefore, upon the Second Advent of the Lord as the True Parent of mankind, all men will come to live harmoniously in the garden as one family.

From this too we may know that today is surely the Last Days. There must be one final gift which history, having thus progressed, is about to present to mankind. This must be the ideology of the macrocosmic nature that can bind all the strangers who now live in turmoil within one world without any true purpose, into one family centred on the same parents.

Doctrine

Mind over Matter: Science and Health with Key to the Scriptures

Here Mary Baker Eddy (1821–1910) expounds succinctly her notion that belief in matter is an illusion. She propounds a version of Idealism or the belief that everything is mental in character, which she saw as a key to understanding scriptures. She places overriding emphasis on Christ's healing activities, and healing was the central motif of the Church of Christ Scientist, founded in Boston in 1879.

The term Christian Science was introduced by the author to designate the scientific system of divine healing.

The revelation consists of two parts:

1. The discovery of this divine Science of Mind-healing, through a spiritual sense of the Scriptures and through the teachings of the Comforter, as promised by the Master.

2. The proof, by present demonstration, that the so-called miracles of Jesus did not specially belong to a dispensation now ended, but that they illustrated an ever-operative divine Principle. The operation of this Princple indicates the eternality of the scientific order and continuity of being.

Christian Science differs from material science, but not on that account is it less scientific. On the contrary, Christian Science is pre-eminently scientific, being based on Truth, the Principle of all science.

Physical science (so-called) is human knowledge – a law of mortal mind, a blind belief, a Samson shorn of his strength. When this human belief lacks organizations to support it, its foundations are gone. Having neither moral might, spiritual basis, nor holy Principle of its own, this belief mistakes effect for cause and seeks to find life and intelligence in matter, thus limiting Life and holding fast to discord and death. In a word, human belief is a blind conclusion from material reasoning. This is a mortal, finite sense of things, which immortal Spirit silences forever.

The universe, like man, is to be interpreted by Science from its divine Principle, God, and then it can be understood; but when explained on the basis of physical sense and represented as subject to growth, maturity and decay, the universe, like man, is, and must continue to be, an enigma.

Adhesion, cohesion and attraction are

properties of Mind. They belong to divine Principle, and support the equipoise of that thought–force, which launched the earth in its orbit and said to the proud wave, 'Thus far and no farther'.

Spirit is the life, substance and continuity of all things. We tread on forces. Withdraw them, and creation must collapse. Human knowledge calls them forces of matter; but divine Science declares that they belong wholly to divine Mind, are inherent in this Mind, and so restores them to their rightful home and classification.

The elements and functions of the physical body and of the physical world will change as mortal mind changes its beliefs. What is now considered the best condition for organic and functional health in the human body may no longer be found indispensable to health. Moral conditions will be found always harmonious and health-giving. Neither organic inaction nor overaction is beyond God's control; and man will be found normal and natural to changed mortal thought, and therefore more harmonious in his manifestations than he was in the prior states which human belief created and sanctioned.

As human thought changes from one stage to another of conscious pain and painlessness, sorrow and joy – from fear to hope and from faith to understanding – the visible manifestation will at last be man governed by Soul, not by material sense. Reflecting God's government, man is self-governed. When subordinate to the divine Spirit, man cannot be controlled by sin or death, thus proving our material theories about laws of health to be valueless.

The seasons will come and go with changes of time and tide, cold and heat, latitude and longitude. The agriculturist will find that these changes cannot affect his crops. 'As a vesture shalt Thou change them and they shall be changed.' The mariner will have dominion over the atmosphere and the great deep, over the fish of the sea and the fowls of the air. The astronomer will no longer look up to the stars – he will look out from them upon the universe; and the florist will find his flower before its seed.

Thus matter will finally be proved nothing more than a mortal belief, wholly inadequate to affect a man through its supposed organic action or supposed existence. Error will be no longer used in stating truth. The problems of nothingness, or 'dust to dust', will be solved, and mortal mind will be without form and void, for mortality will cease when man beholds himself God's reflection, even as man sees his reflection in a glass.

All Science is divine. Human thought never projected the least portion of true being. Human belief has sought and interpreted in its own way the echo of Spirit, and so seems to have reversed it and repeated it materially; but the human mind never produced a real tone nor sent forth a positive sound.

The point at issue between Christian Science on the one hand and popular theology on the other is this: shall Science explain cause and effect as being both natural and spiritual? Or shall all that is beyond the cognizance of the material senses be called supernatural, and be left to the mercy of speculative hypotheses?

I have set forth Christian Science and its application to the treatment of disease just as I have discovered them. I have demonstrated through Mind the effects of Truth on the health, longevity, and morals of men; and I have found nothing in ancient or in modern systems on which to found my own, except the teachings and demonstrations of our great Master and the lives of prophets and apostles. The Bible has been my only authority. I have had no other guide in 'the straight and narrow way' of Truth.

If Christendom resists the author's application of the word Science to Christianity, or questions her use of the word Science, she will not therefore lose faith in Christianity, nor will Christianity lose its hold upon her. If God, the All-in-all, be the creator of the spiritual universe, including man, then everything entitled to a classification as truth, or Science, must be comprised in a knowledge or understanding of God, for there can be nothing beyond illimitable divinity.

The terms Divine Science, Spiritual Science, Christ Science or Christian Science, or Science alone, she employs interchangeably, according to the requirements of the context. These synonymous terms stand for everthing relating to God, the infinite, supreme, eternal Mind. It may be said, however, that the term Christian Science relates especially to Science as applied to humanity. Christian Science reveals God, not as the author of sin, sickness and death, but as Divine Principle, Supreme Being, Mind, exempt from all evil. It teaches that matter is the falsity, not the fact, of existence; that nerves, brain, stomach, lungs, and so forth, have – as matter – no intelligence, life nor sensation.

There is no physical science, inasmuch as all truth proceeds from the divine Mind. Therefore truth is not human, and is not a law of matter, for matter is not a lawgiver. Science is an emanation of divine Mind, and is alone able to interpret God aright. It has a spiritual, and not a material origin. It is a divine utterance – the Comforter which leadeth into all truth.

Christian Science eschews what is called natural science, in so far as this is built on the false hypotheses that matter is its own lawgiver, that law is founded on material conditions, and that these are final and overrule the might of divine Mind. Good is natural and primitive. It is not miraculous to itself.

The term Science, properly understood, refers only to the laws of God and to His government of the universe, inclusive of man. From this it follows that business men and cultured scholars have found that Christian Science enhances their endurance and mental powers, enlarges their perception of character, gives them acuteness and comprehensiveness and an ability to exceed their ordinary capacity. The human mind, imbued with this spiritual understanding, becomes more elastic, is capable of greater endurance, escapes somewhat from itself, and requires less repose. A knowledge of the Science of being develops the latent abilities and possibilities of man. It extends the atmosphere of thought, giving mortals access to broader and higher realms. It raises the thinker into his native air of insight and perspicacity.

Ritual

The Meaning of Meditation: The Hour of God

Sri Aurobindo (1872–1950) was concerned to bring together Western thought, which he had absorbed as a child and young man in England, and Indian religion, which he rediscovered on his return to India. Much of his life was devoted to writing and to being the spiritual focus of the life of the Ashram at Pondicherry, which attracted during and after his lifetime a large number of men and women from India and the West. In the present passage he desribes how self-training through prayer and meditation can achieve the necessary stillness for receiving divine illumination. This was part of his 'integral Yoga' or system of daily living, which uses healthy and creative living as a means of self-perfection; it is thus that mankind evolves upwards.

And what then was gained when Nature passed from the obscurity of the plant kingdom to the awakened sense, desire and emotion and the free mobility of animal life? The gain was liberated sense and feeling and desire and courage and cunning and the contrivance of the objects of desire, passion and action and hunger and battle and conquest and the sex-call and play and pleasure, and all the joy and pain of the conscious living creature. Not only the life of the body which the animal has in common with the plant but a life-mind that appeared for the first time in the earth-story and grew from form to more organized form till it reached in the best the limit of its own formula.

The animal achieved a first form of mind, but could not possess it, because this first organized mind-consciousness was enslaved to a narrow scope, tied to the full functioning of the physical body and brain and nerve, tied to serve the physical life and its desires and needs and passions, limited to the insistent uses of the vital urge, of material longing and feeling and action, bound in its own inferior instrumentation, its spontaneous combinings of association and memory and instinct. It could not get away from them, could not get behind them as man's intelligence gets behind them to observe them; still less could it turn down on them from above as do human reason and will to control, enlarge, re-order, exceed, sublimate.

At each capital step of nature's ascent there is a reversal of consciousness in the evolving spirit. As when a climber turns on a summit to which he has laboured and looks down with an exalted and wider power of vision on all that was once above or on a level with him but is now below his feet, the evolutionary being not only transcends his past self, his former now exceeded status, but commands from a higher grade of self-experience and vision, with a new apprehending feeling or a new comprehending sight and effectuating power in a greater system of values, all that was once his own consciousness but is now below him and belongs to an inferior creation. This reversal is the sign of a decisive victory and the seal of a radical progress in Nature.

The new consciousness attained in the spiritual evolution is always higher in grade and power, always larger, more comprehensive, wider in sight and feeling, richer and finer in faculties, more complex, organic, dominating than the consciousness that was once our own but is now left behind us. There are greater breadth and space, heights before impassable, unexpected depths and intimacies. There is a luminous expansion that is the very sign-manual of the Supreme upon his work.

Mark that each of the great radical steps forward already taken by Nature has been infinitely greater in its change, incalculably vaster in its consequences than its puny predecessor. There is a miraculous opening to an always richer and wider expression, there is a new illuminating of the creation and a dynamic heightening of its significances. There is in this world we live in no equality of all on a flat level, but a hierarchy of ever-increasing precipitous superiorities pushing their mountain shoulders upwards towards the Supreme.

Because man is a mental being, he naturally imagines that mind is the one great leader and actor and creator or the indispensable agent in the universe. But this is an error; even for knowledge mind is not the only or the greatest possble instrument, the one aspirant and discoverer. Mind is a clumsy interlude between Nature's vast and precise subconscient action and the vaster infallible superconscient action of the Godhead.

There is nothing mind can do that cannot be better done in the mind's immobility and thought-free stillness.

When mind is still, then Truth gets her chance to be heard in the purity of the silence.

Truth cannot be attained by the Mind's thought but only by identity and silent vision. Truth lives in the calm wordless Light of the eternal spaces; she does not intervene in the noise and cackle of logical debate.

Thought in the mind can at most be Truth's brilliant and transparent garment; it is not even her body. Look through the robe, not at it and you may see some hint of her form. There can be a thought-body of Truth, but that is the spontaneous supramental Thought and word that leap fully formed out of the Light, not any difficult mental counterfeit and patchwork. The Supramental thought is not a means of arriving at Truth, but a way of expressing her; for Truth in the Supermind is self-found or self-existent. It is an arrow from the Light, not a bridge to reach it.

Cease inwardly from thought and word, be motionless within you, look upward into the light and outward into the vast cosmic consciousness that is around you. Be more and more one with the brightness and the vastness. Then will Truth dawn on you from above and flow in you from all around you.

But only if the mind is no less intense in its purity than its silence. For an impure mind the silence will soon fill with misleading lights and false voices, the echo or sublimation of its own vain conceits and opinions or the response to its secret pride, vanity, ambition, lust, greed or desire. The Titans and the Demons will speak to it more readily than the divine Voices.

Silence is indispensable, but also there is needed wideness. If the mind is not silent, it cannot receive the lights and voices of the supernal Truth or receiving mixes with them its own flickering tongues and blind pretentious babble. Active, arrogant, noisy it distorts and disfigures what it receives. If it is not wide, it cannot house the effective power and creative force of the Truth. Some light may play there but it becomes narrow, confined and sterile; the Force that is descending is cabined and thwarted and withdraws again to its vast heights from this rebellious foreign plane. Or even if something comes down and remains, it is a pearl in the mire; for no change takes place in the nature or else there is formed, only a thin intensity that points narrowly upward to the summits, but can hold little and diffuse less upon the world around it.

Institutional Expression

The Church of the Latter-Day Saints: The Book of Mormon

This chapter, part of the book which Joseph Smith (1805–44) wrote down after his visionary experience of the angel Moroni and receiving the gold plates to translate, contains a vision of the new Jerusalem. This was the charter for Joseph's foundation of the Church of Jesus Christ of Latter-Day Saints and the vision which drew the faithful in their drive to create a new society in the American West.

And verily I say unto you a sign, that ye may know the time when these things shall be about to take place – that I shall gather in, from their long dispersion, my people, O house of Israel, and shall establish again among them my Zion;

And behold, this is the thing which I will give unto you for a sign – for verily I say unto you that when these things which I declare unto you, and which I shall declare unto you hereafter of myself, and by the power of the Holy Ghost which shall be given unto you of the Father, shall be made known unto the Gentiles that they may know concerning this people who are a remnant of the house of Jacob, and concerning this my people who shall be scattered by them;

Verily, verily, I say unto you, when these things shall be made known unto them of the Father, and shall come forth of the Father, from them unto you;

For it is wisdom in the Father that they should be established in this land, and be set up as a free people by the power of the Father, that these things might come forth from them unto a remnant of your seed, that the covenant of the Father may be fulfilled which he hath covenanted with his people, O house of Israel;

Therefore, when these works and the works which shall be wrought among you hereafter shall come forth from the Gentiles, unto your seed which shall dwindle in unbelief because of iniquity;

For thus it behoveth the Father that it should come forth from the Gentiles, that he may show forth his power unto the Gentiles, for this cause that the Gentiles, if they will not harden their hearts, that they may repent and come unto me and be baptized in my name and know of the true points of my doctrine, that they may be numbered among my people, O house of Israel;

And when these things come to pass that thy seed shall begin to know these things – it shall be a sign unto them that they may know that the work of the Father hath already commenced unto the fulfilling of the covenant which he hath made unto the people who are of the house of Israel.

And when that day shall come, it shall come to pass that kings shall shut their mouths; for that which had not been told them shall they see; and that which they had not heard shall they consider.

For in that day, for my sake shall the Father work a work, which shall be a great and a marvellous work among them; and there shall be among them those who will not believe it, although a man shall declare it unto them.

But behold, the life of my servant shall be in my hand; therefore they shall not hurt him, although he shall be marred because of them. Yet I will heal him, for I will show unto them that my wisdom is greater than the cunning of the devil.

Therefore it shall come to pass that whosover will not believe in my words, who am Jesus Christ, which the Father shall cause him to bring forth unto the Gentiles, and shall give unto him power that he shall bring them forth unto the Gentiles, (it shall be done even as Moses said) they shall be cut off from among my people who are of the covenant.

And my people who are a remnant of Jacob shall be among the Gentiles, yea, in the midst of them as a lion among the beasts of the forest, as a young lion among the flocks of sheep, who, if he go through both treadeth down and teareth in pieces, and none can deliver.

Their hand shall be lifted up upon their adversaries, and all their enemies shall be cut off.

Yea, woe be unto the Gentiles except they repent; for it shall come to pass in that day, saith the Father, that I will cut off thy horses out of the midst of thee, and I will destroy thy chariots;

And I will cut off the cities of thy land, and throw down all thy strongholds;

And I will cut off withchcrafts out of thy land, and thou shalt have no more soothsayers;

Thy graven images I will also cut off, and thy standing images out of the midst of thee, and thou shalt no more worship the works of thy hands;

And I will pluck up thy groves out of the midst of thee; so will I destroy thy cities.

And it shall come to pass that all lyings, and deceivings, and envyings, and strifes, and priestcrafts, and whoredoms, shall be done away.

For it shall come to pass, saith thy Father, that at that day whosoever will not repent and come unto my Beloved Son, them will I cut off from among my people, O house of Israel;

And I will execute vengeance and fury upon them, even as upon the heathen, such as they have not heard.

But if they will repent and hearken unto my words, and harden not their hearts, I will establish my church among them and they shall come in unto the covenant and be numbered among this remnant of Jacob, unto whom I have given this land for their inheritance;

And they shall assist my people, the remnant of Jacob, and also as many of the house of Israel as shall come, that they may build a city, which shall be called the New Jerusalem.

And then shall they assist my people that they may be gathered in, who are scattered upon all the face of the land, in unto the New Jerusalem.

And then shall the power of heaven come down among them; and I also will be in the midst.

And then shall the work of the Father commence at that day, even when this gospel shall be preached among the remnant of this people. Verily I say unto you, at that day shall the work of the Father commence among all the dispersed of my people, yea, even the tribes which have been lost, which the Father hath led away out of Jerusalem.

Yea, the work shall commence among all the dispersed of my people, with the Father, to prepare the way whereby they may come unto me, that they may call on the Father in my name.

Yea, and then shall the work commence, with the Father, among all nations, in preparing the way whereby his people may be gathered home to the land of their inheritance.

And they shall go out from all nations; and they shall not go out in haste, nor go by flight, for I will go before them, saith the Father, and I will be their rearward.

Experience

A Black Messiah: Acts of the Nazarites

The son of the Zulu prophet Isaiah Shembe, who in 1911 founded the Nazarite Church or Ama Nazaretha, whose holiest place is the hill Ekuphakameni, compiled the *Acts of the Nazarites*, consisting of conversion and other testimonies. The present passage, from Bengt Sundkler's *Zulu Zion and Some Swazi Zionists* (1976), shows the effects of directly experiencing the charisma and healing powers of Isaiah Shembe. The themes are Biblical but are given new and surprisingly vivid expression in the actual life of the people among whom Shembe moved.

His presence amazed me. He looked like Jesus, and I was thinking, I am not sleeping, nor am I drunk. Furthermore he was so pleasant, speaking in a friendly manner. I have seen Jesus in pictures. Here only the hair was different from that of Jesus. Later he said, 'Let us go.' His Jesus-like appearance began to change and slowly disappeared, and now he looked like a beautiful girl, and I have never seen a girl as beautiful as this one was.

As we walked along, people were acknowledging him and I had to ask him, 'Did Jesus really come on earth?' He said, 'He came for sure, my child, but people did not understand it and they crucified him. Today many do not see him,' and he added, 'Blessed are those who see him.'

Shembe told people to give Mngoma a chair. Mngoma said, 'Never shall I sit on a chair, like my Lord who is also sitting on a chair.' He then gave me a mat.

In a certain Church service later on, Shembe said, 'Today the witchfinder of heaven (*isangoma sasezulwini*) has come, knowing all the acts which people have committed, good and bad. Some among you do good, others do bad things. I am dividing people according to their acts.' Later, Shembe said, 'I, Shembe, am leaving with you two prophets clothed in sackcloth; they are the two olive trees about whom the Book of Revelations (11:4) is speaking. The Lord is leaving and handing over the Church to these two prophets.'

In the morning, there was a Church service, and after that the sick ones came. There was a piece of cloth with the help of which the sick ones were prayed for. The Lord gave it to us in order that we pray with it. There was a woman with a bad demon. Then Shembe called those patients and caught hold of the woman who was as dead, lying down. He said, 'Her spirit is in heaven!' We were very much afraid as we heard that she was dead, and that her spirit was in heaven.

Then I felt that the work of the Lord at that place was indeed spoiled, because they said they offered human sacrifice at Ekuphakameni, and yet they said about Jesus that he was praying for them with the help of Beelzebul. I saw him looking towards heaven and then to that person. That gave me hope, for now I noticed that the woman began to move; the one who was dead had risen.

Shembe now left for another place. As we approached, an old woman was singing praises and saying, 'Now the Saviour has come to liberate me!'

Shembe said, 'We have come here to chase away the war from this place.' Then he produced the piece of cloth and said, 'Let us pray for the sick.'

Many people assembled. The time for baptizing people had come. People said, 'There are crocodiles in that place where we are to be baptized.' They came to a small river. I brought out the word which I did not even know [beforehand] that I was to pronounce. Those who enter this water will find that their sins will remain in it, and the different kinds of illness will remain in that water. Indeed after my sermon, I entered the water and baptized them and these people who had been dragged there by hand-cart were now healed and could walk on their own.

We came from Judia and were on our way to Velabahleke [two different Nazaretha centres]. Near the dip at Emlalazi many came to see Shembe. An old man, Newanga, came and said, 'Man of God, we are dying, we and our children and cattle are killed by the sun. I pray for rain.' The man of God said, 'You have your pastors – why do you not ask them?' He replied, 'They have no rain' (*abanayo imvula*). He said, 'Whom are you asking about rain?' He said, 'I ask you; I see you are man of God, and you will get it.'

Only one day passed, and then very heavy rain fell, continuing for two days all over the country. We left and came to Mkhwanazis, walking along praising Jehova on our dancing drum. As we walked along, a miracle happened; a Ndlanzi girl was bitten by a puff-adder. The man of God bowed down and sucked the wound, getting [the poison] out. The girl was healed and she crossed the river, walking easily on her own feet. May the name of Jehova be praised who gave us his Servant so that we should live through him.

Ethics 1

Self-expression and the Good Life: Twenty-One Precepts

This outline of ethics is the central summary of the Perfect Liberty Kyodan's practical teaching. The Precepts were supposed to have been revealed to the second founder, Miki Tokuchika (*b* 1900), who carried on the earlier work of Miki Tokuharu (1871–1938). Stress is placed on the way in which God is an artist and likewise men have to act in a creative and joyous manner in their daily living. The religion is a kind of modernized Shinto, but was prescribed in its earlier form as Hito no Michi or Way of Man before being re-founded as the Perfect Liberty Kyodan in 1956.

1. Life is art.
2. The whole life of the individual is a continuous succession of self-expression.
3. The individual is a manifestation of God.
4. We suffer if we do not manifest ourselves.
5. We lose our self if we are swayed by our feelings.
6. Our true self is revealed when our ego is effaced.
7. All things exist in mutual relation to one another.
8. Live radiantly as the Sun.
9. All men are equal.
10. Bring mutual happiness through our expressions.
11. Depend on God at all times.
12. There is always a way for each person.
13. There is one way for men, and there is another for women.
14. All things exist for world peace.
15. Our whole environment is the mirror of our mind.
16. All things make progress and develop.
17. Grasp the heart of everything.
18. At every moment man stands at the crossroad of good and evil.
19. Practise at once whatever your first inspiration dictates.
20. Attain the perfect harmonious state of mind and matter.
21. Live in Perfect Liberty.

Ethics 2

United Humanity: Faith of Bahā'ullāh

This is drawn from the writings of 'Abdu'l-Bahā (1844–1921), elder son of the main founder of the faith, Bahā'ullāh, and authorized interpreter of the teachings.

. . Just as the thoughts and hypotheses of past ages are fruitless today, likewise dogmas and codes of human invention are obsolute and barren of product in religion. Nay, it is true that they are the cause of enmity and conducive to strife in the world of humanity; war and bloodshed proceed from them and the oneness of mankind finds no recognition in their observance. Therefore it is our duty in this radiant century to investigate the essentials of divine religion, seek the realities underlying the oneness of the world of humanity, and discover the source of fellowship and agreement which will unite mankind in the heavenly bond of love. This unity is the radiance of eternity, the divine spirituality, the effulgence of God and the bounty of the Kingdom. We must investigate the divine source of these heavenly bestowals and adhere unto them steadfastly. For if we remain fettered and restricted by human inventions and dogmas, day by day the world of mankind will be degraded, day by day warfare and strife will increase and satanic forces converge toward the destruction of the human race.

If love and agreement are manifest in a single family, that family will advance, become illumined and spiritual; but if enmity and hatred exist within it destruction and dispersion are inevitable. This is likewise true of a city. If those who dwell within it manifest a spirit of accord and fellowship it will progress steadily and human conditions become brighter whereas through enmity and strife it will be degraded and its inhabitants scattered. In the same way the people of a nation develop and advance toward civilization and enlightenment through love and accord, and are disintegrated by war and strife. Finally, this is true humanity itself in the aggregate. When love is realized and the ideal spiritual bonds unite the hearts of men, the whole human race will be uplifted, the world will continually grow more spiritual and radiant and the happiness and tranquillity of mankind be immeasurably increased. Warfare and strife will be uprooted, disagreement and dissension pass away and Universal Peace unite the nations and peoples of the world. All mankind will dwell together as one family, blend as the waves of one sea, shine as stars of one firmament and appear as fruits of the same tree. This is the happiness and felicity of humankind. This is the illumination of man, the glory eternal and life everlasting; this is the divine bestowal.

Postscript

Some of the books of religious founders have come to attain the status of authoritative scriptures, and even to be printed in a way bringing out their sacredness. But other literary traditions are in process of formation, especially among the African independent churches. The whole phenomenon of new religions has attracted widespread interest and study among historians and sociologists of religion. Doubtless the spirit bloweth where it listeth, and the more orthodox religious traditions of the world have had to come to terms with these various new flowerings of the religious imagination.

Followers listen to a sermon during one of the great festivals of the Nazarite Church, founded in 1911 by the Zulu prophet Isaiah Shembe (see page 377).

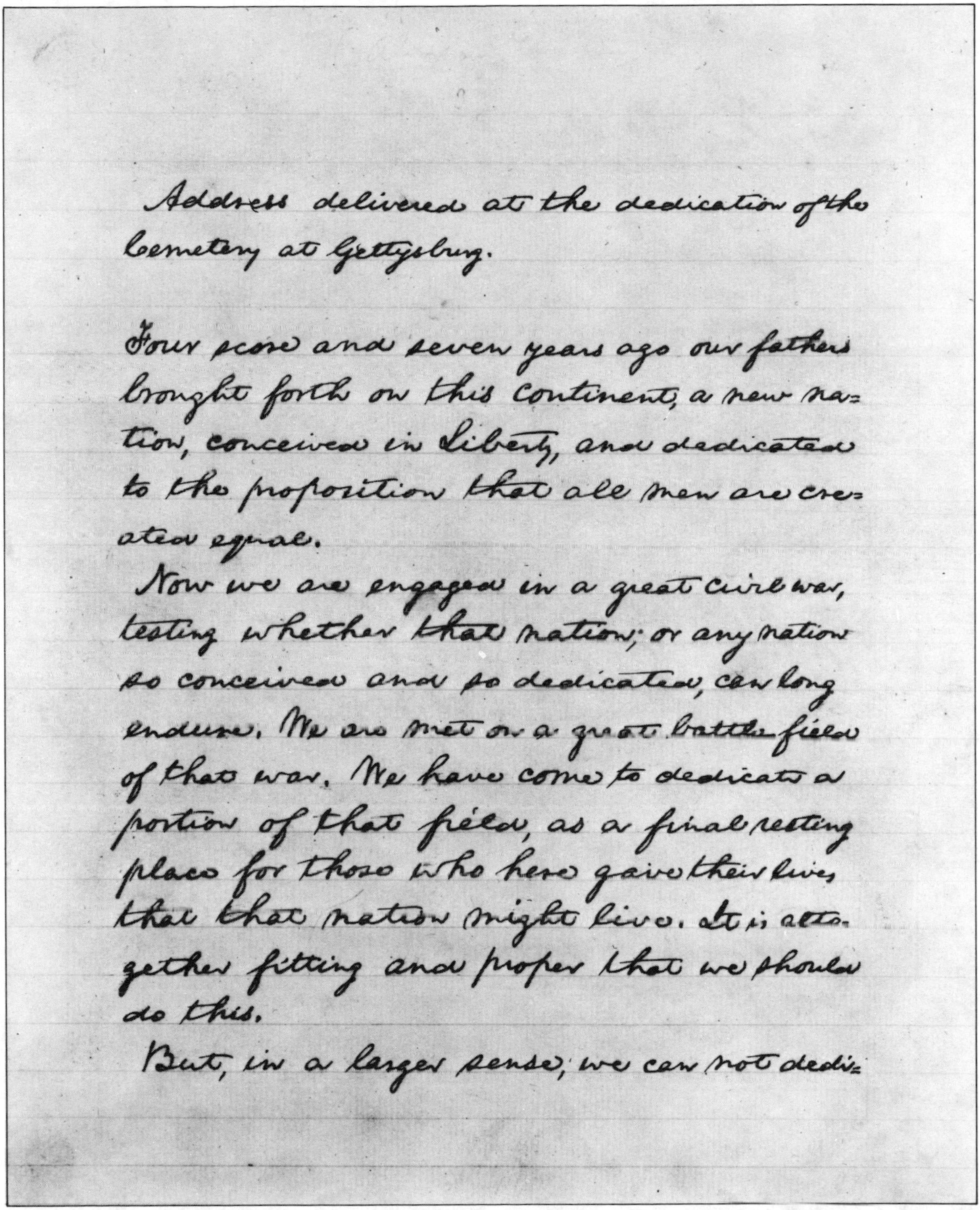
Address delivered at the dedication of the Cemetery at Gettysburg.

Four score and seven years ago our fathers brought forth on this continent, a new nation, conceived in Liberty, and dedicated to the proposition that all men are created equal.

Now we are engaged in a great civil war, testing whether that nation, or any nation so conceived and so dedicated, can long endure. We are met on a great battle field of that war. We have come to dedicate a portion of that field, as a final resting place for those who here gave their lives that that nation might live. It is altogether fitting and proper that we should do this.

But, in a larger sense, we can not dedi-

A manuscript of the Gettysburg Address in Abraham Lincoln's handwriting. The address, delivered on 19 November 1863, has become an integral part of the 'civil religion' of the United States (see page 382).

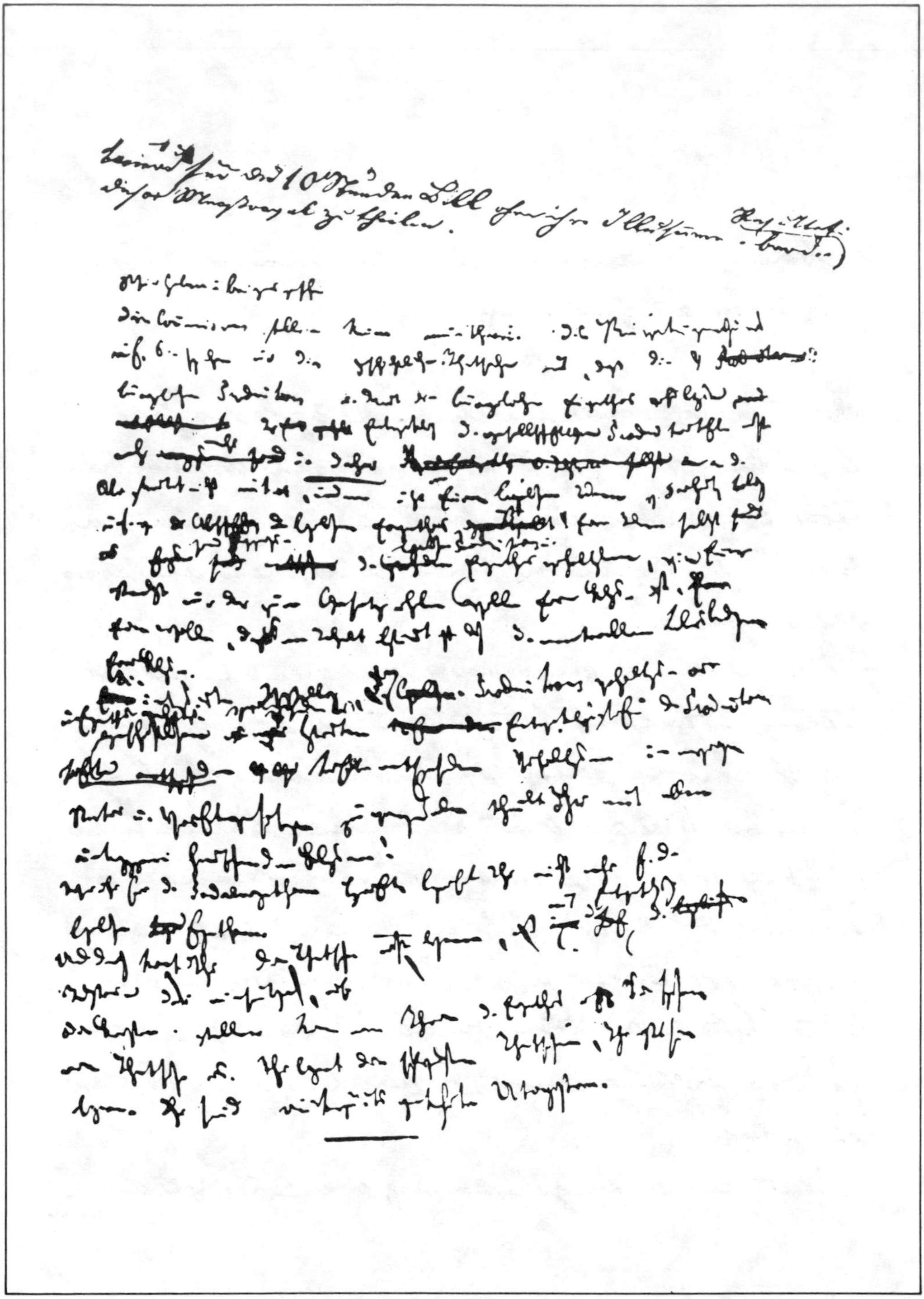

A page from the original manuscript of the Communist Manifesto *(1848), in Karl Marx's handwriting; the two lines at the top are in his wife's hand.*

Secular Worldviews

Introduction

Often modern belief-systems, though they do not regard themselves as being religious and, indeed, are sometimes passionately anti-religious, have some of the features of traditional religion. Such outlooks as humanism, Marxism and nationalism often command deep loyalties, provide an orientation in life and express an ethical viewpoint and a programme for human betterment. They have been called 'quasi-religions', and no account of the human search for spiritual meaning and social salvation can be complete if it ignores these worldviews.

Naturally such secular worldviews do not have sacred texts in the traditional sense. Still, some of their literature is authoritative and some inspiring. In the passages which we include here are some of the most famous pieces of this kind, together with one or two which help to illustrate something of the ethos of secular outlooks.

We begin with something which illustrates the borderline between the secular and the religious, a passage so famous to American citizens because it is used as part of the national remembrance of the dead, and so a passage which takes its place in what is sometimes called 'civil religion'. It is a major feature of the modern world that nationalism and so the sentiment of patriotism is a vital shaping force of life: for many purposes the nation-state has become the central institution determining people's lives. Lincoln's Gettysburg Address combines the themes of national dedication and freedom. It is an important passage for helping Americans to interpret their past, especially because it gave meaning to the tragedies of the Civil War. It is thus a way of re-expressing the sacred narrative of the nation's past. Other nations have other stories, but it is a universal idea that 'our' past has meaning and helps to give us identity and dignity, even in its defeats and disasters.

Of all the ideologies of the modern world, Marxism has the greatest emphasis upon doctrine. The interpretation of the world through a particular philosophy and theory of history and economics is important for practice, and adherence to some version of the doctrine is an important element in the discipline of the various Marxist parties and movements. Part of that interpretation is here expressed in the famous *Communist Manifesto* of Marx and Engels.

Of all 20th-century writers who have tried to express a form of scientific humanism perhaps none has had the intellectual power and lucidity of Bertrand Russell. He summed up his way of dealing with life at its deepest moments in 'A Free Man's Worship'. Next, we include a passage from Mao Zedong, which underlines the importance of the Party as the 'Church' which institutionalizes the revolution, and leads the people to a transformation of society. Note how the themes of nationalism and social revolution are blended here. Religious experience is not necessarily excluded by a secular or non-theistic outlook. As an example of 'secular mysticism' we here have a passage from Richard Jefferies's *The Story of My Heart*.

The themes of national self-determination and human rights are both important in modern ethical attitudes: freedom is often seen as the over-riding quality to be promoted in life. The noble moral ideals of the allied nations after their victory over Nazi Germany and Imperial Japan were expressed in the preamble to the Charter of the United Nations, reproduced here under the heading Ethics.

The tension in modern secular ideologies between individualism and collectivism is illustrated in this selection.

Sacred Narrative

National Sacrifice: Abraham Lincoln's Gettysburg Address

This address, delivered at the dedication of the cemetery at Gettysburg, appears in various versions: the present one is the last, completed sometime after early March 1864. The address was given on 19 November 1863.

Four score and seven years ago our fathers brought forth on this continent a new nation, conceived in Liberty, and dedicated to the proposition that all men are created equal.

Now we are engaged in a great civil war, testing whether that nation, or any nation so conceived and so dedicated, can long endure. We are met on a great battle-field of that war. We have come to dedicate a portion of that field, as a final resting place for those who here gave their lives that that nation might live. It is altogether fitting and proper that we should do this.

But, in a larger sense, we can not dedicate – we can not consecrate – we can not hallow – this ground. The brave men, living and dead, who struggled here, have consecrated it, far above our poor power to add or detract. The world will little note, nor long remember what we say here, but it can never forget what they did here. It is for us the living, rather, to be dedicated here to the unfinished work which they who fought here have thus far so nobly advanced. It is rather for us to be here dedicated to the great task remaining before us – that from these honored dead we take increased devotion to that cause for which they gave the last full measure of devotion – that we here highly resolve that these dead shall not have died in vain – that this nation, under God, shall have a new birth of freedom – and that government of the people, by the people, for the people, shall not perish from the earth.

Doctrine

The New Materialism and History: The Communist Manifesto

The originality of Marx and Engels was to turn German philosophy after Hegel into practical analysis and to propound a materialism in motion: Marxist doctrine as much concerned the development of history through economic forces as it did the constitution of the world and human beings. Thus doctrine in Marxism has always related to a 'myth of history'. When *The Communist Manifesto* was prepared – and it became the most famous socialist document of all time – Marx and Engels were still quite young (they were born in 1818 and 1820 respectively), and its timing (February 1848) was dramatic, for that year was to see many risings and upheavals across the European continent. The text here is the English edition of 1888. We here reproduce the first portion, which dramatically sets forth the condition of the world as perceived by the authors.

A spectre is haunting Europe – the spectre of Communism. All the Powers of old Europe have entered into a holy alliance to exorcize this spectre: Pope and Czar, Metternich and Guizot, French Radicals and German police spies.

Where is the party in opposition that has not been decried as Communistic by its opponents in power? Where the Opposition that has not hurled back the branding reproach of Communism, against the more advanced opposition parties, as well as against its reactionary adversaries?

Two things result from this fact:

I. Communism is already acknowledged by all European Powers to be itself a Power.

II. It is high time that Communists should openly, in the face of the world, publish their views, their aims, their tendencies, and meet this nursery tale of the Spectre of Communism with a Manifesto of the party itself.

To this end, Communists of various nationalities have assembled in London, and sketched the following Manifesto, to be published in the English, French, German, Italian, Flemish and Danish languages.

Bourgeois and Proletarians

The history of all hitherto existing society is the history of class struggles.

Freeman and slave, patrician and plebian, lord and serf, guild-master and journeyman, in a word, oppressor and oppressed, stood in constant opposition to one another, carried on an uninterrupted, now hidden, now open fight, a fight that each time ended either in a revolutionary reconstitution of society at large, or in the common ruin of the contending classes.

In the earlier epochs of history, we find almost everywhere a complicated arrangement of society into various orders, a manifold gradation of social rank. In ancient Rome we have patricians, knights, plebians, slaves; in the Middle Ages, feudal lords, vassals, guild-masters, journeymen, apprentices, serfs; in almost all of these classes, again, subordinate gradations.

The modern bourgeois society that has sprouted from the ruins of feudal society has not done away with class antagonisms. It has but established new classes, new conditions of oppression, new forms of struggle in place of the old ones.

Our epoch, the epoch of the bourgeoisie, possesses, however, this distinctive feature: it has simplified the class antagonisms. Society as a whole is splitting up more and more into two great hostile camps, into two great classes directly facing each other: Bourgeoisie and Proletariat.

From the serfs of the Middle Ages sprang the chartered burghers of the earliest towns. From these burgesses the first elements of the bourgeoisie were developed.

The discovery of America, the rounding of the Cape, opened up fresh ground for the rising bourgeoisie. The East Indian and Chinese markets, the colonization of America, trade with the colonies, the increase in the means of exchange and in commodities generally, gave to commerce, to navigation, to industry, an impulse never before known, and thereby, to the revolutionary element in the tottering feudal society, a rapid development.

The feudal system of industry, under which industrial production was monopolized by closed guilds, now no longer sufficed for the growing wants of the new markets. The manufacturing system took its place. The guild-masters were pushed on one side by the manufacturing middle class; division of labour between the different corporate guilds vanished in the face of division of labour in each single workshop.

Meantime the markets kept ever growing, the demand ever rising. Even manufacture no longer sufficed. Thereupon, steam and machinery revolutionized industrial production. The place of manufacture was taken by the giant, Modern Industry, the place of the industrial middle class by industrial millionaires, the leaders of whole industrial armies, the modern bourgeois.

Modern industry has established the world market, for which the discovery of America paved the way. This market has given an immense development to commerce, to navigation, to communication by land. This development has, in its turn, reacted on the extension of industry; and in proportion as industry, commerce, navigation, railways extended, in the same proportion the bourgeoisie developed, increased its capital, and pushed into the background every class handed down from the Middle Ages.

We see, therefore, how the modern bourgeoisie is itself the product of a long course of development, of a series of revolutions in the modes of production and of exchange.

Each step in the development of the bourgeoisie was accompanied by a corresponding political advance of that class. An oppressed class under the sway of the feudal nobility, an armed and self-governing association in the medieval commune; here independent urban republic (as in Italy and Germany), there taxable 'third estate' of the monarch (as in France), afterward, in the period of manufacture proper, serving either the semi-feudal or the absolute monarch as a counterpoise against the nobility, and, in fact, corner-stone of the great monarchies in general, the bourgeoisie has at last, since the establishment of Modern Industry and of the world market, conquered for itself, in the modern representative State, exclusive political sway. The executive of the modern State is but a committee for managing the common affairs of the whole bourgeoisie.

The bourgeoisie, historically, has played a most revolutionary part.

The bourgeoisie, wherever it has got the upper hand, has put an end to all feudal, patriarchal, idyllic relations. It has pitilessly torn asunder the motley feudal ties that bound man to his 'natural superiors', and has left remaining no other nexus between man and man than naked self-interest, than callous 'cash payment'. It has drowned the most heavenly ecstacies of religious fervour, of chivalrous enthusiasm, of philistine sentimentalism, in the icy water of egotistical calculation. It has resolved personal worth into exchange value, and in place of the numberless indefeasible chartered freedoms, has set up that single, unconscionable freedom – Free Trade. In one word, for exploitation, veiled by religious and political illusions, it has substituted naked shameless, direct, brutal exploitation.

The bourgeoisie has stripped of its halo every occupation hitherto honoured and looked up to with reverent awe. It has converted the physician, the lawyer, the priest, the poet, the man of science, into its paid wage-labourers.

The bourgeoisie has torn away from the family its sentimental veil, and has reduced the family relation to a mere money relation.

The bourgeoisie has disclosed how it came to pass that the brutal display of vigour in the Middle Ages, which Reactionists so much admire, found its fitting complement in the most slothful indolence. It has been the first to show what man's activity can bring about. It has accomplished wonders far surpassing Egyptian pyramids, Roman aqueducts and Gothic cathedrals; it has conducted expeditions that put in the shade all former Exoduses of nations and crusades.

The bourgeoisie cannot exist without constantly revolutionizing the instruments of production, and thereby the relations of production, and with them the whole relations of society. Conservation of the old modes of production in unaltered form was, on the contrary, the first condition of existence for all earlier industrial classes. Constant revolutionizing of production, uninterrupted disturbance of all social conditions, everlasting uncertainty and agitation distinguish the bourgeois epoch from all earlier ones. All fixed, fast-frozen relations, with their train of ancient and venerable prejudices and opinions are swept away, all new-formed ones become antiquated before they can ossify. All that is solid melts into air, all that is holy is profaned, and man is at last compelled to face with sober senses his real conditions of life and his relations with his kind.

Ritual

A Free Man's Worship

Bertrand Russell (1872–1970) was perhaps the most widely-known scientific humanist of the 20th century, and made great contributions to the philosophy of mathematics, general philosophy and ethical thought. He was also concerned with liberation and political causes, such as, in later years, nuclear disarmament. In a celebrated essay in 1909, reprinted in *Mysticism and Logic*, Russell published his thoughts about how a person whose outlook on the cosmos was scientific could come to terms with the alien, godless character of the world in which he found himself. He tried to substitute new attitudes for those which had in traditional religions been expressed in such ritual activities as prayer and worship.

In action, in desire, we must submit perpetually to the tyranny of outside forces; but in thought, in aspiration, we are free, free from our fellow-men, free from the petty planet on which our bodies impotently crawl, free even, while we live, from the tyranny of death. Let us learn, then, that energy of faith which enables us to live constantly in the vision of the good; and let us descend, in action, into the world of fact, with that vision always before us.

When at first the opposition of fact and ideal grows fully visible, a spirit of fiery revolt, of fierce hatred of the gods, seems necessary to the assertion of freedom. To defy with Promethean constancy a hostile universe, to keep its evil always in view, always actively hated, to refuse no pain that the malice of Power can invent, appear to be the duty of all who will not bow before the inevitable. But indignation is still a bondage, for it compels our thoughts to be occupied with an evil world; and in the fierceness of desire from which rebellion springs there is a kind of self assertion which it is necessary for the wise to overcome. Indignation is a submission of our thoughts, but not of our desires; the Stoic freedom in which wisdom consists is found in the submisson of our desires, but not of our thoughts. From the submisson of our desires springs the virtue of resignation; from the freedom of our thoughts springs the whole world of art and philosophy, and the vision of beauty by which, at last, we half reconquer the reluctant world. But the vision of beauty is possible only to unfettered contemplation, to thoughts not weighted by the load of eager wishes; and thus Freedom comes only to those who no longer ask of life that it shall yield them any of these personal goods that are subject to the mutations of Time.

Although the necessity of renunciation is evidence of the existence of evil, yet Christianity, in preaching it, has shown a wisdom exceeding that of the Promethean philosophy of rebellion. It must be admitted that, of the things we desire, some, though they prove impossible, are yet real goods; others, however, as ardently longed for, do not form part of a fully purified ideal. The belief that what must be renounced is bad, though sometimes false, is far less often false than untamed passion supposes; and the creed of religion, by providing a reason for proving that it is never false, has been the means of purifying our hopes by the discovery of many austere truths.

But there is in resignation a further good element: even real goods, when they are unattainable, ought not be fretfully desired. To every man comes, sooner or later, the great renunciation. For the young, there is nothing unattainable; a good thing desired with the whole force of a passionate will, and yet impossible, is to them not credible. Yet, by death, by illness, by poverty, or by the voice of duty, we must learn, each one of us, that the world was not made for us, and that, however beautiful may be the things we crave, Fate may nevertheless forbid them. It is the part of courage, when misfortune comes, to bear without repining the ruin of our hopes, to turn away our thoughts from vain regrets. This degree of submission to Power is not only just and right: it is the very gate of wisdom.

But passive renunciation is not the whole of

wisdom; for not by renunciation alone can we build a temple for the worship of our own ideals. Haunting foreshadowings of the temple appear in the realm of imagination, in music, in architecture, in the untroubled kingdom of reason, and in the golden sunset magic of lyrics, where beauty shines and glows, remote from the touch of sorrow, remote from the fear of change, remote from the failures and disenchantments of the world of fact. In the contemplation of these things the vision of heaven will shape itself in our hearts, giving at once a touchstone to judge the world about us, and an inspiration by which to fashion to our needs whatever is not incapable of serving as a stone in the sacred temple.

Except for those rare spirits that are born without sin, there is a cavern of darkness to be traversed before that temple can be entered. The gate of the cavern is despair, and its floor is paved with the gravestones of abandoned hopes. There Self must die; there the eagerness, the greed of untamed desire must be slain, for only so can the soul be freed from the empire of Fate. But out of the cavern the Gate of Renunciation leads again to the daylight of wisdom, by whose radiance a new insight, a new joy, a new tenderness, shine forth to gladden the pilgrim's heart.

When, without the bitterness of impotent rebellion, we have learnt both to resign ourselves to the outward rule of Fate and to recognize that the non-human world is unworthy of our worship, it becomes posssible at last so to transform and refashion the unconscious universe, so to transmute it in the crucible of imagination, that a new image of shining gold replaces the old idol of clay. In all the multiform facts of the world – in the visual shapes of trees and mountains and clouds, in the events of the life of Man, even in the very omnipotence of Death – the insight of creative idealism can find the reflection of a beauty which its own thoughts first made. In this way mind asserts its subtle mastery over the thoughtless forces of nature. The more evil the material with which it deals, the more thwarting to untrained desire, the greater is its achievement in inducing the reluctant rock to yield up its hidden treasures, the prouder its victory in compelling the opposing forces to swell the pageant of its triumph. Of all the arts, Tragedy is the proudest, the most triumphant; for it builds its shining citadel in the very centre of the enemy's country, on the very summit of his highest mountain; from its impregnable watch-towers, his camps and arsenals, his columns and forts, are all revealed; within its walls the free life continues, while the legions of Death and Pain and Despair, and all the servile captains of tyrant Fate, afford the burghers of that dauntless city new spectacles of beauty. Happy those sacred ramparts, thrice happy the dwellers on that all-seeing eminence. Honour to those brave warriors who, through countless ages of warfare, have preserved for us the priceless heritage of liberty, and have kept undefiled by sacreligious invaders the home of the unsubdued.

But the beauty of Tragedy does but make visible a quality which, in more or less obvious shapes, is present always and everywhere in life. In the spectacle of Death, in the endurance of intolerable pain, and in the irrevocableness of a vanished past, there is a sacredness, an overpowering awe, a feeling of the vastness, the depth, the inexhaustible mystery of existence, in which, as by some strange marriage of pain, the sufferer is bound to the world by bonds of sorrow. In these moments of insight, we lose all eagerness of temporary desire, all struggling and striving for petty ends, all care for the little trivial things that, to a superficial view, make up the common life of day by day; we see, surrounding the narrow raft illuminated by the flickering light of human comradeship, the dark ocean on whose rolling waves we toss for a brief hour; from the great night without, a chill blast breaks in upon our refuge; all the loneliness of humanity amid hostile forces is concentrated upon the individual soul, which must struggle alone, with what of courage it can command, against the whole weight of a universe that cares nothing for its hopes and fears. Victory, in this struggle with the powers of darkness, is the true baptism into the glorious company of heroes, the true initiation into the overmastering beauty of human existence. From that awful encounter of the soul with the outer world, renunciation, wisdom, and charity are born: and with their birth a new life begins. To take into the inmost shrine of the soul the irresistible forces whose puppets we seem to be – Death and change, the irrevocableness of the past, and the powerlessness of Man before the blind hurry of the Universe from vanity to vanity – to feel these things and know them is to conquer them.

This is the reason why the Past has such magical

power. The beauty of its motionless and silent pictures is like the enchanted purity of late autumn, when the leaves, though one breath would make them fall, still glow against the sky in golden glory. the Past does not change or strive; like Duncan, after life's fitful fever it sleeps well; what was eager and grasping, what was petty and transitory, has faded away, the things that were beautiful and eternal shine out of it like stars in the night. Its beauty, to a soul not worthy of it, is unenduarble; but to a soul which has conquered Fate it is the key of religion.

The life of Man, viewed outwardly, is but a small thing in comparison with the forces of Nature. The slave is doomed to worship Time and Fate and Death, because they are greater than anything he finds in himself, and because all his thoughts are of things which they devour. But, great as they are, to think of them greatly, to feel their passionless splendour, is greater still. And such thought makes us free men; we no longer bow before the inevitable in Oriental subjection, but we absorb it, and make it a part of ourselves. To abandon the struggle for private happiness, to expel all eagerness of temporary desire, to burn with passion for eternal things – this is emancipation, and this is the free man's worship. And this liberation is effected by a contemplation of Fate; for Fate itself is subdued by the mind which leaves nothing to be purged by the purifying fire of Time.

United with his fellow-men by the strongest of all ties, the tie of a common doom, the free man finds that a new vision is with him always, shedding over every daily task the light of love. The life of Man is a long march through the night, surrounded by invisible foes, tortured by weariness and pain, towards a goal that few can hope to reach, and where none may tarry long. One by one, as they march, our comrades vanish from our sight, seized by the silent orders of omnipotent Death. Very brief is the time in which we can help them, in which their happiness or misery is decided. Be it ours to shed sunshine on their path, to lighten their sorrows by the balm of sympathy, to give them the pure joy of a never-tiring affection, to strengthen failing courage, to instill faith in hours of despair. Let us not weigh in grudging scales their merits and demerits, but let us think only of their need – of the sorrows, the difficulties, perhaps the blindnesses, that make the misery of their lives; let us remember that they are fellow-sufferers in the same darkness, actors in the same tragedy with ourselves. And so, when their day is over, when their good and their evil have become eternal by the immortality of the past, be it ours to feel that, where they suffered, where they failed, no deed of ours was the cause; but wherever a spark of the divine fire kindled in their hearts, we were ready with encouragement, with sympathy, with brave words in which high courage glowed.

Brief and powerless is Man's life; on him and all his race the slow, sure doom falls pitiless and dark. Blind to good and evil, reckless of destruction, omnipotent matter rolls on its relentless way; for Man, condemned today to lose his dearest, tomorrow himself to pass through the gate of darkness, it remains only to cherish, ere yet the blow falls, the lofty thoughts that ennoble his little day; disdaining the coward terrors of the slave of Fate, to worship at the shrine that his own hands have built; undismayed by the empire of chance, to preserve a mind free from the wanton tyranny that rules his outward life; proudly defiant of the irresistible forces that tolerate, for a moment, his knowledge and his condemnation, to sustain alone, a weary but unyielding Atlas, the world that his own ideals have fashioned despite the trampling march of unconscious power.

Institutional Expression

The Party and Faith: The Foolish Old Man who Removed the Mountains

Mao Zedong wrote this in June 1945. The passage (*Selected Works*, III, 271–2) emphasizes the way in which the Party is the leader in the Chinese Communist struggle. There was an emphasis after the success of Mao in controlling all China in 1949 on the elite party members and cadres (later too the Red Guards) who dynamized the masses. They were like a secular priesthood or religious order. In this famous parable Mao stresses the importance of solidarity with the people and the need for commitment. Mao later feared that the Party might become bureaucratized and alienated from the masses.

We have had a very successful congress.[1] We have done three things. First, we have decided on the line of our Party, which is boldly to mobilize the masses and expand the people's forces so that, under the leadership of our Party, they will defeat the Japanese aggressors, liberate the whole people and build a new-democratic China. Second, we have adopted the new Party constitution. Third, we have elected the leading body of the Party – the Central Committee. Henceforth our task is to lead the whole membership in carrying out the Party line. Ours has been a congress of victory, a congress of unity. The delegates have made excellent comments on the three reports. Many comrades have undertaken self-criticism; with unity as the objective unity has been achieved through self-criticism. This congress is a model of unity, of self-criticism and of inner-Party democracy.

When the congress closes, many comrades will be leaving for their posts and the various war fronts. Comrades, wherever you go, you should propogate the line of the congress and, through the members of the Party, explain it to the broad masses.

Our aim in propagating the line of the congress is to build up the confidence of the whole party and the entire people in the certain triumph of the revolution. We must first raise the political consciousness of the vanguard so that, resolute and unafraid of sacrifice, they will surmount every difficulty to win victory. But this is not enough; we must also arouse the political consciousness of the entire people so that they may willingly and gladly fight together with us for victory. We should fire the whole people with the conviction that China belongs not to the reactionaries but to the Chinese people. There is an ancient Chinese fable called 'The Foolish Old Man who Removed the Mountains'. It tells of an old man who lived in northern China long, long ago and was known as the Foolish Old Man of North Mountain. His house faced south and beyond his doorway stood the two great peaks, Taihang and Wangwu, obstructing the way. He called his sons, and hoe in hand they began to dig up these mountains with great determination. Another greybeard, known as the Wise Old Man, saw them and said derisively, 'How silly of you to do this! It is quite impossible for you to dig up these two huge mountains.' The Foolish Old Man replied, 'When I die, my sons will carry on; when they die, there will be my grandsons, and then their sons and grandsons, and so on to infinity. High as they are, the mountains cannot grow any higher and with every bit we dig, they will be that much lower. Why can't we clear them away?' Having refuted the Wise Old Man's wrong view, he went on digging every day, unshaken in his conviction. God was moved by this and he sent two angels, who carried the mountains away on their backs. Today, two big mountains lie like a dead weight on the Chinese people. One is imperialism, the other is feudalism. The Chinese Communist Party has long made up its mind to dig them up. We must persevere and work unceasingly, and we too will touch God's heart. Our God is none other than the masses of the Chinese people. If they stand up and dig together with us, why can't these two mountains be cleared away?

---

[1] Namely the Seventh National Congress of the Chinese Communist Party.

Experience

Mystical Experience: The Story of My Heart

In his famous book *The Story of My Heart* Richard Jefferies (1848–87) describes an experience which changed his life. He was not in a traditional sense a religious believer, and he is an early exponent of the possibility of religious experience within a secular and atheistic framework of belief. The type of experience he here describes has been called 'panenhenic' – a sense of oneness with the All, rather than the inner quest of the yogi or mystic who looks within. But his emphasis on natural experience has had echoes in the perennial philosophy of Aldous Huxley and others in the 20th century, who have emphasized the world-wide character of mysticism.

The story of my heart commences seventeen years ago. In the glow of youth there were times every now and then when I felt the necessity of a strong inspiration of soul-thought. My heart was dusty, parched for want of the rain of deep feeling; my mind arid and dry, for there is a dust which settles on the heart as well as that which falls on a ledge. It is injurious to the mind as well as to the body to be always in one place and always surrounded by the same circumstances. A species of thick clothing slowly grows about the mind, the pores are choked, little habits become a part of existence, and by degrees the mind is enclosed in a husk. When this began to form I felt eager to escape from it, to throw it off like heavy clothing, to drink deeply once more at the fresh fountains of life. An inspiration – a long deep breath of the pure air of thought – could alone give health to the heart.

There was a hill to which I used to resort at such periods. The labour of walking three miles to it, all the while gradually ascending, seemed to clear my blood of the heaviness accumulated at home. On a warm summer day the slow continued rise required continual effort, which carried away the sense of oppression. The familiar everyday scene was soon out of sight; I came to other trees, meadows, and fields; I began to breathe a new air and to have a fresher aspiration. I restrained my soul till I reached the sward of the hill; psyche, the soul that longed to be loose. I would write psyche always instead of soul to avoid meanings which have become attached to the word soul but it is awkward to do so. Clumsy indeed are all words the moment the wooden stage of commonplace life is left. I restrained psyche, my soul, till I reached and put my foot on the grass at the beginning of the green hill itself.

Moving up the sweet short turf, at every step my heart seemed to obtain a wider horizon of feeling; with every inhalation of rich pure air, a deeper desire. The very light of the sun was whiter and more brilliant here. By the time I had reached the summit I had entirely forgotten the petty circumstances and the annoyance of existence. I felt myself, myself. There was an entrenchment on the summit, and going down into the fosse I walked round it slowly to recover breath. On the south-western side there was a spot where the outer bank had partially slipped, leaving a gap. There the view was over a broad plain, beautiful with wheat, and enclosed by a perfect amphitheatre of green hills. Through these hills there was one narrow groove, or pass, southwards, where the white clouds seemed to close in the horizon. Woods hid the scattered hamlets and farmhouses, so that I was quite alone.

I was utterly alone with the sun and the earth. Lying down on the grass, I spoke in my soul to the earth, the sun, the air, and distant sea far beyond sight. I thought of the earth's firmness – I felt it bear me up; through the grassy couch there came an influence as if I could feel the great earth speaking to me. I thought of the wandering air – its pureness, which is its beauty; the air touched me and gave me something of itself. I spoke to the sea: though so far, in my mind I saw it, green at the rim of the earth and blue in deeper ocean; I desired to have its strength, its mystery and glory. Then I addressed the sun, desiring the soul equivalent of his light and brilliance, his endurance and unwearied race. I turned to the blue heaven over, gazing into its depth, inhaling its exquisite colour and sweetness. The rich blue of the unattainable flower of the sky drew my soul towards it, and there it rested, for pure colour is rest of heart. By all these I prayed; I felt an emotion of the soul beyond all definition; prayer is a puny thing to it, and the word is a rude sign to the feeling, but I know no other.

By the blue heaven, by the rolling sun bursting through untrodden space, a new ocean of ether every day unveiled. By the fresh and wandering air encompassing the world; by the sea sounding on the shore – the green sea white-flecked at the margin and the deep ocean; by the strong earth under me. Then, returning, I prayed by the sweet thyme, whose little flowers I touched with my hand; by the slender grass; by the crumble of dry chalky earth I took up and let fall through my fingers. Touching the crumble of the earth, the blade of grass, the thyme flower, breathing the earth-encircling air, thinking of the sea and the sky, holding out my hand for the sunbeams to touch it, prone on the sward in token of deep reverence, thus I prayed that I might touch to the unutterable existence infinitely higher than deity.

With all the intensity of feeling which exalted me, all the intense communion I held with the earth, the sun and sky, the stars hidden by the light, with the ocean – in no manner can the thrilling depth of these feelings be written – with these I prayed, as if they were the keys of an instrument, of an organ, with which I swelled forth the notes of my soul, redoubling my voice by their power. The great sun burning with light; the strong earth, dear earth; the warm sky; the pure air; the thought of ocean; the inexpressible beauty of all filled me with a rapture, an ecstacy, an inflatus. With this inflatus, too, I prayed. Next to myself I came and recalled myself, by bodily existence. I held out my hand, the sunlight gleamed on the skin and the iridescent nails; I recalled the mystery and beauty of the flesh. I thought of the mind with which I could see the ocean sixty miles distant, and gather to myself its glory. I thought of my inner existence, that consciousness which is called the soul. These – that is, myself – I threw into the balance to weigh the prayer the heavier. My strength of body, mind and soul, I flung into it; I put forth my strength; I wrestled and laboured, and toiled in might of prayer. The prayer, this soul-emotion was in itself – not for an object – it was a passion. I hid my face in the grass, I was wholly prostrated, I lost myself in the wrestle, I was rapt and carried away.

Becoming calmer, I returned to myself and thought, reclining in rapt thought, full of aspiration, steeped to the lips of my soul in desire. I did not then define, or analyse, or understand, this. I see now that what I laboured for was soul-life, more soul-nature, to be exalted, to be full of soul-learning. Finally I rose, walked half a mile or so along the summit of the hill eastwards, to soothe myself and come to the common ways of life again. Had any shepherd accidentally seen me lying on the turf, he would only have thought that I was resting a few minutes; I made no outward show. Who could have imagined the whirlwind of passion that was going on within me as I reclined there! I was greatly exhausted when I reached home. Occasionally I went up the hill deliberately, deeming it good to do so; then, again, this craving carried me away up there of itself. Though the principal feeling was the same, there were variations in the mode in which it affected me.

Sometimes on lying down on the sward I first looked up at the sky, gazing for a long time till I could see deep into the azure and my eyes were full of the colour; then I turned my face to the grass and thyme, placing my hands at each side of my face so as to shut out everything and hide myself. Having drunk deeply of the heaven above and felt the most glorious beauty of the day, and remembering the old, old sea, which (as it seemed to me) was but just yonder at the edge, I now became lost, and absorbed into the being or existence of the universe. I felt down deep into the earth under, and high above into the sky, and farther still to the sun and stars. Still farther beyond the stars into the hollow of space, and losing thus my separateness of being came to seem like a part of the whole. Then I whispered to the earth beneath, through the grass and thyme, down into the depth of its ear, and again up to the starry space hid behind the blue of day. Travelling in an instant across the distant sea, I saw as if with actual vision the palms and coconut trees, the bamboos of India, and the cedars of the extreme south. Like a lake with islands, the ocean lay before me, so clear and vivid as the plain beneath in the midst of the amphitheatre of hills.

With the glory of the great sea, I said; with the

firm, solid, and sustaining earth; the depth, distance and expanse of either; the age, timelessness, and ceaseless motion of the ocean; the stars, and the unknown in space; by all those things which are most powerful known to me, and by those which exist, but of which I have no idea whatever, I pray. Further, by my own soul, that secret existence which above all other things bears the nearest resemblance to the ideal of spirit, infinitely nearer than earth, sun, or star. Speaking by an inclination towards, not in words, my soul prays that I may have something from each of these, that I may gather a flower from them, that I may have in myself the secret and meaning of the earth, the golden sun, the light, the foam-flecked sea. Let my soul become enlarged; I am not enough; I am little and contemptible. I desire a greatness of soul, an irradiance of mind, a deeper insight, a broader hope. Give me power of soul, so that I may actually effect by its will that which I strive for.

Ethics

National Freedoms and Human Rights: Preamble to the UN Charter

The meeting of the victorious nations at San Francisco after the end of World War II set the scene for the creation of a successor body to the League of Nations, incorporating ideals that had been set forth by the war leaders during the war (for instance, in Churchill and Roosevelt's Atlantic Charter). It looked to a new ethical stance among the peoples of the world.

WE THE PEOPLES OF THE UNITED NATIONS DETERMINED

to save succeeding generations from the scourge of war, which twice in our lifetime has brought untold sorrow to mankind, and
to reaffirm faith in fundamental human rights, in the dignity and worth of the human person, in the equal rights of men and women and of nations large and small, and
to establish conditions under which justice and respect for the obligations arising from treaties and other sources of international law can be maintained, and
to promote social progress and better standards of life in larger freedom,
AND FOR THESE ENDS
to practise tolerance and live together in peace with one another as good neighbours, and
to unite our strength to maintain international peace and security, and
to ensure, by the acceptance of principles and the institution of methods, that armed force shall not be used, save in the common interest, and
to employ international machinery for the promotion of the economic and social advancement of all peoples,
HAVE RESOLVED TO COMBINE OUR EFFORTS TO ACCOMPLISH THESE AIMS
Accordingly, our representative governments, through representatives assembled in the city of San Francisco, who have exhibited their full powers found to be in good and due form, have agreed to the present Charter of the United Nations and do hereby establish an international organization to be known as the United Nations.

Postscript

The collectivist secular worldviews represented in varieties of official Marxism have adjusted their authoritative writings from time to time. Thus there have been official Soviet editions not only of Marx and Engels, but also of Lenin and Stalin; in China the *Selected Writings of Mao Zedong* were in process of revision after his death, while during the Cultural Revolution the 'Little Red Book' of excerpts from his writings was a source of inspiration and guidance for activists. New forms of 'civil religion' have emerged in Africa and elsewhere as nationalism has spread. Secular individualism is necessarily more eclectic. Indeed we are here already getting to the very edge of what can be seen as a 'sacred text'. Rather, the secularist looks upon the whole of literature as being available as a source of guidance and inspiration.

Index

This thematic index follows the organization of the text and includes a separate entry for each of the religions discussed in this volume. Common terms are cross-indexed. The pages marked in bold type indicate quotations from specific texts.

Sources

The Powerful Dead

Sacred Narrative 1: J. Duchesne-Guillemin, *The Hymns of Zarathustra*, tr. M. Henning (London: J. Murray, 1952); Sacred Narrative 2, Institutional Expression 2: 'The Creation Epic' and 'The Epic of Gilgamesh', trans. E.A. Speiser, in *Ancient Near East Texts Relating to the Old Testament*, ed. J.B. Pritchard (Princeton: Princeton University Press, 1955); Sacred Narrative 3: *Hesiod's Theogony*, trans. N.O. Brown (New York: Liberal Arts Press, 1953); Sacred Narrative 4: *Latin-American Mythology*, trans. H.B. Alexander, (Boston, 1920); Doctrine 1, Ritual 1, Institutional Expression 1, Experience 1: *Ancient Egyptian Literature*, trans. M. Lichtheim, 2 vols (Berkeley, Los Angeles and London: University of California Press, 1973 and 1975); Doctrine 2: *The Teachings of the Magi*, trans. R.C. Zaehner (London, Allan & Unwin, 1956); Doctrine 3: *Timaeus*, trans. B. Jowett, in *The Collected Dialogues of Plato*, ed. E. Hamilton and H. Cairns (New York: Pantheon Books, 1961); Doctrine 4, Ethics 4: M. Leon-Portilla, *Aztec Thought and Culture: A Study of the Ancient Nahuatl Mind*, trans. J.E. Davis (Norman: University of Oklahoma Press, 1963); Ritual 2: The *Zend-Avesta*, trans. J. Darmesteter, in *Sacred Books of the East*, ed. F.M. Müller (Oxford: Clarendon Press, 1883); Ritual 3: Iamblichus, *On the Mysteries*, in F.C. Grant, ed. and trans., *Hellenestic Religion: The Age of Syncretism* (New York: The Liberal Arts Press Inc., 1953); Ritual 4: B. de Sahguń, *General History of the Things of New Spain according to the Florentine Codex*, Book II, trans. A.J.O. Anderson and C.E. Dibble (Santa Fe: The School of American Research and the University of Utah, 1951); Institutional Expression, 3 Experience 3: Virgil, *Ecologues* and Apuleius, *Metamorphoses* in F.C. Grant, ed. and trans., *Ancient Roman Religion* (New York: The Liberal Arts Press, Inc., 1957); Institutional Expression 4: B. de Sahaguń, *General History of the Things of New Spain*, trans. I. Nicholson, quoted in L. Séjourne, *Burning Water: Thought and Religion in Ancient Mexico* (New York: Vanguard Press, 1957); Experience 2: S.N. Kramer, *The Sumerians: Their History, Culture and Character* (Chicago and London: University of Chicago Press, 1963); Ethics 1, Experience 4: *The Book of the Dead: The Hieroglyphic Transcript of the Papyrus Ani*, trans. E.A. Wallis Budge (1901) vol 2; Ethics 2: 'The Code of Hammurabi', trans. T.J. Meek, in *Ancient Near Eastern Texts Relating to the Old Testament, op. cit.*; Ethics 3: Plotinus, *Enneads*, trans. A.H. Armstrong, Loeb Classical Library (Cambridge and London: Harvard University Press and William Heinemann Ltd, 1906)

Judaism

Biblical quotations: *The Holy Bible, Revised Standard Version*, ed. H.G. May (New York and London: Collins, 1971)

Christianity

Sacred Narrative 1 and 4, Doctrine 1, Ritual 3: The Holy Bible, Authorized Version of 1611; Sacred Narrative 2 and 3, Doctrine 2–5, Ritual 1, 2 and 4, Institutional Expression 1–3, Experience 1–3, Ethics 1–3: *The New English Bible*, (Oxford University Press, 1961 and 1970)

Islam

All Sūras are from *The Koran Interpreted*, trans. A.J. Arberry, 2 vols. (London: Allen & Unwin, 1955) apart from Sūra 52: 29–32 (Sacred Narrative 1), which is from *Islam: Muhammad and his Religion*, ed. A. Jeffrey (New York: Liberal Arts Press, 1958). The following are also from *Islam: Muhammad and his Religion*: Sacred Narrative 1: al-Tabarai, *Ta'rīkh al-Rasūl wa'l-muluk*; Sacred Narrative 2: al-Bāqillānī, *I'jāz al-Qur'ān*; Doctrine 1: Muhammad al-Madanī, *Tasbīh Asmā Allāh al-husnā*; Doctrine 3: Ibn Makhluf, *Kitāb al-'ulūm al–fākhira fī'n-Nazr fī 'Umūr al-Ākhira*; Doctrine 4: Muslim, *Sahīh*; al-Bukhārī, *Sahīh*; Ritual 1: Muhammad Haqqī al-Nāzilī, *Khazīnat al-Asrār*; Ritual 2: Abū al-Rahmān Ahmad al-Nasā'ī, *Sunan*; Ritual 3 and 4: Muslim, *Sahīh*; Ritual 5: Al-Azraqī, *Kitāb Akābar Makka*; Experience 4: Al-Baghawī, *Masābīh al-Sunna*; Experience 5: Al-Suyūtī, *al-La'ālī al-masnū'a*. Other sources are as follows: Sacred Narrative 2: al-Bukhārī, *Al-Sahīh*, in *Islam from the Prophet Muhammad to the Capture of Constantinople*, ed. B. Lewis (New York: Harper & Row, 1974); Sacred Narrative 3: (Ishāq, *Sīrat Rasūl Allāh*), Institutional Expression 1 and 2: *Life of Muhammad*, ed. Ibn Hisham, trans. A. Guillaume (Lahore, Karachi and Dacca: Oxford University Press, 1955); Institutional Expression 3: Muhammad Ali, *Manual of Hadīth* (London and Dublin: Curzon Press, 1944); Ethics 3: Abu Muhammad al-Husayn, *Mishkāt al-Masābīh*, trans. J. Robson (Lahore: Sh. Muhammad Ashraf, 1965) vol. 4

Hinduism

Sacred Narrative 1 (Rgveda), Sacred Narrative 3 (Rgveda), Institutional Expression 3 (Rgveda): R.T.H. Griffith, *The Hymns of the Rig Veda, translated with a Popular Commentary* (1889; repr. Delhi: Motilal Banarsidass, 1973); Sacred Narrative 1 (Manu-Smrti); Institutional Expression 2; *The Laws of Manu*, trans. G. Bühler, in *Sacred Books of the East*, ed. F.M. Müller (Oxford: Clarendon Press, 1886); Sacred Narrative 1 (Brhadāranyaka Upanisad, Chāndogya Upanisad), Doctrine 1, 3, 4 and 5, Experience

3, Ethics 2: *The Thirteen Principal Upanishads*, trans. R.E. Hume, 2nd revised ed. (Oxford: Oxford University Press, 1931); Sacred Narrative 2, Sacred Narrative 3 (Śatapatha-Brāhmana), Ritual 3 and 4: *The Śatapatha-Brāhmana according to the Text of the Madhyandina School*, trans. J. Eggling, in *Sacred Books of the East*, ed. F.M. Müller, vol 12 (1882; repr. Delhi: Motilala Banarsidass, 1972); Sacred Narrative 4 (*Mahābhārata*): W. Doniger O'Flaherty, trans., *Hindu Myths*, (Middlesex: Penguin Books, 1975); Sacred Narrative 4 (Rāmāyana): K. Bolle, *The Freedom of Man in Myth* (Nashville: Vanderbilt University Press, 1968): Sacred Narrative 5: *The Devī-Māhātmyam or Sri Durga-Saptasati*, trans. Swami Jagadisvarananda (Madras: Sri Ramakrishna Math, 1969); Doctrine 2: R.C. Zaehner, ed. and trans., *Hindu Scriptures*, Everyman's Library (London: J.M. Dent, 1966); Doctrine 6 (Commentary on the *Brahmasūtras*): *The Vedanta Sūtras with the Commentary by Śankarākārya*, trans. G. Thibaut, in *Sacred Books of the East*, ed. F.M. Müller, vol 34 (Oxford: Clarendon Press, 1890); Doctrine 6 (Commentary on *Upadeśa-Sahāsrī*): *A Thousand Teachings in Two Parts – Prose and Poetry*, trans. Swami Jagadananda (Madras: Sri Ramakrishna Math, 1970); Doctrine 7: *Rāmānuja on the Bhagavadgītā: A Condensed Rendering of his Gītābhasya with Copious Notes and Introduction*, trans. J.A.B. van Buitenen (Delhi: Motilal Banarsidass, 1968); Ritual 1 (*Rgveda*) Institutional Expression 1, Institutional Expression 3 (*Rgveda*): *The Rig Veda: an Anthology*, trans. W. Doniger O'Flaherty, (Middlesex: Penguin Books, 1981); Ritual 1 (*Yajurveda*, *Taittīrigya Samhitā*) and 2: *The Veda of the Black Yajus School entitled Taittiriya Samhita*, trans. A.B. Keith (1914, repr. Delhi: Motilal Banarsidass, 1967), vol. 1; Ritual 5, Ethics 1: *Agni Purānam, a Prose English Translation*, trans. Manmatha Nath Dutt Shastri (1903; repr. Benares: Chowkhamba Sanskrit Series, vol. 54, 1967); Institutional Expression 3 (*Vaisnava-dharma-Śāstra*): *The Institutes of Vishnu*, trans. J. Jolly, in *Sacred Books of the East*, U.S. ed. vol 8, ed. F.M. Müller (New York: Charles Scribners's Sons, 1900); Experience 1 and 2: *The Bhagavadgītā: A New Translations*, trans. K.W. Bolle, (Berkeley, Los Angeles and London: University of California Press, 1979); Experience 4: J.S.M. Hooper, *Hymns of the Alvars* (Calcutta: Association Press, 1929): Experience 5: *The Gospel of Rāmakrishna* (New York: The Vedanta Society, 1907); Ethics 3: M.K. Gandhi, *An Autobiography*, trans. Mahadev Desai (Ahmedabad: Navajivan, 1927)

Buddhism

Sacred Narrative 1, Ritual 2, Institutional Expression 1 and 2: *Buddhist Texts through the Ages*, ed. E. Conze (London: Faber, 1954); Sacred Narrative 2, Doctrine 1–5, Ritual 1, 3 and 4, Experience 1–3, Ethics 5 and 6: Pali Text Translation Series (London: 1909 onwards); Sacred Narrative 3, Ethics 4: H. Clarke Warren, *Buddhism in Translations*, Harvard Oriental Series, vol. 3 (Cambridge, Mass.: 1915); Sacred Narrative 4, Ethics 1–3: C.H. Hamilton, *Buddhism: A Religion of Infinite Compassion: Selections from Buddhist Literature* (New York, Liberal Arts Press, 1952); Doctrine 6: E. Conze, *Buddhist Wisdom Literature* (London: Allen & Unwin, 1958); Ritual 5, Doctrine 7: L. Stryk, *The World of the Buddha* (New York: Doubleday, 1968)

Jainism

Sacred Narrative 1 and 2, Doctrine 1 and 2, Ritual 2 and 3, Experience 1 and 2, Institutional Expression, Ethics 1 and 2: *Jaina Sūtras*, trans. H. Jacobi, in *Sacred Books of the East*, ed. F.M. Müller (Oxford: Clarendon Press, 1884–95) vols. xxii and xlv; Ritual 1: R.H.B. Williams, *Jaina Yoga: a Survey of the Medieval Sravakacaras* London Oriental Series, vol. 14 (London: Oxford University Press, 1963); Experience 3: P.S. Jaini, *The Jaina Path of Purification* (Berkeley: University of California Press, 1975)

Taoism

Sacred Narrative 1 and 2, Doctrine 1, Experince 3, Ethics 1 and 2: trans. N. Smart; Sacred Narrative 3, Doctrine 2: Wm T. de Bary, Wing-Tsit Chan and B. Watson, *Sources of Chinese Tradition* (New York and London: Columbia University Press, 1960) vol. 1; Sacred Narrative 4, Experience 1: Yu-Lan Fung, *Chuang Tzu, a New Selected Translation* (Shanghai: Commercial Press Ltd, 1933); Ritual: Wing-Tsit Chan, *A Source Book in Chinese Philosophy* (Princeton: Princeton University Press, 1969); Institutional Expression: M. Saso, *The Teachings of the Taoist Master Chuang* (New Haven and London, Yale University Press, 1978); Experience 2 and 4: *Lieh Tzu*, trans. L. Giles (London: Wisdom of the East, 1912)

Confucianism

Sacred Narrative 1, Doctrine 1, Institutional Expression: Wm T. de Bary, Wing-tsit Chan, B. Watson, *Sources of Chinese Tradition* (New York and London: Columbia University Press, 1960); Sacred Narrative 2 and 3, Ritual 2, Ethics 1: *The Analects of Confucius*, trans. A. Waley (London: George Allen and Unwin, 1964); Doctrine 2, Experience 1: *A Source Book in Chinese Philosophy*, trans. Wing-tsit Chan (Princeton: Princeton University Press, 4th ed., 1973); Ritual 1: B. Watson and Hsun Tzu, *Basic Writings of Mo Tzu, Hsun Tzu and Han Fei Tzu* (New York: Columbia University Press, 1963); Experience 2: *The Philosophy of Wang Yang-Ming*, trans. F. Goodrich Henke (New York: Paragon Book Reprint Co., 2nd ed., 1964); Ethics 2: *Mencius*, trans. J. Ware (New York: Mentor Books, 1960)

Shintoism

Sacred Narrative 1 and 3: *Kojiki*, trans. B. Hall Chamberlain, 2nd ed. (Kobe: J.L. Thompson & Co., 1932); Sacred Narrative 2, Ritual: *Nihongi*, trans. W.G. Aston, 1896; Doctrine, Experience, Institutional Expression, Ethics: *Kokutai ni Hongi: Cardinal*

Principles of the National Entity of Japan, trans. J.O. Gauntlett, ed. R. King Hall (Cambridge, Harvard University Press, 1949)

Sikhism

Sacred Narrative, Experience: *Hymns of Guru Nanak*, trans. Khushwant Singh (London: Unesco, Longmans, 1968); Doctrine, Ritual, Institutional Expression: M.A. Macauliffe, *The Sikh Religion: Its Gurus, Sacred Writings and Authors*, 4 vols. (Oxford: Clarendon Press, 1909); Ethics: Gopalk Singh, *The Religion of the Sikhs* (Bombay: Asia Publishing House, 1969)

Small-scale Traditional Religions

Sacred Narrative 1: E. Clews Parsons, *Pueblo Indian Religion* (Chicago: University of Chicago Press, 1939), vol. 1, repr. C.H. Long, *Alpha: The Myths of Creation* (New York: George Braziller, 1963); Sacred Narrative 2: K. Numazawa, 'Background of Myths on the Separation of Sky and Earth from the Point of View of Cultural History', *Scientia*, 88 (1953) repr. Long, *loc. cit.*; Sacred Narrative 3: repr. F.H. Cushing, 'Outlines of Zuñi Creation Myths', *Thirteenth Annual Report of the U.S. Bureau of American Ethnology* (Washington: Smithsonian Institution, 1891–2), repr. Long, *loc. cit.*; Sacred Narrative 4: Teuira Henry, *Ancient Tahiti*, Bernice P. Bishop Museum, Bulletin 48 (Honolulu: Bishop Museum Press, 1928), repr. Long, *loc. cit*; Sacred Narrative 5: T.G.H. Strehlow, *Aranda Traditions* (Melbourne: Melbourne University Press, 1947), repr. Long, *loc. cit*; Sacred Narrative 6: E.S. Craighill Handy, *Polynesian Religion*, Bernice P. Bishop Museum, Bulletin 34 (Honolulu: Bishop Museum Press, 1927), repr. Long, *loc. cit*; Sacred Narrative 7: Uno Holmberg, *Finno-Ugric, Siberian Mythology*, vol. 4 of *The Mythology of All Races* (Boston: Archaeological Institute of America, 1917), repr. Long, *loc. cit*; Sacred Narrative 8: A.E. Jensen, *Das religiöse Weltbild einer frühen Kultur* (Stuttgart: August Schroder Verlag, 1949) trans. J. Campbell, *The Masks of God: Primitive Mythology* (New York: The Viking Press, 1959); Doctrine 1: Jomo Kenyatta, 'Ngai, the High-god of the Gikuyu (Kenya)', *Africa*, 10 (1937); Doctrine 2: J.S. Mbiti, *African Religions and Philosophy* (Garden City, New York: Anchor Books, 1970) quoting T.C. Young, *African Ways and Wisdom* (London, 1937); Doctrine 3: J.R. Walker, *The Sun Dance and other Ceremonies of the Oglala Division of the Teton Dakota*, American Museum of Natural History, Anthropological Papers, 16.2 (1917), repr. Mircea Eliade, ed., *From Primitives to Zen: A Thematic Sourcebook on the History of Religions* (New York and Evanston: Harper and Row, 1967); Ritual 1: T. Koch-Grünberg, *Zwei Jahren unter den Indianen: Reisen in Nordwest-Brasilien, 1903–1905* (Berlin: Ernst Wasmuch A.G., 1910), trans. and repr. J. Campbell, *The Masks of God: Primitive Mythology* (New York: Viking Press, 1959); Ritual 2: W.D. Strong, *Aboriginal Society in Southern California* (Berkeley: University of California Publications in American Archaeology and Ethnology, 1929), vol. 26; Ritual 3: F. Densmore, *Teton Sioux Music* (Washington: Government Printing Office, 1918); Institutional Expression 1: H. Schärer, *Ngaju Religion: The Conception of God among a South Borneo People*, trans. R. Needham (The Hague: Martinus Nijhoff, 1963); Institutional Expression 2: C.M. Bowra, *Primitive Song* (reprint; New York, 1963); Institutional Expression 3: M. Griaule, *Conversations with Ogotemmêli: An Introduction to Dogon Religious Ideas* (Worcester and London: Oxford University Press, 1965); Experience 1: F. Boas, *The Religion of the Kwakiutl Indians*, vol. 2 (New York: Columbia University Press, 1930); Experience 2: F. Densmore, *Teton Sioux Music* (Washibgton: Government Printing Office, 1918); Experience 3: J.G. Neihardt, *Black Elk Speaks: Being the Life Story of a Holy Man of the Oglala Sioux* (Lincoln: University of Nebraska Press, 1932, repr. 1961); Experience 4: J. Mooney, *The Ghost-Dance Religion and the Sioux Outbreak of 1890*, Fourteenth Annual Report, part 2, Bureau of American Ethnology (Washington, 1896); Ethics 1: M. Gusinde, *The Yamana* (New Haven: Human Relations File, 1932)

New Religions

Sacred Narrative: Sun Myung Moon, *Divine Principle* (Holy Spirit Association for the Unification of World Christianity, 2nd ed., 1973); Doctrine: Mary Baker Eddy, *Science and Health* (Boston: Christian Science Publishing Co., 1875); Ritual: *The Essential Aurobindo*, ed. R.A. McDermott (New York: Schocken, 1973); Institutional Expression: *The Book of Mormon*, trans. J. Smith (Manchester: Deseret Enterprises Ltd., 1972); Experience: B. Sundkler, *Zulu Zion and Some Swazi Zionists* (London and Oxford: Oxford University Press, 1976); Ethics: H. Thomsen, *The New Religions of Japan* (Rutland, Vermont and Tokyo: Charles E. Tuttle Co., 1963); Ethics 2: *Selected Writings of Baha'ullah and 'Abdu'l-Baha* (Bahai World Faith, 1960)

Secular Worldviews

Sacred Narrative: Abraham Lincoln, Gettysburg Address (1864 edition); Doctrine: Karl Marx and Frederick Engels, *The Communist Manifesto*, trans. S. Moore, ed. F. Engels, (London, 1888); Ritual: B. Russell, 'A Free Man's Worship' in *Mysticism and Logic* (London: Longmans, 1918); Institutional Expression: Mao Tse-Tung, *Selected Works*, vol. iii; Experience: R. Jefferies, *The Story of My Heart* (London: Longmans, 1883); Ethics: *Charter of the United Nations*

Note: for the sake of consistency, spelling, punctuation and transliteration have in some instances been amended.

Acknowledgements

The authors and publishers gratefully acknowledge permission to publish copyright material from the following:

Anchor Books, New York; Asia Publishing House, Bombay; Bahai World Faith; Charles E. Tuttle Co., Rutland & Tokyo; Chowkhamba Sanskrit Series, Benares; Collins, London; Columbia University Press, New York; Curzon Press, London; J.M. Dent, London; Deseret Enterprises Ltd. Manchester; Doubleday, New York; Faber & Faber, London; George Allen & Unwin, London; George Braziller, New York; Harper & Row, New York; Harvard University Press, Cambridge, Mass: Holy Spirit Association for the Unification of World Christianity; J.L. Thompson, Kobe; John Murray, London; Liberal Arts Press, New York; Longmans, London; Martinus Nijhoff, The Hague; Mentor Books, New York; Motilal Banarsidass, Delhi; Oxford University Press; Pali Text Society, London; Pantheon Books, New York; Paragon Book Reprint Co., New York; Penguin Books, Middlesex; Princeton University Press; Schocken, New York; School of American Research and the University of Utah; Sh. Muhammad Ashraf, Lahore; Sri Ramakrishan Math, Madras; University of California Press, Berkeley; University of Chicago Press; University of Nebraska Press, Lincoln; University of Oklahoma Press, Norman; Vanderbilt University Press, Nashville; Vanguard Press, New York; Viking Press, New York; Yale University Press, New Haven

The publishers have made every effort to trace the copyright holders but if they have inadvertently overlooked any, they will be pleased to make the necessary arrangement at the first opportunity.

The Publishers gratefully acknowledge the following for the illustrations reproduced in this book.

Axel Poignant, facing p.368; Werner Bischof/Magnum from The John Hillelson Agency, facing p.319; *Black Elk Speaks* (1932), facing p.337; Professor Mary Boyce, facing p.44; The British Library, facing p.xiii (OR.1401 f350v–351r), facing p.45 (Add. 15282 f28a), facing p.91 (Facs. 165 p.247), facing p.179 (OR.8837 f60v–61r), facing p.277 (OR.5149 ff39v and 53v); The British Museum, facing p.1; Colorific!/photo Terence LeGoubin, facing p.124, photo Dilip Mehta, facing p.290; Courtesy of The Library of Congress, Washington DC, following p.379; Courtesy of The Church of Jesus Christ of Latter-Day Saints, facing p.369; University of Durham, The Gulbenkian Museum of Oriental Art, facing p.305; Robert Harding Picture Library/photo Jon Gardey, following p.229, photo Robert Harding, facing p.336; Alan Hutchinson Library/photo Sarah Giles, facing p.231, photo Mischa Scorer, following p.379; F.E. Kyte, facing p.329; School of Oriental and African Studies (University of London)/ photo Christopher Barker, following p.317; Ninian Smart, facing p.291, following p.317; Roger Wood, facing p.125; Page from the original manuscript of 1848 of *The Manifesto of the Communist Party* from an English edition of the 1888 translation published in the USSR, facing p.381.